Guatemala

THE ROUGH GUIDE

written and researched by

Mark Whatmore and Iain Stewart

with additional accounts by

Peter Eltringham and Dominique Young

THE ROUGH GUIDES

 We set out to do something different when the first Rough Guide was published in 1982. Mark Ellingham, just out of university, was travelling in Greece. He brought along the popular guides of the day, but found they were all lacking in some way. They were either strong on ruins and museums but went on for pages without mentioning a beach or taverna. Or they were so conscious of the need to save money that they lost sight of Greece's cultural and historical significance. Also, none of the books told him anything about Greece's contemporary life – its politics, its culture, its people, and how they lived.

So with no job in prospect, Mark decided to write his own guidebook, one which aimed to provide practical information that was second to none, detailing the best beaches and the hottest clubs and restaurants, while also giving hard-hitting accounts of every sight, both famous and obscure, and providing up-to-the-minute information on contemporary culture. It was a guide that encouraged independent travellers to find the best of Greece, and was a great success, getting shortlisted for the Thomas Cook travel guide award, and encouraging Mark, along with three friends, to expand the series.

The Rough Guide list grew rapidly and the letters flooded in, indicating a much broader readership than had been anticipated, but one which uniformly appreciated the Rough Guide mix of practical detail and humour, irreverence and enthusiasm. Things haven't changed. The same four friends who began the series are still the caretakers of the Rough Guide mission today: to provide the most reliable, up-to-date and entertaining information to independent-minded travellers of all ages, on all budgets.

We now publish 100 titles and have offices in London and New York. The travel guides are written and researched by a dedicated team of more than 100 authors, based in Britain, Europe, the USA and Australia. We have also created a unique series of phrasebooks to accompany the travel series, along with an acclaimed series of music guides, and a best-selling pocket guide to the Internet and World Wide Web. We also publish comprehensive travel information on our Web site:

www.roughguides.com

HELP US UPDATE

We've gone to a lot of effort to ensure that this new edition of *The Rough Guide to Guatemala* is accurate and up-to-date. However, things change — places get "discovered", opening hours are notoriously fickle, restaurants and rooms raise prices or lower standards, extra buses are laid on or off. If you feel we've got it wrong or left something out, we'd like to know, and if you can remember the address, the price, the time, the phone number, so much the better.

We'll credit all contributions, and send a copy of the next edition (or any other Rough Guide if you prefer) for the best letters. Please mark letters: "Rough Guide Guatemala Update" and send to:
Rough Guides, 62–70 Shorts Gardens, London WC2H 9AB or Rough Guides, 375 Hudson St, 9th floor, New York NY 10014. Or send email to: mail@roughguides.co.uk
Online updates about this book can be found on Rough Guides' Web site at www.roughguides.com

THE AUTHORS

Mark Whatmore, the original author of the Rough Guide to Guatemala, has travelled widely throughout Central America, shooting documentaries in Guatemala and other countries in the region. Now based in the UK and running his own film production company, he spends much of his time researching and travelling abroad.

After two years of travelling the world, **Iain Stewart** ended up in Guatemala and liked it so much that he stayed. Now co-author of the Rough Guides to Guatemala, the Maya World and Central America, he takes every opportunity to return to this part of the world. Based in South London, he combines being a Rough Guide author with his other jobs as a journalist and restaurant critic.

READERS' LETTERS

We would like to thank everyone who has taken the trouble to write in with suggestions, comments and information, including MR Akkan; Joseph Badell; Raphael Birchmeier; Jeroen Boars; D Brown; Ignace Bruyland; AH Bus; Chris Chapman; John Clark; Kathy J Clark; Selena Cunningham; James Flatt; Liza Fourré; Helen Franks; Mercedes García; Ross and Ann Gelbspan; Francisco Girón; John K Graham; Diego Gonzales; Nikolaj Lyngfelot Halberg-Lange; Paul Heesaker; Joe and Mick; Zella King; Toril Kolstoe; Daniella Koss; Sara Lewis; Iris Lohrengel for her excellent Antigua information; Iain Mackay; Fin Mackenzie; Eric B Makino; Kumi Miozobe; Carla Molina; Jake Moore; Gabriella Moretti; Dan Morris; Kevin O'Connor; José Ramon de Castro; Loris Scagliarini; Colin Shadel; Tom Taylor; Thierry and María; Sara D Tuck; Karena Vleck; Nick Warren; FG Worthington; and R Wright.

CONTENTS

PART THREE **CONTEXTS**   **349**

LIST OF MAPS

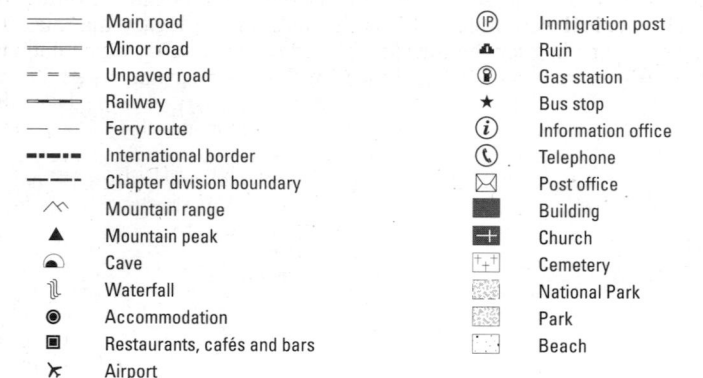

MAP SYMBOLS

=====	Main road	ⓘⓟ	Immigration post
———	Minor road	⚓	Ruin
= = =	Unpaved road	ⓟ	Gas station
▬▬▬	Railway	★	Bus stop
— —	Ferry route	ⓘ	Information office
■-■-■	International border	ⓒ	Telephone
———-	Chapter division boundary	⊠	Post office
⌒⌒	Mountain range	■	Building
▲	Mountain peak	⊞	Church
◠	Cave	⁺₊⁺	Cemetery
⏒	Waterfall	▦	National Park
◉	Accommodation	▨	Park
■	Restaurants, cafés and bars	⌐┘	Beach
✕	Airport		

INTRODUCTION

Spanning the narrow Central American isthmus, Guatemala is a physical and cultural microcosm of Latin America, incorporating an astonishing array of contradictions in a country roughly the size of Ireland. Uniquely, it still has a population which is at least half native American, and the strength of indigenous culture is greater here than perhaps anywhere else on the American continent. More than anywhere, Guatemala is the product of the merger of sophisticated pre-Columbian cultures with Spanish colonialism and the consumerist influences of modern America.

Today, its **Maya** society is a hybrid of pre-Conquest pagan traditions and more recent cultural and religious influences, which combine – above all in the highlands – to form perhaps the most distinctive culture in all of Latin America. Countering this is a powerful **ladino** society of equal strength, a blend of Latin machismo that is decidedly urban and commercial in its outlook. At the edges there is a certain blurring between the two cultures, but the contrast between the hustle of Guatemala City and the murmur of village markets could hardly be more extreme.

Both cultures have left Guatemala with an exceptional wealth of **architectural** and **archeological remains**, and it is this outstanding legacy that makes the country so compelling for the traveller. The Maya civilization, which dominated the entire region from 2000 BC until the arrival of the Spanish, has left its traces everywhere, and Guatemala is scattered with ruins, rising mysteriously out of the rainforest and marking out the more fertile of the highland valleys. These ancient cities, such as the magnificent Tikal, surrounded by pristine jungle, are a fascinating testament to a civilization of great complexity and with a tremendous enthusiam for architectural grandeur. In contrast, the country's *ladino* heritage is typified by the colonial grace and beauty of the former capital, Antigua, with almost every town or large village in the country boasting a whitewashed church, belltower and a classic Spanish-style plaza.

Physically, Guatemala offers an astonishing range of **landscape**, defined by extremes, and by regular earthquakes and volcanic eruptions (though you're unlikely to encounter either of these). In the south, the steamy *ladino*-dominated Pacific coastal plain rises towards a string of magnificent **volcanic** peaks that mark the southern limit of the central highlands. Beyond them lies a series of rolling hills and larger granite peaks, forming the country's heartland, and home to the vast majority of the indigenous population. The scenery here is astonishingly beautiful with unfeasibly picturesque lakes, forests and lush pine-clad hills, dotted with sleepy traditional villages. Further east towards the Caribbean coast, the landscape is more **tropical**, with mangrove swamps, banana plantations and coconut trees dominating. In the north of the country the peaks of the last great **mountain** range, the Cuchumatanes, drop off into the lowlands of Petén – a huge, sparsely populated area of virgin **rainforest**, among the best preserved in Latin America, which harbours a tremendous array of **wildlife**, including jaguar, ocelot, tapir, monkeys, storks and scarlet macaws. Further south, in the **cloudforests**

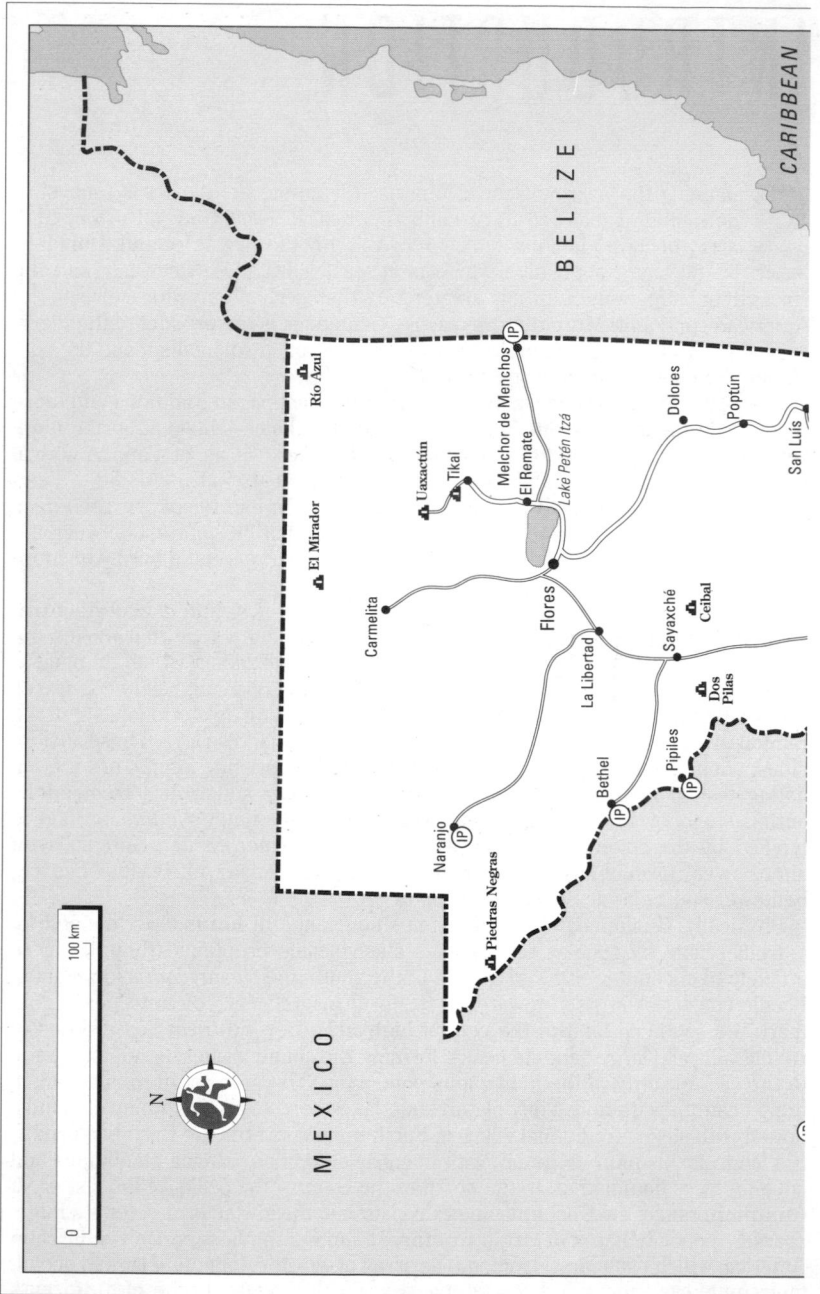

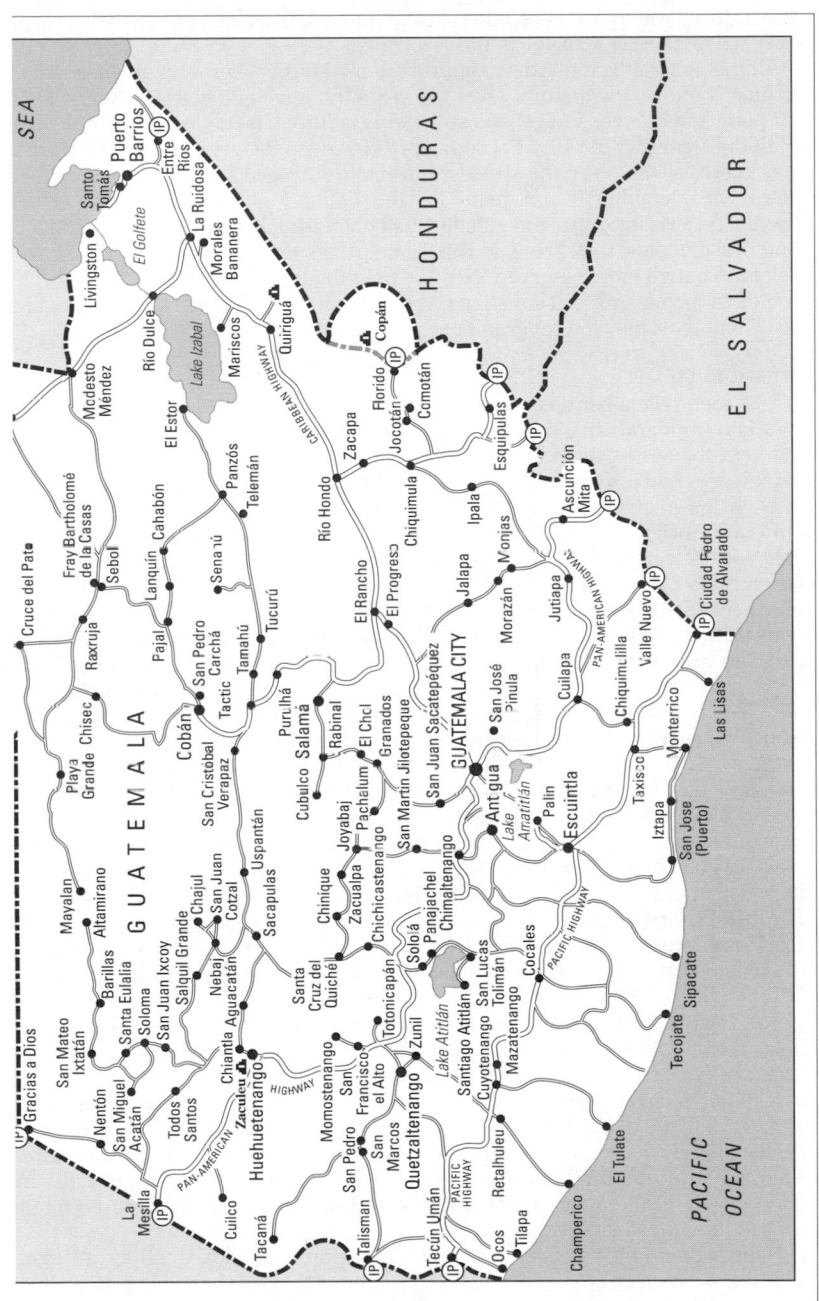

near Cobán, you may glimpse the elusive quetzal, Guatemala's national symbol, or spot a lumbering manatee in the Río Dulce.

All this natural beauty exists against the nagging background of Guatemala's turbulent and bloody **history**. Over the years the huge gulf between the rich and the poor, and between indigenous and *ladino* culture has produced bitter conflict. With the signing of the 1996 Peace Accords between the government and the former guerrillas, however, the armed confrontation ceased and things have calmed down considerably, though many of the country's deep-rooted inequalities remain. As a visitor, you are as safe in Guatemala as almost anywhere else in Latin America, and most travellers find the Guatemalans extraordinarily courteous and helpful. Though more reserved than the neighbouring Mexicans or Salvadorans and often formal in social situations, they are an incredibly friendly people, and you'll find most only too eager to help you out.

Where to go

Whilst each region has its own particular attractions, it is to the Maya-dominated **western highlands** that most travellers head first, and rightly so. The colour, the markets, the fiestas, the culture, and above all the people make it a wholly unique experience. And it seems almost an unfair bonus that all this is set in countryside of such mesmerizing beauty: for photographers, it's heaven. Among the highlights are **Antigua**, the delightful colonial capital whose laid-back atmosphere and café society contrasts with the hectic, fume-filled bustle of the current capital **Guatemala City**, and **Lake Atitlán**, ringed by sentinel-like volcanoes in a setting of exceptional beauty. The shores of the lake are dotted with traditional indigenous villages, as well as a few tranquil low-key settlements, such as **Santa Cruz** and **San Marcos**, where there are just a handful of hotels and some good walking possibilities. More lively is the booming lakeside resort of **Panajachel**, with excellent restaurants, cafés and textile stores, and the bohemian **San Pedro** whose alternative scene and rock-bottom prices attract travellers from all over the world. High up above the lake, the traditional Maya town of **Sololá** has one of the country's best markets (and least-touristy), a complete contrast to the vast twiceweekly affair at **Chichicastenango**, with its incredible selection of weavings and handicrafts. Further west, the sleepy provincial city of **Quetzaltenango (Xela)** makes a good base for exploring the market towns of **Momostenango**, famed for its wool production, and **San Francisco el Alto**, before heading north to **Huehuetanango**, gateway to Guatemala's greatest mountain range, the **Cuchumatanes**. Here, you'll find excellent walking, superb scenery and some of the most isolated and traditional villages in the Maya world, with **Nebaj**, in the Ixil triangle, and **Todos Santos** both making good bases from which to explore.

The **Pacific coast** (usually taken to mean the entire coastal plain) is generally hot and dull, with scrubby, desolate **beaches** backed by a smattering of mangrove swamps. The sole exception is the relaxed seaside village of **Monterrico**, part of a wildlife reserve where you can watch sea turtles coming ashore to lay their eggs. Inland, the region includes some of the country's most productive farmland, devoted purely to commercial agriculture, and dotted with bustling urban centres such as **Esquintla** and **Retalhuleu**. Points of interest are thin on the ground, confined mainly to the pre-Columbian ruins of **Abaj Takalik** and the three minor sites around the town of Santa Lucía.

None of these, however, can compete with the archeological wonders of **Petén**. This unique lowland area, which makes up about a third of the country, is covered with dense rainforest – only now threatened by development – that is alive with wildlife and dotted with superb Maya ruins. The only town of any size is **Flores**, superbly situated on Lake Petén Ixta, from where you can easily reach **Tikal**, the most impressive of all the Maya sites, rivalling any ruin in Latin America. The region's rainforest also hides numerous smaller sites, including **Ceibal**, **Yaxchilán** (just across the border in Mexico) and **Uaxactún**, while adventurous travellers may seek out Petén's more remote ruins, such as the dramatic, pre-Classic **El Mirador** (possibly even larger than Tikal), which requires days of tough travel to reach.

Finally, the **east** of the country includes another highland area, this time with little to offer the visitor, though in the Motagua valley you'll find the superb Maya site of **Quiriguá**, while just over the border in Honduras are the first-class ruins of **Copán**. Further into Honduras are the idyllic **Bay Islands**, whose pristine coral reefs offer some of the finest scuba-diving and snorkelling in the Caribbean. You can also travel up into the rain-soaked highlands of the **Verapaces**, similar in many ways to the central highlands, though fresher and greener. Here, Lake Izabal drains, via the **Río Dulce** through a dramatic gorge, to the Caribbean. At the mouth of the river is the funky town of **Lívingston**, an outpost of Caribbean culture and home to Guatemala's only black community.

When to go

Guatemala enjoys one of the most pleasant climates on earth, with the bulk of the country enjoying warm or hot days with mild or cool evenings year-round. The immediate climate is largely determined by **altitude**. In those areas between 1300 and 1600 metres, which includes Guatemala City, Antigua, Lake Atitlán, Chichicastenago and Cobán, the air is almost always fresh and the nights cool and, despite the heat of the mid-day sun, humidity is never a problem. However, parts of the provinces of Quetzaltenango, Huehuetenango and the Ixil triangle are above this height, so have a cool, damp climate with distinctly cold nights. Low-lying Petén suffers from sticky, steamy conditions most of the year, as do the Pacific and Caribbean coasts, though here at least you can usually rely on the welcome relief of a sea breeze.

The **rainy season** runs roughly from May to October, with the worst of the rain falling in September and October. In Petén, however, the season can extend into December, whilst around Cobán and on the Caribbean coast it can rain at any time of the year. Even at the height of the wet season, though, the rain is usually confined to late afternoon downpours with most of the rest of the day being warm and pleasant. In many parts of the country you can travel without disruption throughout the rainy season, although in the more out-of-the-way places, like the Cuchumatanes, flooding may slow you down by converting the roads into a sea of mud. Also, if you intend visiting Petén's more remote ruins, you'd be well advised to wait until February, as the mud can be thigh deep at the height of the rains.

The **busiest time** for tourists is between December and March, though plenty of people take their summer vacations here in July and August. This is also the period when the language schools and hotels are at their fullest, and many of them hike their prices correspondingly.

PART ONE

THE

BASICS

GETTING THERE FROM NORTH AMERICA

Unless you have time to spare, or are keen to travel overland through Mexico, getting to Guatemala is simplest and cheapest by plane. There are direct flights to Guatemala from Miami, Houston, Washington DC, Chicago, Los Angeles and San Francisco. There are no off-season fares, but flying midweek costs less. All prices quoted below are round-trip.

To Guatemala City, you can get direct flights from **Miami** with American, Iberia and Aviateca; from **Houston** with Continental and Aviateca; from **Los Angeles** with United, Taca and Aviateca; from **Chicago** with United; and from **Washington DC** and **San Francisco** with Taca. All the above flights are daily except Iberia's Miami service, which flies on Tuesdays and Thursdays, Avieteca's Houston service (Tuesdays, Thursdays and Saturdays) and Taca's San Francisco flight (Wednesdays, Fridays and Saturdays). Any of these carriers can organize a connecting flight from elsewhere in the US.

The cheapest **fare** of all from North America is Aviateca's flight from Houston at $245, while American and Aviateca both offer good deals from Miami at around $500. Continental's fare from Houston is around $580. From Los Angeles, Aviateca and Taca both offer fares of around $620 – the same as Taca's fare from San Francisco – while United charges around $820 from LA. From Chicago, United's flight costs around $660, while Taca charges $700 from Washington DC. From New York, you can fly with American via Miami for around $700.

It is also possible to fly **to Mexico City**, which is served by daily flights from most major US cities, and then on to Guatamala, but it is not necessarily cheaper. For example, you'll pay $620 from Los Angeles to Mexico City on Mexicana, then another $287 to fly from Mexico City to Guatemala on Aviateca. To fly from Mexico City on to Guatemala on Mexicana, the price is even higher, at around $375.

There are no direct flights **from Canada** to Guatamala, so you'll have to fly via a US city. The cheapest fare **from Vancouver** is with American, stopping in Dallas and Miami, at CAN $870. Canadian charges CAN$1243 from Vancouver, with stops in Toronto and Miami. **From Toronto**, Canadian charges CAN$1055 for the above flight, though Continental's daily flight via Houston is cheaper at CAN$921.

You can normally cut costs further by going through a **specialist flight agent** – either a **consolidator**, who buys up blocks of tickets from the airlines and sells them at a discount, or a **discount agent**, who in addition to dealing with discounted flights may also offer special student and youth fares and a range of other travel-related services. Bear in mind, though, that penalties for changing your plans can be stiff. Remember too that these companies make their money by dealing in bulk – don't expect them to answer lots of questions. Some agents specialize in charter flights, which may be cheaper than anything available on a scheduled flight, but again departure dates are fixed and withdrawal penalties are high (check the refund policy). If you travel a lot, discount travel clubs are another option – the annual membership fee may be worth it for benefits such as cut-price air tickets and car rental.

AIRLINE NUMBERS

American	☎1-800/433-7300
Aviateca	☎1-800/327-9832
Canadian	☎1-800/426-7000 (US);
	☎1-800/665-1177 (In Canada)
Continental	☎1-800/231-0856
Iberia	☎1-800/772-4642
Mexicana	☎1-800/531-7921
Taca	☎1-800/535-8780
United	☎1-800/538-2929

NORTH AMERICAN DISCOUNT TRAVEL COMPANIES

Airtech, 584 Broadway, Suite 1007, New York, NY 10012 (☎1-800/575-TECH or 212/219-7000). *Standby seat broker; also deals in consolidator fares and courier flights.*

Council Travel, 205 E 42nd St, New York, NY 10017 (☎212/822-2700), plus branches in many other US cities. *Student/budget travel agency.*

Educational Travel Center, 438 N Frances St, Madison, WI 53703 (☎1-800/747-5551 or 608/256-5551). *Student/youth and consolidator fares.*

Skylink, 265 Madison Ave, 5th Fl, New York, NY 10016 (☎1-800/AIR-ONLY or 212/599-0430), plus branches in Chicago, Los Angeles, Toronto, and Washington DC. *Consolidator.*

STA Travel, 10 Downing St, New York, NY 10014 (☎1-800/777 0112 or 212/627-3111), plus branches in the Los Angeles, San Francisco and Boston areas. *Worldwide discount travel firm specializing in student/youth fares. Also offers student IDs, travel insurance, car rental, rail passes, etc.*

Travel CUTS, 187 College St, Toronto, ON M5T 1P7 (☎416/979-2406), plus branches all over Canada. *Specializes in student fares, IDs and other travel services.*

Travelers Advantage, 3033 S Parker Rd, Suite 900, Aurora, CO 80014 (☎1-800/548-1116). *Travel club.*

Worldtek Travel, 111 Water St, New Haven, CT 06511 (☎1-800/243-1723 or 203/772-0470). *Discount travel agency.*

PACKAGES AND ORGANIZED TOURS

There is no shortage of companies operating **tours** and **packages** to Guatemala, the majority of which include visits to wildlife reserves, hikes in the jungle, birdwatching and sight-seeing trips to the Maya ruins. The tours usually last around ten days and cost from US$1000–1300. Some of the companies listed below will tailor-make tours to suit specific requirements, though obviously you will pay more for these.

SPECIALIST TOUR OPERATORS IN THE US AND CANADA

Clark Tours, 310 Lynnway, Suite 304, Lynn, MA 01901 (☎1-800/223-6764 or 617/581-0844). *Land tours of markets and archeological sites.*

Far Horizons, PO Box 91900, Albuquerque, NM 87199-1900 (☎505/343-9400; fax 343-8076). *Archeological and cultural trips.*

GAP Adventures, 264 Dupont St, Toronto, Ontario M5R IV7 (☎1-800/465-5600 or 416/922-8899; fax 922-0822). *Specializes in hiking trips through nature reserves and to the Maya ruins.*

Great Trips, PO Box 1320, Detroit Lakes, MN 56502 (☎1-800/552-3419; fax 218/847-4442). *Trips to Maya ruins, caves and all major archeological sites.*

Guatemala Unlimited, PO Box 786, Berkeley, CA 94701 (☎1-800/733-3350; fax 415/661-6149). *Offers an extensive array of tours to obscure and better known Maya ruins, as well as jungle trekking, river-rafting, mountain-biking and volcano tours.*

South American Journeys, 419 Park Ave South, New York, NY 10016 (☎1-800/434-0540). *Trips to the highlands and archeological sites.*

Tropical Travel, 5 Grogans Park, Suite 102, Woodlands, TX 77380-2190 (☎1-800/451-8017 or 713/688-1985). *Extensive tours around Maya sites, markets, jungle and highlands.*

Toucan Adventure Tours, PO Box 1073, Cambria, CA 93428 (☎805/927-5885; fax 927-0929). *Offers overland adventure tours, including camping, whitewater rafting and canoeing to the rainforest and Maya ruins.*

Tread Lightly Limited, Box 329, Washington Depot, CT 06794 (☎1-800/643-0060; fax 860/868-1718). Web site: *www.treadlightly.com*. *Natural history and cultural travel in Guatemala as well as adventure packages of kayaking, rafting and hiking.*

White Magic Unlimited, PO Box 5506, Mill Valley, CA 94942 (☎1-800/869-9874 or 415/381-8889). *Whitewater rafting and trips to see the Maya sites.*

Winter Escapes, PO Box 429, Erikson, Manitoba, R0J 0P0 (☎204/636-2968; fax 636-2557). *Birdwatching, Maya temple trips, and more general nature and cultural tours.*

GETTING THERE FROM CENTRAL AMERICA AND MEXICO

Guatemala shares boders with four other Central American countries, El Salvador, Honduras, Belize and Mexico. Between **Belize** and Guatemala, there are two border crossings. The first joins **Benque Viejo** in Belize and **Melchor de Mencos** in Guatemala, and is the most direct route to take if you're travelling between Belize City and Petén. A regular bus service connects the crossing to Belize City, and to Flores in Guatemala. The second option is to take one of the ferries and skiffs between **Punta Gorda** (in southern Belize) and **Puerto Barrios** and **Lívingston** in Guatemala (see p.242 for details).

It's also possible to **fly** between Belize and Guatemala: Aerovias, the Guatemalan airline (Guatemala City ☎3325686; fax 3347935), flies between the capitals on Mondays, Wednesdays and Fridays ($100 return; $75 one-way). Tikal Jets (Guatemala City ☎3325070, 3345631 or 3345568; fax 3345631) also flies between Guatemala City and Flores, with a connecting flight on Tropic Air to Belize (Mon–Fri). The flights also connect if you're coming from Belize to Guatemala City, and both are arranged so that you can spend a day at Tikal.

There are three border crossings between **Honduras** and Guatemala. The most used is the **El Florido** crossing that connects the town of Chiquimula in Guatemala with the Copán ruins in Honduras; good minibus services run between the two. The border post at **Agua Caliente** is the best route into Guatemala if you want to visit the town of Esquipulas, while the most adventurous crossing is the excellent **jungle route** that connects Puerto Barrios in Guatemala with Puerto Cortés in Honduras – it's covered in full on p.243.

In addition, **airlines** such as Taca and Aviateca (both Guatemala City ☎3347722; fax 3612159) make the short hop between the two countries, flying from both Tegucigalpa and San Pedro Sula to Guatemala City. A **boat** also connects Omoa in Honduras with Lívingston in Guatemala, leaving Omoa on Tuesdays and Fridays ($36; minimum six people). There may also be the odd ship sailing between Puerto Cortés and Puerto Barrios, check at the port for details.

Between **El Salvador** and Guatemala, the **Valle Nuevo** border post gets by far the most traffic, as it's the fastest route between Guatemala City and San Salvador, but there are a number of other less busy options including the post at **Cuidad Pedro de Alvarado** at the end of the Pacific Highway. **By air**, Taca (see above), Copa (Guatemala City ☎3611567; fax 3342714), Aviateca (see above) and Lacsa (Guatemala City ☎3347722; fax 3612159) connect the two capitals with daily flights.

There are numerous border crossings between **Mexico** and Guatemala, with the main ones being in the south towards the Pacific Coast, at **Tecún Umán** and the **Talismán Bridge**. For Mexico City, however, most traffic uses the Pan-American Highway, which makes a more northerly border crossing at **La Mesilla**. In the jungle region of Peten there are several remote places where you can cross between the two countries (see p.338 and 342), many of which involve isolated river trips over the frontier. From even the most remote border crossings, there are generally good bus connections to Mexico City (at least 24 hours away).

Coming **by air** from Mexico City, there's no shortage of flights to Guatemala City. Both Aviateca and Mexicana have daily services, though fares are not cheap (see p.3 for details).

GETTING THERE FROM THE UK AND IRELAND

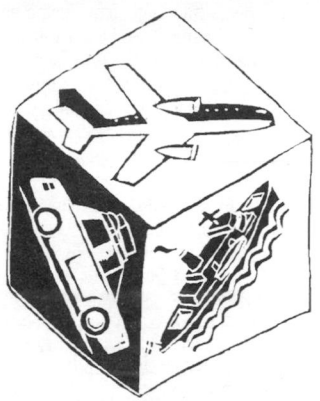

There are no direct flights from London to Guatemala, and it's not all that cheap to fly there, although with a little creative routing it's possible to keep the price down. Fares to Guatemala are always a little higher than those to Mexico City, so you might want to consider travelling overland from there, or even from the USA if you want to see some of Mexico along the way.

For a **scheduled flight** from London to Guatemala City you should expect to pay between £500 and £560 return, if you book through a travel agent or "bucket shop". Official fares, quoted direct by the airlines, are generally much higher. Prices rise slightly in the **high season**, which is July, August and December. There's always some deal available for young people or students,

though don't expect massive reductions. Tickets are usually valid for between three and six months, and you'll probably have to pay more for one that allows you to stay for up to a year. The cheapest tickets are fixed-date returns, but for a little more you can either change the date once you arrive or decide when you'd like to come home once you are there. Some airlines make no charge for changing your return date – it's always worth enquiring.

Scheduled flights to **Guatemala City** from Europe are operated by Iberia via Madrid, KLM via Amsterdam, and Continental via Houston, with other airlines, such as British Airways, offering deals that connect in the US with American airlines. For the **cheapest fares** you'll need to go through an agent, and the more specialized they are the better – see the list of operators below for details. It's also worth looking through the classified ads in magazines and newspapers. In London the most comprehensive lists are in *Time Out* and the *Evening Standard*, while the free weekly magazine *TNT* is also worth checking. Nationally, the *Guardian*, the *Independent*, and the *Observer* all have good classified ads.

A good alternative is to fly to **Mexico City** or **Cancún** and continue overland or by air (see p.3). Several airlines fly from Europe to Mexico City, although only British Airways goes direct, several times a week. Aeroflot, via Moscow, is usually the cheapest, but more comfortable and straightforward routings include Continental from Gatwick via Houston, KLM via Amsterdam, Air France via Paris, and Iberia via Madrid. To Cancún you travel via Miami or Houston. Flying to Mexico you should expect to pay between £50 and £100 less than you would for a flight to Guatemala, through the same agents. Bear in mind, if you're intending to head overland, that Guatemala City is two days' bus journey from Mexico City, while Cancún is about a day from the Guatemalan Petén/Belize border.

If you want to travel through several countries in Central America, or continue into South America, then it's worth considering an "**open jaw**" ticket, which lets you fly into one city and out of another. Engineering one of these can be a little complex, but on some routes you can end up paying not much more than you would for a nor-

AIRLINES	
Aeroflot	☎0171/355 2233
Air France	☎0181/742 6600
American Airlines	☎0345/789789
British Airways	☎0345/222111
Continental	☎01293/567711
Delta	☎0800/414 767
Iberia	☎0171/830 0011
KLM	☎0990/750900
United Airlines	☎0161/ 990 9900

To contact the Central American airlines, call the Central America Corporation on ☎01293/553330.

FLIGHT SPECIALISTS

Bridge the World, 47 Chalk Farm Rd, London NW1 8AN (☎0171/911 0900). *Offers competitively priced fares to all Latin American destinations.*

Campus Travel, 52 Grosvenor Gardens, London SW1W 0AG (Europe ☎0171/730 3402; North America ☎0171/730 2101; worldwide ☎0171/730 8111); 541 Bristol Rd, Selly Oak, Birmingham B29 6AU (☎0121/414 1848); 61 Ditchling Rd, Brighton BN1 4SD (☎01273/570226); 37–39 Queen's Rd, Clifton, Bristol BS8 1QE (☎0117/929 2494); 5 Emmanuel St, Cambridge CB1 1NE (☎01223/324283); 53 Forest Rd, Edinburgh EH1 2QP (☎0131/668 3303); 122 George St, Glasgow G1 1RS (☎0141/5531818); 166 Deansgate, Manchester M3 3FE (☎0161/833 2046); 105–106 St Aldates, Oxford OX1 1DD (☎01865/242067). *Student/youth specialists, with branches also in YHA shops and on university campuses all over Britain.*

Journey Latin America, 14–16 Devonshire Rd, London W4 (☎0181/747 3108). *Specialist with some of the best prices on high-season flights.*

North South Travel, Moulsham Mill Centre, Parkway, Chelmsford, Essex CM2 7PX (☎01245/492882). *Discounted fare agency, with profits going to support projects in the developing world.*

Nouvelles Frontières, 2–3 Woodstock St, London W1R 1HE (☎0171/629 7772). *Offers good deals on flights and has offices throughout Europe.*

STA Travel, 86 Old Brompton Rd, London SW7 3LH, 117 Euston Rd, London NW1 2SX, and 38 Store St, London WC1 (Europe ☎0171/ 361 6161; worldwide ☎0171/ 361 6262); 25 Queens Rd, Bristol BS8 1QE (☎0117/929 4399); 38 Sidney St, Cambridge CB2 3HX (☎01223/366966); 88 Vicar Lane, Leeds LS1 7JH (☎0113/244 9212); 75 Deansgate, Manchester M3 2BW (☎0161/834 0668); 36 George St, Oxford OX1 2OJ (☎01865/792800). *Student/youth specialists with branches also in Birmingham, Canterbury, Cardiff, Coventry, Durham, Glasgow, Warwick, Loughborough, Nottingham and Sheffield.*

Trailfinders, 42–50 Earls Court Rd, London W8 6FT (Europe flights ☎937 5400; long haul and RTW ☎0171/938 3366); 194 Kensington High St, London, W8 7RG (☎0171/938 3232); 58 Deansgate, Manchester M3 2FF (☎0161/839 6969); 254–284 Sauchiehall St, Glasgow G2 3EH (☎0141/353 2224); 22–24 The Priory, Queensway, Birmingham B4 6BS (☎0121/236 1234); 48 Corn St, Bristol BS1 1HQ (☎0117/929 9000). *Worldwide specialists, who offer particularly good deals on flights to Mexico City as part of a round-the-world ticket.*

mal return. For example, a flight from London to Mexico City, returning from Quito and valid for a year, should cost around £550. Journey Latin America is the best first call to sort out the possibilities.

Yet another option is **flying to the USA**, which might well work out cheaper, particularly if you decide to head south overland. From London, **New York** is the cheapest destination, but hardly the most convenient, unless you're planning a tour of the entire continent. **Los Angeles** or **Houston** makes more sense if you plan to continue overland, and **Miami** if you want to fly south, either to Mexico or directly to Guatemala.

Also worth checking out are US **air passes**, which can cover Mexico and are often cheaper if bought in Europe along with a transatlantic ticket. Continental, Delta and United are the most likely candidates.

PACKAGES AND ORGANIZED TOURS

Many companies offer **package tours** to Guatemala and if your time is short, some of them can be exceptionally good value. Among the more interesting operators are Trips, who offer a reasonable degree of comfort on wildlife and archeology tours, and Journey Latin America and Explore Worldwide, both of which organize relaxed overland tours making use of local transport to take in the main sites. Many of the tour operators put on regular slide show/video presentations to give you an idea of what you can expect on their trips; phone the relevant company for details (see below).

All the above tours provide company and a degree of security, but it's worth remembering that there are a large number of **local travel agents** who regularly operate day or overnight trips to all the main places of interest, and are especially useful for those sites that are hard to get to on

SPECIALIST TOUR OPERATORS

Cox and Kings, 45 Buckingham Gate, London SW1E 6AF (fax 0171/630 6038). *Upmarket travel company which offers tours of Guatemala, staying in luxury accommodation.*

Dragoman, 98 Camp Green, Debenham, Stowmarket, Suffolk IP14 6LA (☎01728/861133; fax 861127). *Overland camping expeditions through Central America.*

Encounter Overland, 267 Old Brompton Rd, London SW5 9JA (☎0171/370 6845; fax 0171 244 9737). *Overland truck/camping trips that visit some of Guatemala's more remote corners.*

Exodus, 9 Weir Rd, London SW12 OLT (☎0181/ 673 0859). *Adventure tour operators, taking small groups on a choice of specialist programmes including walking, biking, and overland treks.*

Explore Worldwide, 1 Frederick St, Aldershot GU11 1LQ (☎01252/344161). *A big range of small-group tours, treks and expeditions, with few supplements for single travellers, and an emphasis on small local hotels.*

Guerba Expeditions, Wessex House, 40 Station Rd, Westbury Wilts BA13 3J N (☎01373/826611; fax 858351). *Adventurous tours of Central America including sites in Guatemala.*

Journey Latin America, 14–16 Devonshire Rd, London W4 (☎0181/747 3108). *High-quality tours of Guatemala starting at £1400 for 21 days, as well as good value flights (see above).*

Nouvelles Frontières, 2–3 Woodstock St, London W1R 1HE (☎0171/629 7772). *Runs several tours of Guatemala, with varying degrees of luxury, which depart from points all over Europe.*

Sunvil Discovery, Sunvil House, Upper Square, Old Isleworth, Middlesex TW7 7BJ (☎0181/232 9797). *Offers high-quality tailor-made holidays to various regions of Guatemala.*

Trips, 9 Byron Place, Clifton, Bristol BS8 1JT (☎0117/987 2626; fax 987 2627). *A number of tailor-made itineraries in Latin America, includ-*

your own. See the relevant section in the Guide for details of recommended local companies.

GETTING THERE FROM IRELAND

No airline offers direct **flights from Ireland** to Guatemala. The cheapest way to get there is to take one of the numerous daily flights from Dublin or Belfast to London and then connect with one of the transatlantic flights detailed in the previous section. A return ticket is likely to cost around I£600 in total. From Dublin the other option is to fly direct with Aer Lingus to New York and pick up an onwards flight from there (see p.3). To sort out the various possibilities, contact a reliable travel agent, such as USIT.

TRAVEL AGENTS IN IRELAND

Joe Walsh Tours, 34 Grafton St, Dublin 2 (☎01/676 0991); 69 Upper O'Connell St, Dublin 2 (☎01/872 2555); 8–11 Baggot St Dublin 2 (☎01/676 3053); 117 St Patrick St Cork (☎021/277959) *General budget fares agent, who can arrange flights to Guatemala.*

Maxwell's Travel, D'Olier Chambers, 1 Hawkins St, Dublin 2 (☎01/677 9479; fax 679 3948). *Travel agent offering good deals on flights to Central America.*

Thomas Cook, 11 Donegall Place, Belfast (☎01232/24 23 41); 118 Grafton St, Dublin 2 (☎01/677 1721). *Package holiday and flight agent, with occasional discount offers.*

Trailfinders, 4–5 Dawson St Dublin 2 (☎01/ 677 7666). *Competitive fares out of all Irish airports, as well as deals on hotels, insurance, tours and car rental worldwide.*

USIT, Fountain Centre, College St, Belfast BT1 6ET (☎01232/324073); 10–11 Market Parade, Patrick St, Cork (☎021/270900); 33 Ferryquay St, Derry (☎01504/371888); Aston Quay, Dublin 2 (☎01/6021700); Victoria Place, Eyre Square, Galway (☎091/565177); Central Buildings, O'Connell St, Limerick (☎061/415064); 36–37 Georges St, Waterford (☎051/872601). *Student and youth specialists for flights and train travel.*

World Travel Centre, 35 Pearse St, Dublin 2 (☎01/ 671 7155). *Offers a range of competitively priced flights and holidays.*

AIRLINES IN IRELAND

Aer Lingus
Northern Ireland ☎0645 737747;
Dublin ☎01/705 3333;
Cork ☎021/327155;
Limerick ☎061/474239.
Aeroflot Dublin Airport ☎01/8446166.

British Airways
Belfast ☎0345/222111;
Dublin ☎1800/626747.

British Midland
Belfast ☎0345/554554;
Dublin ☎01/283 8833.
Delta Airlines
Belfast ☎01232/480 526;
Dublin ☎01/676 8080, or ☎1800/768 080.
Iberia Dublin ☎01/677 9846
Ryanair Dublin ☎01/609 7800.
Virgin Atlantic Dublin ☎01/873 3388.

GETTING THERE FROM AUSTRALIA & NEW ZEALAND

There are no direct flights from Australia or New Zealand to Guatemala, so your best bet is to fly to either Los Angeles or Mexico City, with an add-on to Guatemala City. For most airlines, low season is from mid-January to the end of February and October to the end of November, high season is mid-May to the end of August and December to mid-January, and the rest of the year is shoulder season. However, airfares don't vary a huge amount throughout the year, with seasonal differences only working out at about A/NZ$200–300. Fares to Los Angeles and Mexico City are common-rated, while the price you'll pay for the onward fare to Guatemala City varies according to the time

of year (see below). Note that seat availability on flights out of Australia and New Zealand is often limited, particularly in high season, so if you can, book several weeks ahead.

The cheapest fares **from Australia** are on flights which go the long-winded route via Asia. Currently, JAL flies from Sydney, Brisbane and Cairns to Los Angeles and Mexico City, with an overnight stop in Tokyo (included in the fare) from A$1550 in low season, while Garuda flights to Los Angeles, via either Jakarta or Denpasar, and Philippine Airlines, via Manila, both start at around A$1750 in low season. If you don't want to spend the night, Cathay Pacific and Singapore Airlines can get you to Los Angeles from A$1880 (low season), via their home cities of Hong Kong and Singapore respectively. However, for the same price, you can fly direct to Los Angeles on Qantas, Air New Zealand (via Auckland) or United Airlines. All three also offer stopovers in Honolulu, Fiji, Tonga or Papeete, while Air Pacific costs around the same and includes a stopover in Fiji. The above fares are all from east coast cities – on the Pacific route, expect to pay around A$400 more from Perth, and $200 less, on flights via Asia.

From New Zealand, again, the cheapest flight is on JAL via Tokyo, at NZ$1850 in low season and NZ$2250 in high season. Singapore Airlines also offers a good connecting service via Singapore to LA and San Francisco for NZ$2099 in low season to NZ$2499 in high season. However,

AIRLINES

Air Pacific Australia ☎02/9957 0150 & 1800/230 150; New Zealand ☎09/379 2404. *Weekly to LA from Sydney, Melbourne, Brisbane and major New Zealand cities via Nadi in Fiji.*

Air New Zealand Australia ☎13 2476; New Zealand ☎09/357 3000 *Daily from Sydney, Brisbane, Melbourne, Adelaide and Auckland to LA, either direct or via Honolulu/Tonga/Fiji/Papeete.*

Cathay Pacific Australia ☎13 1747; New Zealand ☎09/379 0861*Several flights a week to LA from Sydney, Brisbane and Cairns via Hong Kong.*

Garuda Australia ☎02/9334 9944 & 1800/800 873; New Zealand ☎09/366 1855*Several flights a week to LA from major Australian and New Zealand cities with a stopover in Denpasar or Jakarta.*

JAL Australia ☎02/9272 1111; New Zealand ☎09/379 9906*Several flights a week from* Sydney, Brisbane, Cairns and Auckland to LA and Mexico City via Tokyo.

Philippine Airlines Australia ☎02/9262 3333; No NZ office*Several flights a week to LA from Sydney, Melbourne and Brisbane via Manila.*

Qantas Australia ☎13 1211; New Zealand ☎09/357 8900 & 0800/808 767*Daily to LA from major Australian cities either non-stop or via Honolulu, and daily from Auckland via Sydney.*

Singapore Airlines Australia ☎13 1011; New Zealand ☎09/379 3209*Twice a week to LA from major Australian cities, and once a week from Auckland, via Singapore.*

United Airlines Australia ☎13 1777; New Zealand ☎09/379 3800 *Daily to LA and San Francisco from Sydney, Melbourne and Auckland either direct or via Honolulu.*

DISCOUNT AGENTS

Anywhere Travel, 345 Anzac Parade, Kingsford, Sydney (☎02/9663 0411).

Brisbane Discount Travel, 260 Queen St, Brisbane (☎07/3229 9211).

Budget Travel, 16 Fort St, Auckland, plus branches around the city (☎09/366 0061 & 0800/808 040).

Destinations Unlimited, 3 Milford Rd, Auckland (☎09/373 4033).

Flight Centres 82 Elizabeth St, Sydney (☎13 1600); 205 Queen St, Auckland (☎09/309 6171), plus branches throughout Australia and New Zealand.

Northern Gateway, 22 Cavenagh St, Darwin (☎08/8941 1394).

STA Travel, 702 Harris St, Ultimo, Sydney; 256 Flinders St, Melbourne; other offices in state capitals and major universities (nearest branch ☎13 1776; telesales ☎1300/360 960); 10 High St, Auckland, plus branches in Wellington, Christchurch, Dunedin, Palmerston North, Hamilton and at major universities (☎09/309 0458; telesales ☎09/366 6673). Web site: *www.statravelaus.com.au*; email: *traveller@sta-travelaus.com.au.*

Thomas Cook, 175 Pitt St, Sydney; 257 Collins St, Melbourne, plus branches in other state capitals (local branch ☎13 1771; telesales ☎1800/063 913); 96 Anzac Ave, Auckland (☎09/379 3920).

Tymtro Travel, Level 8, 130 Pitt St, Sydney (☎02/9223 2211 & 1300 652 969).

SPECIALIST AGENTS

Adventure Associates, 197 Oxford St, Bondi Junction (☎02/9389 7466 or 1800 222 141). *Two-to twelve-day jungle, archeological and cultural tours from Guatemala City.*

Adventure Specialists, 69 Liverpool St, Sydney (☎02/261 2927). *Offers a variety of adventure travel options.*

Adventure World, 73 Walker St, N Sydney (☎02/956 7766) with branches in Perth and Auckland. *Short tours to Tikal and Chichicastenango from Guatemala City.*

Contours, 466 Victoria St, N Melbourne (☎03/9329 5211). *Offers a range of cultural and archeological tours.*

Peregrine Adventures, 258 Lonsdale St, Melbourne (☎03/9663 8611), plus offices in Brisbane, Sydney, Adelaide and Perth. *Extended overland/sea adventures through Guatemala, Belize and southern Mexico, and one-week intensive Spanish courses at schools in Quetzaltenango.*

Pride Travel, 254 Bay St, Brighton, Melbourne (☎03/9596 3566 & 1800/061 427). *Gay and Lesbian specialist tour agents offering trips to Guatemala.*

for the same price you can take the much quicker Air New Zealand flight, either non-stop or via Honolulu, Fiji, Tonga or Papeete, or United Airlines, also non-stop or via Honolulu. Fares on Air Pacific, via Fiji, and Qantas, via Sydney, start at around NZ$2150. All the above fares are from Auckland – expect to pay an extra NZ$150 for Christchurch and Wellington departures.

For the add-on fare **from Mexico City to Guatemala City**, which can be bought in conjunction with your main ticket, expect to pay from around A$560/NZ$600 in low season for a restricted, non-refundable, thirty-day Apex fare, to A$1010/NZ$1100 (low season) for a fully refundable economy ticket. From **Los Angeles to Guatemala City**, American Airlines offers a year-round flat-rate fare of A$780/NZ$835, so if you're travelling in high season you may find it cheaper to fly via LA. See Getting There from North America (p.3) for further details of onward travel. Travel agents are usually your best bet for the cheapest fares and also have the latest information on limited special offers – Flight Centres and STA (which give reductions for ISIC card holders and under-26s) offer some of the best deals.

Few **round-the-world tickets** include Guatemala, though with some of the more flexible tickets, such as Cathay Pacific/UA's "Globetrotter", or Air New Zealand/KLM/Northwest's "World Navigator", you can pay a little extra and add it on as a side trip. Both these tickets include open-jaw travel, limited backtracking, side trips, and six stopovers worldwide (with additional stopovers at A$100/NZ$120 each) for A$2699/NZ$3189– A$3299/NZ$3699.

VISAS AND ENTRY REQUIREMENTS

Citizens of the European Union, the USA, Canada, Japan, Switzerland, Norway, Mexico, Israel, Brazil, Australia, New Zealand and all Central American countries do not need a visa, only a valid passport to enter Guatemala. When you arrive at Immigration you may be asked how long you plan to stay, and offered thirty, sixty or ninety days. There is no charge to enter Guatemala, though at the more remote border posts the official may ask for a small sum of money, which is destined straight for his back pocket.

In addition to a valid passport, citizens of some countries – including the Czech Republic, Poland, South Africa and most of the Gulf States – can enter the country with a **tourist card**, if they arrive by air. These are available at the airport, are valid for up to ninety days, and cost $5. If arriving overland, they will need a **visa** ($10). Citizens from other countries including most of Africa and Asia will need visas, wherever they arrive. These must be bought in advance and may take up to a month to process from a Guatemalan consulate.

If you want to extend your visit up to ninety days, you can go to the Immigration department (**Migración**) in Guatemala City (41 C and 17 Av, Zona 8). The process can take a full day, so get there in the morning. You may prefer to use the services of a *tramitador:* an agency that, for a fee, will deal with the red tape for you. Check the *Revue* (see p.29) and noticeboards in Antigua or the capital. Staying any longer than three months is extremely problematic and requires proof of funds as well as a Guatemalan sponsor – most people simply leave the country for 72 hours and enter on a new visa.

GUATEMALAN EMBASSIES AND CONSULATES ABROAD

Australia and New Zealand no representative; contact embassy in Japan.

Belgium Boulevard General Wakis 53, 1030 Brussels (☎02/736 0340; fax 736 61889).

Belize 1 St John St (☎02/33314 and 33150; fax 02/35140).

Canada 130 Albert St, Suite 1010, Ottawa, Ontario KIP 5G4 (☎613/233 7237; fax 2330135).

Japan 38 Kowa Building, Room 905, Nishi-Azabu 412–24, Minato-Ku, Tokyo 106 (☎03/3800-1830; fax 3400-1820).

Mexico Embassy: Av Explanada 1025, Lomas de Chapultepec 11000, Mexico D.F. 4 (☎05/540 7520; fax 202 1142).

Consulates: C Héroes de Chapultepec 354, Chetumal Q.R. (☎983-28585); 2 Av Poniente Norte No. 28, Comitán, Chiapas (☎963-22669; 2 C Oriente 33, Tapachula, Chiapas (☎962-61252).

Netherlands 2E Beukelaan 3, Apeldoorn 7313 (☎55/557421).

South Africa 54 Greenmarket Square, 5th floor Shortmarket St, Cape Town, 8001 (☎21/225786; fax 21/418-1280).

Sweden Wittstockgatan 30, 11527 Stockholm (☎08/660 5229; fax 08/660 4229).

UK 13 Fawcett St, London SW10 9HN (☎0171/351 3042; fax 376 5708).

USA Embassy: 2220 R St NW, Washington DC 20008 (☎202/745-4952; fax 745-1098).

Consulates: 180 N Michigan Ave, Chicago, IL 60601 (☎312/332-1587); 9700 Richmond Ave, Suite 218, Houston, TX 77042 (☎713/953-9531); 2975 Wilshire Blvd, Suite 101, Los Angeles, CA 90010 (☎213/365-9251); 300 Sevilla Ave, Oficina 210, Coral Gables, Miami, FL 33134 (☎305/443-4828); 57 Park Ave, New York, NY 10016 (☎212/686-3837); 10405 San Diego Mission Rd, Suite 205, San Diego, CA 92108 (☎415/282-8127).

Arriving in Guatemala you must go through immigration (*Migración*) and customs (*aduana*), where your passport is stamped. After this you should keep your passport with you at all times, or at least carry a photocopy, as you may be asked to show it.

COSTS AND MONEY

By European or North American standards the cost of living in Guatemala is low, and by Latin American standards the currency, the quetzal, is surprisingly stable. However, fluctuations can and do take place, so we have quoted most prices in the guide in US dollars. The US dollar is the only foreign currency that is accepted throughout the country. Only when the amount is very small or there's a set fee in quetzals – for example, for entrance to minor museums or sites – have we quoted the local currency. Travellers' cheques are the safest way to carry your money, but it's also a good idea to have some dollars in cash, in case you run short of local currency a long way from the nearest bank.

PRICES

Under any circumstances, life in Guatemala is cheaper than in North America and Europe, though of course, what you spend will depend on where, when and how you choose to travel. Peak **tourist seasons**, such as Christmas and Holy Week, tend to push up hotel prices, while certain towns, most notably Guatemala City and the tourist centres of Antigua and Panajachel, are always more expensive. The extremely frugal may be able to get by on around $80 a week. However, by allowing yourself the odd luxury, you can expect to spend around $100 per person per week if you're travelling as a couple, while solo travellers should reckon on $140 a week. On the other hand, for $25 a day you can expect to live well.

The following prices should give you a rough idea of what you might end up paying. Basic **rooms** cost anything from $1.50 to $8 for a single, $3 to $10 double, while you can pay up to $200 a night for a double room in the most luxurious establishments. **Food** prices don't vary quite as much as you might expect; eating a filling meal in a simple *comedor* will cost around $2 anywhere in the country, while in a smarter restaurant you can expect to pay about double that. Anything that is imported will be expensive, so if you have a taste for fancy cheeses, wine or ice cream you'll have to pay for your treats. Fresh produce from the market is very good value – although to get anywhere near the price that locals pay you'll have to bargain in Spanish. Check the fixed-price goods in supermarkets first.

A bottle of Guatemalan **beer** costs a little over $1 in most bars, and half that in a supermarket. Local fire-water, such as the ubiquitous *Quezalteca*, is a lot cheaper, and Guatemalan rum starts at around $3 a bottle. **Cigarettes** cost $1 a pack for local brands, and $1.40 for North American imports; **cigar** smokers will be pleased to find Honduran cigars at bargain rates. If you roll your own, bring a supply of cigarette papers as they are expensive and difficult to obtain in Guatemala.

Travel is probably the greatest bargain, providing you stick to the buses, which charge around 50¢ an hour, although prices vary a little throughout the country. Pullman buses charge up to double this rate. Travelling by car is expensive, and the cost of **renting a car** is higher in Guatemala than it is in the USA, as is the cost of fuel – although both are still cheaper than in Europe.

Generally anything produced in Central America is cheap, anything imported expensive. This applies to most tinned food, American clothing – although plenty of imitations are produced

inside Guatemala – and high-tech goods such as cameras, film and radios. *Caterpillar* boots, made in El Salvador, are about half the price they are in Europe. Almost everything is available at a price, from French wine to canned baby food. A **student card** is not very useful but may occasionally come in handy as a bargaining tool.

CURRENCY

The **quetzal**, named after the endangered, sacred bird, has been one of the most stable currencies in Latin America over the last two decades, defying the nation's inherent instability. A quetzal is divided into 100 centavos. Bank notes come in denominations of Q0.50, Q1, Q5, Q10, Q20, Q50, and Q100. One quetzal is often called simply a *billete* (bill) or *sencillo* (single). Coins include 1, 5, 10 and 25 centavos; the latter is sometimes called a *choco* or *choca*.

At the time of writing the **exchange rate** stands at just over Q6 to $1. Cash and travellers' cheques can be changed easily at banks in the main towns – most are fairly efficient, though you may have to wait for ten minutes or so while they shuffle a few papers. There's a **black market** centred around the main post office in Guatemala City, where street traders will approach you to change money. The rates they offer, however, are only a little better than the banks, so, unless you have a few spare Honduran *lempiras* or Mexican *pesos* to get rid of, you may not find it worth the hassle.

The **US dollar** is the only currency worth bringing with you, though you can change a number of other currencies at the Banco del Quetzal in the Guatemala City airport. There are a few scattered branches of Lloyds Bank in Guatemala (Antigua, Puerto Barrios, Guatemala City and Esquintla) who should accept sterling. If you end up with an abundance of quetzals, you can change them into dollars at the Banco del Quetzal, at either Guatemala City or Flores airports.

CREDIT CARDS, TRAVELLERS' CHEQUES AND MONEY PROBLEMS

Credit cards are fairly widely accepted in Guatemala, except in really small hotels or simple restaurants. You can also use them to get cash, though you'll need travellers' cheques or US$ cash when crossing land borders. Of the credit cards **Visa** is by far the most effective, and will

USEFUL CREDIT CARD NUMBERS

If your credit card is stolen call these collect call numbers to have it cancelled

American Express	☎919/333-3211
Diner's	☎303/790-2433
Discover	☎801/568-0205
Mastercard	☎314/275-6100
Visa	☎703/827-8400

get you money from all Banco Industrial ATMs throughout Guatemala. With **Mastercard** you can get cash from branches of Banco G&T, though as they have few ATMs, this is less useful. **American Express** is not so widely accepted.

Travellers' cheques are a safe way to bring money, as they offer the added security of a refund if they're stolen. To facilitate this you want to make sure that you have cheques issued by one of the big names, which are also more readily accepted. Thomas Cook, with offices at Unitours SA, 7 Av 7–91, Zona 4, Guatemala City (☎3341003), or American Express, Av La Reforma, 9–00, Zona 10, Guatemala City (☎3311311) are probably the most widely recognized. **Personal cheques** are useless in Guatemala.

If you manage to run out of money altogether, then it's not too hard to get someone back home to send money, and in a real emergency you just might persuade your embassy to lend you some. Having **money wired** from home is never convenient or cheap, and should be considered a last resort. Funds can be sent via Western Union (US and Canada ☎1-800/325-6000; UK ☎0800/833

833; Australia ☎1800/649 565; New Zealand ☎09/302 0143; local representative Banco del Agro) or American Express MoneyGram (US and Canada ☎1-800/929-9400; UK ☎0800/894887; Australia ☎1800/230 100; New Zealand ☎0800/262 263; local representative Banco del Café). Both companies' fees depend on the destination and the amount being transferred, and the funds should be available for collection at Amex's or Western Union's local office within minutes of being sent. It's also possible to have money wired directly from a bank in your home country to a bank in Guatemala and Belize, although this is somewhat less reliable because it involves two separate institutions, and can take anywhere between a couple of days and several months. If you go this route, the person wiring the funds to you will need to know the routing number of the bank the funds are being wired to.

TAX

A value added tax of ten percent is levied on all goods and services sold in **Guatemala**, other than market goods – you'll see it marked on bills as I.V.A. All **hotel bills** are subject to twenty percent tax (ten percent IVA, and ten percent to Inguat) though only mid-range and expensive hotels consistently add this. All hotel price codes in the Guide include this tax.

When leaving Guatemala by air you have to pay a **$25 exit tax**, payable in US$ or quetzals. At land borders the official charge is $1, though you may be asked for Q10.

HEALTH

There are no obligatory inoculations to visit Guatemala, but there are several that you should have anyway. Always check with a doctor or travel clinic (see box on p.16) before you set off.

The most important precaution is to make sure you're up to date with your **polio, tetanus** and **typhoid** vaccinations. Gamma-globulin, which protects against **Hepatitis A**, is also recommended, although the effect wears off after about two months. If you plan to stay longer, you should arrange for a booster, or invest in the more costly *Havrix* injections – two jabs (the second two to four weeks after the first) gives a year's protection, a third jab after six months gives five years' protection. If you're planning to spend a long time in rural areas of Guatemala, you may want to think about having a **Hepatitis B** jab. There is currently no significant risk of contracting **cholera** in Guatemala, though children should be immunized against **TB**. Another consideration is

to have a preventative jab against **rabies**, though the risks of contracting the virus in Guatemala are extremely low – if you are bitten by a rabid animal, wash the wound immediately with soap and water or alcohol, and start immunization shots as soon as possible. Finally, if you're arriving from a country where **yellow fever** is endemic, you'll need a vaccination certificate (only available from specialist centres).

Many parts of the country (the highlands, Lake Atitlán, Antigua, Chichicastenango, and the capital) are at high altitude, where there is little risk of **malaria**. However, on the Pacific coast, and in the rainforests of Petén, or other lowland areas, there is a moderate risk of contracting the benign form of the disease, so you may want to take malaria pills. Two weekly Chloroquine tablets are sufficient, and you have to take them for at least a week before you arrive and for another month after you leave the country. Alternatively, you could take Larium (Mefloquine), though some

WATER PURIFICATION

Contaminated water is a major cause of sickness in Guatemala, and even if it looks clean, all drinking water should be regarded with caution. That said, however, it is also essential to increase fluid intake to prevent dehydration. Bottled water is widely available, but always check that the seal is intact.

If you plan to venture off the beaten track, you'll need an appropriate method of treating water, whether your source is tap water or natural groundwater such as a river or stream. **Boiling** it for a minimum of ten minutes (longer at higher altitudes) is sufficient to kill micro-organisms, but is not always practical and does not remove unpleasant tastes.

Chemical sterilization is cheap and convenient, but dirty water remains dirty, and still contains organic matter and other contamination. You can sterilize using chlorine or iodine tablets, but these leave a nasty after-taste (which can be masked with lemon or lime juice) and are not effective in preventing such diseases as amoebic dysentery or giardia. Tincture of iodine is better; add a couple of drops to one litre of water and leave to stand for twenty minutes. Pregnant women, babies and people with thyroid problems should avoid using iodine-based products.

Water filters remove visible impurities and larger pathogenic organisms (most bacteria and cysts). The Swiss-made *Katadyn* filter is expensive but extremely useful (available from outdoor equipment stores, or direct from *Water Works on Wheels*, Oughterard, Co. Galway, Ireland; ☎353/918 2479). However, bear in mind that however fine the filter, it cannot remove viruses, all dissolved chemicals, pesticides and the like. **Purification**, a two-stage process involving filtration and sterilization, gives the most complete treatment. Portable purifiers range from pocket-size units weighing 60g up to 800g. Some of the best water purifiers on the market are made in Britain by *Pre-Mac*, and are available from the British Airways shop on Regent Street (see below), or contact *Pre Mac* (☎01732/460333; fax 460222) for details of local stockists and specialist advice. In North America, contact *Outbound Products*, 1580 Zephyr Ave, Box 56148, Hayward, CA 94545-6148 (☎1-800/663-9262); or 8585 Fraser St, Vancouver, BC V5X 3Y1 (☎604/321-5464). In Ireland, try *All Water Systems Ltd*, Unit 12, Western Parkway Business Centre, Lower Ballymount Road, Dublin 12 (☎01/456 4933).

MEDICAL RESOURCES FOR TRAVELLERS

USA AND CANADA

Canadian Society for International Health, 170 Laurier Ave W, Suite 902, Ottawa, ON K1P 5V5 (☎613/230-2654). *Distributes a free pamphlet, "Health Information for Canadian Travellers".*

Centers for Disease Control, 1600 Clifton Rd NE, Atlanta, GA 30333 (☎404/639-3311; Web site: *www.cdc.gov/travel/travel.html*). *Publishes outbreak warnings, suggested inoculations, precautions and other background information for travellers. Web site is very useful.*

Travel Medicine, 351 Pleasant St, Suite 312, Northampton, MA 01060 (☎1-800/872-8633). *Sells first-aid kits, mosquito netting, water filters and other health-related travel products.*

Travelers Medical Center, 31 Washington Square, New York, NY 10011 (☎212/982-1600). *Consultation service on immunizations and treatment of diseases.*

UK AND IRELAND

British Airways Travel Clinic, 156 Regent St, London W1 (Mon–Fri 9.30am–5.15pm, Sat 10am–4pm; ☎0171/439 9584), no appointment necessary. A walk-in service is also offered at the clinic within Flightbookers, at 177 Tottenham Court Rd, London W1P 0LX (Mon–Fri 9.30am–6.30pm, Sat 10am–2pm; ☎0171/757 2504), though appointments are available at both. There are appointment-only branches at 101 Cheapside, London EC2 (Mon–Fri 9–11.45am & 12.15–4.45pm; ☎0171/606 2977); and at the BA terminal in London's Victoria Station (8.15–11.45am & 12.30–4pm; ☎0171/233 6661). BA also operates around forty regional clinics throughout the country (call ☎0171/831 5333 for the one nearest to you), plus airport locations at Gatwick and Heathrow. *Inoculations, travel associated accessories, including mosquito nets and first-aid kits. Charges start at £8 for the basic injections to £20 and up for the more exotic ones.*

Hospital for Tropical Diseases, St Pancras Hospital, 4 St Pancras Way, London NW1 0PE (☎0171/388 9600). *Travel clinic and recorded message service (☎0839/337733; 49p per min) which gives hints on hygiene and illness prevention as well as listing appropriate immunizations.*

MASTA (Medical Advisory Service for Travellers Abroad), London School of Hygiene and Tropical Medicine. *Operates a pre-recorded 24-hour Travellers' Health Line (☎0891/224100; 50p per min), giving written information tailored to your journey by return of post.*

Travel Medicine Services, P.O. Box 254, 16 College St, Belfast 1 (☎01232/315220; Mon–Fri 9am–4.30pm).

Tropical Medical Bureau, Grafton St Medical Centre, Dublin 2 (☎01/671 9200); and Dun Laoghaire Medical Centre, 5 Northumberland Ave, Dun Laoghaire, Co. Dublin (☎01/280 4996).

AUSTRALIA AND NEW ZEALAND

Auckland Hospital, Park Rd, Grafton (☎09/379 7440).

Travel-Bug Medical and Vaccination Centre, 161 Ward St, N Adelaide (☎08/8267 3544).

Travel Health and Vaccination Clinic, 114 Williams St, Melbourne (☎03/9670 3871).

Travellers' Medical and Vaccination Centre, 7/428 George St, Sydney (☎02/9221 7133); 3/393 Little Bourke St, Melbourne (☎03/9602 5788); 6/29 Gilbert Place, Adelaide (☎08/8212 7522); 6/247 Adelaide St, Brisbane (☎07/3221 9066); 1 Mill St, Perth (☎08/9321 1977). Web site: *www.tmvc.com.au*

Travellers Immunization Service, 303 Pacific Hwy, Sydney (☎02/9416 1348).

---

people experience side effects of depression, disorientation and sleep disturbance – try the drug out before you depart to see if it agrees with you. If you suspect you may have malaria – symptoms include fever of 38°C or above, chills, jaundice and severe headaches – medical help must be sought. If you're days from the nearest clinic or doctor, take 600mg of quinine sulphate three times daily for a minimum of three days followed by three Fansidar tablets taken as a single dose. Another mosquito-carried disease, **dengue fever**, is on the increase in Central America, particularly in lowland rural areas during the rainy season, though it is not widespread in Guatemala. It is carried by a daytime-biting mosquito, and symptoms include high fever, severe headache, extreme pain in bones and joints, and usually a skin rash. There is no treatment for dengue fever,

USEFUL ADDRESSES FOR DISABLED TRAVELLERS

US AND CANADA

Mobility International USA, PO Box 10767, Eugene, OR 97440 (Voice and TDD: ☎541/343-1284). *Information and referral services, access guides, tours and exchange programs. Annual membership $25 (includes quarterly newsletter).*

Society for the Advancement of Travel for the Handicapped (SATH), 347 5th Ave, Suite 610, New York, NY 10016 (☎212/447-7284; www.sittravel.com). *Non-profit travel-industry referral service that passes queries on to its members as appropriate; allow plenty of time for a response.*

Travel Information Service (☎215/456-9600). *Telephone information and referral service.*

Directions Unlimited, 720 N Bedford Rd, Bedford Hills, NY 10507 (☎914/241-1700). *Travel agency specializing in custom-made tours for people with disabilities.*

UK AND IRELAND

Disability Action Group, 2 Annadale Ave, Belfast BT7 3JH (☎01232/491 011). *Provides useful information about access for disabled travellers abroad.*

Holiday Care Service, 2nd floor, Imperial Building, Victoria Rd, Horley, Surrey RH6 7PZ (☎01293/774535; fax 784647; Minicom ☎01293/776943). *Provides free lists of accessible accommodation abroad and information on financial help for holidays.*

RADAR (Royal Association for Disability and Rehabilitation), 12 City Forum, 250 City Rd, London EC1V 8AF (☎0171/250 3222; Minicom ☎0171/250 4119). *A good source of advice on holidays and travel abroad.*

Tripscope, The Courtyard, Evelyn Rd, London W4 5JL (☎0181/994 9294, fax 994 3618). *A registered charity providing a national telephone information service offering free advice on transport and travel for those with a mobility problem.*

AUSTRALIA AND NEW ZEALAND

ACROD (Australian Council for Rehabilitation of the Disabled), PO Box 60, Curtin, ACT 2605 (☎02/6282 4333).

Disabled Persons Assembly, 173–175 Victoria St, Wellington (☎04/811 9100).

---

though the risk of contracting the serious strain is very slim, and normally people shake off the unpleasant side effects after about a week. Obviously, the best solution is to **avoid getting bitten by insects** altogether: cover up arms and legs, use insect repellent containing a high percentage of *Deet*, consider buying a mosquito net if you plan to camp or sleep in a hammock and burn mosquito coils containing pyrethrum (available everywhere).

All this notwithstanding, travelling around Guatemala is generally pretty safe, and the worst thing you are likely to contract is a dose of **diarrhoea**. For most people it's a relatively minor inconvenience, whose effects can be minimized by taking simple precautions, such as eating from clean-looking restaurants and drinking bottled or boiled water (ask for *agua purificada*). If you do get struck down, standard remedies may have some effect, but the best cure is the simplest one: take it easy for a day or two, drink lots of bottled water, and eat only the blandest of foods – papaya is good for soothing the stomach and is also crammed with vitamins. Only if the symptoms last more than four or five days do you need to worry.

More serious is **amoebic dysentery**, which is also endemic in many parts of the region, including Lake Atitlán. The symptoms are more or less the same as a bad dose of diarrhoea but include bleeding. On the whole, a course of *flagyl* (metronidazole or tinidozole) will cure it; if you plan to visit Guatemala's more far-flung corners then it's worth getting hold of some of these, and some advice on their usage, from a doctor before you go.

To avoid the worst stomach problems it's advisable to exercise a degree of caution, particularly during the first week or so, when your system is still adjusting. You should be especially careful with **water**: see the box above. **The sun** can also be a cause of illness, and a high-factor sun cream is vital. Creams are readily available in chemists in Antigua and Guatemala City and cost much less than they do in Europe, and about the same as in North America.

PHARMACIES, DOCTORS AND HOSPITALS

Local pharmacists can sell drugs that in Europe are available only on prescription, but you may not get correct instructions on dosage and the like. For simple medical problems head for the *farmacía*, where you'll find some common brand names and reasonably knowledgeable advice.

If you need the services of a **doctor**, you'll find that many of them were trained in the US and speak good English. Your **embassy** will always have a list of recommended doctors, and some are included in our "Listings" for the main towns. If you have insurance (and it would be madness not to) it's probably better to go to a **private hospital**; Guatemala City and Quetzaltenango have good ones. Even the smallest of villages has a **centro de salud** or *puesto de salud* (health centre) where health care is free, although you can't rely on finding an English-speaking doctor.

If you suspect something is amiss with your insides, it might be worth heading straight for the local **pathology lab** (all the main towns have them), as they can generally detect what's causing your symptoms. In many cases it's better to go to a lab before seeing a doctor, as the doctor will probably send you anyway.

INSURANCE

Medical insurance is a must in Guatemala, as public health care is very basic, and private hospitals are expensive.

You may, however, find that your **bank** or **credit card** (particularly *American Express*) includes a certain level of medical or other insurance, especially if you use it to pay for your trip. This cover can be quite comprehensive, anticipating anything from lost or stolen baggage and missed connections to charter companies going bankrupt; however, certain policies (notably in North America) only cover medical costs.

If you plan to participate in **water sports**, you'll probably have to pay an extra premium; check carefully that any policy you are considering will cover you in case of an accident. Note also that very few insurers will arrange on-the-spot payments in the event of a major expense or loss; you will usually be **reimbursed** only after going home. In all cases of loss or theft of goods, you will have to contact the local police to have a **report** made out so that your insurer can process the claim.

NORTH AMERICAN COVER

Before buying an insurance policy, check that you're not already covered. **Canadian provincial health plans** typically provide some overseas medical coverage, although they are unlikely to pick up the full tab in the event of a mishap. Holders of official **student/teacher/youth cards** are entitled to accident coverage and hospital in-patient benefits – the annual membership is far less than the cost of comparable insurance. **Students** may also find that their student health coverage extends during the vacations and for one term beyond the date of last enrolment. **Homeowners' or renters'** insurance often covers theft or loss of documents, money and valuables while overseas.

After exhausting the possibilities above, you might want to contact a specialist **travel insurance** company; your travel agent can usually recommend one, or see the box below. **Policies** vary: some are comprehensive while others cover only certain risks (accidents, illnesses, delayed or lost luggage, cancelled flights, etc). In particular,

---

TRAVEL INSURANCE COMPANIES IN NORTH AMERICA

Access America ☎1-800/284-8300
Carefree Travel Insurance☎1-800/323-3149
Desjardins Travel Insurance (Canada only) ☎1-800/463-7830
International Student Insurance Service (ISIS), sold by *STA Travel* ☎1-800/777-0112.
Travel Assistance International ☎1-800/ 821-2828
Travel Guard ☎1-800/826-1300
Travel Insurance Services ☎1-800/937-1387

TRAVEL INSURANCE COMPANIES IN THE UK

Columbus Travel Insurance ☎0171/375 0011.
Endsleigh Insurance ☎0171/436 4451.
Liverpool Victoria & Friendly Society ☎01202/292333.
Marcus Hearn ☎0171/739 3444.

---

ask whether the policy pays medical costs up front or reimburses you later, and whether it provides for medical evacuation to your home country. For policies that include lost or stolen luggage, check exactly what is and isn't covered, and make sure the per-article limit will cover your most valuable possessions.

The best **premiums** are usually to be had through student/youth travel agencies – ISIS policies, for example, cost $60 for fifteen days; $110 for a month; $165 for two months; and $665 for a year. These prices do not include coverage for adventure sports of any kind, so if you are planning any underwater activities, make sure you get extra coverage.

Most North American travel policies apply only to items lost, stolen or damaged while in the custody of an identifiable, responsible third party – hotel porter, airline, luggage consignment, etc. Even in these cases you will have to contact the local police within a certain time limit.

COVER IN THE UK AND IRELAND

Comprehensive travel insurance schemes are sold by almost every travel agent (many will offer insurance when you book your flight or holiday) or bank, and by specialist insurance companies. Both Campus Travel and STA offer good policies (see p.7), or you can try any of the companies listed below. If you travel abroad frequently, you may find an annual policy works out to be the best value – Columbus offers annual multi-trip coverage (sixty days maximum per trip) for £90, Endsleigh's annual worldwide policy costs around £81, but is subject to a maximum of 35 days per trip, while cheaper still is the Liverpool Victoria & Friendly Society's worldwide one-year cover for

around £74, with a maximum trip length of ninety days.

If you have a good "all risks" home insurance policy it may well cover your possessions against loss or theft even when overseas, and many private medical schemes also cover you when abroad – make sure you know the procedure and the helpline number.

In **Ireland**, travel insurance is best obtained through a travel specialist such as USIT (see p.8). Their policies cost £44 for six to ten days worldwide coverage and £63 for a month). Discounts are offered to students of any age and anyone under 35.

COVER IN AUSTRALIA AND NEW ZEALAND

You can get **travel insurance** in Australia and New Zealand from most travel agents, some banks, or direct from insurance companies, and it's available for periods ranging from a few days to a year or even longer. All the standard policies are similar in premium and coverage, which includes medical expenses, loss of personal property and travellers' cheques, cancellations and delays, as well as most adventure sports. A standard policy giving coverage for Central America costs around A$100/NZ$120 for two weeks, A$170/NZ$200 for one month, and A$250/NZ$300 for two months.

If you plan to indulge in **high-risk activities** such as mountaineering, bungy-jumping or scuba diving, check the policy carefully to make sure you'll be covered – you may need to buy a tailor-made policy to suit your requirements.

TRAVEL INSURANCE COMPANIES IN AUSTRALIA AND NEW ZEALAND

Cover More ☎02/9202 8000 & 1800/251 881.
Ready Plan Melbourne ☎03/9791 5077 & 1800/337 462; Auckland ☎09/379 3208.

INFORMATION AND MAPS

Information about Guatemala is relatively easy to come by, both inside and outside the country. In addition to the tourist organizations listed below, you can try specialist travel agents (see "Getting There"), and the Internet where you'll find several very useful sites. You could even try the embassies (see p.12), though here you have to struggle to get any real help.

The Guatemalan tourist board, **Inguat**, at 7 Av 1–17, Centro Cívico, Guatemala City, is usually quite helpful if you want to write in advance, although communication will inevitably take a week or two. In addition to the office in Guatemala City, Inguat also has branches in Antigua, Quetzaltenango, Panajachel and Flores. Their information varies though generally the main office, Panajachel and Antigua branches are the most reliable.

For more contextual information in the UK, the **Maya-Guatemalan Indian Centre**, 94a Wandsworth Bridge Rd, London SW6 (☎0171/371 5291), is a useful resource, though they don't answer general travel/tourism queries. This cultural and educational centre allows access to its extensive reference library, video archive and textile collection, all for an annual membership fee of £5. There are also a number of ongoing free exhibitions on various aspects of indigenous life and crafts.

MAPS

The **best map of Guatemala** (1:500,000) is produced by International Travel Map Productions (PO Box 2290, Vancouver, BC, V6B 3W5, Canada), and is also available in the US and the UK. In

MAP OUTLETS

USA AND CANADA
Adventurous Traveler Bookstore, PO Box 1468, Williston, VT 05495 (☎1-800/282-3963).
The Complete Traveler Bookstore, 199 Madison Ave, New York, NY 10016 (☎212/685-9007); and 3207 Fillmore St, San Francisco, CA 92123 (☎415/923-1511).
Map Link Inc, 30 S La Petera Lane, Unit #5, Santa Barbara, CA 93117 (☎805/692-6777).
Open Air Books and Maps, 25 Toronto St, Toronto, ON M5R 2C1 (☎416/363-0719).
Phileas Fogg's Books & Maps, #87 Stanford Shopping Center, Palo Alto, CA 94304 (☎1-800/533-FOGG in California; ☎1-800/533-FOGG elsewhere in US).
Rand McNally, 444 N Michigan Ave, Chicago, IL 60611 (☎312/321-1751); 150 E 52nd St, New York, NY 10022 (☎212/758-7488); 595 Market St, San Francisco, CA 94105 ☎415/777-3131); and 1201 Connecticut Ave NW, Washington, DC 20003 (☎202/223-6751).
For other locations, or for maps by **mail order**, call ☎1-800/333-0136 (ext 2111).
Sierra Club Bookstore, 6014 College Ave, Oakland, CA 94618 (☎510/658-7470).
Travel Books & Language Center, 4931 Cordell Ave, Bethesda, MD 20814 (☎1-800/220-2665).
Traveler's Bookstore, 22 W 52nd St, New York, NY 10019 (☎212/664-0995).
World Wide Books and Maps, 736 Granville St, Vancouver, BC V6Z 1E4 (☎604/687-3320).

UK AND IRELAND
Daunt Books, 83 Marylebone High St, London W1 (☎0171/224 2295).

Easons Bookshop, 40 O'Connell St, Dublin 1 (☎01/873 3811).
Fred Hanna's Bookshop, 27–29 Nassau St, Dublin 2 (☎01/677 1255).
Hodges Figgis Bookshop, 56–58 Dawson St, Dublin 2 (☎01/677 4754).
John Smith and Sons, 57–61 St Vincent St, Glasgow G2 5TB (☎0141/221 7472).
The Map Shop, 30a Belvoir St, Leicester LE1 6QH (☎0116/2471400) Mail order available.
National Map Centre, 22–24 Caxton St, London SW1 (☎0171/222 4945).
Newcastle Map Centre, 55 Grey St, Newcastle-upon-Tyne NE1 6EF (☎0191/261 5622).
Stanfords, 12–14 Long Acre, London WC2 (☎0171/836 1321); 52 Grosvenor Gardens, London SW1W 0AG; 156 Regent St, London W1R 5TA; and 29 Corn St, Bristol BS1 1HT. For mail order maps, call the Long Acre branch.
The Travel Bookshop, 13–15 Blenheim Crescent, London W11 2EE (☎0171/229 5260).
Waterstone's, Queens Bldg, 8 Royal Ave, Belfast BT1 1DA (☎01232/247355).

AUSTRALIA AND NEW ZEALAND
Bowyangs, 372 Little Burke St, Melbourne (☎03/9670 4383).
The Map Shop, 16a Peel St, Adelaide (☎08/8231 2033).
Perth Map Centre, 891 Hay St, Perth (☎08/9322 5733).
Specialty Maps, 58 Albert St, Auckland (☎09/307 2217).
Travel Bookshop, Shop 3, 175 Liverpool St (☎02/9261 8200).

Guatemala, you can usually get a copy from Casa Andinista, 4 C Oriente 5A, Aptdo Postal 343, 03901 Antigua. Inguat also publishes a "tourist map" (1:1,000,000), which although now rather out of date, gives reasonable coverage of Guatemala (and Belize), with a detailed map of the central area and plans of all the main towns. It's sold for $1 at Inguat offices and some shops in Guatemala. Another reasonable map is the free-bie given away by the car rental outlet Hertz, though again it's out of date and many of the newer roads aren't featured.

The only **large-scale maps** of Guatemala (1:50,000) are produced by the Instituto Geográfico Militar, Av de las Americas 5-76, Zona 13, Guatemala City (Mon–Fri 8am–4pm). These cover the country in 250 sections and are accurately contoured, although some aspects are now out of date. You can consult these at the Instituto's offices, and most can be bought for around US$6 without special permission from the Ministry of Defence. A cheaper option, however, is to buy photocopies of most of them from the Casa Andinista in Antigua.

GETTING AROUND

With no trains in Guatemala and only the privileged few being able to afford cars, virtually everyone travels by bus. The buses may be ancient, uncomfortable, fume-filled and overcrowded, but they give you a unique opportunity to talk to ordinary Guatemalans, and by sticking to flights or the sanitized tourist shuttles, you'll be missing out on one of the country's most essential experiences. Buses ply the Pan-American Highway every half-hour or so – some of them quite fast and luxurious – but once you leave the central routes and head off on the byways, things are sure to slow down.

Upgrading the **road network** has been a priority for the present government, and the Pacific Highway is once again the country's fastest road. In addition, the highway to Petén has been tarmacked all the way to Flores, there is a new toll-motorway between Escuintla and Palín, the Caribbean Highway has been upgraded, and numerous smaller roads have been targeted for improvements. Despite these public works, Guatemala's road network is still alarmingly inadequate and you'll often find yourself stuck behind smoking trucks even on the main highways. Fortunately, whatever the pace of your journey, you always have the spectacular Guatemalan countryside outside to wonder at.

BY BUS

Buses are cheap, convenient and can be wildly entertaining. For the most part the service is extremely comprehensive, reaching even the smallest of villages, and the driver will usually stop to pick up passengers anywhere, regardless of how many people are already on board. Though in remote areas many buses leave in the dead of night and travel through the early hours to reach the morning markets, try to avoid travelling after dark, as the risk of robbery is much higher than during daylight hours.

There are two classes of bus. **Second-class** buses, known as *camionetas* to Guatemalans and "chicken buses" to foreigners, are the most common and are easily distinguished by their trademark clouds of thick black noxious fumes. They are open to all and cram their seats, aisles and occasionally even roofs with passengers. These are often old US school buses, their seats designed for the under-fives, so you're liable to have bruised knees after a day or two's travel. While travel by second-class bus may be uncomfortable and frustratingly slow, it is never dull, with chickens clucking, music assaulting your eardrums, and snack vendors touting for business.

Guatemala has hundreds of small bus companies, each determined to outdo the next in the garishness of the paint jobs of their vehicles. Almost all of them operate out of **bus terminals**, usually on the edge of town, and often adjacent to the market; between towns you can hail buses and they'll almost always stop for you. **Tickets** are bought on the bus, and whilst they are always very cheap, gringos do sometimes get ripped off – look and listen to what the locals are paying.

The so-called **pullman** is usually an old Greyhound bus, and is rated as first-class: each passenger will be sure of a seat to him- or herself, and tickets can be bought in advance. These "express" buses are about forty percent more expensive than the regular buses, but quicker, not only because the buses themselves are better, but also because they make fewer stops. Services vary tremendously, with some companies' buses being comfortable and pleasant, while other operators use decrepit buses with cracked windows and bald tyres, and pack in extra passengers standing in the aisles. However, all pullmans have two things in common – speed and, unlikely though it may seem, punctuality.

Pullmans usually leave from the offices of the bus company – addresses are listed in the text – and on the whole they serve only the main routes, connecting the capital with Quetzaltenango, Huehuetenango, the Mexican border, Esquipulas, Puerto Barrios, Cobán and San Salvador. This means that most long journeys can be done at least part of the way by pullman. Note that tickets are sometimes (always in Petén) collected by conductors at the end of the journey, so make sure you don't lose yours.

BY AIR

The **internal flight** you're most likely to take in Guatemala is from the capital to **Flores**. It costs a bargain $60 return and takes only 45 minutes (as opposed to some 12–14 hours on the bus), with five rival airlines offering daily flights. Their addresses and other details can be found in the Petén chapter; tickets can be bought from any travel agent in Guatemala City, Antigua, Quetzaltenango or Flores. There are also flights to Poptún and Playa Grande, and services from Flores and Guatemala City to Belize City, as well as charters to Cópan; again, details are given in the relevant chapters.

BY TRAIN

There are currently **no trains** at all running in Guatemala. Although a fifty-year concession has been granted to an American company, it is very unlikely that services will be resumed in the immediate future, not least because hundreds of people have now built homes alongside the old railway tracks.

BY CAR

On the whole, **driving** in Guatemala is pretty straightforward and it certainly offers unrivalled freedom – traffic is rarely heavy outside the capital, although local driving practices can be alarming at times.

Parking and security constitute the main problems, particularly in the cities where theft and vandalism are common. You should always put your car in a guarded car park – there are plenty in the centre of Guatemala City – or choose a hotel with protected parking space. Even budget hotels often have this facility, and there are appropriate recommendations in the Guide.

Most of the main routes are paved, but beyond this the roads are often extremely rough. **Filling stations** (*gasolineras*), too, are scarce once you venture away from the main roads: **fuel** is extremely cheap by European standards, though marginally more expensive than in the US. Should you break down there'll usually be an enthusiastic local mechanic, but **spare parts** can be a problem, especially for anything beyond the most basic of models. For obscure makes you'd be sensible to bring a basic spares kit. Tyres in particular suffer badly on the burning hot roads and rough dirt tracks. If you plan to head up into the mountains or along any of the smaller roads in Petén then you'll need high clearance and four-wheel drive.

Local **warning signs** are also worth getting to know. The most common is placing a branch in the road, which indicates the presence of a broken-down car. Most other important road signs should be fairly recognizable: you'll see many *Alto* ("stop") signs marking the military checkpoints from more troubled times. Locals usually know which to ignore, but if in doubt it's safest to stop anyway. *Derrumbes* means "landslides", *frene con motor* "brake with motor" (meaning a steep descent) and *tumulos* "bumps in the road", a favourite technique for slowing down traffic.

Renting a car takes some of the worries out of driving but is expensive, costing at least $50 a day (or around $220 a week) by the time you've added the extras. Nonetheless, it can be worth doing if you can get a few people together – even better value if you get a larger group and rent a minibus. If you do rent, make sure you check the details of the insurance, which often does not cover damage to your vehicle at all. Local rental companies are in the "Listings" sections for all the main towns.

HITCHING

If you plan to visit the more remote parts of the country then it is almost inevitable that you'll have to **hitch** a ride from time to time. However, you should always use your common sense, and if you don't feel comfortable about getting in a vehicle – don't. It is also not a good idea for women to hitch alone. Off the main highways private cars are rare, and many of those that do take hitchers run as a bus service, charging all passengers at about the same rate as buses charge. Increasingly, **pick-ups** are supplementing bus services in the mountains –they are often quicker, and you can't beat the open-air views (unless it's raining). In remote areas such as the Ixil triangle, trucks and pick-ups are an essential form of transport for the locals, and you can also try hitching a lift in the numerous MINUGUA (United Nations) four-wheel drives.

BY TAXI

Taxis are available in all the main towns and their rates are fairly low. Outside Guatemala City, metered cabs are non-existent so it's essential to **fix a price** before you set off. Local taxi drivers will almost always be prepared to negotiate a price for a half-day or day's excursion to nearby villages or sites, and if time is short this can be a good way of seeing places where the bus service is awkwardly timed. If you can organize a group this need not be an expensive option, possibly even cheaper than renting a car for the day.

A new innovation on the streets of Guatemala City is three-wheeled Thai **tuk tuks** taxis. Probably the quickest and certainly the most exhilarating way of getting around the city, they charge just Q2.50 a kilometre.

BY BIKE AND MOTORBIKE

Bikes are very common indeed in Guatemala, and cycling has to be one of the most popular sports. You'll be well received almost anywhere if you travel by bike, and if you've got the energy to make your way through the highlands it's a great way to see the country. Since cycling is so popular, most towns will have a repair shop where you can get hold of spare parts, although you still need to carry the basics for emergencies on the road. Mountain bikes make the going easier, as even the main roads include plenty of formidable potholes, and it's a rare ride that doesn't involve at least one steep climb. Second-class buses will carry bikes on the roof, so if you can't face the hills then there's always an easy option. In case you didn't bring you own bike, you can **rent** them

in Antigua or Panajachel: mountain bikes can be rented by the day (about $10), week ($35) or month ($75).

Motorbikes can also be an excellent way of getting around and since many locals ride them it's not too hard to locate parts and expertise. There are rental outlets in Guatemala City, Panajachel and Antigua, charging around $20 a day or $100 for a week.

BY FERRY AND BOAT

Ferries operate on several different routes inside Guatemala. The two major routes take you across Lake Izabal, from Mariscos to El Estor, and between Puerto Barrios and Lívingston. Both of these are daily passenger-only services and very reasonably priced. In addition, there's a twice-weekly service from Puerto Barrios to Punta Gorda in Belize, as well as a very useful connection between Lívingston and Omoa in Honduras.

In Petén, there are a number of regular boat services, including the journey along the Río San Pedro from El Naranjo to the Mexican border and beyond; along the Río Salinas from Sayaxché to Benemerito; on the Río Usumacinta from Bethel to Frontera Corozal; and on Lake Petén Itzá between Flores and San Andrés. Once again, precise details of schedules are given in the relevant chapters of the guide.

Along the Pacific coast the Chiquimulilla canal separates much of the shoreline from the mainland. If you're heading for a beach you'll find a regular **shuttle** of small boats to take you across the canal.

Two of Guatemala's most unmissable **boat trips** are up through the spectacular Río Dulce gorge starting in either Lívingston or the town of Río Dulce, and across Lake Atitlán, usually starting in Panajachel. On almost any of the other navigable waterways you should be able to rent a boat somewhere, though be prepared for hours of patient bargaining, as the boat owners ask serious money for any excursions.

ACCOMMODATION

Guatemalan hotels come in all shapes and sizes, and unless you're really off the beaten track there will usually be a good choice of accommodation to choose from. Though Inguat fixes a maximum price for every hotel room in the country, there are bargains and rip-offs at every level. At the top end of the scale, you can stay in some magnificent colonial hotels decorated with real taste and period detail. In the mid-price bracket, you'll also find some brilliant deals – you can still expect character and comfort, but perhaps without the service and facilities. But Guatemala really is a budget travellers' dream, and you should be able to find a clean double room for under $10 a night in any town in the country.

Accommodation comes under a bewildering assortment of names: *hoteles*, *pensiones*, *posadas*, *hospedajes* and *huespedes*. The names don't always mean a great deal: in theory a *hospedaje* is less formal than a *hotel*, but in prac-

tice the reverse is almost as common. There are no official youth hostels in Guatemala, but you will find the odd dormitory.

Prices for rooms vary as much as anything else. On the whole you can expect the cheapest places to charge $2–5 per person, and to get a reasonable but basic room with its own bathroom for around $10 (a little more in the capital). But price and quality are not always as closely linked as you might expect and, despite rates being officially regulated, it's well worth trying to **haggle** a little, or asking if there are any cheaper rooms. The official prices, set by Inguat, are meant to be displayed in the room, and if you think you've been overcharged you can register a complaint with Inguat, although it's unlikely that much will happen. If travelling in a group you can often save money by **sharing** a larger room, which almost all the cheaper hotels offer.

Prices are at their highest in Guatemala City, where the very cheapest rooms cost around $5, and here it's sometimes difficult to find a single room at all. Many hotels insist on charging solo travellers for the cost of a double regardless. Costs are also higher than average in Antigua and Flores. At fiesta and holiday times, particularly Holy Week and Christmas, rooms tend to be more expensive and harder to find, and the summer tourist season can also be crowded. At these times, particularly if you're going to arrive in Guatemala City at night, it's worth booking a room by phone or fax, but in other parts of the country it's hardly worth it.

When you arrive at a hotel you should always insist on seeing the room before any money changes hands, otherwise they may dump you in the noisiest part of the building and save the good rooms for more discerning customers. In general

ACCOMMODATION PRICE CODES

All accommodation listed in this guide has been graded according to the following price scales. These refer to the price in US dollars of the cheapest double room in high season. Many places, however, will offer reductions at quieter times of the year, particularly those in the more popular tourist centres, where there is plenty of competition. It is always worth negotiating if you think the hotel is not very full.

① Under $5	④ $15–25	⑦ $60–80
② $5–10	⑤ $25–40	⑧ $80–100
③ $10–15	⑥ $45–60	⑨ over $100

the cheaper hotels (①–②) recommended in this book are not the very cheapest – which are often genuinely squalid, although we do list some notable bargains – but one step up. Rooms in these places will be simple, with a shared toilet and bathroom usually at the end of the corridor. In the brackets above this (③ and ④), you can expect a private bathroom, usually with hot water. Rooms in the ⑤ and ⑥ categories should be very comfortable and attractive, while for $80 upwards (⑦, ⑧ and ⑨), you can expect international standards of comfort and luxury, with facilities such as swimming pools, gyms and a good restaurant.

It's only on the Pacific and Caribbean coasts and in Petén, that you'll need a **fan** or **air conditioning**. In the highlands, even the luxury hotels rarely have air-con – many have lovely logwood fires to keep out the winter chill instead. **Mosquito nets** are rarely provided, even in the lowland areas, so if you plan to spend some time in Petén it's well worth investing in one, and it's an essential purchase if you plan to so some jungle trekking.

Campsites are extremely thin on the ground in Guatemala. The main cities certainly don't have them and the only places with any decent formal provision for camping are Panajachel, Poptún and Tikal. However if you decide to set off into the wilds, then a tent is certainly a good idea, although even here it's by no means essential.

Hiking in the highlands usually takes you from village to village, and wherever you go it's possible to find somewhere to sling a hammock or bed down for the night. In villages that don't have hotels you should track down the mayor (*alcalde*) and ask if you can stay in the town hall (*municipalidad*) or local school. If that isn't possible then you'll almost certainly be found somewhere else. If you do take a tent along, the Guatemalan countryside offers plenty of superb spots, although you should always take care where you camp and also try to ask the landowner. In some places, such as Semuc Champey and the ruins of Mixco Viejo, there are thatched shelters where you can sling a hammock or bed down out of the rain.

When it comes to hiking in the jungle you'll need to hire a guide. They usually sleep out in the open, protected only by a mosquito net, so you can either follow suit or use a tent. At most of the smaller Maya sites there are guards who will usually let you sleep in their shelters and cook on their fires. If you plan to use their facilities then bring along some food to share with them.

The other occasion for which a tent is useful is climbing **volcanoes**, which often entails a night under the stars. On the lower cone of Acatenango there's a small hut that provides shelter for sleeping out, but it sometimes fills up at weekends. For renting tents, sleeping bags, stoves and rucksacks, ask at either the Casa Andinista bookshop or the *Albergue Andinista* guesthouse in Antigua, or at Quetzaltrekkers inside the *Casa Argentina* hotel in Quetzaltenango.

COMMUNICATIONS

Keeping in touch with home shouldn't be a problem in Guatemala, and even in small towns you'll find a branch of Telgua, the national phone company, where you can make international phone calls and send or receive faxes. Telgua tariffs are ridiculously high however, and in many places you'll find shops, hotels or travel agencies offering cheaper rates (and no queues). Most of the main tourist destinations now also have an internet café where you can send and recieve email.

MAIL

Outgoing Guatemalan postal services are fairly efficient by Latin American standards, and you can **send mail** easily from even the smallest of towns – though it's probably safer to send anything of importance through a private firm. The regular mail service is also extremely cheap – a postcard costs just Q0.40 to Europe – but not very speedy. Letters generally take around a week to the US, a couple of weeks or more to Europe: to make sure that it won't take any longer get your letters or postcards stamped *via aerea* (air mail).

To receive mail, have it sent to any post office in the country, or to one of the privately owned communications offices (see below). Letters to be picked up from the post office should be addressed to you at the *Lista de Correos*, followed by the Guatemalan town you want to receive the mail at, and of course "Guatemala" at the bottom. Always get the sender to underline your family name. When picking up your mail, you

should also check under all your initials as letters are all too easily misfiled. A small fee is charged by the post office and you'll need some ID. Letters will be only kept at the post office for one month, after which they're returned to the sender.

An efficient, reliable and inexpensive alternative is to have your mail sent to **American Express** in Guatemala City (see p.71 for details). Officially, you need to show either an American Express card or travellers' cheques to use the service, though it's unlikely that they'll actually refuse to hand over any letters.

Sending parcels is not easy, as there are complex regulations about the way in which they should be wrapped. Normally this entails cardboard boxes, brown paper and string, although you can also pack things in a flour sack. (Boxes and sacks can be bought in shops and markets.) The parcel has to be taken to the post office for inspection by the customs department, and is then sealed. Rates for shipment are reasonable, but parcels sent by air are fairly expensive. In the end the whole process is so time-consuming and frustrating that you're almost invariably better off using one of the agencies in Antigua or Panajachel. Try Get Guated Out in Panajachel (see p.150), or Quick Shipping in Antigua (see p.108).

When **receiving parcels**, note that it is unwise to get anyone to send anything valuable or bulky to you through the mail – use a courier service instead, such as UPS, DHL or Federal Express, all of whom operate in Guatemala.

PHONES AND FAXES

Local phone calls in Guatemala are very cheap, but outside Guatemala City there are few payphones: where you do find one you'll need 10, 15 or 25 centavo coins. In the main tourist centres there are plenty of shops, hotels, bars and restaurants that will allow customers to use their phones, though if you are off the beaten path you'll have to rely on the offices of Telgua (formally Guatel), the national phone company. At a Telgua office you tell the operator the number that you want to phone, wait until your name is announced and go to the booth they point out. Afterwards they present you with the bill. Most Telgua offices are open daily from 7am to 10pm, with some staying open until midnight.

USEFUL PHONE NUMBERS

Telephoning overseas from Guatemala
Dial the international access codes ☎00 plus

US ☎1; Canada ☎1; Australia ☎61; New Zealand ☎64; UK ☎44.
International operator ☎171 Directory enquiries ☎124

Telephoning Guatemala from abroad,
the international direct dialling (IDD) code is ☎502.

For **long-distance and international calls**, Telgua charges $9 to call Europe, $6 to the US, and $7 to Canada for a minimum of three minutes. However, if you're in Antigua, Quetzaltenango, Panajachel or Flores, your best bet is to shop around at the various travel agents, shops and hotels that advertise international calls and you'll almost certainly find cheaper rates.

International calls can be direct dialled or you can use the international operator; if you're calling the US you can also use AT&T (☎190), MCI (☎189) or Sprint (☎195), to make regular, collect or credit card calls, avoiding the complications and uncertainties of the Guatemalan phone system. There are similar services for Canada (☎198). If you're calling Australia, you can use Telstra's Telecard or Optus' Calling Card, and for New Zealand there's Telecom's Calling Card, all of which charge your calls back to a domestic account or credit card. For details, call Telstra on ☎1800/626 008, Optus on ☎1300/300 300, or NZ Telecom on ☎04/382 5818.

From Guatemala you can only make **collect calls** (reverse charges) to the USA, Canada, Mexico, Italy, Spain, Japan, Switzerland and other Central American countries – not to Britain.

Faxes can be sent from Telgua offices, or from any number of private businesses, or often cheapest of all, via the Internet (see below).

THE INTERNET

Cyber cafés are mushrooming throughout the country, and you'll find them in Antigua, Flores, Quetzaltenango, Guatemala City, Cobán, Panajachel and Utila in Honduras. However, most Guatemalans have yet to get really excited about the Internet, and there can be problems getting the necessary connections with Guatemala's antiquated phone system.

In addition, many **language schools** are getting online, and offer their students cheaper rates than the cyber cafés for sending and receiving email.

THE MEDIA

For finding out what's happening both inside and outside the country, Guatemala is equipped with several daily papers, a handful of TV channels, and more than enough radio stations. The nation's press is expanding in both volume and coverage and in theory there is little restriction on its freedom, although pressures are still exerted and journalism remains to many in authority a "subversive" profession.

Of the **daily papers**, the most widely read are the *Prensa Libre*, a conservative business-orientated publication, with a reasonable sports section, and *El Grafico*, also to the right of centre, which broadly supports the military and business elite. For a more left-of-centre view, there's the outspoken *El Periódico*, which can be hard to get hold of outside the capital; the *Siglo Veintiuno* which you can buy from almost any newsagent throughout the country; or the afternoon paper *La Hora*, easily available in Guatemala City and Antigua. You should also look out for the **weekly** Huehuetenango-based paper, *El Regional*, which is published in both Spanish and Maya languages, and the monthly news magazine, *La Crónica*, concentrating on Guatemalan politics, current affairs and business news, with a smattering of foreign coverage.

Guatemala also has a substantial **English-language** press, from which travellers can glean useful information, not least about the current security situation. Top of the pile is the excellent, free weekly *Siglo News* – sister paper to the *Siglo Veintiuno*. It has concise, independent coverage of the main news and regional stories, as well as details about forthcoming fiestas and cultural events. Its main rival is the relatively lightweight *Guatemala Weekly*, aimed at the ex-pat

RADIO FREQUENCIES

BBC World Service
Reception is generally quite poor, with the best results being in the evenings. All times are Greenwich Mean Time (GMT):

06.00–08.30:	17.840MHz
08.30–17.00:	17.840 and 15.260 MHz
17.00–23.30:	9.590 MHz

Voice of America
All times are Greenwich Mean Time (GMT):

10.00–02.00:	6.030Mhz, 6.165Mhz and 9.59MHz
00.00–02.00:	5.995Mhz, 9.775MHz and 9.815MHz

American community, which has good coverage of North American sports, excellent news stories courtesy of *Central America Report*, comprehensive listings, a classified section and interesting features on Guatemalan textiles. Again it's free and widely available in hotels, bookstores and cafés and restaurants in the main tourist centres.

The most extensively distributed **monthly** is the *Revue*, published in Antigua (also free), with a "Volcano of the month" column, cultural reports, book reviews, a property section and lots of adverts. It has a distinct regional focus with columns penned from Quetzaltenango, Cobán, Lake Atitlán and even El Salvador. Finally, for businessmen, there's *Business Guatemala* with details of investment opportunities, financial indicators and up-beat reports on the state of the country's economy.

For reliable, in-depth reporting, the long-established *Central America Report* publishes excellent journalistic investigations into controversial news stories such as the plight of street children in Guatemala City, and the discovery of mass graves in Honduras. It's available from info press, whose offices are at 7 Av 2–05 Zona 1, Guatemala City.

As for **foreign publications**, *Newsweek*, *Time* and *The Economist* are all sold in the streets of Guatemala City, particularly on the south side of the main plaza. Some American newspapers are also available, such as *USA Today*, the *Miami Herald*, the *New York Times* and the *Wall Street Journal* – all can be bought from the *Pan-American Hotel*, the *Camino Real*, and the *Sheraton* in Guatemala City. Some are also available in Antigua, and you can read them at the *Instituto Guatemalteco Americano* library at Ruta 4, 4–05, Zona 4, Guatemala City. No British papers are sold in Guatemala although the British Embassy has recent copies.

Guatemala has an abundance of **radio stations**, though variety is not their strong point, with most transmitting a stream of Latin rock and merengue. There is also no shortage of religious stations, too. If you yearn for the voice of the BBC, the World Service transmits a good daily service, as does the Voice of America (see below).

Television stations are also in plentiful supply; viewers can choose from five local channels and over a dozen satellite channels, all of them dominated by American programmes. Many upmarket hotels and some bars in tourist areas (Antigua, for example) also receive US stations direct by satellite or cable, which can be handy for catching up with the news on *CNN*.

EATING AND DRINKING

Food doesn't come high in the list of reasons to visit Guatemala, with most Guatemalans surviving on a strict diet of eggs, beans and tortillas. However, in all the main tourist centres there's more choice, and in Antigua you can feast on numerous different European cuisines, several Asian ones, and even sample Middle Eastern dishes.

WHERE TO EAT

The most important distinction in Guatemala is between the **restaurant** and the ***comedor***. The latter translates as an "eatery", and in general these are simple local cafés serving the food of the poor at rock-bottom prices. In a *comedor* there is often no menu, and you simply ask what's on offer, or look into the bubbling pots. Restaurants, in general, are slightly more formal and expensive. As usual, however, there are plenty of exceptions to this rule: many a restaurant has a very *comedor*-like menu, and vice versa. On the whole you'll find restaurants in the towns, while in small villages there are usually just one or two *comedores*, clustered around the market area. *Comedores* generally look scruffier, but the food is almost always fresh and the turnover is fast.

In the cities you'll also find **fast-food** joints, modelled on the American originals and often owned by the same companies. When you're travelling you'll also come across the local version of fast food: when buses pause they're besieged by vendors offering a huge selection of drinks,

sweets, local specialities and complete meals. Many of these are delicious, but you do need to treat this kind of food with a degree of caution, and bear in mind the general lack of hygiene.

Traditionally, Guatemalans eat a **breakfast** of tortillas and eggs, accompanied by the inevitable beans – and sometimes also a sauce of sour cream. **Lunch** is the main meal of the day, and this is the best time to fill up as restaurants often offer *comidas corridas*, a set two- or three-course meal that sometimes costs as little as a dollar. It's always filling and occasionally delicious. Sometimes the same deal is on offer in the evenings, but usually not, so **evening meals** are likely to be more expensive.

Vegetarians are rarely catered for specifically, except in the tourist restaurants of Antigua and Panajachel and at a handful of places in Guatemala City. It is, however, fairly easy to get by eating plenty of beans and eggs which are always on the menu (although you should check, as beans, especially, are often fried in lard). The markets also offer plenty of superb fruit, and snacks like *tostadas* and *pupusas*.

There are three distinct **types of cooking** in Guatemala, and although they overlap to an extent it's still clear enough which one it is that you're eating.

MAYA CUISINE

The oldest style of cuisine is **Maya cooking**, in which the basic staples of beans and maize dominate. **Beans** (*frijoles*) are the black kidney-shaped variety and are served in two ways: either *volteados*, which are boiled up, mashed, and then refried in a great dollop; or *parados*, which are boiled up whole, with a few slices of onion, and served in their own black juice. For breakfast, beans are usually served with eggs and cream, and at other times of the day they're offered up on a separate plate to the main dish. Almost all truly Guatemalan meals include a portion of beans, and for many highland Maya, beans are the only regular source of protein.

Maize is the other essential, a food which for the Maya (and many other native Americans) is almost as nourishing spiritually as it is physically – in Maya legend, humankind was originally formed from maize. It appears most commonly as the **tortilla**, a thin pancake. The maize is traditionally ground by hand and shaped by clapping it between two hands, a method still in widespread use. The tortilla is cooked on a ***comal***, which is a flat pan of clay placed over the fire, and the very best tortillas are eaten while warm, usually brought to the table wrapped in cloth. For the Maya, the tortilla forms the hub of a meal, with beans or the odd piece of meat to spice it up. The very best warm tortillas have a lovely pliable texture, with a delicate, slightly burnt, smoky taste which will become very much a part of your trip – the smell of them is enough to revive memories years later. Where there's an option local people often serve gringos with bread, assuming they won't want tortillas.

Maize is also used to make a number of traditional **snacks**, which are sold on buses, at markets and during fiestas. The most common of these is the *tamal,* a pudding-like cornmeal package sometimes stuffed with chicken. It's wrapped in a banana leaf and then boiled. Slightly more exciting is the *chuchito,* which is similar but tends to include a bit of tomato and a pinch of hot chilli. Other popular snacks are *chiles rellenos,* stuffed peppers, and *pacaya,* which is a rather stodgy local vegetable.

Chillies are the final essential ingredient of the Maya diet (especially for the Kekchi). They are sometimes placed raw or pickled in the middle of the table in a jar, but also served as a sauce – *salsa picante.* The strength of these can vary tremendously, so treat them with caution until you know what you're dealing with.

Other traditional Maya dishes include a superb range of **stews** – known as *caldos* – made with duck, beef, chicken or turkey; and *fiambre,* which is the world's largest salad, a delicious mix of meat and vegetables traditionally served on the Day of the Dead (November 1), when you can usually find it in restaurants. The best chance to sample traditional food is at a market or fiesta, when makeshift *comedores* serve freshly cooked dishes. A highland breakfast often includes a plate of *mosh,* which is made with milk and oats and tastes rather like porridge. It's the ideal antidote to the early morning chill.

LADINO CUISINE

Guatemala's second culinary style is **ladino food**, which is indebted to the range of cultures that go to make up the *ladino* population. Most of the food has a mild Latin American bias, incorporating a lot of Mexican ideas, but the influence of the United States and Europe is also strongly felt. At its most obvious, *ladino* food includes *bistek* (steak), *hamburguesa* and *chao mein,* all of which are readily available in most Guatemalan towns, with rice and fries (chips) usually provide the carbohydrate. Guatemalan-style *ceviche* (raw fish with spicy salad) is also popular on the coasts. In addition, you'll find a mild **German** influence in the widespread availability of frankfurter-type sausages, and plenty of **Italian**-influenced restaurants offering pasta and pizza. *Ladino*-style cakes and pastries are widely available, but tend to be pretty dull and dry.

CREOLE CUISINE

The final element is the **Creole cooking** found on Guatemala's Caribbean coast. Here, **bananas**, **coconuts** and **seafood** dominate the scene, all of them, if you're lucky, cooked superbly. You have to hunt around to find true Creole cooking, which incorporates the influences of the Caribbean with those of Africa, but it's well worth the effort. Some of the more obvious elements have also penetrated the mainstream; for example, you can get fried plantains (*plátanos fritos*) just about anywhere in the country.

DRINK

To start off the day most Guatemalans drink a cup of hot **coffee**, **chocolate** or **tea** (all of which are usually served with plenty of sugar), but in the highlands you'll also be offered *atol,* a warm, sweet drink made with either rice or maize and sugar. At other times of day, **soft drinks** and beer are usually drunk with meals. Coca-Cola, Pepsi, Sprite and Fanta (all called *aguas*) are common, as are *refrescos,* thirst-quenching water-based drinks with a little fruit flavour added. In many places, you can also get *licuado,* a delicious, thick fruit-based drink with either milk or water added (milk is safer). **Bottled water** (*agua mineral or agua pura*) is almost always available, and it's a good idea to stick to it (see p.15 for further details).

Guatemalan **beers** tend to be bland, unexciting and rarely on draught. One characterless brew has a near monopoly, the ubiquitous *Gallo,* a medium-strength lager-style beer that comes in 33cl- (around $1) or litre- (around $2) bottles. More interesting, but not so widely available, is

A LIST OF FOOD AND DISHES

Basics

Azucar	Sugar	Pescado	Fish
Carne	Meat	Pimienta	Pepper
Ensalada	Salad	Queso	Cheese
Huevos	Eggs	Sal	Salt
Mantequilla	Butter	Salsa	Sauce
Pan	Bread	Verduras/Legumbres	Vegetables

Soups (*Sopas*) and starters

Sopa	Soup	Consome	Consomme
de Arroz	with rice	Caldo	Broth (usually with meat)
de Fideos	with noodles	Ceviche	Raw fish salad, marinated in
de Lentejas	Lentil		lime juice
de Verduras	Vegetable	Entremeses	Hors d'oeuvres

Meat (*Carne*) and Poultry (*Aves*)

Alambre	Kebab	Guisado	Stew
Bistec	Steak	Higado	Liver
Cabrito	Kid	Lengua	Tongue
Carne (de res)	Beef	Milanesa	Breaded escalope
Carnitas	Stewed chunks of meat	Pato	Duck
Cerdo	Pork	Pavo/Guajalote	Turkey
Chorizo	Sausage	Pechuga	Breast
Chuleta	Chop	Pierna	Leg
Codorniz	Quail	Pollo	Chicken
Conejo	Rabbit	Salchicha	Hot dog or salami
Cordero	Lamb	Ternera	Veal
Costilla	Rib	Venado	Venison

Specialities

Chile Relleno	Stuffed Pepper	Quesadilla	Cheese-flavoured sponge
Chuchitos	Stuffed maize dumplings	Taco	Rolled and stuffed tortilla
Enchilada	Flat, crisp tortilla piled with salad or meat	Tamale	Boiled and stuffed maize pudding
Mosh	Porridge	Tapado	Fish stew with plantain and
Pan de Banana	Banana bread		vegetables, served on
Pan de Coco	Coconut bread		Caribbean coast

Moza, a dark brew with a slight caramel flavour. The best of the lagers is *Montecarlo*, an expensive premium beer that is worth the extra quetzal or two, if you can get it. You may also come across *Dorada Draft*, another dull lager brew, and occasionally *Cabra*, which has a little more flavour. Imported beers are rare, though Mexican brands can be found in places like Huehuetenango.

As for **spirits**, rum (*ron*) and *aguardiente*, a clear and lethal sugar cane spirit, are very popular and cheap. *Ron Botran Añejo* is a good rum (around $4 a bottle), while hard drinkers will soon get to know *Quezalteca* and *Venado*, two

Vegetables (*legumbres, verduras*)

Aguacate	Avocado	Lechuga	Lettuce
Ajo	Garlic	Pacaya	Bitter-tasting local vegetable
Casava/Yuca	Potato-like root vegetable	Papas	Potatoes
Cebolla	Onion	Pepino	Cucumber
Col	Cabbage	Plátanos	Plantain
Elote	Corn on the cob	Tomate	Tomato
Frijoles	Beans	Zanahoria	Carrot
Hongos	Mushrooms		

Fruit (*Fruta*)

Ciruelas	Greengages	Melocoton	Peach
Banana	Banana	Melon	Melon
Coco	Coconut	Naranja	Orange
Frambuesas	Raspberries	Papaya	Papaya
Fresas	Strawberries	Piña	Pineapple
Guanabana	Pear-like cactus fruit	Pitahaya	Sweet, purple fruit
Guayaba	Guava	Sandia	Watermelon
Higos	Figs	Toronja	Grapefruit
Limon	Lime	Tuna	Cactus fruit
Mamey	Pink, sweet, full of pips	Uvas	Grapes
Mango	Mango		

Eggs (*Huevos*)

a la Mexicana	Scrambled with mild tomato, onion and chilli sauce	Motuleños	Fried, served on a tortilla with ham, cheese and sauce
Fritos	Fried	Rancheros	Cheese-Fried and smothered in hot chilli sauce
con Jamon	with ham		
con Tocino	with bacon	Revueltos	Scrambled
		Tibios	Lightly boiled

Common terms

A la Parilla	Grilled	Empanado/a	Breaded
Al Horno	Baked	Picante	Hot and spicy
Al Mojo de Ajo	Fried in garlic and butter	Hecado	A sauce for meat made from garlic, tomato and spices
Asado/a	Roast		

Sweets

Crepas	Pancakes	Plátanos al Horno	Baked plantains
Ensalada de Frutas	Fruit salad	Plátanos en Mole	Plantains in chocolate sauce
Flan	Crème caramel		
Helado	Ice cream		

local *aguardientes* available everywhere. If you're after a real bargain, then try locally brewed alcohol (*chicha*), which is practically given away. Its main ingredient can be anything: apple, cherry, sugar cane, peach, apricot and quince are just some of the more common varieties.

Wine is also made in Guatemala, from local fruits or imported concentrates. It's interesting to try, but for something really drinkable stick to the more expensive imports. Chilean wines are the best value with decent bottles available from around $5 in supermarkets, and from double that in restaurants.

OPENING HOURS AND PUBLIC HOLIDAYS

Guatemalan opening hours are subject to considerable local variations, but in general most offices, shops, post offices and museums open between around 8.30am and 5pm, though some take an hour or so break for lunch. Banking hours are extremely convenient, with many staying open until 7pm (and some as late as 8pm) from Monday to Friday, but closing at 1pm on Saturdays. You may not always be able to exchange money after 5.30pm in some places, however, even though the bank is open.

Archeological sites open every day, usually from 8am to 5pm, though **Tikal** is open from 6am to 6pm (until 8pm with permission). Principal public holidays, when almost all businesses close down, are listed below, but each village or town will also have its own fiestas or saints' days when everything will be shut. These can last anything from one day to two weeks.

PUBLIC HOLIDAYS

January 1 New Year's Day

Semana Santa The four days of Holy Week leading up to Easter

May 1 Labour Day

June 30 Army Day, anniversary of the 1871 revolution

August 15 Guatemala City fiesta (Guatemala City only)

September 15 Independence Day

October 12 Discovery of America (only banks close)

October 20 Revolution Day

November 1 All Saints' Day

December 24 From noon

December 25 Christmas

December 31 From noon

FIESTAS, DANCE AND MUSIC

Traditional fiestas are one of the great excitements of a trip to Guatemala, and every town and village, however small, devotes at least one day a year to celebration. The main day is normally prescribed by the local saint's day, though the celebrations often extend to a week or two around that date. On almost every day of the year there's a fiesta in some forgotten corner of the country, and with a bit of planning you should be able to witness at least one. Most of them are well worth going out of your way for.

The **format** of fiestas varies between two basic models. In towns with a largely *ladino* population, fairs are usually set up and the days are filled with processions, beauty contests and perhaps the odd marching band, while the nights are dominated by dancing and salsa rhythms. In the highlands, where the bulk of the population is Maya, you'll see traditional dances, costumes and musicians, and a blend of religious and secular celebration that incorporates elements which predate the arrival of the Spanish. What they all share is an astonishing energy and an unbounded enthusiasm for drink, dance and fireworks, all of which are virtually impossible to escape during the days of fiesta.

One thing you shouldn't expect is anything too dainty or organized: fiestas are above all chaotic, and the measured rhythms of traditional dance and music are usually obscured by the crush of the crowd and the huge volumes of alcohol consumed by participants. If you can join in the mood there's no doubt that fiestas are wonderfully entertaining and that they offer a real insight into Guatemalan culture, *ladino* or indigenous.

Many of the **best fiestas** include some specifically local element, such as the giant kites at **Santiago Sacatepéquez**, the religious processions in **Antigua** and the horse race in **Todos Santos**. The dates of most fiestas, along with their main features, are listed at the end of each chapter. At certain times virtually the whole country erupts simultaneously: Easter Week is perhaps the most important, particularly in Antigua, but both All Saints' Day (November 1) and Christmas are also marked by partying across the land.

DANCE

Dance is the subject of yet another cultural divide. In the nightclubs of Gutemala City and Antigua, it's Latin house, merengue and salsa that get people onto the dance floor, while in more rural parts dancing is usually confined to fiestas. In the highland villages this means traditional dances, heavily imbued with history and symbolism.

The drunken dancers may look out of control, but the process is taken very seriously and involves great expense on the part of the participants, who have to rent their ornate costumes. The most common dance is the **Baile de la Conquista**, which re-enacts the victory of the Spanish over the Maya, while at the same time managing to ridicule the conquistadors. According to some studies, the dance is based in pre-Columbian traditions. Other popular dances are the **Baile de los Gracejos**, the dance of the jesters, the **Baile del Venado**, the dance of the deer, and the **Baile de la Culebra**, the dance of the snake; all of them again rooted in pre-Columbian traditions. One of the most impressive is the **Palo Volador**, in which men swing by

ropes from a thirty-metre pole. Today this is only performed in Chichicastenango, Joyabaj and Cubulco.

MUSIC

Guatemalan **music** combines many different influences, but yet again it can be broadly divided between *ladino* and Maya. For fiestas, bands are always shipped in, complete with a crackling PA system and a strutting lead singer.

Traditional music is dominated by the **marimba**, a type of wooden xylophone that may well have originated in Africa (although many argue that it developed independently in Central America). The oldest versions use gourds beneath the sounding board and can be played by a single musician, while modern models, using hollow tubes to generate the sound, can need as many as seven players. The marimba is at the heart of traditional music, and marimba orchestras play at every occasion, for both *ladino* and indigenous communities. In the remotest of villages you sometimes hear them practising well into the night, particularly around market day. Other important instruments, especially in Maya bands, are the *tun*, a drum made from a hollow log; the *tambor*, another drum traditionally covered with the skin of a deer; *los chichines*, a type of maracas made from hollow gourds; the *tzijolaj*, a kind of piccolo; and the *chirimia*, a flute.

Ladino music is a blend of North American and Latin sounds, much of it originating in Miami, Colombia, the Dominican Republic and Puerto Rico, although there are plenty of local bands producing their own version of the sound. It's fast-moving, easy-going and very rhythmic, and on any bus you'll hear many of the most popular tracks. It draws on **merengue**, a rhythm that originally came from the Dominican Republic, and includes elements of Mexican music and the cumbia and salsa of Colombia and Cuba.

Finally, on the Caribbean coast, you'll hear the sound of **reggae**, which reaches Lívingston from island radio stations. Much of this music comes from the Caribbean islands and is sung in English, although there is also a thriving reggae scene in Central and South America, with the most important bands coming from Belize, Costa Rica, Panamá and Colombia. Reggae has also made it to Guatemala City, where there are a couple of nightclubs popular with people from the Caribbean coast.

SPORTS

Guatemalans have a furious appetite for spectator sports and the daily papers always devote four or five pages to the subject. Football (soccer) tops the bill, and if you get the chance to see a major game it's a thrilling experience, if only to watch the crowd. Otherwise North American sport predominates – baseball, American football, boxing and basketball are all popular.

On a more local level **bullfights**, which are staged in Guatemala City in October and December, draw large crowds. The *matadores* are usually from Spain or Mexico, and entry costs are high. The main bull ring is beside the Parque Aurora in Guatemala City.

Hiking is perhaps the most popular sport among visitors, particularly volcano climbing, which is certainly hard work but almost always worth the effort – unless you end up wrapped in cloud. Guatemala has some 37 volcanic peaks; the tallest is Tajumulco in the west, which at 4220m is a serious undertaking. Among the active peaks Pacaya is an easy climb and a dramatic sight, although as it has been the scene of violent rape and robbery, it should not be attempted alone. Volcano climbing trips are organized by a number of tour groups in Antigua and Quetzaltenango (see p.100 or 173).

As a participatory sport, **fishing** is also popular, with good sea fishing being available on both coasts. On the Pacific side the coastal waters offer sierra mackerel, jack cravelle, yellow and black tuna, snappers, bonito and dorado, with marlin and sailfish further offshore, while the Caribbean side also offers excellent opportunities. In Petén the rivers and lakes are packed with sport fish, including snook, tarpon and peacock bass, and lakes Petexbatún, Izabal and Yaxjá also offer superb fishing, as do the Usumacinta and Dulce rivers. Fishing trips to both coasts and on

the inland waterways are organized by Tropical Tours, 4 C 2–51, Zona 10, Guatemala City (☎3393662), though these trips are expensive, and if you just want to dabble around then you should be able to sort something out with local fishermen in the coastal villages or in Sayaxché or El Estor.

Guatemala's dramatic highland landscape and tumbling rivers also provide some excellent opportunities for **whitewater rafting**, particularly on the rivers Cahabón and Motagua. Three-day trips down the Río Cahabón are organized by Tropical Tours (see above), while Maya Expeditions, 15 C 1–91, Zona 10, Guatemala City (☎3634955; fax 3374646), arranges trips on the Usumacinta, Naranjo, Motagua and Cahabón, giving you the chance to see some really remote areas and visit some of the country's most inaccessible Maya sites. It also organizes Guatemala's only **bungee jump**, every weekend from one of the ravine bridges near the capital or on the Río Dulce bridge.

Scuba diving is another up-and-coming sport in this part of the world, although Guatemala has little to offer compared with the splendours of the neighbouring Belizean or Honduran coastal waters. Nevertheless, there are some diving possibilities here, including Lake Atitlán, the Ipala Lagoon and Lake Izabal, as well as some good Pacific and Caribbean dive sites. Highly recommended for freshwater, high-altitude dives, and excellent instruction are ATI Divers, based in the *Iguana Perdida* hotel in Santa Cruz, Lake Atitlán (see p.160). Dive trips and courses are also offered by Prodiver, 6 Av 9–85, Zona 9, Guatemala City (☎3312738; fax 4782286).

There is also some **surfing** in Guatemala, on the Pacific coast, although if you've come all this way for the waves you may be disappointed; you'll certainly find better breaks in El Salvador or Costa Rica.

CRAFTS, MARKETS AND SHOPS

Guatemalan craft traditions, locally known as *artesanía*, are very much a part of modern Maya culture, stemming from practices that in most cases predate the arrival of the Spanish. Many of these traditions are highly localized, with different regions and even different villages specializing in particular crafts.

ARTESANÍA

The best place to buy Guatemalan **crafts** is in their place of origin, where the quality is usually highest, the prices reasonable, and above all else the craftsmen and women get a greater share of the profit. But if you haven't the time or the energy to travel to remote highland villages, then there are plenty of places where you can find a superb selection from all around the country. The markets in Chichicastenango (Thursday and Sunday) are always good, but you'll also find good-quality *artesanía* in Guatemala City, Antigua, Panajachel and Huehuetenango. In all of these places it's well worth shopping around – and bargaining – as prices can vary wildly.

The greatest craft in Guatemala has to be **weaving**, with styles and techniques that have developed consistently since Maya times and are now practised at an astonishingly high standard throughout the western highlands. Each village has its own traditional designs, woven in fantastic patterns and with superbly vivid colours. One thing to bear in mind is that for the Maya, clothing has a spiritual significance and the pattern is specific to the weaver and the wearer, casting them in a particular social role. If you go into a village and buy local clothing you may well cheapen the value that's placed on it, and it is deeply insulting to offer to buy the clothes that someone is wearing. Having said this there are plenty of indigenous weavers who are very keen to expand their market by selling to tourists, and for them you offer an ideal supplement to a meagre income. All the finest weaving is done on a backstrap loom, and the quality and variety are so impressive that you'll be spoilt for choice. Antigua's Nim Po't, 5 Av Norte (☎ & fax 8322681) sells some of the finest weaving in the country, and is a veritable museum of styles and designs. It's worth a visit even if you're not interested in buying.

Alongside Guatemalan weaving most **other crafts** suffer by comparison. However, if you hunt around you'll also find good ceramics, baskets, mats, silver and jade. The last two are easiest to come by in Antigua, although most of the silver is mined in Alta Verapaz. The others are produced by craftsmen and women in the villages of the highlands, and sold in local markets throughout the country.

MARKETS

For shopping – and simply sightseeing – the **markets** of Guatemala are some of the finest anywhere in the world. Most towns and villages, particularly in the highlands, have weekly markets – some of the larger ones are held twice a week, although one day is always the more important. Traditional markets are the focus of economic and social activity in rural Guatemala, and people come from miles around to sell, buy and have a good time. You really should make the effort to see a few: the mood varies tremendously, from the frenetic tourist markets in Chichicastenango to the calm of San Juan Atitán, but all markets have an air of fiesta about them and incorporate a great deal of chaotic celebration as well as hard-nosed business deals. Above all else markets offer a real glimpse of Maya culture, as they are at the heart of the village economy and social structure.

Prices are almost always lower in markets than in shops or on the streets in tourist areas (although in Chichicastenango bargains are becoming increasingly scarce), but you'll still need to **haggle**. Everyone claims to have perfected a bargaining technique, but few stand a chance against the masters of the market: obvious tips are to have an idea of the shop price of similar items before you start, and always offer way below what's asked and expect to meet somewhere in the middle.

EVERYDAY GOODS

When it comes to everyday **shopping**, you can buy just about everything in Guatemala that you can in the States or Europe – at a price. For **food** you need to look no further than the market, where things are fresh and prices are low, but you should stick to the shops for other things. While basic items are always cheap, imported goods command a high price, and luxuries such as electrical goods and cameras are often very expensive. Print and slide **film** is available in most towns, as is Video 8 and VHS-C, though monochrome film is less common. English-language **books** – a rather limited selection – are sold in Guatemala City and Antigua, but prices are high. For anything out of the ordinary it's a good idea to do your shopping in the capital or Antigua where there's a much greater range on offer. Most of the main tourist centres have a few secondhand bookstores (usually foreign-owned) where you'll be able to exchange novels.

TROUBLE AND SEXUAL HARASSMENT

The problem of personal safety in Guatemala is serious, with a nationwide rise in crime since the end of the guerrilla war and attacks on tourists also on the increase. There is little pattern to these attacks, but some areas can be considered safer than others. There are a few basic precautions that you can take – register with your embassy on arrival, keep informed about the security situation by reading newspapers and the local media, don't travel at night, and always enquire locally before visiting the trouble spots listed below.

CRIME

Though Guatemala attracts around 600,000 tourists a year and more than 99 per cent never have any trouble, it's essential that you try to minimize the chances of becoming a victim. **Petty theft** and **pickpockets** are likely to be your biggest worry, and are most common around bus stations in the main tourist centres, and in Zona 1 and Zona 4 in Guatemala City. A common trick is for someone to spray you or your pack with dirt, ketchup or something similar, which a "passer by" offers to help clean; the bag can then be snatched by an accomplice. Markets and fiestas are also favourite haunts of pickpockets – large gangs sometimes descend on villages for such events. It's never a good idea to flash your money around, and you should avoid leaving cameras and cash in hotel rooms: most hotels will have **a safe** where you can lock your valuables inside a signed-and-sealed envelope.

When **travelling**, there is little danger to your pack if it's on top of a bus, as it's the conductor's responsibility alone to go up the roof and collect the luggage. Be careful in restaurants, though, where leaving your belongings unattended for even a second is a risk. "Bum bags" are possibly the worst possible thing to wear, whether or not you keep your valuables inside – they are a brilliant way of attracting a thief's attention. A much better idea is to keep most of your money, passports, air tickets and cheques in a cotton moneybelt under your clothing, and buy a tiny cloth bag with a zip (available from most markets) that you can put a little cash in for necessities.

Muggings and **violent crime** are on the increase in Guatemala City. There's not too much danger in the daylight hours, providing you don't visit the slum areas, but you should think twice about wandering around after dark, especially if you don't know your way around. Stick to the main streets and use buses and taxis to get around. There have also been some cases of armed robbery in Antigua, which has resulted in a new tourist police presence there. Other **danger zones** that have consistently had security problems are: Zona 1, Guatemala City; the Cerro de la Cruz, overlooking Antigua; the Pacaya volcano;

and the back roads to Lake Atitlán from the Pan-American Highway.

Drivers are perhaps the most likely to run into trouble, and cars left unattended are often relieved of a wing mirror or two. Having North American licence plates will also draw attention to your vehicle.

If you are robbed you'll have to report it to the police, which can be a very long process and may seem like little more than a symbolic gesture. In the end it's worth it, though, as many insurance companies will only pay out if you can produce a police statement.

Bear in mind that **drug offences** are dealt with severely. Even the possession of marijuana could land you in jail, a sobering experience in Guatemala.

POLICE AND SOLDIERS

For Europeans and North Americans expecting to enter a police state, Guatemala may come as something of a surprise. Though undoubtedly you'll see a lot of police and soldiers on the streets there's rarely anything intimidating about their presence, and if you do have any dealings with them you'll probably find them surprisingly helpful. If anything the country is really quite lawless and in most areas there is little effective law enforcement.

Since July 1997 Guatemala's discredited **police** have been replaced by a new civilian force, due to be expanded to 20,000 officers by 1999. They have been trained by the Spanish Civil Guard and experts from the USA, France and Chile, and have a big budget for patrol cars and motorbikes. Officers' monthly pay has doubled (to US$400) and working shifts been reduced in an attempt to cut corruption. Despite these improvements, many observers have little confidence that crime or corruption will be substantially reduced. Antigua also has a new **tourist police** force, partly funded by local business. The officers are being given English lessons, will patrol the streets at night, and escort tourists to danger zones, such as the Cerro de la Cruz. There are plans to expand the force to other tourist towns, such as Panajachel.

Travelling in Guatemala you'll inevitably pass through many **roadblocks** and **checkpoints**, though these are by no means an intimidating experience and in almost all cases it's a routine procedure. It's possible you may be asked to get out of the bus and line up, with men and women separated. If this happens you'll be frisked and have to show your passport, but again it's a routine that Guatemalans have learned to live with.

It's important to **carry your passport** (or a photocopy) at all times, as someone might ask to see it. If for any reason you do find yourself **in trouble with the law**, be as polite as possible and do as you're told. Remember that bribery is a way of life here, and that corruption is widespread. If you do get into a problem with **drugs**, it may be worth enquiring with the first policeman if there is a "fine" (*multa*) to pay, to save expensive negotiations later. At the first possible opportunity get in touch with your embassy and negotiate through them: they will understand the situation better than you. The addresses of embassies and consulates in Guatemala City are listed on p.72.

SEXUAL HARASSMENT

Machismo is very much a part of Latin American culture, and many Guatemalan men consider it their duty to put on a bit of a show to impress the Western gringas. Hassle is usually confined to comments on the street and perhaps the occasional pinch or grab, and unless your Spanish and nerve are up to a duel it's a good idea to ignore such things.

The worst areas are those dominated by *ladino* culture: the Pacific coast, Guatemala City, the eastern highlands and most of the country's *cantinas*. Indigenous society is conditioned into being more deferential so you're unlikely to experience any trouble in the western highlands.

Though there's a strong and growing **women's movement** in Guatemala, compared to other Latin American countries, Mexico, say, there are as yet few places that travellers can depend upon making contact with local feminists.

DIRECTORY

ADDRESSES Almost all addresses are based on the grid system that's used in most towns, with avenidas usually running in one direction (North to South) and calles in the other. All addresses specify the street first, then the block, and end with the zone. For example, the address Av Reforma 3–55, Zona 1 means that house is on Avenida Reforma, between 3 and 4 calles, at no. 55, in Zona 1. Almost all towns have numbered streets, but in some places the old names are also used. In Antigua calles and avenidas are also divided according to their direction from the central plaza – north, south, east or west (*norte, sur, oriente* and *poniente*). *Diagonales* (diagonals) are what you'd expect – a street that runs in an oblique direction.

AIRPORT TAX Has to be paid before departure on all international flights. It's currently set at $25, payable in cash either in quetzals or dollars.

BAGS If you're planning to travel around by bus – and certainly if you're going to do some walking with your gear as well – then a backpack is by far the best option. Guatemalans have a word for backpackers, "*mochileros*", and consider them to be slightly quirky. Whatever you pack your stuff in, make sure it's tough enough to handle being thrown on and off the top of buses. It's a good idea to buy an old sack and string net in a local market, to enclose your bags and make them less of a target for thieves. Better still carry something small enough to fit inside a bus, on the luggage rack, which is both more convenient and safer.

BEGGARS Fairly common, particularly on the streets of the main towns and around church entrances, though they rarely hassle anyone. Local people tend to give a coin or two so you may want to keep some change handy.

CONTRACEPTION Condoms are available from pharmacies (*farmacias*) in all the main towns, though they are so expensive that many Guatemalans can't afford to use them. Some makes of the Pill are available, mostly those manufactured in the States, but these are also pricey, so it's more sensible to bring enough to last for your entire stay. Bear in mind that diarrhoea can reduce the reliability of the Pill (or any other drug) as it may not be in your system long enough to be fully absorbed.

DRUGS Increasingly available as the country is becoming a centre for both shipment and production. Marijuana is readily available and cheap – especially as in recent years Petén has become an area of production, and there is a plentiful supply across the border in Belize. Cocaine is also extremely cheap as it is shipped to the States through Guatemala, and heroin, now produced here, is also to be found on the streets. The drugs problem is viewed increasingly seriously by the government and users will be dealt with harshly. If you're caught, expect to go to jail, or at least pay a hefty fine/bribe in order to avoid it.

ELECTRICITY 110 volts AC in most places, although in isolated spots the current is 220 volts, so ask before you plug in any vital equipment. Anything from Britain will need a transformer and a plug adapter, as may some US appliances. Cuts in the supply and wild fluctuations in the current are fairly common, and in some isolated villages, where they have their own generator, the supply only operates for part of the day (usually the early evening and morning).

EMBASSIES AND CONSULATES Listed on p.72 in the Guatemala City section, where almost every country is represented. In addition there are Mexican consulates in Quetzaltenango and Retalhuleu, and Honduran consulates in Esquipulas and Puerto Barrios.

GAY GUATEMALA Homosexuality is publicly strongly frowned upon – although not theoretically illegal. Macho attitudes incorporate an overwhelming prejudice against gays, and the newspapers occasionally include accounts which might read "the arrest of prostitutes and gays". Discretion is the only answer. There is a small gay community in Guatemala City, but few clubs or public meeting places (see box on p.69). You could also call the low-key gay helpline, OASIS, on ☎2323335 for more details.

LAUNDRY Hotels occasionally offer a laundry service, and most inexpensive places will have somewhere where you can wash and dry your own clothes. In Guatemala City, Quetzaltenango, Panajachel, Huehuetenango and Antigua there are self-service laundries, as well as several places that will do your washing for you – on the whole these are much easier and cost about the same.

METRIC WEIGHTS AND MEASURES See box below.

STUDENT CARDS might get you a discount from time to time, but it's hardly worth struggling to obtain one as there are very few places that offer concessionary rates.

STUDYING SPANISH Guatemala is a great place to study Spanish, with language schools in Antigua, Guatemala City, Huehuetenango and Quetzaltenango among other places. Antigua's branch of the American organization Amerispan (in US: ☎1-800/879-6640; fax 215/985-4524) can match potential students with schools throughout Latin America, and is a useful information and resource centre.

THINGS TO BRING Insect repellent is a must – you can buy it in markets, particularly in Petén, which is where you'll really need it. You can also buy coils that burn through the night to keep the beasts at bay, although if you plan to sleep out there's no substitute for a mosquito net – which you can also buy in the markets in Petén. A torch and alarm clock are worth having for catching those pre-dawn buses, and it's always a good idea to carry toilet paper with you. It's easy enough to buy in Guatemala but it's never there when you need it.

TIME ZONES Guatemala is on the equivalent of Central Standard Time, six hours earlier than GMT. There is very little seasonal change – it gets light around 6am, with sunset at around 6.30pm all year round.

TIPS In upmarket restaurants a ten percent tip is appropriate, but in most places, especially the cheaper ones, tipping is the exception rather than the rule. Taxi drivers are not normally tipped.

TOILETS These are nearly always Western-style (the squat-toilet is rare), with a bucket beside the bowl for your toilet paper. Standards vary greatly throughout the country, but in general the further you are from a city the worse the condition. Public toilets are few and far between; some are filthy, while others are well looked after by an attendant who usually sells toilet paper. The most common name is *baños*, and the signs are *damas* (women) and *caballeros* (men).

VOLUNTEER AGENCIES There's always a demand for volunteers in Guatemala, and several agencies can help you find work. CIAO (Central Index for Appointments Overseas) lists companies looking for professional and semi-skilled volunteers on its excellent website at *www.ciao-directory.org*, while the Central Bureau, 10 Spring Gardens, London SW1A 2BN (☎0171/389 4880), has a section on Guatemala in its book *The*

METRIC WEIGHTS AND MEASURES

1 ounce = 28.3 grams	1 inch = 2.54 centimetres
1 pound = 454 grams	1 foot = 0.3 metre
2.2 pounds = 1 kilogram	1 yard = 0.91 metre
1 pint = 0.47 litre	1.09 yards = 1 metre
1 quart = 0.94 litre	1 mile = 1.61 kilometres
1 gallon = 3.78 litres	0.62 miles = 1 kilometre

Guatemalan Maya also use the ***legua***, a distance of about four miles, which is roughly the distance a person can walk in an hour. ***Yardas*** are yards.

Indigenous fabrics are often sold by the ***vara***, an old Spanish measure of about 33 inches, while land is sometimes measured by the ***cuerda***, a square with sides of 32 *varas*. The larger local units are the ***manzana***, equivalent to three-quarters of a hectare or 1.73 acres, and the ***caballeria*** (45.12 hectares).

Complete Voluntary Service. In Guatemala, El Arco, 5 Av Norte 25B, Antigua (☎8320162), is a good walk-in resource centre, while the Escuela Español Xelaju, 9 C 11–26, Quetzaltenango (☎7612628) runs community projects and encourages its students to help out. Last but definitely not least is the Casa Alianza (see p.50 for details), who need volunteers over-21 who can commit themselves to at least six months helping street children in Guatemala City.

WATER Tap water in the main towns is purified and you can usually taste the chlorine. However, this doesn't mean that it won't give you stomach trouble, and it's always safest to stick to bottled water. For more on water see p.15.

WORK is generally badly paid, and unless you have something special to offer, your best bet is to teach English. The English schools in Guatemala City, in particular, are always on the lookout for new teachers.

CHAPTER ONE

GUATEMALA CITY AND AROUND

C haotic, congested and polluted, **Guatemala City** sprawls, at an altitude of 1350m, across a sweeping highland basin, surrounded on three sides by low hills and volcanic cones. The capital was moved here in 1776, after the seismic devastation of Antigua, but the site – on a natural trade route between the Pacific and the Caribbean – had been of importance long before the arrival of the Spanish. In its early years, the capital grew slowly, and it wasn't until the beginning of this century that it really began to dominate the country. These days, *el capital* is a shapeless, swelling mass, ringed by shanty towns and ranking as the largest city in Central America. It's home to around three million people, a quarter of Guatemala's population, and is the undisputed centre of power, politics, wealth and squalour.

The city has an intensity and vibrancy that are both its fascination and its horror, and for many travellers a trip to the capital is an exercise in damage limitation, struggling through a swirling mass of bus fumes and beggars. The centre is now run-down and polluted – and the affluent middle classes have long since fled to the suburbs – but it does have its share of "sights", including the odd, lonely architectural gem and a couple of good museums. Beyond this, the overwhelming impression has to be the sheer energy of life on the streets, where aspirations focus due north on the materialism of the USA, and an aggressively commercial outlook pervades.

Like it or not – and many travellers don't – Guatemala City is the crossroads of the country, and you'll certainly end up here at some time, if only to hurry between bus terminals or negotiate a visa extension. Once you get used to the pace, though, it can offer a welcome break from life on the road, with a wide variety of restaurants, cinemas, shops and metropolitan culture. And if you really can't take the city, it's easy enough to escape; buses leave every few minutes, day and night.

ACCOMMODATION PRICE CODES

All accommodation listed in this guide has been graded according to the following price scales. These refer to the price in US dollars of the cheapest double room in high season. For more details see p.25.

① Under $5	④ $15–25	⑦ $60–80
② $5–10	⑤ $25–40	⑧ $80–100
③ $10–15	⑥ $45–60	⑨ over $100

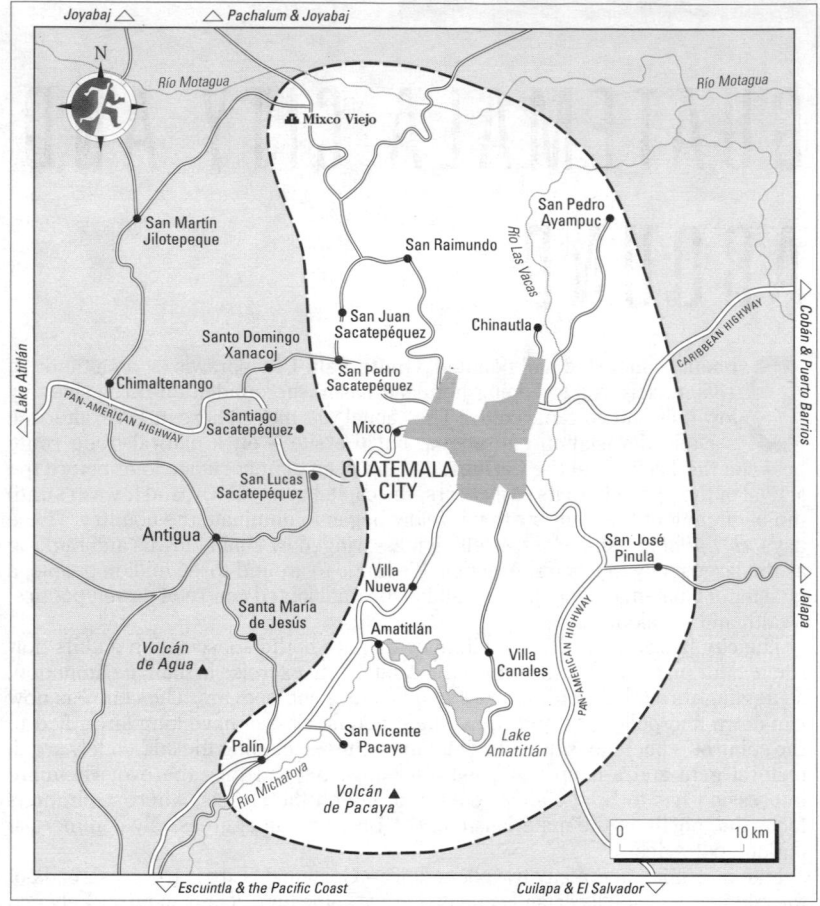

The hills that surround the city have somehow managed to remain unaffected by it, and within an hour or so you'll find yourself in the woods and fresh, mountain air of the highlands. The city basin is hemmed in on three sides by a horseshoe of hills, while to the south, in a narrow gap between the volcanic peaks of Agua and Pacaya, the Río Michatoya and the Pacific Highway cut through to the ocean. Heading out this way you pass **Lake Amatitlán**, a popular weekend resort for those who don't have their own *fincas*. Beyond here a branch road leads up to the village of **San Vicente Pacaya**, from where you can climb the smoking **Pacaya volcano**, the most active of Guatemala's volcanic peaks. The cone's size and appearance aren't particularly impressive, but for the last few years it has been spewing a fountain of sulphurous gas and molten rock that glows red in the night sky. Further down the valley is the village of **Palín**, beyond which you emerge at Escuintla and the Pacific coast, with Puerto San José and the chance of a dip in the ocean just three or four hours from the capital (see chapter 3: The Pacific Coast).

Leaving the city from the opposite side, to the northwest, you travel out through rolling hills and pine forests to the villages of **San Pedro Sacatepéquez** and **San Juan Sacatepéquez**. Both were badly hit by the 1976 earthquake but are now returning to normal and are well worth visiting for their weekend markets. To the north of the villages the road divides, one branch heading northeast over the mountains to **Rabinal**, and the other northwest towards Pachalum, passing the ruins of **Mixco Viejo**, a well-restored but rarely visited site in a spectacular, isolated setting.

GUATEMALA CITY

Guatemala City, an extremely horizontal place, is like a city on its back. Its ugliness, which is a threatened look (the low morose houses have earthquake cracks in their facades; the buildings wince at you with fright lines), is ugliest on those streets where, just past the toppling houses, a blue volcano's cone bulges. I could see the volcanoes from the window of my hotel room. I was on the third floor, which was also the top floor. They were tall volcanoes and looked capable of spewing lava. Their beauty was undeniable; but it was the beauty of witches. The rumbles from their fires had heaved this city down.

Paul Theroux, *The Old Patagonian Express*

Though Theroux's dark impressions remain relevant for much of the city most of the time, Guatemala City is by no means always as black as he implies. It is certainly not somewhere you visit for its beauty or architectural charm, with a few notable exceptions, but a near idyllic climate and the lush greenery of the suburbs give it a certain appeal. Its setting is also dramatic, positioned in a massive highland bowl on a site that was a centre of population and political power long before the arrival of the Spanish. The pre-Conquest city of **Kaminaljuyú**, with its ruins still scattered amongst the western suburbs, was well established here two thousand years ago. In early Classic times (250–550 AD), as a result of an alliance with the great northern power of Teotihuacán (near present-day Mexico City), Kaminaljuyú came to dominate the highlands, and eventually provided the political and commercial backing that fostered the rise of Tikal. The city was situated at the crossroads of the north–south and east–west trade routes, and also controlled the obsidian mine at El Chayal, giving it a virtual monopoly of this essential commodity. To further ensure its wealth, Kaminaljuyú also had access to a supply of quetzal feathers, another highly valued item.

At the height of its prosperity Kaminaljuyú was home to a population of some 50,000. However, following the decline of Teotihuacán and its influence, around 600 AD, it was surpassed by the great lowland centres that it had helped to establish. Soon after their rise, some time between 600 and 900 AD, it was abandoned.

Seven centuries later, when Alvarado entered the country, the fractured tribes of the west controlled the highlands and preoccupied the conquistadors. The nearest centre of any importance was the Pokoman capital of **Mixco Viejo**, about 60km to the northwest. Mainly because of the need to keep a close watch on the western tribes, the Spanish ignored the possibility of settling here, founding their capital instead at Iximché, and later at two separate sites in the Panchoy valley.

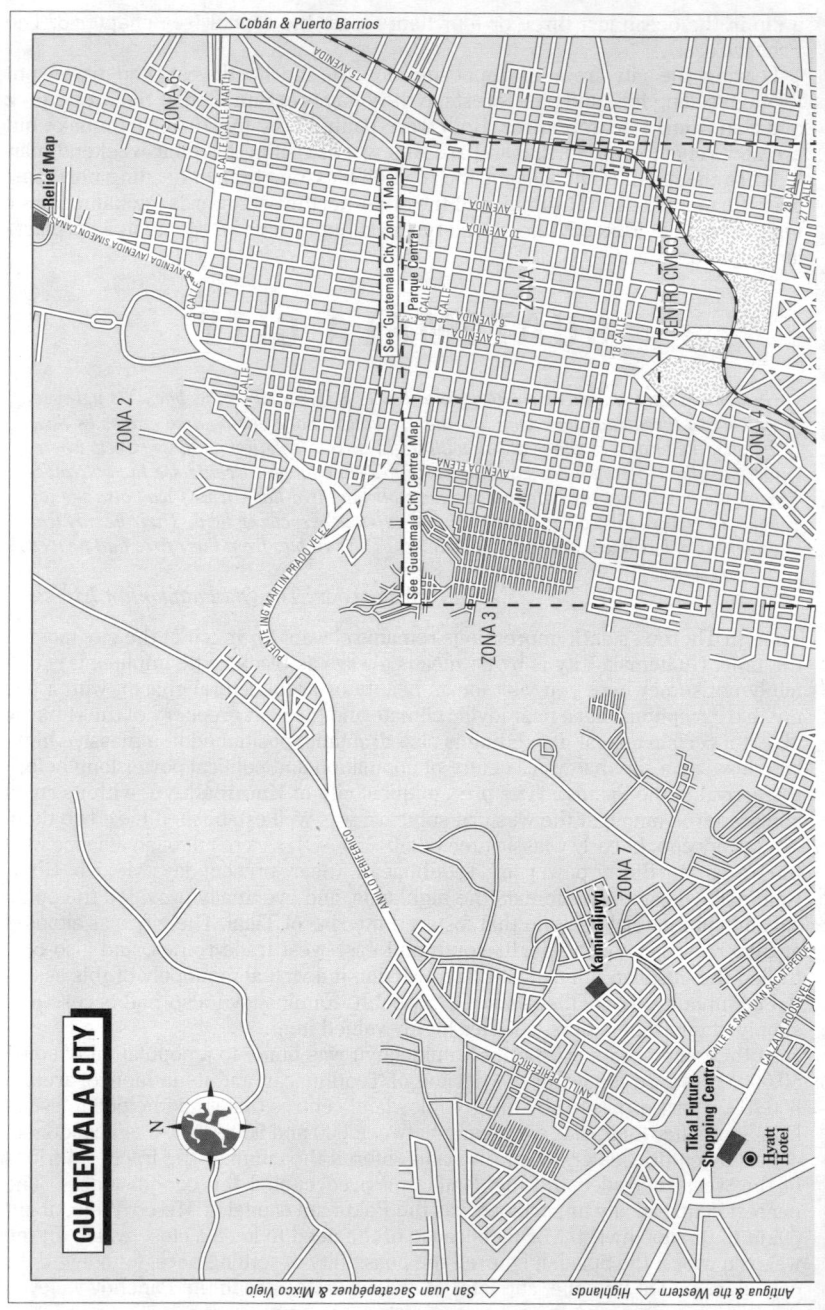

GUATEMALA CITY

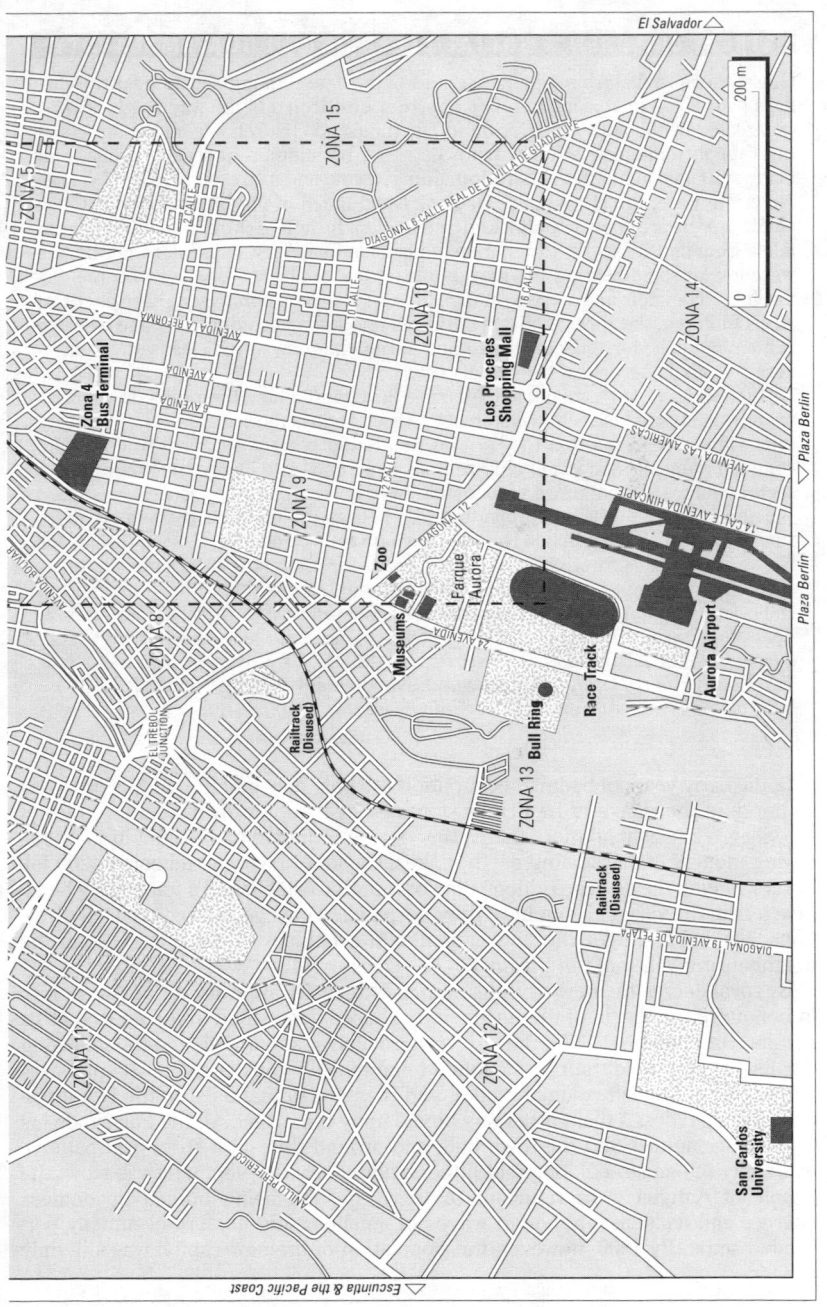

STREET CHILDREN & SOCIAL CLEANSING IN GUATEMALA CITY

One of the most disturbing manifestations of the deteriorating situation for the capital's poor is the increasing number of **street children** and the way in which they are treated by the authorities. Around five thousand children live on the streets of the capital, scratching a living from begging, prostitution and petty crime, and many sniff glue to numb the boredom, hunger, cold and depression. Faced by a rising crime wave, the city's police have directed much of the blame towards these children, who are regularly attacked and beaten. In June 1990, eight children were taken from the streets by armed men in plain clothes. A few days later their bodies were found, some bearing the marks of **torture**. Similar cases have become disturbingly common and despite journalists now giving publicity to the plight of street children, the threats, disappearances and killings continue. In one week in September 1997, forty people, including seven children, were "cleansed" (ie murdered) from the streets of Guatemala City.

Human rights workers and aid agencies have highlighted the problem, which is by no means exclusive to Guatemala within Latin America. In 1997, Amnesty International reported that the "**social cleansing** of so-called 'undesirables' like common criminals and street children has been known to involve members of the security forces. Few of those responsible have been brought to justice".

The main group offering protection and help to the children is **Casa Alianza**, run by the British-born Bruce Harris, who has received countless death threats for his work as well as the 1996 Olof Palme award for promoting international understanding and common security. The organization runs a refuge for the children, and is always on the look out for **volunteers**. You can contact them at Casa Alianza, Apartado Postal, 2704 Guatemala (℡2532965; fax 2533003; email: *bruce@casa-alianza.org*); or at SJO 1039, PO Box 025216, Miami, FL 33102–5216, in the US; or The Coach House, Grafton Underwood, Northants, NN14 3AA in the UK. More information is available on their web site, *www.casa-alianza.org*.

In the early years of Spanish occupation the only new building in this area was a church in the village of La Ermita, founded in 1620. For over a hundred years the village remained no more than a tiny cluster of Indian homes, but in 1773, following months of devastating earthquakes, Captain Mayorga and some 4200 followers, fleeing the disease-ridden ruins of Antigua, established a temporary headquarters in the village. From here they despatched envoys and scouts in all directions, seeking a site for the new capital, and eventually decided to settle in the neighbouring Valley of the Virgin.

By royal decree the new city was named **Nueva Guatemala de la Asunción**, in honour of the Virgin of the Ascension, whose image stood in the church at La Ermita. On January 1, 1776, the city was officially inaugurated, and the following day its "fathers" held their first council to administer construction. The plan was typical of the Spanish colonial model, and identical to that used in the two previous, ill-fated cities. A main plaza was boxed in by the cathedral, the Palacio de los Capitans Generales and the town hall, and around this, on a strict grid pattern, was a city fifteen streets long and fifteen wide. Early development was slow: the people of Antigua were reluctant to leave, despite being bullied by endless decrees and deadlines, although waves of smallpox and cholera eventually persuaded some. By 1800, however, the population of the new capital was still only 25,000.

The splendour of the former capital was hard to re-establish and the new city's growth was steady but by no means dramatic. An 1863 census listed the main structures as 1206 residences, 7 warehouses, 130 shops, 28 churches, 1 slaughterhouse, 2 forts, 12 schools, and 25 fountains and public laundries. The author, Enrique Palacios, concluded that it was "a delightful city and a pleasant place to live". Boddam-Wetham, on the other hand, living here in 1877, claimed that it was "gloomy and dull; owing to the uniformity of the houses ... the regularity of the streets ... and the absence of traffic", adding that "the few signs of life are depressing". When Eadweard Muybridge took some of the earliest photographs in 1875, the city was still little more than a large village with a theatre, a government palace and a fort.

One of the factors retarding the city's growth was the existence of a major rival, Quetzaltenango (Xela). Stimulated by the coffee boom and large numbers of German immigrants, Quetzaltenango competed with the capital in both size and importance, until 1902, when it was razed to the ground by a massive **earthquake**. After this, many wealthy families moved to the capital, finally establishing it as the country's primary city. By then, Guatemala City's population had already been boosted by the exodus from another major earthquake, this time in Antigua. Inevitably, the capital's turn came. On Christmas Eve 1917 Guatemala City was shaken by the first in a series of devastating tremors, and not until early February, after six long weeks of destruction, did the ground stabilize and the dust settle. This time, however, there was nowhere to run; spurred on by the celebrations of a century of independence, and the impetus of the eccentric President Ubico, reconstruction began.

Since 1918 Guatemala City has grown at an incredible rate, tearing ahead of the rest of the country at a pace that still shows little sign of letting up. The flight from the fields, characteristic of all developing countries, is caused by a chronic shortage of land and employment in the countryside, and was exacerbated during the civil war by the army's scorched-earth tactics to combat guerilla groups. According to some estimates, six hundred new *campesinos* arrive in the city every day, many of whom are economic migrants, high on hope and dreams of wealth and prosperity that few will achieve. In some ways the capital is becoming a city of refugees, filled with displaced people, largely Mayan, most of whom feel unwanted and unwelcome here. The deep ravines that surround the city, thought by the original Spanish planners to offer protection from the force of earthquakes, are now filling rapidly with rubbish and shanty towns, while street crime increases daily.

The divisions that cleave Guatemalan society are at their most acute in the capital's crumbling streets. While the wealthy elite sip coffee in air-conditioned shopping malls, Zona 1, the heart of the city, has been left to disintegrate into a threatening, treeless tangle of fume-choked streets, devoid of any kind of life after dark. With glass skyscrapers towering over run-down colonial churches, and shoeless Mayan widows peddling cigarettes and sweets to designer-clad nightclubbers, the contrasts of poverty and extravagance are extreme.

Arrival and information

Although the scale of Guatemala City, with its suburbs sprawled across some nineteen **zones**, can seem overwhelming at first glance, the layout is straightforward and the central area, which is all that you need to worry about, is really quite small. Like almost all Guatemalan towns it's arranged on a strict grid pattern, with **avenidas** running north–south and **calles** east–west.

Broadly speaking, the city divides into two distinct halves. The northern section, centred on **Zona 1**, is the old part of town, containing the central plaza or **Parque Central**, most of the budget hotels, shops, restaurants, cinemas, the post office, and many of the bus companies. This part of the city is cramped, congested and polluted but bustling with activity. The two main streets are 5 and 6 avenidas, both thick with street traders, fast-food joints and neon lights.

To the south, acting as a buffer between the two halves of town, is **Zona 4**, home of the city's main **bus terminal** and the **Centro Cívico**, where you'll find all the main administrative buildings, the tourist office, the central market, and the National Theatre. Further south still, the modern half of the city comprises wealthy **Zonas 9** and **10**, which are separated by the main artery the **Avenida La Reforma**. Here, you'll find exclusive offices, apartment blocks, hotels and shops as well as Guatemala's most expensive nightclubs, restaurants and cafés. Many of the embassies and two of the country's finest museums are also here. Continuing south, the neighbouring **Zonas 13** and **14** hold rich leafy suburbs, and are home to the airport, zoo and more museums and cinemas.

Arrival

Arriving in Guatemala City is always a bit disconcerting, but most of the budget and mid-range hotels are bunched together in central Zona 1, so you'll find that settling in isn't as daunting as it might at first appear. If you're laden with luggage, it's probably not a good idea to take on the bus system, and a taxi is well worth the extra cost (see p.54 for details). For details on using the transport terminals to **move on** from the capital, see p.73. Note that there are currently no **trains** at all running anywhere in Guatemala.

By air

Aurora airport is on the edge of the city in Zona 13, some way from the centre, but close to Zona 10. The domestic terminal, though in the same complex, is separate, and entered by Av Hincapié. Much the easiest way to get to and from the airport is by **taxi**: you'll find plenty of them waiting outside the terminal. The fare

---

ADDRESSES IN GUATEMALA CITY

The system of **street numbering** in the capital may seem a little confusing at first, as the same numbers are given to different streets in different zones. However, once learnt, the system is remarkably logical and simple to use.

When it comes to finding an address, always check for the **zone** first and then the street. For example "4 Av 9–14, Zona 1" is in Zona 1, on 4 Avenida between 9 and 10 Calle, house number 14. Be warned that the same calles and avenidas exist in several different zones.

You may see street numbers written as 1a, 7a, etc, rather than simply 1, 7. This is technically more correct, since the names of the streets are not One Avenue and Seven Street, but First (*primera*), Seventh (*séptima*) and so on. A capital "A" used as a suffix indicates a smaller street between two large ones: 1 Calle A is a short street between 1 and 2 calles.

> **NEW BUS TERMINALS**
>
> Two new **long-distance bus terminals** are currently being built on the outskirts of Guatemala City in order to relieve the congestion and overcrowding of the Zona 4 and Zona 1 terminals. The **Meta del Norte** terminal in Barrio de la Parroquia, Zona 6, will serve the east of the country and Petén, while the **Central de Mayoreo** terminal on Calzada Aguilar Batres, in Zona 12, will be the depot for services to the western highlands and the Pacific coast. Both terminals are expected to be in operation some time in 1999, though the government has had problems persuading the bus companies to relocate from their current central premises. If in any doubt about where your bus will arrive or leave from, check first with the individual bus company, or with the tourist office in Guatemala City (see below).

to Zona 1 costs around $10, to Antigua around $25. **Buses** also leave from directly outside the terminal, across the concrete plaza – take #83 for Zona 1.

The Banco del Quetzal at the airport (Mon–Fri 7am–8pm, Sat & Sun 8am–8pm) gives a better **exchange** rate than you'll get outside the country, and takes most European currencies as well as dollars. If you arrive late at night, however, you'll need a supply of dollar bills to get you into the city and to your accommodation. For tourist **information**, there's an Inguat office (daily 6am–9pm) at the airport, and a Telgua desk, for phone calls, which should be open 24 hours a day.

By bus

If you arrive in the city by second-class bus prepare yourself for the jungle of the **Zona 4 bus terminal**, which has to rate as Guatemala City's most chaotic, fume-filled corner. On the whole, it's only second-class buses from the western and eastern highlands that arrive here, so if you're coming in from the Pacific coast or from Petén you'll be spared, arriving instead at the Zona 1 terminal (see below). However, if you do end up in Zona 4, and decide not to take a taxi – there are always plenty around at the entrance to the terminal – you'll need to walk a couple of blocks to the corner of 2 C and 4 Av, from where local buses go to the centre of town (#17 is one, but always check that the driver is going to *Zona Uno*).

Most of the buses that don't use the Zona 4 terminal will end up somewhere in Zona 1, close enough to walk to a hotel, or at least an inexpensive taxi ride away. The Zona 1 bus terminal is at 18 C and 9 Av, but many companies, especially first-class ones, have their own offices. All the main bus companies, their addresses and bus departure times, are given in "Travel Details", at the end of this chapter on p.80.

Information and maps

The main **tourist office**, Inguat, at 7 Av 1–17, Zona 4 (Mon–Fri 8.30am–4.30pm, Sat 8.30am–1pm; ☎3311333; fax 3318893), has an information desk on the ground floor where you can buy a half-decent **map** of the country and city, or put your questions to the staff – usually someone there speaks English. There's also an Inguat office at the airport (see above). For detailed maps of Guatemala suitable for trekking and exploration, try the Instituto Geografico Militar, Av las Américas 5–76, Zona 13 (Mon–Fri 8am–4pm); bus #65 from the Centro Cívico gets you nearest, or take a taxi. Selected photocopies of these maps, including restricted sheets, are also sold in Antigua at the Casa Andinista bookshop (see p.105 for details).

City transport

In any big city, coping with the public transport system takes time, and Guatemala City is no different; even locals are often baffled by its anarchic web of **bus routes**. To complicate matters further, the city authorities regularly re-route buses in an attempt to control traffic congestion, and most of Zona 1's streets are one-way so buses return along different roads. Add to this the fact that some buses with the same numbers operate along different routes, and confusion reigns. The easiest way to handle it is to accept that getting on the wrong bus isn't the end of the world, and that you can always get off and catch another, or cross the road and go back to where you started. Above all else the buses are cheap, so you'll need some small change to hand. In Zona 1, the most useful streets are **4 Av**, where buses leave for many different parts of the city (destinations are posted on the front of the bus), and **10 Av** for buses #82 and #83. Buses **run** from around 6 or 7am until about 10pm, but try and avoid travelling during the ferocious rush hour (7.30–9am and 4.30–7pm), when many roads throughout the city are jammed solid.

Some routes are covered by a number of new **metro buses**, which are a little cleaner, more modern and a touch more expensive (around Q1) than the ordinary buses. In addition, **minibuses** serve similar routes to the ordinary buses, but tend to be a little more expensive. After 10pm, the minibuses effectively operate as taxis, running along vaguely defined routes until around 1am.

Taxis

If you can't face the complexities of the bus system, or it's late at night, then taxis are a good option and not necessarily that expensive. The excellent new **metered** taxis are comfortable and cheap – *Amarillo* cabs (☎3321515; 24hr) are highly recommended and will pick you up from anywhere in the city; a journey from Zona 1 to Zona 10 will cost $4–5. There are also plenty of **unmetered** taxis around, though you'll have to use your bargaining skills with these. They invariably ask for more than their metered cousins, so always fix the price beforehand.

USEFUL BUS ROUTES

#17 Marked *Kaminaljuyú* – runs along 4 Av in Zona 1, and will take you out west into Zona 7, and to the ruins of Kaminaljuyú.

#71 Connects 10 Av in Zona 1, with the Centro Cívico and the Immigration office, just off Av La Castellana (see p.72 for details) – get off by the big Shell garage just before the flyover.

#82 Starts in Zona 2, then heads along 10 Av, through Zona 1 and the Centro Cívico in Zona 4, then continues down Av La Reforma before turning left at the Obelisco. Ideal for getting between Zonas 1 and 10, this route takes you past many of the embassies, the American Express office, the Popol Vuh and Ixchel museums (see p.63) and the Los Próceres shopping centre.

#83 Shuttles between Zona 1 and the airport.

Terminal Any bus marked *terminal*, and there are plenty of these on 4 Av in Zona 1, will take you to the main bus terminal in Zona 4.

Bolívar or Trébol Any bus with either of these written on will take you along the western side of the city, down Av Bolívar to the Trébol junction.

Accommodation

Accommodation in Guatemala City comes in all shapes and sizes and to suit all pockets, though you'll almost certainly pay more here than in the rest of the country. The majority of the budget choices are conveniently grouped around the centre and eastern side of Zona 1; there are also a few near the two main bus terminals, but these are really for emergency use only (or for very early starts) as the neighbourhoods are neither pleasant nor safe. Bearing in mind that the city is not a great place to be wandering around in search of a room, it's a good idea to call ahead and book. Similiarly, if you arrive after dark, it makes sense to take a taxi. All Zona 1 accommodation is marked on the map on p.60; all accommodation in Zonas 9 and 10 is marked on the map on p.56.

Budget accommodation

Hotel Bristol, 15 C 7–36, Zona 1 (☎2381401). Grim, very basic, but extremely cheap and in a reasonable location. ①.

Hotel Casa Lessing, 12 C 4–35, Zona 1 (☎2381881). Simple budget hotel: the small rooms aren't very exiting, but it's central, clean and friendly. ③.

Hotel Costa del Sol, 17 C 8–17, Zona 1 (☎2321296). Opposite the terminals for Petén, this is really only an option if you're just off the bus and cannot face more travelling. It's basic, but has hot water, and is secure – one of the only places round here that isn't a brothel. ③.

Hotel Fenix, 7 Av 15–81, Zona 1 (☎2516625). Safe and friendly, in a vaguely atmospheric old wooden building. There's a café downstairs and some rooms have private bathrooms. ②.

Hotel Hernani, on the corner of 15 C & 6 Av A, Zona 1 (☎2322839). Comfortable old building with good, clean rooms, all with their own shower. One of the best budget places in town. ②.

Pensión Meza, 10 C 10–17, Zona 1 (☎2323177; fax 2534576). Infamous budget travellers' hang-out, run by the delightful Mario. Fidel Castro and Che Guevara both stayed here, the latter in room 21, although his bed is now in room 10. It's cheap and laid-back, with plenty of 1960s-style ornaments, and has dorms and double rooms, some with private shower. There's a noticeboard, ping pong, music all day and a cheap restaurant next door. ①.

Hotel Monteleone, 18 C 4–63, Zona 1 (☎2382600; fax 2382509). Extremely clean and safe; the rooms are attractively decorated, have good quality matresses and bedside lamps, and come with or without private bath. Right by the terminal for buses to Antigua, it's the best value in the city. ②.

Hotel Posada Real, 12 C 6–21, Zona 1 (☎2381092). A little rough and dark, but still safe and central. All rooms have bathrooms, some have TV. ③.

Hotel San Martin 16 C 7–65 Zona 1 (☎2380319). Very cheap, clean and friendly, one of the best value places at the lower end of the scale. Some rooms have private bath. ②.

Hotel Spring, 8 Av 12–65, Zona 1 (☎2326637; fax 2320107). Excellent value and a safe location, though usually full with Peace Corp volunteers. The rooms, some with private bath, are set around a pretty colonial courtyard, and free mineral water is available. ②–③.

Mid-range accommodation

El Aeropuerto Guest House, 15 C A 7–32, Zona 13 (☎3323086). Pleasant, convenient and very comfortable hotel, just five minutes' walk from the international airport; cross the grass from the terminal and follow the road to the left, or call to be picked up. All rooms have private showers, hot water and fluffy towels. ⑤.

Hotel del Centro, 13 C 4–55, Zona 1 (☎2325547; fax 2300208). Large faded hotel dating from the 1960s. The rooms are not exactly resplendent, with brown carpets and flowery bedspreads, but all have private bathrooms and cable TV. ⑥.

Chalet Suizo, 14 C 6–82, Zona 1 (☎2513786; fax 2320429). Friendly, comfortable and should be very safe, due to its location opposite the police headquarters. Nicely designed, spotlessly clean and all very Swiss and organized, with left luggage and a café that's open all day. No double beds. ④.

Hotel Colonial, 7 Av 14–19, Zona 1 (☎2326722; fax 2328671). Well-situated colonial-style hotel with dark wood, wrought iron and attractive tiles in the lobby. Tasteful and comfortable, but slightly old-fashioned, the rooms come with or without private bathroom. ④.

Hotel Carillon, 5 Av 11–25 Zona 9 (☎ & fax 3324036). This wood-panelled hotel is good value for the location, and has well-appointed rooms. ⑤.

Hotel Excel, 9 Av 15–12, Zona 1 (☎2300140). Clean and safe, but near the red light district; has the advantage of secure parking. ④.

Hotel Fortuna Real, 12 C 8–42, Zona 1 (☎2303378; fax 2512215). Spotless, Chinese-owned hotel in a safe location at the heart of Zona 1. All rooms boast rather bizarre decor, but have TV and private bath and there's a restaurant downstairs. ⑤.

Hotel Hincapié, Av Hincapié 18–77, Zona 13 (☎3327771; fax 3374469). Under the same management as the *Aeropuerto Guest House* and conveniently located for the domestic terminal. Rates include local calls, continental breakfast, and transport to and from the airport. ⑤.

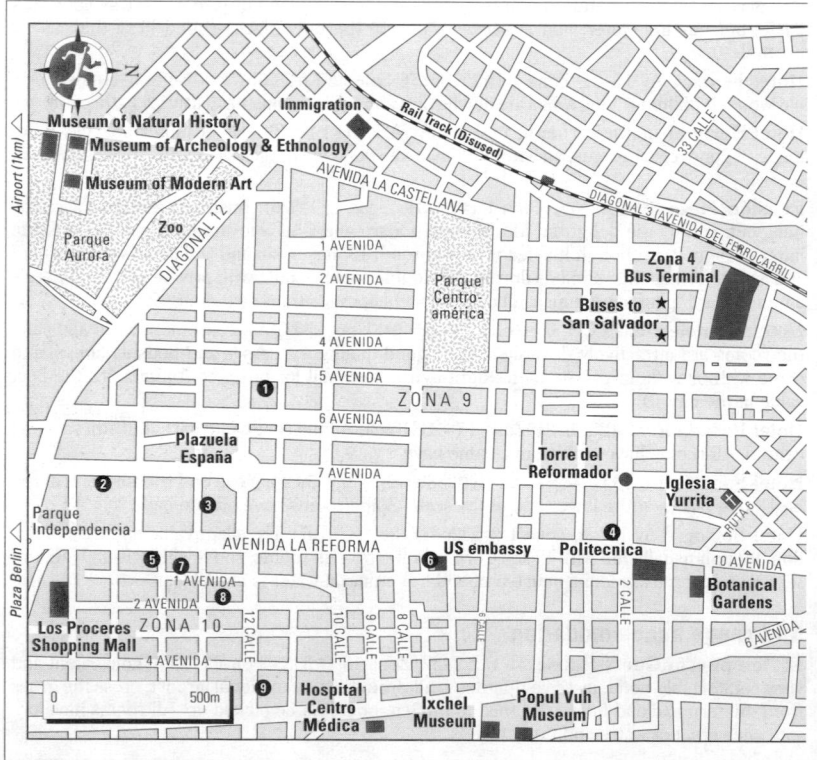

Hotel PanAmerican, 9 C 5–63, Zona 1 (☎2326807; fax 2518749). The city's oldest smart hotel, very formal and civilized, with a strong emphasis on Guatemalan tradition. Cable TV, continental breakfast and airport transfer are included. Even if you can't afford to stay here, drop in for one of the great Sunday breakfasts. ⑤.

Hotel Posada Belén, 13 C A 10–30, Zona 1 (☎2534530; fax 2513478). In a beautiful old building, tucked down a side street, this hotel is supremely quiet and safe and very homely; no children under five. ⑤.

Luxury accommodation

Camino Real, Av La Reforma & 14 C, Zona 10 (☎4484633; fax 3374313). The favoured address for visiting heads of state and anyone on expenses, this hotel continues to lead the luxury category in spite of increasing competition from newer places; rooms start at US$180. ⑨.

La Casa Grande, Av La Reforma 7–67, Zona 10 (☎ & fax 3320914). Elegant villa set slightly back from the road, right next to the US embassy. ⑦.

Hotel Casa Santa Clara, 12 C 4–51, Zona 10 (☎3391811; fax 3320775). Small, beautifully appointed hotel in the heart of the *Zona Viva*, the lively entertainment enclave. It also boasts a good quality Middle Eastern restaurant. ⑦.

Hotel Cortijo Reforma, Av La Reforma 2–18, Zona 9 (☎3322713; fax 3318876). Convenient first-class hotel near the American embassy. ⑦.

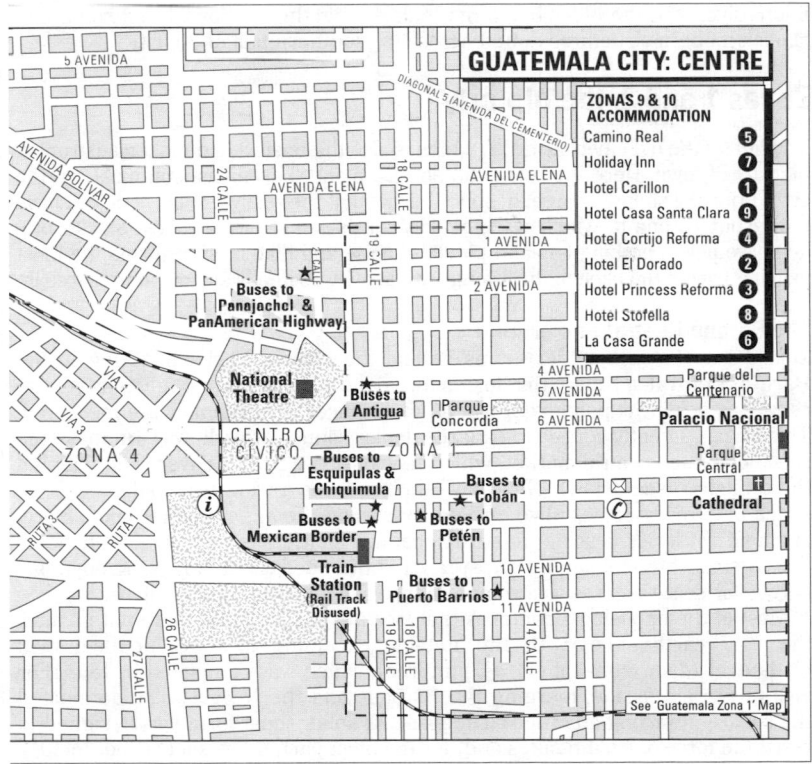

Crowne Plaza Las Américas, Av Las Américas 9–08, Zona 13 (☎3390676; fax 3390690 or 4489071). One of the newest luxury hotels in town, the latest in design and modern services, but you need your own transport or taxi to reach the *Zona Viva*. Rooms start at US$125. ⑨.

Hotel El Dorado, 7 Av 15–45, Zona 9 (☎3317777; fax 3321877). Similar to the *Camino Real*, very luxurious and comfortable. Rooms start at US$140. ⑨.

Holiday Inn, 1 Av 13–22, Zona 10 (☎3322555; fax 3322584). First-class hotel, within walking distance of the city's best upmarket shops, bars and restaurants. Best value in the luxury category. ⑦.

Hotel Princess Reforma, 13 C 7–65, Zona 9 (☎3344545; fax 3344546). Pleasant mid-sized hotel with small pool, sauna, gym and tennis courts. Rooms from US$134. ⑨.

Hotel Ritz Continental, 6 Av A 10–13, Zona 1 (☎2381671; fax 2324659). Huge modern block in the city centre, recently renovated and with all the luxury you'd expect. ⑧.

Hotel Stofella, 2 Av 12–28, Zona 10 (☎3346191; fax 3310823). Small-scale, immaculate business-oriented hotel in the *Zona Viva*. ⑦.

The City

Though few people come to Guatemala City for the sights, there are some places that are worth visiting while you're here. Quite apart from the Ixchel and Popol Vuh **museums**, which are particularly good, some of the city's **architecture** is impressive, with the older buildings huddled together in Zona 1 and some outlandish modern structures dotted across the southern half of the city.

Zonas 1 and 2: the old city

The hub of the old city is **Zona 1**, which is also the busiest and most claustrophobic part of town. Here the two main streets, 5 and 6 avenidas, still make up the city's principal shopping area, despite the fact that the really exclusive places have moved out to Zona 10. Much of the old city consists of squalid, faceless blocks, broken pavements, parking lots and plenty of noise and dirt, but it remains the most exciting part of the capital, throbbing with activity as it falls steadily into disrepair.

The Parque Central and around

Zona 1's northern boundary runs behind the Palacio Nacional, taking in the **Parque Central**, a square that forms the country's political and religious centre, as well as being the point from where all distances in Guatemala are measured. This plaza, currently concealing a large underground car park, was originally the scene of a huge central market, which now operates from a covered site behind the cathedral (see below). Nowadays the square is a windswept, soulless place which only really comes alive on Sundays, when the *huipil* market takes place, and a tide of locals descend to stroll, chat and snack. Next to the giant national flag, a small box containing an **eternal flame** dedicated "to the anonymous heroes for peace" serves as a remembrance site for many Guatemalans.

Most of the imposing structures that face the parque today were put up after the 1917 earthquake, with the notable exception of the blue-tile-domed **Cathedral** (daily 8am–1pm & 3–7pm; free), which was completed in 1868. For years its grand facade, merging the Baroque and the Neoclassical, dominated the square, dwarfing all other structures. Its solid, squat form was designed to resist the force of earthquakes and, for the most part, it has succeeded. In 1917 the bell towers were brought down and the cupola fell, destroying the altar, but the central structure, though cracked and patched over the years, remains intact. Inside there are three main aisles, all lined with arching pillars, austere colonial paintings and intricate altars supporting an array of saints. Some of this collection was brought here from the original cathedral in Antigua when the capital was moved in 1776.

These days, however, the most striking building in the plaza is the **Palacio Nacional**, a solid stone-faced structure facing south towards the neon maze of Zona 1. The palace was started in 1939 under the auspices of President Ubico – a characteristically grand gesture from the man who believed that he was a reincarnation of Napoleon – and completed a year before he was ousted in 1944. For decades the palace housed the executive branch of the government, but it's currently being converted into an interactive **museum** on the history of Guatemala. The interior of the palace is set around two attractive Moorish-style courtyards, with the most impressive rooms being the **Salas de Recepción** (state reception rooms), at the front of the second floor. Along one wall is a row of flags and the country's coat of arms, topped with a stuffed quetzal, while the stained-glass windows represent key aspects of Guatemalan history. Back in the main body of the building the stairwells are decorated with murals, again depicting historical scenes, mixed in with images of totally unrelated events: one wall shows a group of idealized pre-Conquest Indians, and another includes a portrait of Don Quixote.

Opposite the cathedral, the western side of the Parque Central merges into the **Parque del Centenario**, former site of the Palacio de los Capitanes Generales. A long single-storey building intended to be used as the National Palace, it was completed at the end of the nineteenth century, then promptly destroyed in the 1917 earthquake. For the 1921 centenary celebration a temporary wooden structure was set up in its place, but once this had served its purpose it went up in flames. After that it was decided to create a park instead, with a bandstand, gardens and a fountain. Sited on the other side of the Parque del Centenario, the fairly unattractive modern **Biblioteca Nacional** (National Library), holds the archives of Central America.

Around the back of the cathedral is the concrete **Mercado Central** (Mon–Sat 6am–6pm, Sun 9am–noon), with a miserable mini-plaza and car park on its roof. Taking no chances, the architect of this building, which replaced an earlier version destroyed in the 1976 earthquake, apparently modelled the structure on a nuclear bunker, sacrificing any aesthetic concerns to the need for strength. Inside, you'll find textiles, leatherware and jewellery on the top floor; fruit, vegetables, snacks, flowers and plants in the middle; and **handicrafts**, mainly basketry and *típica*, in the basement. Unexpectedly, the market is a good spot to buy traditional weaving, with an astonishing range of cloth from all over the country on offer. It is only visited by a trickle of tourists so prices are reasonable and the traders very willing to bargain. This was once the city's main food market but these days it's just one of many, and by no means the largest.

Two blocks east of the market and one block south along 9 Av, you reach one of the city's less well-known museums, **Museo Nacional de Historia**, 9 C 9–70, Zona 1 (daily 10am–4pm; Q10) which features a selection of artefacts relating to Guatemalan history, including documents, clothes and paintings. Probably the most interesting displays are the photographs by Eadweard Muybridge, who, in 1875, was one of the first people to undertake a study of the country.

GUATEMALA CITY: ZONA 1

ACCOMMODATION

Chalet Suizo	8	Hotel Excel	16	Hotel Posada Belén	17
Hotel Bristol	12	Hotel Fenix	9	Hotel Posada Real	6
Hotel Casa Lessing	3	Hotel Fortuna Real	14	Hotel Ritz Continental	7
Hotel Colonial	10	Hotel Hernani	5	Hotel San Martin	11
Hotel Costa del Sol	15	Hotel Monteleone	1	Hotel Spring	13
Hotel del Centro	2	Hotel Pan American	4	Pensión Meza	18

RESTAURANTS & CAFÉS

Altuna	C
Café Leon	G
Delicadezas Hamburgo	B
Europa Bar	D
Las Cien Puertes	F
Long Wah	A
Rey Sol	E

South around 6 and 7 avenidas

Heading south from Parque Central are **6 and 7 avenidas**, thick with clothes shops, restaurants, cinemas, neon signs and bus fumes. What you can't buy in the shops is sold on the pavements, and *McDonalds*, *Wimpy* and *Pizza Hut* are all very much part of the scene. It's here that most people head on a Saturday night, when the traffic has to squeeze between hordes of pedestrians. By 11pm, though, the streets are largely deserted, left to the cigarette sellers and prostitutes.

Sixth Avenida is the more overwhelming of the two main streets. Halfway along, strangely out of place at the corner of 13 C, is the **Iglesia de San Francisco**, a church famous for its carving of the Sacred Heart, which, like several other of its paintings and statues, was brought here from Antigua. Building began in 1780, but was repeatedly interrupted by seismic activity – it's said that cane syrup, egg whites and cow's milk were mixed with the mortar to enhance its strength. For the most part the church fared well, but in 1917 a tremor brought down one of the arches, revealing that the clergy had used the roof cavity to store banned books.

Another block to the south is the **Police Headquarters**, an outlandish-looking castle built in imitation of medieval battlements. The next block is taken up by

Parque Concordia, a leafy square, where there's always a surplus of shoeshine boys, taxi drivers and lottery tickets – the prizes, usually cars, are sometimes on display in a corner of the park. Concordia is also a favourite spot for street performers and travelling preachers, and at weekends you can watch snake charmers, clowns and rabid evangelicals competing furiously for an audience. More disturbingly, this is where many of Guatemala's street children spend the night (see p.50), and the smell of glue can be overpowering.

Over on 7 Avenida, the **post office** (see p.73) is a spectacular Moorish building with a marvellous arch that spans the road. Less impressive is the nearby **Museo Nacional de Artes y Industrias Populares**, a couple of blocks east on 10 Av 10–72 (Tues–Sun 9am–noon & 2–4pm; Q10), with its small, sadly neglected collection of painting, weaving, ceramics, musical instruments and Indian masks.

Returning to 6 Avenida, heading south from the Parque Concordia, things go into a slow but steady decline as the commercial chaos starts to get out of control. A mass of electrical shops line the road and the pavements become increasingly swamped by temporary stalls, many selling clothes. On the left-hand side of 6 Avenida, beneath the trees, **18 Calle** becomes distinctly sleazy, the cheap food stalls and shoeshine boys now mixed in with grimy nightclubs and "streap-tease" joints. By night the streets are patrolled by prostitutes and the local hotels are protected by prison-like grilles. Night or day it's best avoided, but if you really want to delve into the sleaze take nothing of value and a minimum of cash. At the corner of 18 C and 9 Av, the **eastern bus terminal** is the depot for buses to the Mexican border and Petén, while the surrounding streets are home to a number of bus company offices. On the east side of an open square just off 18 C lie the derelict remains of the **train station**, from where trains used to leave for Tecún Umán and Puerto Barrios. The station was mysteriously burnt down in 1996, with all its documents and records going up in smoke the night before auditors were due to start investigating the finances of the state railway company. Tenders are currently out for a new contract to revive Guatemala's railway system, but for the moment no passenger or freight trains run at all. Further east, past the station, lies **Zona 5**, a run-down residential suburb.

Back on 6 Av, at the junction of 18 C, you'll see the **Tipografía Nacional**, the government's printing press and media centre, a wonderful, crumbling building, where bureaucrats beaver away at their task of disseminating information and propaganda. A little further along 6 Av is the **main food market** (daily 6am–6pm), housed in a vast, multi-coloured hangar. Traders who can afford it pay for a space inside, while those who can't spread themselves along the surrounding streets, which are littered with rubbish and soggy with rotten fruit. At the end of this extended block the character of the city is radically transformed as the ageing and claustrophobic streets of Zona 1 give way to the broad avenues of Zona 4 and the Centro Cívico.

Into Zona 4 – the Centro Cívico

At the southern end of the old city, separating it from the newer parts of town, the **Centro Cívico**, also known as the **Centro Municipal**, marks the boundary between zones 1 and 4. At this point the avenidas from the north merge at a couple of roundabouts, from where they fan out into the more spacious southern city. Bunched around these junctions a collection of multi-storey office blocks house the city's main administrative buildings, including the main office of Inguat (see p.53).

Overlooking the concrete sprawl of the Centro Cívico, a block or so to the west, is the **National Theatre**, the city's most prominent and unusual structure. Built on top of the **San José Fortress**, and still surrounded by the original battlements, it's designed along the lines of a huge ship, painted blue and white, with portholes as windows. Finding an entrance that isn't locked is not always easy, but it's well worth the effort for the superb **views** across the city. The building is also home to the little-visited **Military Museum** (Mon–Fri 8am–6pm), a strange homage to the Guatemalan army. Reached through the main theatre gate, this small collection of weapons and uniforms is really only of interest to would-be commandants.

North to Zona 2 and the Parque Minerva

North of the old city centre is Zona 2, bounded by a deep-cut ravine that prevents the sprawl from spreading any further in this direction. Right out on the edge is the **Parque Minerva,** also known as the Hipodromo del Norte (daily 8am–5pm; Q2), a park and sports complex, where fairs take place on public holidays and fiestas. Its main point of interest, however, is a **relief map of the country**, which covers 2500 square metres and has a couple of special viewing towers. The map was finished in 1905 and designed to have running water flowing in the rivers, although the taps are usually shut off. Its vertical scale is out of proportion to the horizontal, making the mountains look incredibly steep. It does nonetheless give you a good idea of the general layout of the country, from the complexity of the highlands to the sheer enormity of Petén. To get to the Parque Minerva, take bus #1 from anywhere along 5 Av in Zona 1.

The new city

The southern half of the city is far more spacious, though while you may have more room to breathe, the air is no less noxious. Roughly speaking, the new city divides into two, split down the middle by 7 Avenida. The eastern half, centred on Avenida La Reforma, is the smartest part of the city, with banks, hotels, restaurants, boutiques and walled residential compounds being the natural habitat of Guatemala's wealthy elite. The western half of the new town, incorporating the bus terminal, zoo and airport, is less exclusive.

The east: around 7 Avenida and Avenida La Reforma

Heading to the south of the Centro Cívico and into Zona 4 proper, 6 Av runs into the modern city, with Ruta 6 branching off to the east, towards Av La Reforma, crossing 7 Av beside the landmark **Edificio El Triangulo**. From here, 7 Av heads south beneath the illuminated **Torre del Reformador**, at the junction of 2 C. Guatemala's answer to the Eiffel Tower, this steel structure was built along the lines of the Parisian model, in honour of President Barrios, who transformed the country between 1871 and 1885; a bell in the top of the tower is rung every year on June 30 to commemorate the Liberal victory in the 1871 revolution.

Pushing its way southeast, Ruta 6 passes the **Iglesia Yurrita**, an outlandish building designed in an exotic neo-Gothic style that belongs more to horror movies than to the streets of Guatemala City. It was built as a private chapel by a rich philanthropist; his house, in the same style, stands alongside. The church, also known as **Nuestra Señora de las Angustias**, is usually open to the public (Tues–Sun 7am–noon & 4–6pm), and is well worth a look as the inside is just as wild as the exterior.

Ruta 6 meets Av La Reforma at a busy roundabout marked by the Cine Reforma, which has been both a cinema and an evangelical church, but is now a theatre and music venue. On the opposite side of Av La Reforma are the **Botanical Gardens** (Mon–Fri 8am–5pm; free) of the San Carlos University; the entrance is on 0 C. Inside you'll find a beautiful, small garden with a selection of species, all neatly labelled in Spanish and Latin. There's also a small, but not terribly exciting, **Natural History Museum** housing a collection of stuffed birds, including a quetzal and an ostrich, along with geological samples, wood types, live snakes, some horrific pickled rodents and a small library that includes books in English.

Far more interesting, however, are the two privately owned **museums** on the campus of the University Francisco Marroquin, reached by following 6 C Final off Av La Reforma, heading east. **Museo Ixchel** (Mon–Fri 8am–5.50pm, Sat 9am–12.50pm; $2) is a striking, purpose-built edifice designed loosely along the lines of a Maya temple. Probably the capital's best museum, the Ixchel is dedicated to Maya culture, with particular emphasis on traditional weaving. It contains a stunning collection of hand-woven fabrics, including some very impressive examples of ceremonial costumes, with explanations in English. There's also information about the techniques, dyes, fibres and weaving tools used, and the way in which costumes have changed over the years. Although the collection is by no means comprehensive, and the costumes lose some of their impact and meaning when taken out of the villages where they're made, this is a fascinating exhibition. The building also houses a large library, and permanent exhibitions of paintings by Guatemalan artist Andrés Curruchich, who painted scenes of rural life around San Juan Comalapa (see p.117), and Carmen Peterson, who depicted traditional costumes on canvas. Also worth a look is the impressive collection of miniature *huipiles*, next to the café.

Right next door on the third floor of the *auditorio* building, is the city's other private museum, the excellent **Popol Vuh Archeological Museum** (Mon–Fri 9am–5pm, Sat 9am–1pm; $2). Standards here are just as high as at the Ixchel, but this time the subject is archeology, with an outstanding collection of artefacts from sites all over the country. The small museum is divided into Preclassic, Classic, Postclassic and Colonial rooms and all the exhibits are of top quality. The Preclassic room contains some stunning ceramics, stone masks and *hongo zoomorfo* (sculptures shaped like mushroom heads), while highlights of the Classic room include an altar from Naranjo, some lovely incense burners, and a model of Tikal. In the Postclassic room is a replica of the Dresden code, one of only three extant pre-Conquest Maya books, while the Colonial era is represented by assorted ecclesastical relics and processional crosses.

Back on Avenida La Reforma heading south, you pass the **Politecnica**, built in the style of a toy fort and still in use by the military. Beyond this is the smart part of town, where you'll find leafy streets filled with boutiques and travel agents, the American embassy (see p.72), banks, office blocks, sleek hotels and the offices of American Express (see p.71). While there's a steady flow of traffic along Av La Reforma, the surrounding area has clearly escaped the Third World, with quiet streets and mown lawns. A little to the east, around 10 C and 3 Av, is the so-called **Zona Viva**, a tight bunch of up-market hotels, restaurants and nightclubs.

Out to the west side of Av La Reforma, **Plazuela España** sits at the junction of 7 Av and 12 C. Now marked by a fountain, this crossroads was once the site of a statue of King Carlos III of Spain, torn down when independence was declared. At the four corners of the plaza you can still see some superb, tiled benches dating from colonial times.

To get to Av La Reforma from Zona 1, take bus #82 from 10 Av, past the Iglesia Yurrita, and all the way along Av La Reforma. La Reforma is a two-way street, so you can return along the same route.

Zona 14

Heading further south into Zona 14, the end of Av La Reforma is marked by a giant roundabout known as **Parque Independencia**, or **Obelisco Plaza**, at the junction with 20 C. Straight ahead, beyond this point the road continues as **Avenida las Américas**, where things become even more exclusive, with many of the large walled compounds belonging to embassies. Heading down Av las Américas you'll pass the Instituto Geografico Militar on the right (see p.52), and two cinema complexes, including Guatemala's best movie house, the Cine Magic Place (see p.70). At the southern end of the avenida, behind a statue of Pope John Paul II, is the **Plaza Berlin**, whose once stunning view of Lake Amatitlán and the Pacaya volcano has now been obscured by new building. Running parallel to Av las Américas, 14 C – better known as **Avenida Hincapié** – gives access to the **domestic air terminal**, opposite the junction with 18 C.

To the east, the main highway to the border with El Salvador runs out through Zonas 10 and 15. As the road leaves the city it climbs a steep hillside and passes through one of the most exclusive and expensive residential districts in the country, where every house has a superb view of the city below, and most are ringed by ferocious fortifications. Out beyond this, at the top of the hill, is Guatemala's main (if not only) motor-racing track.

West of 6 Avenida

Out to the west of 6 Av it's quite another story, and while there are still small enclaves of upmarket housing, and several expensive shopping areas, things are really dominated by transport and commerce. A disused railway track, lined with bedraggled slums, runs out this way, with the airport, the bullring, the zoo and the infamous Zona 4 bus terminal all rubbing shoulders. Of these, you're most likely to be visiting the **Zona 4 Bus Terminal**, at 1 C and 4 Av, the country's most impenetrable and intimidating jungle, a brutal swirl of petty thieves, hardware stores, bus fumes and sleeping vagrants.

Around the terminal the largest **market** in the city spreads across several blocks. If you can summon the energy it's a real adventure to wander through this maze of alleys, but don't carry too much money as it's a risky part of town. To get to the bus terminal from Zona 1, take any of the buses marked "terminal" from 4 Av or 9 Av, all of which pass within a block or two.

Behind the bus terminal, the railway tracks head off towards the coast, and behind these is **Avenida Bolívar**, an important traffic artery that runs out to the **Trébol junction**, where it meets the main highways from the western highlands and the Pacific coast. Up above the bus terminal here, just off Av Bolívar, is the **Santuario Expiatorio**, also known as the Iglesia Santa Cecilia de Don Bosco, a superb modern church designed (by a then unqualified Salvadorean architect) in the shape of a fish. It's part of a church-run complex that includes clinics and schools, and is well worth a browse, above all for the fantastic mural running down the side of the interior which depicts the Crucifixion and Resurrection with vivid realism.

Further to the south in **Zona 13**, the **Parque Aurora** houses the city's remodelled **zoo** (Tues–Sun 9am–5pm; Q8), where you can see African lions, Bengal tigers, crocodiles, giraffes, Indian elephants, hippos, monkeys and all the Central and South American big cats including some well-fed jaguar. Most of the larger animals have a reasonable amount of space, many smaller animals do not. To get here, take bus #63.

On the other side of the Parque Aurora, reached along 7 Av, is a collection of state-run **museums** (all Tues–Fri 9am–4pm, Sat & Sun 9am–noon & 1.30–4pm). The best of these is the **Museum of Archeology and Ethnology** ($5), with a selection of Maya artefacts to rival the Popul Vuh. The collection includes some fantastic stelae, as well as a display on Indian culture, with traditional masks and costumes. There are several vast pieces of Maya stonework on show, some of them from the more remote sites such as Piedras Negras. In comparison, the city's **Museum of Modern Art** (Q10) is a little disappointing and seems rather neglected. It's not worth a special trip, but if you're in the area you might as well drop in to see some impressively massive murals as well as an abundance of twee images of Indian life. The works cover the last couple of centuries of Guatemalan art, taking in most of the modern movements. Suffering from a similar neglect, the **Museum of Natural History** (Q10) features a range of mouldy-looking stuffed animals from Guatemala and elsewhere and a few mineral samples. Beside the park, there's a **bullring**, where fights still take place from October to December, as well as a running track, while to the south is the **Aurora airport**. Ambitious plans are afoot to remodel the whole Parque Aurora area, including massive reforestation, to make the complex more appealing for tourists. To get here take bus #63 from 4 Av or #83 from 10 Av.

The final point of interest in the southern half of the city is the **Ciudad Universitária**, the campus of San Carlos University, in Zona 12. A huge, purpose-built complex, it is heavily decorated with vivid political graffiti. The San Carlos University, originally founded in Antigua by Dominican priests in 1676, is probably the best in Central America; it has an autonomous constitution and is entitled to five percent of the government's annual budget. The university also has a long history of radical dissent and anti-government protest and students here have been victims of repression and political killing on several occasions – many right-wing politicians still regard the campus as a centre of subversion. Buses marked "Universitária" travel along 4 Av through Zona 1 to the campus.

Zona 7: the ruins of Kaminaljuyú

Way out on the western edge of the city, beyond the stench of the rubbish dump, is the long thin arm of Zona 7, a well-established but run-down part of town that wraps around the ruins of **Kaminaljuyú** (Mon–Fri 8am–4pm, Sat 8am–1pm). Archeological digs on this side of the city have revealed the astonishing proportions of a Maya city that once housed around fifty thousand people and includes more than three hundred mounds and thirteen ball courts. Unlike the massive temples of the lowlands, these structures were built of adobe, and most of them have been lost to centuries of erosion and a few decades of urban sprawl. Today the archeological site, incorporating only a tiny fraction of the original city, is little more than a series of earth-covered mounds, a favourite spot for football and romance. A couple of sections have been cut into by archeologists, and by peering through the fence you can get some idea of what lies beneath the grassy exterior, but it's virtually impossible to get any impression of Kaminaljuyú's former scale and splendour.

To get to the ruins, buses #29 or #72 from the Parque Central, running along C de San Juan Sacatepequez, will drop you close by, or any bus from Zona 1 with a *Kaminaljuyú* sign in the windscreen will take you directly to the site.

A history of Kaminaljuyú

Despite its nondescript appearance, Kaminaljuyú, once the largest Maya city in the Guatemalan highlands, is a particularly important site. Its history falls neatly into two sections: a first phase of indigenous growth, and a later period during which migrants from the north populated the site.

In the Late Preclassic era, 400 BC to 100 AD, the city had already grown to huge proportions, with some two hundred flat-topped **pyramids**, the largest reaching a height of about 18m. Beneath each of these lay entombed a member of the nobility; a few have been unearthed to reveal the wealth and sophistication of the culture. The corpses were wrapped in finery, covered in cinnabar pigment and surrounded by an array of human sacrifices, pottery, jade, masks, stingray spines, obsidian and quartz crystals. A number of carvings have also been found, proving that the elite of Kaminaljuyú were fully literate at a time when other Maya had perhaps no notion of writing. Many of the gods, the ceramic styles and hieroglyphic forms from these early days at Kaminaljuyú are thought to predate those found at later centres such as Tikal and Copán. But the power of the city, pre-eminent during the Late Preclassic era, faded throughout the second and third centuries, and the site may even have been abandoned.

Kaminaljuyú's renaissance took place shortly after 400 AD, when the Guatemalan highlands suffered a massive influx of migrants from the north and fell under the domination of Teotihuacán in central Mexico. The migrants seized the city of Kaminaljuyú and established it as their regional capital, giving them control of the obsidian mines and access to the coastal trade routes and the lowlands of Petén. With the weighty political and economic backing of Teotihuacán the city once again flourished, as the new rulers constructed their own temples, tombs and ball courts. Numerous artefacts have been found from this period, including some pottery that's thought to have been made in Teotihuacán itself, along with endless imitations of the style. Kaminaljuyú's new-found power also played a crucial role in shaping the lowlands of Petén: it was only with the backing of the great Teotihuacán-Kaminaljuyú alliance that Tikal was able to grow so large and so fast. This role was considered of such importance that some archeologists suggest that Curl Nose, one of the early rulers at Tikal (who ascended to power in 387 AD), may actually have come from Kaminaljuyú. The fortunes of Kaminaljuyú itself, however, were so bound up with those of its northern partner that the fall of Teotihuacán around 600 AD weakened and eventually destroyed the city.

Eating, drinking and entertainment

Despite its role as the country's economic centre, Guatemala City isn't a great place for indulging. Most of the population hurry home after dark and it's only the very rich who eat, drink and dance until the small hours. There are, however, **restaurants** everywhere in the city, invariably reflecting the type of neighbourhood they're in, most concentrating on quantity rather than quality. Movie-watching is hugely popular, with a good selection of cinemas; nightclubs and bars are concentrated in Zona 10.

Restaurants and cafés

When it comes to eating cheaply in Guatemala City, stick to **Zona 1**, where the restaurants tend to reflect the fact that most people have little money to spare. At **lunchtime** you'll find set-price, three-course menus all over the central zone for less than $2 a head including a *fresco* drink; try the area west of the Parque Central or around the post office, in particular. There's a cluster of **Chinese** restaurants on 6 C, between 4 and 3 avenidas, a patch that ranks as the city's Chinatown, while a few **Italian** restaurants have also sprung up, as have a couple of specifically **vegetarian** places, despite the fact that this is a city obsessed with meat eating. If you're trying to cut costs, cheap and filling food is sold from stalls around all the bus stations and markets, and on many of the streets in the centre. In the smarter parts of town, particularly **Zonas 9** and **10**, the emphasis is more on upmarket cafés and glitzy dining, and there is more choice here with Mexican, Middle Eastern, Chinese and Japanese options.

Fast food is widely available with plenty of choice, the vast majority being US chains. There's a *McDonald's* at 10 C 5–56, Zona 1, and 7 Av 14–01, Zona 9, and a *Pizza Hut* at 6 Av & 12 C Zona 1 (home delivery ☎2303394). Home-grown breeds include *Burger Shops*, 6 Av 13–40, Zona 1, and the slightly cheaper *Pollo Campero*, the Guatemalan version of *KFC*, with branches throughout the city.

Zona 1

A Guy From Italy, 12 C 6–23. Part of a city-wide pizza and pasta chain, serving tasty, good value Italian food. Slightly more upmarket than *Piccadilly* (see below).

Altuna, 5 Av 12–31. Spanish/Basque food with an emphasis on fish and seafood, served in a wonderfully civilized atmosphere. It's not cheap, at around $20 a head, but worth every cent for the old-fashioned ambience and service.

Café Astoria, 10 C 6–72. Very German deli and café, with excellent sausages and ham on offer.

Las Cien Puertes, Pasaje Aycinena, 9 C between 6 & 7 Avenidas. Funky restaurant/bar (see also "Bars and clubs", p.70) in a beautiful, run-down colonial arcade, serving the most imaginative cooking in Guatemala. Highly recommended.

Delicadezas Hamburgo, 15 C 5–34. A hybrid of Guatemalan and German food; the set meals are particularly good value. They also do a good deal at breakfast, offering a number of set menus from cornflakes to beans and eggs.

Europa Bar, 11 C 5–16. The most popular expat hang-out in Zona 1, inauspiciously located beneath a multi-storey car park. Primarily a bar, with CNN and North American sports on the tv, but there are also cheapish eats. The owner, Judy, is a mine of local information, and you can trade US$ here, and make local calls. Closed Sun.

Fu Lu Sho, 6 Av & 12 C. Popular, inexpensive Chinese restaurant with Art Deco interior, opening onto the bustle of 6 Av.

Café León 8 Av 9–15. Spanish-owned café in the heart of things, ideal for *café solo* and *churros*.

Long Wah, 6 C 3–75, west of the National Palace in Chinatown. Good Chinese restaurant, not at all expensive.

Mundial, 6 Av & 15 C. Good, quiet Chinese restaurant, where you can get decent food at reasonable prices.

Rey Sol, south side of Parque del Centenario. "Aerobic" breakfasts, and a good selection of vegetarian dishes and fruitshakes. The shop sells wholemeal bread, granola and veggie snacks.

Selecta, 14 C 6–24, Zona 1. Inexpensive set meals with no frills – a good diner, especially at lunchtime.

Tao Restaurant, 5 C 9–70. The city's best value three-course vegetarian lunch. There's no menu; you just eat the meal of the day at tiny tables round a plant-filled courtyard.

Zonas 9 and 10

Los Alpes, 10 C 1–09, Zona 10. A haven of peace, this café serves superb pastries and a fine range of drinks making it the best place to relax in the city. Closed Mon.

Los Antojitos, Av La Reforma 15–02, Zona 9. Good, moderately priced Central American food – try the *chile rellenos* or guacamolé.

Antro's, 4 Av 15–53, Zona 10. Excellent vegetarian restaurant with some Middle Eastern dishes. Not too puritanical, and serves "unhealthy" drinks like beer and espresso. Closed Sun.

El Arbol de la Vida, 7 Av 13–56, Zona 9. The city's best vegetarian restaurant, serving reasonably priced dishes in a friendly relaxed, atmosphere.

Burger Warehouse, 4 Av 15–70, Zona 10. One of Zona 10's best budget options, serving well-priced burgers, fried chicken dishes and pitchers of beer.

El Gran Pavo, 6 C 3–09, Zona 9, and 15 Av 16–72, Zona 10. Massive portions of genuine, moderately priced Mexican food in a decidedly Mexican atmosphere. Also in Zona 1, at 13 C 4–41.

Estro Armonico, 15 C 1–11, Zona 10. Fancy food at fancy prices; rare delights such as lamb and duck in unusual sauces.

Jake's, 17 C 10–40, Zona 10. Lunch and dinner from an international menu, very strong on fish and with terrific sweets. Pleasant, candle-lit atmosphere, excellent service, and correspondingly high prices. Closed Sun and Mon.

Luigi's Pizza, 4 Av 14–20, Zona 10. Very popular, moderately priced Italian restaurant, serving delicious pizza, pasta and baked potatoes.

Maitreya's Deli, 13 C 4–44, Zona 10. Top quality, delicious sandwiches, freshly prepared in-house, with a wide range of drinks and full meals also offered. Expensive.

Olivadda 12 C 4–51, Zona 10. Very smart, pretty authentic Middle Eastern fare. Feast on falafel, humous and tabolleh for around $10 a head.

Palace, 10 C 4–40, Zona 10. Pasta and snack dishes as well as cakes and pastries served in a cafeteria atmosphere.

Patsy, Av La Reforma 8–01, Zona 10. Very handy for trips to the Popol Vuh or Ixchel museums. A full range of sandwiches, burgers and pastries is on offer.

Piccadilly, Plazuela España, 7 Av 12–00, Zona 9. One of the most popular continental restaurants with tourists and Guatemalans alike. A decent line-up of pastas and pizzas is served along with huge jugs of beer, all at moderate prices. Also in Zona 1, on 6 Av & 11 C.

Puerto Barrios, 7 Av 10–65, Zona 9. Excellent, pricey seafood in a boat-like building.

Pumpernik's, 2 Av 13–17, Zona 10, inside the Vivacentro building. Good for early-morning breakfasts (from 7am), as well as American-style snacks and meals.

Señor Tenedor, 15 C 3–52, Zona 10. Expensive, gourmet deli, for those who crave imported food and don't mind paying for it.

Sushi, 2 Av 14–63, Zona 10. Very popular, new Japanese restaurant, which bizarrely advertises itself as a "rock café" too.

Tu Tu Tango, 2 Av 14–74, Zona 10. International menu covering everything from fish to pasta, steak to mango mousse. Welcoming atmosphere, and excellent service. Closed Sun.

Vesuvio Pizza, 18 C 3–36, Zona 10. Huge pizzas cooked in traditional, wood-burning ovens with plenty of mouth-watering toppings.

Zona 13

Café de la Libre, 7 Av & 13C, Zona 13. Pleasant, if pricey, vegetarian place next to Librería del Pensativo. Good lunch specials.

Drinking and nightlife

Despite appearances, Guatemala City quietens down very quickly in the evenings, and **nightlife** is not one of its strengths. What little action there is divides into two distinct types: in the southern half of the city in the **Zona Viva** (Zona 10), there's a cluster of western-style nightclubs and bars, while in Zona 1 strip clubs and sleazy bars are all that's on offer. If you crave the low life, then stroll on down 18 C, to the junction with 9 Av, and you're in the heart of the Zona 1 **red light district**, where there are plenty of truly sleazy bars and clubs. As you head towards the newer part of town, the nightclubs take on a more Western flavour.

Techno has now hit Guatemala, though you'll be lucky to get anything other than the standard, commercial, handbag strain. Drum and bass, trip-hop and other mutations have yet to reach Central America, and most city DJs spin a mix of pan-Latin American sounds and Eurohouse, with the merengue of the Caribbean often being spiced up by raggamuffin vocals. Cheesy *ladino* house music is currently very big, and there are also special clubs for **salsa** fanatics. Clubbing in Zona 10 is anything but an egalitarian experience: it's where the shoulder-padded wealthy have fun, but there's very little elsewhere. Ecstasy and amphetamines are almost unknown – when the rich indulge, they powder their noses with Columbian substances instead.

The city's greatest **reggae club** is *La Gran Comal*, on Via 4 between 6 Av and Ruta 6, Zona 4. Radiating rhythm, it's relaxed, but not as worn out as the clubs of Zona 1. It's a favourite haunt of black Guatemalans from Lívingston and the Caribbean coast, and well worth a visit.

Bars and clubs

La Bodeguita del Centro, 12 C 3–55, Zona 1 (☎2302976). Large, leftish venue with live music, comedy, poetry and all manner of arty events; also serves food. Definitely worth a visit for the *Che* memorabilia alone. Free entry in the week, around $4 cover on weekends.

Camino Real Hotel, Av La Reforma & 14 C, Zona 10. The bar and *El Jaguar* disco in this *Zona Viva* hotel, just off Av La Reforma, have more of a Western flavour than other clubs.

Carlos and Charlie's, 3 Av & 12 C, Zona 10. Flashy hang-out for the city's wealthy. Drinks are expensive, and there are queues at the weekend.

Crocodilo's, in the Gran Centro Los Próceres shopping mall, 16 C and 2 Av, Zona 10. A restaurant that doubles up as a cocktail bar, with a daily happy hour 6–9pm.

GAY GUATEMALA CITY

Guatemala City's small **gay** scene is mostly underground and concentrated around a couple of (almost entirely male) clubs. *El Metropole*, 6 C & 3 Av, Zona 1, is small and friendly and plays great dance and house music; it's particularly good fun on Thurs, Fri and Sat nights. *Pandora's Box*, Via 3 & Ruta 3, Zona 4, is the city's largest gay club, and plays average music, but still has a great atmosphere. There are no specifically lesbian clubs or bars in the city. For more information about the gay scene, contact OASIS on ☎2323335.

Danny's Mariscobar, Av Las Américas 8–24, Zona 13. A new bar to liven up this posh residential area. Live bands every Sat.

El Establo, Av La Reforma 14–34, Zona 9. Cosy bar with polished wood interior, bookstore, good food and pool tables round the back.

Jarro Café Cantina, 3 Av & 13 C, Zona 10. Small bar, a little pricey, but packed at weekends.

Kahlua, 15 C & 1 Av, Zona 10. Currently the most happening place in town with two floors, a split-level dance floor and even a chill-out room. During public holidays the street outside is sometimes sealed off and people spill out of the club to party al fresco. The music is by no means innovative, but a reasonable blend of dance and Latin pop is usually on offer.

Las Cien Puertes, Pasaje Aycinena, 9C between 6 & 7 Avenidas, Zona 1. Great bar in a beautiful, run-down colonial arcade. Plays good Latin sounds, and charges very moderate prices. Also serves excellent food (see Restaurants and cafés, p.67).

La Quinta, 5 Av between 13 & 14 calles, Zona 1. In the centre of Zona 1, this club typifies this part of town – weary and middle-aged. But at least there's usually live music, and you can buy (overpriced) food and drink.

Shakespeare's Pub, 13 C 1–51, Zona 10. Small basement bar catering to middle-aged North Americans, most of them expats.

Stratus, 13 C & 3 Av. Upmarket club, aimed at a slightly older crowd. Formal dress is required and a strict door policy is sometimes enforced. Expensive.

Tapocia Azul, 3 Av & 13 C. Stylish English-owned bar, with a cool atmosphere and great food.

El Zócalo, corner of 18 C & 4 Av, Zona 1. Slightly rougher than *La Quinta*, but in much the same mould.

Cinemas

Most movies shown in Guatemala City are in English with Spanish subtitles. Often they're the very latest releases from the States, which tend to arrive in Central America before they reach Europe. There are four **cinemas on 6 Av** between the main plaza and the Parque Concordia, and the following is a selection of the others scattered throughout the city. The best for sound quality is the *Magic Place* (see below). Programmes are listed in the two main newspapers, *El Grafico* and *Prensa Libre*.

Cine Las Américas, Av las Américas, between 8 & 9 calles, Zona 13.
Cine Bolívar, Av Bolívar & 35 C, Zona 8.
Cine Capitol, 6 Av & 12 C, Zona 1.
Cine Capri, 8 C & 3 Av, Zona 1.
Cine Lido, 11 C 7–34, Zona 1.
Cine Lux 11 C & 6 Av, Zona 1.
Cine Magic Place Av las Américas, Zona 13.
Cine Palace, opposite the Capitol.
Cine Plaza, 7 Av 6–7 C, Zona 9.
Cines Taurus, Leo and Aires, 9 C & 4 Av, Zona 1.
Cine Tikal Futura, Tikal Futura, Calzada Roosevelt, Zona 11.
Cine Tropical, Av Bolívar 31–71, Zona 8.

Listings

Airlines Airline offices are scattered throughout the city, with many along Av La Reforma. It is fairly straightforward to phone them and there will almost always be someone in the office who speaks English.

Aerolineas Argentinas, 10 C 3–17, Zona 10 (☎3311567; fax 3346662); Aerovias, Av Hincapié and 18 C, Zona 13 (☎3325686; fax 3347935), and at the airport, 2nd floor (☎3327470; fax 3347935); Air Canada 12 C 1–25 Zona 10 (☎ 3353341); Air France, Plaza Panaméricana, Av La Reforma 9–00, Zona 9 (☎3340043; fax 3314918); American Airlines, Av La Reforma 15–54, Zona 9 (☎3347379; fax 3346080), also in Tikal Futura shopping centre (☎3347379); Aviateca (also for Taca, Lacsa and Nica), Av Hincapié 12–22, Zona 13 (☎3347722; fax 3612159), also at the *Hotel Ritz Continental* (☎2381415); British Airways, 6th floor of Edificio Inexa, 1 Av 10–81, Zona 10, (☎3327402; fax 3347935); Continental, Edificio Geminis 10, Torre Norte, 12 C 1–25, Zona 10, (☎3313341; fax 3353444); Copa, 1 Av 10–17, Zona 10 (☎3611567; fax 3342714); Delta, Centro Ejecutivo building, 15 C 3–20, Zona 10 (☎3370642; fax 3370588); Iberia, Av La Reforma 8–60, Zona 9 (☎3370911; airport ☎3325517; fax 3343715); KLM, Edificio Plaza Maritima, 6 Av 20–25, Zona 10 (☎3370222, fax 3370227, airport ☎3325972); Lacsa, see Aviateca above; LanChile, Edificio Plaza Panamericana, Av La Reforma 9–00, Zona 9 (☎3312070; fax 3312079); Lufthansa, Diagonal 6 10–61, Zona 10 (☎3392990; fax 3392994); Mexicana, Edificio Edyma, 13 C 8–44, Zona 10, (☎3336001; fax 3336096); Nica, see Aviateca above; TWA, Av La Reforma 12–81, Zona 10 (☎3346240; fax 3346241); Taca, see Aviateca above; Tapsa, Av Hincapié and 18 C, Zona 13 (☎3314860; fax 3345572) and at the airport, 2nd floor (☎3326034); Tikal Jets, Av Hincapié and 18 C, Zona 13 (☎3325070, 3345631 or 3345568; airport ☎3346855; fax 3345631); United Airlines, Edificio El Reformador, Av La Reforma 1–50, Zona 9 (☎3322995; fax 3323903); Varig, 8th floor, Edificio Plaza Panamericana, Av La Reforma 9–00, Zona 9 (☎3340043; fax 3323003).

American Express Main office in the Banco del Café, Av La Reforma 9–00, Zona 9 (☎3340040; fax 3311928; Mon–Fri 8.30am–4.30pm). The office, which includes mail service, is in the basement, and the bank on the first floor. Take bus #82 from 10 Av, Zona 1.

Baggage There's no central left-luggage facility, so you'll have to entrust any baggage to your hotel.

Banks and exchange Opening hours vary wildly, with some banks shutting as early as 3pm, and others staying open until after dark. At the airport, Banco Del Quetzal (Mon–Fri 7am–8pm, Sat & Sun 8am–8pm) gives a good exchange rate and takes most European currencies. For cashing travellers' cheques, try any of the following: Banco Industrial, 7 Av 11–52, Zona 1 (Mon–Fri 8.30am–7pm, Sat 8.30am–5.30pm), which also gives Visa cash advances with passport; Banco del Quetzal (Mon–Fri 8.30am–8pm, Sat 9am–1pm) and Banco Promotor (Mon–Fri 9am–4pm), opposite each other on 10 C, between 6 & 7 avenidas, Zona 1; Lloyds Bank, 8 Av 10–67, Zona 1 (Mon–Fri 9am–3pm) will change sterling travellers' checks. At Credomatic, in the gallery of shops next to *Europa Bar* on the corner of 5 Av & 11 C, you can get Visa and Mastercard cash advances (Mon–Fri 8.30am–7pm, Sat 9am–1pm), though you'll need to show your passport. Back in Zona 1, concentrated around the post office on 7 Av between 12 & 13 calles, there's a legal black market which at times offers a better rate than the banks, although only for cash. Take care dealing with the hustlers around here – it's probably best avoided unless you need to get or get rid of Central American currencies.

Books For a reasonable selection of English and French fiction, try Arnel, a musty old bookshop in the basement of the Edificio El Centro on 9 C, corner of 7 Av, in Zona 1. Also worth a browse are Librería del Pensativo, Edificio La Cúpula, 7 Av & 13 C, Zona 9 (Mon–Fri 10am–7pm, Sat 10am–1.30pm); Geminis, 6 Av 7–24, Zona 9; and Sol y Luna, on 12C & 3 Av, Zona 1 (next to the *Bodeguita*). A selection of secondhand English books can be bought from the *El Establo* café, Av La Reforma 14–34, Zona 10, and the *Europa Bar*, on 11 C 5–16, Zona 1, but generally the bookshops in Antigua are better.

Camera repairs Foto Sittler, 12 C 6–20, Zona 1, offers a three-month guarantee on its work; or try La Perla, 9 C & 6 Av, Zona 1.

Car and motorbike rental Renting a car in Guatemala is expensive and you should keep a sharp eye on the terms, particularly when it comes to insurance. All the companies listed below rent jeeps for a little under $100 a day, and also have slightly cheaper cars (for around $70) and minibuses. Ahorrent, Bvd Liberación 4–90, Zona 9 (☎3320544 or 3615661; fax 3615621); Avis, 12 C 2–73, Zona 9 (☎3312734; fax 3321263); Budget, Av La Reforma 15–00, Zona 9 (☎3322591; fax 3342571); Dollar, at the airport (☎3317185); Hertz, 7 Av 14–76, Zona 9

(☎3322242; fax 3317924); National Car Rental, 14 C 1–24, Zona 10 (☎3664670; fax 3370221); Rental, 12 C 2–62, Zona 10 (☎3610672; fax 3342739) – the only company to rent motorbikes; Tabarini, 2 C A 7–30, Zona 10 (☎3319814; fax 3341925); Tally, 7 Av 14–60, Zona 1 (☎2514113; fax 2531749); Thrifty, Av Reforma and 11 C, Zona 9 (☎3321130; fax 3321207); and Tikal, 2 C 6–56, Zona 10 (☎3324721).

Dentist Central Dentist de Especialistas, 20 C 11–17, Zona 10 (☎3371773) is the best dental clinic in the country, and superb in emergencies. Prices are reasonable.

Doctors Your embassy should have a list of bilingual doctors, but for emergency medical assistance, there's the Centro Médico, a private hospital with 24-hour cover, at 6 Av 3–47, Zona 10 (☎3323555). They can also provide booster vaccinations.

Embassies Most of the embassies are in the southeastern quarter of the city, along Av La Reforma and Av las Americas, and they tend to open weekday mornings only. All embassies and consulates should be listed in the blue pages of the phone book, which often also lists opening hours. Argentina, 2 Av 11–04, Zona 10 (Mon–Fri 9am–1pm & 2–4pm; ☎3314969); Belgium, 14 C A 13–39, Zona 10 (Mon–Fri 8am–1pm; ☎3681817); Belize, Suite 803, 8th Floor, Edificio El Reforma, Av La Reforma 1–50, Zona 9 (Mon–Fri 9am–1pm & 2–5pm; ☎3345531 or 3311137); Bolivia, 7 Av 15–13, Zona 1 (Mon–Fri 10am–noon & 3–4pm; ☎2320483); Brazil, 18 C 2–22, Zona 14 (Mon–Fri 9am–1pm; ☎3370949); Canada, Edificio Edyma Plaza, 13 C 8–44, Zona 10 (Mon–Thurs 8am–4.30pm, Fri 8am–1.30pm; ☎3336102); Chile, 14 C 15–21, Zona 13 (Mon–Fri 8.30am–1pm; ☎3321149); Colombia, 12 C 1–25, Zona 10 (Mon–Fri 9am–1pm; ☎3353602); Costa Rica, 3rd floor, Galerias Reforma, Torre 1, Av La Reforma 8–60, Zona 9 (Mon–Fri 9am–2pm; ☎ & fax 3320531); Denmark, 7 Av 20–36, Zona 1 (Mon–Fri 9am–noon; ☎2327039); Ecuador, 4 Av 12–04, Zona 14 (Mon–Fri 9am–1pm; ☎3372902); El Salvador, 4 Av 13-60 Zona 10 (Mon–Fri 8am–2pm; ☎3662240); France, 11th floor, 16 C 4–53, Zona 10 (Mon–Fri 9am–noon; ☎3370647); Germany, Edificio Plaza Maritima, 20 C 6–20, Zona 10 (Mon–Fri 9am–noon; ☎3370028); Honduras, 9 Av 16–34, Zona 10 (Mon–Fri 9am–2pm; ☎3374344); Italy, 5 Av 8–59, Zona 14 (Mon–Fri 8.30am–12.30pm; ☎3374588); Israel, 13 Av 14–07, Zona 10 (Mon–Fri 9am–2pm; ☎3336951); Mexico, 15 C 3–20, Zona 10 (Mon–Fri 9am–1pm & 3–6pm; ☎3337254–8); Netherlands, 4th floor, 12 C 7–56, Zona 9 (Mon–Fri 8.30am–12.30pm; ☎3313505); Nicaragua, 10 Av 14–72, Zona 10 (Mon–Fri 9am–1pm; ☎3680785); Norway, 6 Av 11–77, Zona 10 (Mon–Fri 9am–noon; ☎3329296); Panama, 5 Av 15–45, Zona 10 (Mon–Fri 8.30am–1.30pm; ☎3372445); Peru, 2 Av 9–67, Zona 9 (Mon–Fri 9am–1pm; ☎3318558); Spain, 6 C 6–48, Zona 9 (Mon–Fri 8am–2pm; ☎3343757); South Africa, 10 Av 6–20, Zona 10 (Mon–Fri 9am–noon & 2–5pm; ☎3341531); Sweden, 8 Av 15–07, Zona 10 (8am–1pm & 2–4pm; ☎3336536); Switzerland, 4 C 7–73, Zona 9 (Mon–Fri 9–11.30am; ☎3313726); United Kingdom, 7th floor, Torre II, 7 Av 5–10, Zona 4 (Mon–Fri 9am–noon & 2–4pm; ☎3321604); United States, Av La Reforma, 7–01, Zona 10 (Mon–Fri 8am–5pm; ☎3311541); Venezuela, 8 C 0–56, Zona 9 (Mon–Fri 9am–1pm; ☎3316505).

Emergencies Police ☎120; Fire ☎123; Red Cross ☎125.

Film Colour transparency and both colour and monochrome print film is easy to buy, though expensive. There are several camera shops on 6 Av in Zona 1.

Immigration The main immigration office (*Migración*) is at 41 C 17–36, Zona 8 (☎4751302; fax 4751289; Mon–Fri 8am–4pm). Come here to extend your tourist card up to ninety days, or extend your visa for a month. Take bus #71 from 10 Av in Zona 1 or 6 Av in Zona 4.

Language courses At least five schools in Guatemala City teach Spanish; the best is probably the IGA (the Guatemalan American Institute), on Ruta 1 and Via 4, Zona 4 (☎3310022; fax 3344392). Easy, Blvd Los Proceres 9–67, Zona 10 (☎3373970; fax 3659150), also gets good reports, though generally speaking, you're better off learning Spanish in Antigua, Quetzaltenango or Huehuetenango.

Laundry The best is Lavandería Obelisco, Av La Reforma 16–30, next to Samaritana super-market (Mon–Fri 8am–6.45pm, Sat 8am–5.30pm), which charges around $3 for a wash and dry. Lavandería Internacional, 18 C 11–12, Zona 1, is another good bet, although they may insist that you pay for a complete service wash including ironing. Lavandería Pichola, 18 C 11–60, Zona 1, is cheaper and more basic; or there's a do-it-yourself place at 4 Av 13–89, Zona 1, which costs much the same and takes a lot longer.

Libraries The best library for English books is in the IGA (the Guatemalan American Institute) at Ruta 1 and Via 4, Zona 4. There's also the National Library, on the west side of the Parque Central, another big library alongside the main branch of the Banco de Guatemala, and specialist collections at the Ixchel and Popol Vuh museums.

Newspapers Guatemalan newspapers are sold everywhere on the streets, but European ones are hard to come by. Copies of *Time, Newsweek* and *The Economist* are usually on sale on the south side of the main plaza, and the British Embassy often has copies of the *Times, Independent* and *Guardian.* American papers are fairly readily available: both the *Hotel Panamerican,* 9 C 5–63, Zona 1, and *El Dorado,* in Zona 4, sell US papers, as do some of the street sellers in the centre. *Central American Report* is available from 9 C A 3–56, Zona 1.

Phones You can make long-distance phone calls and send international telegrams from the Telgua office, on the corner of 8 Av & 12 C (daily 7am–midnight), one block from the post office.

Police The main police station is in a bizarre castle-like structure on the corner of 6 Av & 14 C, Zona 1. In an emergency dial ☎120.

Post office 7 Av and 12 C (Mon–Fri 9am–5.30pm). Also has a *Lista de Correos* in Room 110 on the ground floor, where they will hold mail for you, though American Express (see above), runs a more efficient service for receiving mail.

Travel agents There are plenty in the centre and along Av La Reforma in Zonas 9 and 10. Flights to Petén can be booked through all of them. Some of the best include Clarke Tours, 7th floor, Las Margaritas Torre 2, Diagonal 6 10–01, Zona 10 (☎3392888; fax 3392909), which operates city tours and organizes trips to many parts of the country; Discovery Tours, Edificio Plaza Del Sol, 12 C 2–04, Zona 9 (☎3392281; fax 3392285); Maya Expeditions, 15 C 1–91, Zona 10 (☎3634955; fax 3634164), which specializes in ecotourism and adventure trips; Mesoamerica Explorers, 7 Av 13–01, Zona 9 (☎3325045), which organizes nature and archeological trips around Petén and Alta Verapaz; and Tropical Tours, 4 C 2–51, Zona 10 (☎3393662; fax 3315921). For flight tours to Copán/Honduras, as well as to Quiriguá, Caracol, Tikal, Ceibal, Yaxchilan, Zaculeu and Palenque, try Jungle Flying, Hangar 21, domestic airport, Av Hincapié and 18 C, Zona 13 (☎3604917 or 3607223; fax 3314995), which

MOVING ON FROM GUATEMALA CITY

During the day, **bus #83** goes past the **airport**. Remember that there's a $25 **departure tax** on all international flights, payable in either quetzales or dollars.

For the **domestic terminal** take the #65 bus from Zona 1, which heads south on 6 Av in Zona 9 and down Av Las Americas. Alight at the corner of 18 C, easily recognized by the large globe and sculpture of Christopher Columbus on your left. The easiest way to get to the airport, however, is by taxi (around $10 from Zona 1); if you're **leaving** for Petén you'll certainly want to do this as departures are mostly in the early morning, when the bus service is poor.

To get to the **Zona 4 bus terminal** from the centre of town, take any bus marked *terminal*: you'll find these heading south along 4 Av in Zona 1. From here second-class buses run to all parts of the country, with departures every minute of the day. If you're setting out to find a bus, remember that only some of them leave from the terminal itself, while others park in the streets around. There's no real pattern to this, but people are always keen to help, and if you look lost someone will eventually point you in the right direction.

At the corner of 18 C and 9 Av is the **eastern bus terminal**, from where pullman buses head to Puerto Barrios, Esquipulas and the Mexican border (via the Pacific coast); the surrounding streets are home to the offices of several bus companies, including Monja Blanca for Cobán, and Fuente del Norte who will take you to Petén. For a rundown of bus companies, routes and frequencies, see the Travel Details at the end of this chapter.

is excellent if you've little time but plenty of money (around $200 per person for a day-trip to Copán/Honduras).

Credit cards Cash advances from Credomatic, 7 Av 6–26, Zona 1 (☎3318027; Mon–Fri 8am–7pm, Sat 9am–1pm).

Work Hard to come by; the best bet is teaching at one of the English schools, most of which are grouped on 10 and 18 calles in Zona 1. Check the classified sections of the *Siglo News*, *Guatemala Weekly* and *Revue*.

AROUND GUATEMALA CITY

Leaving the capital in any direction, you'll quickly escape its polluted, hectic atmosphere. Only two destinations are suited to day-trips from the city, while the rest of the surrounding hills are easily explored using other towns as a base.

To the south the main road runs to Escuintla and the Pacific coast, passing through a narrow valley that separates the cones of the Pacaya and Agua volcanoes. Out this way is **Lake Amatitlán**, a popular weekend resort just half an hour from the capital. A few kilometres to the south of the lake is the village of **San Vicente Pacaya**, from where you can climb Pacaya itself, one of Guatemala's three active cones, currently very lively, spouting smoke, gases, rocks and a plume of lava.

To the northwest of the capital, the villages of **San Juan Sacatepéquez** and **San Pedro Sacatepéquez**, both have impressive markets, while further northwest lie the ruins of **Mixco Viejo**, the ancient capital of the Pokoman Maya.

South of the city

Heading out through the southern suburbs, the **Pacific highway** runs past the clover-leaf junction at El Trébol and leaves the city through its industrial outskirts. The land to the south of the capital is earmarked for new housing projects, but as yet the skeletal ground plan has drawn only one or two takers, and elaborate advertising posters on empty lots sing the merits of suburban life. Further south lies the small town of **Villa Nueva**, a place a lot older than its name suggests, beyond which the valley starts to narrow, overshadowed by the volcanic cones of Agua and Pacaya.

Lake Amatitlán

A few kilometres east of the highway, **Lake Amatitlán** nestles at the base of the Pacaya volcano, encircled by forested hills. It's a superb setting, but one that's been sadly undermined by the abuses the lake has suffered at the hands of holidaymakers. In the not-too-distant past its delights were enjoyed by a handful of the elite, whose retreats dotted the shoreline, but since then bungalows have proliferated at an astonishing rate, and the waters of the lake are grossly polluted. The wealthy have moved on, seeking their seclusion at Río Dulce and Lake Atitlán, while here at Amatitlán the weekends bring buses from the capital every ten minutes or so, spewing out families who spend the day eating, drinking, barbecuing, boating and swimming. If you want to enjoy the view and some peace and quiet, then come during the week, but if you want to watch Guatemalans at play drop by on a Sunday.

Where the road arrives at the lakeshore, the beach is lined with grimy *comedores* and *tiendas*. Taking a **boat trip** across the lake is a popular pastime, as is a dip in the thermal baths which are reputed to cure rheumatism and arthritis. Considerably more healthy than the black waters of the lake, are the pools, where during daylight hours you can pay a small fee to take a dip in cleaner waters. High above the lake, to the north, is the **Parque de las Naciones Unidas** (the United Nations Park, formerly the Parque El Filón), reached from the lakeside by an Austrian-made bubble-lift that looks strangely out of place so far from the ski slopes. The trip up there, and the park itself, offer incredible views of the lake and the volcanic cones. The lift operates on Saturday and Sunday only.

A kilometre or so from the lake but closer to the highway is the village of **AMATITLÁN**, where you'll find a seventeenth-century church housing El Niño de Atocha, a saintly figure reputed to have miraculous powers, as well as a collection of **hotels** and **restaurants**, including the *Hospedaje Don Leonel*, 8 C 3–25 (②), and *Hospedaje Kati* (②), which also serves good simple food.

Buses run from the capital to Lake Amatitlán every fifteen minutes or so, from 20 C and 3 Av in Zona 1 and return from the plaza in Amatitlán and the lakeshore. The journey takes around 45 minutes.

The Pacaya volcano

Heading further down the valley towards the Pacific coast, a branch road leaves the main highway to the left (east), heading into the hills to the village of **SAN VICENTE PACAYA**. From here you can climb the **Pacaya volcano**, one of the smallest and most impressive of Guatemala's peaks. At a height of just 2250m, Pacaya is the country's most dramatically active volcano, spitting out clouds of rock and ash. The current period of eruption began in 1965, although colonial records show that it was also active between 1565 and 1775. Today it certainly ranks as the most accessible and exciting volcano in Central America, and a trip to the cone is a unforgettable experience.

The route

Whether you decide to go with a guide or not, you'll follow the track from the main highway, winding up through lush coffee plantations and clouds of dust to

---

SAFETY ON THE PACAYA VOLCANO

Before setting out on the climb to the peak of Pacaya, you should bear in mind that the volcano has been the scene of a number of **attacks**, rapes, murders and robberies. The most serious incidents to date took place in early 1991, since when things have quietened down, though robberies are still regularly reported, and tours now come complete with armed guards. While most people climb the volcano without encountering any trouble, it is worth checking the current security situation with your embassy, or at the tourist offices in Guatemala City or Antigua, and keeping an eye on the Antigua noticeboards, where recent incidents are usually publicized. There are a number of self-appointed teams of guides who operate with armed guards out of Antigua (see p.100), which should make it safer, but a lot of these shadowy operations are far too disorganized to be recommended. And, even with a guide, safety is by no means guaranteed.

the village of San Vicente. It's a fairly miserable place, but if you're planning to climb the cone and make it back down the same day, then you may want to find somewhere to stay. There's no hotel in the village and people don't seem particularly friendly, but it's worth asking around for a room anyway – if you don't succeed you can always try one of the villages higher up.

To climb the volcano you need to rejoin the dirt road (which actually bypasses San Vicente) and then turn left at the fork after 100m or so. You'll come to a second bedraggled village, **Concepción El Cedro**, where you want to keep straight on, walking up the track to the right of the church. This track heads around to the left as it leaves the village, and then climbs in a narrow rocky gully, coming out at the village of **San Francisco**, the last settlement and the highest point accessible to motor vehicles. Here, about an hour from the start, you'll pass the last *tienda* and your last chance of finding a bed for the night – ask in the *tienda* and they'll point you towards someone with a room to rent.

From San Francisco the path is a little harder to follow, but it's only another couple of hours to the top. After you pass the *tienda* the path goes up to the right, beside an evangelical church, above which you need to head diagonally across the open grassland – bearing to the left. From this left-hand corner a clear-cut path heads on towards the cone, and where it first forks you should go left, along a path that climbs diagonally. After a while this meets a barbed-wire fence, where you turn sharply to the right and continue up through a thickish forest. From here you head straight on for a kilometre or so (moving diagonally across the hill) until the path goes over a hump, and then down the other side. On the second hump you turn to the left, onto a smaller path, which you follow up through the woods and the slippery cinder until you reach the top.

Scrambling up through the forest you suddenly emerge on the lip of an exposed ridge from where you can see the cone in all its brutal beauty. In front of you is a massive bowl of cooled lava, its fossilized currents flowing away to the right, and opposite is the cone itself, a jet black triangle that occasionally spouts molten rock and sulphurous fumes. From here you can head on around to the left, across lava fields and between the charred stumps of trees. The path runs around the lip of the bowl to a concrete post, and then up the side of the cone, which is a terrifying but thrilling ascent, eventually bringing you face to face with the eruptions. The ascent certainly shouldn't be attempted when Pacaya is highly active – check with your guide about the state of the eruptions before setting out.

The best time to watch the eruptions is **at night**, when the sludge that the volcano spouts can be seen in its full glory as a plume of brilliant orange. But to see this you need either to camp out at one of several good sites near the top or find somewhere to stay in one of the villages, which is possible but not that easy: you just have to ask around. A much simplier option is to pay $15 and join a tour in Guatemala City (see p.73) or Antigua (see p.100).

Buses leave the Zona 4 terminal in Guatemala City daily at 7am and 3.30pm for San Vicente, from where it's a further ninety-minute walk to San Francisco, though infrequent buses and pick-ups also travel this route.

On towards the coast: Palín

Continuing towards the coast the main highway passes through **PALÍN,** whose name derives from the word *palinha*, meaning water that holds itself erect, a reference to a nearby waterfall. Home to a tiny pocket of Pokoman-speaking Maya, the town was once famous for its weaving, but these days the only *huipiles* you'll see are the purples of the village of Santa María de Jesús, connected to Palín by a rough back road. The original Palín *huipiles* were particularly short, exposing the women's breasts when they raised their arms, and it's said that President Ubico, witnessing this when a woman tried to sell pineapples to his train, ordered that they be lengthened.

The best time to visit Palín is for its Wednesday morning **market**, which takes place under a magnificent ceiba tree in the plaza. Buses pass through every ten minutes or so, heading between the capital and the coast, so it's worth stopping off even if you just happen to be passing. Guatemala's first **motorway** starts just outside of town, connecting Palín with the southern town of Esquintla, and very much a key part of President Arzú's commitment to upgrade the country's road network. If you're travelling independently, it's worth paying the small toll to ensure a speedy journey to and from the south coast, and to avoid the slow lorries that line the old road.

Northwest of the city

To the northwest of the capital lies a hilly area that, despite its proximity, is little tainted by the influence of the city. Here the hills are still covered by pine forests, and heading out this way you'll find a couple of interesting villages, both badly scarred by the 1976 earthquake but with markets well worth visiting. Further afield are the **Mixco Viejo** ruins, impeccably restored but seldom visited.

San Pedro Sacatepéquez and San Juan Sacatepéquez

Leaving the city to the northwest you travel out through the suburb of Florida. Once you escape the confines of the city the road starts to climb into the hills, through an area that's oddly uninhabited. To the south of the city the high ground has been colonized by the rich, but here there are only one or two mansions, hidden in the forest.

The first of the two villages you come to is **SAN PEDRO SACATEPÉQUEZ**, where the impact of the earthquake is still painfully felt. The Friday market here is by far the smaller of the two, but still worth a browse. Another 6km takes you over a ridge and into the village of **SAN JUAN SACATEPÉQUEZ**. As you approach, the road passes a number of makeshift greenhouses where flowers are grown, an industry that has become the local speciality. The first carnation was brought to Guatemala by Andrés Stombo some sixty years ago. He employed the three Churup brothers, all from San Juan, and seeing how easy it was they all set up on their own. Since then the business has flourished, and there are flowers everywhere in San Juan.

By far the best time to visit is for the Friday market, when the whole place springs into action and the village is packed. Keep an eye out for the *huipiles* worn in San Juan, which are unusual and impressive, with bold geometric designs of yellow, purple and green. **Buses** to both villages run every half-hour or so from the Zona 4 terminal in Guatemala City.

Mixco Viejo

Beyond San Juan the road divides, one branch heading north to El Chol and Rabinal (one bus a day takes this route, leaving the Zona 4 terminal in Guatemala City at 5am), the other branch going northwest towards **Mixco Viejo** and **Pachalum**. Heading out along this western route the scenery changes dramatically, leaving behind the pine forests and entering a huge dry valley. Small farms are scattered here and there and the *Politecnica*, Guatemala's military academy, is also out this way. Several hours beyond San Juan, in a massive valley, are the ruins of Mixco Viejo.

The ruins

MIXCO VIEJO was the capital of the Pokoman Maya, one of the main pre-Conquest tribes. The original Pokoman language has all but died out – it's now spoken only in a few isolated areas and in the villages of Mixco and Chinautla – and the bulk of their original territory is swamped by Cakchiquel speakers. The site itself is thought to date from the thirteenth century, and its construction, designed to withstand siege, bears all the hallmarks of the troubled times before the arrival of the Spanish. Protected on all sides by deep ravines, it can be entered only along a single-file causeway. At the time the Spanish arrived, in 1525, this was one of the largest highland centres, with nine temples, two ball courts, and a population of around nine thousand.

The Spanish historian Fuentes y Guzmán actually witnessed the conquest of the city, so for once there's a detailed account. At first Alvarado sent only a small force, but when this was unable to make any impact he launched an attack himself, using his Mexican allies, two hundred Indians from Tlaxcala. With a characteristic lack of subtlety he opted for a frontal assault, but his armies were attacked from behind by a force of Pokoman warriors who arrived from Chinautla. The battle was fought on an open plain in front of the city, and by sunset the Spanish cavalry had won the day, killing some two hundred Pokoman warriors, although the city remained impenetrable. According to Fuentes y Guzman the Pokoman survivors then pointed out a secret entrance to the city, allowing the Spanish to enter virtually unopposed and to unleash a massacre of its inhabitants. The survivors were resettled at a site on the edge of the city, in the village of Mixco Viejo, where Pokoman is still spoken.

Today the site has been impressively restored, with its plazas and temples laid out across several flat-topped ridges. Like all the highland sites the structures are fairly low – the largest temple reaches only about 10m in height – and devoid of decoration. It is, however, an interesting site in a spectacular setting, and during the week you'll probably have the ruins to yourself, which gives the place all the more atmosphere.

Getting there

Mixco Viejo is by no means an easy place to reach, and if you can muster enough people it's worth **renting a car** (see p.71). Alternatively, Swiss Travel, in the *Chalet Suizo* in Guatemala City, can organize **tours** of the site (see p.56). If you're determined to travel by **bus** there is one leaving the Zona 4 terminal in Guatemala City at 9.30am, which passes the site on the way to Pachalum. Make sure that the one you take will pass *las ruinas*, as there are buses that go to the village without doing so; also make sure you don't get on a bus saying *Mixco*, which is not the

FIESTAS

Despite its modern appearance Guatemala City has some firmly established traditions, including one or two fiestas. Also listed below are some of those in the surrounding villages, which aren't necessarily covered in the text but may well be worth visiting if you're around at fiesta time.

JANUARY
The fiesta year in the region around Guatemala City starts from the 1st to 4th in the village of **Fraijanes**. There's also a fiesta in **San Pedro Ayampuc** some time in the month, on a different date each year.

MARCH
Villa Canales has its fiesta from the 6th to 14th, while **San Pedro Pinula** celebrates from the 16th to 20th, with the main day on the 19th. **San José del Golfo** has a fiesta from the 18th to 20th, its main day also being the 19th.

APRIL
The only April fiesta is in **Palencia**, from the 26th to 30th.

MAY
May 1, Labor Day, is marked in the capital by marches and protests, while the fiesta in **Amatitlán** is from the 1st to 7th, with the main day on the 3rd.

JUNE
San Juan Sacatepéquez has a June fiesta from the 22nd to 27th, with the main day on the 24th.

JULY
Palín has a traditional fiesta from the 24th to 30th, which climaxes on its final day.

AUGUST
Mixco, an interesting Pokoman village on the western side of town, has its fiesta on the 4th, while the main **Guatemala City** fiesta, involving all sorts of parades and marches, is on the 15th.

NOVEMBER
San Catarina Pinula celebrates from the 20th to 28th, with the main day on the 25th.

DECEMBER
The year ends with a fiesta in **Chinautla**, from the 4th to 9th, with the main day on the 6th, and **Villa Nueva**, where they have a fiesta from the 6th to 11th, which climaxes on its final day.

right place at all (see below). If you opt to travel by bus, then you'll have to **hitch** back on a truck to San Juan Sacatepequez, which may be very slow going, unless you're prepared to hang around until 3am when the bus returns. Far better to **camp** at one of the attractive sheleters overlooking the ruins.

travel details

BUSES

Guatemala City is at the transport heart of the country with even the smallest of villages being connected to the capital. Hence there are literally thousands of buses into and out of the city. Most of these are covered in the "Travel Details" of other chapters, but the following are the main services of the main **bus companies**. Their addresses and departure times are as follows.

The western highlands

Antigua (1hr). Departures every 15min from 18 C and 4 Av in Zona 1 (5.30 am–7pm).

Chichicastenango (3hr 30min) and **Santa Cruz del Quiché** (4hr). Second-class buses leave from the Zona 4 terminal every 30min (4am–4pm).

Huehuetenango (5hr) **and La Mesilla**. There are a few regular pullman services, the best being Los Halcones, 7 Av 15–27, Zona 1 (☎2381979), whose buses leave at 7am, 2pm and 5pm. Velásquez, 20C 1–37 Zona 1 (☎4736005), also runs hourly buses (7.30am–5.30pm), with the morning departures continuing on to the Mexican border at La Mesilla.

Lake Atitlán and **Panajachel** (3hr). Transportes Rebuli runs hourly second-class buses (6am–4pm) from 21 C 1–54, Zona 1. Alternatively take any bus going to the western highlands from the Zona 4 terminal, and then change buses at the Los Encuentros junction.

Quetzaltenango (4hr). Several companies run first-class buses: Líneas Américas, 2 Av 18–74, Zona 1 (☎2321432) has six departures a day at 5.15am, 9am, 12.15pm, 3.15pm, 4.40pm and 7.30pm; Transportes Alamo 21 C 1–14 Zona 1 (☎2532105) has departures at 8am, 10am, 12.45pm, 3pm and 5.45pm; Transportes Marquensita, 1 Av 21–31, Zona 1 (☎2300067 or 2535871), runs first-class pullmans at 6am, 6.30am, 8.40am, 11am, noon, 3.30pm, 4pm and 5pm that continue on to San Marcos; Galgos, 7 Av 19-44 Zona 1 (☎2534868), runs six pretty decrepit pullmans a day, but are probably best avoided. In addition, nine second-class San Juanera buses leave from the Zona 4 terminal between 7am and 4.15pm.

San Marcos (5hr). All first-class Transportes Marquensita buses (see above) to Quetzaltenango continue on to San Marcos, plus eight second-class services from the Zona 4 terminal between 4.30 and 2.30pm.

San Pedro la Laguna (3hr 30min). Ruta Mendez runs four buses a day between 9.30am and 1pm from junction of 21 C and 5 Av, Zona 1.

Cobán and the Verapaces

Cobán (4–5hr). Services, calling at all points en route, including the Biotopo and Tactic, are run by the efficient Transportes Escobar y Monja Blanca, from their terminal on 8 Av 15–16, Zona 1 (☎2381409). Hourly departures 4am–5pm.

Salamá (3hr 30min), **Rabinal** (4hr 30min) and **Cubulco** (5hr). Transporte Dulce María, 19 C and 9 Av, Zona 1 (☎2500082), runs hourly buses (5am–5pm). Alternatively, you can take any bus between Cobán and the capital and get off at La Cumbre de Santa Elena, from where minibuses run to Salamá.

The Pacific coast and the Mexican border

The bus service to this part of the country is one of the best, with most companies being conveniently sited on the edge of Zona 1, outside the old train station at the junction of 19 C and 9 Av. You'll nearly always be able to turn up and go. Buses to **Tecún Umán** and **Talisman** (5hr) run between 2am and around 8pm passing through all main towns in the coastal region between **Esquintla** (1hr) and the border, where you can change buses for smaller places off the main highway. Try Chinita, on 9 Av 18–38 Zona 1 (☎2519144); Fortaleza, 19 C 8–70 Zona 1 (☎2303390); or Galgos, 7 Av 19–44 Zona 1 (☎2323661 & 2534868), who also continue over the border into Tapachula, Mexico at 7.30am and 1.30pm.

Monterrico (4hr 30min) buses leave from the Zona 4 bus terminal every 30min (10am–noon).

The Motagua Valley, the Caribbean, Petén and Copán

Petén buses are run by Fuente del Norte, 7 C 8–46, Zona 1 (☎2513817 or 2383894), close to the main area of budget hotels. There are seven buses daily (12hr) and you need to buy your ticket in advance. The best bus north is the Línea Dorada which leaves daily at 7.30pm (10hr) from 16 C 10–55, Zona 1 (☎2329658), or try Máxima, which leaves twice daily from 9 Av 17–28, Zona 1 (☎2322495).

Puerto Barrios (5hr), **Zacapa, Chiquimula** (3hr) **and Esquipulas** (4hr). Hourly buses, most of them pullmans, leave from the train station terminal at 19 C and 9 Av in Zona 1. Litegua, at 15C 10–40 Zona 1 (☎2327578), provides the best service to Puerto Barrios with 19 daily departures. Rutas Orientales (☎2537882 & 2512160) runs hourly buses to Esquipulas (4am–6pm), calling at Zacapa and Chiquimula. In addition, Izabal Adventure Tours, 2nd floor, Edificio La Galeria, 7 Av 14–44, Zona 9 (☎3340323; fax 3343701) runs a private tourist shuttle-bus between the capital, Río Dulce and Puerto Barrios, which is faster, air-conditioned and not that much more expensive than the standard bus.

For **Copán** in Honduras take any bus to Chiquimula (see above), where you can change to a bus for El Florido on the border (9 daily; 6am–4.30pm, 2hr).

The eastern highlands and San Salvador

For all towns between the capital and the border with El Salvador, second-class buses leave from the terminal in Zona 4. Several companies run a direct service to the Terminal Occidente in **San Salvador**: Melva International buses leave hourly (5.30am–2.30pm with the final bus at 4.15pm; 5hr) from 3 Av 1–38, Zona 9 (☎3310874 or 3316323), a block or so from the main Zona 4 terminal; Tica Bus services leave 11 C 2–72, Zona 9 (☎3611773 or 3314279), daily at 12.30pm; and King Quality operates the very smartest buses from 16 C 1–30, Zona 10 (☎3612516 or 3612493) at 6.30am and 3.30pm every day. To other parts of the eastern highlands, there are regular departures from the Zona 4 terminal, and to **Jalapa** (hourly 4am–6pm) from 22 C 1–20, Zona 1.

To other Central American countries

Tica Bus, 11 C 2–72, Zona 9 (☎3611773 or 3314279), has daily departures at 12.30pm to Panama City, via San Salvador, Tegucigalpa, Managua and San José. The whole trip takes three days and two nights, the first night spent in Salvador, the second in Managua. For Belize, take any of the buses to Petén (see above) and change in Flores (10–12hr); see p.316 for details of buses from Flores to Belize.

PLANES

There are frequent **international flights** from Guatemala City's Aurora airport to Mexico, Central America and North America, and four daily flights to **Flores** in Petén, the only other international airport in the country. Three of these leave at around 7am, and one at about 4pm. Tickets for the 50-min flight can be bought from virtually any travel agent in the capital (see p73), and cost around $60 return.

TRAINS

There are currently no trains in Guatemala.

CHAPTER TWO

THE WESTERN HIGHLANDS

Guatemala's **western highlands**, stretching from the outskirts of Guatemala City to the Mexican border, are perhaps the most beautiful and captivating part of the country. The region is defined by two main features, a chain of awesome volcanoes that line its southern side, and the high mountain ranges that form the northern boundaries. The greatest of these are the **Cuchumatanes**, whose granite peaks rise to some 3600m. Strung between the two is a series of spectacular twisting ridges, lakes, gushing streams and deep valleys.

It's an astounding landscape, blessed with tremendous fertility but cursed by instability. Of the thirteen cones that loom over the western highlands, three volcanoes are still active: **Pacaya**, **Fuego** and **Santiaguito**, all oozing plumes of sulphurous smoke and occasionally spewing out showers of molten rock. Two major **fault lines** also cut through the area, making earthquakes a regular occurrence. The most recent major quake occurred around **Chimaltenango** in 1976 – it left 25,000 dead and around a million homeless. But despite its sporadic ferocity the landscape is outstandingly beautiful, with irrigated valleys and terraced hillsides carefully crafted to yield the maximum potential farmland.

The highland landscape is controlled by many factors, all of which affect its appearance. Perhaps the most important is **altitude**. At lower levels the vegetation is almost tropical, supporting dense forests, **coffee**, **cotton**, **bananas** and **cacao**, while higher up the hills are often wrapped in cloud and the ground is sometimes hard with frost. Here trees are stunted by the cold, and **maize** and potatoes are grown alongside herds of grazing sheep and goats. The seasons also play their part. In the rainy season, from May to October, the land is superbly green, with young crops and lush forests of **pine**, **cedar** and **oak**, while during the dry winter months the hillsides gradually turn to a dusty yellow.

ACCOMMODATION PRICE CODES

All accommodation listed in this guide has been graded according to the following price scales. These refer to the price in US dollars of the cheapest double room in high season. For more details see p.25.

① Under $5	④ $15–25	⑦ $60–80
② $5–10	⑤ $25–40	⑧ $80–100
③ $10–15	⑥ $45–60	⑨ over $100

The Maya highlands

The western highlands are home to one of the American continent's largest groups of surviving indigenous people, the **Maya**, who have lived here continuously for the last two thousand years. The Maya still form the vast majority of the population in this region, and despite the Spanish Conquest, their society, languages and traditions remain largely unchanged. Maya life and culture is strongly separate from the world of *ladinos*, and their history is bound up with the land on which they live. In the days of Classic Maya civilization (300–900 AD) the western highlands was a peripheral area, with the great developments taking place in the lowlands to the north. Apart from the city of **Kaminaljuyú**, on the site of modern Guatemala City, little is known about the highlands at this time, and there are no archeological remains that date from the Classic period.

Towards the end of the eleventh century the area was colonized by the **Toltec**, who moved south from what is now central Mexico and conquered the Maya of the western highlands, installing themselves as an elite ruling class. Under Toltec rule a number of rival empires emerged, each speaking a separate language and based around a ceremonial centre. (For a detailed rundown of the different groups, see p.354.)

Even today the highlands are divided up along traditional tribal lines. The **Quiché** language is spoken by the largest number, centred on the town of Santa Cruz del Quiché and reaching west into the Quetzaltenango valley. The highlands around Huehuetenango are **Mam**-speaking, the **Tzutujil** occupy the southern shores of Lake Atitlán, and the **Cakchiquel** are to the east. **Smaller tribal groups**, such as the Ixil and the Aguateca, also occupy clearly defined areas in the Cuchumatan mountains, with distinct languages and costumes.

The Spanish highlands

Though pre-Conquest life was certainly hard, the **arrival of the Spanish** in 1523 was a total disaster for the Maya population. In the early stages, **Alvarado** and his army of just a few hundred men, met with a force of Quiché warriors in the Quetzaltenango basin and defeated them in open warfare. Legend has it that Alvarado himself slew the great Quiché warrior **Tecún Umán** in hand-to-hand combat. The defeated Quiché took the Spanish to their capital, Utatlán, hoping to negotiate some kind of deal. Alvarado, however, was not to be seduced by such subtlety and promptly burnt the city along with many of its inhabitants. The next move was made by the **Cakchiquel**, who formed an alliance with the Spanish, hoping to exploit the newcomers' military might to overcome former rivals. As a result the Spanish made their first permanent base at the site of the Cakchiquel capital **Iximché**. But in 1527 the Cakchiquel, provoked by demands for tribute, rose up against the Spanish and fled to the mountains, from where they waged a campaign of guerrilla war against their former allies. The Spanish then moved their capital into the Almolonga valley, to a site near the modern town of Antigua, from where they gradually brought the rest of the highlands under a degree of control.

However, the damage done by Spanish swords was nothing when compared to that of the **diseases** they introduced. Waves of smallpox, typhus, plague and measles swept through the indigenous population, reducing their numbers by as much as ninety percent in the worst hit areas. The population was so badly devastated that it only started to recover at the end of the seventeenth century, and didn't get back to pre-Conquest levels until the middle of the twentieth century.

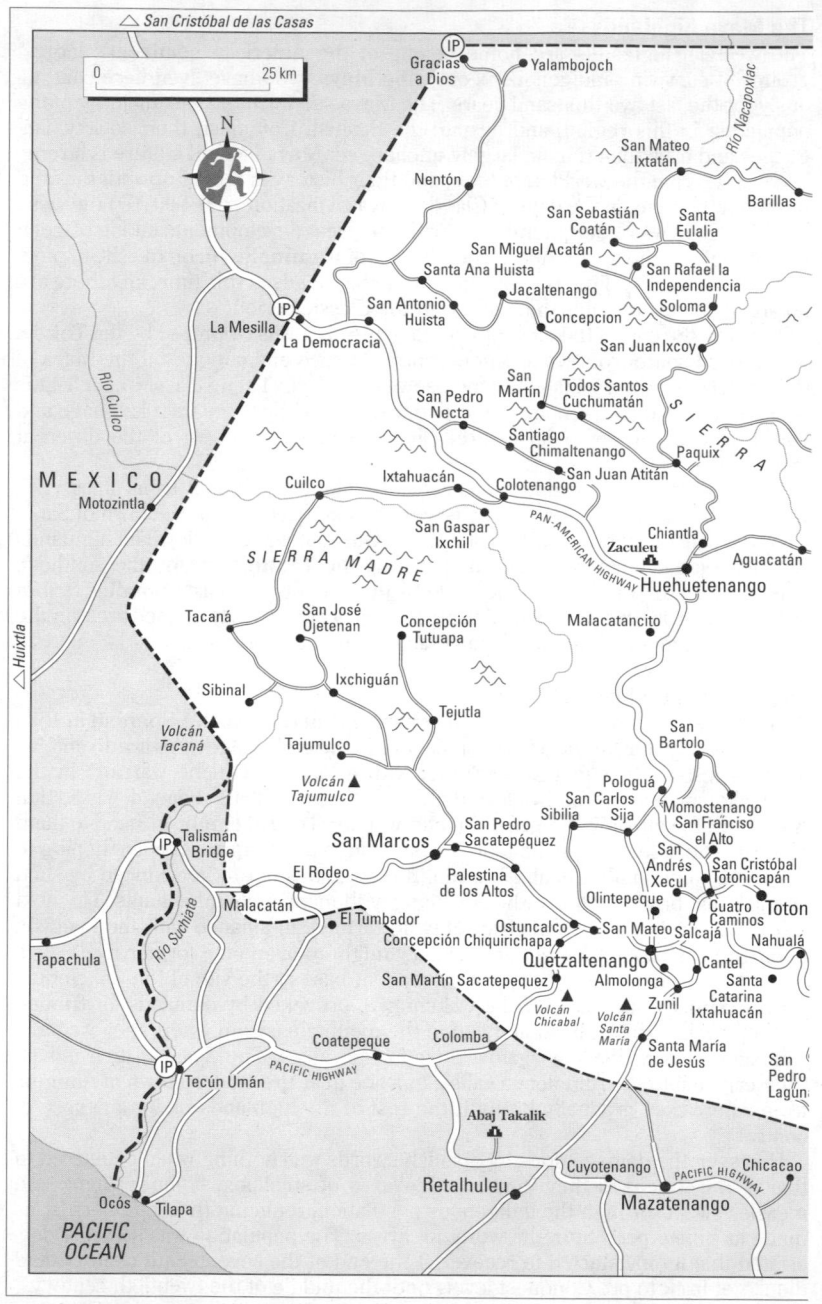

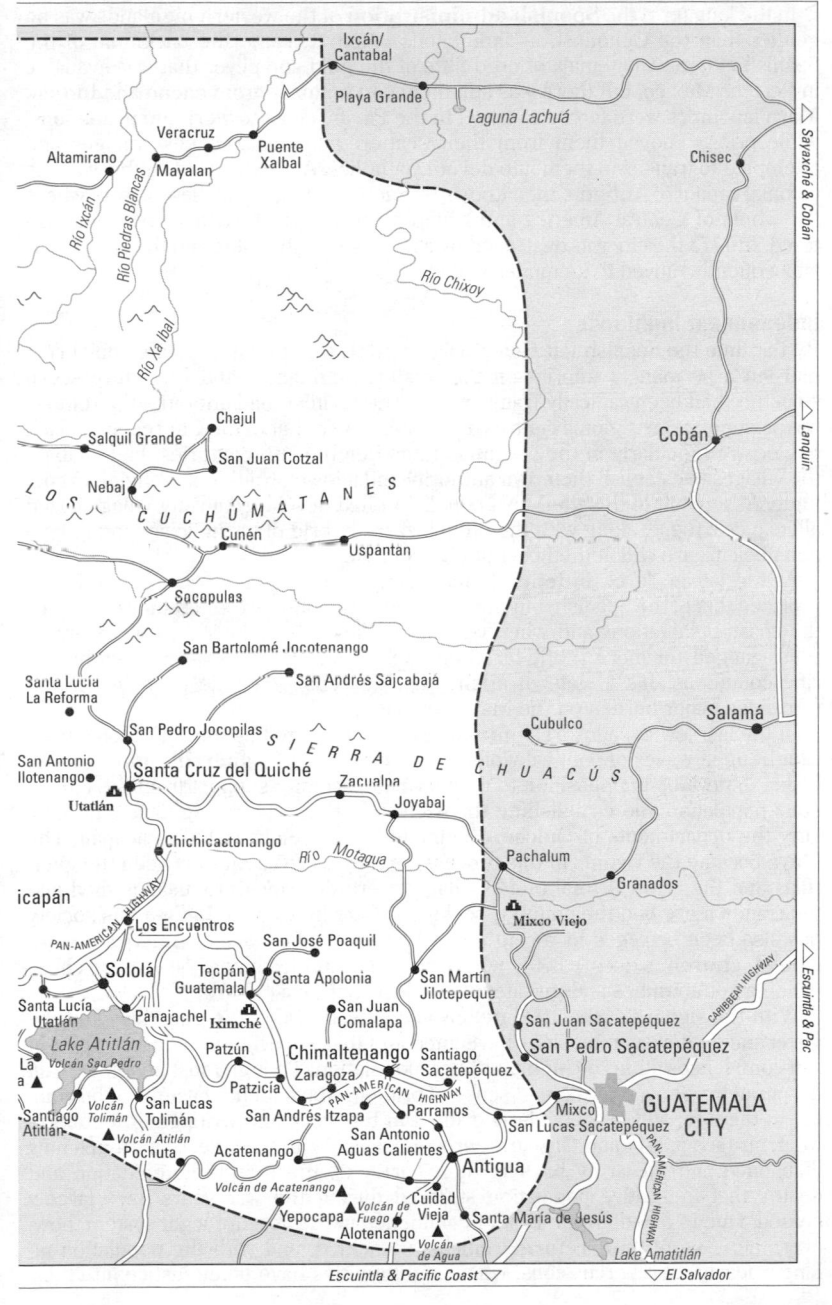

In the long term the **Spanish administration** of the western highlands was no gentler than the Conquest, as indigenous labour became the backbone of the Spanish empire. Guatemala offered little of the gold and silver that was available in Peru or Mexico, but there was still money to be made from **cacao** and **indigo**. Maya labourers were forced to travel to the Pacific coast to work the plantations, while priests moved them from their scattered homes into new villages and attempted to transform them into devout Catholics. At the heart of all this was the colonial capital of **Antigua**, then known as Santiago de los Caballeros, from where the whole of Central America and Chiapas (now part of Mexico) was administered. In 1773 the city was destroyed by a massive earthquake, and the capital was subsequently moved to its modern site.

Independent highlands

By the time the Spanish left Guatemala, in 1821, three centuries of colonial rule had left a permanent imprint on the western highlands, and the entire social structure had been radically transformed. The Spanish had attempted to remove the power of large regional centres, replacing it with that of the Church, but a lack of clergy, particularly in the seventeenth and eighteenth centuries, had enabled the villages to establish their own authority and allowed traditional religion to continue. As a result of this the Maya population had developed strong village-based allegiances: these, along with the often bizarre hybrid of Catholicism and indigenous beliefs, are still at the heart of highland life.

At the village level, **independence** brought little change. *Ladino* authority replaced that of the Spanish, but the indigenous people were still required to work the coastal plantations and when labour supplies dropped off they were simply press-ganged (or more subtly lured into debt) and forced to work, often in horrific conditions. It's a state of affairs that has changed little even today, and remains a major burden on the Maya population.

In the last few decades fresh pressures have emerged as the Maya have been caught up in waves of political violence. In the late 1970s **guerrilla movements** began to develop in opposition to military rule, seeking support from the indigenous population and establishing themselves in the western highlands, particularly the departments of Quiché, Huehuetenango, Sololá and Totonicapán. The Maya became the victims in this process, as they were caught between the guerrillas and the army. A total of 440 villages were destroyed; thousands died and thousands more fled the country, seeking refuge in Mexico. Indigenous society has also been besieged in recent years by a holy tidal wave of American **evangelical churches** (see p.379), whose influence undermines local hierarchies, dividing communities and threatening to destroy Maya culture.

With the signing of the 1996 **peace accords** between the guerrillas and the government, however, tensions have lifted and there is evidence of a new spirit of self-confidence within the highland Maya population. Though most people remain desperately poor, a reawakened sense of pride in Maya identity seems to be coming to the fore, and is particularly evident in the work and writings of Rigoberta Menchú (see p.391) and Gaspar Pedro Gonzáles. With the guerrilla groups now disbanded and the army back in their barracks, the threats, intimidation and deaths that the native population suffered during the war years have largely ceased. Due to a nationwide lack of confidence in the corrupt legal system, however, the issue of **land reform** remains untackled, and with the population no longer fearful of repercussions, whole communities have taken justice into their

MARKET DAYS

Throughout the western highlands **weekly markets** are the main focus of economic and social activity, drawing people from the area around the town or village where they're held. Make an effort to catch as many market days as possible – they're second only to local fiestas in offering a glimpse of a way of life unchanged for centuries.

Monday
Antigua; Chimaltenango; Santa Barbara; San Juan Atitán; Zunil.

Tuesday
Acatenango; Comalapa; Chajul; El Tejar; Olintepeque; Patzún; Salcajá; San Andrés Semetabaj; San Antonio Ilotenango; San Lucas Tolimán; San Marcos; San Pedro Jocopilas; Totonicapán; Yepocapa.

Wednesday
Almolonga; Chimaltenango; Colotenango; Cotzal; Huehuetenango; Momostenango; Palestina de Los Altos; Patzicía; Sacapulas; San Sebastián.

Thursday
Aguacatán; Antigua; Chichicastenango; Chimaltenango; El Tejar; Jacaltenango; La Libertad; Nebaj; Panajachel; Patulul; Patzite; Patzún; Sacapulas; San Juan Atitán; San Luis Jilotepeque; San Mateo Ixtatán; San Miguel Ixtahuacán; San Pedro Necta; San Pedro Pinula; San Pedro Sacatepéquez; San Rafael La Independencia; Santa Barbara; Santa Cruz del Quiché; Soloma; Tajumulco; Tecpán; Totonicapán; Uspantán; Zacualpa.

Friday
Chajul; Chimaltenango; Jocotenango; San Francisco el Alto; San Andrés Itzapa; San Lucas Tolimán; Santiago Atitlán; Sololá; Tacaná.

Saturday
Antigua; Almolonga; Colotenango; Cotzal; Ixchiguan; Malacatán; Nentón; Palestina de los Altos; Patzicía; Santa Clara La Laguna; Santa Cruz del Quiché; Sumpango; Todos Santos; Totonicapán; Yepocapa.

Sunday
Acatenango; Aguacatán; Cantel; Chichicastenango; Chimaltenango; Cuilco; Huehuetenango; Jacaltenango; Joyabaj; La Libertad; Malacatancito; Momostenango; Nebaj; Nahualá; Ostuncalco; Patzite; Nentón; Panajachel; Parramos; Patzún; Sacapulas; San Bartolo; San Carlos Sija; San Cristóbal Totonicapán; San Juan Comalapa; San Luis Jilotepeque; San Martín Jilotepeque; San Mateo Ixtahuacán; San Miguel Acatán; San Miguel Ixtahuacán; San Pedro Necta; San Pedro Sacatepéquez; Santa Barbara; Santa Cruz del Quiché; Santa Eulalia; Sibilia; Soloma; Sumpango; Tacaná; Tecpán; Tejar; Tucuru; Uspantán; Yepocapa; Zacualpa.

own hands to resolve local disputes. Suspected thieves have been lynched, peasants have squatted *finca* farmland and angry mobs have stormed the municipal buildings of local administrations. Travellers in the region are unlikely to be affected by these incidents; indeed, the more remote highland areas are some of the safest parts of the country for travellers, as tightly controlled communual life regulates behaviour and outsiders are easily spotted.

Even in a climate of institutionalized racism and bitter poverty **Maya society** remains largely intact: traditional structures are still in place, local languages still spoken, native costume still worn, and certain isolated villages still use the 260-

day Tzolkin Maya calendar. It is this unique culture, above all else, that is Guatemala's most fascinating feature. Maya society is inward-looking and conservative, operating, in the face of adversity, on its own terms. Rejecting *ladino* commercialism, the Maya see trade as a social function as much as an economic one, with life centring on the village and its own civil and religious hierarchy, and subsistence farming of maize and beans remaining at the heart of Maya existence.

Visiting Maya **villages** during the week, you may find them almost deserted – their permanent populations are generally small, though they may support five or ten times as many scattered rural homesteads. It's on **market** and **fiesta** days however, when the villages fill to bursting, and you can most clearly sense the values of the Maya world – in the subdued bustle and gossip of the market or the intense joy of celebration.

Where to go

Travelling in the western highlands you're spoilt for choice, with beautiful verdant scenery yielding up atmospheric highland **villages** of adobe houses and whitewashed colonial churches at every turn. Of course, **Antigua**, the most impressive colonial city in Central America, is the highlight of the region, not only for its ruins, but also for its picturesque setting and tranquil atmosphere. In addition to the colourful market towns and spectacular mountainscapes for which the region is famed, there are a few **historical sites**, such as the pre-Conquest cities of Iximché, Utatlán and Zaculeu, which, although they don't bear comparison to Tikal and the lowland sites, are nevertheless fascinating in their own way.

Travelling west from Guatemala City, Antigua is the first unmissable place of interest, where it's easy to settle into the relaxed pace of things, sample the cosmopolitan restaurant scene, climb the giant volcanoes which overshadow the city, visit the surrounding villages, and take in the colonial ruins. Northwest of here lies the department of **El Quiché**, with the well-known market at **Chichicastenango** and the ruins of **Utatlán**, near the departmental capital of **Santa Cruz del Quiché**. To the south of Quiché, **Lake Atitlán** is the jewel of the western highlands, ringed by volcanoes and some of the country's most traditional villages, and reached via the colourful market town of **Sololá**, and **Panajachel**, a booming lakeside resort. To the north are the wildly beautiful peaks of the **Cuchumatanes**, between which nestle the towns of the **Ixil triangle**, remote and intensely traditional communities at the end of a tortuous bus journey. Heading on to the west you pass the strongly traditional town of **Nahualá** and go up over the mountains to Guatemala's second city, **Quetzaltenango** (Xela), an ideal base for visiting local villages or climbing the near-perfect volcanic cone of **Santa María**. Beyond this, the border with Mexico is marked by the departments of **San Marcos** and **Huehuetenango**, both of which offer superb mountain scenery, dotted with isolated villages, the pick of which is the traditional **Todos Santos**.

The **Pan-American Highway** runs through the middle of the western highlands so it's easy enough to get around. There's a constant flow of buses along this main artery, some branching off onto minor roads to more remote areas. Travelling on these roads can sometimes be a gruelling experience, particularly in northern Huehuetenango and Quiché, but the scenery makes it well worth the discomfort. The most practical plan of action is to base yourself in one of the larger places and then make a series of day trips to markets and fiestas, although even the smallest of villages will usually offer some kind of accommodation.

ANTIGUA AND AROUND

Superbly situated in a sweeping highland valley, suspended between the cones of Agua, Acatenango and Fuego volcanoes is one of America's most enchanting colonial cities, **ANTIGUA**. In its day this was one of the great cities of the Spanish empire, ranking alongside Lima and Mexico City and serving as the administrative centre for the *Audiencia de Guatemala*, which encompassed all of Central America and Mexican Chiapas. Spanish architects and Maya labourers constructed a classically designed city of elegant squares, churches, monasteries and grand houses, whose magnificent colonial legacy ensures Antigua's continuing prosperity as one of Guatemala's premier tourist attractions.

Antigua was actually the third capital of Guatemala. The Spanish settled first at the site of **Iximché** in July 1524, so that they could keep a close eye on their Cakchiquel allies. In November 1527, when the Cakchiquel rose up in defiance of their new rulers, the capital was moved into the Almolonga valley, to the site of **Ciudad Vieja**, a few kilometres from Antigua. In 1541, however, shortly after the death of Alvarado, this entire town was lost beneath a massive mud slide. Only then did the capital come to rest in Antigua, known in those days as *La Muy Noble y Muy Leal Ciudad de Santiago de los Caballeros de Goathemala*. Here, despite the continued threat from the instability of the bedrock – the first earthquake came after just twenty years – it settled and began to achieve astounding prosperity.

As the heart of colonial power in Central America, Antigua grew slowly but steadily. One by one the religious orders established themselves, competing in the construction of schools, churches, monasteries and hospitals. Bishops built grand palaces that were soon rivalled by the homes of local merchants and corrupt government officials. When the English friar Thomas Gage visited Antigua in 1627, he was shocked by the wickedness of Spain's empire:

> *Great plenty and wealth hath made the inhabitants as proud and vicious as are those of Mexico. Here is not only idolatry, but fornication and uncleanliness as public as in any place of the Indies. The mulattoes, Blackamoors, mestizos, Indians, and all common sort of people are much made on by the greater and richer sort, and go as gallantly apparelled as do those of Mexico. They fear neither a volcano or mountain of water on the one side, which they confess hath once poured out a flood and river executing God's wrath against sin there committed, nor a volcano of fire, on the other side, roaring with and threatening to rain upon them Sodom's ruin and destruction.*

The city reached its peak in the middle of the eighteenth century, after the 1717 earthquake prompted an unprecedented building boom, and the population rose to around fifty thousand. By this stage Antigua was a genuinely impressive place, with a university, a printing press, a newspaper, and streets that were seething with commercial and political rivalries. But as is so often the case in Guatemala, **earthquakes** brought all of this to an abrupt end. For the best part of a year the city was shaken by tremors, with the final blows delivered by two severe shocks on September 7 and December 13, 1773. The damage was so bad that the decision was made to abandon the city in favour of the modern capital: fortunately, despite endless official decrees, there were many who refused to leave and Antigua was never completely deserted.

Since then the city has been gradually repopulated, particularly in the last hundred years or so. As Guatemala City has become increasingly congested, many of

TOURIST CRIME IN ANTIGUA AND LAKE ATITLÁN

While there is no need to be paranoid, visitors to the heavily touristed areas around Antigua and Lake Atitlán should be aware that **crime against tourists** – including robbery and rape – is a problem. Pay close attention to security reports from your embassy and follow the usual precautions. In particular, avoid walking alone, especially at night or to isolated spots during the day. If you want to visit viewing spots such as the *cruce* overlooking Antigua, inform the tourist police (see p.108) and they will accompany you or even give you a ride there on one of their motorbikes. Though there have been very few attacks on people hiking around Lake Atitlán recently, it's still safer to walk in a group. Similarly, don't amble around Panajachel alone late at night. In the more remote highlands, where foreigners are a much rarer sight, attacks are extremely uncommon.

the conservative middle classes have moved to Antigua. They've been joined by a large number of resident and visiting foreigners attracted by the city's relaxed and sophisticated atmosphere, lively cultural life, the benign climate and largely traffic-free streets.

In recent years concern has mounted for the fate of the city's ancient architecture. Antigua was the first planned city in the Americas, originally built on a rigid grid pattern, with neatly cobbled streets and grand buildings. Of this tremendous colonial legacy, some buildings now lie in atmospheric ruin, others are steadily decaying, and yet more have been restored as hotels or restaurants. Local **conservation** laws have been brought in to protect the streets from the intrusion of overhanging signs, extensions to houses are subject to tight planning controls and every effort is being made to preserve the architectural grandeur of the past.

Antigua

Once regarded as the cultural, religious and political centre of the country, these days **ANTIGUA** is a haven of tranquillity. Offering a welcome break from the unrelenting energy of the capital, it has become the country's foremost tourist destination, a favoured hang-out for travellers to refuel and recharge. It's almost inevitable that you'll run into someone here that you met in a bar in Mexico City or on a beach in Honduras. Aside from the lively bar scene and a great choice of restaurants, the main attraction is the relaxed ambience and the beauty of Antigua itself. Another factor is the city's **language schools**, some of the best and cheapest in all Latin America, drawing students from around the globe. The expats, including English, Italians, Americans, South Americans, Swiss and Germans, contribute to the town's cosmopolitan air, mingling with locals selling their wares in the streets and the middle-class Guatemalans who come here at weekends to eat, drink and enjoy themselves. The downside of this settled, comfortable affluence is perhaps a loss of vitality – it's a great place to wind down and eat well for a few days if you've been travelling hard, but after a while this civilized, isolated world can seem almost a little too smug and comfortable. After a few days of sipping cappuccinos and munching cake, you could almost forget that you're in Central America at all.

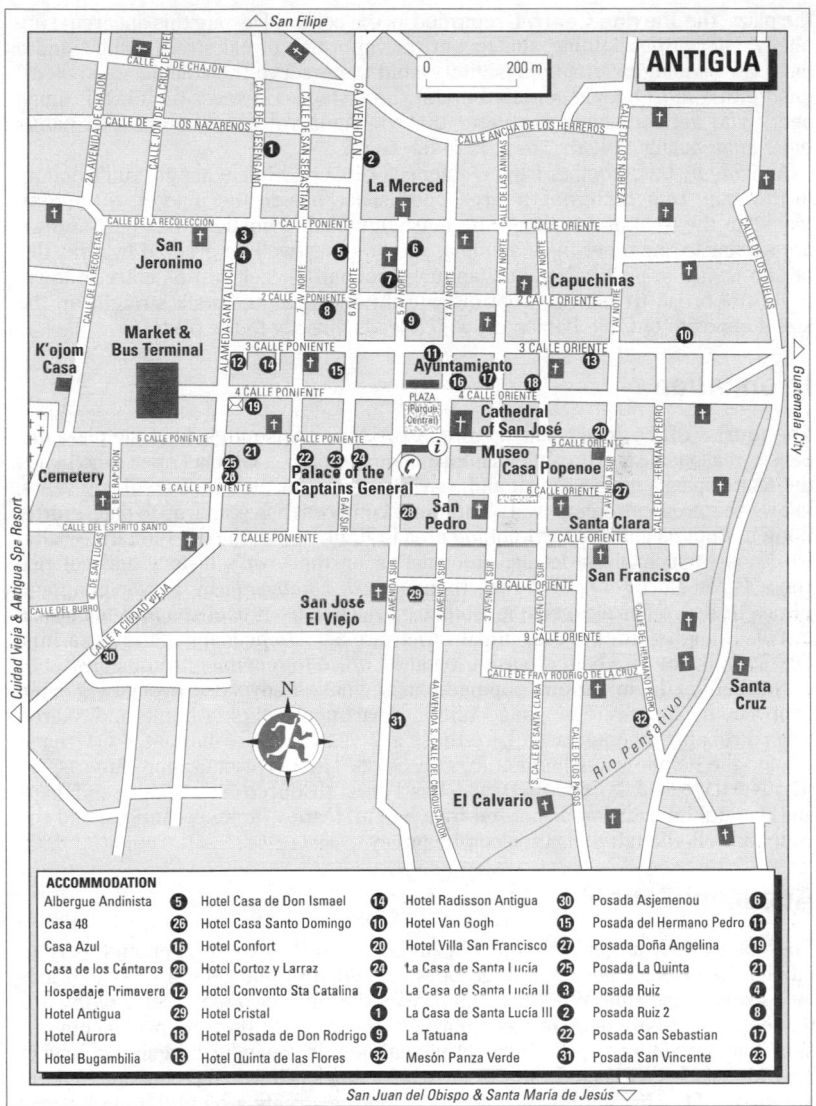

ACCOMMODATION

Albergue Andinista	⑤	Hotel Casa de Don Ismael	⑭	Hotel Radisson Antigua	㉚	Posada Asjemenou	⑥
Casa 48	㉖	Hotel Casa Santo Domingo	⑩	Hotel Van Gogh	⑮	Posada del Hermano Pedro	⑪
Casa Azul	⑯	Hotel Confort	⑳	Hotel Villa San Francisco	㉗	Posada Doña Angelina	⑲
Casa de los Cántaros	⑳	Hotel Cortoz y Larraz	㉔	La Casa de Santa Lucía	㉕	Posada La Quinta	㉑
Hospedaje Primavera	⑫	Hotel Convento Sta Catalina	①	La Casa de Santa Lucía II	③	Posada Ruiz	④
Hotel Antigua	㉙	Hotel Cristal	—	La Casa de Santa Lucía III	②	Posada Ruiz 2	⑧
Hotel Aurora	⑱	Hotel Posada de Don Rodrigo	⑨	La Tatuana	㉒	Posada San Sebastian	⑰
Hotel Bugambilia	⑬	Hotel Quinta de las Flores	㉜	Mesón Panza Verde	㉛	Posada San Vincente	㉓

San Juan del Obispo & Santa María de Jesús ▽

Arrival

Antigua is laid out on the traditional grid system, with *avenidas* running north–south, and *calles* east–west. Each street is numbered and has two halves, either a north and south (*norte/sur*) or an east and west (*oriente/poniente*), with the plaza, the **Parque Central**, regarded as the centre. Despite this apparent simplicity, poor street lighting, the recent revival of use of old street names, and a local law banning overhanging signs – a bid to preserve the colonial character – ensure that most people get lost here at some stage. However the town is small and if you get confused, remember that the Agua volcano, the one that hangs most immediately over the town, is to the south.

Arriving by bus, whether from Guatemala City or Chimaltenango, you'll end up in the main **bus terminal**, a large open space beside the market, three long blocks to the west of the plaza. The noise, fumes and bustle of this part of town are similar to any other in Guatemala, and you may well be greeted by a hustler or two trying to push a hotel or language school. To get to the centre of town, cross the broad tree-lined street outside the terminal and walk straight up the street opposite (4 Calle Poniente), which leads directly to the plaza.

Information

The **tourist office** (daily 8am–6pm; ☎8320763) on the south side of the plaza dispenses reasonable if overcautious information. Benjamen García Lopez, who heads the team, speaks good English and, having worked in the office for thirty years, knows the area extremely well. The most comprehensive and up-to-date **guidebook** to Antigua and the surrounding area is *Antigua For You*, by Barbara Balchin De Koose, which gives detailed information on the town's history and colonial ruins. If you can't get hold of that, then *Antigua Guatemala* by Trevor Long and Elizabeth Bell ranks alongside it. Both are available from bookshops in town (see p.105). Though **guides** of the human variety are often to be found in the plaza, hustling for business, it's better to ask the tourist office to recommend someone.

Noticeboards in various popular tourist venues advertise everything from happy hours to private language tuition, apartments, flights home and shared rides. Probably the most useful are those at *Doña Luisa's* restaurant, 4 C Oriente 12, and the Rainbow Reading Room, 7 Av Sur 8. The US organization, Amerispan, 6 Av Norte 40 (☎ & fax 8320164), also has a great resource centre with good maps and general information dispensed by a helpful team who know Antigua and the country well, though their trips can be pricey.

Accommodation

There are nearly a hundred hotels in Antigua, and they come in enough permutations to suit every pocket, though be warned that rooms get scarce (and prices increase) around Holy Week (see p.95). Would-be guides often greet arriving bus passengers with offers of a hotel; be aware, though, that they get paid a commission if you take a room, so if you arrive with one in tow your bargaining powers have already been affected. Only at very busy times is it worth taking one of them up. Many of the budget hotels are situated in the streets around the market and bus terminal, and so can be noisy; hotels located in all other parts of the city are much more tranquil.

Budget accomodation

Albergue Andinista, 6 Av Norte 34 (☎ & fax 8323343). Secure rooms and apartments, a little bare but serviceable, plus luggage storage and volcano tours run by Guatemala's most experienced volcano guide (see p.100). ③.

Hotel Bugambilia, 3 C Oriente 19 (☎8325780). Decent option, clean and safe. Though other places may offer more attractive rooms for the price, the location is quiet and the owners very helpful and hospitable. Snacks are available, and English is spoken. ③.

Casa 48, 6 C Poniente 48 (no phone). Near-legendary budget guest house, clean and one of the cheapest places in town. Offers good deals for single travellers. ①.

Hotel la Casa de Don Ismael, 3 C Poniente 6 (☎8321932). A very quiet location, attractive rooms and nice touches like towels and soap provided, make this a role model for budget hostels. There's a lovely little garden, free mineral water and tea or coffee in the morning. No private bathrooms, but the communal ones are brightly painted and spotless. Very fair prices. ②.

La Casa de Santa Lucía, Alameda Santa Lucía 5 (☎8326133). Secure, spacious and attractive rooms decorated with dark wood, all with bathrooms and hot water. Best value in town in this price category, hence very popular. You'll have to ring the bell to get in; guests are given a key. ③.

La Casa de Santa Lucía II, Alameda de Santa Lucía Norte 21; **La Casa de Santa Lucía III**, 6 Av Norte 43A (no phones). Almost carbon copies of the original. Spacious rooms all with hot showers and both extremely well priced. Neither are signposted. Ring the bell for entry. ③.

Hotel Cristal, Av del Desengano 25 (☎8324177). Good-value family-run hotel with pleasant balcony overlooking a flower-filled courtyard. Rooms with or without private bath – hot water and use of kitchen included. The only drawback is its site on the main road out of town – the whole building shakes as buses thunder past, so it's not the place to stay if you're worried about earthquakes. ②.

Posada Doña Angelina, 4 C Poniente 33 (☎8325173). Popular budget option close to the bus terminal, so, though handy, it's not the most tranquil place in town. The rooms are a bit gloomy, but there's plenty of them, and some have private bath. ②.

Hospedaje Primavera, 3 Callejón Poniente 2 (no phone). Good budget bet, with tidy rooms, in a quiet setting. It's run by nice people and is good value. ②.

Posada La Quinta, 5 C Poniente 19 (no phone). Clean, safe place run by a friendly family but close to the bus station, so be prepared for some noise and active streetlife. ②.

Posada Ruiz, Alameda Santa Lucía 17; **Posada Ruiz 2**, 2 C Poniente 25 (no phones). No frills, small rooms but extremely cheap rates, just a short stumble from the bus terminal. *Ruiz 2* is marginally better, and there is a mini travellers' "scene" in the courtyard in the evenings. ①.

Hotel Villa San Francisco, 1 Av Sur 15 (☎8323383). Well-run, Swiss-owned hotel with secure, pleasant rooms, a rooftop terrace and very competitive email, fax and phone services. Also home to Maya Mountain Bike Tours (see p.107). ②.

Mid-range accommodation

Posada Asjemenou, 5 Av Norte 31 (☎8322670, fax 8322832). Comfortable rooms with a colonial feel, set nicely around a tranquil courtyard. Very good value, either with or without private bathroom. ④.

Hotel Aurora, 4 C Oriente 16 (☎ & fax 8320217). Attractive, colonial building with rooms set around a lovely grassy courtyard and fountain. It's a little old-fashioned, but comfortable enough; breakfast is included. ⑥.

Hotel Confort, 1 Av Norte 2 (☎8320566). Attractive family-run guest house with pleasant garden in a quiet street. Though the rooms are attractive, none come with private bath. ④.

Hotel Convento Santa Catalina, 5 Av Norte 28 (☎8323080; fax 8323079). Scruffy rooms that are well overpriced. Earplugs are essential at weekends when the neighbouring *Casbah* disco fires up. ⑥.

Hotel Cortez y Larraz, 6 Av Sur 3 (☎8230276). Very friendly family-run affair, but the rooms, though clean and tidy, are a little uninspiring. ④.

Posada del Hermano Pedro, 3 C Oriente 3 (☎8322089; fax 8322087). Recent conversion of a historic colonial mansion, which has been accomplished with sensitivity and taste. Character, comfort and location are all very good, and when the rooftop bar opens, the views will be stunning. ⑥.

Posada San Sebastian, 3 Av Norte 4 (☎ & fax 8322621). Charming establishment where all the delightful rooms are individually decorated with antiques; there's a gorgeous little bar and the location is very convenient. Excellent value. ⑥.

Posada San Vincente, 6 Av Sur 6 (☎8323311). Friendly guest house in a quiet part of town, away from the main tourist bustle. The rooms are far from beautiful but all come with bathroom and hot water; bikes are available for rent. ④.

La Tatuana, 7 Av Sur 3 (☎8320537). Extremely good value, this small hotel has many imaginative touches; the rooms are artistically decorated and all have a private bathroom. Complimentary fresh coffee is always available. ④.

Hotel Van Gogh, 6 Av Norte 14 (☎ & fax 8320376). Homely place with choice of attractive rooms, a nice bar/TV lounge with log fires in winter, a café, and email and fax services. Special weekly and monthly rates are available. ④.

Luxury accommodation

Hotel Antigua, 8 C Poniente 1, 5 Av Sur (☎8320288; fax 8320807). Antigua's oldest luxury hotel, with tasteful colonial decor and a ruined church practically on the premises. It also has a pool, excellent restaurant, beautiful gardens – and pleasant rooms with open fires to ward off the chill of the night. $132, including breakfast. ⑨.

Antigua Spa Resort, San Pedro El Panorama, on road to Cuidad Viejo (☎8323960; fax 8323968). Central America's only hotel spa offers a sumptuous environment, volcano views and very attractive rooms with pine furnishings and log fires. There are first-class exercise facilities, a lovely pool, and lots of opportunities for indulgence in the form of herbal wraps, milk almond baths and body massages. ⑨.

Casa Azul, 4 Av Norte 5 (☎8320961; fax 8320944). Huge, atmospheric rooms in a converted colonial mansion in one of the best locations in town, just off the plaza. It's equipped with a full range of facilities, including sauna, jacuzzi and a small swimming pool. ⑧.

Casa de los Cántaros, 5 Av Sur 5 (☎8320674; fax 8320609). Splendid American-owned colonial house harbouring three gorgeous rooms straight out of *Elle Decoration*, all set around a stunning garden – peace and tranquillity guaranteed. There's a library, and TV room, and breakfast is included. ⑦.

Hotel Casa Santo Domingo, 3 C Oriente 28 (☎8320140; fax 8320102). Guatemala's most atmospheric hotel, this spectacular former convent has been sympathetically converted, with rooms and corridors displaying ecclesiastical art and holy paraphernalia. There's no lack of luxury and the entire place has the air of a colonial museum, with rooms costing around $150 double, though off season, prices can be almost half. ⑨.

Mesón Panza Verde, 5 Av Sur 19 (☎ & fax 8322925). Small, quality hotel with immaculate, imaginative decor in a colonial-style building that also harbours one of Antigua's premier retaurants. The suites are huge and supremely comfortable, some with four-poster beds, and the service is faultless. It's in the southern quarter of town, away from the main tourist drag, so you can be sure of peace and quiet. Breakfast included. ⑦.

Hotel Posada de Don Rodrigo, C del Arco, 5 Av Norte 17 (☎ & fax 8320291). Spacious, old-fashioned but comfortable rooms set around attractive courtyards; also has a decent restaurant and a nice wood-panelled bar. Rates are not the best value in this category, however, and the central location means it tends to get swamped by day-trippers. ⑦.

Hotel Quinta de las Flores, Calle del Hermano Pedro 6 (☎8323721; fax 8323726). A little out of town, but the attractive, tastefully decorated rooms and the spectacular garden, with swimming pool and many rare plants, shrubs and trees, make it one of the most delightful spots in Antigua – a wonderful place to relax. ⑦.

Hotel Radisson Antigua, 9 C, south of town on the road to Ciudad Vieja (☎8320291 & 8320387; fax 8320237). Although it looks like a whitewashed army base from the outside, this

---

SEMANA SANTA IN ANTIGUA

Antigua's **Semana Santa (Holy Week) celebrations** are perhaps the most extravagant and impressive in all Latin America. The celebrations start with a procession on Palm Sunday, representing Christ's entry into Jerusalem, and continue through to the really big processions and pageants on Good Friday. On Thursday night the streets are carpeted with meticulously drawn patterns of coloured sawdust, and on Friday morning a series of processions re-enacts the progress of Christ to the Cross accompanied by sombre music from local brass bands. Setting out from La Merced, Escuela de Cristo and the village of San Felipe, teams of penitents wearing peaked hoods and accompanied by solemn dirges and clouds of incense carry images of Christ and the Cross on massive platforms. The pageants set off at around 8am, the penitents dressed in either white or purple. After 3pm, the hour of the Crucifixion, they change into black.

It is a great honour to be involved in the procession, but no easy task as the great cedar block carried from La Merced weighs some 3.5 tonnes, and needs eighty men to lift it. Some of the images displayed date from the seventeenth century and the procession itself is thought to have been introduced by Alvarado in the early years of the Conquest, imported directly from Spain.

Check the exact details of events with the tourist office who should be able to provide you with a map detailing the routes of the processions. During Holy Week hotels in Antigua are often full, and the entire town is always packed on Good Friday. But even If you have to make the trip from Guatemala City or Panajachel, it's well worth coming here for, especially on the Friday.

---

large concrete structure holds more than 100 rooms and boasts every luxury, including two tennis courts, a pool, gym and a disco. The corporate, impersonal design and edge of town location means that you may forget you're in Antigua at all. Rooms cost around $140 a double. ⑨.

The City

In accordance with its position as the seat of colonial authority in Central America, Antigua was once a centre of secular and religious power, trade and, above all, wealth. Here the great institutions competed with the government to build the country's most impressive buildings. Churches, monasteries, schools, hospitals and grand family homes were constructed throughout the city, all with tremendously thick walls to resist earthquakes. Today Antigua has an incredible number of ruined and restored **colonial buildings**, and although these constitute only a fraction of the city's original architectural splendour, they do give an idea of its former extravagance. Mentioned below are only some of the remaining examples; armed with a map from the tourist office you could spend days exploring the ruins (most charge a small entrance fee). However, the prospect of visiting the lot can seem overwhelming; if you'd rather just see the gems, make La Merced, Las Capuchinas, the Casa Popenoe and San Francisco your targets.

The Parque Central

As always, the focus of the colonial city was its central plaza, the **Parque Central**. Old prints show it as an open expanse of earth, which in the rainy season turned into a sea of mud. For centuries it served as the hub of the city, bustling with constant activity: a huge market spilled out across it, cleared only for bullfights, military parades, floggings and public hangings. The calm of today's shady Parque Central is relatively recent, and the fountain, originally set to one side so as not to interfere with the action, was moved to the centre in 1936.

The most imposing of the surrounding structures is the **Cathedral of San José**, on the eastern side. The first cathedral was begun in 1545, using some of the vast fortune left by Alvarado's death. However, the execution was so poor that the structure was in a constant state of disrepair, and an earthquake in 1583 brought down much of the roof. In 1670 it was decided to start on a new cathedral worthy of the town's role as a capital city. For eleven years the town watched, as conscripted Maya laboured and the most spectacular colonial building in Central America took shape. The scale of the new cathedral was astounding: a vast dome, five naves, eighteen chapels, and a central chamber measuring 90m by 20m. Its altar was inlaid with mother-of-pearl, ivory and silver, and carvings of saints and paintings by the most revered of European and colonial artists covered the walls.

The new cathedral was strong enough to withstand the earthquakes of 1689 and 1717, but its walls were weakened and the 1773 earthquake brought them crashing to the ground. Today, two of the chapels have been restored as the **Church of San José**, which opens off the Parque Central, and inside it is a figure of Christ by the colonial sculptor Quirio Cataño, who also carved the famous Black Christ of Esquipulas (see p.258). Behind the church, entered from 5 C Oriente, are the remains of the rest of the structure, a mass of fallen masonry, rotting beams, broken arches and hefty pillars, cracked and moss-covered. Buried beneath the floor are some of the great names of the Conquest, including Alvarado, his wife Beatriz de la Cueva, Bishop Marroquín and the historian Bernal Díaz del Castillo.

Along the entire south side of the Parque Central runs the squat two-storey facade of the **Palace of the Captains General**, with a row of 27 arches along each floor. It was originally built in 1558, but as usual this first version was destroyed by earthquakes and in 1761 it was rebuilt, only to be damaged again in 1773, and finally restored along the lines of the present structure. The palace was home to the colonial rulers and also housed the barracks of the dragoons, the stables, the royal mint, law courts, tax offices, great ballrooms, a large bureaucracy, and a lot more besides. Today it contains the local government offices, the headquarters of the Sacatepéquez police department and the tourist office.

Directly opposite, on the north side of the plaza, is the **Ayuntamiento**, the city hall, also known as the *Casa del Cabildo* or town house. Dating from 1740, its metre-thick walls balance the solid style of the Palace of the Captains General. Unlike most others, this building survived earlier rumblings and wasn't damaged until the 1976 earthquake, although it has been repaired since. The city hall was abandoned in 1779 when the capital moved to its modern site, but it later housed the police headquarters; now that they've moved across the plaza the building is again used by the city's administration.

The Ayuntamiento also holds a couple of museums. The first of these is the **Museo de Santiago** (Tues–Fri 9am–4pm, Sat & Sun 9am–noon & 2–4pm; Q10), which holds a collection of colonial artefacts, including bits of pottery, a sword said to have been used by Alvarado, some traditional Maya weapons, portraits of stern-faced colonial figures, and some paintings of warfare between the Spanish and the Maya. At the back of the museum is the old city jail, beside which there was a small chapel where condemned prisoners passed their last moments before being hauled off to the gallows in the plaza. Also under the arches of the city hall is the **Museo del Libro Antiguo** (same hours as above; Q10), in the rooms that held the first printing press in Central America. This arrived here in 1660, from Puebla de los Angeles in Mexico, and churned out the first book three years later. A replica of the press is on display alongside some copies of the works produced on it.

South and east of the plaza

Across the street from the ruined cathedral, in 5 C Oriente (Calle de La Universidad), is the **Seminario Tridentino**, one of the great colonial schools. It was founded at the start of the seventeenth century for some fifteen students, and later expanded to include the Escuela de Guadalupe, a special school for indigenous Maya of high birth, so that local people could share in the joys of theology. The structure is still in almost perfect condition, but it's now divided up into several separate homes, so the elaborate stucco doorway is all you'll get to see.

A little further up the same street is the **University of San Carlos Borromeo**, which now houses the **Museo de Arte Colonial** (Tues–Fri 9am–4pm, Sat & Sun 9am–noon & 2–4pm; $4). The founding of a university was first proposed by Bishop Marroquín in 1559, but met with little enthusiasm as the Jesuits, Dominicans and Franciscans couldn't bear the thought of a rival to their own colleges. It wasn't until 1676 that the plan was authorized, using money left by the bishop, and classes began in 1681 with seventy students applying themselves to everything from law to the Cakchiquel language. For a while only pure-blooded Castilians were admitted, but entry requirements were later changed to include a broader spectrum of the population. After the 1751 earthquake the university's original building was beyond repair and the rector of the Seminary donated the house next door to his own. Since then the university has moved to Guatemala City, and in 1832 this building became a grammar school, and then, in 1936, a museum. The deep-set windows and beautifully ornate cloisters make it one of the finest architectural survivors in Antigua. The museum contains a good collection of dark and brooding religious art, sculpture, furniture, murals depicting life on the colonial campus, and a seventeenth-century map of Antigua by the historian Antonio de Fuentes y Guzmán.

Further up 5 C Oriente, between 1 and 2 avenidas, is the house that once belonged to Bernal Díaz del Castillo, one of the soldiers who served under Alvarado in Mexico and Guatemala, and who, in his later years, wrote an account of the Conquest. Just around the corner, on 1 Av Sur, is the **Casa Popenoe** (Mon–Sat 2–4pm; $1), a superbly restored colonial mansion, which not only gives a welcome break from church ruins, but also an interesting insight into domestic life in colonial times. The house, set around a well-tended, grassy courtyard, was originally built in 1634 by the Spaniard Don Luis de las Infantes Mendoza, who came to Antigua to serve as the supreme court judge. Needless to say it was badly damaged over the years and eventually abandoned, until 1932, when Doctor Wilson Popenoe, a United Fruit company scientist, began its comprehensive restoration. Dr Popenoe and his wife Dorothy painstakingly sifted through the rubble and, piece by piece, restored the building to its former glory, filling it with an incredible collection of colonial furniture and art. Among the paintings are portraits of Bishop Marroquín and the menacing-looking Alvarado himself. Every last detail has been authentically restored, down to the original leather lampshades painted with religious musical scores and the great wooden beds decorated with a mass of accomplished carving. The kitchen and servants' quarters have also been carefully renovated, and you can see the bread ovens, the herb garden and the pigeon loft, which would have provided the original occupants with their mail service. A narrow staircase leads up from the pigeon loft to the roof, from where there are spectacular views over the city and volcanoes. Dr Popenoe died in 1972, but two of his daughters still live in the house.

A block to the south, on 6 C Oriente, two churches face each other at opposite ends of a palm tree-lined plaza, frequented by street vendors, washerwomen and fast-food friers. At the western end is the **San Pedro Church** and hospital. Originally built in 1680, and periodically crammed full of earthquake victims, the church was finally evacuated in 1976 when one of the aftershocks threatened to bring down the roof. Reconstruction was completed in 1991 and the facade now has a polished perfection that's strangely incongruous in Antigua. At the other end of the plaza is the convent and church of **Santa Clara**, founded in 1699 by nuns from Puebla in Mexico. In colonial times this became a popular place for well-to-do young ladies to take the veil, as the hardships were none too hard, and the nuns earned a reputation for their cooking, by selling bread to the aristocracy. The huge original convent was totally destroyed in 1717, as was the second in 1773, but the current building was spared in 1976 and its ornate facade remains intact.

Walking around the front of the church down 2 Av Sur and then left, along 7 C Oriente, you arrive at **San Francisco** (daily 8am–6pm), one of the few ruined churches to have come back into service. The latest phase of its reconstruction began in 1960 and is still the subject of much controversy. The nave has been restored in its entirety, but the ornate mouldings and sculpture have been left off, so although you get a rough idea of its former splendour, it would actually have been considerably more decorative. One of the oldest churches in Antigua, the earliest building on this site was begun in 1579 by the Franciscans, the first religious order to arrive in the city. It grew into a vast religious and cultural centre that included a school, a hospital, music rooms, a printing press and a monastery, covering four blocks in all. All of this, though, was lost in the 1773 earthquake. The **ruins** of the monastery, which are among the most impressive in Antigua, are surrounded by pleasant grassy verges with good picnicking potential (daily 8am–6pm).

Inside the church are buried the remains of **Hermano Pedro de Betancourt** (a Franciscan from the Canary Islands who founded the Hospital of Belén in Antigua), and pilgrims from all over Central America come here to ask for the benefit of his powers of miraculous intervention. Hundreds of little plaques and photographs, as well as a handful of disused crutches, all clustered around the shrine, give thanks for miracles performed. Hermano Pedro's remains have been moved around several times over the years, most recently in October 1990, some 323 years after his death, when he was put into a newly built Chapel of the True Cross, on the north side of the altar. Across the nave, on the south side of the church, there is a **museum** dedicated to Hermano Pedro (daily 8am–noon & 2–4pm; $1), featuring clothes, sandals and a moneybag that belonged to him.

Heading out of town to the south, in the direction of the Agua volcano, you can follow the **Stations of the Cross**, twelve little chapels (all now in assorted states of disrepair) signifying Christ's route to crucifixion at Calvary. Along the way you pass the cracked remains of **Nuestra Senora de Los Remedios** and at the far end is **El Calvario**, a small functioning church with magnificently thick walls.

Outside the church, sunk in the middle of the road and looking oddly out of place, stands a beautifully carved stone fountain.

North of the Parque Central

Setting out northwards from the Parque Central, along 4 Av Norte, you'll find the hermitage of **El Carmen**, down to the right past the first block. This was originally one of the city's great churches, first built in 1638 and rebuilt many times since: the top half of the facade finally collapsed in 1976 but the remains hint at its former glory and you can look in at the rubble-filled nave. Back on 4 Av and another block to the north lies the church and convent of **Santa Teresa**, originally founded by a Peruvian philanthropist for a group of Carmelite nuns from Lima. These days it serves as the city jail.

A block further to the east, at the junction of 2 C Oriente and 2 Av Norte, is the site of **Las Capuchinas** (Tues–Sun 9am–5pm; Q10), the largest and most impressive of the city's convents, whose ruins are some of the best preserved but least understood in Antigua. The Capuchin nuns, who came from Madrid, were rather late on the scene, founding the fourth convent in the city in 1726. They were only granted permission by the colonial authorities on the condition that the convent would exact no payment from its novices. The Capuchin order was the most rigorous in Antigua. Numbers were restricted to 25, with nuns sleeping on wooden beds with straw pillows. Once they had entered the convent the women were not allowed any visual contact with the outside world; food was passed to them by means of a turntable and they could only speak to visitors through a grille.

The ruins are the most beautiful in Antigua, with fountains, courtyards and massive earthquake-proof pillars. The tower or "retreat" is the most unusual feature, with eighteen tiny cells set into the walls of its top floor, each having its own independent sewage system. Two of the cells have been returned to their original condition to demonstrate the harshness of the nuns' lives. The lower floor is dominated by a massive pillar that supports the structure above and incorporates seventeen small recesses, some with stone rings set in the walls. Theories about the purpose of this abound: as a warehouse, a laundry room, a communal bath, a pantry, or even a torture chamber.

A couple of blocks to the west, spanning 5 Av Norte, is the **arch of Santa Catalina**, which is all that remains of the original convent founded here in 1609. By 1697 it had reached maximum capacity with 110 nuns and six novices, and the arch was built in order that they could walk between the two halves of the establishment without being exposed to the pollution of the outside world. Somehow it managed to defy the constant onslaught of earthquakes and was restored in the middle of the nineteenth century.

Walking under the arch and to the end of the street, you reach the church of **La Merced**, which boasts one of the most intricate and impressive facades in the entire city. It has been beautifully restored, painted mustard yellow and white, and crammed with plaster moulding of interlaced patterns. Look closely and you'll see the outline of a corn cob, a design not normally seen on Catholic churches and probably added by the original Maya labourers. The church is still in use, but the cloisters and gardens lie ruined, exposed to the sky. In the centre of one of the courtyards is a fountain surrounded by four pools that's known as the *Fuente de Pescados*; the pools were used by the Mercedarian brothers for breeding fish. The colonial fountain in front of the church is worth a look for its superbly preserved carved decoration.

Further out to the northeast along 1 Av Norte, the badly damaged ruins of the churches of **Santa Rosa**, **Candelaria** and **Nuestra Señora de los Dolores del Cerro** are of interest to ruined church buffs only.

West of the Parque Central

The last of the ruins lie over to the west of the plaza, towards the bus station. At the junction of 4 C Poniente and 6 Av Norte stands **La Compañia de Jesús**, an educational establishment and church that was operated by the Jesuits until the King of Spain, feeling threatened by their tremendous and growing power, expelled them from the colonies in 1767. Earlier this century the market moved here from the plaza, and was housed in the cloisters until the 1976 earthquake: nowadays most of the ruins are closed off, though a number of rather touristy *artesanía* stalls have recently moved back in.

Turning to the right in front of the bus station, walk to the end of the tree-lined Alameda Santa Lucía, and you reach the spectacular remains of **San Jeronimo**, a school built in 1739. Well-kept gardens are woven between the huge blocks of fallen masonry and crumbling walls. Down behind San Jeronimo a cobbled road leads to the even more chaotic ruin **La Recolección**, where the middle of the church is piled high with the remains of the roof and walls. Recolectos friars first arrived here and asked for permission to build in 1685, but it wasn't until 1701 that they started the church, and a further fourteen years before it was finished. Only months after its completion, the church was brought to the ground by a huge earthquake. This second version was destroyed in 1773 and has been steadily decaying ever since.

On the southern side of the bus station, along Av Alameda de Santa Lucía, is an imposing monument to **Rafael Landivar** (1731–93), a Jesuit composer who is generally considered the finest poet of the colonial era. Along with the other members of his order he was banished from the Americas in 1767. Behind the bus station at C de Recolección 55 is the **K'ojom Casa de la Música** (Mon–Fri 9am–12.30pm & 2–5pm, Sat closes at 4pm; $1), a small but delightful museum devoted to indigenous music, with some fascinating photographs of Maya life. Also on show is a short documentary film on the history of Maya music.

VOLCANO TOURS FROM ANTIGUA

A number of outfits in Antigua run guided tours to climb the **Pacaya volcano** near Guatemala City (see warning, p.75). These trips cost $12–15 per person, and enable you to visit the volcano at night without having to camp out. They leave Antigua in the early afternoon to climb the volcano, coming back down in the dark and returning to Antigua at around 11pm. Though the spectacle is astounding there is an element of danger involved and not just from falling rocks and ash – a number of cowboy outfits offer trips to Pacaya and set up "robberies" of their own tourists. Though there is a small risk whoever you go with, some of the most reliable companies include Quetzal Volcano Expeditions, who advertise in *Dona Luisa's*; Gran Jaguar Tours, 4 C Poniente 30 (☎8322712); and Adventuras Vacacionales, 5 Av Sur 11B (☎8323352). Avoid Popeye and Yaxcha Expeditions.

For more serious volcano climbing, Daniel Ramírez Ríos, at *Albergue Andinista*, 6 Av Norte 34 (see p.92), is the best and most experienced volcano guide in the country. He knows all the peaks well, speaks good English, and can rent out camping equipment.

Walking back to the plaza along 5 C Poniente, you'll pass the **Iglesia de San Agustín**, the remains of a vast convent complex that once occupied about half the block but has stood derelict since the earthquake of 1773, after which the Augustinians followed the government in the exodus to Guatemala City.

Eating

In Antigua the choice of food is even more cosmopolitan than the population, and you'll be able to munch your way around the world in a number of authentic **restaurants** for a few dollars a time, or dine in real style for around half what it would cost back home. The only thing that seems hard to come by is an authentic Guatemalan *comedor*, which may be a relief if you've been subsisting on eggs and beans in the mountains. Because Antigua boasts such a wide variety of restaurants to suit every budget we have categorized them according the price of a full meal with drinks: in places marked inexpensive you'll pay under $5, moderate is $5–10, and expensive refers to places charging more than $10.

If you're after a takeout, the best **deli** is *Deliciosa*, 4 Av Norte 10D, where you'll find lots of gourmet treats and some decent wine. For the best **coffee** in town, if not the country, *Tostaduria Antigua*, 6 Av Sur 12 A, near the corner with 6 C is the place to pick up some to take home. The tiny shop is suffused with the aroma of roasting beans and the owner will let you taste before you buy.

Cafés

Bagdad Café, 1 C Poniente 9. A simple courtyard café that bakes its own bread and serves healthy snacks, tasty sandwiches and cakes. Also has email, fax and phone facilities.

Bagel Barn, 5 C Poniente 2, just off the plaza. A good spot for a coffee and cake pit stop as well as tasty, if pricey, bagels, sandwiches and homemade soup; takeouts are also available.

C@fe.net, 2 Av Norte 6B, inside the *Mistral* restaurant/bar. Surfing and coffee, with internet connections and email services.

La Cenicienta, 5 Av Norte 7. Bizarre Guatemalan attempt to re-create a Victorian tearoom – fine for quiche, cakes and sweet snacks though the coffee is very weak. No smoking.

Café Condesa, west side of plaza, through the Casa de Conde bookshop. Extremely civilized spot to enjoy an excellent breakfast, coffee and cake, or a full lunch. A gurgling fountain and period charm set a nice tone for the long, lazy Sunday brunches favoured by Antiguan society.

Cookies Etc, 3 Av Norte & 4 C Oriente. Fourteen varieties of cookie on offer, as well as breakfasts and free coffee refills. Takeouts available.

Cybermannia, 5 Av Norte 25B. Internet café run by helpful staff. Has full facilities, fibre-optic links, modern machines and email.

Delicias de Natura, 7 C Poniente 11. Tiny but extremely agreeable café with the finest croissants, *pain au chocolat* and tarts in Antigua. A mini-shop also sells baguettes and French cheeses.

Café la Fuente, in La Fuente centre, 4 C Oriente 14. Vegetarian restaurant/café where you can eat stuffed aubergine and falafel, or sip coffee in one of the nicest courtyards in the city.

Jugocentre Peroleto, Alameda Santa Lucía 36. Brilliant hole-in-the-wall cabin serving excellent healthy, cheap breakfasts, fruit juices and yummy cakes.

Café Opera, 6 Av Norte 17. Expensive café with lavish wall-to-wall operatic paraphernalia, comfortable seating and a tiled floor. Superb, strong coffee, croissants, ice cream and sandwiches are on offer, accompanied by the odd dose of loud opera. Closed Wed.

Pasteleria Okrassa, 6 Av Norte 29. Great for croissants, cinnamon rolls and heathy drinks – try the raspberry juice.

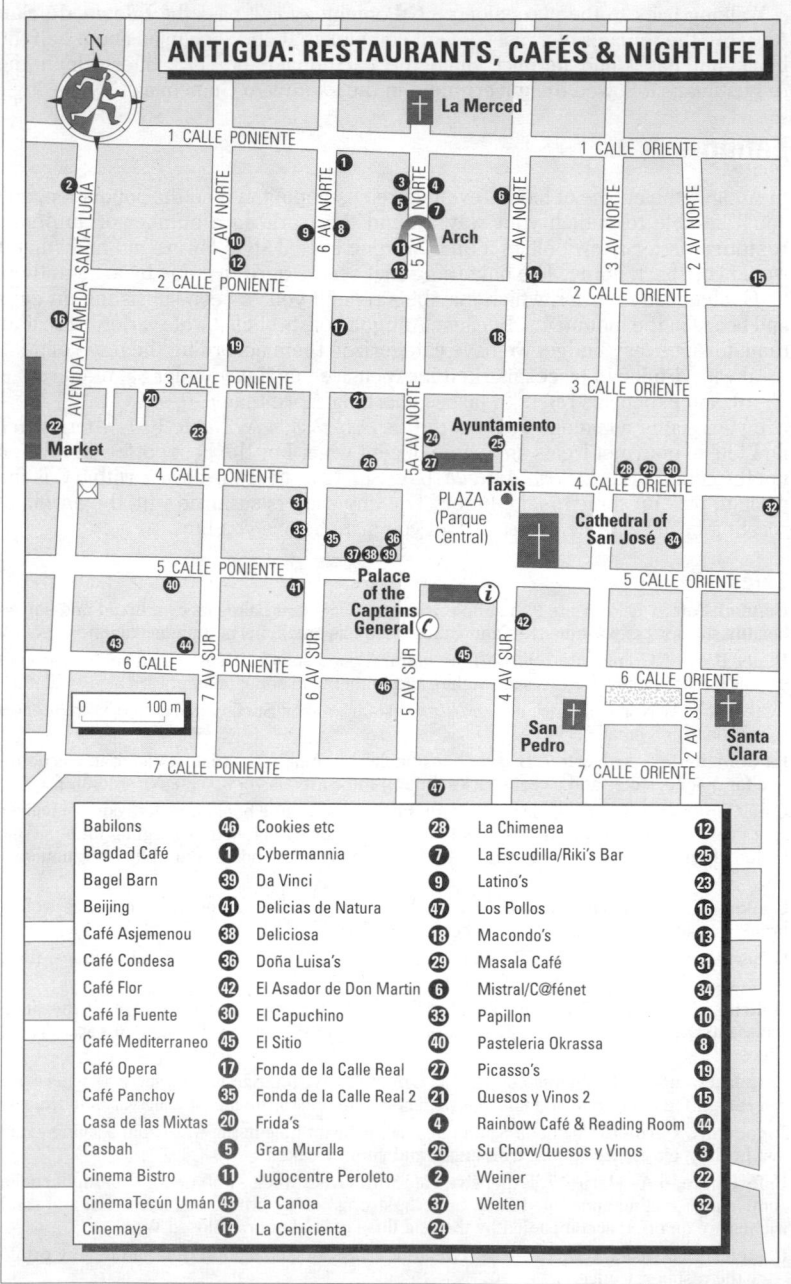

ANTIGUA: RESTAURANTS, CAFÉS & NIGHTLIFE

Babilons	㊻	Cookies etc	㉘	La Chimenea	⑫
Bagdad Café	❶	Cybermannia	❼	La Escudilla/Riki's Bar	㉕
Bagel Barn	㊴	Da Vinci	❾	Latino's	㉓
Beijing	㊶	Delicias de Natura	㊼	Los Pollos	⑯
Café Asjemenou	㊳	Deliciosa	⑱	Macondo's	⑬
Café Condesa	㊱	Doña Luisa's	㉙	Masala Café	㉛
Café Flor	㊷	El Asador de Don Martin	❻	Mistral/C@fénet	㉞
Café la Fuente	㉚	El Capuchino	㉝	Papillon	⑩
Café Mediterraneo	㊺	El Sitio	㊵	Pasteleria Okrassa	❽
Café Opera	⑰	Fonda de la Calle Real	㉗	Picasso's	⑲
Café Panchoy	㉟	Fonda de la Calle Real 2	㉑	Quesos y Vinos 2	⑮
Casa de las Mixtas	⑳	Frida's	❹	Rainbow Café & Reading Room	㊹
Casbah	❺	Gran Muralla	㉖	Su Chow/Quesos y Vinos	❸
Cinema Bistro	⑪	Jugocentre Peroleto	❷	Weiner	㉒
Cinema Tecún Umán	㊸	La Canoa	㊲	Welten	㉜
Cinemaya	⑭	La Cenicienta	㉔		

Restaurants

El Asador de Don Martín, 4 Av Norte 16. One of the most luxurious restaurants in the country, suberbly set in colonial surroundings with beautiful dining rooms, a nice bar area, a lovely garden and a roof terrace offering some of the finest views in Antigua. It has three ambitious menus, huge wine list and assured service. Expect to pay around $25 for a three-course meal with wine, but well worth the splurge. Expensive.

Beijing, 6 Av Sur and 5 C Poniente. Antigua's best Chinese and East Asian food prepared with a few imaginative twists. Good noodle dishes, soups and Vietnamese spring rolls, as well as friendly service and tasteful decor. Moderate.

Café-Pizzeria Asjemenou, 5 C Poniente 4. A favourite for its near-legendary breakfasts; it's also very strong on pizza and calzone but service can be distracted. Daily 9am–10pm. Moderate.

El Capuchino, 6 Av Norte 12. Old-fashioned Italian with rows of flowery plastic chairs and caged birds; not exactly the most appealing place in town, but a reasonable bet for pizza and pasta, and the cheap lunchtime set meals. Closed Mon. Moderate.

Casa de las Mixtas, 3 C Poniente & 7 Av Norte. A basic *comedor*, but with interesting decor and cooking that is executed with more flair than most. Open early until 7.30pm. Inexpensive.

Cevicheria Peroleto, Alameda Santa Lucía 36. Popular with Guatemalans, this place specializes in Peruvian pickled fish and shrimps. Inexpensive.

Da Vinci, 6 Av Norte 32. Attractive, modish restaurant serving good Italian and international dishes – try the spaghetti San Marcos. Moderate.

Doña Luisa's, 4 C Oriente 12. One of the most popular places in town, frequented by foreigners and locals alike. The setting is relaxed but the simple menu could do with a revamp – a basic line-up of chilli con carne, baked potatoes, salads and hamburgers is looking a little tired. The adjoining shop sells bread and pastries baked on the premises. Moderate.

La Escudilla, 4 Av Norte 4. Tremendous courtyard restaurant, usually extremely busy on account of its excellent value and good quality food, with plenty of tasty choices for vegetarians. The delicious salads are unequalled in Antigua, the pasta is good, and the $3 all-day/all-night set meal is exceptional value. The only problem is the kitchen can't always cope with the demand, so expect a wait when busy. Inexpensive.

Café Flor, 4 Av Sur 1. Highly commended restaurant serving Thai, Indonesian and Indian food. The cuisine may not be a hundred percent authentic, but dishes are well executed and the atmosphere relaxed and convivial. Closed Sun. Moderate.

La Fonda de la Calle Real, upstairs at 5 Av Norte 5. Antigua's most famous restaurant, with a smarter new branch in a beautiful colonial house at 3 C Poniente 7. Both serve excellent, flavoursome food, creatively prepared, with Guatemalan specialities including *pepián* (spicy meat stew) and *caldo real* (chicken soup). Closed Wed. Moderate to expensive.

Frida's, 5 Av Norte 29. The best Mexican food in town, including a tasty selection of enchiladas, fajitas and all the other favourites. There's usually a lively buzz about the place, which is decorated with 1950s US artefacts. Closed Mon. Moderate.

Caffé Mediterraneo, 6 C Poniente 6A. Real Italian cooking, with fresh pasta, bruschetta and decent wine. Very civilized and popular with Antigua's resident foodies. Closed Tues. Moderate.

Gran Muralla, 4 C Poniente 18. Very Guatemalan *comedor* that dispenses generous portions of steaks, pasta and vaguely Chinese food at low prices. Inexpensive.

Masala Café, 6 Av Sur 14a. Authentic Japanese and Thai food, with special menus at lunchtime and for Sunday breakfast. Closed Wed. Moderate.

Café Panchoy, 6 Av Norte 1B. Good value cooking with a Guatemalan flavour – top steaks, excellent margaritas, and some traditional favourites like *chiles rellenos*. The tables are nicely set round a central kitchen. Closed Tues.

Panza Verde, 5 Av Sur 19. One of Antigua's most exclusive restaurants, exemplary European cuisine, professional service and a nice setting with well-spaced tables grouped around the courtyard garden of this beautiful little hotel. Try the trout or sea bass *meuniere*. Closed Sun and Mon evening. Expensive.

Papillon, 7 Av Norte 13B. The place to go for crêpes, savoury and sweet, plus other Gallic treats such as *croque monsieur*. Closed Sun and Mon. Inexpensive.

Los Pollos, Av Alamada Santa Lucía & 2 C Poniente. The restaurant everyone loves to hate, home to assorted nocturnal Antiguan low life. The soggy fries and deep-fried chicken may not seem that tempting, but wait until you stumble out of a bar at midnight. Open 24 hours. Inexpensive.

Quesos y Vino, 5 Av Norte 32. Very stylish Italian-owned restaurant with a reliable reputation for good homemade pasta and pizza, and wines from Europe and South America. Another branch, at 2 C Oriente, is more atmospheric, and serves the same menu in a stunning location. Moderate.

Rainbow Café, 7 Av Sur 8. A favourite travellers' hangout, which attracts a relaxed bohemian crowd. Great vegetarian menu of creative salads and pasta dishes, epic smoothies and decent cappuccinos matched by friendly, prompt service. It's also home to one of Antigua's best travel agents, a good secondhand bookshop, and regular musical jams. Moderate.

Su Chow, 5 Av Norte 38. Good Chinese food, cooked and served by a charming Belizean family. Inexpensive.

Weiner, Alameda Santa Lucía 8. Especially good for a well-priced, filling breakfast, this restaurant also does lunchtime specials, serves good coffee and herbal teas and has an extensive selection of bottled European beers. Moderate.

Welten, 4 C Oriente 21. Exclusive restaurant spread over a covered patio and a number of rooms. The international menu with a marked European influence is let down by an exorbitantly priced wine list. Expensive.

Drinking and nightlife

Evening activity is somewhat curtailed in Antigua by a "dry law", which forbids the sale of alcohol after 1am, though there are plenty of places that flout this regulation. Those listed below on 5 and 7 Av Norte are particularly popular with the gringo crowd and all open up around 7pm. For a more genuinely Guatemalan atmosphere, try one of the simple bars on Alameda de Santa Lucía.

For more elevated pursuits, the **Proyecto Cultural el Sitio**, 5 C Poniente 15 (☎8323037), is Antigua's premier cultural venue, hosting concerts, plays in Spanish and English, exhibitions and movies. Check *Revue,* a free monthly magazine, or *Guatemala Weekly* newpaper for details of current events; both are widely available throughout town.

Bars and live music

Babilons, 6 C Poniente & 5 Av Sur. Large bar, popular with Guatemalan rich kids; nicely laid out but often lacking real ambience.

La Chimanea, 7 Av Norte 7. One of the more popular bars with a dauntingly eclectic music selection – expect everything from Rod Stewart to Black Sabbath.

Latino's, 7 Av Norte 16. A touch rougher than *Picasso's*, with things really warming up when it hosts the odd live music night.

Macondo's, 5 Av Norte & 2 C Poniente. Probably the closest Antigua has to a pub, though the constant visual barrage of music videos spoils things somewhat. Closed Mon.

Mistral, 2 Av Norte 6B. Upstairs bar that also serves reasonable food – it's the best place to catch up on US sports or CNN news.

Picasso's, 7 Av Norte 16. Good drinking hole that can get quite lively in high season. Usually closed Sun.

Riki's Bar, 4 Av Norte 4. Unquestionably the most happening place in town, due to its excellent location inside *La Escudilla*, the jazz-only policy and the unrivalled happy hour (7–9pm). All these combine to make it crammed full most nights.

Clubs

Antigua is not at the cutting edge of the global **clubbing** scene, and raving in the western sense isn't really on the agenda. However, it is possible to have a good time as there are a couple of venues which can get very lively. The weekend starts early in Antigua, with Thursday being a busy night and Friday and Saturday really packing in the punters.

La Canoa, 5 C Poniente 4. A small, unpretentious club playing mainly Latin sounds. Merengue is the main ingredient, with a dash of salsa and reggae; they also play a few tracks of western and latin pop/rock. If you visit more than once you'll soon recognize all the tunes in the DJ's box, but *La Canoa* is still a fun night out. Good mix of locals and foreigners and reasonable drink prices. Entry $2 at weekends; free in the week.

La Casbah, 5 Av Norte 30. Primarily attracting a well-heeled young crowd from Antigua and Guatemala City, and considered positively subversive by the old school (including the tourist office), the *Casbah* is undeniably pretentious but with a positive edge. The venue, in the ruins of an ancient church, is spectacular and the music matches the site with deep, bassline-driven dance mixes, "handbag" house, and a smattering of hot Latin tunes; drinks are expensive. Entry $4 at weekends; free in the week.

Cinemas

There is no longer a movie theatre in Antigua, but a number of small video cinemas geared to Western tastes show different films on a daily basis – *Trainspotting, Salvador* and *Reservoir Dogs* are on almost permanently. Look out also for Spanish-language films, which can be an entertaining supplement to your tuition. Fliers with weekly listings are posted on noticeboards all over town. The only cinemas are **Cinemaya**, 2 C Oriente 2; **Cinema Bistro**, 5 Av Norte 28; **Cinema Tecún Umán**, 6 C Poniente 34a; and **Proyecto Cultural El Sitio**, 5 C Poniente 15.

Listings

Banks and exchange There are a multitude of banks in Antigua, all offering similar exchange rates. Banco Industrial, 5 Av Sur 4, just south of the plaza (Mon–Fri 8.30am–7pm, Sat 8am–5pm) will change travellers' cheques and also has a 24-hour ATM for Visa card holders. Banco del Agro is on the north side of the plaza (Mon–Fri 9am–8pm, Sat 9am–6pm), and Lloyds, in the northeast corner of the plaza (Mon–Fri 9am–5pm), will change sterling travellers' cheques. If you're stuck for cash on a Sunday, two shops close to the plaza will change your dollar bills: Central, 4C Poniente & 5 Av Norte, and Utatlán, on 5 Av Norte & 2 Poniente.

Books Casa Andinista, 4 C Oriente 5A, has an interesting selection of English and Spanish books on Guatemala and Latin America, travel guides and a book rental service; Casa de Conde, on the west side of the plaza, has the widest selection of English books; Un Poco de Todo, also on the west side of the plaza, sells some English books on Guatemala and Central America, as well as Spanish textbooks and a few secondhand books in English, Spanish and German; Librería del Pensativo, 5 Av Norte 29, is the best Spanish-language bookshop in town, with an impressive selection of cultural and political titles; while the Rainbow Reading Room, 7 Av Sur 8 (daily 9am–9pm), has by far the largest selection of secondhand books, including some quality fiction – they also have a tearoom and bar (see above).

Camping equipment Ask at Casa Andinista, 4 C Oriente 5A, or *Hotel Villa San Francisco*, 1 Av Sur 15 (☎ 8323383), about tent and sleeping bag rental.

Car rental Avis, 5 Av Norte 22 (☎ & fax 8322692); and Budget in the *Hotel Radisson*, 9 C, south of town on the road to Ciudad Vieja (☎8320011); in the *Hotel El Carmen*, 3 Av Norte 9 (☎8323850 & fax 8323847) and Tabarini, 2C Poniente 19A (☎ & fax 8323091), all have similar

STUDYING SPANISH IN ANTIGUA

Antigua's **language school** industry is big business, with a couple of dozen established schools, and many more less reliable set-ups, some operating in the front room of someone's house. Whether you're just stopping for a week or two to learn the basics, or settling in for several months in pursuit of total fluency, there can be no doubt that this is one of the best places in Latin America to learn Spanish: it's a beautiful, relaxed town, lessons are cheap and there are several superb schools. In addition, Guatemalan Spanish is clearly pronounced and has few local dialects. The only major drawback is that there are so many other students and tourists here that you'll probably end up spending your evenings speaking English. If this worries you then you might want to consider studying in a less touristy town – Quetzaltenango, Huehuetenango, Cobán and nearby Chimaltenango all have Spanish schools and fewer visitors.

Before making any decisions, you could drop into **Amerispan**, 6 Av Norte 40 (☎ & fax 8320164; in USA ☎1-800/879-6640; fax 215/985-4524), which selects schools throughout Latin America to match the needs and requirements of students, and provides advice and support.

CHOOSING A SCHOOL

Though you can sign up for tuition only, most schools offer a weekly package that includes up to eight hours' one-on-one tuition a day and full board with a local family. Prices vary tremendously, from $170 a week for the above deal at the top schools, down to as little as $70 at a smaller school, though most schools will negotiate, particularly in the low season. Generally speaking you get what you pay for, with the more expensive schools offering the best programmes and most professional teachers.

The enthusiasm and aptitude of your teacher, of course, is paramount, and, even in the better schools, the quality of teaching staff can vary widely. If you are not happy

prices: cars from around $60 a day, jeeps from $80, including unlimited mileage and insurance.

Cigars and cigarettes There's an incredible selection of cigars, cigarettes and rolling papers on sale at the International Smoke Shop, 4 C Poniente 38B.

City tours Geovanny, at Monarcas, 6 Av Norte 34 (☎8323343), leads fascinating tours looking at the Maya influence on Antiguan architecture and the flora around the city; author Elizabeth Bell (☎8320140, ex 341) also leads excellent historical walking tours around the town.

Cultural centre El Sitio, 5 C Poniente 15 (☎8323037), has an active theatre, art gallery ad library (see libraries below), and regularly hosts exhibitions and concerts – see the *Revue* or *Guatemala Weekly* for details of current events.

Dentist Doctor De La Cruz, 3 Av Norte 2–3 C.

Doctor Doctor Aceituno, who speaks good English, has a surgery at 2 C Poniente 7 (☎8320512).

Email Scores of offices, cafés, hotels and language schools will send email – try *Cybermannia*, on 5 Av Norte 25B (☎8320162); *C@fe.net*, 2 Av Norte 6B, inside the *Mistral* restaurant/bar; *Conexion*, 4 C Oriente 14, inside La Fuente centre; or *Hotel San Francisco*, 1 Av Sur 15 (☎8323383).

Gym La Fábrica, C Del Hermano Pedro 16 (☎8320486), has excellent facilities, including running machines, weights, and dance, aerobics, step and martial arts classes. Very reasonable daily, weekly, monthly or annual rates (Mon–Sat 6am–10pm).

Horse riding Rolando Pérez, Colonia San Pedro El Panorama, Casa 28, on the southern outskirts of Antigua (☎8322809), takes tours lasting anything from a couple of hours to a few days.

with your teacher, ask for another; some programmes offer a different teacher each week. Before choosing a school, check how many other students will be sharing your house, as some schools pack as many as ten foreigners in with one family. It is also possible for students and teachers to go private, having met through a school: this brings the price down and enables the teacher to earn more, although it should only be done with the utmost discretion. Expect to pay $5 an hour for a private lesson. The tourist office in Antigua has a list of "approved schools", but this is as much a product of bribery and influence as a reflection of professional integrity. Note that the *Rigoberta Menchú* school has a bad reputation and has no connection at all with Rigoberta or her foundation. The following schools are well established, recommended and towards the top end of the price scale:

Tecún Umán Linguistic School, 6 C Poniente 34 (☎ & fax 8312792);
Projecto Lingüístico Francisco Marroquín, 7C Poniente 31 (☎8322886);
Centro Lingüístico Maya, 5 C Poniente 20 (☎ & fax 8320656);
Instituto Antigüeno de Español, 1 C Poniente 33 (☎8322685);
Christian Spanish Academy, 6 Av Norte 15 (☎ & fax 8320367);
Sevilla, 1 Av Sur 8 (☎ & fax 8320442);
San José El Viejo, 5 Av Sur 34 (☎8323028; fax 8323029).

The following are little less expensive, but still professional and recommended:
APPE, 6 C Poniente 40 (☎8320720);
La Unión, 1 Av Sur 21 (☎ & fax 8320424);
Probigua, 6 Av Norte 41B (☎ & fax 8320860).

Finally, if you'd rather study with a private teacher, try one of the following:
Julia Solis – see noticeboard in *Doña Luisa's* at 4 C Oriente 12;
Rossalinda Rosales, 1 C Poniente 17;
Gladys de Porras, 7 Av Sur 8.

Hospital 24-hour emergency service at the Santa Lucía Hospital, Calzada Santa Lucía Sur 7 (☎8323122 or 2300003).

Laundry There are numerous *lavanderías* all over town, with a heavy concetration on 6 C Oriente & 6 C Poniente, south of the plaza. One of Antigua's most efficient is the Rainbow Laundry on 6 Av Sur 15 (Mon–Sat 7am–7pm), where a typical wash costs around $2.

Library La Biblioteca Internacional de Antigua, in the El Sitio cultural centre on 5 C Poniente 15 (☎8322037), has an extensive collection of English fiction, biography, travel, art, geography and reference books. Temporary/monthly memberships are available. CIRMA (*Centro de Investigaciones Regionales de Mesoamerica*) is a research centre and library with facilities for students of Central America, whose work it also publishes. The library and reading room are to one side of a gorgeously peaceful courtyard at 5 C Oriente 5.

Massage There are always a handful of alternative therapists at work in Antigua – Gerald Katt is recommended (☎8327396), or keep an eye on the noticeboards. For more luxurious surroundings drop into the *Antigua Spa Resort*, on the road to the Cuidad Viejo (☎8323960).

Motorbike rental Jopa, 6 Av Norte 3 (☎8320794), is the most established and professional place in town. Prices for a 200cc bike are around $15 (4hr), $22 (24hr), $100 (week) or $250 (month) including insurance, helmet and unlimited mileage. Credit card deposit is required.

Mountain bikes The *Posada San Vincente*, 6 Av Sur 6 (☎ & fax 8323311) and Aviatur, 5 Av Norte 27 (☎ & fax 8322642), charge around $8 a day or $25 a week. For a better quality bike, or accompanied bike tours in the beautiful countryside around Antigua, Maya Mountain Bike Tours, based in the *Hotel Villa San Francisco*, 1 Av Sur 15 (☎8323383), is highly recommended.

Police The main police headquarters is in the Palace of the Captains General on the Parque Central. The tourist police is just off the Parque Central, on 4 Av Norte.

Pool hall 3 C Poniente 4–5 A, is very much a male-dominated institution although tourists of either sex are welcome, providing they can handle the smell. Alternatively, try *Bar Fenix*, on 6 Av Norte 33.

Post office Alameda de Santa Lucía, opposite the bus terminal (Mon–Fri 8am–4.30pm). DHL, at 6 C Sur 16 (☎8323718 or 8323732), and Quick Shipping, 3 Av Norte 26 (☎8322595), will also send parcels.

Phones The cheapest place in town to make international phone calls is at the CSA language school, 6 Av Norte 15 (☎8323922). The Telgua office, half a block south of the plaza on 5 Av Sur (7am–10pm), is a last resort, as rates are high and you'll have to queue for the pleasure.

Rafting Area Verde Expeditions, 4 Av Sur 8 (☎ & fax 8323863), runs a variety of dramatic whitewater trips which are highly recommended. Try also Maya Expeditions, 15 C1–91, Zona 10, Guatemala City (☎3634965).

Shopping If you're interested in seeing *huipiles* from more than one hundred villages, head for Kaslan Po't, 4 C Oriente 14, or Nim Po't, 5 Av Norte 29, which sell some of the finest *huipiles* in the country at reasonable prices. Frank Mays, the owner and curator of what is in effect a museum of contemporary Maya weaving, has an extensive collection of complete costumes, as well as books on Maya culture, and can advise how to choose a *huipil*. La Fuente centre, at 4 C Oriente 14, has a number of upmarket clothing and handicraft stores, while Al Pie del Volcán, on 4 Av Norte 7, also sells quality handicrafts. For the most fun and the lowest prices, check out the open-air market in the palm-tree-lined plaza on 6 C Oriente 2–3 Av Sur, or the stalls at the junction of 4C Poniente and 6 Av Norte.

Swimming pool *Hotel Antigua*, 8 C Poniente 1 & 5 Av Sur, has a reasonably sized pool, which non-guests can use for $4 a day. There are also two beautiful but chilly spring-fed pools (daily 7am–4pm; $1) at El Pilar, on the edge of town on the road to Santa Mariá de Jesús. Past the Stations of the Cross you come to a large school on the left; follow the track that cuts off to the left just before it.

Taxis (☎8320526). Drivers loiter around on the east side of the plaza close to the cathedral.

Travel agents There are dozens of travel agents in Antigua, of which the following are the most professional and reliable: Adventure Travel Center Viareal, 5 Av Norte 25B (☎ & fax 8320162), is an excellent agent, particularly for adventure and sailing trips; Aventuras Vacacionales, 1 Av Sur 11B (☎ & fax 8323352), offers boat tours of Lake Izabal and the Río Dulce, and a very popular catamaran five-day trip to the Belizean reef; Monarcas, 6 Av Norte 34 (☎ & fax 8323343) is a highly recommended specialist agency with some fascinating Maya culture and ecology tours, as well as trips to Semuc Champey and Copán; the Rainbow Travel Center, 7 Av Sur 8 (☎8324202/3/4/7; fax 8324206), has some of the best deals in town, is fully computerized and has friendly and efficient staff; Tivoli, 5 Av Norte 10A, on the west side of the plaza (☎8323041), is another recommended all-rounder; Turansa, 5C Poniente 11B (☎ & fax 8323316) and in the *Hotel Radisson* (☎ & fax 8322928) is somewhat smarter and operates many of the tourist shuttles as well as organizing one-day tours of Guatemala City.

Around Antigua: villages and volcanoes

The countryside surrounding Antigua is superbly fertile and breathtakingly beautiful. The valley is dotted with small villages, ranging from the *ladino* coffee centre of Alotenango to the traditional indigenous village of Santa María de Jesús. None is more than an hour or two away and all make interesting day-trips. For the more adventurous, the **volcanic peaks** of Agua, Acatenango and Fuego offer strenuous but superb hiking. When walking anywhere around Antigua, however, keep in mind our warnings about **crimes against tourists** (see p.90) and take no risks with your safety.

MOVING ON FROM ANTIGUA

The bus terminal is beside the market at the western end of 4 C Poniente (also known as C del Ayuntamiento). **Local buses** to the villages within the valley leave from the rear of the terminal. The main bus schedule is as follows:

To Guatemala City (1hr). A constant flow of buses leaves for the capital from 4am to 7pm, except on Sunday, when the first one leaves at 6am.

Chimaltenango (40min). Every twenty minutes from 5am to 7pm. From here, there are frequent daytime buses heading west to Quetzaltenango, Lake Atitlán and Huehuetenango.

Escuintla via El Rodeo (2hr 30min). Buses leave at 7am and 12.30pm. Alternatively, you can travel via Guatemala City.

Panajachel (2hr 30 min). Buses leave daily at 7am. Alternatively, take a bus to Chimaltenago and change there.

Yepocapa and **Acatenango** (both 40min). Buses leave in the late afternoon, around 3 or 4pm.

SHUTTLES

Bus services between Antigua, Guatemala City, Panajachel and Chichicastenango are supplemented by several "tourist shuttle" services, the best of which are organized by the Turansa and Adventure Travel Viareal travel agencies (see Listings, p.108, for details). Although a lot more expensive than the public bus, these shuttles are more comfortable and travel direct so are much quicker. There are frequent airport and Guatemala City shuttles for around $7; Chichicastanango (around $12) is well served on market days (Thursday and Sunday); and there are less frequent services to Panajachel (around $18). For Copán in Honduras (around $35), try Monarcas (see p.108). Shuttles to the Río Dulce (around $25) and Monterrico ($25) run at weekends when there is enough demand. Just about any travel agent in Antigua will book you a shuttle; recommended agencies are detailed in Listings on p.108.

San Felipe de Jesús

The nearest of the villages, **SAN FELIPE DE JESÚS**, is so close that you can walk there: just a kilometre or so north of Antigua following 6 Av Norte (or catch one of the minibuses from the bus terminal). San Felipe has a small Gothic-style church housing a famous image of Christ, Jesus Sepultado, said to have miraculous powers. Severely damaged in the 1976 earthquake, the church has been well restored since, and there's a fiesta here on August 30 to celebrate the anniversary of the arrival of the image in 1670. The village's other attraction is a **silver workshop**, where silver mined in the highlands of Alta Verapaz is worked and sold. To find the workshop, follow the sign to the *Platería Típica La Antigüeña*.

San Antonio Aguas Calientes

To the south of Antigua the Panchoy valley is a broad sweep of farmland, overshadowed by three volcanic cones and covered with olive-green coffee bushes. A single, poorly maintained road runs out this way, eventually reaching Escuintla and the Pacific coast, and passing a string of villages as it goes.

The first of these, a couple of kilometres from Antigua, is the village of **SAN ANTONIO AGUAS CALIENTES**, set to one side of a steep-sided bowl beneath the peak of Acatenango. San Antonio is famous for weaving, characterized by its complex floral and geometric patterns, and on the stalls in the plaza you can find a complete range of the local output. This is also a good place to learn the traditional craft of back-strap weaving; if you're interested, the best way to find out about possible tuition is by simply asking the women in the plaza.

Adjoining San Antonio is the village of **SANTA CATARINA**, which has a superb ruined colonial church. Out on the edge of the village there's also a small **swimming pool** (Tues–Sun 9am–6pm) – the perfect place for a chilly dip. To get to the pool, walk along San Antonio's main street until you come to the plaza in Santa Catarina and continue up the street that goes up the far side of the church. Turn left at the end and you'll come to the pool, on the right, in five minutes or so. **Minibuses** from the terminal in Antigua run a regular service to San Antonio and Santa Catarina.

Ciudad Vieja and Alotenango

Three kilometres beyond San Antonio is **CIUDAD VIEJA**, a scruffy and unhurried village with a distinguished past: it was near here that the Spanish established their second capital, Santiago de los Caballeros, in 1527. Today, however, there's no trace of the original city, and all that remains from that time is a solitary tree, in a corner of the plaza, which bears a plaque commemorating the site of the first mass ever held in Guatemala. The plaza also boasts an eighteenth-century colonial church that has recently been restored.

The Spanish settled at first near the Cakchiquel capital of Iximché. Within a year, however, the Cakchiquel had turned against them, and the Spanish decided to base themselves elsewhere, moving their capital to the valley of Almolonga, 35km to the east between the Acatenango and Agua volcanoes. Here, on St Celia's Day 1527, in a landscape considered perfect for pasture and with plentiful supplies of building materials, the first official capital, **Santiago de los Caballeros**, was founded. The new city was built in a mood of tremendous confidence, with building plots distributed according to rank and the suburban sites given over to Alvarado's Mexican allies. Within twenty years things had really started to take shape, with a school, a cathedral, monasteries, and farms stocked with imported cattle. But while the bulk of the Spaniards were still settling in, their leader, the rapacious **Alvarado**, was off in search of action. His lust for wealth and conquest sent him to Peru, Spain and Mexico, and in 1541 he set out for the Spice Islands, travelling via Jalisco, where he met his end, crushed to death beneath a rolling horse. When news of his death reached his wife **Doña Beatriz**, at home in Santiago, she plunged the capital into an extended period of mourning, staining the entire palace with black clay, inside and out. She went on to command the officials to appoint her as her husband's replacement, and on the morning of September 9, 1541, became the first woman to govern in the Americas. On the official declaration she signed herself as *La sin ventura Doña Beatriz*, and then deleted her name to leave only *La sin ventura* (the unlucky one) – a fateful premonition.

Following the announcement of Alvarado's death the city had been swept by storms, and before the night of Beatriz's inauguration was out an earthquake added to the force of the downpour. A tremor shook the surrounding volcanoes and from the crater of the Agua volcano a great wave of mud and water slid down, accelerating as it surged towards the valley floor, sweeping away the capital, and killing Doña Beatriz. Today the exact site of the original city is still the subject of some debate, but the general consensus puts it about 2km to the east of Ciudad Vieja, though it's probable that one of the suburbs would have reached out as far as the modern village.

A further 10km down the valley, the ragged-looking village of **ALOTENANGO** is dwarfed by the often steaming, scarred cone of the Fuego volcano, which has been in a state of constant eruption since the arrival of the Spanish. A path leads from the village up the volcano, but it's extremely hard to find and follow, so unless you're with a guide it's a lot easier to climb Acatenango instead, using La Soledad as a starting point (see below).

Beyond Alotenango a rough dirt road continues down the valley to **Escuintla** (see p.224), passing through the village of El Rodeo. One, and sometimes two buses a day connect Antigua and Escuintla (2hr 30min), leaving Antigua at 7am and 12.30pm.

To get to Ciudad Vieja or Alotenango, there's a steady stream of **buses** leaving from outside the terminal in Antigua (opposite the post office): the last one returns from Alotenango at around 7pm.

Acatenango and Fuego volcanoes

To the south of Antigua, just a short way beyond Ciudad Vieja, a dusty dirt track branches off to **SAN MIGUEL DUEÑAS**, a dried-out, scrappy-looking sort of place where the roads are lined with bamboo fences and surrounded by coffee *fincas*. There's little to delay you in San Miguel itself, but you may well find yourself passing through on your way to La Soledad, the best starting point for climbing the Acatenango and Fuego volcanoes. **Buses** head out to San Miguel every half-hour or so from the terminal in Antigua, but once you progress beyond the village, traffic becomes scarce even at the best of times. If you're making for the volcanoes then you will have to either take a taxi from Antigua to La Soledad or walk for a couple of hours up the road from San Miguel Dueñas.

Climbing Acatenango

The trail for **Acatenango** starts in **LA SOLEDAD**, an impoverished village perched on an exposed ridge high above the valley. Walking up the road from San Miguel Dueñas, you come upon a cluster of bamboo huts, with a soccer field to the right. Here you'll find a small *tienda* and the last tap – so fill up on water. A short way beyond the *tienda* a track leads up to the left, heading above the village and towards the wooded lower slopes of Acatenango. It crosses another largish trail and then starts to wind up into the pine trees. Just after you enter the trees you have to turn onto a smaller path that leads away to the right; 100m or so further on, take another small path that climbs to the left. This brings you onto a low ridge, where you meet a thin trail that leads to the left, away up the volcano – this path eventually finds its way to the top, somewhere between six and nine hours away. At times it's a little vague, but most of the way it's fairly easy to follow.

There are two other important spots on the ascent, the **campsites**, which are also the easiest places to lose the trail. The first, a beautiful grassy clearing, is about ninety minutes up – the path cuts straight across, so don't be tempted by the larger track heading off to the right. Another ninety minutes above this is the second campsite, a little patch of level ground in amongst the pine trees. You're now about halfway to the top.

The trail itself is an exhausting climb, a thin line of slippery volcanic ash that rises with unrelenting steepness through the thick forest. Only for the last 50m or so does it emerge above the tree line, before reaching the top of the lower cone. Here there's a radio mast and a small yellow hut, put up by the Guatemalan Mountaineering Club, where you can shelter for the freezing nights – though at weekends it may be full. To the south, another hour's gruelling ascent, is the main cone, a great grey bowl that rises to a height of 3975m. From here there's a magnificent view out across the valley below. On the opposite side is the Agua volcano, and to the right the fire-scarred cone of Fuego. Looking west you can see the three cones that surround Lake Atitlán, and beyond that the Santa María volcano, high above Quetzaltenango.

When it comes to getting down again, the direct route towards Alotenango may look invitingly simple but is in fact very hard to follow. It's easiest to go back the same way that you came up.

Climbing Fuego

In the unlikely event that you have any remaining energy you can continue south and climb the neighbouring cone of **Fuego** (3763m). The cone is certainly impressive and when the English friar Thomas Gage saw it in 1678, he was inspired to make a comparison with the Agua volcano:

> *This volcano or mountain (whose height is judged full nine miles to the top) is not so pleasing to the sight, but the other which standeth on the other side of the valley opposite unto it is unpleasing and more dreadful to behold. For here are ashes for beauty, stones and flints for fruits and flowers, baldness for greenness, barrenness for fruitfulness. For water whisperings and fountain murmurs, noises of thunder and roaring of consuming metals; for running streams, flashingly of fire; for tall and mighty trees and cedars, castles of smoke rising in height to out-dare the sky and firmament; for sweet and odiferous and fragrant smells, a stink of fire and brimstone, which are still in action striving within the bowels of that ever burning and fiery volcano.*

All this may seem a little exaggerated when you look across at Fuego's gently smoking cone, and from the top of Acatenango it looks comfortingly close. Walking down and up the dip between the two peaks, however, does take a good few hours, and you should be wary of getting too close to Fuego's cone as it oozes overpowering sulphur fumes and occasionally spits out molten rock. Descending from Fuego is fairly problematic, too, as the trail that leads down to Alotenango is very hard to find. The bottom of the gully, though it may look tempting, is impassable – the actual trail is on the Fuego side of this dip. The only way to be really sure of a trouble-free descent is to go back over Acatenango and down the way you came up.

Fuego can also be climbed by a direct ascent from the village of Alotenango, but the climb is very hard going and the trail difficult to follow. Hire a guide if you plan to take this route.

San Juan del Obispo, Santa María de Jesús and the Agua volcano

East of Antigua the dirt road to Santa María de Jesús runs out along a narrow valley, sharing the shade with acres of coffee bushes. Before it starts to climb, the road passes the village of **SAN JUAN DEL OBISPO**, invisible from the road but marked by what must rank as the country's finest bus shelter, beautifully carved in local stone. The village is unremarkable in itself, although it does offer a good view of the valley below. What makes it worth a visit is the **Palacio de Francisco Marroquín**, who was the first Bishop of Guatemala. The place is currently home to about 25 nuns, and if you knock on the great wooden double doors one of them will come and show you around.

Marroquín arrived in Guatemala with Alvarado and is credited with having introduced Christianity to the Maya, as well as reminding the Spaniards about it from time to time. On the death of Alvarado's wife he assumed temporary responsibility for the government, and was instrumental in the construction of Antigua. He died in 1563, having spent his last days in the vast palace that he'd built for himself here in San Juan. The palace, like everything else in the region, has been badly damaged over the years, and serious reconstruction only began in 1962. The interior, arranged around two small courtyards, is spectacularly beautiful and several rooms still contain their original furniture. Attached to the palace is a fantastic church and chapel with ornate wood carvings, plaster mouldings and austere religious paintings.

There are regular **buses** to San Juan from the market in Antigua (7.30am–6pm; 20min) terminating in the churchyard. Alternatively you could catch one heading for Santa María de Jesús and ask them to drop you here.

Santa María de Jesús

Up above San Juan the road arrives in **SANTA MARÍA DE JESÚS**, starting point for the ascent of the Agua volcano. Perched high on the shoulder of the volcano, the village is some 500m above Antigua, with magnificent views over the Panchoy valley and east towards the smoking cone of Pacaya. It was founded at the end of the sixteenth century for the Maya transported from Quetzaltenango: they were given the task of providing firewood for Antigua and the village earned the name *Aserradero*, lumber yard. Since then it has developed into a farming community where the women wear beautiful purple *huipiles*, although the men have recently abandoned traditional costume. The village has a certain scruffy charm, with the only place **to stay** being the *Hospedaje Oasis* (②), just off the plaza on the road into town; it's a friendly, clean institution that serves meals – beans, eggs and tortillas – as simple as the rooms.

Buses run from Antigua to Santa María every hour or so from 6am to 5pm, and the trip takes thirty minutes. Beyond Santa María, the road continues down the east side of the volcano to the village of Palín (see p.76), on the Guatemala City–Escuintla highway. No buses cover this route, but there's a chance that you might be able to hitch a lift on a truck.

The Agua volcano

Agua is the easiest and by far the most popular of Guatemala's big cones to climb: on Saturday nights sometimes hundreds of people spend the night at the summit. It's an exciting ascent with a fantastic view to reward you at the top. The trail starts in Santa María de Jesús (see above) – to reach it, head straight across the plaza, between the two ageing pillars, and up the street opposite the church doors. Take a right turn just before the end, and then continue past the cemetery and out of the village. From here on it's a fairly simple climb on a clear path, cutting across the road that goes some of the way up. The climb can take anything from four to six hours, and the peak, at 3766m, is always cold at night: there is shelter (though not always room) in a small chapel at the summit, however, and the views certainly make it worth the struggle.

Antigua to Chimaltenango

As an alternative to the main highway from Guatemala City, a second, smaller road connects Antigua with the Pan-American Highway, this time intersecting it at **Chimaltenango** (see p.116). On its way out of town the road passes through the suburb of **JOCOTENANGO**, where locally produced coffee beans are processed and which is also notorious for its brothels and gang violence. In colonial times Jocotenango was the gateway to Antigua, where official visitors would be met to be escorted into the city. There's a magnificent, crumbling church on the plaza.

Another 4km brings you to **SAN LORENZO EL TEJAR**, which has some superb hot springs. To reach the springs turn right in the village of **San Luís Las Carretas**, and then right again when the road forks: they're at the end of a narrow valley, a couple of kilometres from the main road. If you want to bathe in the sulphurous waters you can either use the cheaper communal pool or for a dollar or so rent one of your own – a little private room with a huge tiled tub set in the floor. The baths are open daily from 6am to 5pm, except Tuesday and Friday afternoons, when they are closed for cleaning.

From San Luís the main road climbs out of the Panchoy valley through Pastores and Parramos, a couple of dusty farming villages, after which a dirt track branches to **SAN ANDRÉS IZTAPA**, one of the many villages badly hit by the 1976 earthquake. Tragically San Andrés also hit the headlines at the end of 1988, when it was the scene of the largest massacre since the return of civilian rule. On a hillside above the nearby hamlet of El Aguacate, 22 corpses were found in a shallow grave. Blame was passed back and forth between the army and the guerrillas, but nothing has been proved by either party.

Today, however, San Andrés' main claim to fame is as home to the cult of San Simón, or Maximón (see box below). To pay San Simón a visit, head for the cen-

---

THE WICKED SAINT OF SAN ANDRÉS IZTAPA

San Andrés shares with the western highland villages of Zunil (see p.176) and Santiago Atitlán (see p.153) the honour of revering **San Simón** or Maximón, the wicked saint, whose image is housed in a pagan chapel in the village. You'll find it surrounded by drunken men, cigar-smoking women and hundreds of burning candles, each symbolizing a request. Uniquely in Guatemala, this San Simón attracts a largely *ladino* congregation and is particularly popular with prostitutes. Inside the dimly lit shrine, the walls are adorned with hundreds of plaques from all over Guatemala and Central America, thanking San Simón for his help. For a small fee, you may be offered a *limpia*, or soul cleansing, which involves one of the resident women beating you with a bushel of herbs, while you share a bottle of local firewater, *aguadiente*, with San Simón and the attendant, who will periodically spray you with alcohol from her mouth. If you want to sample the San Simón experience, you have to do so between sunrise and sunset, as he is believed to sleep at other times – indeed above the entrance to his *casa* is a sign saying "San Simón 6am–6pm".

tral plaza from the dirt road into the village, turn right when you reach the church, walk two blocks, then up a little hill and you should spot street vendors selling charms, incense and candles. If you get lost, ask for the *Casa de San Simón*. The other point of interest in the village is the particularly intricate weaving of the women's *huipiles*. The patterns are both delicate and bold, similar in many ways to those around Chimaltenango. San Andrés' Tuesday market is also worth a visit.

To get to San Andrés Iztapa, take any **bus** heading to Chimaltenango from the terminal in Antigua (every 20min 5.30am–7pm; 40min). Get the driver to drop you off where the dirt road leaves the highway, from where you can hitch or walk for thirty minutes to the village. Alternatively catch one of the hourly buses to San Andrés Iztapa from the market in Chimaltenango (6am–5pm; 20min).

After the turning for San Andrés, the main road drops through pine trees into the bottom of a dip and to the **Laguna de Los Cisnes**, a small boating lake surrounded by cheap *comedores* and swimming pools, popularly known as *Los Aposeutos*. The lake is very popular with the people of Antigua and Chimaltenango, who flood out here every weekend and public holiday. Above the lake is the local army base, and beyond that the Pan-American Highway and **Chimaltenango**, 19km and 45 minutes from Antigua.

The Pan-American Highway

The serpentine **Pan-American Highway** forms the main artery of transport in the highlands, cutting right through the region from Guatemala City in the east to the border with Mexico in the west. As you travel around, the highway and its junctions will inevitably become familiar, since wherever you're going it's invariably easiest to catch the first local bus to the Pan-American and then flag down one of the buses heading along the highway.

There are three major junctions on the Pan American which you'll soon get to know well. The first of these is **Chimaltenango**, an important town and capital of its own department, from where you can also make connections to or from Antigua. Continuing west, **Los Encuentros** is the next main junction, where one road heads off to the north for Chichicastenango and Santa Cruz del Quiché and another branches south to Panajachel and Lake Atitlán. Beyond this the highway climbs high over a mountainous ridge before dropping to **Cuatro Caminos** (p.179), from where side roads lead to Quetzaltenango, Totonicapán and San Francisco el Alto. The Pan-American Highway continues on to Huehuetenango before it reaches the Mexican border at La Mesilla. Virtually every bus travelling along the highway will stop at all of these junctions and you'll be able to buy fruit, drink and fast food from an army of vendors, some of whom will storm the bus looking for business, others being content to dangle their wares at your window from the street.

From Guatemala City to Chimaltenango

Heading out to the west from Guatemala City along the Pan-American Highway to Chimaltenango, you travel through one of the central highland valleys, where a number of large villages are devoted to market gardening. The villages themselves are particularly scruffy, but their fields are meticulously neat and well taken care of, churning out a wide range of vegetables for both the domestic and export markets.

Leaving Guatemala City, the first place you pass is **MIXCO**, a village now absorbed into the capital's suburban sprawl. Founded in 1525 to house Pokoman refugees from Mixco Viejo, Mixco still has a large Maya population. Next along the way is **SAN LUCAS SACATEPÉQUEZ**, just before the turning for Antigua. The village dates back to before the Conquest but these days bears the scars of the 1976 earthquake and serves the weekend needs of city dwellers, with cheap *comedores* and family restaurants lining the highway.

Beyond this is **SANTIAGO SACATEPÉQUEZ**, whose centre lies a kilometre or so to the north of the highway. The road to Santiago actually branches off the highway at San Lucas Sacatepéquez – and buses shuttle back and forth along the branch road. (Alternatively, you can walk to Santiago from a point overlooking it on the highway, 2km west of San Lucas.) The best time to visit Santiago is on November 1, for a local fiesta to honour the **Day of the Dead**, when massive paper kites are flown in the cemetery to release the souls of the dead from their agony. The festival is immensely popular, and hundreds of Guatemalans and tourists come every year to watch the spectacle. The kites, made from paper and bamboo, are massive circular structures, measuring up to 6–7m in diameter. Teams of young men struggle to get them aloft while the crowd looks on with bated breath, rushing for cover if a kite comes crashing to the ground.

At other times of the year, there are **markets** in Santiago on Tuesday and Sunday and the town has a small local **museum** (Mon–Fri 9am–4pm, Sat & Sun 9am–noon & 2–4pm), just below the plaza, which is crammed with tiny Maya figurines, clay fragments and pots, all donated by local people from their homes and fields. Also on display is the Guatemalan peso, dating from 1909, a traditional costume from 1901, small paper kites and a stuffed quetzal.

Beyond the entrance to Santiago the Pan-American Highway goes on past Sumpango, and through El Tejar, famous for its bricks, before reaching Chimaltenango.

Chimaltenango and around

CHIMALTENANGO was founded by Pedro de Portocarrero in 1526, on the site of the Cakchiquel centre of Bokoh, and was later considered as a possible site for the new capital. It has the misfortune, however, of being positioned on a continental divide: it suffered terribly from the earthquake in 1976, which shook and flattened much of the surrounding area. Today's town, its centre just to the north of the main road, is dominated by that fact, and like so much of the region its appearance testifies to rapid and unfinished reconstruction, with dirt streets, breeze block walls and an air of weary desperation. But it remains busy, a regional centre of transport and trade whose prosperity is boosted by the proximity of the capital.

The town's plaza is an odd mix of architectural styles, with a police station that looks like a medieval castle, a church that combines the Gothic and the Neoclassical, and a superb colonial fountain positioned exactly on the continental divide – half the water drains to the Caribbean, the other half to the Pacific. Chimaltenango's second focal point is the Pan-American Highway itself, which cuts through the southern side of the town, dominating it with an endless flow of trucks and buses. The town extracts what little business it can from this stream of traffic, and the roadside is crowded with cheap *comedores*, mechanics' work-shops, and sleazy bars that become brothels by night.

The **post office** (Mon–Fri 8am–4.30pm), Banco de Occidente (Mon–Fri 9am–7pm, Sat 9am–1pm), and Telgua (7am–midnight) are all on the plaza, and if you want **to stay** here the *Hotel La Predilecta*, a block to the south on 9 C (②), has pleasant, simple rooms and safe parking. The best place **to eat** is at *La Casa de las Legendas* at Km 56 on the Pan-American Highway, where you can choose from an excellent selection of grilled meats and Guatemalan specialities. Chimaltenango is also home to a good Spanish school, the Spanish and Maya Language School of Chimaltenango, 9C final, Lote 23, Quintas Los Aposentos 1 (☎ & fax 8391492), where you can live and study away from the gringo scene of Antigua. **Buses** passing through Chimaltenango run to all points along the Pan-American Highway: for Antigua they leave every twenty minutes between 5.30am and 6.30pm from the market in town – though you can also wait at the turn-off on the highway. To get here from Guatemala City, take any bus heading to the west-ern highlands from the Zona 4 bus terminal.

San Martín Jilotepeque

To the north of Chimaltenango a rough dirt road runs through 19km of plunging ravines and pine forests to the village of **SAN MARTÍN JILOTEPEQUE**. The village itself remains badly scarred by the 1976 disaster, but the sprawling Sunday market is well worth a visit and the weaving here, the women's *huipiles* especial-ly, is some of the finest you'll see – with intricate and ornate patterning, predom-inantly in reds and purples.

Buses to San Martín leave the market in Chimaltenango every hour or so from 4am to 2pm; the last one returns at about 3pm. The trip takes around an hour. To the north of San Martín the road continues to **Joyabaj** (see p.130). One bus a day covers this route, leaving the capital in the morning and passing through San Martín around 12.30pm; the return bus leaves Joyabaj early the following day.

San Juan Comalapa, Patzicía and Patzún

Heading west from Chimaltenango, a series of turnings lead off the Pan-American Highway to interesting but seldom-visited villages. The first of these, 16km to the north of the road, on the far side of a deep-cut ravine, is **SAN JUAN COMALA-PA**. The village was founded by the Spanish, who brought together the popula-tions of several Cakchiquel centres: a collection of eroded pre-Columbian sculp-tures is displayed in the plaza. There's also a small monument to Rafael Alvarez Ovalle, a local man who composed the Guatemalan national anthem. Like so many of the villages in this area, Comalapa's appearance still suffers from the impact of the 1976 earthquake, its plaza overshadowed by the crumbling facade of the ruined church.

In the last few decades the villagers of Comalapa have developed something of a reputation as **folk artists**, and there are several galleries in the streets around the plaza where their work is exhibited and sold. The whole thing started with Andrés Curuchich (1891–1969), who painted simple scenes documenting village life, such as fiestas, funerals and marriages, with a clarity that soon attracted the attention of outsiders. Throughout the 1950s he became increasingly popular, exhibiting in Guatemala City, and later as far afield as Los Angeles and New York, and was awarded Guatemala's highest civilian honour, the Order of the Quetzal.

Inspired by his example and the chance of boosting their income, forty to fifty painters are now working here, including two or three women – although success is considerably more difficult for them as painting is generally perceived as a man's task. There is a permanent exhibition devoted to the paintings of Andrés Curuchich at the Museo Ixchel in Guatemala City (see p.63). Comalapan **weaving** is also of the highest standards, using styles and colours characteristic of the Chimaltenango area. Traditionally the weavers work in silk and an untreated natural brown cotton called *cuyuxcate*, although these days they increasingly use ordinary cotton and synthetic fibres.

As ever, the best time to visit is for the **market**, on Tuesday, which brings the people out in force. **Buses** to Comalapa run hourly from Chimaltenango (1hr) and the service is always better on a market day. There's nowhere to stay in the village and the last bus back leaves at 3 or 4pm.

Patzicía and Patzún: a route to the lake

Further to the west another branch road runs down towards Lake Atitlán, connecting the Pan-American Highway with several small villages. At the junction with the main road is **PATZICÍA**, a ramshackle sprawl still reeling from the impact of the 1976 earthquake. Despite its bedraggled appearance the village has a history of independent defiance, and in 1944 it was the scene of a Maya uprising that left some three hundred dead. Villagers were led to believe that Maya people throughout Guatemala had risen up against their *ladino* rulers, and charged through the village killing any they could set hands on. Armed *ladinos*, arriving from the capital, managed to put down the uprising, killing the majority of the rebels. Ironically enough, over a hundred years earlier, in 1871, the Declaration of Patzicía was signed here, setting out the objectives of the liberal revolution.

PATZÚN, 11km from the main highway heading towards Lake Atitlán, also suffered terrible losses in 1976. A monument in the plaza remembers the 172 who died, and a new church stands beside the shell of the old one, somehow making an even more poignant memorial. Traditional costume is still worn here and the colourful Sunday market is well worth a visit. Outside the twin churches the plaza fills with traders, with the majority of the women dressed in the brilliant reds of the local costume.

Beyond Patzún it's possible to continue all the way to the small village of Godínez, high above the northern shore of Lake Atitlán, and from there along the road to Panajachel and San Lucas Tolimán. A couple of buses a day make this trip but the road is fairly rough and often closed by landslides. If you're considering this route you should also bear in mind that it has been the scene of a number of armed robberies, roadblocks and attacks on tourists. **Buses** to Patzún leave the Zona 4 terminal in Guatemala City every hour or so, and you can pick them up in Chimaltenango or at the turning for Patzicía.

Back at Patzicía, a second branch road leaves the Pan-American Highway to head south, past huge coffee plantations, to the villages of **Acatenango** and **Yepocapa**. It's a fairly obscure part of the country and there's no very good reason to travel this way, although there are several daily buses as far as Acatenango and one that goes all the way through to the Pacific coast, heading back to the capital via Escuintla. Buses or trucks heading for Yepocapa pass also through La Soledad, on the lower slopes of the Acatenango volcano, which is the starting point for a climb to the cone (see p.111). The **bus** that covers the round trip,

Guatemala City–Chimaltenango–Acatenango–Yepocapa–Escuintla, leaves the capital daily at 5am, passing through Chimaltenango at 6am and Patzicía at around 7.30am.

Tecpán and the ruins of Iximché

The small town of **TECPÁN** lies just a few hundred metres south of the Pan-American Highway, ninety minutes or so from Guatemala City. This may well have been the site chosen by Alvarado as the first Spanish capital, to which the Spanish forces retreated in August 1524, after they'd been driven out of Iximché. Today it's a modest place of little interest, though it has a substantial number of restaurants and guest houses that cater for a mainly Guatemalan clientele; travellers, however, are unlikely to do more than pass through on the way to the ruins. Tecpán again suffered severely in the 1976 earthquake, and in the centre a new church stands alongside the cracked remains of the old one.

The **ruins of Iximché** (daily 8am–5pm; foreigners $4, Guatemalans Q2), the pre-Conquest capital of the Cakchiquel, are about 5km south, on a beautiful exposed hillside site, protected on three sides by steep slopes and surrounded by pine forests. From the early days of the Conquest the Cakchiquel allied themselves with the conquistadores, so the structures here suffered less than most at the hands of the Spanish. Since then, however, time and weather have taken their toll and the majority of the buildings, originally built of adobe, have disappeared, leaving only a few stone-built pyramids, clearly defined plazas and a couple of ball courts. Nevertheless the site, which housed a population of around ten thousand, is strongly atmospheric, and its grassy plazas, ringed with pine trees, are marvellously peaceful, especially during the week, when you may well have the place to yourself.

The Cakchiquel were originally based further west, around the modern town of Chichicastenango, and the Cakchiquel language is still spoken throughout the central highlands and along the eastern side of Lake Atitlán. But when their villages came under the control of the Quiché, the Cakchiquel were the first to break away, moving their capital to Iximché in order to establish their independence. They founded the new city in about 1470 and from that time on were almost continuously at war with other tribes. Despite this, they managed to devote a lot of energy to the building and rebuilding of their new capital, and trenches dug into some of the structures have revealed as many as three superimposed layers. War may, in fact, have helped the process, as most of the labour was done by slaves captured in battle. When the Spanish arrived, the Cakchiquel were quick to join forces with Alvarado in order to defeat their old enemies, the Quiché. Grateful for the assistance, the Spanish established their first headquarters near here on May 7, 1524 – possibly Tecpán. The Cakchiquel referred to Alvarado as *Tonatiuh*, the son of the sun, and as a mark of respect he was given the daughter of a Cakchiquel king as a gift.

On July 25 the Spanish renamed the new settlement **Villa de Santiago**, declaring it their new capital. But within months the Cakchiquel had risen in rebellion, outraged by Alvarado's demands for tribute. Alvarado retaliated by burning Iximché, and forcing the Cakchiquel to flee into the mountains from where they waged a guerrilla war against the Spanish until 1530. The Spanish capital was moved from Tecpán to the greater safety of Ciudad Vieja, a short distance from Antigua (see p.110). For 450 years the ruins slumbered peacefully until the predominantly Maya organization the CUC (Peasant Unity Committee) met here in February 1980 and issued the **Declaration of Iximché**. Provoked by the massacre of their leaders during a peaceful occupation of the Spanish embassy in Guatemala City, the declaration identified this atrocity as the latest episode in more than four centuries of state-sponsored genocide against the Maya race. The storming of the embassy led to the outraged Spanish government breaking off diplomatic relations with Guatemala for five years.

The ruins of Iximché are made up of four main plazas, a couple of ball courts and several small pyramids. In most cases only the foundations and lower parts of the original structures were built of stone, while the upper walls were of adobe, with thatched roofs supported by wooden beams. You can make out the ground plan of many of the buildings, but it's only the most important all-stone structures that still stand. The most significant buildings were those clustered around courts A and C, which were probably the scene of the most revered rituals. On the sides of **Temple 2** you can make out some badly eroded murals, the style of which is very similar to that used in the codices.

It's thought that the site itself, like most of the highland centres, was a ceremonial city used for religious rituals, and, indeed, Maya worship still takes place here down a small trail through the pine trees behind the final plaza. The site was thought to have been inhabited only by the elite, with the rest of the population living in the surrounding hills and coming to Iximché only to attend festivals and to defend the fortified site in times of attack. Archeological digs here have unearthed a number of interesting finds, including the decapitated heads of sacrifice victims, burial sites, grinding stones, obsidian knives, a flute made from a child's femur, and large numbers of incense burners. There was surprisingly little sculpture, but most of it was similar to that found in the ruins of Zaculeu and Mixco Viejo, both of which were occupied at around the same time.

Getting to Iximché

To get to Iximché, take any bus travelling along the Pan-American Highway between Chimaltenango and Los Encuentros, and ask to be dropped at Tecpán, from where you can walk to the site. From Guatemala City any of the buses going to Sololá, Quiché or Xela will do: they leave the Zona 4 terminal about every thirty minutes, and pass through Chimaltenango. If you're coming from Los Encuentros take any bus heading for Guatemala City.

To get to the ruins simply walk through Tecpán and out the other side of the plaza, passing the *Centro de Salud*, and follow the road through the fields for about 5km, an hour or so on foot. With any luck you'll be able to hitch some of the way, particularly at weekends when the road can be fairly busy. You can **camp** at the site, but bring your own food, as the small shop sells little apart from drinks – Iximché's shady location is perfect for a picnic or barbeque. If you're not planning to camp, be back on the Pan-American Highway before 6pm to be sure of a bus out.

EL QUICHÉ

At the heart of the western highlands, sandwiched between the Verapaces and Huehuetenango, is the **Department of El Quiché**. Like its neighbours, El Quiché encompasses the full range of Guatemalan scenery. In the south, only a short distance from Lake Atitlán, is a section of the sweeping central valley, a fertile and heavily populated area that forms the upper reaches of the Motagua valley. To the north the landscape becomes increasingly dramatic, rising first to the **Sierra de Chuacús**, and then to the massive, rain-soaked peaks of the **Cuchumatanes**, beyond which the land drops away into the inaccessible rainforests of the **Ixcán**.

The department takes its name from the greatest of the pre-Conquest tribal groups, the **Quiché**, for whom it was the hub of an empire. From their capital **Utatlán**, which stood just west of the modern town of Santa Cruz del Quiché, they overran much of the highlands and were able to demand tribute from most of the other tribes. Although by the time the Spanish arrived their empire was in decline, they were still the dominant force in the region and challenged the conquistadors as soon as they entered the highlands, at a site near Quetzaltenango. They were easily defeated though, and the Spanish were able to negotiate alliances with former Quiché subjects, playing one tribe off against another, and eventually overcoming them all. Today these highlands remain a stronghold of Maya culture and the department of El Quiché, scattered with small villages and mountain towns, is the scene of some superb fiestas and markets.

For the Spanish, however, this remote mountainous terrain, with little to offer in the way of plunder, remained an unimportant backwater: only in later years, when large-scale commercial farming began on the Pacific coast, did it grow in importance as a source of cheap labour. This role has had a profound impact on the area for the last two hundred years and has forced the population to suffer horrific abuses. Perhaps not surprisingly the region became a noted centre of guerrilla activity in the late 1970s, and subsequently the scene of unrivalled repression.

For the traveller El Quiché has a lot to offer, in both the accessible south and the wilder north. **Chichicastenango**, one of the country's most popular destinations, is the scene of a vast twice-weekly market and remains a relatively undisrupted centre of Maya religion. Beyond this, at the heart of the central valley, is the departmental capital of **Santa Cruz del Quiché**, stopping off point for trips to a string of smaller towns and to the ruins of **Utatlán**. Further to the north the paved road ends and the mountains really begin. Travelling here can be hard work but the extraordinary scale of the scenery makes it all well worthwhile. Isolated villages are set in superb highland scenery, sustaining a wealth of indigenous culture and occupying a misty, mysterious world of their own. Passing over the Sierra de Chuacús, and down to the Río Negro, you reach **Sacapulas** at the base of the **Cuchumatanes**. From here you can travel across the foothills to Cobán or Huehuetenango, or for real adventure up into the mountains to the three towns of the **Ixil triangle – Nebaj**, **Chajul** and **Cotzal**.

The road for Chichicastenango and the department of El Quiché leaves the Pan-American Highway at the **Los Encuentros** junction. From here it descends the southern volcanic ridge and runs into the central valley, a land suspended between the volcanoes and the mountains.

Chichicastenango

Heading north from Los Encuentros, the road drops down through dense, aromatic pine forests, into a deep ravine housing a tributary of the river Motagua.

Just beyond the bridge over the river, a sign marks the spot where Jorge Carpio, newspaper owner and cousin of the president, was shot and killed on July 3, 1993. The assassination was seen as a warning to President Ramiro de León Carpio (see p.369) not to challenge the established power structure dominated by the army, landowners and big business. Carpio, a former human rights ombudsman, did little to upset the status quo for the rest of his presidential term.

The road begins a tortuous ascent from the valley floor around endless switchbacks until it reaches **CHICHICASTENANGO**, 17km from the Los Encuentros junction. Known as Guatemala's "Mecca del turismo", this compact and traditional town of cobbled streets, adobe houses and red-tiled roofs has its day-to-day calm shattered on a twice-weekly basis by the **Sunday** and **Thursday markets** – Sunday is the busiest. As the town is conveniently placed a short hop from the Pan-American Highway, the market attracts a myriad of tourists and commercial traders on day trips out of Antigua, Panajachel, Guatemala City, as well as Maya weavers from throughout the central highlands. For many years the market and town managed to coexist happily, but recently the invasion of outsiders has begun to dominate and now threatens to undermine Chichicastenago's unique identity – you may find yourself embroiled in one of the country's very few traffic jams out-

side the capital, as traders, tourists and locals all struggle to reach the town centre.

The market is by no means all that sets Chichicastenango apart, however, and for the local Maya population it's an important centre of culture and religion. Long before the arrival of the Spanish this area was inhabited by the Cakchiquel, whose settlements of Patzak and Chavier were under threat from the all-powerful Quiché. In a bid to assert their independence, the Cakchiqueles abandoned the villages in 1470 and moved south to Iximché (see p.119), from where they mounted repeated campaigns against their former masters. Chichicastenango itself was founded by the Spanish in order to house Quiché refugees from Utatlán to the north, which they conquered and destroyed in 1524. The town's name is a Nahuatl word meaning "the place of the nettles", accorded it by Alvarado's Mexican allies.

Over the years Maya culture and folk Catholicism have been treated with a rare degree of respect in Chichicastenango, although inevitably this blessing has been mixed with waves of arbitrary persecution and exploitation. Today the town has an incredible collection of Maya artefacts, parallel indigenous and *ladino* governments, and a church that makes no effort to disguise its acceptance of unconventional pagan worship. Traditional weaving is also adhered to in Chichicastenango and the women wear superb, heavily embroidered *huipiles*. The men's costume of short trousers and jackets of black wool embroidered with silk is highly distinguished, although it's very expensive to make and these days most men opt for western dress. However, for fiestas and market days a handful of *cofradías* (elders of the religious hierarchy) still wear the traditional clothing.

Chichicastenango's appetite for religious fervour is evident during the **fiesta** of Santo Tomás, from December 14 to 21. While it's not the most spontaneous of fiestas it's certainly spectacular, with attractions including the *Palo Volador* (in which men dangle by ropes from a twenty-metre pole), a live band or two, a massive procession, traditional dances, clouds of incense, gallons of *chicha*, and endless deafening fireworks. On the final day, all babies born in the previous year are brought to the church for christening. Easter, too, is celebrated here with tremendous energy and seriousness.

Arrival and information

There's no bus station in Chichi, so the corner 5 C and 5 Av operates loosely as a terminal. **Buses** heading between Guatemala City and Santa Cruz del Quiché pass through here every half hour, stopping for a few minutes to load up passengers. In Guatemala City buses leave every thirty minutes from the terminal in Zona 4, from 4am to about 5pm. Coming from Antigua, you can easily connect with these buses in Chimaltenango, while on market days, a shuttle service runs the whole route. From Panajachel you can take any bus up to Los Encuentros and change there, or, on market days there are several direct buses, supplemented by a steady flow of tourist shuttles.

If you're bitten by market fever and need to **change money** there's no problem in Chichi, even on a Sunday. Try Banco Ejercito, on 6 C (Tues–Sun 9am–5pm) or, almost opposite, Banco Industrial (Mon 10am–2pm, Wed–Sun 10am–5pm). *Hotel Santo Tomás* (see below) can also change money. The **post office** (Mon–Fri 9am–5.30pm) and **Telgua** (daily 7am–8pm) are both on 6 Av, up behind the church.

CHICHICASTENANGO'S MARKET

There's been a **market** at Chichicastenango for hundreds, if not thousands, of years, and despite the twice-weekly invasions the local people continue to trade their wares. On market days Chichicastenango's streets are lined with stalls and packed with buyers, and the choice is overwhelming, ranging from superb quality Ixil *huipiles* to wooden dance masks, and including pottery, gourds, machetes, belts and a gaudy selection of recently invented "traditional" fabrics. You can still pick up some authentic and beautiful weaving, but you need to be prepared to wade through a lot of trash and to haggle hard – easier said than done, but your chances are better before 10am when the tourist buses arrive from the capital, or in the late afternoon once things have started to quieten down. The best of the stuff from the local villages is held in the centre of the plaza and is far more interesting than the bulk of the stalls, at least if you haven't come to buy. Prices are pretty competetive here, but for a real bargain you need to head further into the highlands, while Panajachel is a better bet for *típica* clothes.

For a brilliant vantage point over a typical Maya market, head for the indoor balcony on the upper floor of the **Centro Comercial** building on the north side of the plaza. You'll be able to gawp down on the villagers below as they haggle and chat over bunches of spring onions and pick out costumes from all over the highlands. At this vegetable market, you'll see *huipiles* from the Atitlán villages of San Antonio and Santa Catarina and from even as far away as Nebaj; the funky "space cowboy" shirts and pants are worn by men from the Sololá area.

Accommodation

Accommodation can be in short supply on Saturday nights in Chichicastenango, before the Sunday market, but you shouldn't have a problem on other days. Hotel prices can also be inflated on market days, though at other times you can usually negotiate a good deal.

Hotel Bella Vista, 4 Av, heading north out of town (☎2041097). New small-scale pensión, with spotless rooms and immaculate bathrooms that are shared with one other room. ③

Hotel Chugüilá, 5 Av 5–24 (☎ & fax 7561134). Attractive rooms, some with fireplaces, are scattered on different levels around the hotel, which overflows with greenery and pot plants. Secure parking. ④.

Hospedaje El Salvador, 5 Av 10–09 (☎7561329). Best budget deal in town, with a vast warren of rooms, a bizzare colour scheme, and cheap prices. There is hot water, but you may have to insist that they turn it on. ②.

Hospedaje Girón, 6 C 4–52 (☎7561156). Rooms are pretty, clean and well priced, and come either with or without private bath. A good deal, especially for single travellers. ③.

Maya Inn, 8 Calle A & 3 Av (☎7561176; fax 7561212). Chichi's oldest tourist hotel offers very comfortable rooms, with old-fashioned period charm. Though their character is undeniable, prices are a bit steep. ⑧.

Hotel Pascual Abaj, 5 Av & 3 C (☎7561055). The decor certainly won't win any design awards, but the rooms are serviceable enough and all have private bathrooms and hot water. Front rooms are a little noisy due to passing buses. ②.

Hotel Posada Belen, 12 C 5–55 (☎7561244). Half the rooms have private bathrooms, half don't, but none are especially attractive even though the views from the back are good. ②.

Hospedaje Santa Marta, 5 Av, past the arch. Very basic, but clean. Will suffice if all else in town is full, though there's no hot water and no single rooms. ②.

Hotel Santo Thomás, 7 Av 5–32 (☎7561061; fax 7561306). Very comfortable, well-appointed rooms all set around two colonial-style courtyards. Rooms 29–37 are the ones to book if you can – they have great mountain views. Also has a restaurant, swimming pool, sauna and jacuzzi. ⑦.

Hotel Villa Grande, just before town, off the Los Encuentros road (☎561053; fax 7561140). Monstrous new concrete hotel, designed to cater for tour groups. Built into the hillside so consequently the views are good. All luxuries, including a restaurant and pool. ⑧.

The Town

Though most visitors come here to see the market, Chichicastenango also offers an unusual insight into traditional religious practices in the highlands. At the main **Santo Tomás Church**, in the southeast corner of the plaza, the Quiché Maya have been left to adopt their own style of worship, blending pre-Columbian and Catholic rituals. The church was built in 1540 on the site of a Maya altar, and rebuilt in the eighteenth century. It's said that indigenous locals became interested in worshipping here after Francisco Ximénez, the priest from 1701 to 1703, started reading their holy book, the Popul Vuh (see below). Seeing that he held considerable respect for their religion, they moved their altars from the hills and set them up inside the church. Today, this ancient, unique hybrid of Maya and Catholic worship still takes place in the church.

Before entering the building it's customary to make offerings in a fire at the base of the steps or burn incense in perforated cans, a practice that leaves a cloud of thin, sweet smoke hanging over the entrance. Inside is an astonishing scene of avid worship. A soft hum of constant murmuring fills the air, as the faithful kneel to place candles on low level stone platforms for their ancestors and the saints. For these people the entire building is alive with the souls of the dead, each located in a specific part of the church. The place of the "first people", the ancient ancestors, is beneath the altar railing; former officials are around the middle of the aisle; common people to the west in the nave; and deceased native priests beside the door. Alongside these, and equally important, are the Catholic saints, who receive the same respect and are continuously appealed to with offerings of candles and alcohol. Last, but by no means least, certain areas within the church, and particular patterns of candles, rose petals and *chicha*, are used to invoke specific types of blessings, such as those for children, travel, marriage, harvest or illness. Don't enter the building by the front door, which is reserved for *cofrades* and senior church officials, but through the **side door**. It's deeply offensive to take **photographs** inside the building – don't even contemplate it.

Beside the church is a former monastery, now used by the parish administration. It was here that the Spanish priest Francisco Ximénez became the first outsider to be shown the **Popol Vuh**, the holy book of the Quiché. His copy of the manuscript is now housed in the Newberry Library in Chicago: the original was lost some time later in the eighteenth century. The text itself was written in nearby Utatlán shortly after the arrival of the Spanish, and is a brilliant poem of over nine thousand lines that details the cosmology, mythology and traditional history of the Quiché. Broadly speaking it's split into two parts; the first is an account of the creation of man and the world, culminating in an epic struggle beween the wizard twins Hunahpú and Xbalanqué and the Death Lords of the Maya underworld, with the twins ultimately triumphing and the cycle of creation being born. The second part describes the wanderings of ancestors of the Quiché as they migrate south and settle in the highlands of Guatemala. The opening lines give an impression of the book's importance, and the extent to which it sets out to preserve a threatened cultural heritage:

> *This is the beginning of the Ancient World, here in this place called Quiché. Here we shall ascribe, we shall implant the ancient word, the potential and source of everything done in the citadel of Quiché.*
>
> *And here we shall take up the demonstration, revelation, and account of how things were put in shadow and brought to light....We shall write about this amid the preaching of God, in Christendom now. We shall bring it out because there is no longer a place to see it, a Council book.*

Translation by Dennis Tedlock

On the south side of the plaza, the **Rossbach Museum** (Tues, Wed, Fri & Sat 8am–noon & 2–4pm, Thurs & Sun 8am–1pm & 2–4pm; Q1) houses a wide-ranging collection of pre-Columbian artefacts, mostly small pieces of ceramics that had been kept by local people in their homes, some as much as two thousand years old. The collection is based on that of Ildefonso Rossbach, an accountant-turned-priest who served in Chichicastenango from 1894 until his death in 1944. Most of the pieces here were donated to him by local people.

Across the plaza, opposite Santo Tomás is **El Calvario**, a smaller chapel reserved for the use of indigenous people. Inside there's a large image of Christ in a glass case that's paraded through the street during Holy Week. The steps are the scene of incense-burning rituals and the chapel is considered good for general confessions and pardons.

The cemetery and the shrine of Pascual Abaj

The town **cemetery**, down the hill behind El Calvario, offers further evidence of the strange mix of religions that characterizes Chichicastenango. The graves are marked by anything from a grand tomb to a small earth mound, and in the centre is an Indian shrine where the usual offerings of incense and alcohol are made. At the back, in a large yellow building, is entombed the body of Father Rossbach.

The churches and cemetery are certainly not the only scenes of Indian religious activity, and the hills that surround the town, like so many throughout the country, are topped with shrines. The closest of these, less than a kilometre from the plaza, is known as **Pascual Abaj**. The site is regularly visited by tourists, but it's important to remember that these ceremonies are deeply serious and you should still keep your distance and be sensitive about taking any **photographs**. The shrine is laid out in a typical pattern with several small altars facing a stern pre-Columbian sculpture. Offerings are usually overseen by a *brujo*, a type of shaman, and range from flowers to sacrificed chickens, always incorporating plenty of incense, alcohol and incantations. In 1957, during a bout of religious rivalry, the shrine was raided and smashed by reforming Catholics, but the traditionalists gathered the scattered remains and patched them together with cement and a steel-reinforcing rod.

To get to Pascual Abaj, walk down the hill beside the Santo Tomás church, take the first right, 9 Calle, and follow this as it winds its way out of town. You'll soon cross a stream and then a well-signposted route takes you through the courtyard of a workshop making wooden masks. If a ceremony is in progress you may be able to pick out Pascual Abaj by a thin plume of smoke. Continue to follow the path uphill for ten minutes through a dense pine forest to the shrine.

> ### MOVING ON
>
> If you're **heading south** from Chichicastenango, it's often quickest to catch the first bus as far as Los Encuentros and make a connection there. Direct buses head **to Guatemala City** every thirty minutes or so (3hr), the last one leaving at around 6.30pm, and seven buses daily head westwards to Quetzaltenango between 6am and 3pm (2hr 30min). **For Antigua**, catch a Guatemala City-bound bus and change at Chimaltenango, except on market days when you can get a direct shuttle, if funds permit. If you're **heading north**, take the first bus to Santa Cruz del Quiché (every 30min; 30min), from where buses go to Nebaj and the mountains.

Eating

If you've come from Panajachel or Antigua, the dining scene here may seem rather dull. What is on offer is simple, good value Guatemalan *comedor* nosh, which means lots of *pollo frito, carne asada* and *huevos y frijoles*. Even at the smarter restaurants, such as the *Hotel Santo Tomás* or the *Maya Inn*, the food is unlikely to excite real gastronauts. The plaza on **market day** is the place for some authentic highland food – try one of the makeshift *comedores*, which sell cauldrons of stew, rice and beans.

Tapena, opposite the Hotel Chugüilá. Simple well-priced Guatemalan food served in pleasant surroundings.

Café La Villa de Los Cofrades, in the Centro commercial on 5 Av, on the north side of the plaza. Good set meals – soup, salad, fries, bread and a main dish cost under $4. The breakfasts are also superb and the people-watching here is unrivalled.

Restaurant La Villa de Los Cofrades, upstairs on the corner of 6 C & 5 Av. Similar set-up to the café below, but a little smarter. Portions are big and tables overlook the action on the street.

Buenadventura, upper floor, inside the Centro Commercial, on the north side of the plaza. Birds-eye view of the vegetable market, with simple, no-nonsense food and the cheapest breakfasts in town.

La Fonda del Tzijolaj, upper floor in the Centro Comercial, on the north side of the plaza. The name's unpronounceable, but the food is probably the best in town and the balcony views of the church of Santo Thomás and the market are excellent. Try the *chiles rellanos*.

Comedor Gumarcaj, 7 Av, opposite the *Hotel Santo Tomás*. Very simple, very cheap and very friendly *comedor* that serves up a mean *pollo y papas* and lush *licuados*.

Santa Cruz del Quiché and around

The capital of the department, **SANTA CRUZ DEL QUICHÉ**, lies half an hour north of Chichicastenango. A good paved road connects the two towns, running through pine forests and ravines, and past the **Laguna Lemoa**, a lake which, according to local legend, was originally filled with tears wept by the wives of Quiché kings after their husbands had been slaughtered by the Spanish. Santa Cruz del Quiché itself is a pretty uneventful place where not a lot happens. It is, however, the transport hub for the department and the most direct route to the Ixil Triangle, as well as being the only practical place to base yourself for a visit to the nearby ruins of **Utatlán**.

The Town

Dominating the central **plaza** of Santa Cruz del Quiché is a large colonial church, built by the Dominicans with stone from the ruins of Utatlán. The clock tower beside it is also said to have been built from Utatlán stone, stripped from the temple of Tohil. In the middle of the plaza a defiant statue of the Quiché hero Tecún Umán stands prepared for battle. His position is undermined somewhat by an ugly urban tangle of hardware stores, *panaderías* and trash that surrounds the plaza, as well as the spectacularly ugly, looming presence of the breeze block, tin-roofed **market** building. The market here takes place on the same days as in Chichicastenango – Thursday and Sunday – and sprawls over most of the area south and east of the plaza, spreading down to the bus station. Palm weaving is a local speciality, and Maya people can often be seen threading a band or two as they walk through town. Many of the palm hats on sale throughout the country were put together here, but if you want to buy you'll have to look hard and long to find one that fits a gringo head.

Practicalities

The **bus terminal**, a large open affair, is about four blocks south and a couple east of the central plaza. Connections are generally excellent from Quiché, with a stream of second-class **buses** to Guatemala City leaving every thirty minutes between 3.30am and 5pm (3hr 30min); all pass through Chichicastanango (30min) and Los Encuentros (1hr). Other points in the highlands are equally well served, with regular services to Nebaj between 8.30am and 4pm (every 1hr 30min; 4hr), hourly buses to Joyabaj from 6am to 4pm (2hr 30min), four daily buses to Uspantán between 9am and 2pm (5hr), and regular buses to Quetzaltenango leaving between 3am and 1pm (3hr). If you're heading for anywhere outside the department then it's generally easiest to take any bus to Los Encuentros and change there.

There's a limited range of **hotels** in Quiché, with the cheapest being right beside the bus terminal. The best budget deal in town is the brand new *Posada San Antonio*, 2 Av, two blocks from the terminal (②), with smallish but clean rooms (and hot water), while *Hotel Maya Quiché*, 3 Av 4–19 Zona 1 (☎7551464; ③), is a friendly place, with big clean rooms that come with or without bathrooms. Slightly more upmarket is the *Hotel Rey K'iche*, 8 C 0–39 Zona 5, two blocks north, and one block east of the bus terminal (☎2325834; ④) – it's well run, extremely clean and welcoming and has 26 rooms, most with cable TV and private bathroom.

For **food**, there's not much choice here and very little to get excited about. Most restaurants and cafés are grouped around the plaza, where you'll also find a number of bakeries that sell a pretty uninspiring range of dry pastries and cakes. In the morning, between the church and clock tower, you'll find a señora dispensing freshly squeezed orange juice for a few quetzals a glass. The smartest place in town is *El Torito Steakhouse*, 7C 1–73, just southwest of the plaza, a real carnivore's delight, specializing in steaks and meat platters, served with soup as a starter. The sausages are very tasty here, the fried chicken's good and the whole place is bedecked in kitsch cowboy decor. On the west side of the plaza, *La Pizza de Ciro* does reasonable pizzas, and the friendly *Café La Torré* serves coffee, snacks and delicious cheesecake. Finally, for friendly service, cheap breakfasts and no-nonsense *comedor* grub, there's *Restaurante Las Rosas*, on 1 Av 1–28.

There are two **banks** which will change travellers' cheques: Banco Industrial, at the northwest corner of the plaza (Mon–Fri 8.30am–5.30pm, Sat 8.30am–12.30pm), who also give cash to Visa card holders, and Banco G&T, 6 A 3–00 (Mon–Fri 9am–7pm, Sat 9am–1pm), who won't. If you're heading into the Ixil Triangle, you may need to stock up on **film** in which case Kodak and Fuji both have shops one block northeast of the church where you can buy slide film.

The ruins of Utatlán (K'umarkaaj)

Early in the fifteenth century, riding on a wave of successful conquest, the Quiché king Gucumatz (Feathered Serpent) founded a new capital, K'umarkaaj. A hundred years later the Spanish arrived, renamed the city **Utatlán**, and then destroyed it. Today the **ruins** (daily 8am–8pm; $2) can be visited, about 4km to the west of Santa Cruz del Quiché.

According to the Popol Vuh, Gucumatz was a lord of great genius, assisted by powerful spirits: "The nature of this king was truly marvellous, and all the other lords were filled with terror before him.... And this was the beginning of the grandeur of the Quiché, when Gucumatz gave these signs of his power. His sons and his grandsons never forgot him." And there's no doubt that this was once a great city, with several separate citadels spread across neighbouring hilltops. It housed the nine dynasties of the tribal elite, including the four main Quiché lords, and contained a total of 23 palaces. The splendour of the city embodied the strength of the Quiché empire, which at its height boasted a population of around a million.

By the time of the Conquest, however, the Quiché had been severely weakened and their empire fractured. They first made contact with the Spanish on the Pacific coast, suffering a heavy defeat at the hands of Alvarado's forces near Quetzaltenango, with the loss of their hero Tecún Umán. The Quiché then invited the Spanish to their capital, a move that made Alvarado distinctly suspicious. On seeing the fortified city he feared a trap and captured the Quiché leaders, Oxib-Quch and Belcheb-Tzy. His next step was characteristically straightforward: "As I knew them to have such a bad disposition to service of his Majesty, and to ensure the good and peace of this land, I burnt them, and sent to burn the town and destroy it."

The site

Utatlán is not as immediately impressive as some of the Petén ruins, but its dramatic situation, surrounded by deep ravines and pine forests, the stunning views across the valley and its fascinating historical significance make up for the lack of huge pyramids and stellae. There has been little restoration since the Spanish destroyed the city, and only a few of the main structures are still recognizable, most buried beneath grassy mounds and shaded by pine trees. The small **museum** has a scale model of what the original city may once have looked like.

The central plaza is almost certainly where Alvarado burned alive the two Quiché leaders, in the year 1524. Nowadays it's where you'll find the three remaining **temple buildings**, the Great Monuments of Tohil, Auilix and Hacauaitz, which were simple pyramids topped by thatched shelters. In the middle of the plaza there used to be a circular **tower**, the Temple of the Sovereign Plumed Serpent, but these days just its foundations can be made out. The only other feature that is still vaguely recognizable is the **ball court**, which lies beneath grassy banks to the south of the plaza.

Perhaps the most interesting thing about the site today is that *brujos*, traditional Indian priests, still come here to perform religious rituals, practices that pre-date the arrival of the Spanish by thousands of years. The entire area is covered in small burnt circles – the ashes of incense – and chickens are regularly sacrificed in and around the plaza.

Beneath the plaza is a long constructed **tunnel** that runs underground for about 100m. Inside are nine shrines, the same number as there are levels of the Maya underworld, Xibalbá. At each shrine devotees pray, but it is the ninth one, housed inside a chamber, that is most actively used for sacrifice, incense and alcohol offerings. Why the tunnel was constructed remains uncertain, but local legends suggest that it was dug by the Quiché to hide their women and children from the advancing Spanish whom they planned to ambush at Utatlán. Others believe it represents the seven caves of Tula mentioned in the Popul Vuh (see p.125). Whatever the truth, today the tunnel is the focus for Maya rituals and a favourite spot for sacrifice, the floor carpeted with chicken feathers, and candles burning in the alcoves at the end. To get to the tunnel follow the signs to *la cueva* (the cave); the entrance is usually littered with empty incense wrappings and *aguadiente* liquor bottles. If a ceremony is taking place you'll hear the mumbling of prayers and smell incense smoke as you enter, in which case it's wise not to disturb the proceedings by approaching too closely.

To **get to** Utatlán from Santa Cruz de Quiché you can walk or take a taxi (expect to pay around $8 for a return trip, with an hour at the ruins). It's a pleasant forty-minute hike, heading south from the plaza along 2 Av, then turning right down 10 C, which will take you all the way out to the site. You're welcome to **camp** close to the ruins, but here there are no shower facilities or food available.

A rough road continues west from the ruins to San Antonio Ilotenango and from there to Totonicapan. A fair amount of traffic passes along this back route, which takes in some superb high ground.

East to Joyabaj

An astonishingly good paved road runs east from Santa Cruz del Quiché, beneath the impressive peaks of the **Sierra de Chuacús**, through a series of interesting villages set in beautiful rolling farmland. The first of the villages is **CHICHÉ**, a sister village to Chichicastenango, with which it shares costumes and traditions, though the market here is on Wednesday. Next is **CHINIQUE**, followed by the larger village of **ZACUALPA**, which has Thursday and Sunday markets in its beautiful broad plaza. The village's name means "where they make fine walls", and in the hills to the north are the remains of a pre-Conquest settlement. There's a *pensión* down the street beside the church should you want to stay here.

The last place out this way is the small town of **JOYABAJ**, again with a small archeological site to its north. During the colonial period Joyabaj was an important staging post on the royal route to Mexico, but all evidence of its former splendour was lost when the earthquake in 1976 almost totally flattened the town and hundreds of people lost their lives: the crumbling facade of the colonial church that stands in front of the new prefabricated version is one of the few physical remains. In recent years the town has staged a miraculous recovery, however, and it is now once again a prosperous traditional centre: the Sunday **market**, which starts up on Saturday afternoon, is a huge affair well worth visiting, as is the **fiesta** in the second week of August – five days of unrelenting celebration that

IAN OSBORNE, FOOTPRINTS

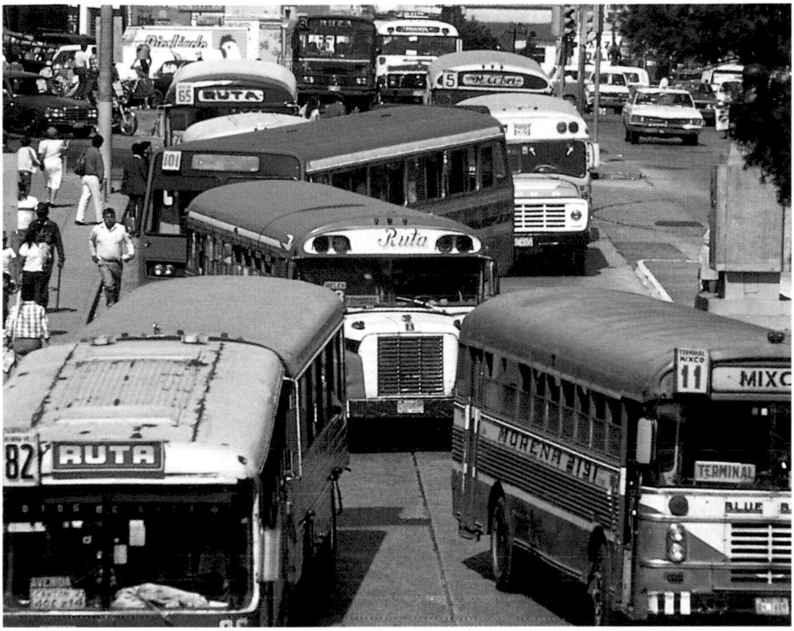

Guatemala City buses

IAN OSBORNE, FOOTPRINTS

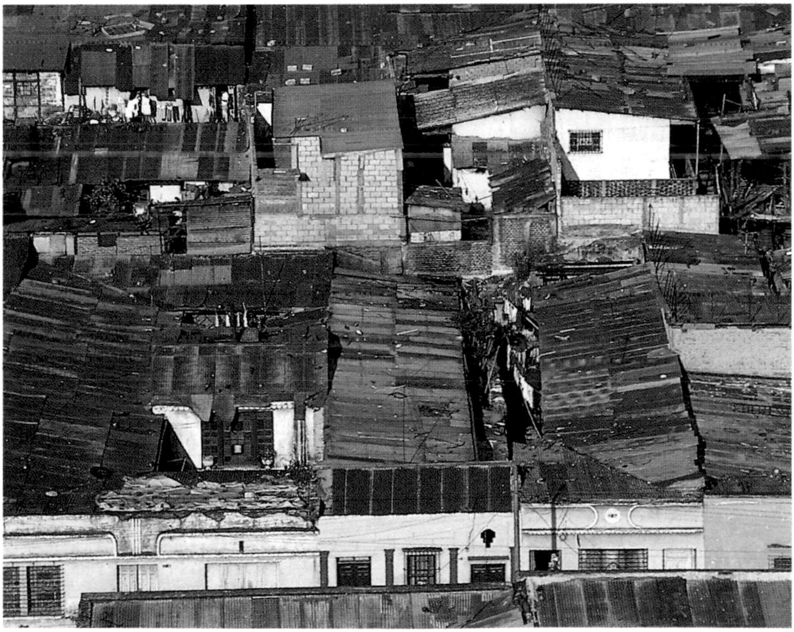

Rooftops, Guatemala City

Evangelical baptists, Lake Atitlán

Todos Santos costume

Dance of the Conquistadors, Panzós fiesta

Sololá market

Farmer, Santiago Atitlán

JAMIE MARSHALL, GUATEMALAN INDIAN CENTRE

Nebaj costume

KRYSTYNA DEUSS, GUATEMALAN INDIAN CENTRE

Semana Santa, Antigua

IAIN STEWART

Sololá costume

IAIN STEWART

Festival dancer from San Juan Atitán

IAIN STEWART

San Francisco el Alto market

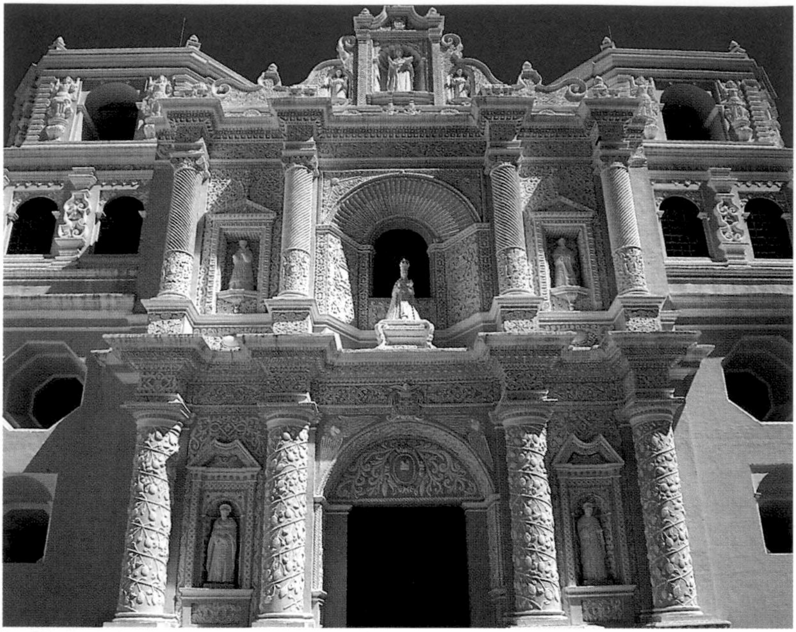

La Merced, Antigua

Laké Atitlán

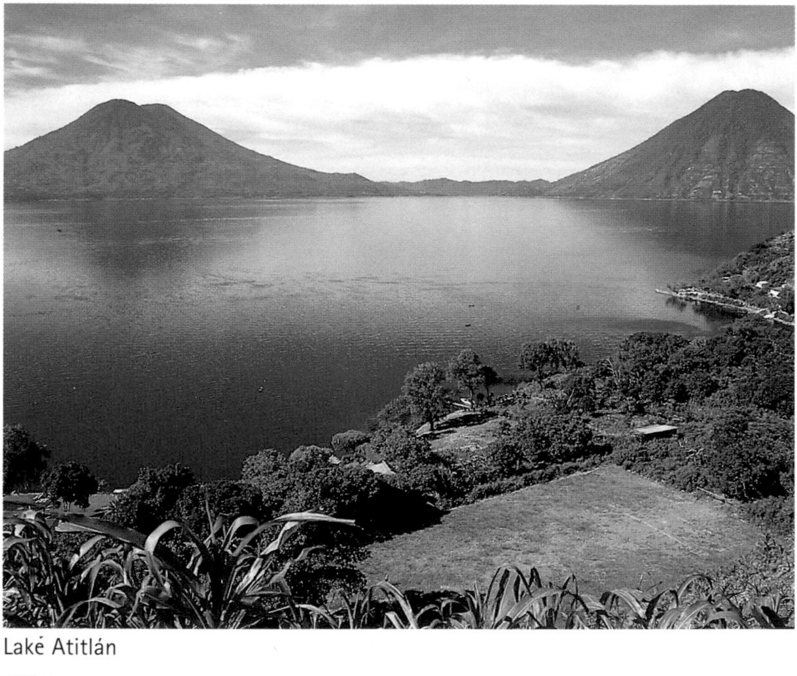

includes some fantastic traditional dancing and the spectacular *Palo Volador*, in which "flying" men or *ángeles* spin to the ground from a huge wooden pole; a pre-Conquest ritual now performed in only three places in the country. Though the fiesta is in many ways a hybrid of Maya and Christian traditions, the *ángeles* symbolize none other than the wizard twins of the Popul Vuh (see p.125) who descend into the underworld to do battle with the Lords of Death.

While the town may have recovered economically, the remote **Maya villages** beyond are still suffering great hardship through lack of any services – from roads to hospitals. Many inhabitants have survived terrible massacres during the early 1980s and have received little assistance rebuilding their lives. You may, therefore, be interested in supporting a **local development project** run by fifteen indigenous community councils, under the auspices of the non-governmental, rural development organization SCDRYS (*Sociedad Civil para el Desarollo Rural Replicable y Sostenible*), based in Quetzaltenango (see p.168). A language centre has been set up, called the XOY Centre, in Joyabaj, where students can live with and learn Spanish or Quiché from locally trained teachers for $110 per week. For further information, phone ☎7630407.

It's possible to **walk** from Joyabaj, over the Sierra de Chuacús, to Cubulco in Baja Verapaz. It's a superb but exhausting hike, taking at least a day, though it's perhaps better done in reverse (as described on p.289).

Practicalities

Buses run between Guatemala City and Joyabaj, passing through Santa Cruz del Quiché, every hour or so (8am–2.30pm from the capital and 5am–3pm from Joyabaj). There's a good but very basic **pensión**, the *Hospedaje Mejia* (①), on the plaza in Joyabaj, and plenty of scattered **comedores** – one of the best is just off the main street beside the filling station.

For Panajachel and connections to the Pacific coast, **buses** leave Joyabaj twice daily in the morning, heading for Cocales. It's also possible to get back to the capital along two rough and seldom-travelled routes. The first of these is **via San Martín Jilotepeque** on the daily bus that leaves Joyabaj at 2am; the second option takes you **to Pachalum**, although you'll have to rely on sporadic truck traffic as there is no longer a bus service on this route. There's nowhere to stay in Pachalum but onward buses leave for the capital at 2am, passing the ruins of Mixco Viejo – and the driver may let you sleep in the bus while you wait.

To the Cuchumatanes: Sacapulas and Uspantán

The land to the north of Santa Cruz del Quiché is sparsely inhabited and dauntingly hilly. About 10km out of town, the single rough road in this direction passes through San Pedro Jocopilas, and from there struggles on untarmacked, skirting the western end of the Sierra de Chuacús and eventually dropping to the isolated town of **SACAPULAS**, two hours from Quiché. Set in a spectacular position on the river Negro beneath the dusty foothills of the Cuchumatanes, Sacapulas has a small colonial church, and a good market is held every Thursday and Sunday beneath a huge ceiba tree in the plaza. Some of the women still wear impressive *huipiles* and tie their hair with elaborate pom-poms, similar to those of Aguacatán.

Since long before the arrival of the Spanish, **salt** has been produced here in beds beside the Río Negro, a valuable commodity that earned the town a degree of importance. Legend has it that the people of Sacapulas originally migrated from the far north, fleeing other savage tribes. The town's original name was Tajul, meaning "hot springs", but the Spanish changed it to Sacapulas, "the grassy place", as they valued the straw baskets made locally. Along the river bank, downstream from the bridge, there are several little pools where warm water bubbles to the surface, used by local people for washing. On the opposite bank trucks and buses break for lunch at some ramshackle *comedores* and fruit stalls.

Getting to Sacapulas is not hard – you can catch any of the **buses** that leave Santa Cruz del Quiché for Uspantán or Nebaj. Leaving Sacapulas is more difficult, as buses to Quiché leave at the ungodly hours of 1am and 3am, with another passing through from Nebaj at 9am – after this, you'll have to hitch. There are also buses to Huehuetenango at 3am, 4am and 5.30am and to Uspantán at 11am, 1pm, 2pm and 4pm. All services in this remote region are erratic and subject to delays and cancellations and sometimes they even leave early. Hitchhike whenever possible and expect to pay the same rate as you would on the bus.

At least if you get stuck, there's a reasonable place to **stay**; the *Restaurant Río Negro*, on the south side of the bridge, offers basic but clean rooms (①). The cook, Manuela, serves good **meals** (menus in English and Spanish) and excellent banana, pineapple and papaya milkshakes. *Panadería Karla*, near the square, does good choco-bananas and the street *comodores* serve tasty *tamales* and *enchiladas*.

East to Uspantán, and on to Cobán

East of Sacapulas a dirt road rises steeply, clinging to the mountainside and quickly leaving the Río Negro far below. As it climbs, the views are superb, with tiny riverside Sacapulas dwarfed by the sheer enormity of the landscape. Eventually the road reaches a high valley and arrives in **USPANTÁN**, a small town lodged in a chilly gap in the mountains and often soaked in steady drizzle. The only reason you're likely to end up here is in order to get somewhere else, and with the buses for Cobán and San Pedro Carchá leaving at 3am and 3.30am the best thing to do is go to bed. (The return buses leave San Pedro Carchá for Uspantán at 10am and noon.) There are two friendly *pensiones*, the *Casa del Viajero* (①), and the *Galindo* (①). **Buses** for Uspantán, via Sacapulas, leave Quiché at 9am, 11am, noon and 2pm, returning at 7pm, 11.30pm, 1am and 3am – a five-hour trip.

The Ixil triangle: Nebaj, Chajul and Cotzal

High up on the spine of the Cuchumatanes, in a landscape of steep hills, bowl-shaped valleys and gushing rivers, is the **Ixil triangle**. Here the three small towns of Nebaj, Chajul and Cotzal, remote and extremely traditonal, share a language spoken nowhere else in the country. This triangle of towns forms the hub of the **Ixil-speaking region**, a massive highland area which drops away towards the Mexican border and contains at least 100,000 inhabitants. These lush and rain-drenched hills are hard to reach and notoriously difficult to control, and today's relaxed atmosphere of highland Maya colour and customs conceals a bitter history of protracted conflict. It's an area that embodies some of the very best and worst characteristics of the Guatemalan highlands.

On the positive side is the beauty of the landscape and the strength of indigenous culture, both of which are overwhelming. When Church leaders moved into the area in the 1970s they found very strong communities in which the people were reluctant to accept new authority for fear that it would disrupt traditional structures, and women were included in the process of communal decision-making. Counterbalancing these strengths are the horrors of the human rights abuses that took place here over the last decades, which must rate as some of the worst anywhere in Central America.

Before the **Conquest** the town of Nebaj was a sizeable centre, producing large quantities of jade and possibly allied in some way to Zaculeu (see p.190). The Spanish Conquest was particularly brutal in these parts, however. After several previous setbacks, the Spaniards eventually managed to take Nebaj in 1530, and by then they were so enraged that not only was the town burnt to the ground but the survivors were condemned to slavery as punishment for their resistance. In the years that followed, the land was repeatedly invaded by the Lacandon Indians from the north and swept by devastating epidemics. Things didn't improve with the coming of independence, when the Ixil were regarded as a source of cheap labour and forced to work on the coastal plantations. It is estimated that between 1894 and 1930 six thousand labourers migrated annually to work on the harvest, suffering not only the hardship of the actual work, but also exposure to a number of new diseases. Many never returned, and even today large numbers of local people are forced to migrate in search of work, and conditions on many of the plantations remain appalling (see p.214). In the late 1970s and early 1980s, the area was hit by waves of horrific violence (see p.134) as it became the main theatre of operation for the **EGP** (the Guerrilla Army of the Poor). Caught up in the conflict, the people have suffered enormous losses, with the majority of the smaller villages destroyed by the army and their inhabitants herded into "protected" settlements. With the peace accords, a degree of normality has returned to the area, and new villages are beginning to spring up on the old sites.

Despite this terrible legacy, the fresh green hills are some of the most beautiful in the country and the three towns are friendly and accommodating, with a relaxed and distinctive atmosphere in a misty world of their own.

Nebaj

NEBAJ is the centre of Ixil country and by far the largest of the three settlements, a beautiful old town of white adobe walls and cobbled streets. The weaving done here is unusual and intricate, its greatest feature being the women's *huipiles*, which are a mass of complex geometrical designs in superb greens, yellows, reds and oranges, worn with brilliant red *cortes* (skirts). The women also wear superb headcloths decorated with "pom-pom" tassles that they pile up above their heads, though few men still wear traditional dress preferring to buy secondhand american clothes from the market. The men's ceremonial jackets, which are dusted down for fiestas, are formal-looking and ornately decorated, modelled on those worn by Spanish officers. (The finest red cloth, often used in both the jackets and the women's sashes, originates in Germany and keeps its colour incredibly well.) The people of Nebaj are keen to establish a market for their weaving, but most of them can't afford to travel as far as Chichicastenango, and so as soon as you arrive in town you'll probably be hassled by an army of young girls, desperate to sell their clothing. You'll also find an excellent shop, selling goods produced by the Ixil weaving co-op, on the main square.

Nebaj's plaza is the focal point for the community and houses the major shops, municipal buildings, and the police station. There's little to do in the town itself, though the small **market**, a block to the east of the church, is worth investigation. It's fairly quiet most days, but presents the best photographic opportunities in town as Nebajeños go about their daily business. On Thursday and Sunday the numbers swell and traders visit from out of town selling secondhand clothing, stereos from Taiwan and Korea and chickens, eggs, fruit and vegetables from the highlands. If you're in town for the second week in August you'll witness the **Nebaj fiesta**, which includes processions, dances, drinking and fireworks.

Practicalities

Getting to Nebaj is straightforward with **buses** leaving Santa Cruz del Quiché every ninety minutes between 8.30am and 4pm, and arriving at the brand new bus terminal close to the market on 7 C four hours later. There is also a daily service from Huehuetenango which leaves there at 11.30am (6hr). **Leaving** Nebaj is more problematic, with the schedules being designed to get locals to the early morning market, so buses leave at 11pm and 1am for Quiché and at 1.45am to Huehuetenango. There should also be a morning bus to Quiché at 7am, but don't

---

THE EGP IN THE IXIL TRIANGLE

Of the entire western highlands the Ixil triangle was one of the areas most devastated by the bitter **civil war** of the late 1970s and early 1980s. During this period the entire area became a desperate battleground and by the time the dust settled virtually all the smaller villages had been destroyed, 15–20,000 people had been killed and tens of thousands more displaced.

The severity of the violence is a measure of the success of the **EGP** (*Ejército Guerrillero de los Pobres* – The Guerrilla Army of the Poor), who fought the army in northern Quiché for more than two decades. The EGP first entered the area in 1972, when a small group of guerrilla fighters (some of whom had been involved in the 1960s guerrilla campaign) crossed the Mexican border to the north and began building links with local people. At the time there was little military presence in the area and they were able to work swiftly, impressing the Ixil Maya with their bold plans for political and social revolution. In 1975 they opened their military campaign by assassinating Luis Arenas, the notorious owner of Finca La Perla, to the north of Chajul, where hundreds of labourers were kept in a system of debt bondage. The EGP shot Arenas in front of hundreds of his employees as he was counting the payroll. According to the EGP, "shouts of joy burst from throats accustomed for centuries only to silence and lament, and with something like an ancestral cry, with one voice they chanted with us our slogan, "*Long live the poor, death to the rich.*"

These early actions prompted a huge response from the **armed forces**, who began killing, kidnapping and torturing suspected guerrillas and sympathizers. The organization was already well entrenched, however, and the army's brutality only served to persuade more and more people to seek protection from the guerrillas. By late 1978 the EGP were regularly occupying villages, holding open meetings and tearing down the debtors' jails. In January 1979 they killed another despised local landowner, Enrique Brol, of the Finca San Francisco near Cotzal, and the same day briefly took control of Nebaj itself, summoning the whole of the town's population, including the western travellers staying at *Las Tres Hermanas*, to the central plaza, while they denounced the barbaric inequalities of life in the Ixil.

count on it and, as usual in these parts, all the timetables are subject to frequent changes, so check at the terminal before you want to leave. **Getting around** the Ixil triangle has become much easier in the last few years, with two late morning buses running to Chajul (1hr 15min) and one to Cotzal (1hr) on Thursdays and Sundays. Pick-ups, the odd truck and develoment agency four-wheel drives also supplement the buses between Nebaj and Chajul and Cotzal. On market days in Chajul (Tues and Fri) and Cotzal (Wed and Sat), there are also early morning buses leaving Nebaj.

The range of **accomodation** in Nebaj is fairly limited and you'll find little in the way of luxury, although what there is has an inimitable charm and some of the lowest prices in the country. There are few street signs in Nebaj, so you'll have to rely on the gang of children who act as guides and present themselves to new arrivals. The two cheapest options are the brand new *Hospedaje Ilebal Tenam*, three minutes from the plaza on the Chajul/Cotzal road (①), which has simple but very clean rooms and baking hot showers, and the *Hospedaje Las Tres Hermanas*, a block northwest of the plaza (①). Despite its damp rooms, ancient mattresses and a shabby appearance, this is one of Guatemala's most famous and characterful hotels, which put up a virtual who's who of international and

---

Predictably, the army responded with a wave of horrific attacks on the civilian population. Army units swept through the area, committing random atrocities, burning villages and massacring thousands of their inhabitants, including women and children. Neverthless, the strength of the guerrillas continued to grow and in 1981 they again launched an attack on Nebaj, which was now a garrison town. Shortly afterwards the army chief of staff, Benedicto Lucas García (the president's brother), flew into Nebaj and summoned a meeting of the entire population. In a simple speech he warned them that if they didn't "clean up their act" he'd bring five thousand men "and finish off the entire population."

President Lucas Garcia was overthrown by a military coup in early 1982 and the presidency of **General Ríos Montt** saw a radical change in the army's tactics. Ríos Montt used civilian patrols to ensure the loyalty of the people and placed them in the front line of the conflict. Villagers were given ancient M1 rifles and told to protect their communities from the guerrillas. Meanwhile, the army began aggressive sweeps through the highlands, but instead of burning villages and terrorizing the population they brought people back into Nebaj to be fed and eventually settled in new "model" villages. This new approach revealed that many people of the Ixil were in fact determined to remain neutral and had only taken sides in order to ensure their survival. Relatively quickly, whole communities adapted to the new situation and rejected contact with the guerrillas.

The guerrillas were hit extremely hard and for a brief period responded with desperate acts. On June 6, 1982, guerrillas stopped a bus near Cotzal and executed thirteen civil patrol leaders and their wives; eleven days later a guerrilla column entered the village of Chacalté, where the new civil patrol had been particularly active, and killed a hundred people, wounding another thirty-five.

The army's offer of amnesty, twinned with a continuous crackdown on the guerrillas, soon drew refugees out of the mountains: between 1982 and 1984 some 42,000 people turned themselves in, fleeing a harsh existence under guerrilla protection. By 1985 the guerrillas had been driven back into a handful of mountain strongholds in Xeputul, Sumal and Amachel, all to the north and west of Chajul and Cotzal.

Guatemalan journalists during the troubles of the 1970s and 1980s. Slightly more upmarket is the functional and friendly *Hotel Ixil*, on the main road south out of town (②), with large, bare rooms which are a little on the damp side, though the setting in an old colonial house around a courtyard is nice. The smartest place in town is the new *Hotel Posada de Don Pablo*, one block west of the plaza (③), with spotless, pine-trimmed rooms, comfortable beds, private bathrooms and safe parking.

As for **eating**, the best *comedor* in town is *Irene's*, just off the main square, and there are several others in the plaza. The *Maya-Inca*, on 5 C, is owned by a friendly Peruvian/Guatemalan couple and serves delicious Peruvian and local dishes, though the portions are small. In addition, you can always get something to eat at the market. Nebaj's **bank**, *Bancafe*, 2 Av 46, near the market (Mon–Fri 8.30am–4pm, Sat 8am–1pm), exchanges both cash and travellers' cheques.

Walks around Nebaj

In the hills that surround Nebaj there are several beautiful **walks**, with one of the most interesting taking you to the village of **Acul**, two hours away. Starting from the church in Nebaj, cross the plaza and turn to the left, taking the road that goes downhill between a shop and a *comedor*. At the bottom of the dip it divides, and here you take the right-hand fork and head out of town along a dirt track.

Just after you pass the last houses you'll see some pre-Columbian burial mounds to your right. These are still used for religious ceremonies, and if you take a close look you'll find burnt patches marking the site of offerings. Since the mounds are usually planted with maize they can be a bit difficult to spot, but once you get up higher above the town they're easier to make out.

Beyond this the track carries on, switchbacking up a steep hillside, and heads over a narrow pass into the next valley, where it drops down into the village. **ACUL** was one of the original so-called "model villages" into which people were herded after their homes had been destroyed by the army, and despite the spectacular setting – and the efforts of the United Nations, amongst others, to improve the standard of living – it's a sad and weary place. If you walk on through the village and out the other side you arrive at the Finca San Antonio, a bizarre Swiss-style chalet set in a neat little meadow. An Italian family have lived here for more than fifty years, making some of the country's best cheese, and visitors are welcome to have a look around – especially if they buy some produce. José Azzari who founded the *finca* died in 1990, at the ripe old age of 99.

A second, shorter walk takes you to a beautiful little **waterfall**, La Cascada de Plata, about an hour from Nebaj. Take the road to Chajul and turn left just before it crosses the bridge, a kilometre or two outside Nebaj. Don't be fooled by the smaller version you'll come to shortly before the main set of falls.

A third half-day circular walk climbs up the steep eastern edge of the natural bowl that surrounds Nebaj to the village of **Cocop** and back to the main Nebaj–Cotzal road. Starting from *Bancafe*, on 2 Av, in the centre of town, continue until the end of the road, turn right, and then first left downhill to the bridge. Cross the bridge, and continue walking until you reach the pueblo of Xemamatzé on the edge of Nebaj. This village used to be home to a huge internment camp where Ixil villagers who had surrendered to the army were subject to lengthy "repatriation" treatment before being allowed to return to their native villages. In Xemamatzé take the well-trodden trail uphill just after the *Pepsi tienda* sign, which climbs steadily for about an hour to 2300m. Back across the valley there are spectacular views towards Nebaj. When you eventually come to a maize field, bear left and continue round the mountain. The path grips the side of the slope and twists and turns, then gradually starts to descend as the small village of Cocop comes into view below. The village has recently been rebuilt on old foundations, after it was razed to the ground during the civil war, and 98 villagers were massacred by the army. Today it's a pretty little settlement in a delightful position beside a gurgling river, with a single shop where you can buy a warm, fizzy drink. To head back, walk straight ahead from the shop past the Emmanuel church for a lovely hour's stroll along the V-shaped valley through sheep-filled meadows. At the end of the trail is the village of Río Azul on the main Cotzal–Nebaj road from where you can wait for a pick-up, truck or bus, or hike back to Nebaj in an hour an a half.

West to Salquil Grande

Another possible excursion from Nebaj takes you to the village of **SALQUIL GRANDE**, 23km to the west. A road runs out this way, through the village of Tzalbal, and across two huge and breathtaking valleys. New villages, built to replace those burnt to the ground by the army, pepper the hillsides, their tin roofs still clean and rust-free. They are inhabited by people who spent the war years either starving in the mountains or shut away in the refugee camps of Nebaj. **Trucks** run out to Salquil Grande from the market in Nebaj at around 6am on most days, and certainly for the Tuesday market. There's nowhere to stay in the village but the trucks usually return a couple of hours later. Continuing west from Salquil Grande, a very rough road runs some 44km to join up with the main Huehuetenango to Barillas road, a spectacular way of reaching the Paquix junction for the turn-off for Todos Santos.

The landscape around Salquil Grande is supremely beautiful and best enjoyed on foot. A good hike takes you to the little village of **Parramos Grande** in around two hours. Starting from the statue of a soldier on the edge of Salquil Grande, you want to take the path to the right and when this divides take a left through the *milpa*, heading downhill. Along the way you pass a couple of beautiful waterfalls, so if the sun's shining you can always pause for a chilly dip.

San Juan Cotzal and Chajul

To visit the other two towns in the Ixil triangle it's best to coincide your visit with **market** days when there is more traffic on the move (Cotzal's is on Wednesday and Saturday; Chajul's on Tuesday and Friday). On market days, regular morning **buses** leave Nabaj for the two towns from 4am. Buses should return daily to Nebaj from San Juan Cotzal at 6am and 1am, and from Chajul at 11.30am and 12.30pm. In addition, a truck usually leaves Chajul at 3.30pm, though you'll have to share the covered trailer with firewood and vegetables. Pick-ups supplement the buses, as do aid agency and MINUGUA (United Nations) four-wheel drives. Sunday is also a good day to travel because villagers from the other two Ixil towns visit Nebaj for its weekly market, heading back after 10am.

SAN JUAN COTZAL is the closer town to Nebaj, an hour to ninety minutes away depending on the state of the road. The town is beautifully set in a gentle dip in the valley, sheltered beneath the Cuchumatanes and often wrapped in a damp blanket of mist. In the 1920s and 1930s this was the largest and busiest of the three Ixil towns, as it was from here that the fertile lands to the north were colo-

WALKING FROM COTZAL TO CHAJUL

Though there is a newish unpaved road beween Cotzal and Chajul it's also possible to hike (approx 2hr 30min) an indirect route through some beautiful Ixil scenery before joining the road for the last two or three kilometres. From Cotzal church take the road downhill that leaves Cotzal for the *Finca San Francisco*, passing a school and a football pitch on your right. Just before the bridge, leave the road and take the path that follows the Río Tichum for about five minutes, until you reach another bridge. Cross the second bridge and take the left-hand path uphill through maize fields; the right-hand path leads to the village of Xepalma. After thirty minutes you'll reach a ridge, marking the border between two municipalities, from where you can see the white bulk of Chajul's church. Continue down a muddy path through woodland and you'll come to a large fenced-off field. Turn to the left and follow the fence until you reach a large path; turn right here and you'll shortly reach the Cotzal–Chajul road. From here, it's about an hour to Chajul: turn right and follow the road down a small valley before climbing very steeply to the village.

nized. Once a road reached Nebaj in the 1940s, however, Cotzal was somewhat eclipsed, although there is still a higher concentration of *ladinos* here. Cotzal attracts very few Western travellers, so you may find many people assume you're an aid worker or attached to a fundamentalist church.

There is little to do in the town itself but there is some great hill walking closeby. If you want to **stay** there is a small, very basic unmarked *pensión* called *Don Polo* (②), two blocks from the church, or you may find the *farmacía* in the corner of the plaza will rent you a room (①). *La Maguey* **restaurant**, in a front room a block behind the church, serves up reasonable, if bland, food.

Last but by no means least of the Ixil settlements is **CHAJUL**, made up almost entirely of old adobe houses, with wooden beams and red-tiled roofs blackened by the smoke of cooking fires. It is also the most traditional and least bilingual of the Ixil towns. The streets are usually bustling with activity: you'll be met by an army of small children, and the local women gather to wash clothes at the stream that cuts through the middle of the village. Here boys still use blowpipes to hunt small birds, a skill that dates from the earliest of times but is now little used elsewhere. The women of Chajul dress entirely in red, filling the streets with colour, and wear earrings made of old coins strung up on lengths of wool. The traditional red jackets of the men are a rare sight these days. Make sure you visit the shop run by the local weaving co-operative, called *Va'l Vaq Quyol,* between the church and the market, where you will find some of the best quality, handmade textiles in the country at very decent prices.

The colonial church, on the plaza, a huge old structure full of gold leaf and massive wooden beams, is home to the **Christ of Golgotha** and the target of a large pilgrimage on the second Friday of Lent – a particularly good time to be here. The two angels that flank the image were originally dressed as policemen, after a tailor who'd been cured through prayer donated the uniforms so that his benefactor would be well protected. Later they were changed into army uniforms, and recently they've been toned down to look more like boy scouts.

Chajul's plaza was the place where Rigoberta Menchú, in her autobiography (see p.391), describes the public execution of her brother at the hands of the army. According to Menchú, her brother and several other suspected communists and labour organizers were brought before the town's population by the army, all showing signs of hideous torture. She describes the commander delivering an anti-communist lecture then ordering the prisoners to be burnt alive. Although there is no doubt that atrocities took place, painstaking investigation by author David Stoll, and evidence by EGP member Mario Payeras, contradicts Menchú's version of events – eye witnesses testify that the prisoners were machine-gunned, the date of the killings is in dispute, as is the fact that Menchú was there at all. Though the show trial execution was horrific enough under any circumstances, the reliablity of Menchú's account has undoubtedly come into question.

The dirty *Hospedaje Cristina* (①) is a depressing option if you need somewhere to **stay** for the night – ask instead at the post office, where one of the workers rents out rooms. Other families also now rent out beds in their houses to the steady trickle of travellers that come to Chajul; they will find you.

Beyond the triangle: the Ixcán

To the north of the Ixil triangle is a thinly populated area known as the **Ixcán**, which drops away towards the Mexican border to merge with the Lacandon rainforests. Again this area, formerly an EGP stronghold, was heavily fought over until the mid 1990s. The Ixcán has long been one of Guatemala's great untamed frontiers. In the 1960s and 1970s land-hungry migrants from Quiché and Huehuetenango began moving into the area to carve out new farms from the forest. After a few years of extreme hardship and assisted by Maryknoll missionaries, they established thriving communities. The land yielded two crops a year and produced an abundance of fruit, coffee and cardamom. The settlers built health clinics and churches, established a system of radio communication and a transport network and began applying for collective land titles. However, in the early 1970s the EGP moved into the area and the 1980s saw it devastated by bitter fighting, in which virtually every village was burnt to the ground and thousands fled to Mexico.

Now many refugees and ex-guerrillas have returned to the northern Ixcán and there are a number of resettlement camps. The rough route across the very northern part of Ixcán from Playa Grande to Barillas is covered on p.302, though currently no routes link this road with the Ixil.

LAKE ATITLÁN

Lake Como, it seems to me, touches the limit of the permissibly picturesque; but Atitlán is Como with the additional embellishments of several immense volcanoes. It is really too much of a good thing. After a few days of this impossible landscape one finds oneself thinking nostalgically of the English Home Counties.

Aldous Huxley, *Beyond the Mexique Bay* (1934).

Whether or not you share Huxley's refined sensibilities, there's no doubt that Lake Atitlán is astonishingly beautiful, and most people find themselves captivated by its scenic excesses. Indeed the effect is so overwhelming that a handful of gringo devotees have been rooted to its shores since the 1960s. The lake, just three hours from Guatemala City and a few kilometres south of the Pan-American Highway, rates as the country's number one tourist attraction. It's a source of national pride, and some Guatemalans claim that it ranks with the Seven Wonders of the World.

The water itself is an irregular shape, with three main inlets. It measures 18km by 12km at its widest point, and shifts through an astonishing range of blues, steely greys and greens as the sun moves across the sky. Hemmed in on all sides by steep hills and massive volcanoes, it's at least 320m deep and has no visible outlet, draining as it does through an underground passage to the Pacific coast. In the morning the surface of the lake is normally calm and clear, but by early afternoon the *xocomil*, "the wind that carries away sin", blows from the coast, churning the surface and making travel by boat a hair-raising experience. A north wind, say the Maya, indicates that the spirit of the lake is discarding a drowned body, having claimed its soul.

If the physical beauty of the lake is so captivating, the most astonishing aspect of Atitlán is the strength of Maya culture still evident in the lakeside villages. Despite the holiday homes and the thousands of tourists that venture

TOURIST CRIME AROUND LAKE ATITLÁN

Sadly, **crime against tourists**, including armed robbery and rape, is not unknown in the Atitlán area. Visitors, and particularly women, should avoid walking alone, especially at night. If you do plan to walk between the lakeside villages, check first with the tourist office in Panajachel for the latest information (see p.145). Note that incidents are extremely rare outside Panajachel in the more islolated settlements.

here each year, many of the villages in the region remain intensely traditional – **San Antonio Palopó, Santiago Atitlán** and **Sololá**, in the hills above the lake, are some of the very few places in the entire country where Maya men still wear the native *traje* costume. Around the southwestern shores, from Santiago to San Pedro, the indigenous people are **Tzutujil** speakers, the remnants of one of the smaller pre-Conquest tribes, whose capital was on the slopes of the San Pedro volcano. On the other side of the water, from San Marcos to Cerro de Oro, **Cakchiquel** is spoken, marking the western barrier of this tribe.

There are thirteen villages on the shores of the lake, with many more in the hills behind, ranging from the cosmopolitan resort-style **Panajachel** to tiny, isolated **Tzununá**. The villages are mostly subsistence farming communities, and it's easy to hike and boat around the lake staying in a different one each night. The lakeside area has been heavily populated since the earliest of times, but it's only relatively recently that it has attracted large numbers of tourists. For the moment things are still fairly undisturbed, except in Panajachel, and the beauty remains overwhelming, though some of the new pressures are decidedly threatening. The fishing industry, once thriving on the abundance of small fish and crabs, has been crippled by the introduction of **black bass**, which eat the smaller fish and water birds and are, moreover, much harder to catch. These fish stick to the deeper water and have to be speared by divers – their introduction was intended to create a sport-fishing industry. The increase in population has also had a damaging impact on the shores of the lake, as the desperate need to cultivate more land leads to deforestation and accompanying soil erosion.

Beginning in the early 1990s the shores suffered through yet another invasion, as the wealthy Guatemala City crowd abandoned the blackened waters of Lake Amatitlán and moved across to Atitlán. Weekend retreats are still springing up around the shores and Saturday afternoons see the waters dotted with speedboats and skiers. In 1955 the Atitlán basin was declared a national park to preserve its wealth of cultural and natural characteristics, but this seems to have had little effect on development.

You'll probably reach the lake through Panajachel, a small town on the northern shore which is now dominated by tourism. It makes a good base for exploring the surrounding area, either heading across the lake or making day trips to **Chichicastenango, Nahualá, Sololá** and **Iximché**. Panajachel has an abundance of cheap hotels and restaurants and is well served by buses. To get a sense of a more typical Atitlán village, however, travel by boat to Santiago or San Antonió Polopó, while for an established travellers' scene and a surplus of cheap hotels, try **San Pedro**. **Santa Cruz** and **San Marcos** are the places to head for if you're seeking real peace and quiet and some good hikes.

Sololá and around

A couple of kilometres to the west of Los Encuentros, at the El Cuchillo junction, the road for Panajachel branches off the Pan-American Highway. Dropping towards the lake it arrives first at **SOLOLÁ**, the departmental capital and the gateway to the lake, which is perched on a natural balcony some 600m above the water. Overlooked by the majority of travellers, Sololá is, nonetheless, a fascinating place and the **Friday market** (there's also a smaller one on Tuesdays) is one of Central America's finest, a mesmeric display of colour and commerce. Aldous Huxley described the market here as "a walking museum of fancy dress". From as early as 5am the plaza is packed, drawing traders from all over the highlands, as well as thousands of Sololá Maya, the women covered in striped red cloth and the men in their outlandish shirts, woollen aprons and wildly embroidered trousers. Weaving is a powerful creative tradition in the lives of Sololá Maya and each generation develops a distinctive style based upon previous designs.

The town itself isn't much to look at: a wide central plaza with a recently restored clock tower on one side and a modern church on the other. In common with only a few other places in the country, Sololá has parallel indigenous and *ladino* governments, and is one of Guatemala's largest Maya towns. Tradition dominates daily life here and the town is said to be divided into sections, each administered by a Maya clan, just as it was before the Conquest. Little is known about the details of this system, though, and its secrets are well kept. The town's symbol, still to be seen on the back of the men's jacket, is an abstraction of a bat, referring to the royal house of Xahil, who were the rulers of the Cakchiquel at the time of the Conquest. The pre-Conquest site of **Tecpán-Atitlán**, which was abandoned in 1547 when Sololá was founded by the Spanish, is to the north of town.

Another interesting time to visit Sololá is on Sunday, when the **cofradías**, the elders of the Indian religious hierarchy, parade through the streets in ceremonial costume to attend the 10am Mass. They're easily recognizable, carrying silver-tipped canes and wearing broad-brimmed hats with particularly elaborate jackets. Inside the church the sexes are segregated, and the women wear shawls to cover their heads.

Sololá practicalities

There are several simple **hotels** in Sololá: the *Hotel Santa Ana*, a block uphill from the plaza at 6 Av 8–35, has plain rooms around a pleasant courtyard (②); there's the similar *Hotel Paisaje*, also a block above the plaza at 9 C between 6 and 7 avenidas (②); and the *Hotel La Posada del Viajero*, on the plaza, is again basic but a bit overpriced (②). The first two have *comedores*, and there are a few other simple **places to eat** scattered around town, although you can always eat in the market during the day.

There's a **post office** (Mon–Fri 8am–4.30pm) on the plaza and a Banco G&T at 9 C and 5 Av (Mon–Fri 9am–5.30pm, Sat 10am–2pm). For **bus** times refer to the Panajachel schedules, as all buses travelling between Panajachel and Los Encuentros pass through Sololá. There are also minibuses that run regularly between Sololá and Los Encuentros. The last bus to Panajachel passes through Sololá at around 6pm.

Nearby villages

Several other villages can be reached from Sololá, most of them within walking distance. About 8km to the east is **Concepción**, an exceptionally quiet farming village with a spectacularly restored colonial church. The restoration was completed in 1988 and the facade is still a shiny white. The walk out there, along a dirt track skirting the hills above Panajachel, offers superb views across the lake.

Four kilometres to the west of Sololá, along another dirt road and across a deep-cut river valley, **San José Chacayá** has a tiny colonial church with thick crumbling walls but little else. Another 8km further along the track is **Santa Lucía Utatlán**, which can also be reached along a dirt track that branches off the Pan-American Highway. From Santa Lucía the road continues around the lake, set back from the ridge of hills overlooking the water, to Santa María Visitación and **Santa Clara La Laguna**. The latter is connected by a steep trail to San Pablo La Laguna on the lakeshore below: if you're planning to walk to San Pablo via Santa Clara set out early as it's a full day's hike.

On the hillside below Sololá is **San Jorge La Laguna**, a tiny hamlet perched above the lake, whose inhabitants have been chased around the country by natural disasters. The village was founded by refugees from the 1773 earthquake in Antigua and the original lakeside version was swept into the water by a landslide, persuading the people to move up the hill.

Panajachel

Ten kilometres beyond Sololá, separated by a precipitous descent, is **PANAJACHEL**. Over the years what was once a small Maya village has become something of a resort, with a sizeable population of long-term foreign residents, whose numbers are swollen in the winter by an influx of North American seasonal migrants and a flood of tourists. Back in the 1960s and 1970s, Panajachel was the premier Central American hippie hang-out and developed a bad reputation among some sections of Guatemalan society as a haven for drug-taking gringo drop-outs. Today, however, "Pana" is much more integrated into the tourism mainstream and is as popular with Guatemalans (and Mexicans and Salvadoreans) as Westerners. The lotus-eaters and crystal-gazers have not all deserted the town, though – many have simply reinvented themselves as capitalists, owning restaurants and exporting handicrafts. There is much talk about Lake Atitlán being one of the world's few "vortex energy fields", which attracts a perennial population of healers, therapists and masseurs to Panajachel.

Not so long ago (although it seems an entirely different age) Panajachel was a quiet little village of **Cakchiquel** Maya, whose ancestors were settled here after the Spanish crushed a force of Tzutujil warriors on the site. In the early days of the Conquest the Franciscans established a church and monastery in the village, using it as the base for their regional conversion campaign. Today the old village has been enveloped by the new building boom, but it still retains a traditional feel, and most of the Maya continue to farm in the river delta behind the town. The Sunday market, bustling with people from all around the lake, remains oblivious to the tourist invasion.

For travellers Panajachel is one of those inevitable destinations, and although no one ever owns up to actually liking it, everyone seems to stay for a while. The old village is still attractive and although most of the new building is fairly nondescript, its lakeside setting is superb. The main **daytime activity** is hanging out, either wandering the streets, shopping, eating and drinking, or at the **public beach**, where you can swim and sunbathe, or rent a kayak and explore the lake

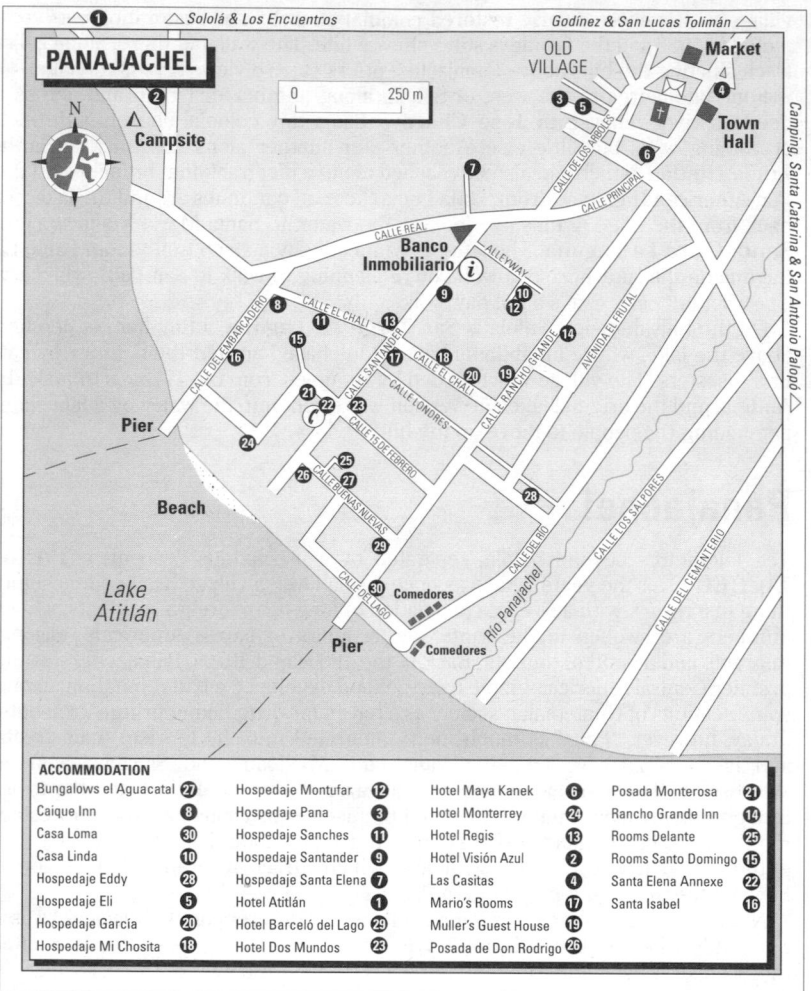

PANAJACHEL

Sololá & Los Encuentros

Godínez & San Lucas Tolimán

OLD VILLAGE

Market

Town Hall

Camping, Santa Catarina & San Antonio Palopó

Campsite

N

0   250 m

Banco Inmobiliario

ALLEYWAY

CALLE REAL

CALLE DE LOS ÁNGELES

CALLE PRINCIPAL

CALLE EL CHALÍ

CALLE DEL EMBARCADERO

CALLE SANTANDER

CALLE EL CHALÍ

CALLE LONDRES

CALLE RANCHO GRANDE

AVENIDA EL FROTAL

Pier

CALLE 15 DE FEBRERO

Beach

CALLE BUENAS NUEVAS

CALLE DEL RÍO

CALLE LOS SALPORES

CALLE DEL CEMENTERIO

Lake Atitlán

CALLE DEL LAGO

Comedores

Río Panajachel

Pier

Comedores

ACCOMMODATION

Bungalows el Aguacatal **27**	Hospedaje Montufar **12**	Hotel Maya Kanek **6**	Posada Monterosa **21**
Caique Inn **8**	Hospedaje Pana **3**	Hotel Monterrey **24**	Rancho Grande Inn **14**
Casa Loma **30**	Hospedaje Sanches **11**	Hotel Regis **13**	Rooms Delante **25**
Casa Linda **10**	Hospedaje Santander **9**	Hotel Visión Azul **2**	Rooms Santo Domingo **15**
Hospedaje Eddy **28**	Hospedaje Santa Elena **7**	Las Casitas **4**	Santa Elena Annexe **22**
Hospedaje Eli **5**	Hotel Atitlán **1**	Mario's Rooms **17**	Santa Isabel **16**
Hospedaje García **20**	Hotel Barceló del Lago **29**	Muller's Guest House **19**	
Hospedaje Mi Chosita **18**	Hotel Dos Mundos **23**	Posada de Don Rodrigo **26**	

for a few hours (mornings are usually calmer). The water, however, is said to be much cleaner on the other side of the lake around San Pedro (see p.155) or Santa Cruz (see p.159). You can also pay a few dollars to use the swimming pool and private beach at *Vision Azul* (see below), in the bay before Panajachel.

Weaving from all over Guatemala is sold with daunting persistence in the streets here. Much of it is of the very highest standards with the weavers themselves travelling down from places like Todos Santos, Nebaj and Chajul to sell their wares. Prices can be high, so bargain hard. The main **market** day is Sunday, when the old village is alive with activity, although things are also busy on Saturday.

Panajachel also makes a comfortable base for exploring the lake and the central highlands. The markets in **Nahualá** on Sunday and **Chichicastenango** on Thursday and Sunday are both within an hour or two's travel, and the ruins at **Utatlán** and **Iximché** can also be visited as day trips.

Arrival and information

Arriving in Panajachel, the bus drops you beside the Banco Inmobiliario, very close to the main drag, C Santander, which runs down to the lakeshore. Straight ahead, up Calle Principal, is the old village. The town is fairly easy to find your way around, though you may find some of Panajachel's streets have been renamed – we have stuck to the older names here, as these are more commonly used. The **Inguat** office is on C Santander (Mon–Sat 9am–5pm; ☎7621392), and has boat and bus schedules posted on its door.

Accommodation

The streets of Panajachel are overflowing with cheap **hotels**, and there are huge numbers of **rooms** to let. Some of the latter look as if they've been left over from the 1960s, their walls adorned with trippy poetry and bizarre drawings. If you're in a group, and planning to stay for a while, then check the noticeboards for **houses to rent**; the Delante bookstore (see Listings) is an excellent place check first, and also has six rooms to rent (on a weekly basis only) in a extremely quiet location, ideal for bookworms.

If you have a tent, first choice is the new **campsite** (☎7622479; $2 per person), on the corner of the road to Santa Catarina and C del Cementerio, over the river bridge. Here, there are kitchen and storage facilities as well as sleeping bags and tents for rent. Second choice is a nice lakeside plot at the *Hotel Visión Azul* (☎ & fax 7621426; $8 for two), where there are also full hook-up facilities, and you get free use of the pool and private beach. Finally you can take your chances on the public beach over the Río Panajachel, where you'll usually find a cluster of fellow campers, but security can be a problem here.

Budget accommodation

Las Casitas, C Principal, at the back of the old village, near the market (☎7621224). Very clean, friendly, safe and quiet rooms, all with private bathrooms and hot water. ③.

Hospedaje Eddy, down an alleyway off Av el Frutal. Friendly atmosphere, double beds and run by a lovely Maya lady. ①.

Hospedaje Eli, Callejón del Pozo, off C de los Arboles (☎7620148). Eight clean, cheap rooms overlooking a pretty garden in a quiet location. ①.

Hospedaje García, C El Chali (☎7622187). Plenty of perfectly reasonable budget rooms and the hot water is reliable. ②.

Casa Linda, down an alley off the top of C Santander. Popular backpackers' retreat where the central garden is undeniably beautiful but the rooms, though clean, are a shade pricey. ②.

Casa Loma, C Rancho Grande (☎7621447). New place near the lake with very inviting pine-trimmed rooms, plus a kitchen and TV if required. Best value in town in this price category. ③.

Mario's Rooms, C Santander (☎7621313) Plenty of basic, clean rooms, some with private bathrooms. Hot water on request for a few quetzals. ②. **Hospedaje Pana**, Callejón del Pozo, off C de los Arboles. Ten clean rooms around a salmon pink courtyard; also has a gym. ①.

TRANSPORT AROUND PANAJACHEL

Panajachel has no terminal – all **buses** arrive and leave from outside the Banco Inmobiliario. Throughout the day **minibuses** shuttle between Panajachel and Los Encuentros, and much of the time it's easier to catch one of these and flag down another bus on the Pan-American Highway. All schedules can be checked at the Inguat office.

Guatemala City (3hr 30min). Rébuli runs nine buses daily from 5am to 2.30pm.

Antigua (3hr). One Rébuli bus daily at 10.45am, or get a minibus to Los Encuentros and catch a bus there via Chimaltenango.

Chichicastenango (1hr 30min). On market days (Thursdays and Sundays), there are seven direct buses starting at 6.30am, and a number of tourist shuttles. On other days take the first bus to Los Encuentros and change there, where there are connections every twenty minutes during daylight hours.

Cocales for Pacific Highway and Tapachula, Mexico (2hr 30min). Buses leave at 6am, 8am, 9.30am, noon & 2pm.

Huehuetenango (4hr). There are no direct services, so take the first bus to Los Encuentros and change there.

Quetzaltenango (2hr 30min). Morales runs buses from Monday to Saturday at 5.30am, 6.15am, 7.30am, 9.30am, 1pm and 2pm. On Sundays there are fewer services, so it may be quicker to get the first bus to Los Encuentros, and change there.

San Antonio Palopó (45min). Buses run daily at 9.15am, and there's also an hourly pick-up from the corner of Calle Principal and the road to Santa Catarina.

San Lucas Tolimán (1hr 30min). Direct services at 6.45am and 4pm, or you can take a bus heading for Cocales and hitch or walk the 2km from the junction.

Santa Catarina (30min). Buses run daily at 9.15am, and there's also hourly pick-up from the corner of Calle Principal and the road to Santa Catarina.

SHUTTLE SERVICES

Antigua (2hr 30min) A tourist shuttle operated by Turansa in Antigua (see p.108) will pick you up from your hotel in Panajachel on Wednesday, Friday and Saturday at 7.30am; the return bus leaves Antigua at 3.30pm. Tickets are available from hotels and shops in Antigua and Panajachel.

Hotel Maya Kanek, C Principal, near the church (☎7621104). Comfortable rooms (all with private showers), set around a cobbled courtyard that doubles as a car park.③.

Hospedaje Mi Chosita, C El Chali. Very bare, small but clean wooden rooms with paper-thin walls. Run by a friendly family, and has a good laundry service. ②.

Hospedaje Montufar, down an alley, off the top of C Santander, next to Casa Linda (☎7620406). Quiet location, spotless rooms and an extremely friendly family. Doubles and triples available. ②.

Hospedaje Pana, Callejón del Pozo, off C de los Arboles. Ten clean rooms around a salmon pink courtyard; also has a gym. ①.

Hospedaje Sanches, C El Chali. Quiet position and the clean rooms are a little larger than most. ①.

Hospedaje Santa Elena, down a path off Calle Real. Very basic bare rooms at correspondingly cheap rates. ①.

Guatemala City (3hr). Shuttles are operated by Panajachel Tourist Services, C Santander, next to the *Hotel Regis* (☎ & fax 7622246).

Chichicastango (1hr). Numerous companies on C Santander offer early morning market day services.

BOATS

There are two **piers** in Panjachel. The pier near the *Hotel Barceló del Lago* serves Santa Catarina, San Antonio Palopó, San Lucas Tomilán, Santiago Atitlán and lake tours. The second pier at the end of C del Embarcadero is for all villages on the northern side of the lake, Santa Cruz, San Marcos, San Juan and San Pedro. Confusing matters somewhat, some of the boats for the northern lakeside start from the *Hotel Barceló del Lago* pier, but all will call at the C del Embarcadero pier to pick up passengers. Unfortunately, rip-offs are the rule for tourists – you'll be asked for triple or quadruple what the locals normally pay, and may well be charged more for the last boat of the day. The Inguat office has a list of boat schedules and prices; we've listed these semi-official rates, that are more expensive than the local price.

Tours of the lake run by the Santa Fe company leave the *Hotel Barceló del Lago* pier at 8.30am; tours run by Santiago depart at 10.30am. Both visit San Pedro, Santiago Atitlán and San Antonio Palopó with plenty of time in each village, returning to Panajachel at 3.30pm and 5pm respectively. Price per person, $7.

Panajachel to Santiago (1hr; $1.20) Boats leave at 5.45am, 8.35am, 9.30am, 10.30am, 1pm, 3pm and 4.30pm, returning at 6am, 7am, 11.45am, 12.30pm, 2pm, 3pm and 4.30pm.

Panajachel to San Pedro (1hr 30min; $1.20). Boats leave at 6am, 7am, 8.20am, 10am, 11am, noon, 2pm, 3pm, 4pm, 6pm, 7pm, returning at 4.45am, 5.30am, 6am, 8am, 8.45am, 10am, noon, 12.30pm, 2pm, 3.45pm and 5pm.

Panajachel to San Antonio (40min; $1.60) Boats leave at 9.30am and 2pm, returning at 1pm.

Panajachel to Santa Catarina (20min; $1.60). Boats leave at 9.30am and 2pm, returning at 1.30pm.

Panajachel to San Lucas (1hr 30min; $2.50) Boats leave at 9.30am and 2pm, returning at noon and 4pm.

Santiago to San Pedro (40min; 80¢). Boats leave at 7am, 9am, 10am, 11am, noon, 1pm, 2pm, 3.30pm and 5pm, returning nine times daily from 6am until 3pm.

Santa Elena Annexe, C 15 de Febrero. Safe, pleasant and ramshackle with an abundance of children and parrots. One of the cheapest places in Pana, though hot showers are extra. ①.

Hospedaje Santander, C Santander (☎7621304). Leafy courtyard, friendly owners and clean, cheap rooms, some with private bathrooms. Recommended. ①.

Rooms Santo Domingo, down a path off C Monterrey. One of the very cheapest places in town set well away from the hustle. Wooden rooms all face a charming little garden or there are more expensive options upstairs with private baths. ①.

Mid-range accommodation

Bungalows el Aguacatal, C Buenas Vistas (☎7621482). These twin-bedroom pre-fab cabins, which sleep four are a good option for families or small groups (some have kitchens). They are just off the beach, but it's essential to book ahead at weekends when prices rise too. ④.

Caique Inn, C del Embarcadero (☎7621205 & fax 7622053). Tranquil position away from the crowds, with a decent-sized swimming pool, and pleasant garden. Large, comfortable rooms with fireplaces. ⑥.

Posada Monterosa, C Monterrey (☎7620055). A new small place which has spotless rooms with bathrooms and safe car parking. ④.

Hotel Monterrey, C Monterrey, on the lakeshore (☎ & fax 7621126). Very faded first-class hotel, which, despite grotty carpets and classic 1970s decor, has a pretty garden and the best private beach. ⑤.

Muller's Guest House, C Rancho Grande (☎7622442; Guatemala City fax 3344294). Extremely tasteful Swiss-owned luxury guest house with quality modern European furnishings and a garden. Recommended. ⑤.

Hotel Dos Mundos, C Santander (☎ & fax 7622078). Italian-owned hotel, just off the main drag, offering comfortable rooms set in a private garden, where there's also a small swimming pool. The attached *Lanterna* restaurant is recommended for authentic Italian cuisine at moderate prices. ⑤.

Rancho Grande Inn, C Rancho Grande (☎7621554; fax 7622247). A longstanding Panajachel institution with very attractive, nicely appointed bungalows, superbly kept gardens and helpful staff. Breakfast included. ⑤.

Hotel Regis, C Santander 3-47 (☎7621149; fax 7621152). Age-old establishment, whose individual bungalows are pleasant and come with cable TV, but best of all are the lovely outdoor thermal pools set in verdant gardens. ⑤.

Santa Isabel, C del Embarcadero (☎7621462). Three well-spaced comfortable bungalows in a relaxing enviroment. ④.

Luxury accommodation

Hotel Atitlán, on the lakeside, 1km west of centre (☎ & fax 7621441& 7621416). Panajachel's nicest hotel with a stunning lakeside location, colonial charm, lovely gardens and a swimming pool. Rooms are very comfortable and tastefully decorated, and cost around $120 double. ⑨.

Hotel Barceló del Lago, right on the lakeshore (☎ 7621555, fax 7621562). Luxury colossus complete with pool, jacuzzi and gym. Has a very corporate "international" flavour, though great volcano views help remind you you're in Guatemala; rooms cost around $110 for a double. ⑨.

Hotel Posada de Don Rodrigo, C Santander, facing the lake (☎ & fax 7622322 or 7622329). Colonial-style hotel where the rooms, though on the small side, have a little more character than most. Pity the staff, forced to wear ridiculous mock traditional uniforms. Right in the heart of things, with the pool and ugly waterslide overlooking the lake. ⑧.

Eating, drinking and entertainment

Panajachel has an abundance of **restaurants**, all catering to the cosmopolitan tastes of its floating population – you'll have no trouble finding tasty Chinese, Indian, Italian, Mexican and Mediterranean dishes. For really cheap and authentically Guatemalan food there are plenty of *comedores* on and just off the beach promenade and around the market.

Cafés and restaurants

Bombay, in the shopping arcade just past *Al Chisme*, C Los Arboles. Eclectic vegetarian food which, despite the name, has nothing Indian about it. Especially good are the *gado-gado*, epic pitta bread sandwiches (try the falafel), and organic coffee. Closed Mon.

Las Chinitas, halfway down C Santander. Excellent pan-Asian cuisine served on a pretty patio. The moderately priced menu includes dishes influenced by Indonesia, China, Thailand and Japan. Closed Mon.

Al Chisme, C Los Arboles. Very popular with gringos: a smart, European-style restaurant and bar adorned with black and white photographs of former customers. Delicious food including sandwiches, crêpes, steaks, curried shrimps and pasta, but all a little pricey. Closed Wed.

Circus Bar, C Los Arboles. Pizza is the speciality here but it also does steaks, salads and pasta and a daily set menu. Prices are moderate and there's live music in the evenings.

Comedor Costa Sur, near church in old town. Clean and attractive *comedor*, bedecked with loud Mexican blankets. Great breakfasts, lunchtime dishes and *licuados*.

Deli, C Principal, **Deli 2** and **Delicafé**, both on C Santander. Excellent range of salads, sandwiches, pastries, bagels, cakes, wine and tea. *Deli* and *Deli 2* have nice gardens and classical music.

Restaurante Jhanny, halfway down C Rancho Grande. Ignore the fairy lights and head inside for a superb Guatemalan-style *menú del día* ($2.50), at tables arranged around a little garden.

The Last Resort, C el Chali. One of the most popular places in Panajachel, it looks vaguely like an English pub but serves the best American buffet breakfasts in town. Also has a vast menu of pasta, steaks and vegetarian dishes, all served in huge portions.

Libelula, C Santander. Painted aquamarine, this café looks like a beach bar but serves healthy snacks like houmous and falafel sandwiches and tremendous (if pricey) smoothies.

Mario's, C Santander. A limited range of low cost food, including huge salads, delicious yoghurt and pancakes.

Sevananda, in the shopping arcade, just past *Al Chisme*, C Los Arboles. Popular vegetarian restaurant in the same arcade as the *Bombay*, serving Indian and Thai curries, tempeh and tofu burgers. Closed Sun.

La Terraza, above Inguat, at the top of C Santander. The finest restaurant on the lake and one of the best in the country, serving a captivating collection of European- and Asian-influenced cuisine. Expensive.

Yalanki, C Santander. Panajachel's best streetside bar/café with tasty snacks, barbequed meat, beer and good music.

Nightlife

There are three **video bars** each showing English-language films: the *Grapevine* on C Santander, one in the *Carrot Chic* restaurant at the top end of C los Arboles, and *Café Cinema*, on the same street. The best place for **drinking** is *The Last Resort*, on C el Chali, where you can also play table tennis, or *Ubu's Cosmic Cantina*, behind the *Sevananda* restaurant on C los Arboles, with a big screen for sports fans, movies buffs and news addicts. C los Arboles acts loosely as Panajachel's *Zona Viva* (Lively zone), and it's along here that you'll also find the long-running *Circus Bar* and the new *El Aleph* bar/café, both of which have good **live music**. Also along this road but on the other side is the long-established *Chapiteau* **nightclub**. Finally there's a **pool hall** in the old village, near the post office.

Listings

Alternative therapies The Rituales y Reliquias Wellness Center, in Los Patios Plaza, C Santander, offers healing services, classes and spiritual tours, including "authentic channelling" and "emotional-release meditation".

Bicycle rental Moto Servicio Quiché, C los Arboles and C Principal, rents mountain bikes for $1 an hour, $5 a day.

Banks Banco Inmobiliario is at the junction of C Santander and C Principal (Mon–Fri 9am–7pm Sat 9am–noon); Banco Industrial, on C Santander, has a 24-hour ATM for Visa card holders; the AT Travel Agency and *Hotel Regis,* both on C Santander, will advance money on Mastercard.

Books Delante, down an alley off C Buenas Vistas, has a comprehensive selection of secondhand titles; Galería Bookstore, upper floor, C Los Arboles, stocks a reasonable selection of secondhand books and a few interesting new books in English.

Doctor Dr Edgar Barreno speaks good English; his surgery is down the first street that branches to the right off C Los Arboles (☎7621008).

Email *C@fenet*, at street level in the same building as Telgua, near the junction of C Santander and C del Chali, will send and receive email.

Health Food The Centro Naturista, C los Arboles 27 (Mon–Sat 9am–noon only) has a good selection of healthy essentials.

Language schools In general Panajachel isn't a particularly good place to study but Panatitlán, C de la Navidad 0-40 (fax 7621426), and EEP, C 14 de Febrero (☎7622637; fax 7621196) both have reasonable reputations.

Laundry Lavanderia Automatico, C los Arboles (Mon–Sat 7.30am–6pm) charges $4 for a full load washed, dried and folded.

Motorbikes Moto Servicio Queche, C los Arboles and C Principal, rents 185cc bikes for $6 an hour; $25 for 24 hours; $100 for the week

Phones and faxes Check first with businesses up and down C Santander for the best rates, many advertise discounted calls; otherwise there's always Telgua (daily 7am–midnight), near the junction of C Santander and C del Chali.

Police On the plaza in the old village (☎7621120).

Post office In the old village, down a side street beside the church (Mon–Fri 8am–4.30pm). For a long-established and reliable parcel service, try Get Guated Out, upstairs inside the Comercial El Pueblito on C Los Arboles (☎ & fax 7622015).

Shopping Panajachel has dozens of shops and stalls selling a huge range of ethnic trousers, shirts, waistcoats and *huipiles*, on C Santander alone.

Taxis Usually wait outside the post office, or you can call one on ☎7621571.

Water sports Canoes, kayaks and windsurfers can be rented on the main beach. Scuba divers can dive the lake with ATI Divers (see p.160).

Around the lake

The villages that surround the lake are all easily accessible. For an afternoon's outing, head along the shore southeast of Panajachel to **San Antonio** and **Santa Catarina Palopó**. If you want to spend a day or two exploring the area then it's well worth crossing the lake to **Santiago**, and going on to **San Pedro**. It's perfectly feasible to walk round the whole lake in four to five days; alternatively, you could cut out a section or two by catching a boat between villages. Perhaps the finest **walking** is on the western side, between San Pedro and Santa Cruz (around a six-hour hike). These southern and western shores are by far the most beautiful and it would be a shame to visit the lake without seeing them.

The eastern shore

There are two roads around the lake's eastern shore from Panajachel: one clings to the shoreline while the other runs parallel up along the ridge of hills. Beside the lake, backed up against the slopes, are a couple of villages, the first of which, **SANTA CATARINA PALOPÓ**, is just 4km from Panajachel. The people of Santa Catarina used to live almost entirely by fishing and trapping crabs, but these days the black bass has put an end to all that and they've turned to farming and migratory work, with many of the women travelling to Panajachel and Antigua to peddle their weaving. The womens' *huipiles* here are unusual in that they have dazzling zigzags in vibrant shades of turquoise or purple, though the traditional design was predominantly red with tiny geometric designs of people and animals. The changes are partly due to an American who visited the village in the 1970s and commissioned a *huipil* to be made in purple, blue and green as opposed to the traditional colours. These new shades became very popular in the village and are now worn almost universally.

On the outskirts of the village, much of the shoreline has been bought and developed by the wealthy, and great villas, ringed by impenetrable walls and razor wire, have come to dominate the view. Very much a part of this invasion is the new hotel *Villa Santa Catarina* (☎7621291; ⑦), which has opened on the lakeshore, complete with 32 rooms, two banqueting halls, a pool and superb views of the lake. Continuing on around the lake you'll pass the currently closed *Hotel Bella Vista,* and then just as the steep profile of San Antonio comes into view the road dips, and there is a beautiful secluded little beach almost hidden among the reeds. San Antonio is a further 2km from here.

Two kilometres on from the beach, **SAN ANTONIO PALOPÓ** is a larger and more traditional village, squeezed in beneath a steep hillside. The village is on the tour group itinerary, which has encouraged the inhabitants to become a bit pushy, eager to sell their weavings. Despite the persistant sales techniques, San Antonio is quite interesting and certainly traditional. The hillsides above the village are well irrigated and terraced, reminiscent of rice paddies, and most of the villagers still wear the traditional *traje*. The whitewashed central church is worth a look: just to the left of the entrance are two ancient bells, one almost completely cracked in two, while inside is a model of the birth of Jesus, San Antonio-style, with Joseph wearing the village costume.

The best way to visit the two villages is on foot. Catch a bus from Panajachel towards Godínez, and get off at the *mirador* about a kilometre before Godínez. From here you can enjoy some of the best lake views of all, and there are various paths that lead to San Antonio (about a thirty-min walk) through vegetable terraces of spring onions and tomatoes. It's a ninety minute walk from San Antonio, through Santa Catarina, back to Panajachel, though you may well be able to hitch some of this distance in a pick-up. If you do plan to travel this way, check the current situation with the tourist office in Panajachel before setting out, as the area around Godínez has been the scene of a number of robberies and attacks on tourists. Alternatively, you can stick to the lower road that runs through the villages themselves. A single **bus** leaves Panajachel for San Antonio at 9.15am, but a number of pick-ups also ply this route (approximately every hour, with the last one returning to Panajachel from San Antonio at 5pm).

If you decide **to stay** in San Antonio there are two options: the fairly upmarket *Hotel Terrazas del Lago* (☎7621288; ⑤), down by the water, has beautiful views, although the owner, Feliks, a Polish expatriate, tends to be a little picky about when he serves meals. Otherwise you can stay in the very simple but clean *pensión* (①) owned by Juan Lopez Sanchez near the entrance to the village. For **food**, the *comedor* below the church serves a decent cheap meal.

The higher road – to Godínez and beyond to San Lucas Tolimán

The higher of the two roads heads back into the delta behind Panajachel, before climbing up above the lake to **SAN ANDRÉS SEMETABAJ**, where there's a fantastic ruined colonial church. A path opposite the church's main entrance leads back to Panajachel, winding down through fields and coffee bushes – a nice walk of an hour or so. Beyond San Andrés the road curves around the edge of the ridge, offering an incredible sweeping view of the lake below and the irregular cone of the Tolimán volcano opposite, and arriving eventually in Godínez. A short way before is the *mirador* mentioned above, from where paths leads down to the lakeside village of San Antonio Palopó.

At **GODÍNEZ**, a ramshackle and wind-blown village, the road divides, one way running out to the Pan-American Highway (through Patzicía and Patzún – best avoided, this is a dangerous road for attack and robbery), and the other on around the lake to the village of **SAN LUCAS TOLIMÁN** in the southeast corner. Set apart from the other villages in many ways, this is probably the least attractive of the lot. The surrounding land is almost all planted with coffee, which dominates the flavour of the place. The indigenous people take a poor second place to the sizeable *ladino* population, and the easy-going atmosphere of the lake is tempered by the influence of the Pacific coast. The setting, however, is as spectacular as always. The village is at the back of a small inlet of reed beds, with the Tolimán **volcano** rising above. Both the Tomilán and Atitlán volcanoes can be climbed from here, though taking a guide is recommended as the trails are difficult to find – ask at your hotel or the town hall. The main **market** day here is on Friday, which is certainly the best time to drop by, although unfortunately it clashes with the market in Santiago.

If you need somewhere **to stay**, there's the pretty, comfortable *Hotel Villa Real Inter* on 7 Av 1–84 (☎7220102; ③) with hot showers, safe parking and a restaurant, or the *Hotel Brisas del Lago*, down by the lake (③), which has similar facilities. For a good, cheap deal, the best place is the friendly, clean and good value *Cafetería Santa Ana* (①). There are a number straightforward places to **eat**, of which *Café Tomilán* is perhaps the best. San Lucas is the junction of the coast road and the road to Santiago Atitlán, and a regular flow of **buses** thunder through in both directions. On the whole, buses head out towards Cocales and the coast in the early morning, with the last bus at about 2.30pm. The return buses make their way back to Santiago in the afternoon with the last one passing through San Lucas at around 5.30pm. There are also five daily buses between here and Panajachel (1hr 30min) running mostly in the morning – the last one leaves at 2pm. **Boats** leave San Lucas for Panjachel at noon and 4pm (1hr 30min; $2.50) calling in at San Antonio and Santa Catarina on the way. There is sometimes also an early morning service, but always check schedules at the dock first.

Santiago Atitlán

On the other side of the lake, **SANTIAGO ATITLÁN** is set to one side of a sheltered horseshoe inlet, overshadowed by the cones of the San Pedro, Atitlán and Tolimán volcanoes. It's the largest and most important of the lakeside villages, and also one of the most traditional, being the main centre of the Tzutujil-speaking Maya. At the time of the conquest the Tzutujil had their fortified capital, **Chuitinamit-Atitlán**, on the slopes of San Pedro, while the bulk of the population lived spread out around the site of today's village. Alvarado and his crew, needless to say, destroyed the capital and massacred its inhabitants, assisted this time by a force of Cakchiquel Maya, who arrived at the scene in some three hundred canoes.

Today Santiago is an industrious but relaxed sort of place, in a superb setting, and if you're planning a trip around the lake it's probably best to spend the first night either here or in San Pedro. During the day the town becomes fairly commercial, its **main street**, which runs from the dock to the plaza, lined with weaving shops. There's nothing like the Panajachel overkill, but the persistence of underage gangs can still be a bit much, particularly during the Friday morning **market**. By mid-afternoon, once the ferries have left, things revert to normal and the whole village becomes a lot more friendly.

There's little to do in Santiago other than stroll around soaking up the atmosphere, though the old colonial Catholic **church** is worth a look for its interesting Maya religious detail. The huge altarpiece, carved when the church was under *cofradía* control, culminates in the shape of a mountain peak and a cross, which symbolizes the Maya world tree. In the middle of the floor is a small hole which villagers believe to be the centre of the world. The church is also home to a stone memorial commemorating Father Stanley Rother, an American priest who served in the parish from 1968 to 1981, and was a committed defender of his parishioners in an era when in his own words, "shaking hands with an Indian has become a political act". Branded a communist by President García, he was assassinated by a paramilitary death squad. His body was returned to his native Oklahoma for burial, but not before, with his family's consent, his heart was removed and buried in the church of Santiago Atitlán.

HOLY SMOKE

Easter celebrations are particularly special in Santiago, and as Holy Week draws closer the town comes alive with expectation and excitement. **Maximón** maintains an important role in the proceedings. On the Monday of Holy Week his image is taken to the lakeshore where it is washed, on the Tuesday he's dressed, and on the Wednesday the image is housed in a small chapel in the plaza. Here he waits until Good Friday, when the town is the scene of a huge and austere religious procession, the plaza packed out with everyone dressed in their finest traditional costume. Christ's image is paraded solemnly through the streets, arriving at the church around noon, where it's tied to a cross and raised above the altar. At around 3pm it's cut down from the cross and placed in a coffin born by penitents, who emerge from the church for a symbolic confrontation in the plaza between Christ and Maximón, who is carried out of an adjoining chapel by his bearer.

The presence of Maximón, decked out in a felt hat and Western clothes, with a cigar in his mouth, is scorned by reforming Catholics and revered by the traditionalists. The precise origin of the saint is unknown, but he's also referred to as San Simón, Judas Iscariot and Pedro de Alvarado, and always seen as an enemy of the church. Some say that he represents a Franciscan friar who chased after young Indian girls, and that his legs are removed to prevent any further indulgence. "Max" in the Mam dialect means tobacco, and Maximón is always associated with *ladino* **vices** such as smoking and drinking; more locally he's known as *Rij Laj*, the powerful man with a white beard. Throughout the year he's looked after by a *cofradía*; if you feel like dropping in to pay your respects to him ask for "*La Casa de San Simón*", and someone will show you the way. Take along a packet of cigarettes and a bottle of *Quezalteca* for the ever-thirsty saint and his minders, who will ask you to make a contribution to fiesta funds. For details on visiting San Simón in Zunil and for a warning about the gravity of the process, see p.176.

As is the case in many other parts of the Guatemalan highlands, the Catholic Church in Santiago is locked in bitter rivalry with several evangelical sects, who are building churches here at an astonishing rate. Their latest construction, right beside the lake, is the largest structure in town. Folk Catholicism also plays an important role in the life of Santiago and the town is well known as one of the few places where Maya still pay homage to **Maximón**, the drinking and smoking saint (see p.153).

The traditional **costume** of Santiago, still worn a fair amount, is both striking and unusual. The men wear long shorts which, like the women's *huipiles*, are white- and purple-striped, intricately embroidered with birds and flowers. The women also wear a *xk'ap*, a band of red cloth approximately 10m long, wrapped around their heads, which has the honour of being depicted on the 25 centavo coin. Sadly this headcloth is going out of use and on the whole you'll probably only see it at fiestas and on market days, worn by the older women.

Around Santiago: volcanoes and the nature reserve

The land around Santiago is mostly volcanic, with only the odd patch of fertile soil mixed in with the acidic ash. Farming, fishing and the traditional industry, the manufacture of *cayucos* (canoes), are no longer enough to provide for the population, and a lot of people travel to the coast, or work on the coffee plantations that surround the volcano. The Tolimán and Atitlán **volcanoes** can both be climbed from here (or San Lucas Tomilán), but you'll need up to a couple of days to make it to the top of the latter. It's always best to take a guide to smooth the way as there have been robberies. If you're looking for a guide, ask in the hotel *Chi-Nim-Ya* (see below), or at one of the restaurants.

If you're here for the day then you can walk out of town along the track to San Lucas Tolimán, or rent a **canoe** and paddle out into the lake – just ask around at the dock. To the north of Santiago is a small island which has been designated as a **nature reserve**, originally for the protection of the *poc*, or **Atitlán grebe**, a flightless water bird. The *poc* used to thrive in the waters of the lake but two factors have now driven it into extinction: the overcutting of the reeds where it nests and the introduction of the fierce black bass, which eat the young birds – although the reserve is surrounded by an underwater fence to keep out the marauding fish. Despite the disappearance of the *poc*, the island is still a beautiful place to spend an hour or two and is an interesting destination if you're paddling around in a canoe.

Practicalities

Daily **boats** to Santiago leave from Panajachel seven times a day betwen 5.45am and 4.30pm, returning between 6am and 4.30pm – the trip takes about an hour (see p.147 for full details). The village is also well connected by **bus** to most places except Panajachel; buses depart six times daily between 2.30am and 2pm from Santiago's central plaza and head via San Lucas Tolimán and Cocales to Guatemala City.

Thanks to the steady flow of tourists, Santiago offers the full range of **accommodation**. A longstanding favourite among backpackers is the *Hotel Chi-Nim-Ya* (☎7217131; ②), a two-storey, old wooden building on the left as you enter the village from the lake. Some of its comfortable rooms come with superb views and private bath. For those on a really tight budget, the *Pensión Rosita* (①), beside the church, offers simple rooms, hot water and a *comedor*. Higher up the scale, the good value *Hotel Tzutuhil*, in the centre of the village (☎7217174; ②), is a five-

---

THE EXPULSION OF THE ARMY FROM SANTIAGO ATITLÁN

Santiago Atitlán's recent history, like that of so many Guatemalan villages, is marked by trouble and violence. The village has assumed a unique role, however, as the first in the country to successfully **expel the armed forces**. Relations between the army and the village had been strained since a permanent base was established there in the early 1980s, when the ground above the village was used extensively by ORPA guerrillas. The army accused the villagers of supporting the insurgents and attempted to terrorize the population into subservience. Throughout the 1980s villagers were abducted, tortured and murdered – a total of around three hundred were killed over eleven years.

Under civilian rule the guerrilla threat dropped off considerably and the people of Santiago grew increasingly confident and resentful of the unnecessary army presence. Matters finally came to a head on the night of December 1, 1990, when two drunken soldiers shot a villager. The men fled to the army base on the outskirts of the village but were followed by an unarmed crowd that eventually numbered around two thousand. The six hundred soldiers inside the garrison clearly believed they were about to be overwhelmed and opened fire on the crowd, killing thirteen people, including three children, and wounding another twenty. After this incident some twenty thousand villagers signed a petition calling for the expulsion of the army from Santiago and, after intense international pressure, the army finally withdrew, shutting down the base.

Difficulties then arose with the police, when, on December 6, the local civil patrol discovered a group of policemen on a suspicious night-time mission. A mob soon surrounded the police station and the police were similarly forced to leave. New recruits were sent from Guatemala City to replace them, however, but for two weeks the residents refused to sell them any food and it was a month before they agreed to allow them to use the public toilet – for a monthly fee of $4.

In June 1991, Santiago's example was followed by neighbouring San Lucas Tolimán, where the killing of a community leader by a soldier led to the army's expulsion. Other villages, in more sensitive areas, have also taken steps, but have yet to succeed. In Joyabaj a mass rally in February 1992 denounced the presence of the army base as a "physical and moral danger" to the community, and early in 1993 villagers in Chajul called for the removal of the army base there.

---

storey concrete building with spectacular views from the top floor and a restaurant, while the *Posada de Santiago*, on the lakeshore 1km south of the village (☎ 7028462; fax 7217167; ⑤) is a fine American-owned luxury hotel and restaurant with rooms in stone cabins, each with its own log fire.

There are three **restaurants** at the entrance to the village, just up from the dock. The *Buen Samaritano* is the cheapest, then comes the *Restaurant Regiemontano* and finally the slightly smarter *Restaurant El Gran Sol*. In the centre of the village you can eat at the *Hotel Tzutuhil*, or if you really want to dine in style, then head out to the restaurant in the *Posada de Santiago*.

San Pedro La Laguna

Around the other side of the San Pedro volcano is the village of **SAN PEDRO LA LAGUNA**, which has now usurped Panajachel to become the pivotal centre of Guatemala's travelling scene. This isn't Goa, but more than anywhere else in Guatemala, it has a distinctive bohemian feel about it. Despite a rather maniacal

evangelical presence, things seem very mellow in San Pedro, though it has not always been so. Crack cocaine arrived here in the early 1990s, and the locals got so fed up with wasted gringos that they wrote to a national newspaper demanding that the freaks leave their village. Today things have settled down again, and the mostly evangelical locals and the travellers seem to rub along reasonably well together.

Again, the setting is spectacular, with the San Pedro volcano rising to the east and a ridge of steep hills running behind the village. To the left of the main beach, as you look towards the lake, a line of huge white boulders juts out into the water – an ideal spot for an afternoon of swimming and sunbathing. Tradition isn't as powerful here and only a few elderly people, mostly men, wear the old costume, although there is a sense of permanence in the narrow cobbled streets and old stone houses. The people of San Pedro have a reputation for driving a hard bargain when trading their coffee and avocados, and have managed to buy up a lot of land from neighbouring San Juan, with whom there's endless rivalry. They're also famed for the *cayucos* (canoes) made from the great cedar trees that grow on the slopes of the San Pedro volcano.

The **San Pedro volcano**, which towers above the village to a height of some 3020m, is largely coated with tropical forest and can be climbed in four to five hours. Any of the underage guides will be able to show you the trail (Andres Adonias Cotuc Cite, who makes a living collecting wood on the volcano, is highly recommended); get an early start in order to see the views at their best and avoid the worst of the heat. The peak itself is also ringed by forest, which blocks the view over San Pedro, although an opening on the south side gives excellent views of Santiago. If you'd rather do something a little more relaxing, **horses** can be rented for around $2.50 an hour, and **canoes** for a great deal less, or you could just soak yourself at the **thermal baths** (open late afternoon and early evening), whose American owner also serves great organic food.

Accommodation

San Pedro has some of the cheapest accomodation in Latin America, with a number of basic, clean guest houses that almost all charge less than $2 a person per night. There's nothing in the way of luxury. If you plan to stay around for a while then you might want to consider **renting a house**, which works out incredibly cheap.

Posada Casa Domingo. Very simple, basic rooms in a quiet hotel, with magnificent volcano views over the neighbouring maize fields. ①.

Casa Elena, turn left after Nick's Place. Six simple rooms all with twin beds, some right on the lakeshore. Owned by a nice Maya family. ①.

Hotel Puerto Bello, turn left after Nick's Place. Excellent budget hotel with really cheap rates, hot showers and a friendly owner. A good deal for solo travellers. ①.

Hotel Sakari. The smartest place in town – modern and clean with four tiled rooms all with private bath and hot water. ①.

Hospedaje San Francisco. Clean rooms, a nice little patio and good long-term rates. ①.

Hotel San Pedro, up the road from the Santaigo pier, next door to the *Villa Sol*. Clean rooms grouped around a central courtyard, some with private bath. ②.

Hotel Ti'Kaaj, close to the Santiago pier. The rooms may be the same as everywhere else, but the setting is better in a beautiful garden filled with orange trees and hammocks. ①.

Hotel Valle Azul, turn right at the Panajachel pier. Ugly new double-decker addition to the lakeshore. However, views are exellent from the rooms, which are plain, clean and good value, some also with private bathrooms. ①.

Hotel Villa Sol, beside the Santiago pier. Twin deck concrete block with plain clean rooms, some with bathroom. Palm trees and a nice lawn add a little green relief. ②.

Hospedaje Xocomil. Spotless rooms grouped around a little garden, plus reliable hot water. ①.

Eating and drinking

The steady flow of gringo travellers has given San Pedro's **cafés** and **restaurants** a decidedly international flavour and most places are excellent value for money. Vegetarians are well catered for, and there are a few typical Guatemalan *comedores* in the centre of the village and by the Santiago pier. For **drinks**, most people head to *Nick's Place*, *Tort's Bar* (happy hour 6–8pm) or the *Ti'Kaaj*.

Comedor Francés. Very reasonably priced gallic fare – coq-au-vin is less than $2 and the crêpes are delicious.

Restaurant al Mesón, close to the Panajachel pier. Thatched *cabañas* shelter a good restaurant serving chicken platters and sandwiches. A great daytime haunt for sitting on the grassy verges and watching the boats come and go.

Nick's Place, prime position by the Panajachel pier. Free movies upstairs and good value grub (chicken and chips costs $2) make this the most popular place in the village.

Pinocchio, between the two piers. Well-established Italian place where you can feast on bruscetta and pasta.

Restaurant Rosalinda. Excellent *comedor*, serving fresh lake fish, grilled meats and with a warm welcome.

Restaurant Ti'Kaaj, opposite the eponymous hotel. Stunning views of the lake and volcanoes from the upper floor, and a lovely garden out front too. Great breakfasts, pasta, and a nice bar.

Comedor Ultima Cena, in the centre of the village. Not just *comedor* nosh, but also pizza and pancakes.

Restaurant Valle Azul. Nice position overlooking the lake, popular for daytime snacks and drinks.

Moving on

The last **boat** to Panajachel leaves at 5pm, though you'll be charged double the usual fare as it's the last; for a detailed schedule see p.147. Two early morning **buses** to Guatemala City (4hr) and one to Quetzaltenango (2hr 30min) struggle along the road that runs along the ridge above the western shore of the lake. Though these journeys make interesting trips, they are hardly the most convenient or comfortable way to travel – you're better off getting the boat to Panajachel and taking a bus from there.

The western shore

The **western side** of the lake is the only part that remains largely inaccessible to cars. From San Pedro a rough dirt road runs as far as Tzununá, from where a spectacular path continues all the way to Sololá. Most of the boats between San Pedro and Panajachel call at all the villages en route but the best way to see this string of isolated settlements is **on foot**; it makes a fantastic day's walk. Most of the way a narrow strip of level land is wedged between the water and the steep hills behind, but where this disappears the path is cut into the slope with dizzying views of the lake below. At several of the villages along the way *tiendas* sell Coke and biscuits, so there's no need to carry water. To walk from San Pedro to Santa Cruz takes between five and six hours, so you might want to take a boat as far as San Marcos (most boats between Panajachel and San Pedro call in here), and walk from there to Santa Cruz – the most interesting section – and finish the day by returning to Panajachel by boat. If you want some real peace and quiet this is the section of the lake to head for and there are some excellent **places to stay** in both San Marcos and Santa Cruz.

From San Pedro you follow a dirt road for 2km to **SAN JUAN LA LAGUNA**, which sits at the back of a sweeping bay surrounded by shallow beaches – the area is known as *Aguas Cristalinas*. The village of San Juan specializes in the weaving of *petates*, mats made from lake reeds, and is home to a large weaving co-op called *Las Artesanas de San Juan*, which you can look round; if you walk from the dock, it's signposted on the left. There are plenty of simple places to eat in San Juan – *Comedor Chi Nimaya*, close to the dock, has tasty *carne asada* and good views of the lake, while *Pizzeria Robert* serves pizza and pasta as well as the usual *comedor* food.

Leaving the lakeside here, a trail leads high up above the village to Santa Clara La Laguna, which is connected to Sololá by a seldom-used road. The lakeside road, however, runs on through coffee plantations to **SAN PABLO LA LAGUNA**, where the traditional speciality is the manufacture of rope from the fibres of the maguey plant; you can sometimes see great lengths being stretched and twisted in the streets.

After San Pablo the villages start to shrink, starting with **SAN MARCOS LA LAGUNA**, about two hours' walk from San Pedro. Tranquil San Marcos, little more than a few houses and **hotels** loosely clustered around a small, ancient church, has a decidedly "New Age" feel, thanks to the presence of the *Pirámides* yoga and meditation retreat (fax 7622080; $8 per person per day including courses and accommodation). The grounds of the retreat are beautiful, the *cabañas* are comfortable and the vegetarian food delicious. San Marcos has a number of other accommodation possibilities, including the excellent *Posada Schumann*, just off the lake (☎3604049, 3392683 in Guatemala City; cellular phone 2022216; ④), which is solar-powered and has three beautiful stone bungalows with stupendous volcano and lake views, and four rooms; there's also a sauna and a good restaurant. *Hotel Paco Real* (fax 7629168; ②) has a good choice of well-priced chalets and rooms, and hot water in the immaculate communal bathrooms, while *Hotel la Paz* (☎7029168; ④) has three nice bungalows under the shade of a giant mango tree (bargain for a good rate), a good vegetarian restaurant and a sauna. Although there are no *comedores* in San Marcos, all the above hotels have **restaurants**, and there's a brilliant gringo-run **bakery** that bakes wholemeal bread. To get to any of the places listed above from the jetty, turn left (west) and walk along the lakeshore path for 300m, then turn to the right by the signposts beside the *Posada Schumann*.

Beyond San Marcos, the villages en route have a greater feeling of isolation, and you'll find the people surprised to see outsiders and eager for a glimpse of passing gringos. Nowhere is this more true than in **TZUNUNÁ**, the next place along the way, where the women run from oncoming strangers, sheltering behind the nearest tree in giggling groups. They wear beautiful red *huipiles* striped with blue and yellow on the back. The village originally sat at the lakeside, but after it was badly damaged by a flood in 1950 the people rebuilt their homes on the higher ground. Here the road indisputably ends, giving way to a narrow path cut out of the steep hillside, which can be a little hard to follow as it descends to cross small streams and then climbs again around the rocky outcrops.

The next village is **Jaibalito**, a ragged-looking place lost amongst the coffee bushes, from where a glorious, easy-to-follow path grips the steep hillside for another couple of hours to **SANTA CRUZ LA LAGUNA**. Set well back from the lake on a shelf 100m or so above the water, Santa Cruz is the largest of the villages that line the western shore. There isn't much to see here apart from a fine sixteenth century church, and most people spend their time walking, swimming or just chilling out with a book. On the shore, opposite a line of wooden jetties, the *Iguana Perdida* (①–②) has fairly basic **accommodation**, ranging from a dorm to twin-bed doubles with lake views, but with the most convivial atmosphere in Lake Atitlán. Its gorgeous, peaceful site overlooking the lake and volcanoes, and the socializing and storytelling really make the place – evening dinner is a three-course communal affair for $5. The *Iguana* is also home to Lake Atitlan's only **dive school**, ATI Divers, a professional PADI outfit that trains all levels from non-divers up to assistant instructor level. Next door, the *Hotel Arca de Noé* (④) is slightly more expensive and comfortable with attractive rooms and excellent home cooking. Just behind the *Iguana*, the *Hospedaje García* (②) has simple, clean rooms and, on the other side, the *Posada Abaj* (③) has the one of the finest gardens on the lake, good food and comfortable rooms, though it can lack a little atmosphere. There are **no phones** in Santa Cruz; use the communal fax number instead (7621196), and try and book a few days ahead.

Beyond Santa Cruz there are two ways to reach Panajachel, whether by boat or on foot. Boats travelling between Panajachel and San Pedro stop here, or you can rent a boat to Panajachel for around $4. The path that runs directly to Panajachel is very hard to follow, and distraught walkers have been known to spend as long as seven hours scrambling through the undergrowth. Alternatively, you could walk up through the village to Sololá, along a spectacular and easy-to-follow path that takes around three hours, and from there catch a bus back to Panajachel.

If you want to do this walk in the other direction – **from Sololá to San Pedro** – you should head west out of Sololá along the dirt road towards San José Chacayá, and as you come up out of the river valley, about 1km out of Sololá, follow the track branching off to the left. The track can be very hard to find as there are many leaving Sololá in this direction, so ask around before committing yourself to any particular direction. The trail eventually brings you to Santa Cruz, from where you simply follow the shoreline, although this is a hell of a hike for one day and you'd be better off catching a boat from Panajachel to Santa Cruz.

The Pan-American Highway: Los Encuentros to Cuatro Caminos

Heading west from the Los Encuentros junction to Cuatro Caminos and the Quetzaltenango valley, the Pan-American Highway runs through some fantastic high mountain scenery. The views alone are superb, and if you have a Sunday morning to spare then it's well worth dropping into Nahualá for the market. **LOS ENCUENTROS** itself is an all-important staging point on the Pan-American Highway and typical of the junctions along the way, with wooden *comedores*, an army base, and a team of enthusiastic sales people who besiege waiting buses. Here a branch road heads north to Chichicastenango, while the main highway continues west towards Quetzaltenango, Huehuetenango and the Mexican border. Only a kilometre or so beyond this turning, at the **EL CUCHILLO** junction, a second road runs south to Sololá, Panajachel and the shores of Lake Atitlán.

These junctions are likely to feature heavily in your travels as it's here that you transfer from one bus to another on routes between Panajachel, Chichicastenango and the rest of the country. There are direct buses to and from all of these places, but if their schedule doesn't coincide with yours then it's easier to take any bus to the junction and intercept one going your way – all buses stop here and their destinations are yelled by the driver's assistant, touting for business. The last buses to Chichicastenango, Panajachel and Guatemala City pass through Los Encuentros at around 7pm; if you miss those you'll have to negotiate with a taxi.

Nahualá

West of Los Encuentros and El Cuchillo the Pan-American Highway runs through some spectacular and sparsely inhabited countryside. The only place of any size before Cuatro Caminos is **NAHUALÁ**, a small and intensely traditional town a kilometre or so to the north of the highway, at the base of a huge, steep-sided and intensely farmed bowl. The unique atmosphere of isolation from and indifference to the outside world make Nahualá one of the most impressive and unusual Quiché towns.

The town itself is not much to look at, a sprawl of cobbled streets and adobe houses, but the inhabitants of Nahualá have a reputation for fiercely preserving their independence and have held out against *ladino* incursions with exceptional tenacity. At the end of the nineteenth century the government confiscated much of their land, as they did throughout the country, and sold it to coffee planters. In protest, the entire male population of Nahualá walked the 150km to Guatemala City and demanded to see President Barrios in person, refusing his offers to admit a spokesman and insisting that they all stood as one. Eventually they were allowed into the huge reception room where they knelt with their foreheads pressed to the floor, refusing to leave until they were either given assurances of their land rights or allowed to buy the land back, which they had done twice before. The action managed to save their land that time, but since then much of it has gradually been consumed by coffee bushes all the same.

On another occasion, this time during the 1930s under President Ubico, *ladinos* were sent to the town as nurses, telegraph operators and soldiers. Once again the Nahualáns appealed directly to the president, insisting that their own people should be trained to do these jobs, and once again their request was granted. Ubico also wanted to set up a government-run drink store, but the villagers chose instead to ban alcohol, and Nahualáns who got drunk elsewhere were expected to confess their guilt and face twenty lashes in the town's plaza.

These days the ban's been lifted, and if you're here for the fiesta on November 25 you'll see that the people are keen to make up for all those dry years. However, only a handful of *ladinos* live in the town, and the indigenous Maya still have a reputation for hostility, with rumours circulating about the black deeds done by the local shaman. You don't have much to worry about if you drop in for the **Sunday market**, though, as this is one time that the town is full to bursting and the people seem genuinely pleased to welcome visitors. There is also a smaller market on Thursdays.

The town's **weaving** is outstanding: the *huipiles*, designed in intricate geometrical patterns of orange on white, particularly impressed the Spanish because they featured a double-headed eagle, the emblem of the Hapsburgs who ruled Spain at the time of the Conquest. The men wear bright yellow and pink shirts with beautifully embroidered collars, short woollen skirts, huge hats and leather sandals very similar to those of the ancient Maya.

To **get to Nahualá** take any bus along the Pan-American Highway between Los Encuentros and Cuatro Caminos, and get off at the *Puente Nahualá*, from where it's a kilometre or so up the path behind the old bus shelter. There's a very basic *pensión* (①) in the centre of town, but it's easier to visit on a day trip from Chichicastenango, Panajachel or Quetzaltenango.

Santa Catarina and the Alaskan heights

Beyond Nahualá the road continues west, climbing a mountainous ridge and passing the entrance road to **SANTA CATARINA IXTAHUACAN**, a sister and bitter rival of Nahualá, 8km to the other side of the highway. The costumes and traditions of the two places, which are together known as the **Pueblos Chancatales**, are fairly similar, and they're both famous as producers of *metates*, the stones used for grinding corn. These days much corn-grinding is done by machine and they've turned to making smaller toy versions and wooden furniture – both of which you'll see peddled by the roadside.

As it continues west, the road climbs above Santa Catarina, coming out on a flat plateau high up in the hills and into the most impressive section of the Pan-American Highway. Known as **Alaska**, this exposed tract of land, where the men of Nahualá farm wheat and graze sheep, shines white with frost in the early mornings. At 3000m, almost on a level with the great cones, the view is of course fantastic – this is one of the highest points anywhere on the Pan-American Highway (second only to the Cerro de la Muerte in Costa Rica, which reaches 3300m). Away to the east a string of volcanoes runs into the distance, and to the west the Totonicapán valley stretches out below you.

Further on, as the road drops over the other side of the ridge, the Quetzaltenango valley opens out to the left, a broad plain reaching across to the foot of the Santa María volcano. At the base of the ridge the highway arrives at the Cuatro Caminos crossroads, the crucial junction of the extreme western highlands. Turning right here leads to Totonicapán, left to Quetzaltenango, and straight on for Huehuetenango and the Mexican border.

QUETZALTENANGO AND AROUND

To the west of Lake Atitlán the highlands rise to form a steep-sided ridge topped by a string of forested peaks. On the far side of this is the **Quetzaltenango basin**, a sweeping expanse of level ground that forms the natural hub of the western highlands. The Quetzaltenango basin is perhaps the most hospitable area in the region, encompassing a huge area of fertile farmland that has been densely populated since the earliest times. Originally it was part of the Mam kingdom, administered from their capital **Zaculeu** (at a site adjacent to the modern city of Huehuetenango), but sometime between 1400 and 1475 the area was overrun by the Quiché, and was still under their control when the Spanish arrived. Today the western side of the valley is Mam-speaking and the east Quiché. It was here that the conquistador Pedro de Alvarado first struggled up into the highlands, having already confronted one Quiché army on the coast and another in the pass at the entrance to the valley. Alvarado and his troops came upon the abandoned city of Xelajú (near Quetzaltenango) and were able to enter it without encountering any resistance. Six days later they fought the Quiché in a decisive battle on the nearby plain, massacring the Maya warriors – legend has it that Alvarado himself killed the Quiché king Tecún Umán in hand-to-hand combat. The old city was then abandoned and the new town of Quetzaltenango established in its place. The name means "the place of the quetzals" in Nahuatl, the language spoken by

Alvarado's Mexican allies. Quetzals may well have existed here then, but the name is more likely to have been chosen because of the brilliant green quetzal feathers worn by Quiché nobles and warriors, including, no doubt, Tecún Umán himself.

It's easy to spend a week or two exploring this part of the country; making day trips to the markets and fiestas, basking in hot springs, or hiking in the mountains. Nowadays the valley is heavily populated, with three major towns: the departmental capital of **Quetzaltenango** (Xela) – the obvious place to base yourself, with bus connections to all parts of the western highlands – and the textile centres of **Salcajá** and **San Francisco Totonicapán**. In the surrounding hills are numerous smaller towns and villages, mostly indigenous agricultural communities and weaving centres. To the south, straddling the coast road, are **Almolonga**, **Zunil** and **Cantel**, all overshadowed by volcanic peaks, where you'll find superb natural hot springs. To the north are **Totonicapán**, capital of the department of the same name, and **San Francisco el Alto**, a small market town perched on an outcrop overlooking the valley. Beyond that, in the midst of a pine forest, lies **Momostenango**, the country's principal wool-producing centre. Throughout this network of towns and villages Maya culture remains strong, based on a simple rural economy that operates in a series of weekly markets, bringing each town to life for one day a week. Leaving Quetzaltenango you can head west to the rather neglected, little-visited department of **San Marcos** – a potential route to **Mexico** by the coastal crossing, and the home of the country's highest volcano, Tajumulco. You could also follow the Pan-American Highway to **Huehuetenango**, and cross into Mexico from there.

Set in some of the finest highland scenery, the area offers excellent **hiking**. The most obvious climb is the **Santa María volcano**, towering above Quetzaltenango itself. It's just possible to make this climb as a day trip, but to really enjoy it, and increase your chances of a good view from the top, you should plan to take two days, camping on the way. If you haven't the time, energy or equipment for this then try instead the hike to **Laguna Chicabal**, a small lake set in the cone of an extinct volcano. The lake is spectacularly beautiful, and can easily be reached as a day trip from Quetzaltenango, setting out from the village of **San Martín Sacatepéquez**.

Quetzaltenango (Xela)

Totally unlike the capital, and only a fraction of its size, Guatemala's second city, **QUETZALTENANGO (XELA)**, has the subdued provincial atmosphere that you might expect in the capital of the highlands, its edges gently giving way to corn and maize fields. Bizarre though it may seem, Quetzaltenango's character and appearance is vaguely reminiscent of a Northern English industrial town – grey, cool, slightly dour and culturally conservative. Ringed by high mountains, and bitterly cold in the early mornings, the city wakes slowly, only getting going once the warmth of the sun has made its mark. The main plaza, heavily indebted to Neoclassicism, is a monument to stability, with great slabs of grey stone that look reassuringly permanent, defying a history of turbulence and struggle. The heart of town has the calm order of a regional administrative centre, while its outskirts are ruffled by the bustle of a Maya market and bus terminal. Locally, the city is usually referred to as Xela (pronounced "shey-la"), a shortening of the Quiché

name of a nearby pre-Conquest city, Xelajú. Meaning "under the ten", the name is probably a reference to the surrounding peaks.

A brief history

Under colonial rule Quetzaltenango flourished as a commercial centre, benefiting from the fertility of the surrounding farmland and good connections to the port at Champerico. When the prospect of independence eventually arose, the city was set on deciding its own destiny. After the Central American Federation broke with Mexico in 1820, Quetzaltenango declared itself the capital of the independent state of **Los Altos**, which incorporated the modern departments of Huehuetenango, Sololá, San Marcos and Totonicapán. But the separatist movement was soon brought to heel by President Carrera in 1840, and a later attempt at secession, in 1848, was put down by force. Despite having to accept provincial status, the town remained an important centre of commerce and culture, consistently rivalling Guatemala City. The coffee boom at the end of the last century was particularly significant, as Quetzaltenango controlled some of the richest coffee land in the country. Its wealth and population grew rapidly, incorporating a large influx of German immigrants, and by the end of the nineteenth century Quetzaltenango was firmly established as an equal to Guatemala City.

All this, however, came to an abrupt end when the city was almost totally destroyed by the massive **1902 earthquake**. Rebuilding took place in a mood of high hopes; all the grand Neoclassical architecture dates from this period. A new rail line was built to connect the city with the coast, but after this was washed out in 1932–33 the town never regained its former glory, gradually falling further and further behind the capital.

Today Quetzaltenango has all the trappings of wealth and self-importance: the grand imperial architecture, the great banks, and a list of famous sons. But it is completely devoid of the rampant energy that binds Guatemala City to the all-American twentieth century. Instead the city finds itself suspended in the late nineteenth century, with a calm, dignified air that borders on the pompous. *Quezaltecos* have a reputation for formality and politeness, and pride themselves on the restrained sophistication of their cultured semi-provincial existence. If the chaos of Guatemala City gets you down then Quetzaltenango, relaxed and easy-going, is an ideal antidote, though pollution is still a problem and there's little to detain you in the town itself for more than a day or two.

Arrival and information

Unhelpfully for the traveller, virtually all buses arrive in and depart from nowhere near the centre of Quetzaltenango. If you arrive by **second class bus** you will almost certainly end up in the chaotic **Minerva bus terminal** on the western side of the city, on the northern side of the Parque Minerva, just off 6 C. It's quite a way from the centre, so you'll need to catch a local bus to and from the plaza. Local buses heading into town stop on the other side of the road, on 4 C. Separating the two is a large covered market: walk down the passage that runs through the middle of this, and on the south side cross a large patch of open ground to reach the road. Any of the small buses going to the left will take you to the plaza – look out for a "parque" sign on the front of the bus. Local buses run Mon–Sat 6am–9pm, Sun 8am–9pm, and charge 50 centavos – you need to have some change to hand.

First-class or pullman buses come and go from the office of the particular company. Líneas Américas is on 7 Av 3-33, in Zona 2, just off Calzada Independencia, on the eastern side of town (☎7612063 & 7614587); Alamo is on 14 Av 3-60, Zona 3 (☎7612964); while the Galgos terminal is at C Rodolfo Robles 17-43, Zona 1 (☎7612248). An extremely useful transport hub is a roundabout called the **rotunda** at the far end of Calzada Independencia, where virtually all long-distance buses stop on their way to and from the city.

The official **tourist office** (Mon–Fri 8am–1pm & 2–5pm, Sat 8am–noon; ☎7614931) is on the main plaza. Here you can pick up a map of the town and get information on trips to the surrounding villages. In addition, the owners of Casa Iximulew travel agency, 15 Av 5 C, Zona 1 (☎7635270; fax 7651308), are always keen to point tourists in the right direction and know the area very well; they have a full bus timetable and also run tours to the villages and volcanos around Xela.

Orientation and city transport

Quetzaltenango is laid out on a standard grid pattern, somewhat complicated by a number of steep hills. Basically, **avenidas** run north–south, and **calles** east–west. The oldest part of the city, focused around the plaza, is made up of nar-

QUETZALTENANGO TRANSPORT CONNECTIONS

As the focus of the western highlands, Quetzaltenango is served by literally hundreds of buses. **Getting to Quetzaltenango** is fairly straightforward: there are direct pullmans from Guatemala City, and at any point along the Pan-American Highway you can flag down a bus to take you to Cuatro Caminos, from where buses leave for Quetzaltenango every twenty minutes (the last at around 7pm). Coming from the coast you can catch a bus from the El Zarco junction, Mazatenango or Retalhuleu. **Leaving the city**, there are plenty of direct buses, but it's often easier to head for the Cuatro Caminos junction and go on from there

PULLMAN BUSES

Líneas Américas has daily buses to Guatemala City at 5.15am, 9.45am, 11.15am, 1.15pm, 3.45pm & 8pm. Buses from Guatemala City to Quetzaltenango run at 5.15am, 9am, 12.15pm 3.15pm, 4.40pm and 7.30pm. The Guatemala City office is at 2 Av 18–74, Zona 1 (☎2320219).

Alamo has buses to Guatemala City from Monday to Saturday at 4.30am, 5.45am, 8am, 10.15am and 2.30pm. On Sundays, buses leave at 8am, 2pm, 2.30pm and 3pm. From Guatemala City, buses leave daily from their terminal at 21 C 1–14, Zona 1 (☎2320219) at 8am, 10am 12.45pm and 3pm, with an extra service at 5.45pm on Mondays to Saturdays.

Galgos has daily services at 3.30am, 4.15am, 8.30am, 10am, 11.45am, 2.30pm and 4.30pm. In Guatemala City buses leave from 7 Av 19–44, Zona 1 (☎2534868) at 5.30am, 8.30am, 11am, 12.45pm, 2.30pm, 5pm, and 7pm. On Sundays, it's essential to book ahead for services to Guatemala City. See p.165 for details of bus terminals in Quetzaltenango.

row twisting streets, while in the newer part, reaching out towards the Minerva terminal and sports stadium, the blocks are larger. The city is also divided up into **zones**, although for the most part you'll only be interested in 1 and 3, which contain the plaza and the bus terminal respectively.

When it comes to **getting around** the city, most places are within easy walking distance (except the bus terminal). To get to the Minerva terminal you can take any bus that runs along 13 Av between 8 C and 4 C in Zona 1. To head for the eastern half of town, along 7 Av, catch one of the buses that stops in front of the Casa de la Cultura, at the bottom end of the plaza. You pay the driver; have some small change handy.

Accommodation

Once you've made it to the plaza you can set about looking for somewhere to stay. Most of the **hotels** in town are a little gloomy, even at the top end of the market, and not especially good value for money. However all the places listed below are within ten minutes walk of the centre.

Pensión Altense, 9 C 8-48 (☎7612811). Slightly pricier than the real budget joints, but has plenty of clean rooms all with private bathrooms. ③.

Casa Argentina, 12 Diagonal 8-37 (☎7612470). Probably the best budget place in town, with friendly owners who are an excellent source of information. It has very comfortable rooms (most with cable TV), a reasonable dorm, a kitchen and is home to Quetzaltrekkers (see listings). ②.

SECOND-CLASS BUSES

Buses for **Zunil** (25min), **San Francisco el Alto** (45min) and **Totonicapán** (1hr) leave every thirty minutes between 8am and 6pm from the corner of 11 C and 9 Av, Zona 1, and all pass the rotunda on their way out of town. From the main Minerva terminal in Zona 3 there are daily buses about every thirty minutes to **Huehuetenango** (6.15am–5.45pm; 2hr 30min), **Mazatenango** (5.30am–5.30pm; 2hr), **Retalhuleu** (5.45am–5.45pm; 1hr 20min), **Coatepeque** (5am–5.45pm; 1hr 45min), and hourly services to **San Marcos** (7am–5pm; 2hr). In addition to the first class services (see above), second class buses leave the terminal for **Guatemala City** every thirty minutes (3am–4.30pm; 4hr).

There are also buses from the Minerva terminal to **Panajachel** at 6.15am, 8am, 10am, 11am, 11.30am, noon, 1pm, 2.15pm and 3.15pm (2hr 30min), and one to **San Pedro la Laguna** at noon (2hr 30min). Services to **Momostenango** leave hourly (2hr; 8am–4pm). For all but the Pacific destinations and San Marcos, you can also catch these buses at the *rotunda*, though you are unlikely to get a seat as they are usually full by this stage.

Heading for **Santa Cruz del Quiché** and **Chichicastenango**, you can catch any bus going to Guatemala City and change at the Los Encuentros junction, though fairly regular buses leave from the terminal between 6.30am until 4pm.

For **Antigua**, catch any Guatemala City-bound bus and change at Chimaltenango.

To the Mexican border at Talismán (3hr 30min). It's possible to travel via San Marcos to the border in a day, but the quickest route is to take a bus heading for the coast or Coatepeque, and intercept a pullman on the Coastal Highway.

To the Mexican border at La Mesilla. The easiest way is to take a direct bus to Huehuetenango and catch another from there to the border or simply take any bus to Cuatro Caminos and change there.

Pensión Bonifaz, northeast corner of the plaza (☎7612182; fax 7612850). Founded in 1935, this hotel has character and comfort, a decent restarant and a quirky bar. Very much the backbone of Quetzaltenango society, with an air of faded upper-class grandeur, but still the best place in town. ⑥.

Hotel del Campo, Carretera a Cantel Km 224, 4km from the town centre (☎ 7611663, fax 7610074). Big, modern hotel with swimming pool and a decent restaurant. Though it's good value, it's only really an option if you have your own transport. ⑤.

Hotel Casa Florencia, 12 Av 3–61 (☎7612811). The lobby isn't going to win any design awards but the nine rooms are comfortable enough and all come with private bath. Cheap breakfasts too. ④.

Casa International, 3C 10-24 (☎7612660) Excellent budget choice, safe and friendly. Has a kitchen and hot water, but it can be difficult to get a room. ②.

ACCOMMODATION PRICE CODES

All accommodation listed in this guide has been graded according to the following price scales. These refer to the price in US dollars of the cheapest double room in high season. For more details see p.25.

① Under $5	④ $15–25	⑦ $60–80
② $5–10	⑤ $25–40	⑧ $80–100
③ $10–15	⑥ $45–60	⑨ over $100

Casa Kaehler, 13 Av 3–33 (☎7612091). Lovely place with spotless rooms around a leafy courtyard; hot showers and some private baths. Very secure – knock on the door to get in but be sure to book ahead, as it's always popular. ②.

Hotel Modelo, 14 Av A 2–31 (☎7612529; fax 7631376). Civilized and quiet but a bit gloomy for the price, and decidedly old-fashioned. The nicest rooms face a small garden courtyard, or try the better value seperate annexe on the same street. ④.

Hotel Radar 99, 13 Av 3-27. Poky rooms but friendly cheap and just off the plaza. ①.

Hotel Río Azul, 2 C 12–15 (☎ & fax 7630654). At the top end of the budget range: spotless, friendly and all rooms have private bathroom. ③.

Pensión San Nicolas, 12 Av 3-16 (☎7616864). Ramshackle, pretty dirty and the beds are ancient, but it's conviently located and very cheap. ①.

Hotel Villa Real Plaza, northwest corner of the plaza, 4 C 12–22 (☎7614045; fax 7616780). The city's second hotel and a modern(ish) rival to the *Bonifaz*. Comfortable enough, but lacks atmosphere. ⑥.

Staying with a Maya family

Quetzaltenango is the base for **SCDRYS** (*Sociedad Civil para al Desarrollo Rural Replicable y Sostenible*), 7 C 7–18, between 24 & 25 Av, Zona 3 (☎7630409; fax 7616873). Managed by Douglas Sandoval, this non-profit organization is run in

STUDYING SPANISH IN XELA

Xela is now one of the most popular places in the world to **study Spanish**, having literally dozens of language schools, many of a very high standard. Though the days are long gone when schools could boast about the absense of foreigners in the town, Xela is still less visited than Antigua and its relatively large population (120,000) means that you shouldn't have to share a family home with other gringos.

Many schools claim to fund community and enviromental projects, like supporting village libraries and clean water programmes. However, whilst most genuinely do assist development work, there are cowboys whose financial aid never gets through to the people they claim to support. Always ask to see evidence of the projects they profess to be involved with before you enrol. Virtually all schools have a student liaison officer who speaks English to act as a go-between for students and teachers.

All the schools below offer intensive Spanish classes and the chance to live with a local family (usually with full-board). In addition, they often run trips to places of interest around Xela and hold lectures on local political and social issues. For four or five hours' individual tuition from Monday to Friday and seven nights' full-board accomodation in a family, you can expect to pay around $120 a week, often a little more in July and August. The following schools are all well established, employ professional teachers and put on activities after classes. In addition, the tourist office has a list of officially recognized language schools.

Casa de Español Xelajú, 9C 11-26, Zona 1 (☎7612628).
Desarrollo del Pueblo, 20 Av 0-65, Zona 1 (☎7622932; ☎ & fax 7616754).
English Club International Language School, Diagonal 4 9-71 (☎7632198). Also offers lessons in Mam and Quiché.
Escuela Juan Sisay, 15Av 8-38, Zona 1 (☎ & fax 763 1684).
Guatemalensis, 19 Av 2-14, Zona 1 (fax 7632198).
La Paz, 2C 19-30, Zona 1 (☎7614243).
Popwuj, 1C 17-72, Zona 1(☎7618286).
Projecto Lingüístico Quetzalteco de Español, 5C 2-40, Zona 1 (☎7612620). Also has branches in Todos Santos and on the Pacific slope.

association with Maya community leaders in remote areas of the departments of Quiché, Huehuetenango and Quetzaltenango, and provides an excellent opportunity to spend time with an indigenous family, either as a language student in Joyabaj (see p.131), or simply as a **guest** of a particular village. Expect to pay approximately $80–100 per person per week, less if there are several of you. The money is paid direct to the *alcalde* (mayor) of the community, who distributes 30 percent to your host family, 20 percent to the community, 25 percent to aid projects, 15 percent to SCDRYS and 10 percent for administration.

The City

There aren't many things to do or see in Quetzaltenango, but if you have an hour or two to spare then it's well worth wandering through the streets, soaking up the atmosphere and taking in the museums. The hub of the place is, obviously enough, the **central plaza**, officially known as the **Parque Centro América**. A mass of false Greek columns, banks and shoeshine boys, with an atmosphere of wonderfully dignified calm, the plaza is the best place to appreciate the sense of self-importance that accompanied the city's rebuilding after the 1902 earthquake. The buildings have a look of defiant authority, although there's none of the buzz of business that you'd expect. The Greek columns were probably intended to symbolize the city's cultural importance and its role at the heart of the liberal revolution, but today many of them do nothing more than support street lights. The northern end of the plaza is dominated by the grand Banco del Occidente, complete with sculptured flaming torches. On the west side is Bancafé, and the impressive but crumbling **Pasaje Enriquez**, which was planned as a sparkling arcade of upmarket shops, spent many years derelict, but has now been partially renovated. Inside you'll find Xela's most hip spot, the *Salon Tecún Bar*, a friendly place for meeting other travellers.

At the bottom end of the plaza, next to the tourist office, is the **Casa de la Cultura** (Mon–Fri 8am–noon & 2–6pm, Sat 9am–1pm; $1), the city's most blatant impersonation of a Greek temple, with a bold grey frontage that radiates stability and strength. The main part of the building is given over to an odd mixture of local **museums**. On the ground floor, to the left-hand side, you'll find a display of assorted documents from the liberal revolution and the State of Los Altos, sports trophies, and a museum of marimba. Upstairs there are some interesting Maya artefacts, a display about local industries and a fascinating collection of old photographs.

Along the eastern side of the plaza is the **Cathedral**, with a new cement version set behind the spectacular crumbling front of the original. There's another unashamed piece of Greek grandeur, the **Municipalidad** or town hall, a little further up. Take a look inside at the courtyard, which has a neat little garden set out around a single palm tree. Back in the centre of the plaza are rows and circles of redundant columns, a few flowerbeds, and a monument to President Barrios, who ruled Guatemala from 1873 to 1885.

In the bottom corner of the plaza, between the cathedral and the Casa de la Cultura, the old **Mercadito** still functions, although nowadays it's eclipsed by the larger market near the bus terminal in Zona 3. Beside it, there's a grim three-storey shopping centre, the **Centro Comercial Municipal**.

Beyond the plaza

Away from the plaza the city spreads out, a mixture of the old and new. 14 Av is the commercial heart, complete with pizza restaurants and neon signs. At the top of 14 Av, at the junction with 1 C, stands the **Teatro Municipal** (currently undergoing restoration), another spectacular Neoclassical edifice. The plaza in front of the theatre is dotted with busts of local artists, including Osmundo Arriola (1886–1958), Guatemala's first poet laureate, and Jesus Castillo, "the re-creator of Maya music" – another bid to assert Quetzaltenango's cultural superiority.

Further afield, the city's role as a regional centre of trade is more in evidence. Out in Zona 3 is the **La Democracia Market**, a vast covered complex with stalls spilling out onto the streets. A couple of blocks beyond the market stands the modern **Church of San Nicolás**, at 4 C and 15 Av, a bizarre and ill-proportioned neo-Gothic building, sprouting sharp arches.

There's another Greek-style structure right out on the edge of town, also in Zona 3. The **Minerva Temple** makes no pretence at serving any practical purpose, but was built to honour President Barrios's enthusiasm for education.

Beside the temple is the little **zoo** (Tues–Sun 9am–5pm; free), doubling as a childrens' playground. Crammed into the tiny cages are a collection of foxes, sheep, birds, monkeys (who are, for some reason, sponsored by Toyota), wild boar and big cats, including a pair of miserable-looking lions, who have miraculously managed to raise a family. Below the temple comes the sprawling **market** and **bus terminal**, and it's here that you can really sense the city's role as the centre of the western highlands, with indigenous traders from all over the area doing business, and buses heading to or from every imaginable village and town. To get to this side of the city take any of the local buses that run along 13 Av between 8 C and 4 C in Zona 1.

Eating, drinking and entertainment

There are more than enough **restaurants** to choose from in Quetzaltenango, with four reasonable pizza places on 14 Av alone. Note that very few places open before 8am in the morning, so forget early breakfasts. Xela is very sleepy after dark and **nightlife** is not easy to come by – those determined to party till late will have to catch a taxi to the best **clubs** which are all out of town.

Restaurants and cafés

Artura's Restaurant, 14 Av 3–09, Zona 1. Dark and fairly cosy atmosphere, where there's traditional, moderately priced food and a separate civilized bar for drinking.

Café Baviera, 5 C 12 50, Zona 1. Spacious pine-panelled coffee house dripping with photographic nostalgia, a block from the plaza. Quality cakes and unquestionably the best coffee in town. Daily 8am–8pm.

Café Berna, 16 Av 3–25, Zona 3, on the Parque Benito Juarez. Enduring café, which sells great cakes, milkshakes and snacks. Daily 8am–10pm.

Blue Angel Video Café, 7 C 15–22, Zona 1. Another popular gringo hang-out, an intimate, friendly place which serves great vegetarian food. The small library offers well-thumbed paperbacks and the daily video programme is not bad. Daily 2.15pm–11pm.

Pensión Bonifaz, corner of the plaza, Zona 1. A sedate and civilized spot for a cup of tea and a cake, or a full meal, and for rubbing shoulders with the town's elite. Expensive.

Cardinali's, 14 Av 3–41, Zona 1. Without doubt the best Italian food outside the capital and better pizza than anywhere in Antigua, at reasonable prices. Make sure you're starving when you eat here because the portions are huge. They also have a bakery, which is less reliable, near the municipal theatre at 14 Av and 1C.

Deli Crêpe, 14 Av, Zona 1. Looks a bit gloomy from the outside but wait till you try the *licuardos*, pancakes and delicious sandwiches.

Helados La Americana, 14 Av 4–41, Zona 1. The best ice-cream and candy in town.

Pan y Pasteles, 18 Av & 2 C, Zona 1. Xela's best bakery, run by Mennonites, whose fresh pastries and breads are sold to all the finest restaurants. Tues & Fri only 10am–4pm.

Pizza Rica, 14 Av 2–52, Zona 1. Pretty authentic, inexpensive homemade pizza and pasta.

La Polonesa, 14 Av 4-55, Zona 1. An unbeatable section of set lunches (with daily specials) all at under $2 and served on nice solid wooden tables.

El Rincón de los Antojitos, 15 Av and 5 C, Zona 1. Despite being run by a French–Guatemalan couple, this friendly little restaurant has a far from cosmopolitan menu but does offer inexpensive Guatemalan specialities such as *pepian* (spicy chicken stew) and *hilachas* (beef in tomato sauce). Excellent vegetarian pies and snacks. Mon–Fri 8am–1pm & 2–7pm.

Royal Paris, 2 C 14 A–32, Zona 1. Simple, unpretentious restaurant set in a very pleasant, covered courtyard. The menu is international. Daily 9am–11pm.

Shanghai, 4 C 12–22, Zona 1. Some of the best Chinese food in town, half a block from the plaza, and not too expensive.

Sagrado Corazon, 9 C 9-00, Zona 1. Excellent little *comedor,* great value breakfasts, meals and very friendly service.

Drinking and nightlife

There's not much to do in the evenings in Quetzaltenango, and the streets are generally quiet by about 9pm. A few of the **bars**, though, are worth visiting. At the popular *Tecún*, on the west side of the plaza, you can down *cuba libras* or sip lager on tap, while listening to the latest sounds. At the more sedate *Don Rodrigo*, 1 C and 14 Av, you'll find leather-topped bar stools, draught beer and good but pricey sandwiches, while the popular bar, *Zodiaco's*, at 13 Av & 9 C, is also worth checking out. The *Greenhouse Café Teatro*, 12 Av 1-40 (☎7630271), has a lively cultural programme including theatre, dance, poetry readings, while *Aladino's*, 20 Av 0–66, Zona 3, attracts a good mix of Guatemalans and travellers, with its great music and good food.

On the edge of town there are a couple of **nightclubs**. The best music is at *Loro's*, past the Minerva terminal – a taxi is essential – where they play Latin sounds and house music. It's popular with rich Guatemalans and the drinks are expensive. The vast *Garage Club*, Centro Commercial Ciani, Boulevard Minerva is another option for merengue, salsa, commercial house and Latin rock, and drinks here are more reasonably priced.

Quetzaltenango is a good place to catch movies, with a number of **cinemas**: the new screen inside the shopping mall Plaza Polonco, just off the central plaza shows pure Hollywood, while Cadore, at 7 C & 13 Av, is good for violence, horror and soft porn. There's also the Roma, a beautiful old theatre at 14 Av A–34, and the Alpino, at 4 C and 24 Av, part of a new complex in Zona 3 near the bus terminal. For art-house films, try the excellent Paraiso, on 14 Av, very close to the Teatro Municipal, which shows English-language films with Spanish subtitles.

Listings

Banks Banco Inmobiliario, Banco del Occidente and Bancafé (the latter has the longest opening hours; Mon–Fri 8.30am–8pm, Sat 10am–2pm) are all in the vicinity of the plaza and will change travellers' cheques. Banco Industrial, also on the plaza, has an ATM for Visa credit cards. For cash, you get the best rate at the Banquetzal, on 14 Av, Zona 1.

Bike and car rental Guatemala Unlimited, 12 Av & 1C, Zona 1 (☎7616043), rents out cars, as well as mountain bikes for around $6 a day. Alternatively, try the Vrisa bookstore (see below).

Books Vrisa, 15 Av 3–64, opposite Telgua, has over 3000 used titles, plus a newsroom which sells *Newsweek*, and *The Economist*. It also has a useful message board, expresso coffee, and bike rental.

Camera repairs Try Fotocolor, 15 Av 3–25, or one of the several shops on 14 Av that sell a good range of film.

Doctors Cohen and Molina at the Policlinica, A C 13–15, speak some English; for real emergencies, the Hospital Privado is at C Rudolfo Robles 23–51, Zona 1.

Email Maya Communications, above the Tecún Bar on the central plaza (daily 10am–7pm; ☎ & fax 7612832) offers email facilities as well as all other communication services.

Laundry At MiniMax, 14 Av & 1 C, Zona 1 (Mon–Sat 7am–7pm), it's $2 for a wash and dry; or try Quick Wash 'n' Dry, 7 C 13–25 A, Zona 1 (Mon–Sat 8am–6pm).

Mexican consulate 9 Av 6–19, Zona 1 (Mon–Fri 8–11am & 2.30–3.30pm). A Mexican tourist card costs $1. Hand in the paperwork in the morning and collect in the afternoon.

Phones The Telgua office is just opposite the post office at the junction of 15 Av and 4 C (7am–10pm daily).

Post office at the junction of 15 Av and 4 C (Mon–Sat 8am–4.30pm). The Shipping Center, 15 Av 3–51, Zona 1 (Mon–Fri 9am–5.45pm, Sat 9am–noon; ☎ & fax 7632104), also offers mail and parcel services, as well as courier, phone and fax facilities.

Travel agents Casa Iximulew, 15 Av & 5 C, Zona 1, runs trips to most of the volcanoes around Xela and to Zunil and Fuentes Georginas. Alternatively, try Agencia de Viajes Guatemala Unlimited, 12 Av and 1 C, Zona 1 (☎ & fax 7616043).

Hiking tours Quetzaltrekkers, based inside the *Casa Argentina* (see p.166), runs regular hikes to the Tajumulco volcano, Central America's highest mountain, and an amazing three-day trek between Todos Santos (see p.198) and Nebaj (see p.133).

Olintepeque and the old road towards Huehuetenango

To the north of Quetzaltenango, perched on the edge of the flat plain, is the small textile-weaving town of **OLINTEPEQUE**. According to some accounts this was the site of the huge and decisive battle between the Spanish and Quiché warriors, and legend has it that the Río Xequijel, the "river of blood", ran red during the massacre of the Quiché. These days, however, it's better known as a peaceful little village with a small colonial church and a market on Tuesdays. **Buses** for Olintepeque (20min) leave from the Minerva terminal in Quetzaltenango every thirty minutes.

Olintepeque was a staging post on the old road to Huehuetenango, and although only local traffic heads this way nowadays you can still follow the route. Leaving Olintepeque the road climbs the steep hillside onto a plateau, arriving at the village of **SAN CARLOS SIJA**, 22km from Quetzaltenango and the hub of a fertile and isolated area. There's nowhere to stay in San Carlos, but five buses a day connect it with Quetzaltenango – leaving from the Minerva terminal – the last returning at about 4pm. The only real reason to come out here is for the wonderful views, or to visit the small Sunday market. Heading on from San Carlos, you can hitch a ride to the Pan-American Highway, just 10km away, where there's plenty of traffic to Quetzaltenango via Cuatro Caminos or on to Huehuetenango. The old road itself continues more or less due north, rejoining the Pan-American Highway about 40km before Huehuetenango – but there's very little traffic.

The Santa María volcano

Due south of Quetzaltenango, the perfect cone of the **Santa María volcano** rises to a height of 3772m. From the town only the peak is visible, but seen from the rest of the valley the entire cone seems to tower over everything around. The view from the top is, as you might expect, spectacular, and if you're prepared to sweat out the climb you certainly won't regret it. It's possible to climb the volcano as a day trip, but to really see it at its best you need to be on top at dawn, either sleeping on the freezing peak, or camping at the site below and climbing the final section in the dark by torchlight. Either way you need to bring enough food, water and stamina for the entire trip, and you should be acclimatized to the altitude before attempting it. For more **information** on climbing Santa María, or any of the volcanoes in the region, contact Casa Iximulew (see p.173), or Natán Hardeman, who can be found at *Aladino's* bar in Quetzaltenango most nights (see p.172), or emailed at the Inter-American School (*IAS@uvg.edu.gt*).

Climbing the cone

To get to the start of the climb you need to take a local bus to **Llanos del Pinal**, a twenty-minute ride: buses leave every hour or so between 7am and 5.30pm from the Minerva terminal in Quetzaltenango. The village is set on a high plateau beneath the cone, and the bus driver will drop you at a crossroads from where you head straight down the road towards the right-hand side of the volcano's base. After passing a small plaque dedicated to the Guatemalan Mountaineering Club, the track bears up to the left, quickly becoming a rocky trail. At the end of a confined rocky stretch, a few hundred metres in length, the path crosses a more open grassy area and then curves further around to the left. All the way along this first section painted arrows mark the way – those signs painted with a fierce "NO" mean exactly what they say and you should backtrack until you find an alternative.

As you push on, the path continues to climb around to the left, up a rocky slope and under some trees, arriving at a flat and enclosed grassy area about the size of small football pitch. There's a grass bank to the right, a wooded area to the left, and a big boulder at the other end. This point is about ninety minutes to two hours from the start, and is an ideal place to **camp** if you want to make the final ascent in the hours before dawn. The path cuts off to the right from here, leaving from the start of this level patch of grass. (Another path heads across the grass, but this isn't the one for you.) From here on, the route is a little harder to follow, but it heads more or less straight up the side of the cone, a muddy and backbreaking climb of two or three hours: avoid the tempting alternative that skirts round to the right.

At the top the cone is a mixture of grass and volcanic cinder, usually frozen solid in the early morning. The highest point is marked by an altar where the Maya burn copal and sacrifice animals, and on a clear day the **view** will take your breath away – as will the cold if you get here in time to watch the sun rise. In the early mornings the Quetzaltenango valley is blanketed in a layer of cloud, and while it's still dark the lights of the city create a patch of orange glow; as the sun rises, its first rays eat into the cloud, revealing the land beneath. To the west, across a chaos of twisting hills, are the cones of Tajumulco and Tacaná, marking the Mexican border. But most impressive is the view to the east. Wrapped in the early morning haze are four more volcanic cones, two above Lake Atitlán and two more above Antigua. The right-hand cone in this second pair is Fuego, which sometimes emits a stream of smoke, rolling down the side of the cone in the early morning. If you look south, you can gaze down over the smaller cone of **Santiaguito**, which has been in constant eruption since 1902. Every now and then it spouts a great grey cloud of rock and dust hundreds of metres into the air.

South towards the coast: Almolonga to Zunil

The most direct route from Quetzaltenango to the coast takes you through a narrow gash in the mountains to the village of **ALMOLONGA**, sprawled around the sides of a steep-sided, flat-bottomed valley just 5km from Quetzaltenango.

Almolonga is Quiché for "the place where water springs", and streams gush from the hillside, channelled to the waiting crops. This is the market garden of the western highlands, where the flat land is far too valuable to live on and is parcelled up instead into neat, irrigated sections.

In **markets** throughout the western highlands the women of Almolonga corner the vegetable trade; it's easy to recognize them, dressed in their bold, orange zigzag *huipiles* and wearing beautifully woven headbands. The village itself has markets on Wednesday and Saturday – the latter being the larger one – when the plaza is ringed by trucks and crammed with people, while piles of food and flowers are swiftly traded between the two. The Almolonga market may not be Guatemala's largest, but it has to be one of the most frenetic, and is well worth a visit.

A couple of kilometres beyond the village lie **Los Baños**, where about ten different operations offer a soak in waters heated naturally by the volcano: two good ones are *Fuentes Saludable* and *El Recreo* (daily 5am–10pm). For a dollar you get a private room, a sunken concrete tub, and enough hot water to drown an elephant. In a country of lukewarm showers it's paradise, and the baths echo to the sound of indigenous families who queue barefoot for the pleasure of a good scrub. Below the baths is a communal pool, usually packed with local men, and a *pila* where the women wash their clothes in warm water. Below the road between the baths and the village there's a warm swimming pool known as *Los Chorros* – follow the sign to *Agua Tibia* – which you can use for a small fee.

If on the other hand you'd prefer to immerse yourself in steam, then this too emerges naturally from the hillside. To get to the **vapores**, as they're known, get off the bus halfway between Quetzaltenango and Almolonga at the sign for Los Vahos, and head off up the track. Take the right turn after about a kilometre, follow this track for another twenty minutes, and you'll come to the steam baths. Here you can sweat it out for a while in one of the cubicles and then step out into the cool mountain air, or have a bracing shower to get the full sauna effect.

Buses run to Almolonga from Quetzaltenango every twenty minutes, leaving from the Minerva terminal in Zona 3 and stopping to pick up passengers at the junction of 10 Av and 10 C in Zona 1. They pause in Almolonga itself before going on to the baths, and, although the baths stay open until 10pm, the last bus back is at around 7pm. Beyond Los Baños the road heads through another narrow gully to join the main coast road in Zunil. A few of the buses for Zunil also pass this way.

Cantel, Zunil and the Fuentes Georginas

Most buses to the coast avoid Almolonga, leaving Quetzaltenango via the **Las Rosas** junction and passing through **CANTEL FÁBRICA**, an industrial village built up around an enormous textile factory. The factory's looms produce a range of cloths, using indigenous labourers, German dyes, English machinery and a mixture of American and Guatemalan cotton. The village was originally known as Chuijullub, a Quiché word meaning "on the hill", and this original settlement (now called Cantel – Cantel Fabrica simply means "Cantel Factory") can still be seen on a height overlooking the works.

A kilometre beyond Cantel on the road to Zunil is the **Copavic glass factory**, one of Guatemala's most successful cooperatives. Copavic uses one hundred percent recycled glass and exports the finished product all over the world. Visitors are welcome to see the glass blowers in action (Mon–Fri 8am–1pm), or visit the

VISITING SAN SIMÓN IN ZUNIL

Zunil's reputation for the worship of **San Simón** is well founded, and as in Santiago Atitlán (see p.153) with a minimum of effort you can pay a visit to the man himself. Every year on November 1, at the end of the annual fiesta, San Simón is moved to a new house; discreet enquiries will locate his current home. Here his effigy sits in a darkened room, dressed in Western clothes, and guarded by several attendants, including one whose job it is to remove the ash from his lighted cigarettes – this is later sold off and used to cure insomnia, while the butts are thought to provide protection from thieves. San Simón is visited by a steady stream of villagers, who come to ask his assistance, using candles to indicate their requests: white for the health of a child, yellow for a good harvest, red for love and black for an enemy. The petitioners touch and embrace the saint, and just to make sure that he has heard their pleas they also offer cigarettes, money and rum. The latter is administered with the help of one of the attendants, who tips back San Simón's head and pours the liquid down his throat, presumably saving a little for himself. Meanwhile, outside the house a small fire burns continuously and more offerings are given over to the flames, including whole eggs – if they crack it signifies that San Simón will grant a wish.

If you **visit San Simón** you will be expected to contribute to his upkeep (50¢). While the entire process may seem chaotic and entertaining, it is in fact deeply serious and outsiders have been beaten up for making fun of San Simón, so proceed with caution.

David Dickinson

factory shop (Mon–Fri 8am–5pm & Sat 8am–noon), which sells a fine selection of glasses, vases, jugs and other assorted goods.

Further down the valley is **ZUNIL**, another centre for vegetable growing. As at Almolonga, the village is split in two by the need to preserve the best land. The plaza is dominated by a beautiful colonial church with an intricate silver altar protected behind bars. The women of Zunil wear vivid purple *huipiles* and carry incredibly bright shawls, and for the Monday market the plaza is awash with colour. Just below the plaza, there's a **textile cooperative** (Mon–Sat 8.30am–5pm, Sun 2–5pm), where hundreds of women market their beautiful weavings. Zunil is also one of the few remaining places where **Maximón** (or San Simón), the evil saint, is still worshipped (see above). In the face of disapproval from the Catholic Church, the Maya are reluctant to display their Judas, who also goes by the name Alvarado, but his image is usually paraded through the streets during Holy Week, dressed in Western clothes and smoking a cigar. At other times of the year you can meet the man himself (see above box).

In the hills above Zunil are the **Fuentes Georginas**, a spectacular set of luxurious hot springs, state-owned and named after the dictator Jorge Ubico (1931–44). A turning to the left off the main road, just beyond the entrance to the village, leads up into the hills to the baths, 8km away. You can walk it in a couple of hours, or rent a truck from the plaza in Zunil for about $5, though if you're not staying the night you'll have to pay another $5 for the return trip. The baths are surrounded by fresh green ferns, thick moss and lush forest, and to top it all there's a restaurant and bar beside the main pool. You can swim in the pool for $1 or rent a **bungalow** for the night (②), complete with bathtub, double bed, fireplace and barbecue. In the rainy season it can be cold and damp, but with a touch of sunshine it's a fantastic place to spend the night.

Buses to Cantel and Zunil run from Quetzaltenango's Minerva bus terminal every thirty minutes or so, with the last bus back from Zunil leaving at around 6pm. All buses to and from the coast also pass through this way. Just below Zunil the road from Almolonga meets with the main coastal highway, so you can easily walk between the two villages, a trek of little more than half an hour, although some buses do use this route when heading between Quetzaltenango and Zunil.

West to Ostuncalco, and towards the coast via San Martín Sacatepéquez

Heading west from Quetzaltenango, a good paved road runs 15km along the valley floor, through **San Mateo**, to the prosperous village of **SAN JUAN OSTUN-CALCO**, the commercial centre for this end of the valley. The large Sunday market draws people from all the surrounding villages; here you can see the furniture made locally from wood and rope, painted in garish primary colours. The village's other famous feature is the *Virgen de Rosario*, in the church, which is reputed to have miraculous powers. Barely 2km away, on the far side of the coast road, is the quiet, traditional village of **CONCEPCIÓN CHIQUIRICHAPA**, which hosts a very local market on Thursday, attended by only a few outsiders and conducted in hushed tones.

Buses and minibuses run every thirty minutes between Quetzaltenango and Ostuncalco. If you find yourself enchanted by the place, there's a very relaxed **guest house** at the entrance to the village: *Ciprés Inn*, 6 Av 1–29 (☎7616174; ③), a beautiful wooden house that looks like it ought to be in New England, and which boasts huge double beds, a restaurant and a garden. Beyond the village the road splits, one branch running to Coatepeque on the coast, and the other over a high pass north to San Marcos and San Pedro Sacatepéquez. The road to the coast climbs into the hills and through a gusty pass before winding down to **SAN MARTÍN SACATEPÉQUEZ**, also known as San Martín Chile Verde, an isolated Mam-speaking village set in the base of a natural bowl and hemmed in by steep, wooded hills. The village was abandoned in 1902 when the eruption of the Santa María volcano buried the land beneath a metre-thick layer of sterile pumice stone, killing thousands. These days both the people and fertility have returned to the land, and the village is once again devoted to farming. The men of San Martín wear a particularly unusual costume, a long white tunic with thin red stripes, ornately embroidered around the cuffs and tied around the middle with a red sash; the women wear beautiful red *huipiles* and blue *cortes*.

A three- to four-hour hike from San Martín brings you to **Laguna Chicabal**, a spectacular lake set in the cone of the Chicabal volcano which is the site of Maya religious rituals. To get there, head down the side of the church and turn right onto the track at the end, which takes you out of the village. Once the track has crossed a small bridge take the path that branches off to the right, and follow this as it goes up and over a range of hills, then drops down and bears around to the left – several kilometres from the village. Beyond the lip the path carries on under a ridge and then crosses a flat pass before disappearing into the trees. Just as it enters the trees, take the smaller path that branches off to the right: this goes up through the forest and curves around to the right before finally cutting up to the left and crossing over into the cone itself. All of a sudden you come into a different world, eerily still, disturbed only by the soft buzz of a hummingbird's wings or the screech of parakeets. From the rim the path drops precipitously, through thick, moist forest, to the water's edge, where charred crosses and bunches of fresh-cut flowers mark the site of ritual sacrifice. On May 3 every year *brujos* from several different tribes gather here for ceremonies to mark the fiesta of the Holy Cross: at any time, but on this date especially, you should take care not to disturb any ceremonies that might be taking place – the site is considered holy by the local Maya. Note also that fog can be a problem in February, making it easy to get lost.

San Martín can be visited either as a day trip from Quetzaltenango or on the way to the coast – if you want to **stay**, the woman who runs the *Centro de Salud* has a room that she rents out (①). **Buses** run along the road between Coatepeque (for the coast) and Quetzaltenango every hour or so, with the last passing San Martín in both directions at about 5pm. From Quetzaltenango buses for Coatepeque leave from the Minerva terminal in Zona 3.

Quetzaltenango to Cuatro Caminos

Between the Cuatro Caminos junction and Quetzaltenango, lined along the road is the small *ladino* town of **SALCAJÁ**, one of Guatemala's main commercial weaving centres, producing much of the cloth used in the dresses worn by Maya women. The lengths of fabric are often stretched out by the roadside, either to be prepared for dyeing or laid out to dry, and on market day they're an exceptionally popular commodity.

Salcajá's other claim to fame is that (according to some historians at least) it was the site of the first Spanish settlement in the country, and its church is therefore regarded as the first Catholic foundation in Guatemala. If you're staying in Quetzaltenango and travelling out to the surrounding villages then the sight of Salcajá will become familiar as you pass through heading to and from Cuatro Caminos. But the ideal time to stop off is for the market on Tuesday.

A few kilometres beyond Salcajá the main road turns sharply to the right, beside a filling station. At this point a dirt track branches off to the left, running to the edge of the valley and the village of **SAN ANDRÉS XECUL**. Bypassed by almost everything, and enclosed on three sides by steep dry hills, it is to all appearances an unremarkable farming village – but two features set it apart. The first is little more than rumour and hearsay, set in motion by the artist Carmen Petterson when she was painting here in the 1970s. She claimed to have discovered that a "university" for *brujos* was operating in the village, attracting young students of shamanism from Quiché villages throughout the country. There's little sign of this in the village itself, though, except perhaps for an atmosphere that's even more hushed and secretive than usual. The second feature is the **village church**, a beautiful old building with incredibly thick walls. Its facade is painted an outrageous mustard yellow, with vines dripping plump, purple fruit, and podgy little angels scrambling across the surface. Less orthodox religious ceremonies are conducted at hundreds of small altars in the hills, one of which is up a hill just above the smaller painted church.

A few daily **buses** leave the Minerva terminal in Quetzaltenango for San Andrés; it's easier, though, to take any bus as far as the filling station beyond Salcajá and hitch a ride from there.

Cuatro Caminos and San Cristobal Totonicapán

At **CUATRO CAMINOS** the Pan-American Highway is met by the main roads from Quetzaltenango and Totonicapán. This is the most important junction in the western highlands and you'll find all the usual characteristics of Guatemalan road junctions, including the cheap motels, the hustlers, the outrageously priced fruit and the shanty-like *comedores*. More importantly, up until about 7pm there's a stream of **buses** heading for Quetzaltenango, Huehuetenango, Guatemala City and smaller villages along the way. Wherever you are, this is the place to make for in search of a connection.

One kilometre to the west, the *ladino* town of **SAN CRISTOBAL TOTONICAPÁN** is built at the junction of the Sija and Salamá rivers. Similar in many ways to Salcajá, San Cristobal is a quiet place that holds a position of importance in the world of Maya tradition as a source of fiesta costumes, which can be rented from various outfitters. If you'd like to see one of these you can drop in at 5 C 3–20, where they rent costumes for around $50 a fortnight, depending on age and quality. The colonial church, on the other side of the river, has been restored by the local wheat-growers' association and contains some fantastic ancient altars, including ornate silverwork and images of the saints. Look out especially for the silver figure of St Michael. The market here is on Sunday. **Buses** going to San Francisco el Alto pass the village – they leave from the rotunda in Quetzaltenango.

San Francisco el Alto and Momostenango

From a magnificent hillside setting, the small market town of **SAN FRANCISCO EL ALTO** overlooks the Quetzaltenango valley. It's worth a visit for the view alone, with the great plateau stretching out below and the cone of the Santa María volcano marking the opposite side of the valley. At times a layer of early morning cloud fills the valley, and the volcanic cone, rising out of it, is the only visible feature.

An equally good reason for visiting the village is the **Friday market**, the largest weekly market in the country. Traders from every corner of Guatemala make the trip, many arriving the night before, and some starting to sell as early as 4am by candlelight. Throughout the morning a steady stream of buses and trucks fills the town to bursting; by noon the market is at its height, buzzing with activity.

The town is set into the hillside, with steep cobbled streets connecting the different levels. Two areas in particular are monopolized by specific trades. At the very top is an open field used as an animal market, where everything from pigs to parrots changes hands. The teeth and tongues of animals are inspected by the buyers, and at times the scene degenerates into a chaotic wrestling match, with pigs and men rolling in the dirt. Below this is the town's plaza, dominated by textiles. These days most of the stalls deal in imported denim, but under the arches and in the covered area opposite the church you'll find a superb selection of traditional cloth. (For a really good view of the market and the surrounding countryside, pay the church caretaker Q1 and climb up to the church roof.) Below, the streets are filled with vegetables, fruit, pottery, furniture, cheap *comedores* and plenty more. By early afternoon the numbers start to thin out, and by sunset it's all over – until the following Friday.

San Francisco practicalities

There are plenty of **buses** from Quetzaltenango to San Francisco, leaving every twenty minutes or so from the rotunda; the first is at 6am, with the last bus back leaving at about 5pm. If you'd rather stay in town, the cheapest **accommodation** is at the *Hospedaje Central* (①) on the main street, a roughish sort of place that fills with market traders. The *Hotel Vista Hermosa*, 3 Av 2–22, a block or so below the plaza (☎7384030, ②), looks smartish from the outside but is run-down, though, as its name suggests, some of the front rooms have magnificent views. Finally, the newest hotel in town is the *Hotel Galaxia* (①), which is very neat, clean and hospitable, some of the rooms having private bathrooms and views to rival the *Vista Hermosa*. San Francisco goes to bed at around 7.30pm, so if you're stuck here for an evening you might want to see what's showing at the Cine García. Nearby, there's a Banco G&T, which may be persuaded to change travellers' cheques.

Momostenango

Above San Francisco a dirt road continues over the ridge, dropping down on the other side through lush pine forests. The road is deeply rutted, and the journey painfully slow, but within an hour you arrive in **MOMOSTENANGO**. This small, isolated town is the centre of wool production in the highlands, and *Momostecos* travel throughout the country peddling their blankets, scarves and rugs. Years of experience have made them experts in the hard sell and given them a sharp eye for tourists. The wool is also used in a range of traditional costumes, including the short skirts worn by the men of Nahualá, and San Antonio Palopó, and the jackets of Sololá. The ideal place to buy Momostenango blankets is in the **Sunday market**, which fills the town's two plazas.

A visit at this time will also give you a glimpse of Momostenango's other feature: its rigid adherence to tradition. Opposite the entrance to the church, people make offerings of incense and alcohol on a small fire, muttering their appeals to the gods. The town is famous for this unconventional folk-Catholicism, and it has been claimed that there are as many as three hundred Maya **shamans** working here. Momostenango's religious **calendar**, like that of only one or two other villages, is still based on the 260-day *Tzolkin* year – made up of thirteen twenty-day months – that has been in use since ancient times. The most celebrated ceremony is *Guaxaquib Batz*, "Eight Monkey", which marks the beginning of a new year. Originally this was a purely pagan ceremony, starting at dawn on the first day of the year, but the Church has muscled in on the action and it now begins with a Catholic service the night before. The next morning the people make for Chuitmesabal (Little Broom), a small hill about 2km to the west of the town. Here offerings of broken pottery are made before age-old altars (Momostenango means "the place of the altars"). The entire process is overseen by *brujos*, shamans responsible for communicating with the gods. At dusk the ceremony moves to Nim Mesabal (Big Broom), another hilltop, where the *brujos* pray and burn incense throughout the night.

As a visitor, however, even if you could plan to be in town at the right time, you'd be unlikely to see any of this, and it's best to visit Momostenango for the market, or for the fiesta on August 1. If you decide to stay for a day or two then you can take a walk to the *riscos*, a set of bizarre sandstone pillars, or beyond to the **hot springs** of Pala Chiquito. The springs are about 3km away to the north, and throughout the day weavers work there washing and shrinking their blankets – it's always best to go early, before most people arrive and the water is discoloured by soap.

Practicalities
By far the best place **to stay** in Momostenango is the *Hotel Estiver*, 1 C 4–15, Zona 1 (☎7365036; ②), with clean rooms, some with private bathrooms, great views from the roof and safe parking. The hotel is also the place to get in touch with ADIFAM, a development agency that concentrates on educating children in the municipality and is in need of Spanish-speaking volunteers (they can also be emailed on *momos@guate.net*). The very basic *Hospedaje Paclom* (①) is a distant second best, but you'll have to hike to the hot springs for a wash because there are no showers here. For **food**, head to any of the many small *comedores* on the main plaza. You can also **study Quiché** in Momostenango at the Kuinik Ta'ik Language School, whose office is at the *Hotel Estiver* (or you could email them, also on *momos@guate.net*).

Buses run here from Quetzaltenango, passing through Cuatro Caminos and San Francisco el Alto on the way. They leave the Minerva terminal in Quetzaltenango every hour or so from 10am to 4pm, and from Momostenango between 6am and 3pm. On Sunday a special early morning bus leaves Quetzaltenango at 6am: you can catch this at the rotunda.

Totonicapán

TOTONICAPÁN, capital of one of the smaller departments, is reached down a direct road leading east from Cuatro Caminos. Surrounded by rolling hills and pine forests, the town stands at the heart of a heavily populated and intensely farmed region. There is only one point of access and the valley has always held out against outside influence, shut off in a world of its own. In 1820 it became the scene of one of the most famous **Maya rebellions**. The early part of the nineteenth century had been marked by a series of revolts throughout the area, particularly in Momostenango and Totonicapán; the largest of these erupted in 1820, sparked by demands for tax. The indigenous people expelled all of the town's *ladinos*, crowning their leader Atanasio Tzul the "king and fiscal king", and making his assistant, Lucas Aquilar, president. His reign lasted only 29 days before it was violently suppressed.

Today, Totonicapán is a quiet place whose faded glory is ruffled only by the Tuesday and Saturday markets, which fill the two plazas to bursting. Until fairly recently a highly ornate traditional costume was worn here. The women's *huipiles* were some of the most elaborate and colourful in the country, and the men wore trousers embroidered with flowers, edged in lace, and decorated with silver buttons. Today, however, all this has disappeared and the town has instead become one of the chief centres of commercial weaving. Along with Salcajá it produces much of the *jasped* cloth worn as skirts by the majority of indigenous women: the machine-made *huipiles* of modern Totonicapán are used throughout the highlands as part of the universal costume. On one side of the old plaza is a workshop where young men are taught to weave on treadle looms, and visitors are always welcome to stroll in and take a look around. This same plaza is home to the municipal theatre, a grand Neoclassical structure echoing that in Quetzaltenango.

There are good connections between Totonicapán and Quetzaltenango, with buses shuttling back and forth every thirty minutes or so. Totonicapán is very quiet after dark, but if you want to stay, the best **hotel** is the *Hospedaje San Miguel*, 8 Av & 3 C, one block from the plaza (②). It's pretty comfortable and some rooms have bathrooms, but prices rise before market days. The *Pensión Blanquita*, at 13 Av and 4 C (①), is a friendly and basic alternative, opposite the filling station. **Buses** for Totonicapán leave Quetzaltenango passing the rotunda and Cuatros Caminos en route. Entering the village you pass one of the country's finest *pilas* (communal washing places), ringed with Gothic columns.

The Department of San Marcos

Leaving Quetzaltenango to the west, the main road heads out of the valley through San Mateo and Ostuncalco and climbs a massive range of hills, dropping down on the other side to the village of Palestina de Los Altos. Beyond this it weaves through a U-shaped valley to the twin towns of **San Marcos** and **San Pedro Sacatepéquez**. These towns form the core of the country's westernmost department, a neglected area that once served as a major trade route and includes Guatemala's highest volcano and a substantial stretch of the border with Mexico. There's little to detain you in either place, but they make useful bases for a trip into the mountainous countryside to the north.

San Pedro Sacatepéquez and San Marcos

SAN PEDRO SACATEPÉQUEZ is the larger and busier of the two towns, a bustling and unattractive commercial centre with a huge plaza that's the scene of a market on Thursday and Sunday. In days gone by this was a Maya settlement, famed for its brilliant yellow weaving, in which silk was used. Over the years the town has been singled out for some highly questionable praise: in 1543 the King of Spain, Carlos V, granted the headmen special privileges as thanks for their assistance during the Conquest, and in 1876 the town was honoured by President Rufino Barrios, who with a stroke of his pen raised the status of the people from Maya to *ladinos*.

A dual carriageway road connects San Pedro with its sister town of San Marcos, 2km west. Along the way, a long-running dispute about the precise boundary between the two towns has been solved by the construction of the departmental headquarters at **La Union**, halfway between the two. The building, known as the **Maya Palace**, is an outlandish and bizarre piece of architecture that goes some way to compensate for the otherwise unrelenting blandness of the two towns. The structure itself is relatively sober, but its facade is covered in imitation Maya carvings. Elaborate decorative friezes run around the sides, two great roaring jaguars guard the entrance, and above the main doors is a fantastic clock with Maya numerals and snake hands. The **buses** that run a continuous shuttle service between the two towns can drop you at the Maya Palace. A few kilometres away there's a spring-fed **swimming pool**, where you can while away an hour or two: to get there walk from the plaza in San Pedro down 5 C in the direction of San Marcos, and turn left in front of the Templo de Candelero along 2 Av. Follow this road through one valley and down into a second, where you take the left turn to the bottom. The pool – marked simply *Agua Tibia* – is open from 6am to 6pm, and there's a small entrance fee.

SAN MARCOS, officially the capital of the department, once stood proud and important on the main route to Mexico, but these days articulated lorries roar along the coastal highway and the focus of trade has shifted to San Pedro, leaving San Marcos to sink into provincial stagnation.

Practicalities

Most of the activity and almost all the transport are based in **San Pedro**. The cheapest **place to stay** is the *Pensión Mendez*, a very basic place at 4 C and 6 Av (①). The *Hotel Samaritano*, 6 Av 6–44 (②), is a clean but characterless modern building, though definitely better than the *Hotel Bagod*, on 5 C and 4 Av (①). Finally, the newish *Hotel Tacana*, 3 C 3–22 (②), is good value, and some of its rooms have private showers. In **San Marcos** the *Hotel Palacio*, on 7 Av, opposite the police station (①), is an amazing old place, its rooms decaying and very musty with peeling wallpaper. There's also a relatively luxurious hotel, the *Pérez*, at 9 C 2–25 (☎7601007; ③), a very dignified and longstanding establishment that's excellent value and has its own restaurant.

There are plenty of cheap **comedores** in San Pedro, fewer in San Marcos. For real Italian food in San Pedro, head for *La Cueva de los Faraones*, at 5C 1-11, or in San Marcos, try *Mah Kik* behind the Chevron station, an elegant, subdued and fairly expensive place. Both towns have **cinemas**: the Cine T-manek on the plaza in San Pedro, and the Cine Carua, beside the *Hotel Pérez* in San Marcos. There are **banks** on both plazas.

Second-class **buses** run hourly from San Pedro to Malacatán, Quetzaltenango (both 1hr 30min) and Guatemala City, between 5am and 5pm, from a small chaotic terminal one block behind the church. *Marquensita* pullmans go direct from San Marcos to Guatemala City, passing through the plaza in San Pedro eight times daily from 2.30am until 4pm.

To Tacaná and the high country

To the northwest of San Pedro is some magnificent high country, strung up between the Tajumulco and Tacaná volcanoes and forming an extension of the Mexican Sierra Madre. A rough dirt road runs through these mountains, connecting a series of isolated villages that lie exposed in the frosty heights.

Leaving San Pedro the road climbs steeply, winding up through thick pine forests and emerging onto a high grassy plateau. Here it crosses a great boggy expanse to skirt around the edge of the Tajumulco **volcano**, whose 4220-metre peak is the highest in Guatemala. It's best climbed from the roadside hamlet of Tuchan, from where it's about four hours to the summit – not a particularly hard climb as long as you're acclimatized to the altitude. Quetzaltrekkers, in Quetzaltengo (☎ 7612470; see p.166 for full details), conducts tours up Tajumulco.

Up here the land is sparsely inhabited, dotted with adobe houses and flocks of sheep and goats. The rocky ridges are barren and the trees twisted by the cold.

At this altitude the air is thin and what little breath you have left is regularly taken away by the astonishing views which – except when consumed in the frequent mist and cloud – open up at every turn. The village of **IXCHIGUÁN**, on an exposed hillside at 3050m, is the first place of any size, surrounded by bleak rounded hills and in the shadow of the two towering volcanic cones. Buses generally stop here for lunch, giving you a chance to stretch your legs and thaw out with a steaming bowl of *caldo*.

Moving on, the road climbs to the **CUMBRE DE COTZIL**, a spectacular pass which reaches some 3400m and marks the highest point on any road in Central America. From here on it's downhill all the way to the scruffy village of **TACANÁ**, a flourishing trading centre that signals the end of the road – 73km from San Marcos and less than 10km from the Mexican border. Cross-border ties are strong and at the end of 1988 the inhabitants threatened to incorporate themselves into Mexico if the road to San Pedro wasn't paved, claiming that this had been promised to them by the Christian Democrats in the run-up to the 1985 election. Up above the village, spanning the border, is the **Tacaná volcano** (4064m), which can be climbed from the village of Sibinal. It last erupted in 1855, so it should be safe enough. Unless you're setting out to climb one of the volcanoes there's not much to do out this way, but the bus ride alone, bruising though it is, offers some great scenery. Three **buses** a day leave the terminal in San Pedro for Tacaná, at 9am, 11am and noon, returning at 3am, 5am and 11am. The trip takes about five hours, and there is also a bus service to Sibinal and Concepción Tutuapa – at similar times. In Tacaná the best **hotel** is the *Hotel El Trebol*, on the entrance road (①), where they also do good food. Right in the village, you'll also find the *Hospedaje Los Angeles* (①) and the *Pensión Celajes Tacanecos* (①).

Heading on from Tacaná, pick-ups provide links with Cuilco (from where there are regular buses to Huehuetenango) and to a remote crossing point on the Mexican border called Niquimiul.

Towards the Mexican border

The main road through San Pedro continues west, through San Marcos and out of the valley. Here it starts the descent towards the Pacific plain, dropping steeply around endless hairpin bends and past acre after acre of coffee bushes. Along the way the views towards the ocean are superb. Eventually you reach the sweltering lowlands, passing through San Rafael and El Rodeo with their squalid shacks for plantation workers. About an hour and a half out of San Pedro you arrive in **MALACATÁN**, a relatively sedate place by coastal standards. If you get stuck here on your way to or from the border, try the *Pensión Lucía* (☎7769415;②) or the *Hotel América* (①), both on the plaza, or *Hotel Don Arturo*, 5 C & 7 Av (☎7769169; ④), for somewhere more comfortable. Contrary to popular belief, there is no Mexican consul in Malacatán, but if you need to change money, you can do so at a branch of the Banco del Café (Mon–Fri 8.30am–noon & 2–5.30pm).

Buses between Malacatán and San Marcos run every hour from 5am to 5pm. There are trucks and minibuses every half hour from Malacatán to the border at Talisman, and plenty of pullmans pass through on their way between the border and the capital.

HUEHUETENANGO AND THE CUCHUMATANES

The **department of Huehuetenango**, slotted into the northwest corner of the highlands, is a wildly beautiful part of the country that's bypassed by the majority of visitors. The area is dominated by the mountains of the **Cuchumatanes**, but also includes a limestone plateau in the west and a strip of dense jungle to the north. The vast majority of this is inaccessible to all but the most dedicated of hikers, but with adequate time and a sense of adventure, this can be one of the most rewarding and spectacular parts of the country.

The **Pan-American Highway**, cutting through from Cuatro Caminos to the Mexican border, is the only paved road in the department, and if you're heading through this way you'll get a glimpse of the mountains, and perhaps a vague sense of the isolating influence of this massive landscape. With more time and energy to spare, a trip into the mountains to **Todos Santos**, or even all the way out to **San Mateo Ixtatán**, reveals an exceptional wealth of Maya culture. It's a world of jagged peaks and deep-cut valleys, where Spanish is definitely the second language and traditional costume is still rigidly adhered to. Heavily populated before the Conquest, the area has pre Columbian ruins scattered throughout the hills, with the largest at **Zaculeu**, immediately outside **Huehuetenango**, a lively town with good budget hotels and some decent restaurants and cafés.

Despite the initial devastation, the arrival of the Spanish had surprisingly little impact in these highlands with some of the communities remaining amongst the most traditional in Guatemala. A visit to these mountain villages, either for a market or fiesta (and there are plenty of both), offers one of the best opportunities to see Maya life at close quarters.

Heading on from Huehuetenango you can be at the **Mexican border** in a couple of hours, reach Guatemala City in five or six, or use the back roads to travel across the highlands through **Aguacatán** towards Santa Cruz del Quiché, Nebaj or Cobán.

From Cuatro Caminos to Huehuetenango

Heading northwest from Cuatro Caminos, the Pan-American Highway climbs steadily, passing the entrance to San Francisco el Alto and stepping up out of the Xela valley onto a broad plateau thick with fields of wheat and dotted with houses. The only village along the way is **POLOGUÁ**, where they have a small weekly market, a *pensión* – the *Pologuita* (①) – and a fiesta from August 21 to 27.

About a kilometre before the village, a dirt track leads north to **SAN BARTOLO**, a small agricultural centre down amongst the pine trees, some 12km from the road. The place is virtually deserted during the week, but on Sundays the farmers who live scattered in the surrounding forest gather in the village for the market. There's a small unmarked *pensión* and some thermal springs a couple of kilometres away. Another track, branching from the first a couple of kilometres before San Bartolo, connects the village with Momostenango, which is about two hours' walk. From Quetzaltenango to San Bartolo there are three daily buses, all returning between 6am and 6.30am.

Beyond Pologuá the road turns towards the north and leaves the corn-covered plateau, crossing the crest of the hills and skirting around the rim of a huge sweeping valley. To the east a superb view opens out across a sea of pine forests, the last stretch of levellish land before the mountains to the north. Way out there in the middle is Santa Cruz del Quiché and closer to hand, buried in the trees, lies Momostenango. Once over the ridge the road winds its way down towards Huehuetenango. The first place inside the department is the *ladino* village of **Malacatancito**, where Mam warriors first challenged the advancing Spanish army in 1525.

Huehuetenango

In the corner of a small agricultural plain, 5km from the main road at the foot of the mighty Cuchumatanes, **HUEHUETENANGO**, capital of the department of the same name, is the focus of trade and transport for a vast area. Nonetheless, its atmosphere is provincial and relaxed. The name is a Nahuatl word meaning "the place of the old people", and before the arrival of the Spanish it was the site of one of the residential suburbs that surrounded the Mam capital of Zaculeu (see p.190). Under colonial rule it was a small regional centre with little to offer other than a steady trickle of silver and a stretch or two of grazing land. The supply of silver dried up long ago, but other minerals are still mined, and coffee and sugar have been added to the area's produce.

Arrival and information

Like all Guatemalan towns, Huehuetenango, known simply as Huehue, is laid out on a grid pattern, with avenidas running one way and calles the other. It's fairly

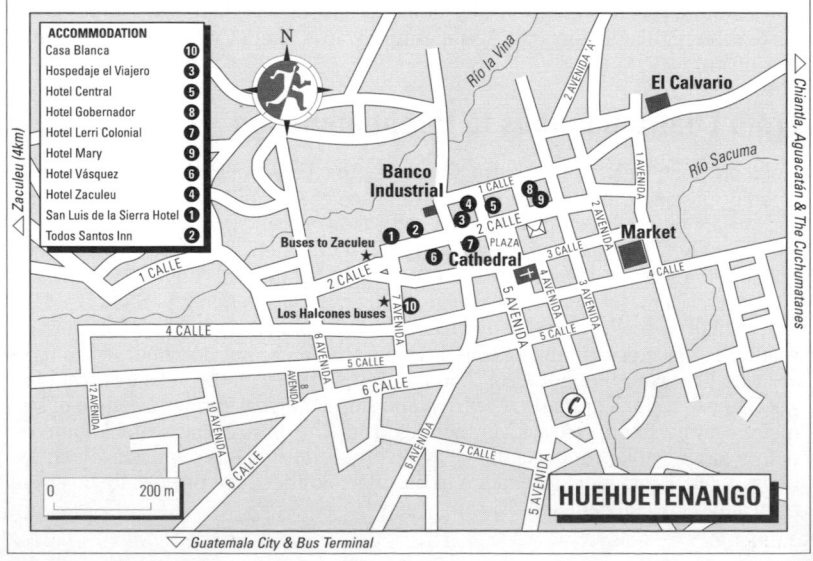

small so you shouldn't have any real problems finding your way around, particularly once you've located the plaza.

Most buses arrive at the **bus terminal**, halfway between the Pan-American Highway and town. Minibuses make constant trips between the town centre and the bus terminal, or you can take the larger bus, heading for **Chiantla**, just beyond Huehue, via the town centre.

You'll probably be coming to **Huehuetenango** from elsewhere in the highlands, in which case you might be able to pick up a direct bus somewhere along the Pan-American Highway – or you can catch any bus to Cuatro Caminos, where you'll be able to get one to Huehuetenango. There's also a regular service, with hourly departures, from the terminal in Quetzaltenango.

Coming direct **from Guatemala City** the best way to travel is by pullman. Los Halcones runs buses at 7am, 2pm and 5pm from its offices at 7 Av 15–27, Zona 1, Guatemala City. Also highly recommended is Transportes Velasquez, 20 C 1–37, Zona 1 (☎4736005) in Guatemala City, who runs pullmans to Huehuetenango eleven times a day from 5.20am until 5.30pm, with an extra service on Fridays at 6.30pm. Five of the morning departures continue on to the Mexican border at La Mesilla. There are also second-class departures every hour from the main bus terminal in Zona 4. Coming **from the Mexican border** at La Mesilla, there's a bus every hour from 4am to 4pm.

Accommodation

Huehuetenango has a good range of **hotels**, most of which are good value and attractive, though there are no luxury options. Most of the real cheapies are scruffy, chaotic places clustered around 1 Av, and geared mainly towards market traders.

Casa Blanca, 7 Av 3–41 (☎ & fax 7642586). The town's most upmarket hotel, built in colonial style. The fine restaurant on a spacious garden terrace is well worth a visit in its own right. ⑤.

Hotel Central, 5 Av 1–33 (☎7641197) Classic budget hotel, with large, scruffy rooms in a creaking old wooden building. There are no singles or private baths, but it has a fantastic *comedor*. ①.

Hotel Gobernador, 4 Av 1–45 (☎ & fax 7641197). Formerly known as the Astoria this is an excellent budget hotel run by a very friendly family. It has attractive rooms, with or without bath, hot showers and a good *comedor*. ②.

Hotel Lerri Colonial, 2 C 5–49 (☎7641526). Formerly known as *Roberto's*, this place is basic but reasonable enough for the price. Some rooms have private showers. ②.

Hotel Mary, 2 C 3–52 (☎7641618; fax 7641228). Central with small but pleasant rooms, some with a private shower and loads of steaming hot water. ②.

San Luis de la Sierra Hotel, 2 C 7-00 (☎ & fax 7641103). New in 1997, this place has nice modern rooms all with cable TV and private bathrooms, and some with good views of the Cuchumatanes mountains. Safe parking, too. ④.

Todos Santos Inn, 2 C 6–74 (☎7641241). The best budget hotel in town. Rooms seem far too attractive for the price and come with bedside lights for reading and good hot water. Excellent deal for single travellers. ②.

Hotel Vásquez, 2 C 6–67 (☎7641338). Cell-sized rooms around a bare courtyard, but clean, safe, and with secure parking. ②.

Hospedaje El Viajero, 2 C 5–36. Cheap but very rough – a lot like the market traders' hotels on 1 Av. ①.

Hotel Zaculeu, 5 Av 1–14 (☎7641086; fax 7641575). Large, comfortable hotel and something of an institution, though in need of refurbishment. Some of the older rooms surrounding a leafy courtyard are a bit musty and gloomy, while those in the more expensive new section are larger and more spacious. All come with cable TV and private bathroom. There's also parking and a reasonable restaurant. ④.

The Town

Today's Huehuetenango has two quite distinct functions – and two contrasting halves – each serving a separate section of the population. The large majority of the people are *ladinos*, and for them Huehuetenango is an unimportant regional centre far from the hub of things, a mood summed up in the unhurried atmosphere of the attractive **plaza** at the heart of the *ladino* half of town, where shaded walkways are surrounded by administrative offices. Overlooking it, perched above the pavements, are a shell-shaped bandstand, a clock tower and a grandiose Neoclassical church, a solid whitewashed structure with a facade that's crammed with Doric pillars and Grecian urns. In the middle of the plaza there's a **relief map** of the department with flags marking the villages. The details are vague and the scale a bit warped, but it gives you an idea of the mass of rock that dominates the region, and the deep river valleys that slice into it.

A few blocks to the east, the town's atmosphere could hardly be more different. Here the neat little rows of arches are replaced by the pale green walls of the **market**, hub of the Maya part of town, where the streets are crowded with traders, drunks and travellers from Mexico and all over Central America. This part of Huehuetenango, centred on 1 Av, is always alive with activity, its streets packed with people from every corner of the department and littered with rotten vegetables.

Eating, drinking and entertainment

Most of the better **restaurants** are, like the accommodation, in the central area, around the plaza. **Films** are shown two or three times a week at the cinema on 3 C, half a block west of the plaza.

Las Brasas, 4 Av 1–55 . Reasonably good Chinese food and steaks, but a bit overpriced.

La Cabana del Café, 2C opposite *Hotel Vásquez*. Wooden café with an excellent range of coffees (including cappuccino), great cakes and a few snacks.

Café Jardin, 4 C and 6 Av. Friendly place serving inexpensive but excellent breakfasts, milkshakes, pancakes and the usual chicken and beef dishes. Open 6am–11pm.

Hotel Central, 5 Av 1–33. Very tasty, inexpensive set meals, including a particularly good breakfast served from 7am.

La Fonda de Don Juan, 2 C 5–35. Attractive place with good if pricey pizzas, though the pasta portions are tiny.

Maxi Pizza, 2 C, just off the plaza. Does just what you'd expect and does it fairly well.

Mi Tierra, 4 C 6-46. Superb new restaurant with attractive decor including plants and a fountain, a good atmosphere and an imaginative menu. Great for house salads, *churrascos,* cheesecake, and the beer's cheap. Closed Wed.

Pizza Hogareña, 6 Av 4–45, next to *Hotel Mary*. Delicious sandwiches, *churrascos*, fish, huge salads, pasta, fruit juices and pizzas.

Restaurante Rincón, 6 Av A 7–21. Under the same management as the *Pizza Hogareña* and offering the same food.

Listings

Banks Banco G&T is on the plaza (Mon–Fri 9am–8pm, Sat 10am–1pm); Banco del Café, a block to the south (Mon–Fri 8.30am–8pm, Sat 9am–3pm); and there's a Banco del Ejercito at the junction of 5 Av & 4 C (Mon–Fri 9am–7pm, Sat 9am–1pm). Note that you may have problems getting cash or changing travellers' cheques on a Saturday.

Language schools Huehuetenango is a good place to learn Spanish as you don't rub shoulders with many other gringos. As almost everywhere, schools offer a package of tuition and accommodation with a family for around $110 a week. One of the best is El Portal, 1 C 1–64, Zona 3 (☎ & fax 7641987), closely rivalled by Fundacion 23, 6 Av 6–126, Zona 1 (☎7641478), and Xinabajul, 6 Av 0-69 (☎ & fax 7641518). Abesaida Guevara de López gives good private lessons (☎ 7642917).

Laundry The best is in the Turismundo Commercial Centre at 3 Av 0–15 (Mon–Sat 9.30am–6.30pm).

MOVING ON FROM HUEHUETENANGO

All transport, except to the village of St Juan Atitán and the Zaculeu ruins, leaves from the **main bus terminal** on the edge of town. To get there from the town centre, take either a minibus or the Chiantla bus from the *parada servicio urbano* just past the *Café Jardin*, or on 6 Av, between 2 and 3 C. The terminal is well laid out, each bus company with its own office, so you can easily get the latest timetable information; don't believe the times painted on the walls, though. Note also that it is standard practice to buy your ticket from the office, before boarding the bus, even for second-class buses. Generally, there are more buses in the mornings to all destinations.

Buses to the **Mexican border** (2hr) leave every half hour from 5.30am onwards, with the last one departing at 7pm. For Coatepeque and the Mexican border at Tecún Umán, 17 buses leave daily between 3am and 4.45pm. For anywhere along the **Pacific Highway**, Velasquez buses leave at 3.30am, 7.15am, 8.30am, 10.30am and 2.30pm and travel this alternative route to Guatemala City. There are buses every half hour to **Quetzaltenango** (2hr), with the first one leaving at 4.30am, and the last at 6pm. To **Guatemala City** (6hr), there are hourly departures from 2.15am to 4pm plus the luxury Los Halcones buses that leave from their own terminal on 7 Av 3-62 (☎7642251) at 7am, 2pm and 5pm. If you want to go to **Antigua**, take a capital-bound bus and change at Chimaltenango; for **Lake Atitlán** or **Chichicastenango** change at Los Encuentros.

More remote destinations are also served. Heading north, into the **Cuchumatanes mountains**, there are buses for **Barillas** (7hr) at 5am, 9.30am, 10am and 10pm, as well as regular departures to San Miguel Acatán, Soloma and San Mateo Ixtatán (see p.195 for details). The **Todos Santos** (3hr) buses leave at 3am, 12.30pm, 1pm and 3pm with afternoon buses often continuing on to San Martín and Jacaltenango. Buses for **Nentón** (4hr 30min) leave at 5am, 5.30am, 9.30am, 12.30pm and 1.20pm, with the 5am, 12.30pm and 1.20pm departures continuing on to **Gracias a Dios** (7hr 30min), in the isolated northwest. You should always check these schedules, however, prior to your planned day of departure.

To the west, buses head for isolated **Cuilco** (3–4hr) at 5am and 2pm. Heading east and northeast, there are eight buses for **Aguacatán** (1hr 15min) leaving daily at 6am, 7am, 11am, noon, 1.30pm, 2.15pm, 2.45pm and 3.30pm, and one daily (which also stops at Aguacatán) to **Sacapulas** (4hr) at 12.45pm, where you can make daily connections south, for Quiché and Chichicastenango. A daily direct bus to **Nebaj** (6hr), departing at 11.30am, also goes via Aguacatán and Sacapulas.

Mexican consulate In the Farmacía El Cid, on the plaza at 5 Av and 4 C (8am–noon & 2–7pm). They'll charge you $1.80 for a tourist card that's usually free at the border though few nationalities now need one.

Phones Telgua is currently at 4 Av 6–54 (7am–10pm), though it has plans to revert back to its former address next to the post office.

Post office 2 C 3–54 (Mon–Fri 8am–4.30pm).

Shopping Superb weaving is produced throughout the department and can be bought in the market here or at Artesanias Ixquil, on 5 Av 1–56, opposite the *Hotel Central*, where both the prices and quality are high. If you have time, though, you'd be better advised to travel to the villages and buy direct from the producers.

Zaculeu

A few kilometres to the west of Huehuetenango are the ruins of **ZACULEU**, capital of the **Mam**, who were one of the principal pre-Conquest highland tribes. The site (daily 8am–6pm; $5) includes several large temples, plazas and a ball court, but unfortunately it has been restored with an astounding lack of subtlety (or accuracy). Its appearance – more like an ageing film set than an ancient ruin – is owed to a latter-day colonial power, the **United Fruit Company**, under whose auspices the ruins were reconstructed in 1946 and 1947; the company is, of

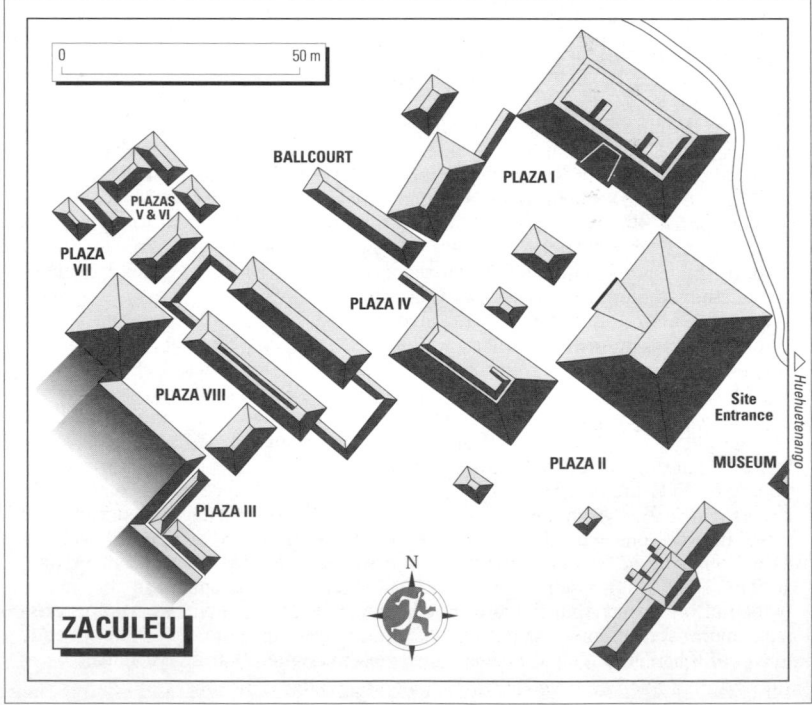

course, notorious for its heavy-handed practices throughout Central America, and the Zaculeu reconstruction is no exception. The walls and surfaces have been levelled off with a layer of thick white plaster, leaving them stark and undecorated. There are no roof-combs, carvings or stucco mouldings, and only in a few places does the original stonework show through. Even so, the site does have a peculiar atmosphere of its own and is worth a look: surrounded by trees and neatly mown grass, with fantastic views of the mountains, it's an excellent spot for a picnic.

Not all that much is known about the early history of Zaculeu as no Mam records survived the Conquest, but the site is thought to have been a religious and administrative centre housing the elite, while the bulk of the population lived in small surrounding settlements or scattered in the hills. Zaculeu was the hub of a large area of Mam-speakers, its boundaries reaching into the mountains as far as Todos Santos and along the Selegua and Cuilco valleys, an area throughout which Mam remains the dominant language.

To put together a history of the site means relying on the records of the Quiché, a more powerful neighbouring tribe. According to their mythology, the Quiché conquered most of the other highland tribes, including the Mam, some time between 1400 and 1475: the Popol Vuh tells that "our grandfathers and fathers cast them out when they inserted themselves among the Mam of Zakiulew". The Quiché maintained their authority under the rule of the leader Quicab, but following his death in 1475 the subjugated tribes began to break away from the fold. As a part of this trend the Mam managed to reassert their independence, but no sooner had they escaped the clutches of one expansionist empire than the **Spanish** arrived with a yet more brutal alternative.

For the first few months the Spaniards devoted themselves to conquering the Quiché, still the dominant force in the highlands. But once they'd achieved this they turned their attention to the Mam, especially after being told by Sequechul, leader of the Quiché, that a plan to burn the Spanish army in Utatlán had been suggested to his father by **Caibal Balam**, king of the Mam. In answer to this, Pedro de Alvarado despatched an army under the command of his brother Gonzalo to mete out punishment. They were met by about five thousand Mam warriors near the village of Malacatancito, and promptly set about a massacre. Seeing that his troops were no match for the Spanish, Caibal Balam withdrew them to the safety of Zaculeu, where they were protected on three sides by deep ravines and on the other by a series of walls and ditches. The Spanish army settled outside the city, preparing themselves for a lengthy siege, while Gonzalo offered the Maya a simple choice – they either became Christians "peacefully" or faced "death and destruction".

Attracted by neither option they struggled to hold out against the invading force. At one stage a relief army of eight thousand arrived from the mountains, but again they were unable to ruffle Gonzalo's well-disciplined ranks. Finally, in mid-October, after about six weeks under siege, his army starving to death, Caibal Balam surrendered to the Spanish. With the bitterest of ironies a bastardized version of his name has been adopted by one of Guatemala's crack army regiments – the "Kaibils", who have been held responsible for numerous massacres during the 1970s and early 1980s.

Excavations at the site have unearthed hundreds of burials carried out in an unusual variety of ways; bodies were crammed into great urns, interred in vaults and even cremated. These burials, along with artefacts found at the site, including pyrite plaques and carved jade, have suggested links with the site at Nebaj.

There's a small **museum** on site (daily 8am–noon & 1–6pm) with examples of some of the burial techniques used and some interesting ceramics found during excavation.

To get to **Zaculeu** from Huehuetenango, take one of the pick-ups or buses that leave from 7 Av between 2 and 3 calles – make sure it's a Ruta 3 bus heading for Ruinas Zaculeu (not Zaculeu central).

Chiantla

The village of **CHIANTLA** is backed right up against the mountains, 5km to the north of Huehuetenango. The main point of interest here is the colonial church, built by Dominican friars, which is now the object of one of the country's largest pilgrimages, annually on February 2, in honour of its image of the **Virgen del Rosario**. Legend has it that the image of the Virgin was given to the church by a Spaniard named Almengor, who owned a silver mine in the hills. Not only did the mine proceed to yield a fortune, but on his last visit to it, just after Almengor had surfaced, the entire thing caved in – thus proving the power of the Virgin. She is also thought to be capable of healing the sick, and at any time of the year you'll see people who've travelled from all over Guatemala asking for her assistance. A mural inside the church depicts a rather ill-proportioned Spaniard watching over the Maya toiling in his mines, while on the wall opposite the Maya are shown discovering God. The precise connection between the two is left somewhat vague, but presumably the gap is bridged by the Virgin. **Buses** from Huehuetenango to Chiantla travel between the main bus terminal and Chiantla every fifteen minutes between 6am and 6.30pm. You can catch one as it passes through the town centre, or wait at the *calvario* (by the junction of 1 Av and 1 C), instead of heading out to the terminal.

The Cuchumatanes

The **Cuchumatanes**, rising to a frosty 3837m just to the north of Huehuetenango, are the largest non-volcanic peaks in Central America. The mountain chain rises from a limestone plateau close to the Mexican border, reaches its full height above Huehuetenango, and falls away gradually to the east, continuing through northern Quiché to form part of the highlands of Alta Verapaz. Appropriately enough the name translates as "that which was brought together by great force", from the Mam words *cucuj*, to unite, and *matan*, superior force.

The mountain scenery is magnificent, ranging from wild, exposed craggy outcrops to lush, tranquil river valleys. The upper parts of the slopes are barren, scattered with boulders and shrivelled cypress trees, while the lower levels, by contrast, are richly fertile, cultivated with corn, coffee and sugar. Between the peaks, in the deep-cut valleys, are hundreds of tiny villages, isolated by the enormity of the landscape. This area had little to entice the Spanish, and even at the best of times they only managed to exercise vague control, occasionally disrupting things with bouts of religious persecution or disease, but rarely maintaining a sustained presence. Following the initial impact of the Conquest, the people were, for the most part, left to revert to their old ways, and their traditions are still very powerful today, showing through in the fiestas, costumes and folk-Catholicism.

More recently the mountains were the scene of bitter fighting between the army and the guerrillas. In the late 1970s and early 1980s the area was struck by a wave of violence and terror that sent thousands fleeing across the border to Mexico. These days things have calmed down, and some families have returned from exile, although many still remain in refugee camps on the other side of the border. It is, however, generally **safe** to travel into the mountains, discovering some of the country's most spectacular scenery and fascinating villages. A single rough road runs through the range, climbing the steep south face, crossing the exposed central plateau and dropping into the isolated valleys to the north. Travel here is not easy – distances are large, hotels and restaurants basic at best, buses are packed and frequent cloudbursts often make the roads impassable – but if you can summon the energy it's an immensely rewarding area, offering a rare glimpse of Maya life and some of the country's finest fiestas and markets. The mountains are also ideal for hiking, particularly if you've had enough of struggling up volcanoes.

The most accessible of the villages in the vicinity, and the only one yet to receive a steady trickle of tourists, is **Todos Santos**, which is also one of the most interesting. At any time of year the Saturday market here is well worth visiting, and the horse race fiesta on November 1 has to be one of the most outrageous in Guatemala. From here, you can walk over the hills to **San Juan Atitán** and **Santiago Chimaltenango**, or head on down the valley to **San Martín** and **Jacaltenango**. Further into the mountains are the villages of **Soloma** and **San Mateo Ixtatán**, both of which have markets on Thursday and Sunday. Another good hike takes you from **San Miguel Acatán** along the edge of the hills to Jacaltenango. Beyond San Mateo Ixtatán the road comes to an end a few kilometres past **Barillas**, a *ladino* town from where the jungle lowlands beyond are being colonized.

Huehuetenango to Barillas

Heading north out of Huehuetenango, the road for the mountains passes through Chiantla before starting to climb the arid hillside, and as the bus sways around the switchbacks, the view across the valley is superb. In the distance you can sometimes make out the perfect cone of the Santa María volcano, towering above Quetzaltenango some 60km to the south.

At the top of the slope the road slips through a pass into the *región andina*, a desolate grassy plateau suspended between the peaks, strewn with boulders and segregated with neat earth walls. At this height the air is cool, thin and fresh, the ground often hard with frost and occasionally dusted with snow. In the middle of the plain is the *Comedor de los Cuchumatanes*, where buses stop for a chilly lunch before pressing on through Paquix, junction for the road to Todos Santos. Shortly before the road reaches the *comedor* a rough track branches off to the east, climbing through the mountains for 44km to Salquil Grande – the road is often impassable, but if you're in search of an unpredictable adventure it makes a spectacular trip.

Beyond Paquix the road runs through a couple of magical valleys, where great grey boulders lie scattered among ancient-looking oak and cypress trees, their trunks gnarled by the bitter winds. A few families manage to survive the rigours of the altitude, collecting firewood and tending flocks of sheep. Sheep have been grazed here since they were introduced by the Spanish, who prized this wilder-

THE MAYA PRIESTS OF THE CUCHUMATANES

The high peaks and rugged terrain of the Cuchumatanes guard one of the country's most traditional Maya cultures. Ethnographer Krystyna Deuss has been studying Maya rituals in these remote communities for more than ten years, focusing her attention on the prayer-makers, who occupy a position parallel to that of local priests. Here she explains their role and some of the key rituals surrounding their office.

Some of the purest **Maya rituals** today can be found among the Kanjobal of the northwestern Cuchumatanes. The office of *alcade resador* (chief prayer-maker) still exists here and the 365-day *Haab* calendar is used in conjunction with the 260-day *Tzolkin*. The former ends with the five days of *Oyeb ku*, when adult souls leave the body; the return of the souls on the fifth day brings in the new year. As this always falls on a day of *Watan, Lambat, Ben* or *Chinax*, these four day lords are referred to as the "Year Bearers" or "Chiefs". Depending on the community, the *Haab* year begins either at the end of February or the beginning of March, coinciding with the corn planting season.

The duty of the **alcade resador** is to protect his village from evil and ensure a good harvest by praying for rain at planting time and for protection against wind, pest and disease while the corn is maturing. His year of office – during which he and his wife must remain celibate – begins on January 1, the day all the voluntary municipal officials change, and in the towns of Santa Eulalia, Soloma and San Miguel Acatán where traditions are particularly strong, he lives in a house which has been especially built for him. Traditionalists regularly visit to ask for prayers and to leave gifts of corn, beans, candles and money. On the altar of the house stands the **ordenanza**, a chest that not only contains religious icons but also ancient village documents, a throwback to the time when religious and civil authorities worked as one. The chest now serves both as a symbol of authority and as a

ness as the best pasture in Central America, though you are unlikely to find lamb on a menu up here or anywhere in Guatemala.

Continuing north the road gradually winds down off the plateau, emerging on the other side at the top of an incredibly steep valley. Here the track clings to the hillside, cut out of the sheer rock face that drops hundreds of metres to the valley floor. This northern side of the Cuchumatanes contains some of the most dramatic scenery in the entire country, and the road is certainly the most spine-chilling. A little further down, as if to confirm your worst fears, the rusting wreck of a bus lies a hundred metres or so beneath the road.

The first village reached by the road is **SAN JUAN IXCOY**, an apple-growing centre drawn out along the valley floor. There's no particular reason for breaking the journey here, but there is a small *pensión* (①), where you can get a bed and a meal. In season, around the end of August, passing buses are besieged by an army of fruit-sellers. This innocent-looking village has a past marked by violence. On the night of July 17, 1898, following a dispute about pay, the Maya of San Juan murdered the local labour contractor, and in a desperate bid to keep the crime secret they slaughtered all but one of the village's *ladino* population. The authorities responded mercilessly, killing about ten Maya for the life of every *ladino*. In local mythology the revolt is known as *la degollación*, the beheading.

Over another range of hills and down in the next valley is **SOLOMA**, largest, busiest and richest of the villages in the northern Cuchumatanes, with a popula-

sacred object, and can only be opened by the *alcade resador*, in private, once a year. The *resador's* whole day is spent in prayer: at his home altar before the *ordenanza*, in church and at sacred village sites marked by crosses. Prayers for rain are often accompanied by the ritual sacrifice of turkeys whose blood is poured over the candles and incense destined to be burned at the sacred places the following day. These ceremonies are not open to the general public.

Festivals more in the public domain happen on January 1 when the incumbent *resador* hands over to his successor. In **Soloma** after an all-night vigil the *ordenanza* is carried in procession to the middle of the market square and put on a makeshift altar under a pine arch. When the incoming group arrives there are prayers and ritual drinking and they receive their wooden staffs of office, after which the outgoing *resador* (usually a man in his sixties or seventies) is free to leave for his own home. The new *resador's* group stays in the marketplace praying, collecting alms and drinking until 3pm, when they carry the *ordenanza* back to the official residence in a somewhat erratic procession. Notwithstanding a further night of vigil and ceremonial drinking, at 7am the following morning, the *resador* sets out on his first prayer-round to the sacred mountains overlooking the town.

In **San Juan Ixcoy** the year-end ceremonies differ in that the new *resador* is not appointed in advance. Here the outgoing group carries the *ordenanza* to a small chapel outside the church on the night of the 31st and leaves it in the care of a committee of traditionals. The usual all-night vigil with prayers, ritual drinking and collecting alms continues throughout the following day while everyone waits anxiously for a candidate to turn up. As the office of *resador* is not only arduous, and with dwindling support from the community, also expensive, the post is not always filled on January 1. The *ordenanza* sometimes stays locked in the chapel for several days before a volunteer (usually an ex-prayer maker) takes on the office again rather than let the *ordenanza* and the tradition be abandoned.

Krystyna Deuss – The Maya-Guatemalan Indian Centre, London

tion of around three thousand. Its flat valley floor was once the bed of a lake, and the steep hillsides still come sliding down at every earthquake or cloudburst. Soloma translates (from Kanjobal, the dominant language on this side of the mountains) as "without security", and its history is blackened by disaster; it was destroyed by earthquakes in 1773 and 1902, half burnt down in 1884, and decimated by smallpox in 1885. The long white *huipiles* worn by the women of Soloma are similar to those of San Mateo Ixtatán and the Lacandones, and are probably as close as any in the country to the style worn before the Conquest. These days they are on the whole donned only for the **market** on Thursday and Sunday, which again is by far the best time to visit.

About four hours from Huehuetenango, Soloma makes a good place to break the trip. The *Río Lindo* is a good, friendly **hotel** (②) that also does food, or there's the cheaper *Hotel Central* (①), and, as a last resort, the *Hospedaje San Juan* (①). Flor Solomera **buses** leave the terminal in Huehuetenango at 9.30am and 10pm; San Pedrito buses leave Huehuetenango terminal at 10am and 5pm; and Autobuses del Norte leave from the terminal in Huehuetenango at 3pm and 4.30pm. Rutas Barillenses also run services; check at the bus terminal for details. Buses going on to San Rafael La Independencia, San Sebastian Coatan and Barillas also pass through. Check all schedules first in the Huehue terminal.

Leaving Soloma the road climbs again, on a steadily deteriorating surface, over another range of hills, to the hillside village of Santa Eulalia. Beyond, past the junction to San Rafael La Independencia, it heads through another misty, rock-strewn forest and emerges on the other side at **SAN MATEO IXTATÁN**, the most traditional, and quite possibly the most interesting, of this string of villages. Little more than a thin sprawl of wooden-tiled houses on an exposed hillside, it's strung out beneath a belt of ancient forest and craggy mountains. The people here speak **Chuj** and form part of a Maya tribe who occupy the extreme north-west corner of the highlands and some of the jungle beyond; their territory borders that of the Lacandon, a jungle tribe never subjugated by the Spanish, who constantly harassed these villages in colonial times. The only industry is the manufacture of salt from some communally owned springs in the hills, and life at these heights is hard at the best of times. The only time to visit, other than for the fiesta on September 21, is on a market day, Thursday or Sunday. For the rest of the week the village is virtually deserted. The women here wear unusual and striking *huipiles*, long white gowns embroidered in brilliant reds, yellows and blues, radiating out from a star-like centre. The men wear short woollen tunics called *capixay*, often embroidered with flowers around the collar and quetzals on the back. Below the village is a beautiful Maya ruin, the unrestored remains of a small pyramid and ball court, shaded by a couple of cypress trees. If you decide to **stay**, there are several extremely basic *pensiónes* – don't expect sheets – the best of which is the *El Aguila* (①), run by the very friendly family who also operate the *Comedor Ixateco*. To the northwest of San Mateo a road cuts high across the mountain and is the start of a beautiful hike to Yalambojoch (see below).

Beyond San Mateo the road drops steadily east to **BARILLAS**, a *ladino* frontier town in the relative warmth of the lowlands. Further on still, the land slopes into the Usumacinta basin through thick, uninhabited jungle. Rough tracks penetrate a short distance into this wilderness (and a local bus runs out as far as San Ramón), opening it up for farming, and eventually a road will run east across the **Ixcán** (the wilderness area that stretches between here and the jungles of Petén) to Playa Grande (see p.302). The cheapest place **to stay** in Barillas is the *Tienda las Tres Rosas* (①), and the best, the *Hotel Monte Cristo* (①) costs not much more.

Pullman buses to Barillas, passing through all the villages en route, are operated by Flor Solomera and leave Huehuetenango at 10pm and 9.30am, taking around four hours to reach Soloma and at least eight hours to Barillas. San Pedrito, Autobuses del Norte and Rutas Barillenses also run services (see above). All buses leave from Huehue main bus terminal, and it's well worth buying your ticket in advance as they operate a vague system of seat allocation. It's a rough and tortuous trip, the buses usually filled to bursting and the road invariably appalling. Buses leave Barillas for Huehuetenango at 5am, 6am, 10am, 11am, 11.45am and 11.30pm.

Hiking from San Mateo to Yalambojoch

The great forested peaks looming to the west of San Mateo Ixtatán are in fact a narrow spur of the Cuchumatanes and can easily be crossed in day. In a matter of hours you're up on top of the ridge, in a misty world of forest and high pasture, while over on the other side you soon drop onto a low-lying limestone plateau from where you can catch a bus back to Huehuetenango.

The main road from San Mateo to Barillas heads on around the side of the mountain, dipping into a narrow gulley. At the bottom of this dip – less than a kilometre east of the centre of San Mateo – another road branches off to the left, climbing into the hills. Following this you pass right over the spine of the

Cuchumatanes, through high alpine pastures and beautiful pine and white oak forests, the older trees draped in mosses, ferns and bromeliads. Sadly, the trees are being cut down at a phenonemal rate to provide firewood for the nearby villages, although this does mean you may be able to catch a ride on one of the lumber lorries.

After a couple of hours' walk you emerge from the forest at the top of a huge, steep-sided valley, beside the tiny settlement of **Chizbazalum**. Sticking with the road, you want to cross the top of the valley, which drops away beneath you. Individual houses, maize fields and herds of sheep are scattered across this enormous landscape and many of the young shepherds are armed with blowpipes, a tradition probably inherited from the lowland Indians to the north. (The only other area that hunters use blowpipes is in Chajul in the Ixil triangle, where they were heavily influenced by Lacandon Indians.) The focus of this dispersed community is the village of **Patalcal**, where the road divides – you want to bear right and head up and onto the next shoulder. The road pushes out along this high ridge, but again it splits and you need to branch right. Here too the high ground is forested, but the trail soon starts to drop again, zigzagging down towards the village of Bulej – five or six hours' walk from San Mateo. If it's a clear day the views are superb, with the Mexican plateau mapped out below and the Lagunas de Montebello catching the light.

BULEJ itself is a remote settlement that acts as a centre for the surrounding farming communities of scattered wooden buildings and fruit trees. If you happen to be here in June then the entire place will be in bloom, while in August it is awash with pears and apricots. You shouldn't have any trouble finding a place to stay here and there is a shop on the main square selling soft drinks and biscuits. If you decide to press on, then it's another couple of hours of steep descent to the village of **YALAMBOJOCH**, which is right down on the plateau and the point you finally meet up with the road from Huehuetenango. The recent history of Yalambojoch is bound up with that of Finca San Francisco, a smaller village along the road some 3km to the east. In 1982 the army massacred around three hundred people in San Francisco (see *Contexts*) and the entire population of the surrounding area fled for their lives, crossing the border into Mexico. After more than a decade people started to return, and life in Yalambojoch is beginning to return to normal. Despite all this horror you'll find the people warm and welcoming, and although they are very poor you shouldn't have any trouble finding somewhere to stay. The village of **FINCA SAN FRANCISCO** is itself also well worth a look – just follow the road to the east. Along the way you can stop off for a chilly dip in a beautiful crystal-clear stream, and in the village itself there is a small Maya temple, which is also the site of a plaque commemorating those who died in the massacre.

Transportes Chiantlequita **buses** connect Yalambojoch and Huehuetenango. They leave the bus terminal in Huehuetenango at 5am, 12.30pm and 1.20pm, passing through Yalambojoch after about seven hours, before spending the night at Finca Gracias a Dios, metres from the Mexican border. The next morning two buses leave Gracias a Dios at 3am and one at 7am for the journey back to Huehuetenango and pass though Yalambojoch.

San Rafael La Independencia, San Miguel Acatán and on foot to Jacaltenango

Between Santa Eulalia and San Mateo Ixtatán a branch road cuts off to the left, heading over the spine of the Cuchumatanes and curving around the other side to **SAN RAFAEL LA INDEPENDENCIA**, a small village perched on a cold outcrop. In San Rafael you'll find a couple of *comedores* and a Thursday market but probably nowhere to stay: however, if you ask in the office of the bus company they'll usually be able to find you a concrete floor on which you can spend the night. There are **buses** to San Rafael from Huehue at 3pm and 4.30pm, which return at 3am and 9am. From San Rafael you can walk on down the valley, following the road or taking the path towards the larger village of **SAN MIGUEL ACATÁN**. Here there's a couple of *comedores,* a Sunday market and a small *pensión* in the house behind the Municipalidad. **Buses** leave Huehuetenango for San Miguel at 12.30am, 1pm and 1.30pm returning at noon, 4am and 8.30am. Confirm all schedules in Huehuetenango before you travel, as the poor roads in this region affect services and punctuality.

From San Miguel Acatán, a spectacular walk takes you along the edge of the mountains to Jacaltenango (see p.201). Setting out from San Miguel, cross the river and follow the trail that bears to the right as it climbs the hill opposite. At the fork, halfway up, take the higher path that crosses the ridge beside a small shelter. On the other side it drops down into the head of the next valley. Here you want to follow the path down the valley on the near side of the river, and through the narrow gorge to an ancient wooden bridge. Cross the river and climb up the other side of the valley, heading down towards the end of it as you go. The path that heads straight out of the valley runs to Nentón, and the other path, up and over the ridge to the left, heads towards **Jacaltenango**. Along the way there are stunning views of the rugged peaks of the southern Cuchumatanes and the great flat expanse that stretches into Mexico – on a clear day you can see the Lagunas de Montebello, a good 50km away, over the border. On the far side of the ridge the path eventually drops down to Jacaltenango through the neighbouring village of San Marcos Huista: some eight or nine tough but worthwhile hours in all from San Miguel.

Todos Santos

If you turn off at the **Paquix** junction, about 20km from Huehuetenango, you can follow a road heading west to **TODOS SANTOS**. This western road slopes down through **La Ventosa**, a narrow gulley lined with pine and cedar trees, where almost immediately you'll begin to see the traditional red costume of Todos Santos: the men in their red-and-white striped trousers, black woollen breeches and brilliantly embroidered shirt collars; the women in dark blue *cortes* and superbly intricate purple *huipiles*. Further down, at the bottom of the steep-sided, deep-cut river valley, is the village itself – a single main street with a few *tiendas*, a plaza, a church, a language school and a loose collection of houses and corn fields. Above the village flocks of sheep are grazed and below it the crops are farmed. It's a fairly typical highland village, but Todos Santos is better known than most because of the work of writer Maud Oakes (whose *The Two Crosses of Todos Santos* was published in 1951) and photographer Hans Namuth, who has been recording the faces of the villagers for more than forty years.

As usual, most of the people the village serves don't actually live here. The immediate population is probably around twelve hundred, but there are perhaps ten times that many in the surrounding hills who are dependent on Todos Santos for trade, supplies and social life. This population is more than the land can support, and many travel to the coast in search of work. All over the country you'll

---

LEARNING SPANISH IN TODOS SANTOS

Todos Santos is home to one of Guatemala's most interesting **language schools**, the Proyecto Lingüístico de Español/Mam Todos Santos. Despite the fact that Spanish is the second language here, and students get little chance to practise it with their Mam-speaking host families, if you're looking for **cultural exchange** you'll find the course highly rewarding – especially if you don't mind very basic living conditions. Courses consist of five hours' tuition a day and accommodation with a local family, all for around $120 a week: a percentage of the profits go to local development projects. Reservations can be made through Proyecto Lingüístico Quezalteco de Español, 5 C 2–40, Zona 1 (or Apdo Postal 114), Quetzaltenango (☎7612620).

---

see them, always dressed in *traje* – traditional costume. However, there's one event that brings them all home, the famous November 1 **fiesta** for All Saints (*todos santos*). For three days the village is taken over by unrestrained drinking, dance and marimba music. The event opens with an all-day horse race, which starts out as a massive stampede. The riders tear up the course, thrashing their horses with live chickens, pink capes flowing out behind them. At either end of the run they take a drink before burning back again. As the day wears on some riders retire, collapse, or tie themselves on, leaving only the toughest to ride it out. On the second day, "The Day of the Dead", the action moves to the cemetery, with marimba bands and drink stalls setting up amongst the graves for a day of intense ritual that combines grief and celebration. On the final day of the fiesta the streets are littered with bodies and the jail packed with brawlers. You can see some of the community's historic costumes, tools, and traditional idols, if the local **museum**, just off the main square ($1 donation), has reopened.

If you can't make it for the fiesta then the Saturday **market**, although nothing like as riotous, also fills the village, and the night before you might catch some marimba. During the week the village is fairly quiet, although it's a pleasant and peaceful place to spend some time and the surrounding scenery is unbelievably beautiful. Moreover, since the **language school** opened in Todos Santos, a small but lively "gringo scene" has developed, revolving around *Comedor Katy* and the school's evening events. This is either a bonus or spoils the whole place – depending on your point of view.

Todos Santos is one of the few places where people are still said to use the 260-day *Tzolkin* calendar, which dates back to Maya times. Above the village – follow the track that goes up behind the *Comedor Katy* – is the small Maya site of **Tojcunanchén**, where you'll find a couple of mounds sprouting pine trees. The site is occasionally used by *brujos* for the burning of incense and the ritual sacrifice of animals.

Practicalities

Buses leave Huehuetenango for Todos Santos from the main bus terminal at 12.30pm and 3pm – get there early to save your seat and buy a ticket. Some carry on through the village to Jacaltenango and pass through Todos Santos on the way back to Huehuetenango at 4am and 10.30am. Ask around for the latest schedule.

New places **to stay** are springing up all over the village, but one of the best is *Hospedaje Casa Familiar* (②), 30m above the main road past *Comedor Katy*. There are breathtaking views from its terrace café, which is the best place in town for breakfast, and hot showers cost $1 a time. Another good place is the *Hospedaje las*

Ruinas, a couple of minutes' walk further uphill on the right (①), which is run by a friendly family, and has a *chuc* (a traditional smoke sauna). The two hotels in the village, *Hospedaje La Paz* (①) and *Las Olguitas* (①), are both very inexpensive, rather rough and best avoided. The best place **to eat** is at the delightful *Comedor Katy,* heading left up the hill, though the *Casa Familiar* and *Las Olguitas* both do good meals. The new wooden gringo-geared restaurant/café, *Ixcanac,* on the left as you enter the centre of town, serves spaghetti, good *currasco* and wine, and shows films. If you want to take a *huipil* home with you, you'll find an excellent co-op selling good quality weavings next to the *Casa Familiar.*

Hikes from Todos Santos

The scenery around Todos Santos is some of the most spectacular in all Guatemala and there's no better place to leave the roads and set off on foot. In a day you can walk across to **San Juan Atitán**, and from there continue to the Pan-American Highway or head on to **Santiago Chimaltenango**. From the highway you'll be able to catch a bus back to Huehuetenango for the night, and if you make it to Santiago you shouldn't have any problem finding somewhere to stay. This is the more interesting walk, particularly if you set out early on a Thursday morning and arrive in San Juan before the market there has finished.

Alternatively, you can walk down the valley from Todos Santos to **San Martín** and on to **Jacaltenango**, a route which offers superb views. There's a hotel in Jacaltenango, so you can stay the night and then catch a bus back to Huehuetenango in the morning.

Walking to San Juan Atitán

The village of **SAN JUAN ATITÁN** is around five hours from Todos Santos, across a beautiful isolated valley. The walk follows the path that bears up behind the *Comedor Katy,* passes the ruins and climbs steeply above the village through endless muddy switchbacks, bearing gradually across to the right. You reach the top of the ridge after about an hour and if the skies are clear you'll be rewarded by an awesome view of the Tajumulco and Tacaná volcanoes. Here the path divides: to the right are the scattered remains of an ancient cloud forest and a lovely grassy valley, while straight ahead is the path to San Juan, dropping down past some huts, through beautiful forest. The route takes you up and down endless exhausting ridges, through lush forests, and over a total of five gushing streams, only the first and third of which are bridged.

Beside the first stream is an idyllic spot where a family have set up home – they may allow you to **camp** here especially if you share your rations. Between the fourth and fifth streams, about three hours' from Todos Santos, you'll find an ideal place for a **picnic** overlooking the valley. Having crossed the thinly inhabited valley the path swings up to the left and on to the top of another pass, about three and a half hours from Todos Santos. From here you can see the village of San Juan, strung out along the steep hillside in a long thin line, though it is still more than an hour's walk away. To head down into the village follow one of the left-hand trails that goes out along the hillside and then drops down amongst the houses. There are several paths to choose from – all cross a series of deep ravines before emerging onto the main track that runs through the village.

Built on treacherously unstable land, San Juan is regularly hit by landslides that sweep whole houses into the valley below. The government has proposed that the entire village be moved, but the people have so far resisted this idea. It's an intensely traditional place: all the men wear long woollen coats (similar in style to the habits worn by Spanish friars), red shirts and plain white trousers. The high-backed sandals worn by both the men and the women, and also by a lot of people in Todos Santos, are a style depicted in ancient Maya carving – they are also worn in some of the villages around San Cristóbal de las Casas in Chiapas, Mexico.

Like most of these mountain villages, San Juan is a pretty quiet place, active only on market days, Monday and Thursday. The central square has a giant palm tree and a pretty garden, and from the marketplace, below the health centre, there are spectacular views across the valley.

If you want to **stay**, the *Hospedaje San Diego*, on the hill above the plaza (①), makes a very basic but friendly place to rest, and the family may cook you supper on request. Alternatively, there's the *Hospedaje Jimenez*, beside the church (①). For food, the small *comedor* beneath the *San Diego* serves up reasonable meals, but watch out for the fearsome *picante* sauce. Next morning you can catch a pick-up to Huehuetenango at 6am (1hr), in time to catch the morning bus for Todos Santos, or walk back. From Huehuetenango, the pick-ups for San Juan leave from outside the *Cafeteria Tucaná*, 2 C 2–15, around noon. Get there early for a space. In this direction the journey takes a good two hours.

On to Santiago Chimaltenango

SANTIAGO CHIMALTENANGO makes a good alternative destination. If you want to go straight here from Todos Santos, turn right when you reach the top of the pass overlooking San Juan, head along the side of the hill and over another pass into a huge bowl-like valley. The village lies on the far side. If you're coming from San Juan, follow the track straight through the village and you'll come to the same pass in just over an hour. From the top of the pass, follow the main track down into the valley as it bears around to the right, towards the village – about one and a half hours from the top. Although not as traditional as the other villages of the region, Santiago is nevertheless a beautiful old place, a compact mass of narrow cobbled streets and adobe houses.

Ask at the main terminal in Huehuetenango for information on buses to and from Santiago Chimaltenango, otherwise you will have to walk on down the valley through coffee plantations to the village of San Pedro Necta, and beyond to the Pan-American Highway, which should take two or three hours. *Mini Trenda La Benedicion* below the market is a friendly **place to stay** (①).

From Todos Santos to San Martín and Jacaltenango

Heading down the valley from Todos Santos the road arrives at the one-street village of **SAN MARTÍN**, three hours away. It is inhabited entirely by *ladinos*, but has a Friday market that attracts indigenous people from the land all around, including many from Todos Santos. A little beyond the village the road down the valley divides, with a right fork that leads 11km around the steep western edge of the Cuchumatanes. On a clear day there are spectacular views, reaching well into Mexico. At the end of the old road, on a rocky outcrop, is the poor and ragged village of **CONCEPCIÓN**, from where a new road plunges to Jacaltenango, the final destination of one of the Todos Santos buses, which returns from there to Huehuetenango at about 3am.

Perched on a plateau overlooking the limestone plain that stretches out across the Mexican border, **JACALTENANGO** is the heart of an area that was once very traditional, inhabited by a small tribe of Jacaltec speakers. However, in recent years the surrounding land has been planted with coffee and waves of *ladinos* have swelled the population of the town. Today the place has a calm and prosperous feel to it. There are two *pensiones* – one in the large *tienda* on the corner of the plaza and the other up the hill opposite it – and plenty of cheap *comedores* along the side of the market, which is at its busiest on Sunday.

The town can also be reached by a branch route that leaves the Pan-American Highway close to the Mexican border. A **bus** usually leaves Huehuetenango for Jacaltenango at 12.30pm, but you should always check the timetable at the terminal.

East to Aguacatán

To the east of Huehuetenango, a dirt road turns off at Chiantla to weave along the base of the Cuchumatanes, through dusty foothills, to **AGUACATÁN**. This small agricultural town is strung out along two main streets, shaped entirely by the dip in which it's built. The village was created by Dominican friars, who in the early years of the Conquest merged several smaller settlements inhabited by two distinct peoples. The remains of one of the pre-Conquest settlements can still be seen a couple of kilometres to the north, and minute differences of dress and dialect linger – indeed the village remains loosely divided along pre-Columbian lines, with the Chalchitec to the east of the market and the Aguatec to the west. The language of Aguateca (used by both) is spoken only in this village and its immediate surrounds, by a population of around 15,000. During the colonial period gold and silver were mined in the nearby hills, and the Indians are said to have made bricks of solid gold for the king of Spain, to persuade him to let them keep their lands. Today the town is steeped in tradition and the people survive by growing vegetables, including huge quantities of garlic, much of it for export.

Aguacatán's vast Sunday **market** gets under way on Saturday afternoon, when traders arrive early to claim the best sites. On Sunday morning a steady stream of people pours down the main street, cramming into the market and plaza, and soon spilling out into the surrounding area. Around noon the tide turns as the crowds start to drift back to their villages, with donkeys leading their drunken drivers. Despite the scale of the market its atmosphere is subdued and the pace unhurried: for many it's as much a social event as a commercial one.

The traditional costume worn by the women of Aguacatán is unusually simple: their skirts are made of dark blue cotton and the *huipiles*, which hang loose, are decorated with bands of coloured ribbon on a plain white background. This plainness, though, is set off by the local speciality – the *cinta*, or headdress, in which they wrap their hair, an intricately embroidered piece of cloth combining blues, reds, yellows and greens.

Aguacatán's other attraction is the source of the **Río San Juan**, which emerges from beneath a nearby hill, fresh and cool. The source itself, bubbling up beneath a small bush and then channelled by concrete walls, looks a bit disappointing to the uninitiated (though as far as cavers and geologists are concerned, it's a big one), but if you have an hour or two to kill it's a good place for a chilly swim – for which you have to pay a small fee. To get there walk east along the main street out of the village for about a kilometre, until you see a sign directing you down a track to the left. Follow this round a sharp bend to the left and then take the right turn, towards the base of the hills. From the village it takes about twenty minutes.

Eight daily **buses** run from Huehuetenango to Aguacatán passing by the Calvario in Huehuetenango, at the junction of 1 Av and 1 C; the first bus leaves at 6am and the last at about 2.45pm. The 25-kilometre journey takes around an hour. In Aguacatán the best place **to stay** is the simple *Hospedaje Aguateco* (①), with small rooms off a courtyard. If that's full try the *Hospedaje La Paz* (①). **Beyond Aguacatán** the road runs out along a ridge, with fantastic views stretching out below. Eventually it drops down into the Chixoy valley, to the riverside town of **Sacapulas** (p.131).

West to the Mexican border

From Huehuetenango the Pan-American Highway runs for 79km through the narrow Selegua valley to the Mexican border at **La Mesilla**. Travelling direct this takes about two and a half hours on one of the buses that thunder out of Huehuetenango every hour or so between 5am and 6pm. Along the way, just off the main road, are some interesting traditional villages, largely oblivious to the international highway that carves through their land. Most are best reached as day trips out of Huehuetenango.

The first of these, 20km from Huehuetenango, is **San Sebastián Huehuetenango**, a quiet little place barely 200m north of the highway. The village was the site of a pre-Conquest centre, and of a settlement known as Toj-Jol, which was swept away by the Río Selegua in 1891. Further on the road runs through a particularly narrow part of the valley known as **El Tapón**, the cork, and past a turning for San Juan Atitán (12km) and another for San Rafael Petzal, 2km from the main road. Beyond this it passes roads that lead to Colotenango, Nentón and Jacaltenango.

You pass one last roadside village, La Democracía, before reaching the border at **LA MESILLA**. If you get stuck here, there's **accommodation** at the new *Hotel Maricruz* (②), which is clean with private bathrooms and a restaurant, or at the cheaper *Hospedaje Marisol* (②). The two sets of customs and immigration are 3km apart; taxis run between the immigration points, and on the Mexican side you can pick up buses via the border settlement of **Ciudad Cuauhtemoc** to **Comitán**, or even direct to **San Cristóbal de las Casas**. Heading into Guatemala, the last bus leaves La Mesilla for Huehuetenango at around 4pm, and wherever you're aiming for in Guatemala, it's best to take the first bus to Huehue and change there.

Colotenango, San Ildefonso Ixtahuacán and Cuilco

The most important of the villages reached from the highway is **COLOTENAN-GO**, perched on a hillside 1km or so south from the main road. The municipality of Colotenango used to include San Rafael and San Ildefonso, until 1890 when they became villages in their own right. Ties are still strong, however, and the red *cortes* worn by the women of all three villages are almost identical. Colotenango remains the focal point for the smaller settlements, and its Saturday market is the largest in the Selegua valley. From early Saturday morning the plaza is packed, and the paths that lead into the village are filled with a steady stream of traders, indigenous families, cattle, chickens, reluctant pigs and the inevitable drunks. Here you'll see people from all of the surrounding villages, most of them wearing traditional costume. The village is also worth visiting during Holy Week, when elaborate and violent re-enactments of Christ's Passion take place (the bravest of villagers takes the role of Judas, and is shown no mercy by the rest), and for its fiesta from August 12 to 15.

To get to Colotenango from Huehuetenango take any bus heading towards the Mexican border, and ask the driver to drop you at the village. They'll usually leave you on the main road just below, from where you have to cross the bridge and walk up the hill. The journey from Huehuetenango takes around 45 minutes.

On to San Ildefonso and Cuilco

Behind Colotenango a dirt road goes up over the hills and through a pass into the valley of the Río Cuilco. Here it runs high above the river along the top of a ridge, with beautiful views up the valley: below you can make out the tiny village of San Gaspar Ixchil, which consists of little more than a church and a graveyard.

Another few kilometres brings you to the larger village and mining centre of **SAN ILDEFONSO IXTAHUACÁN**. Similar in many ways to Colotenango, it has a large and traditional Maya population. In 1977 the place achieved a certain notoriety after its miners were locked out of the mine because they'd tried to form a union. In response to this they decided to walk the 260km to Guatemala City in order to put their case to the authorities. At the time this was a bold gesture of defiance and it captured the imagination of the entire nation. When they eventually arrived in the capital 100,000 people turned out to welcome them.

Beyond San Ildefonso the road slopes down towards the bottom of the valley and crosses the river before arriving at **CUILCO**, a sizeable *ladino* town 36km from the Pan-American Highway that marks the end of the road. The Mexican border is just 15km away, and the town maintains cross-border trade links both inside and outside the law. Beyond today's village are the ruins of an earlier settlement known as **Cuilco Viejo**. Cuilco has also earned itself something of a reputation, although this time it's for producing heroin. As a result of the successful anti-drug campaigns in Mexico, poppy growers have moved across the border, and the American Drug Enforcement Agency has estimated that the area may provide enough opium to supply three times the number of heroin addicts in the US.

Buses run between Huehuetenango and Cuilco at 5am and 2pm, returning at 7am and 8.30am, so if you come out this way you'll probably end up having to stay: the *Hospedaje Osorio* (①) is on the main street. If the roads are in reasonable condition, trucks and pick-ups run south from Cuilco to the mountain village of Tacaná, from where there is a regular bus service to San Pedro.

North to Nentón and Jacaltenango

A short distance before the border, from the roadside village of **Camoja Grande**, a dirt road leads off to the north, running parallel to the border. It heads across a dusty white limestone plateau to the village of **Nentón**, and right up into the extreme northwest corner of the country, to **Gracias a Dios** and Yalambojoch. Although there are **buses** (two a day to Jacaltenango, three to Gracias a Dios), the only reason to venture out this way would be to walk back into the Cuchumatanes or use the remote **border crossing** into Mexico at Gracias a Dios. It's a ten-minute walk from Gracias a Dios to Carmixan in Mexico and bus services do connect.

Halfway between the Pan-American Highway and Nentón, at the junction of Cuatro Caminos, a branch road heads east towards the mountains, through lush foothills, passing the entrance to **Santa Ana Huista**. It then continues through rich coffee country to **San Antonio Huista** – with the *Pensión Victoria* (①) should you want to stay – and ends up in Jacaltenango, from where you can walk to Todos Santos (see p.198).

FIESTAS

The **western highlands** are the home of the traditional Guatemalan fiesta. Every village and town, however small, has its own saint's day, around which a fiesta is based that can last anything from a day to two weeks. All of these involve traditional dances that mix pre-Columbian moves with more modern Spanish styles, and each fiesta has its own speciality, whether it's a horse race or a firework spectacular.

JANUARY

January is a particularly active month, kicking off in **Santa María de Jesús**, near Antigua, where they have a fiesta from the 1st to 5th, with the main action on the first two days. In **El Tumbador**, in the department of San Marcos, there's a fiesta from the 3rd to 8th, and in **San Gaspar Ixchil**, a tiny village on the road to Cuilco in the department of Huehuetenango, they have their fiesta from the 3rd to 6th. In **Sibilia**, in the department of Quetzaltenango, there's a fiesta from the 9th to 15th, with the main day on the 13th, and **Santa María Chiquimula**, near Totonicapán, has its fiesta from the 10th to 16th, in honour of the Black Christ of Esquipulas. **Nentón**, to the northwest of Huehuetenango, has a fiesta from the 13th to 16th, and **La Libertad**, to the west of Huehuetenango, from the 12th to 16th. In the central highlands **Chinique**, east of Santa Cruz del Quiché, has a very traditional fiesta from the 12th to 15th, with the final day as the main day. **Colomba**, in the department of Quetzaltenango, has one from the 12th to 16th. The village of **San Antonio Ilotenango**, west of Santa Cruz del Quiché, has its fiesta from the 15th to 17th (the main day). **San Sebastián Coatan**, in the department of Huehuetenango, has a fiesta from the 18th to 20th. **El Tejar**, on the Pan-American Highway near Chimaltenango, has a fiesta from the 18th to 20th, with the final day being the main day, and **Santa Lucía La Reforma**, in the department of Totonicapán, has its fiesta from the 19th to 21st. The village of **Ixtahuacán**, on the road to Cuilco in the department of Huehuetenango, has a traditional fiesta from the 19th to 24th. **San Pablo La Laguna**, on the shores of Lake Atitlán, has a fiesta from the 22nd to 26th, with the main day on the 25th. **San Pablo**, in the department of San Marcos, has its fiesta from the 23rd to 27th. The village of **Chiantla**, just north of Huehuetenango, celebrates from January 28 to February 2, with the final day as the main day, and finally **Jacaltenango**, to the west of Huehuetenango, also has a fiesta that starts on the 28th and goes on until February 2.

FEBRUARY

The celebratory season in February starts in **Cunén**, in the department of Quiché, with a fiesta from the 1st to 4th, with the main day on the 2nd. **Ostuncalco**, in the department of Quetzaltenango, has a fiesta on the 8th. **Santa Eulalia** in Huehuetenango has its fiesta from the 8th to 13th, with the main day on the 8th, and **Patzité**, in Quiché, has a fiesta from the 6th to 10th, in which the main action is also on the 8th. **Antigua**'s fiesta celebrates the first Friday in Lent, as does **Palestina de Los Altos**, in the department of San Marcos.

Continues over

MARCH

In March things start off in **San Jose El Rodeo**, in the department of San Marcos, where they have a fiesta from the 14th to 20th, with the main day on the 19th. **La Democracía**, between Huehuetenango and the Mexican border, has a moveable fiesta sometime during the month. **San Jose Poaquil**, near Chimaltenango, has a fiesta on the 19th. The second Friday in Lent is marked by fiestas in **Chajul** and **La Democracía**. Holy Week is celebrated throughout the country but with extreme fervour in **Antigua**: here the main processions are marched over carpets of painted sawdust and involve huge numbers of people engulfed in clouds of incense. **Santiago Atitlán** is also worth visiting during Holy Week to see Maximón paraded through the streets, usually on the Wednesday.

APRIL

San Marcos has its fiesta from the 22nd to 28th, with the main day on the 25th, **San Jorge La Laguna** celebrates on the 24th, and **San Marcos La Laguna** on the 25th. **Barillas**, far to the north of Huehuetenango, has a fiesta from April 29 to May 4, and both **Zacualpa** and **Aguacatán** have moveable fiestas to mark forty days from Holy Week. **Zacualpa** also has a moveable fiesta at some stage during the month. Finally **La Esperanza**, in the department of Quetzaltenango, has its fiesta from April 30 to May 4.

MAY

Cajola, a small village in the department of Quetzaltenango, has its fiesta from the 1st to 3rd, with the final day as the main day. **Uspantán** has a busy and traditional fiesta from the 6th to 10th, with the main day on the 8th. **Santa Cruz La Laguna**, on the shores of Lake Atitlán, has its fiesta from the 8th to 10th, with the main day on the last day, as does **Santa Cruz Balanya**, in the department of Chimaltenango. **Patzún** has a fiesta on the 20th.

JUNE

Things start to hot up again in June, starting in **San Antonio Palopó**, to the east of Panajachel, which has a fiesta from the 12th to 14th, with the main day on the 13th. The same days are celebrated in **San Antonio Huista**, while **San Juan Ixcoy**, in the department of Huehuetenango, has its fiesta from the 21st to 25th, with the main day on the 24th. **Olintepeque**, a few kilometres from Quetzaltenango, has its fiesta from the 21st to 25th. Towards the end of the month there are two very interesting fiestas high up the mountains: the first, at **San Juan Cotzal**, a very traditional village to the north of Nebaj, lasts from the 22nd to 25th, with the main day on the 24th; the second, in remote **San Juan Atitán** near Huehuetenango, runs from the 22nd to 26th, with the main day on the 24th. **Comalapa**, near Chimaltenango, has a fiesta on the 24th; **San Juan la Laguna**, on the shores of Lake Atitlán, from the 23rd to 26th, with the main day on the 24th; **San Pedro Sacatepéquez** from the 24th to 30th; and the isolated village of **Soloma**, to the north of Huehuetenango, from the 26th to 30th, with the main day on the 29th. At the end of the month three villages share the same dates: **Yepocapa** in the department of Chimaltenango, **San Pedro Jocopilas** to the north of Santa Cruz del Quiché, and **San Pedro La Laguna** on Lake Atitlán all have fiestas from the 27th to 30th, with the main day on the 29th. Finally in **Almolonga**, near Quetzaltenango, there's a fiesta from the 28th to 30th, with the main day on the 29th. Corpus Christi celebrations, held throughout Guatemala in June, are particularly spectacular in **Patzún**.

JULY

In July things start off in **Santa María Visitación**, near Sololá, where they have a fiesta from the 1st to 4th, with the main day on the 2nd. In **Huehuetenango** there's a fiesta from the 12th to 17th, and in **Momostenango** from July 21 to August 4 – a traditional celebration that is worth going out of your way for, especially on the 25th. The village of **Tejutla**, high above San Marcos, has a fiesta from the 22nd to 27th, with the main day on the 25th, as does **San Cristóbal Totonicapán**, in the department of Totonicapán. **Chimaltenango** has a fiesta from the 22nd to 27th, with the main day on the 26th; **Malacatancito**, a small *ladino* town on the border of the department of Huehuetenango, celebrates from the 23rd to 26th, with the last day as the main day. **Santiago Atitlán's** fiesta, from the 23rd to 27th, is most enjoyable on the 25th; and **Antigua** has a one-day fiesta on the 25th in honour of Santiago. **Patzicía** has a fiesta from the 22nd to 27th, with the main day on the 27th, and **Santa Ana Huista**, in the department of Huehuetenango, has its fiesta from the 25th to 27th, with the main day on the 26th. Finally **Ixchiguan**, in the department of San Marcos, has a fiesta from the 29th to 31st, with the final day the main day.

AUGUST

August is a particularly good month for fiestas and if you're in the central area you can visit three or four of the very best. The action starts in **Sacapulas**, which has a fiesta from the 1st to 4th, with the last day as the main day. **Santa Clara La Laguna** has its fiesta from the 10th to 13th, with the main day on the 12th. **Joyabaj** has its fiesta from the 9th to 15th, with the last day as the main day. This is the first of August's really special fiestas and sees Joyabaj filled with Indians from throughout the valley: traditional dances here include the *Palo Volador*, in which men swing from a huge pole. The second major fiesta is in **Sololá**, from the 11th to 17th, with the main day on the 15th. The next is in **Nebaj**, where the fiesta is from the 12th to 15th, with the main day on the last day. In **Colotenango**, near Huehuetenango, they have a fiesta from the 12th to 15th, with the final day as the main day. **Cantel**, near Quetzaltenango, has a fiesta from the 12th to 18th, the main day on the 15th, and **Tacaná** has a fiesta from the 12th to 15th, the main day on the 15th. In **Santa Cruz del Quiché** there's a fiesta from the 14th to 19th, with the main day on the 18th, and in **Jocotenango** the fiesta is for a single day on the 15th. **San Bartolo** has its fiesta from the 18th to 25th, climaxing on the 24th, while **Salcajá** has a fiesta from the 22nd to 28th, with the principal day the 25th. **Sipacapa**, in the department of San Marcos, has its fiesta from the 22nd to 25th, and **Sibinal**, in the same department, has its fiesta from the 27th to 30th, with the main day on the 19th.

SEPTEMBER

The fiesta in **Quetzaltenango** lasts from the 12th to 18th, with the main day on the 15th. **San Mateo**, to the west of Quetzaltenango, has a fiesta on the 21st, **San Mateo Ixtatán**, to the north of Huehuetenango, from the 17th to 21st, with the last day the main day, and the departmental capital of **Totonicapán** from the 24th to 30th, with the main day on the 29th. **San Miguel Acatán**, in the department of Huehuetenango, has a fiesta from the 25th to 30th, with the main day also on the 29th. Finally **Tecpán** has its fiesta from September 26 to October 5.

Continues over

OCTOBER

The action in October starts up in **San Francisco el Alto**, which has its fiesta from the 1st to 6th, with its main day on the 4th. **Panajachel** has a fiesta from the 2nd to 6th, which also has its main day on the 4th. **San Lucas Tolimán**, on the shores of Lake Atitlán, has its fiesta from the 15th to 20th, with the main day on the 18th. Finally the fiesta in **Todos Santos**, one of the best in the country, starts on October 21 and continues into the first few days of November. The 29th is the main day and features a wild and alcoholic horse race.

NOVEMBER

The 1st is the scene of intense action in **Todos Santos** and in **Santiago Sacatepéquez**, where they fly massive paper kites in the village cemetery. **San Martín Jilotepeque** has its fiesta from the 7th to 12th, with the main day on the 11th. **Malacatancito**, in the department of Huehuetenango, has a fiesta from the 14th to 18th, with the last day as the main day. **Nahualá** has a very good fiesta from the 23rd to 26th, with the main day on the 25th. **Santa Catarina Ixtahuacán**, in the department of Sololá, has its fiesta from the 24th to 26th, with the principal day on the 25th. **Zunil** has a fiesta from the 22nd to 26th, again with the chief action on the 25th, and **Santa Catarina Palopó** has a fiesta on that day. Finally **Cuilco**, **San Andrés Semetabaj**, **San Andrés Itzapa** and **San Andrés Xecul** all have their fiestas from November 27 to December 1. The main day in Cuilco is on the 28th, and in all the San Andréses on the 30th.

DECEMBER

Santa Barbara, in the department of Huehuetenango, has its fiesta from the 1st to 4th. **Huehuetenango** has a fiesta from the 5th to 8th, again with the last day as the main one, as does **Concepción Huista**, in the department of Huehuetenango. **Concepción**, in the department of Sololá, has its fiesta from the 7th to 9th, and **Malacatán**, in the department of San Marcos, has a fiesta from the 9th to 14th. **Santa Lucía Utatlán**, in Sololá, has its fiesta from the 11th to 15th, with the main day on the 13th. **Chichicastenango** has its fiesta from the 13th to 21st, with the last day as the main day. This is another very large and impressive fiesta, with an elaborate procession and a mass of fireworks. Chichicastenango's sister village, **Chiché**, has its fiesta from the 25th to 28th, with the last day as the main day. From the 7th December men dressed as devils chase around highland towns, particularly in those around Quetzaltenango, and the night of the 7th is celebrated with bonfires throughout the country – The Burning of the Devil.

travel details

BUSES

Travel in the western highlands is fairly straightforward. Along the **Pan-American Highway** there's an almost constant stream of buses heading in both directions: certainly between about 8am and 6pm you should never have to wait more than twenty minutes. The major towns are generally just off the highway, and it's the main connections to these that are covered below: other, more local schedules have been given in the text. The best way to explore the western highlands is to base yourself in one of these main towns and make a series of day trips into the surrounding area.

Antigua and Chimaltenango

To Antigua Direct buses **from Guatemala City** (1hr) run every 15min from 18 C and 4 Av in Zona

1 (Mon–Fri 5.30am–7pm); the service is less regular at weekends, when the first buses leave at around 6am. Buses **from Chimaltenango** (the junction for the rest of the highlands; 40min) leave every 20min (5.30am–7pm). Two daily buses also leave **from Escuintla** (2hr 30min) at 6.30am and noon.

From Antigua Buses **to Guatemala City** run every 15min (Mon–Fri 4am–7pm, Sat & Sun 7am–7pm), and more expensive tourist shuttles also connect Antigua with the city and the airport. Buses **to Chimaltenango** (40min) leave every 20min (5am–7pm), from where you can get regular connections **to Chichicastenango and Quiché, Panajachel, Quetzaltenango and Huehuetenango**. Buses to **Patzicía** and **Patzún** pass through Chimaltenango every hour or so.

Santa Cruz del Quiché and Chichicastenango

To Santa Cruz del Quiché via Chichicastenango. Buses leave **from Guatemala City** every 30min (4am–4pm; 3hr 30min) from the terminal in Zona 4. Along the way they can be picked up in Chimaltenango or at **Los Encuentros**, the junction for this part of the country.

From Santa Cruz del Quiché Buses leave the main bus terminal for **Nebaj** (4hr) at 8.30am, 10am, 11.30am, 1pm, 2.30pm and 4pm. Buses to **Uspantán** (5hr), which all pass through **Sacapulas** (2hr), leave Quiché at 11am, 1pm, 2pm and 4pm returning at 1am, 3am and 9am. **From Uspantán** there are buses for **San Pedro Carchá**, a few kilometres from Cobán (5hr), at 3am and 3.30am, returning at 10am and noon. **From Sacapulas** to **Huehuetenango** (5hr) there are buses at 3am, 4am and 5.30am. Direct buses from Santa Cruz to **Quetzaltenango** (3hr) leave hourly between 3am and 1pm; at other times go to Los Encuentros and change there. Buses to **Joyabaj** (2hr) pass through Santa Cruz (hourly; 9am–5pm). The last bus back from Joyabaj leaves at 4pm.

Lake Atitlán

Buses **to Panajachel** (3hr 30min) via **Sololá** are run by the Rebuli company, whose offices in Guatemala City are at 21 C 3–24, Zona 1. There are direct buses between Guatemala City and Panajachel (hourly; 6am–4pm); at other times you can travel via Los Encuentros. There is one daily bus at 7am from Antigua to Panajachel (3hr), which returns at 10.45am. **From Panajachel** there are departures to **Quetzaltenango** (2hr 30min) at 5.30am, 6.15am, 7.30am, 9.30am, 1pm and 2pm, and five buses a day to **Cocales** (2hr 30min) between 6am and 2pm, via **San Lucas Tolimán**. Seven direct buses to **Chichicastenango** leave Panajachel on market days (Thurs and Sun) from 6.30am; on other days there are less frequent direct buses and it's usually quicker to change at Los Encuentros.

There are also direct buses six times daily (from 2.30am and 2pm) between Guatemala City and **Santiago Atitlán** along the coastal highway, but this is a very slow route.

To get to **Nahualá** from Lake Atitlán, take any bus heading along the Pan-American Highway to the west of Los Encuentros.

Quetzaltenango

Pullman buses **to Quetzaltenango** (4hr) via Chimaltenango, Los Encuentros and Cuatro Caminos **from Guatemala City** are run by a number of companies: Líneas Américas buses leave from 2 Av 18–74, Zona 1, Guatemala City, at 5.15am, 9am, 12.15pm, 3.15pm, 4.40pm and 7.30pm, and from 7 Av 3–33, Zona 2, Quetzaltenango, at 5.15am, 9.45am, 11.15am, 1.15pm, 3.45pm and 8pm. For details of Alamo and Galgos buses, see p.80.

From Quetzaltenango Second-class buses leave hourly from the Minerva terminal in Zona 3, for San Pedro, San Marcos, Retalhuleu, Mazatenango, Huehuetenango and Guatemala City. Details of buses to the smaller towns are given in the relevant chapters. From Quetzaltenango **to the Mexican border** (2hr), it's quickest to take a bus to Mazatenango or Coatepeque, and then catch another from there.

San Marcos

Transportes Marquensita runs pullman buses **to San Marcos** from 21 C 12–41, Zona 1, **Guatemala City** (5hr 30min) at 6am, 6.30am, 8.40am, 11am, noon, 3.30pm, 4pm and 5pm, as well as additional second-class services throughout the day. Eight pullmans plus extra second-class buses make the return journey to Guatemala City between 2.30am and 4pm.

From San Marcos There are hourly buses to **Quetzaltenango** (1hr 30min), and **Malacatán** (1hr 30min), from where regular buses leave for the Mexican border at Talisman bridge.

Huehuetenango

Los Halcones pullman buses **to Huehuetenango** leave daily at 7am, 2pm and 5pm, from 7 Av 15–27, Zona 1, **Guatemala City** (5hr 30min), returning from Huehue at 4.30am, 7am and 2pm. Transportes Velasquez runs 11 buses daily from 20 C 1–37, Zona 1, Guatemala City to Huehuetenango at 5.20am, 7.30am, 8.30am, 9.30am, 10.30am, 11.30am, 12.15pm, 2.30pm, 3.30pm, 4.30pm and 5.30pm (plus a 6.30pm departure on Fridays).

Second-class buses to Huehuetenango run from Zona 4 terminal in Guatemala City and the Minerva terminal in **Quetzaltenango** every hour or so.

From Huehuetenango, there are buses to the border at **La Mesilla** every 30min or so until 7pm.

CHAPTER THREE

THE PACIFIC COAST

A chain of volcanoes divides the cool air of the mountains from a sweltering strip of low-lying, tropical, *ladino* land, some 300km long and on average 50km wide. Known simply as **La Costa Sur** this featureless yet supremely fertile coastal plain – once a wilderness of swamp, forest and savannah – is today a land of vast *fincas*, indifferent commercial towns and small seaside resorts scattered along an unrelentingly straight, black sand shoreline.

Prior to the arrival of the Spanish, the Pacific coast was similar in many ways to the jungles of Petén, and certainly as rich in wildlife and archeological sites. However, while the jungles of Petén have lain undisturbed, the Pacific coast has been ravaged by development. Today its large-scale agriculture – including sugar cane, palm oil, cotton and rubber plantations – accounts for a substantial proportion of the country's exports. Only in some isolated sections, where mangrove swamps have been spared the plough, can you still get a sense of the way it once looked: a maze of tropical vegetation. Little, if any, of the original dry tropical forest remains, although in several areas, including the **Monterrico Reserve**, the unique swampy coastal environment is protected, offering a refuge to sea turtles, iguanas, crocodiles and an abundance of bird life.

As for the archeological sites, they too have largely disappeared, though you can glimpse the extraordinary art of the **Pipil** (see below) around the town of Santa Lucía Cotzumalguapa. Totally unlike the sites in the highlands and Petén – and nowhere near as spectacular – these ceremonial centres, almost lost in fields of sugar cane, reveal a hotchpotch of carvings, some of which are still regularly used for religious rituals. However, the one site in the area that ranks with those elsewhere in the country is **Abaj Takalik**, outside Retalhuleu. For a fascinating insight into the Preclassic era of the Pacific littoral, the ruins are well worth a detour on your way to or from Mexico, or as a day trip from Xela or Retalhuleu. The site is only in the early stages of excavation, but already its significance has been clearly established. In addition, recent discoveries at **La Nueva**, near the border with El Salvador, prove that the area is hiding a lot more archeological secrets, and that the Maya World extended further than had been originally thought.

The main attraction of the region should be the **coastline**, though sadly much of it is mosquito-ridden and full of filthy palm huts, pig-pens and garbage, with dangerous currents and poor surfing conditions. The hotels are some of the country's worst, so if you're desperate for a quick dip and a fresh shrimp feast, you're far better off taking a day trip from the capital or from Quetzaltenango. The one glorious exception is the nature reserve of **Monterrico**, which harbours an attractive village and maybe the country's finest beach, with a superb stretch of clear, clean sand.

The main transport link in this region is the **coastal highway** (CA2), the country's fastest and busiest road. It is the usual route for pullman buses speeding

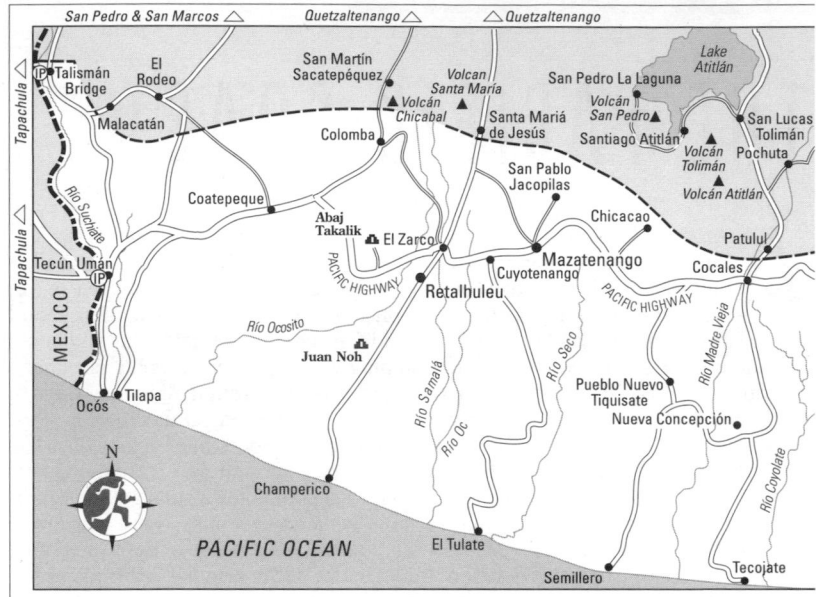

between Guatemala City and the Mexican border, so travel is normally swift and comfortable.

Some history

The earliest history of the Pacific coast remains something of a mystery, with the only hints offered by the remnants of two distinct languages: **Zoquean**, still spoken by a tiny population on the Mexico–Guatemala border, and **Xincan**, which is thought to have been spoken throughout the eastern area but can now only be heard in an isolated part of the Zacapa department. However, the extent to which these languages can be seen as evidence of independent tribes, and how the tribes might have developed the coast, remains mere speculation. It's generally held that the cultural sophistication of the peoples to the north – in what is now Mexico – spread along the Pacific coast, giving birth to the **Ocós** and **Iztapa** cul-

---

ACCOMMODATION PRICE CODES

All accommodation listed in this guide has been graded according to the following price scales. These refer to the price in US dollars of the cheapest double room in high season. For more details see p.25.

① Under $5	④ $15–25	⑦ $60–80
② $5–10	⑤ $25–40	⑧ $80–100
③ $10–15	⑥ $45–60	⑨ over $100

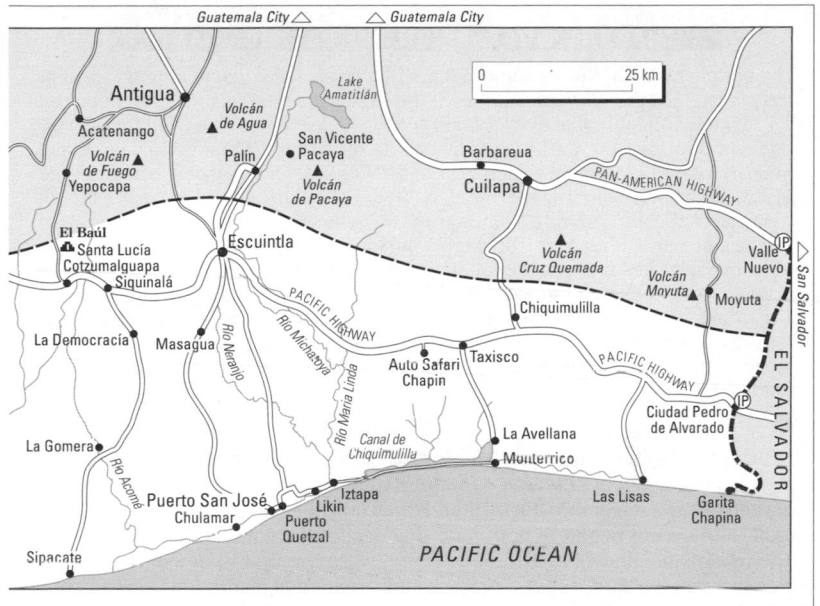

tures, which thrived here some time around 1500 BC. These were small, village-based societies that had developed considerable skills in the working of stone and pottery. It's also generally believed that great cultural developments, including writing and the basis of the Maya calendar, reached the southern area via the Pacific coast.

What is certain is that some time between 400 and 900 AD the entire coastal plain was overrun by the **Pipil**, who migrated south from the Central Highlands and Veracruz area of Mexico, possibly driven out by the chaos that followed the fall of Teotihuacán. (The Pipil language is actually an antiquated form of Nahuatl, the official language of the Aztec empire.) These migrants brought with them their architectural styles and artistic skills, and the remains of their civilization show that they used a foreign calendar and worshipped the gods familiar in Mexico. The Pipil built half a dozen sites, all compact ceremonial centres with rubble-filled pyramids. Their main produce was cacao, from which they extracted the beans to make a chocolate drink and to use as a form of currency. But by the time of the Conquest the ever-expanding tribes of the highlands had started to encroach upon the coastal plain, with the Mam, Quiché, Tzutujil and Cakchiquel all claiming a slice of the action.

The first Spaniards to set foot in Guatemala did so on the Pacific coast, arriving overland from the north. Alvarado's first confrontation with Quiché warriors came here in the heat of the lowlands, before he headed up towards Quetzaltenango. Once they'd established themselves, the Spanish despatched a handful of Franciscans to convert the coastal population, and were faced with a long, hard fight from the Pipil. In **colonial times** the land was mostly used for the

MIGRANT WORKERS ON THE PACIFIC COAST

Though the towns of the Pacific coast are quintessentially *ladino* in temperament and climate, it's the Maya people from the highlands who form the backbone of the region's agricultural activity. Families and whole communities fled the repression and bullets of the civil war to live along the coast in semi-permanent exile, while thousands more arrive each year to provide essential seasonal labour. In the past the Maya were forcibly recruited, but today the shortage of land in the mountains drives them to migrate "voluntarily" for several months a year in search of employment. In addition to working in burning conditions for a pittance, many economic migrants face ritual exploitation from the *finca* henchmen who routinely underpay and overcharge workers for food and drink, pharmacy bills and tool hire. Malaria and pesticide poisoning are also rife. One of the best and most harrowing accounts of life on a *finca* can be read in the autobiography of Rigoberta Menchú (see p.391), whose family buried two brothers during their days on the south coast.

production of indigo and cacao, and for cattle ranching, but the inhospitable climate and accompanying disease soon took their toll, and for much of that era the coast remained a miserable backwater. It was only after **independence** that commercial agriculture began to dominate this part of the country. The lower slopes of the mountains, known as the *Boca Costa*, were the first to be covered in huge coffee plantations; later, rubber, banana and sugar cane plantations spread across the land below. By 1880 the area was important enough to justify the construction of a railway (now disused) to connect Guatemala City with Puerto San José, and subsequently extended all the way to the Mexican border.

Today the coastal strip is the country's most intensely farmed region, where entire villages are effectively owned by vast *fincas*. Much of the nation's income is generated here and the main towns are alive with commercial activity, ringed by the ostentatious homes of the wealthy and dominated by the assertive machismo of *ladino* culture.

Crossing the border

Approaching the coast from the Mexican border, you face some of the very worst that the region has to offer. Breathless and ugly **Coatepeque** is typical of the towns you'll find, though **Retalhuleu** is somewhat more attractive and sedate. If you plan to spend any time on the coast, aim for the area south of Escuintla, but if you just want to head for the beach then **El Tulate** and **Champerico** are both within easy reach of Quetzaltenango and the border.

Tecún Umán and the Talismán Bridge

The coastal border with Mexico is the busiest of Guatemala's frontiers, with two crossing points, Talismán and Tecún Umán, both open 24 hours. Tourist cards for either country can be obtained at the immigration posts, but if you require a visa you'll need to get hold of one beforehand – there's a Guatemalan consulate in Tapachula on the Mexican side, and Mexican consulates in Retalhuleu, Quetzaltenango, Huehuetenango and Guatemala City.

The northernmost of the two crossings is the **Talismán Bridge** also referred to as El Carmen, where the customs and immigration posts face each other from opposite banks of the Río Suchiate. This tends to be the more relaxed of the two as there's nothing here but a few huts and a couple of basic *pensiones*, and it's also marginally better for first-class buses to Guatemala City. There's little difference on the Mexican side, as both crossings are thirty minutes from Tapachula and well connected by a stream of minibuses. On the Guatemalan side, a regular flow of trucks, minibuses and buses leaves for **Malacatán**, where you'll find hotels and buses for San Marcos and the western highlands. If you're heading for Guatemala City, there's usually a bus waiting at the border – if not go to Malacatán and catch one from there.

The **Tecún Umán** crossing, on the edge of the dusty and bustling border town of Ciudad Tecún Umán, is favoured by most Guatemalans and all commercial traffic. The town has an authentic frontier flavour with all-night bars, lost souls, contraband and moneychangers, and its streets are almost permanently choked by a chaos of articulated lorries and buses, with cycle rickshaws snaking through the traffic. Everything and everyone is on the move, mostly trying to get out as soon as possible. If you do get stuck, there are plenty of cheap **hotels** and restaurants – the *Hotel Vanessa 2* is one of the best and has rooms with fans (②), while the *Vanessa 1* is cheaper still (②). Otherwise, you could try the *Hospedaje Marcel 2* (②), or the *Hotel Don José*, 2 C 3–42 (☎7768164; ②). Once again there's a steady stream of buses connecting the border with Guatemala City, Coatepeque and Retalhuleu.

South to the beach: Ocós and Tilapa

South of Tecún Umán a rough dirt road, running parallel to the border, bounces through clouds of thick white dust and past endless palm-oil plantations to **OCÓS** on the beach. The village is one of the most forlorn and miserable in the country, with sand streets that run past rows of squalid palm huts. Before the Conquest this was the site of a Mam settlement called Ucez, and prior to that it was part of the so-called Ocós culture, a network of small fishing and farming villages, which was one of the earliest civilizations on the Pacific coast, existing here from 1250 to 1150 BC. There is no evidence of this nowadays, however, and if you do end up in Ocós you'll probably want to leave immediately, as the only accommodation in town is horrific.

The quickest way out is to take the boat across the Río Naranjo to the simple resort town of **TILAPA**, a much better bet for spending an hour or two by the sea. It has a decent beach largely devoid of rubbish, as well as a row of *comedores* dispensing good, fresh prawns and fish, and Gallo beer. The coastline here forms part of the **Reserva El Manchón**, which covers some 30km of prime turtle-nesting beach and extends around 10km inland to embrace a belt of swamp and mangrove, which is home to crocodiles, iguanas, kingfishers, storks, white herons, egrets and an abundance of fish. If you're interested in exploring you shouldn't have any trouble finding a boatman willing to take you on a tour of the canals and lagoons. A resident Peace Corps worker looks after the reserve, and is a good source of local information (just ask for the "gringo").

Although the only *pensión* is very basic, with reed mats to sleep on, you may choose **to stay** here rather than risk returning late to Quetzaltenango, as robberies and attacks have been reported after dark along the paved road that connects with the coastal highway. **Buses** run between Tilapa and Coatepeque every hour or so from 5am to 6pm, and several times a day between Coatepeque and Ocós.

The coastal highway: Coatepeque and Retalhuleu

As you head east from the Mexican border, **COATEPEQUE** is the first place of any importance on the main road. In many ways typical of the coastal strip, this furiously busy, purely commercial town is where most of the coffee produced locally is processed. The action is centred on the **bus terminal**, an intimidating maelstrom of sweat, mud and energetic chaos: buses run every thirty minutes from here to the two border crossings, hourly between 4am and 5pm to Quetzaltenango (via Santa María and Zunil), and hourly from 2.30am to 6pm to Guatemala City. Local buses also run regularly to **Colomba**, which is in the coffee-producing foothills of the highlands, with some continuing onto Quetzaltenanago via San Martín Sacatepéquez (approximately hourly).

Coatepeque practicalities

The best place to **stay** in Coatepeque is the *Hotel Villa Real*, 6 C 6–57 (☎7751308; fax 7751939; ④), a modern hotel with clean rooms and secure parking. A bit cheaper is the family-run *Hotel Baechli*, 6 C 5–35 (☎7751483; ④), which has plain rooms with fans and TV plus secure parking, while the *Hotel Lee*, on 4 Av (③), just below the plaza, is basic, but also offers secure parking. At the budget end of the market, there's the *Europa* (②), at 6 C & 4 Av, just off the plaza, and the *Pensión La Batalla* (①), both just below the bus terminal on 2 C.

For **changing money**, there are branches of the Banco del Occidente (Mon–Fri 9am–7pm, Sat 9am–1pm), and Bamex, on the central plaza (Mon–Fri 8.30am–8pm, Sat 9am–1pm), with several more banks nearby. The **Telgua** office (daily 7am–10pm) for long-distance and local phone calls, is on 5 Av, at the corner of 7 C, and there's a **cinema** a short distance from the plaza, down the hill on 4 Av.

Retalhuleu

Beyond Coatepeque lies the most densely populated section of the Pacific strip, where a branch road leads to **RETALHULEU**, the largest town in this western section. The town is usually referred to as **Reu**, pronounced "Ray-oo", which is what you should look for on the front of buses. Set away from the highway, and surrounded by the walled homes of the wealthy, Retalhuleu has managed to avoid the worst excesses of the coast, protected to some extent by a combination of wealth and tradition. It was founded by the Spanish in the early years of the Conquest, when they merged the villages of Santa Catarina Sacatepéquez and San Antonio. Indian women from these two villages maintained, until recently, the tradition of wearing no blouse – though they were banned from appearing topless in public. This traditionalism marks a real division in the town between a *ladino* population said to be proud of a lineage untainted by Indian blood, and the Indians who have repeatedly risen up against their control.

Today, however, things seem astonishingly peaceful and Retalhuleu is something of an oasis of civilization in the chaos of life on the coast. Its plaza epitomizes all this, with towering Greek columns on a shiny white *municipalidad*, a covered bandstand and an attractive colonial church. The mood is relaxed and easy-going and in the warmth of the evening young couples nestle in the bushes, birds squawk in the trees and BMWs glide through the streets. If you have time to kill, pop into the local **Museum of Archeology and Ethnology** in the *municipalidad* (Tues–Sun 9am–noon & 2–6pm; $1). Rooms are divided into Preclassic, Classic and Postclassic Maya periods, and display an amazing collection of anthropomorphic figurines, mostly heads. Many show a strong Mexican influence in their design, with large ear-plugs a common feature. Upstairs a fascinating collection of ancient photographs, dating back to the 1880s, provides an excellent historic record of the town's changing streetscapes and industries, deomonstrating to what extent its leading citizens tried to create a bourgeois haven among the festering plantations.

Retalhuleu practicalities

Budget **accommodation** is in short supply in Retalhuleu. The cheapest place in town is the *Hotel Pacífico,* close to the market on 7 Av between 9 and 10 calles (☎7711178; ①). It's scruffy and fanless but better than the only other budget choice, the rough *Hotel Hillman*, on 7 Av (①). Slightly pricier is the *Hotel Astor*, 5 C 4–60 (☎7710475; ③), which has rooms with fan, TV and bath, set around a pleasant courtyard, and is very good value for money. Across the road, the *Hotel Modelo* (☎7710256; ③) makes an old-fashioned but decent alternative, with the same facilities for a little less. If you want a bit of luxury, try the modern *Hotel Posada de Don José*, 5 C 3–67 (☎7710180; ④), which has good rooms, a reasonable restaurant and a pool.

The **plaza** is the main hub of activity: here you'll find three **banks** – including the Banco del Agro, and the Banco Industrial, with a 24-hour Visa ATM – and the **post office** (Mon–Fri 8am–4.30pm). The town's best **restaurants** are also on the plaza – try *Cafetería La Luna* for breakfast and other meals, or *El Volován* for cakes and pastries – as is the Cinc Moran. The Telgua office (daily 7am–10pm) is just around the corner on 5 C & 4 Av.

Buses running along the coastal highway almost always pull in at Retalhuleu, and stop at the bus terminal on the southern side of town. To get to the terminal you can either walk, or catch a ride with any bus going south through town along 7 Av. There's an hourly service to and from Guatemala City, the Mexican border and Quetzaltenango, and there are also regular buses to Champerico and El Tulate. Retalhuleu has the only **Mexican consulate** on the Pacific coast, on the eastern edge of town at 5 C and 3 Av (Mon–Fri 4–6pm).

Abaj Takalik

The area around Retalhuleu was heavily populated before the arrival of the Spanish and has been the scene of a number of recent archeological digs, casting new light on the development of early Maya civilization and in particular the formative influence of other cultures from the north. Near El Asintal, a small village 15km to the east of Retalhuleu, the site of **Abaj Takalik** (daily 9am–4pm; $4), currently being excavated, has already provided firm evidence of an **Olmec** influence reaching the area in the first century AD. Excavations have unearthed enormous stelae, several of them very well preserved, dating the earliest monuments to around 126 AD. The only part of the nine-square-kilometre site that has been cleared so far is on the property of the *Finca Margarita*, and does not reveal the main plazas. But the remains of two large **temple platforms** have been excavated and what makes a visit to this obscure site really worthwhile are the carved sculptures and stelae found around their base. In particular, you will find rare and unusual representations of frogs and toads – and even an alligator (monument 66). The finest carving, though, is a giant Olmec head, showing a man of obvious wealth with great hamster cheeks. A kilometre away, close to a river bank, there are two more stelae which are still regularly used for pagan religious worship.

To **get to Abaj Takalik**, take a local bus from Reu to El Asintal, from where it's a four-kilometre walk through coffee and cacao plantations. If in your own transport, take the highway towards Mexico and turn right at the sign. Note that after the village of El Asintal the unpaved track is very rough and best negotiated by four-wheel drive or high clearance vehicles only.

The El Zarco junction

Between Retalhuleu and Cuyotenango is the **El Zarco** junction, from where one of the country's most scenic roads heads up into the highlands towards Quetzaltenango. The stunning hour-and-a-half ride climbs more than 2000m from tropical lowland past dense forests, skirting the Santa María volcano and the village of Zunil. Although you can catch a direct bus to Quetzaltenango from Mazatenango, Coatepeque and Retalhuleu, it's generally quicker to take any bus to El Zarco and change – you shouldn't have to wait more than about twenty minutes at the speed bump.

Champerico

South from Retalhuleu a paved road reaches to the beach at **CHAMPERICO**, which, though it certainly doesn't feel like it, is the country's third port. Founded in 1872, it was originally connected to Quetzaltenango by rail and enjoyed a brief period of prosperity based on the export of coffee. In 1934 Aldous Huxley passed through, but was distinctly unimpressed: "Then suddenly, vast and blank, under a glaring white sky, the Pacific. One after another, with a succession of dreary bumps, the rollers broke on a flat beach." Huxley was fortunate enough to board a steamer and escape what he called "the unspeakable boredom of life at Champerico". If anything, things have got worse, as barely any trade passes through the port these days, and the rusting pier, the only feature to disturb the coastline, will doubtless soon sink beneath the waves. Champerico still supports a handful of fishermen, but spends most of its time waiting for the weekend, when hordes of weary city dwellers descend on the coast. The **beach** is much the same as anywhere else, although its sheer scale is impressive (watch out for the dangerous undertow). When you tire of testing your strength against the fury of the surf, plenty of places serve delicious **meals** of shrimp or fish, including the *Restaurant Monte Limar*, where the portions are big and the prices small.

The most atmospheric **hotel** in Champerico is the *Miramar*, 2 C & Av Coatepeque (☎7737231; ②), a lovely old building with, dark windowless rooms, hot water, and a Spanish owner. It also has a fantastic dark wood **bar**, the best place is town to take on your thirst. The *Martita*, just over the street (②), is nothing special, or there's the *Hospedaje Buenos Aires* (①), a very seedy little boarding house.

Buses from Champerico run directly to Quetzaltenango, passing through Retalhuleu, every couple of hours, from 4am to 3pm. Coming the other way, there are direct buses from 7am, though you are better off grabbing the first bus to Retalhuleu and changing there. If you're heading anywhere else, catch a bus from Champerico to Retalhuleu and then another along the coastal highway. The last bus to Retalhuleu leaves Champerico at 6pm.

Cuyotenango, El Tulate, Mazatenango and Cocales

Beyond Retalhuleu the highway runs east to **CUYOTENANGO**, one of the older towns along the way. It started life as the site of a pre-Conquest Cakchiquel village before becoming an important colonial town. The narrow streets and some of the older buildings bear witness to this distinguished past, but the thunder of the highway, which cuts right through the town, overwhelms all else, and its larger neighbours have long since consumed any importance that Cuyotenango once held.

Another branch road turns off for the beach here, heading 45km south to **EL TULATE**, where the village and the ocean are separated from the mainland by a narrow expanse of mangrove swamp. The beach itself, lined with palm trees, is another featureless strip of black sand, and the only places to stay are on the reed mattresses in the shacks adjoining the open-air restaurants. However, the fried seafood is good, and the isolation of the village is a definite bonus. **Buses** to El Tulate run every hour or so from Mazatenango and Retalhuleu, with the last bus back to Mazatenango at 4pm, and the last to Retalhuleu at 5pm: small boats meet the buses to ferry their passengers from the end of the road to the village.

Back on the highway, the next stop is **MAZATENANGO**, another seething commercial town. There are two sides to "Mazate", as it's generally known. The main street, which runs down the side of the market, past the filling stations and bus terminal, is characteristic of life along the coastal highway, redolent of diesel fumes and cheap commercialization. The other half of town, centred on the plaza, is quieter, calmer and more sophisticated, with long shaded streets. There's no particular reason to linger in Mazatenango, but if you do find yourself here for the night, budget **accommodation** options include the *Hotel Costa Rica*, 1 Av & 2 C, on the corner opposite the filling stations (①), and the *Hotel Sarah*, beside the old train station, which offers good-value simple rooms with private bath (②). If you want somewhere more comfortable to stay, head for the *Hotel Alba*, on the main highway heading for Mexico (☎8720264; ④), which has the advantage of secure parking. For **food**, try *Maxim's*, 6 Av 9–23, which specializes in barbecued meat and Chinese dishes, or *Croissants Pastelería*, on the plaza, for coffee and cakes. There are a couple of cinemas in Mazatenango and plenty of **banks**.

Buses can be caught at the small terminal above the market on the main street, or outside the filling stations, which is where most of the pullmans stop. They run regularly in both directions along the coastal highway, and to Quetzaltenango, El Tulate, Chicacao and Pueblo Nuevo Tiquisate, every hour or so from 8am to 4pm.

East to Cocales

Continuing east from Mazatenango the main road passes the junction for Chicacao, a coffee centre with close links to Santiago Atitlán (see p.152), and **PUEBLO NUEVO TIQUISATE**, once the local headquarters of the all-powerful United Fruit Company, whose banana plantations stretched almost as far as its political influence. The company, now owned by Del Monte, planted huge numbers of bananas in this area after its plantations on the Caribbean coast were hit by disease, although modern techniques have enabled many to be switched back to their original locations. If you want to **stay** overnight before heading south to the coast, your best bet is the *Hotel El Viajero* (☎8847189; ③), which has simple but decent rooms with fan and TV, plus secure parking. From here you can either drive, hitch or take a local bus to Semillero or Tecojate. The better beach is at **Semillero**, and the branch road heading this way offers an interesting glimpse of sugar cane plantations and the very different houses of the workers (dormitories) and managers (great wooden houses on stilts, painted a neat New England-style green and white).

About 30km beyond Mazatenango is **COCALES**, a crossroads from where a road runs north to San Lucas Tolimán and Lake Atitlán, and south to the agricultural centre of **NUEVA CONCEPCIÓN**. Concepción is an inconspicuous little town that catapulted into the headlines in the 1980s as the home parish of Guatemala's most radical and controversial priest, **Padre Andrés Girón**, who founded the country's first significant land reform movement since the Arbenz government (1949–54). During the civil war, Girón spoke out eloquently on behalf of *campesinos* and led fifteen thousand peasants in a four-day march to Guatemala City. He received numerous death threats for his troubles but, undeterred, has since entered politics.

From Cocales, **buses** run to **Santiago Atitlán**, **Panajachel** and **San Lucas Tolimán**. If you're heading this way you can wait for a connection at the junction, but don't expect to make it all the way to Panajachel unless you get here by mid-day. The best option is take the first pick-up or bus to Santiago and catch a boat from there to other points around the lake. The last bus to Santiago Atitlán leaves Cocales at around 4pm but plenty of pick-ups also run this route.

Santa Lucía Cotzumalguapa and around

Another 23km brings you to **SANTA LUCÍA COTZUMALGUAPA**, a pretty uninspiring Pacific town a short distance north of the highway. The main reason to visit is to explore the **archeological sites** that are scattered in the surrounding cane fields, though you should bear in mind that getting to them is not easy unless you rent a taxi.

Santa Lucía Cotzumalguapa

Pullman **buses** passing along the highway will drop you at the entrance road to town ten minutes' walk from the town centre, while second-class "direct" buses from the capital go straight into the terminal, a few blocks from the plaza. Buses to Guatemala City leave the terminal hourly from 3am to 4pm, or you can catch a pullman from the highway.

As usual, the **plaza** is the main point of interest. Santa Lucía's shady square is home to one of the country's ugliest structures, a horrific green and white concrete municipal building. Just off the plaza, you'll find several cheap and scruffy **hotels**: the *Pensión Reforma*, 4 Av 4–71 (①), true to its name, is owned by some friendly but fearsome Catholics – the light switches are outside the rooms and if there's any suggestion of immoral activities they'll switch your light on; even the bathrooms are separate sex. Around the corner on 5 Calle, another budget option, *Hospedaje El Carmen* (①), has thirteen tiny but clean rooms. The nearest upmarket place is the *Caminotel Santiaguito* (☎8825435; ④), a slick motel on the main highway, with a swimming pool and restaurant. Alternatively, there's the *El Camino,* across the road from here (☎8825316; ③), but it's quite expensive for what you get.

For **food**, the *Comedor Lau* on 3 Av serves reasonable Chinese meals, or there's a huge new *Pollo Campero* on the north side of the plaza. *Sarita* on 3 Av does great ice-creams, while *Cevicheria La Española*, on 4 Av, a block south of the plaza, is the best bet for a drink. The only other non-sleazy night-time entertainment is watching a film at the *Cine Victoria* on 3 Av. The *Kodak Club,* also on 3 Av, stocks slide film, and at least three **banks** will change your travellers' cheques – Banco Corpativo, on the plaza, accepts most varieties.

Sites around Santa Lucía Cotzumalguapa

A tour of the **sites** around Santa Lucía Cotzumalguapa can be an exhausting and frustrating process, taking you through a sweltering maze of cane fields. Doing the whole thing on foot is certainly the cheapest way, but also by far the hardest. Note that wandering about the cane fields alone is never a good idea, though if you are determined to, do so in the mornings when, as locals would say, "the thieves are still sleeping". You're far better off taking a round trip by taxi instead – you'll find plenty in the plaza in varying degrees of decrepitude – and if you bargain well it need not be prohibitively expensive (reckon on around $10 all in). Make sure the trip includes all the sites and fix a firm price beforehand. If you only want to see one of the sites, choose **Bilbao**, just a kilometre or so from the centre of town, and featuring some of the best carving. The sites are covered below, with directions, in the best order for visiting them on foot, but it's still fairly easy to get lost. If you do, just ask for *las piedras*, as they tend to be known locally.

Bilbao
Bilbao lies just north of Santa Lucía Cotzumalguapa. In 1880, more than thirty Late Classic stone monuments were removed from this site, and nine of them, probably the very finest of the Pacific coast stelae, deemed far too good to waste on Guatemala, were shipped to Germany. One was lost at sea and the others are currently on display in the Dahlem Museum in Berlin. Four sets of stones are still visible in situ, however, and two of them, both beautifully preserved slabs of black volcanic rock, perfectly illustrate the magnificent precision of the carving.

To get to the site, walk uphill from the plaza along 4 Av, and bear right at the end, where a dirt track takes you past a small red-brick house and along the side of a cane field. About 200m further on is a fairly wide path leading left into the cane for about 20m. This brings you to two large stones carved in bird-like patterns, with strange circular glyphs arranged in groups of three: the majority of the glyphs are recognizable as the names for days once used by the people of southern Mexico. Numbers are expressed only by dots and circles, without the bar that was used by the Maya to represent five. This is further evidence that the Pipil, who carved these stones some time between 400 and 900 AD, had more in common with the tribes of the far north than with those of the Guatemalan highlands or Petén.

The same cane field contains two other sets of stones, reached along similar paths further up this side of the field. The first of them is badly eroded, so that it's only possible to make out the raised border and little or nothing of the actual carving. But the second is the best of the lot, a superbly preserved set of figures and interwoven motifs. The Mexican migrants who were responsible for all this shared with the Maya a fascination for the ball game, and on this stone a player is depicted, reaching up to decidedly Mexican divinities – a fairly clear indication that the game was regarded as a form of worship. The player is wearing a heavy protective belt, which would have been made from wood and leather, and you can clearly make out several birds and animals, as well as pods of cacao beans – which were used as currency.

There's one final stone hidden in the cane, which can be reached by heading back down the side of the field and turning right at the bottom, along the other side. Here you will come across yet another entrance, opposite *Casa No. 13,* which brings you to the last carving, another well-defined set of figures. The face of this stone has been cut into, presumably in an attempt to remove it.

Finca El Baúl

The second site is also out on the northern side of town, though somewhat further afield in the grounds of the **Finca El Baúl**. The *finca* is about 5km from Santa Lucía Cotzumalguapa and has its own collection of artefacts, as well as a small but fascinating site out in the cane fields. To get there from the last of the Bilbao stones, walk on beyond *Casa No. 13* and onto the tarmacked road (if you're coming out of town this is a continuation of 4 Av). At the T-junction straight ahead of you turn to the right and follow the road for some 4km until it comes to a bridge. Cross this and take the right-hand fork for another kilometre or so, passing all the houses. Once out here a dirt track crosses the road, and you want to turn right along this to the base of a small hill. The site is on top of this hill, but you need to walk round to the other side to find the path up. Once there you'll see the two stones: one flat and carved in low relief, the other a massive half-buried stone head, with wrinkled brow and patterned headdress. The site has a powerful, mysterious atmosphere and is still used for religious ceremonies and by women seeking children and safe birth. In front of the stones is a set of small altars on which local people make animal sacrifices, burn incense and leave offerings of flowers. The faces of the stone figures are smeared and stained with wax dripped from candles. El Baúl makes an ideal shaded spot for a picnic lunch, with fine vistas towards the twin peaks of volcanos Agua and Fuego to the north.

The next place of interest is the *finca* itself, a few kilometres away. This can be reached by continuing down the dirt track that exits the site, crossing a tarmacked road and walking through the sugar cane for about after ten minutes until you emerge onto another road; here you should turn right for the *finca's* main building. At the gate, explain to the guards that you're here to see *el museo*, then walk beyond the rows of shanty-like huts to the huge furnace, behind which the main administration building is protected by further armed guards. Ask in here to see the collection, which is housed in a special compound under lock and key: despite the fierce-looking security measures they're always willing to oblige. The carvings include some superb heads, a stone skull, a massive jaguar and many other interesting pieces jumbled together. Alongside all this antiquity is the *finca's* old steam engine, a miniature machine that used to haul the cane along a system of private tracks. A visit is also interesting for the rare glimpse it offers of a working *finca*, where about nine hundred people are employed. They even have their own bus service laid on from town, which you may be able to hitch a ride on – buses leave from the *Tienda El Baúl*, a few blocks uphill from the plaza in Santa

Lucía Cotzumalguapa, four or five times a day, the first at around 7am and the last either way at about 6pm.

Finca Las Ilusiones
The remaining site is on the other side of town, at the **Finca Las Ilusiones**, home to another private collection of artefacts and some stone carvings. To get there walk east along the highway for about a kilometre, out beyond the two Esso stations and past a small football field to the north of the road. After this a track leads off to the left (north) to the *finca* itself. Outside the buildings you'll see some copied carvings and several originals, including some fantastic stelae. The building to the left houses a small museum – ask around for the man who looks after the key. Inside is a tiny room crammed with literally thousands of small stone carvings and pottery fragments. There are more carvings leant against the walls of a private courtyard, reached by crossing the bridge and turning to the left. If you manage to get a peep you'll see many figures with the flattened foreheads that are so common in Maya art, while others that look like nothing you'd expect to find in the Maya heartland.

La Democracía and the coast at Sipacate

Heading east from Santa Lucía Cotzumalguapa the coastal highway arrives next at Siquinalá, a run-down sort of place that straddles the road, from where another branch road heads to the coast. Along the way, 9km to the south, **LA DEMOCRACÍA** is of particular interest as the home of another collection of archeological relics. To the east of town lies the archeological site of **Monte Alto**, and many of the best pieces which have been found there are now spread around the town plaza under a vast ceiba tree. These so-called "fat boys" are massive stone heads with simple, almost childlike faces. Some are attached to smaller rounded bodies and rolled over on their backs clutching their swollen stomachs. The figures resemble nothing else in the Maya world, but are strikingly similar to the far more ancient Olmec sculptures found near Villahermosa in the Gulf of Mexico. In academic circles debate still continues to rage about the precise origins of these traits, but for the moment even less is known about these relics than about the sites around Santa Lucía Cotzumalguapa. However, it seems likely that they predate almost all other archeological finds in Guatemala. The faces of the "fat boys", with their bizarre, almost Buddha-like appearance of contentment, could well be as much as four thousand years old. Also on the plaza, the town **museum** (Tues–Sun 8am–noon & 2–5pm) houses carvings, ceremonial yokes worn by ballgame players, pottery, grinding stones and a few more carved heads.

The road continues further south to **La Gomera**, a mid-sized agricultural centre where buses usually wait for a while, and beyond to the coast at **Sipacate**. The beach here is separated from the village by the black waters of the Chiquimulilla Canal, across which boats ferry a constant stream of passengers. In recent years the branch road heading this way has fallen into such a state of disrepair that the journey of several hours to reach Sipacate really isn't worth it. If you are determined to visit, *La Costa* (②), in the village, is the best place **to stay**, but avoid the badly maintained and overpriced *Rancho Carillo* on the beach itself (④).

Buses to Sipacate and La Democracía from both Guatemala City and Santa Lucía Cotzumalguapa pass through Siquinalá. However, the direct buses from Guatemala City are extremely slow, so if you want to head down this way the best thing to do is catch a bus to Siquinalá and wait outside the market there for one heading for La Democracia and Sipacate. Note that the trip from the main highway to Sipacate can take as long as three hours, with the last bus back to the highway leaving at 5pm.

East from Escuintla towards El Salvador

The eastern section of the Pacific coast is dominated by **Escuintla**, the region's largest town, and **Puerto San José**, formerly its most important port. If you're heading for the coast from Guatemala City this is probably the route you'll take, and it's a fairly easy day trip. Neither town is particularly attractive, however, and you're unlikely to stay more than a single night, if that. Further to the east is **Monterrico**, an impressive beach where you'll find the coast's most important wildlife reserve, a protected area of mangrove swamps that's home to some superb birdlife. Beyond that the coastal highway runs to the border with El Salvador, with branch roads heading off to a couple of small seashore villages.

Escuintla

At the junction of the two principal coastal roads, **ESCUINTLA** is the largest and most important of the Pacific towns. There's nothing to do here but you do get a good sense of what life on the coast is all about, dominated as it is by a heady cocktail of pace, energy, squalour, dirt and commerce. Escuintla lies at the heart of the country's most productive region, both industrially and agriculturally, and the department's resources include cattle, sugar, cotton, light industry and even a small Texaco oil refinery. The town is also one of the oldest on the Pacific coast, built on the site of a pre-Conquest Pipil settlement. Its modern name is a contraction of the Pipil word *Isquitepeque*, meaning "the hill of the dogs", a name given to the village because of the dog-like animals the Pipil kept for meat. These days there's no doubt about the commercial bustle of Escuintla's streets, but they look as though the inhabitants, swept up in all this hubbub, have completely forgotten about the town itself, leaving it to crumble around them. One side of the plaza is taken up by the mossy ruins of an old school, and the entire town is in a state of advanced decay.

Below the plaza, a huge, chaotic daily **market** sprawls across several blocks, spilling out into 4 Av, the main commercial thoroughfare, which is also notable for a lurid blue mock-castle that functions as the town's police station.

Practicalities

There are plenty of cheap **hotels** near 4 Av, most of them sharing the general air of dilapidation. The *Hospedaje El Centro,* on 3 Av, a block behind the market (①) is one of the better cheap places, with *Hospedaje Oriente,* 4 Av 11–30 (①) being slightly more upmarket. For more luxury, the *Hotel Izcuintla,* 4 Av 6–30 (③), offers overhead fans and private baths, while *Hotel Costa Sur,* 4 Av and 12 C (☎8881819; ③), is recommended, not least for its air-conditioning and secure parking. For real peace and quiet, head for the *Hotel La Villa* (☎8880395; ④), a very dignified hotel a few blocks from the bustle of the town centre at 3 Av 3–21. If money is no object, you could try the rather overpriced motel *Sarita* on Avenida Centroamérica, at the junction of the coastal highway and the Guatemala City road (☎8880482; fax 8881959; ⑥), which has a nice pool.

Again, 4 Av is the place to head if you're looking for something **to eat** – it is lined with restaurants offering anything from Guatemalan seafood feasts to the inevitable *ch'ao mein* and burgers, with the best deal being the Q10 lunch specials at *Pizzeria al Macarone*, 4 Av 6–103. For true burger-junkies, there's a giant *McDonalds*, a kilometre away from the centre on 1 Av. **Banks** are plentiful, and include Banco Industrial, at 4 Av and 6 C, Lloyds, at 7 C 3–07, and Banco de Occidente and Banco Immobiliario, both on 4 Av. Escuintla also has a couple of **consulates** – El Salvador is on 16 C 3–20, and Honduras is on 6 Av 8–24. There are two **cinemas** in town – the Rialto at 5 C & 3 Av, and the Lux on 7 C, opposite the bank.

Buses to Escuintla leave the Treból junction in Guatemala City every thirty minutes or so from 4am to 7pm. In Escuintla, they leave at the same times from 8 C & 2 Av. Services to other destinations depart from one of two other terminals: for places **en route to the Mexican border**, buses run through the north of town and stop by the Esso station opposite the Banco Uno (take a local bus up 3 Av); buses for the **coast road and inland route to El Salvador** are best caught at the main terminal on the south side of town, at the bottom of 4 Av (local bus down 4 Av). From the latter, buses leave every thirty minutes for Puerto San José and Iztapa, hourly for the eastern border, and daily at 6.30am and noon for Antigua, via El Rodeo.

To the coast: Puerto San José

South from Escuintla the coast road heads through acres of cattle pasture to **PUERTO SAN JOSÉ**, another run-down and redundant port. In its prime San José, which opened as a port in 1853, was Guatemala's main shipping terminal, funnelling goods to and from the capital, but it has now been made virtually redundant by Puerto Quetzal, a container port a few kilometres to the east (and connected to Escuintla by a new fast road, which is sure to accelerate further the decline of San José). Today both town and port are somewhat sleazy and the main business is local tourism: what used to be rough sailors' bars pander to the needs of day-trippers from the capital who fill the beaches at weekends.

The shoreline is again separated from the mainland, by the **Canal de Chiquimulilla**, which starts near Sipacate, west of San José, and runs as far as the border with El Salvador, cutting off all the beaches in between. For the most part it is nothing more than a narrow strip of water, but in some places it fans out into a maze of mangrove swamps, providing a home for a wide array of wildlife.

In San José the main resort area is on the other side of the canal, directly behind the beach. This is where all the bars, restaurants and hotels are, most of them crowded at weekends with big *ladino* groups feasting on seafood and playing the jukebox until the small hours. The hotels are not so enjoyable, catering as they do to a largely drunken clientele. Prices are usually high and standards low – in the cheapest digs you'll be lucky if you get a sheet, and will have to make do with a bare reed mat. You're better off sampling the delights of San José as a day trip from the capital, but if you do need **to stay**, the best deal is at the *Casa San José Hotel*, on Av del Comercio (☎7765587; ③), where you'll find a pool and restaurant, or for a cheaper option, there's the basic *Viñas de Mar*, right on the beach (②). If you want to spend a few days on the coast then head along to Iztapa, or to Monterrico.

Buses between the plaza in San José and the Zona 4 bus terminal in Guatemala City run every hour or so all day, with most services continuing on to Iztapa.

Chulamar and Likin

Leaving San José and following the coast in either direction you come upon the beach resorts of the rich. Guatemala's wealthy elite abandoned Puerto San José to the day-trippers long ago, establishing instead their own enclaves of holiday homes in pale imitation of California. The first of these is **CHULAMAR**, about 5km west of Puerto San José, reached only by private car or taxi. Here you'll find another strip of sand separated from the land by the muddy waters of the canal. On the beach there's a single upmarket **hotel**, *Hotel Santa María del Mar* (☎8811293; ⑤), and a string of small *cabañas* (④).

East of San José, past the container terminal at **Puerto Quetzal**, is the second of the resorts, **BALNEARIO LIKIN**. Here a complete residential complex has been established, based around a neat grid of canals and streets. The ranks of second homes have speedboats and swimming pools, and the entire compound comes complete with an armed guard. There are no buses to Likin itself but any of those going from San José to Iztapa will drop you at the entrance. Like all these places it's deserted during the week, when there are no boats to shuttle you to the beach, but at weekends you can drop by to watch the rich at play.

Iztapa and along the coast to Monterrico

Further east the road comes to an end at **IZTAPA**, another old port that now serves the domestic tourist industry. Of all the country's redundant ports Iztapa is the oldest, as it was here that the Spanish chose to harbour their fleets. In the early days Alvarado used the port to build the boats that took him first to Peru and then on the trip to the Spice Islands from which he never returned. In 1839 the English explorer and diplomat John Lloyd Stephens passed through on his way to Nicaragua, and found the inhabitants far from happy: "The captain of the port as he brushed them away (the swarming moschetoes), complained of the desolation and dreariness of the place, its isolation and separation from the world, its unhealthiness, and the misery of a man doomed to live there." While for some this might be a fitting description of the entire Pacific coast, there are certainly places that it fits better than Iztapa these days. If not exactly beautiful, the village is at least one of the nicer Pacific beach resorts, smaller and quieter than San José but with none of the elitism of Likin or Chulamar. The beach itself, a bank of black sand, is on the other side of the Chiquimulilla canal, and a handful of boatmen provide a regular shuttle service to and from the village.

There are also several reasonable **hotels**, another rarity in this part of the country. The *Sol y Playa Tropical* (④) is the most luxurious, a family hotel set around a small pool, whose rooms each have private baths. The *Hotel Brasilia*, 1 C 4–27 (③), has fewer pretensions to class, its basic second-floor rooms looking down over a huge bar and dance floor. The cheapest deal in town is the smaller, gringo-run *Pollo Andra* (②), which has simple rooms with fans. **Buses** run from the Zona 4 bus terminal in Guatemala City to Iztapa every hour or so (5am–5pm).

Beyond Iztapa the path of the coast road is blocked by the mouth of the **Río Naranjo**, but it is possible to continue along the coast as far as Monterrico by catching a boat across the river and then a bus on the other side. You have to walk a little way east to the edge of Iztapa, and when you reach the river bank look for a boatman to ferry you across – there are usually plenty of canoes and their owners are all too willing to earn a quetzal or two (overcharging gringos is common and often unavoidable, although it's worth attempting to bargain). On the other side is the village of **Pueblo Viejo**; it's important to make sure that this is where you're being taken, or you might end up on the beach. From Pueblo Viejo three buses a day should go to **Monterrico** – usually at 11.30am, 1.30pm and 4pm, although the buses are old and the schedule uncertain at the best of times. Buses leave Monterrico for Pueblo Viejo at 5.30am, 11am and 2pm.

Monterrico: the beach and nature reserve

The setting of **MONTERRICO** is one of the finest on the Pacific coast, with the scenery reduced to its basic elements: a strip of dead straight sand, a line of powerful surf, a huge empty ocean and an enormous curving horizon. The village is friendly and relaxed, separated from the mainland by the waters of the Chiquimulilla canal, which weaves through a fantastic network of mangrove swamps. Mosquitoes can be a problem during the wet season.

Beach apart, Monterrico's chief attraction is the **nature reserve** (known as the Biotopo Monterrico-Hawaii), which embraces the village, the beach – an important turtle nesting ground – and a large slice of the swampland behind, forming a total area of some 2800 hectares. Sadly, however, the protected status the reserve officially enjoys does not prevent mounds of domestic rubbish being dumped, nor the widespread theft of turtle eggs. That said, it's well worth making your way to Monterrico, if only for the fantastically beautiful ocean, and it is certainly the best place to spend time by the sea.

Getting to Monterrico

There are two ways to **get to Monterrico**: either the slower route by ferry and bus from Iztapa (see above) or from Taxisco (see p.230) on the coastal highway, where trucks and buses run the 17km south to La Avellana. From here, boats shuttle passengers (Q3) and cars ($8) back and forth to Monterrico on the opposite side of the mangrove swamp. There's a steady flow of traffic between Taxisco and La Avellana, with the last bus leaving Taxisco at 6pm and La Avellana at 4.30pm – though if you don't want to wait for a bus it's usually easy enough to hitch a ride with a truck or a car. There are also direct buses between La Avellana and the Zona 4 bus terminal in Guatemala City, which take around three and a half hours, leaving La Avellana at 4am, 6am and 7.30am, and Guatemala City every thirty minutes between 10am and noon – if these buses fail to show up, just get on any bus heading for Taxisco and change there.

On **arrival** at the dock, follow the meandering dirt track through some coconut palms towards the slumbering, tropical village centre. You'll pass a couple of *tiendas,* a pharmacy, a football pitch and plenty of pigs, chickens and dogs. Continue past a group of open-air restaurants and you'll soon hear the pounding of the Pacific and see what all the fuss is about – **Baule beach**.

Accommodation

There's a pretty good range of **accomodation** with almost everthing concentrated right on the beach. All the hotels, except the *Pig Pen*, *Sagastume* and the *Paradise*, are to the left as you face the ocean. As there are **no phones** in Monterrico it isn't easy to book in advance; you'll do best if you try those that have reservations numbers in Guatemala City. As with most places on the coast, prices can increase by around fifty per cent at **weekends**, and finding a bed may involve trudging through the sand from place to place.

THE TURTLES OF MONTERRICO

The huge, sparsely populated expanses of beach around Monterrico are prime nesting sites for three types of **sea turtle**, including the largest of them all, the giant leatherback. The reserve was originally established to protect the turtles from the soup pot and to curb the collection of the eggs, which are considered an aphrodisiac. Further dangers to the turtles include being hunted for their shells, drowned inside fishing nets and poisoned by pollution, especially plastic bags that resemble jellyfish, a favourite food. Turtles almost always nest in the dark, and on a moonless night in egg-laying season you have a good chance of seeing one in Monterrico.

Leatherback *Dermochelys coriace*. The gargantuan leatherback is by far the largest of the world's turtles, growing to more than 2m in length and weighing up to 900 kilos. Named *baule* in Spanish, the leatherback gives the beach at Monterrico its name. It feeds almost exclusively on jellyfish, diving as deep as a kilometre beneath the sea in search of its prey. As its name suggests, it is the only turtle not to have a hard exterior shell, instead it has a layer of black, soft, rubbery skin. The leatherback frequents tropical and Arctic waters from Malaysia to Scotland and makes one of the longest migrations of any creature on earth. The species, which has been around for 200 million years, is in severe danger of extinction. It nests at Monterrico between mid-October and February.

Olive Ridley *Lepidochelys olivacea*. Spread throughout the tropical waters of the Pacific, Atlantic and Indian oceans, the Olive Ridley is the most numerous of the world's eight species and also one of the smallest, typically 80cm long and weighing around 35 kilos. Olive Ridleys gather in huge numbers off favoured beaches to mate, then the females return en mass to nest. They are common visitors at Monterrico during their nesting season beween July and November.

East Pacific Black Turtle *Chelonia Agassizi* The East Pacific black turtle nests only on the Pacific coast between California and Ecuador, and is not found anywhere else in the world. It reaches more than a metre in length and has a characteristic dark heart-shaped shell. Some scientists believe it to be a subspecies of the

Hotel Baule Beach, next door to the *Kaiman* (Guatemala City ☎4736196; fax 4713390). The most enduring gringo guest house on the entire Pacific coast, run by American Nancy Garver, a former Peace Corps volunteer, who was so enchanted by Guatemala that she decided to stay. All rooms have their own bathroom and mosquito net, there's a pool, and decent grub is available, including fresh shrimp, fish and beef. It's a good deal for single travellers. ③.

Johnny's Place, the first place you come to along the beach (Guatemala City ☎3326973). Self-catering bungalows sleeping up to four, with three small pools. ④.

Kaiman Inn, the second place you come to as you head east along the beach. Here large rooms have mosquito nets and fans. There's also a pool and an erratic Italian restaurant that is sometimes excellent and sometimes ordinary, depending on who's wearing the apron. ④.

Hotel El Mangle, behind the *Baule Beach* (Guatemala City ☎3603336). Five simple rooms all with private bathroom. Serves as a reasonable overflow if other possibilities are full, but has no pool or food. ④.

Paradise Hotel, 2km outside the village, on the road heading for Iztapa (Guatemala City ☎4784202; fax 4784595). Most easily reached with your own transport. Spacious bungalows with two double beds and private bath, plus a pool. The restaurant, though decent, charges silly prices. ⑦.

Pez de Oro, last place as you head east along the beach (Guatemala City ☎3683684). The nicest cottages on the beach. Well-spaced, comfortable and tastefully decorated with a small

more common green turtle, which shares a similar shell outline and can be found throughout the tropics. Its nesting season at Monterrico is the same as that of the Olive Ridleys, from July to November.

All the species of turtle use similar **nesting** techniques, hauling themselves up the beach, laboriously digging a hole about 50cm deep with their flippers, and with great effort depositing a clutch of a hundred or so soft, ping-pong-ball-sized eggs. They then bury the cache and race back into the ocean. The eggs of the two smaller turtles take around fifty days to hatch, those of the leatherback 72. When their time comes, the tiny turtles, no larger than the palm of your hand, use their flippers to dig their way out and make a mad dash for the water, desperately trying to avoid the waiting seabirds. Once in the water they have a very hazardous existence for the first few years of their lives, with only one in a hundred making it to maturity.

Watching a turtle lay her eggs at Monterrico should be a memorable experience, but the presence of the local *hueveros* (egg collectors) will probably ensure that it's not. In season Baule beach is lined with sentries on the lookout for turtles, scanning the waves with torches every minute or so for signs of the marine visitors. When a turtle comes ashore these human vultures leave the creature undisturbed until all its eggs have been laid, then a *huevero* will pick it up (unless it's a leatherback) and dump the exhausted beast elsewhere before delving straight into the nest. Most foreign witnesses are content to take a photo and touch the bewildered creature before it claws its way back to the ocean, though you shouldn't use flash photography as it can upset and disorientate the sensitive turtles. Other braver souls who have challenged the *hueveros* have been threatened with machetes.

Officially the taking of eggs is outlawed, but informally a deal has been done so that out of each clutch of eggs collected, a dozen are donated to the turtle hatchery at the reserve headquarters, from where five thousand baby turtles are released a year. It's hoped that this deal will ease relations between the local community, who sell the eggs for $2 a dozen, and the conservation aims of the reserve. The turtles themselves are no longer killed and eaten.

swimming pool. The restaurant (being Italian owned) is very good, with excellent pasta and wine by the glass. ⑤.

Pig Pen, 2m down the beach on the righthand side. Excellent budget base with the cheapest beds in town. Rooms are bare but clean, and have facilities for cooking your own food. Alternatively hook up a hammock for a dollar a night. ①.

Hotel Sagastume, turn right just before you reach the beach, and it's 20m down the track on the left. Six pleasant rooms with en-suite showers. ④.

Hotel San Gregorio, on a dirt track behind *Johnny's Place* (Guatemala City ☎2517326). Ugly new multi-storey hotel whose high walls enclose a private world of modern rooms set around a large pool. ⑤.

The Biotopo Monterrico-Hawaii

Monterrico's **mangrove swamp** is a bizarre and rich environment, formed as rivers draining from the highlands find their path blocked by the black sands of the beach and spill out into this enormous watery expanse before finally finding their way to the sea through two estuaries, 30km to the east and west of the village. These dark, nutrient-rich waters are superbly fertile, and four distinct types of mangrove form a dense mat of branches, interspersed with narrow canals, open lagoons, bullrushes and water lilies. The tangle of roots acts as a kind of marine nursery, offering small fish protection from their natural predators, while above the surface the dense vegetation and ready food supply provide an ideal home for hundreds of species of bird and a handful of mammals, including racoons, iguanas, alligators and opossums.

At any time of day a trip into the swamp is an adventure, taking you through a complex network of channels and beneath a dense canopy of vegetation. The best way to go is in a small *cayuco*, and there are always plenty of children hanging around the dock in Monterrico who'll be willing to take you on a trip into the wilds, or you can rent a larger boat with an engine – but you won't see as much. You shouldn't expect to encounter the anteaters and racoons, whichever way you travel, but you probably will see a good range of bird life, including kingfishers, white herons and several species of duck, with the Palmilla lagoon being a particuarly good spot. Failing all else the trip is well worth it just to watch the local fishermen casting their nets.

At the **headquarters** of the Monterrico reserve (daily 8am–noon & 2–5pm), beside the *Hotel Baule Beach*, there is a shaded section of sand where the turtle eggs are reburied (see below). Once the turtles hatch they are released from buckets directly into the ocean, so that they can avoid the attentions of sea birds. You can also see some baby turtles kept in tanks, as well as a dusty collection of jars filled with pickled fish and crustaceans. The reserve and research project, run by the government body CECON and the University of San Carlos, is urgently in need of funding, Spanish-speaking volunteers, and contacts with overseas universities. If you're interested in helping out, write to CECON USAC, Reserva Natural, Monterrico, 06024 Taxisco, Santa Rosa.

A short **trail** runs from the headquarters along the edge of the reserve, past enclosures of alligators and green iguanas which are also bred for release into the wild. If you turn to the right down the dirt road at the end of the trail you'll pass a shrimp farm on the right before the track eventually meets the beach. It's a good stroll for birdwatching, particularly in the early morning and evening.

East to Hawaii

Further along the beach, about 5km to the east of Monterrico, is isolated **HAWAII**, accessible only by boat. This is another relaxed fishing village where the ocean life has attracted a handful of regular tourists, notably wealthy Argentinians from Guatemala City who have built second homes on the beach. Locals live by fishing and farming and there is a large turtle project, where up to ten thousand turtles are released each year. You can visit on a day-trip from Monterrico, by renting a boat from the dock.

Eating and drinking

When it comes to **eating** in Monterrico you can either dine at any of the hotels on the beach, or at one of the *comedores* in the village, the best of which is the *Divino Maestro*, where they do excellent shrimp, fish, beef, chicken and a superb shark steak with rosemary. For a **drink** and relaxed socializing with great music, head for the *Pig Pen* (see above), run by a friendly Canadian, Michael, who can point you in the right direction if you wish to rent surfboards and boats or find a guide.

From Escuintla to El Salvador

Heading east from Escuintla the coastal highway brings you to **TAXISCO**, a quiet farming centre set to the north of the main road. From here a branch road runs to **La Avellana**, from where you can catch a boat to Monterrico. If you're heading for Monterrico then take a bus as far as Taxisco and hitch from there or ask around in the plaza. **Buses** to Taxisco leave from the Zona 4 terminal in Guatemala City, calling at Escuintla and usually going on to the El Salvador border. If you get stuck in Taxisco, make for the recently refurbished *Hotel Jereson*, on the main street (③).

Shortly before it reaches Taxisco the highway passes one of Guatemala's most unusual and neglected tourist sights, the **Club Auto Safari Chapín** (Tues–Sun 9.30am–5pm; $3). Central America's only safari park lies about a kilometre south of the highway (at Km 87.5) on land owned by one of the great *fincero* families, whose older generation were enthusiastic big-game hunters, covering the walls of the main hacienda with the heads and skins of animals from every corner of the globe. Their children, however, developed a strong resistance to these exploits and insisted on bringing their animals home alive. The end result is a safari park that includes giraffes, hippos, a pair of black rhinos, African lions, pumas, deer, tapir, antelope, coyotes and a superbly comprehensive collection of Central American animals, snakes and birds. Sadly, their elephant died after he was fed a piece of plastic and the tapir died of old age, but aside from these mishaps the animals are active and well cared for and every species, except for the black rhino, has been successfully bred here in captivity.

The park is set up and managed in a very Guatemalan style, catering almost exclusively to domestic tourists, who like to make a day of it, picnicking, feasting in the restaurant and swimming in the pools. The entrance fee entitles you to a swim and a trip through the park in a minibus, although you can drive yourself if you have a car. There is also a small walk-through zoo, laid out around a lake, which is largely devoted to Central American wildlife.

Beyond Taxisco is **CHIQUIMULILLA**, from where another branch road heads up into the eastern highlands, through acres of lush coffee plantations, to the town of Cuilapa. Chiquimulilla is another fairly nondescript town that serves as a market centre for the surrounding area, but you might easily end up here in order to change buses – if you get stuck, try the *Hotel San Carlos*, Barrio Santiago (☎8850187; ②). The town is in the heart of *ladino* cowboy country and superb **leather goods**, including machete cases and saddles, are handcrafted in the market, so you may want to do a little shopping. From the small bus terminal, a block or so from the plaza, there's a steady flow of traffic to both the border and Guatemala City, with departures every hour or so. There are also hourly buses to Cuilapa, departing from the other side of the market.

Heading on towards the border, the highway is raised slightly above the rest of the coastal plain, giving great views towards the sea. A few kilometres south of the road, archeological digs at a long-forgotten Maya site called **La Nueva** have recently yielded some fascinating stellae and evidence that more than five thousand people lived here between the years 250 and 900 AD. A short distance before the border the road divides, one branch running to the seashore village of **LAS LISAS**, which is another good spot for spending time by the sea. Like all of these villages Las Lisas is separated from the mainland by the murky waters of the Chiquimulilla canal, again bridged by a shuttle service of small boats. On the sandbank itself the village follows a standard pattern, with a collection of scruffy huts and palm trees behind a beautiful black sand beach. It's a great place to relax for an afternoon but accommodation is high in price and very low in quality. **Buses** run between Las Lisas and Chiquimulilla hourly from 9am to 4pm (1hr 30min).

FIESTAS

Ladino culture dominates on the Pacific coast – despite the presence of a massive migrant labour force – so fiestas here tend to be more along the lines of fairs, with parades, fireworks, sporting events and heavy drinking. You'll see very little in the way of traditional costume or pre-Columbian dances, although marimba bands are popular even here and many of the fiestas are still based on local saints' days. Nevertheless, there's no doubt that the people of the coast like to have a good time and know how to enjoy themselves. Allegiances tend to be less local than those of the Indian population and national holidays are celebrated as much as local ones.

JANUARY
The year kicks off in **Taxisco** from the 12th to 15th, with a fiesta in honour of the Black Christ of Esquipulas: events include bullfighting and plenty of macho bravado. In **Colomba** (a few kilometres from Coatepeque) a fiesta takes place from the 12th to 16th which honours the same Black Christ and also involves bullfighting. In **Cuyotenango** there's a fiesta from the 11th to 18th, with the main day on the 15th – unlike most coastal fiestas this one includes some traditional dancing.

FEBRUARY
A moveable fiesta takes place in **Tecún Umán** some time during the month.

MARCH
Holy Week is celebrated everywhere in a combination of religious ritual and secular partying, while in **Coatepeque** there's a local fiesta from the 11th to 19th, with the main day on the 15th. In **Puerto San José** the fiesta is from the 16th to 22nd, with the principal day on the 19th, and **Ocós** has a fiesta some time during the month on an unfixed date.

APRIL
Chiquimulilla has a fiesta from April 30 to May 4.

JULY
Coatepeque has a one-day fiesta on the 25th, in honour of Santiago Apostol.

AUGUST
The port of **Champerico** holds a fiesta in honour of El Salvador del Mundo, from the 4th to 8th, with the main day on the 6th.

OCTOBER
Iztapa's fiesta takes place from the 20th to 26th. The 24th is the main day.

NOVEMBER
1 November, All Saints' Day, is celebrated throughout the country, and people gather in cemeteries to eat and drink and to honour the dead. In **Siquinalá** they have a local fiesta from the 23rd to 26th.

DECEMBER
Retalhuleu has a fiesta from the 6th to 12th; the main day is the 8th. **Chicacao**'s fiesta, from the 18th to 21st, includes traditional dancing as the town has close links with Santiago Atitlán. **Escuintla** has a fiesta from the 6th to 15th, with the main day on the 8th, and in **Santa Lucía Cotzumalguapa** the main fiesta is held on the 25th. Finally it's the turn of **La Democracía** on the 31st.

The border with El Salvador

The coastal highway finally reaches the border with El Salvador at **CIUDAD PEDRO DE ALVARADO**, a quiet and easy-going crossing point. Most of the commercial traffic and all the pullman buses use the highland route to El Salvador, and consequently things are fairly relaxed here. Should you get stuck for the night, *Hospedaje Yesina* (①) is right opposite the immigration post, and there's a selection of basic hotels and *comedores* on the El Salvador side of the border. There are second-class buses to and from the Zona 4 terminal in Guatemala City every hour or so between 1am and 4pm, all of them going via Escuintla. There's also another branch road from here to the coast, ending up at a couple of small seaside villages, Garita Chapina and Barra de La Gabina.

travel details

BUSES

Buses are certainly the best way to get around on the Pacific coast, and the main highway, from Guatemala City to the Mexican border, is served by a constant flow of pullmans. Heading in the other direction, to the border with El Salvador, there are no pullmans but there is a regular stream of second-class buses. On either of these main routes you can hop between buses and expect one to come along every thirty minutes or so, but if you plan to leave the highways then it's best to travel to the nearest large town and find a local bus from there. If you're heading up into the highlands take any bus to the relevant junction and wait for a connection there – **El Zarco** for buses to Quetzaltenango and **Cocales** for Lake Atitlán – but set out early.

The coastal highway

Guatemala City to the Mexican border (5hr). There are buses every thirty minutes or so calling at all the main towns along the coastal highway, including **Escuintla**, **Santa Lucía Cotzumalguapa**, **Cocales**, **Mazatenango**, **Retalhuleu** and **Coatepeque**. The bulk of these leave from the terminal at 19 C and 9 Av, in Zona 1 (watch your bags carefully if you are waiting around here). The main companies to the borders at **Talismán** and **Tecún Umán** are Fortaleza del Sur (hourly, 4.30am–7pm; ☎2303390) and Chinita (11 daily, 9am–6.30pm; ☎2519144), both with offices on 19 C between 8 and 9 avenidas, Zona 1, Guatemala City. In addition, Galgos, 7 Av 19–44, Zona 1 (☎2534868), runs two buses daily (7.30am and 1.30pm) to **Tapachula** in Mexico, via Talismán.

Coatepeque to: Retalhuleu (50min); Tecún Umán (40min).

Cocales to: Escuintla (30min).

Escuintla to: Guatemala City (1hr).

Retalhuleu to: Cocales (50min); Mazatenango (30min).

The **Mexican border to Quetzaltenango**. You have to branch off the coastal highway at one of two junctions: either travel to **Malacatán** and then up through **San Marcos**, or come along the coast road and catch a direct bus to Quetzaltenango from the El Zarco junction, Retalhuleu, Coatepeque or Mazatenango. If you're coming from the Talismán border it's easy enough to find a truck or bus to Malacatán, and from there, there are hourly buses to San Marcos, but if you're coming from Tecún Umán it's more straightforward to travel via Retalhuleu, from where there are hourly buses to Quetzaltenango between 6.30am and 5pm.

Branching off the coastal highway

To Ocós and Tilapa. From Coatepeque to Tilapa (hourly; 2hr), and to Ocós (3 or 4 daily; 2hr): boats connect the two.

To Champerico. From Retalhuleu (hourly; 1hr 20min); from Quetzaltenango (hourly from 7am–noon; 2hr 45min).

To Escuintla. Buses leave from El Trebol or the Zona 4 terminal in Guatemala City (every 30min; 1hr), returning from 8 C and 2 Av in Escuintla every 30min until 7pm. From Escuintla there are also two daily direct buses down a very slow road to Antigua (over 2hr). All buses to Puerto San José pass through Escuintla.

To Puerto San José. Buses leave from the Zona 4 terminal in Guatemala City (hourly; 2hr), most of which go on to Iztapa (30min from San José), and return from there.

To Monterrico. Buses leave **Pueblo Viejo** at 11.30am, 1pm and 4pm (2hr) and return from Monterrico at 5.30am, 11am and 2pm. Monterrico is better reached from **Taxisco**, by taking a bus or truck to La Avellana and a boat from there. Buses from Taxisco run hourly (6am–6pm).

To Taxisco (3hr) **and Chiquimulilla** (3hr 30min). There are buses every hour or so from the Zona 4 terminal in Guatemala City, many of which go on to the border with El Salvador at Cuidad Pedro de Alvarado (1hr from Chiquimulilla).

To Las Lisas (1hr). There are buses from Chiquimulilla (hourly 9am–4pm), most of which start from the Zona 4 terminal in Guatemala City.

To Ciudad Pedro de Alvarado (4hr 30min). There are buses every hour or so from the Zona 4 terminal in Guatemala City, which travel via Escuintla and Taxisco. Buses from the border to Guatemala City leave hourly from 6am to 4pm.

CHAPTER FOUR

EAST TO THE CARIBBEAN

Connecting Guatemala City with the Caribbean is the **Motagua valley**, a broad corridor of low-lying land that separates the Sierra del Espíritu Santo, marking the border with Honduras, from the Sierra de Las Minas. In fact the valley starts in the central highlands, around Santa Cruz del Quiché, cutting east through a particularly arid section of the mountains and meeting the Caribbean Highway at the El Rancho junction, where the river is surrounded by desert. From here on, the valley starts to take its true form, opening out into a massive flood plain with the parallel ridges rising on either side. The land is fantastically fertile and lush with vegetation at all times of the year, and the air is thick with humidity.

ACCOMMODATION PRICE CODES

All accommodation listed in this guide has been graded according to the following price scales. These refer to the price in US dollars of the cheapest double room in high season. For more details see p.25.

① Under $5   ④ $15–25   ⑦ $60–80
② $5–10   ⑤ $25–40   ⑧ $80–100
③ $10–15   ⑥ $45–60   ⑨ over $100

This final section, dampened by tropical heat and repeated cloudbursts, was densely populated in Maya times, when it formed the southern limit of their civilization. The valley served as an important trade route, connecting the highlands with the Caribbean coast just as it does today, and it was also one of the main sources of jade. Following the decline of the Maya civilization the area lay disease-infested and virtually abandoned until the end of the nineteenth century. Its revival was part of the masterplan of the United Fruit Company, who cleared and colonized the land, planting thousands of acres with bananas and reaping massive profits. At the height of its fortune the company was powerful enough to bring down the government and effectively monopolized the country's trade and transport. Today bananas are still the main crop, though cattle are becoming increasingly important, and the Caribbean Highway, thundering through the valley, is also a vital resource, carrying the bulk of foreign trade from both Guatemala and El Salvador.

For the traveller the Motagua valley is the main route to and from Petén, and most people get no more than a fleeting glimpse of it through a bus window. But two of the greatest Maya sites are in this area: **Quiriguá**, just 4km from the main road, and **Copán**, across the border in Honduras (a side trip of a day or two).

The region to the north of the Motagua valley is dominated by the sub-tropical **Río Dulce** and **Lake Izabal**, a vast expanse of freshwater ringed by isolated villages, swamps, hot springs and caves. The largely unpopulated shores of the lake are home to a tremendous variety of **wildlife** (most of it threatened), including alligators, iguanas and turtles, as well as large numbers of migratory birds and resident parrots and toucans; there is excellent sport fishing in the lake, too. From Lake Izabal, you can sail to the Caribbean through **El Golfete**, another large freshwater expanse where there's a manatee nature reserve. Beyond here, the Río Dulce runs through spectacular gorges, with jungle towering overhead, to the coast at **Lívingston**, a laid-back seaside town, and home to one of Guatemala's few communities of black Garífuna people. Also on the Caribbean coast, and connected to Livingston by ferry, is the faded, slightly seedy port of **Puerto Barrios**, jumping-off point for the jungle route into Honduras and the stunning **Bay Islands**, a string of cayes with fantastic diving opportunities.

Also covered in this chapter is the **eastern highlands**, a seldom visited part of the country that shares little with the highlands of the west. Its dry *ladino* lands are dominated by ancient, eroded volcanos and hot, dusty towns. Though the scenery is superb, there is little for the traveller here, save the beautiful isolation of the **Ipala volcano** with its stunning crater lake, and the curious holy town of **Esquipulas**, home of the famous Black Christ, the scene of Central America's largest annual pilgrimage.

THE MOTAGUA VALLEY

The highway to the Caribbean is also the main route to Cobán, until the road divides at the **El Rancho junction** beneath the parched hills of the upper Motagua: here a branch road climbs into the rain-soaked highlands of the Verapaces while the main highway continues to the Caribbean coast. Heading on down the Motagua valley for another 20km or so the land is bleak, dry and distinctly inhospitable, with the road keeping well to the left of the river and bypassing the villages that line the railway. The first place of any note is the **Río Hondo junction**, a smaller version of El Rancho, where the road divides, with one arm heading south to Esquipulas and the three-way **border** with Honduras and El Salvador and the main branch continuing on to the coast. Here you'll find an army of food sellers swarming around every bus that stops and a line of *comedores*, as well as a number of motels scattered around. Río Hondo is home to the large Valle Dorada water park (daily 8am–6pm; $6 per day), which makes it a popular weekend retreat for Gutemalans: if you stay at the *Valle Dorada* motel, at Km 149 (☎9412542; fax 9412543; ⑤), you get free use of the slides and pools. For a cheaper bed, try *Hotel el Atlantico* (☎9347160; fax 9347041, ⑤) with nice bungalows and a pool, or the simpler *Hotel Santa Cruz* (☎ & fax 9347112; ②), both at Km 126.

On down the valley the landscape starts to undergo a radical transformation; the flood plain opens out and the cacti are gradually overwhelmed by a profusion of tropical growth. It is this supremely rich flood plain that was chosen by both the Maya and the United Fruit Company, to the great benefit of both. Here the broad expanse of the valley is overshadowed by two parallel mountain ranges; to the northwest the **Sierra de las Minas**, and over on the other side, marking out the Honduran border, the **Sierra del Espíritu Santo**.

The ruins of Quiriguá

Of one thing there is no doubt; a large city once stood there; its name is lost, its history unknown; and no account of its existence has ever before been published. For centuries it has lain as completely buried as if covered with the lava of Vesuvius. Every traveller from Yzabal to Guatimala has passed within three hours of it; we ourselves had done the same; and yet there it lay, like the rock-built city of Edom, unvisited, unsought, and utterly unknown.

John Lloyd Stephens (1841).

In 1841 John Stephens was so impressed with the ruins at **Quiriguá** that he planned to take them home, using the Río Motagua to float the stones to the Caribbean so that "the city might be transported bodily and set up in New York". Fortunately, the asking price was beyond his means and the ruins remained buried in the rain forest until 1909, when the land was bought by the United Fruit Company.

Today things are somewhat different: the ruins themselves are partially restored and reconstructed, and banana plantations stretch to the horizon in all directions. Few travellers visit Quiriguá, which is a shame because whilst it can't compete with the enormity of Tikal, it does have some of the finest of all Maya carving. Only nearby Copán comes close to matching the magnificent stelae, altars and zoomorphs that are covered in well-preserved and superbly intricate glyphs and portraits.

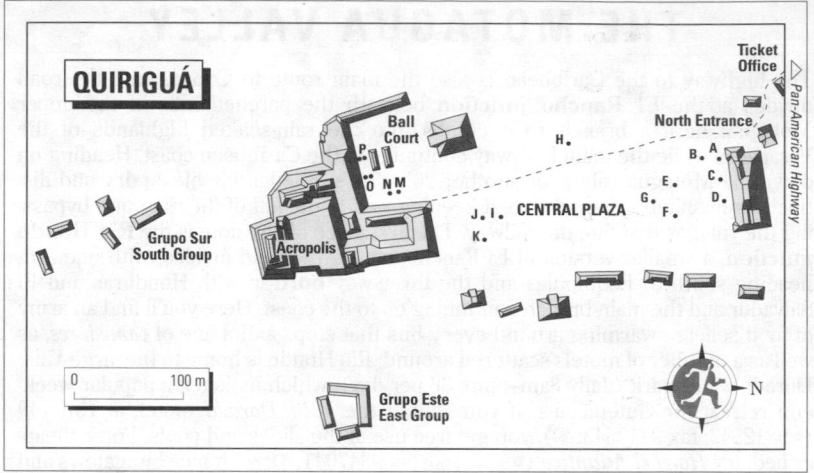

The site is surrounded by a dense patch of lush rain forest, and weather conditions are decidedly **tropical**; cloudbursts are the rule and the buzz of mosquitoes is almost uninterrupted – take repellent.

A brief history of Quiriguá

Quiriguá's history starts a short distance from the existing site, near the hospital, where two stelae and a temple have been unearthed, marking the site of an earlier ceremonial centre. From there it moved to a second location nearby, where another stela has been found, before finally settling at the main site you see today.

The **early history** of Quiriguá is still fairly vague, and all that is certain is that at some time during the Late Preclassic period (250 BC–300 AD) migrants from the north, possibly Putun Maya from the Yucatán peninsula, established themselves as the rulers here. Thereafter, in the Early Classic period (250–600 AD), the centre was dominated by Copán and doubtless valued for its position on the banks of the Río Motagua, an important trade route, and as a source of jade, which is found throughout the valley. At this stage the rulers themselves may well have come from Copán, just 50km away, and there certainly seem to have been close ties between the two sites: the architecture, and in particular the carving that adorns it, makes this very clear.

In the Late Classic period (600–900 AD) Quiriguá really started to come into its own. The site's own name glyph is first used in 731, just six years after its greatest leader, **Cauac Sky**, ascended to the throne. As a member of the longstanding Sky dynasty, Cauac Sky took control of a city that was already embarked upon a campaign of aggressive expansion, and in the process of asserting its independence from Copán. In 737 matters came to a head when he captured Eighteen Rabbit, Copán's ruler, thus making the final break (see p.262). For the rest of his sixty-year reign the city experienced an unprecedented building boom: the bulk of the great stelae date from this period and are decorated with Cauac Sky's portrait. For a century Quiriguá dominated the lower Motagua valley and its highly prized resources. Cauac Sky died in 771 and was succeeded 78 days later by his son, Sky Xul, who ruled for nineteen years until being usurped by Jade Sky, who took the throne in 790. Under Jade Sky Quiriguá reached its peak, with fifty years of extensive building work, including a radical reconstruction of the acropolis. But from the end of Jade Sky's rule, in the middle of the ninth century, the historical record fades out, as does the period of prosperity and power.

The ruins

Entering the site beneath the ever-dripping trees you emerge at the northern end of the **Great Plaza**. To the left-hand side of the path is a badly ruined pyramid and directly in front of this are the **stelae** for which Quiriguá is justly famous. The nine stelae in the plaza are the tallest in the Maya world and their carving is arguably the best. The style, similar in many ways to that of Copán, always follows a basic pattern, with portraits on the main faces and glyphs covering the sides. As for the figures, they represent the city's rulers, with Cauac Sky depicted on no fewer than seven (A, C, D, E, F, H and J). Two unusual features are particularly clear: the vast headdresses, which dwarf the faces, and the beards, a fashion that caught on in Quiriguá thirty years after it became popular in Copán. Many of the figures are shown clutching a ceremonial bar, the symbol of office, which has at one end a long-nosed god – possibly Chaac, the rain god – and at the other the head of a snake. The glyphs, crammed into the remaining space, record dates and events during the reign of the relevant ruler.

Largest of the stelae is E, which rises to a height of 8m and weighs 65 tonnes – it was originally sunk about 3m into the ground and set in a foundation of rough stones and red clay, but was reset in 1934 using concrete. The stelae are carved out of an ideal fine-grained sandstone, from a quarry about 5km from the site. The stones were probably rolled to the site on skids, set up, and then worked by sculptors standing on scaffolding. Fortunately for them the stone was soft once it had been cut, and fortunately for us it hardened with age.

Another feature that has earned Quiriguá its fame are the bizarre **zoomorphs**, six blocks of stone carved with interlacing animal and human figures. Some, like the turtle, frog and jaguar, can be recognized with relative ease, while others are either too faded or too elaborate to be accurately made out. The best of the lot is P, which shows a figure seated in Buddha-like pose, interwoven with a maze of others. The zoomorphs are usually referred to as altars and thought to be connected with the stela altar complexes at Tikal, but their size and shape make this seem unlikely.

Around the plaza are several other interesting features. Along the eastern side are some unrestored structures that may have been something to do with Quiriguá's role as a river **port** – since the city's heyday the river has moved at least 1km from its original course. At the southern end of the plaza, near the main zoomorphs, you can just make out the shape of a **ball court** hemmed in on three sides by viewing stands, although the actual playing area is still buried beneath tons of accumulated soil. The **Acropolis** itself, the only structure of any real size that still stands, is bare of decoration. Trenches dug beneath it have shown that it was built on top of several previous versions, the earliest ones constructed out of rough river stones. Apart from these central structures there are a few smaller unrestored complexes scattered in the surrounding forest, but nothing of particular interest.

Quiriguá practicalities

The **ruins** (daily 7.30am–5pm; $4) are situated some 70km beyond the junction at Río Hondo, and 4km from the main road, reached down a dirt track that serves the banana industry. All **buses** running between Puerto Barrios and Guatemala City pass by – just ask the driver to drop you at the ruins and you'll end up at the entrance road, about four hours from Guatemala City, from where there's a fairly regular bus service to the site itself, as well as a number of motorbikes snd pickups that shuttle passengers back and forth. The entrance to the ruins is marked by a couple of cheap *comedores* and a car park. To get back to the main road, wait until a bus or motorbike turns up. Buses, often packed with plantation workers, are the most likely to stop at the barrier – some go only as far as the road, others all the way to Morales and Bananera.

There's nowhere to stay at the ruins themselves, but there are two **hotels** in the village – also known as **Quiriguá** – about halfway between the site and the main road. To get there ask to be dropped off at the rail line (which crosses the dirt track about 1km from the main road) and walk south along the tracks for a further kilometre; by car the village is reached by a separate entrance road off the main road. Nowadays it's a ramshackle and run-down sort of place, strung out along the railway track, but in the past it was famous for its hospital of tropical diseases, run by the United Fruit Company. This imposing building still stands on the hill above the track, now a state-run workers' hospital. Up beside the hospital is the plaza, where you'll find the surprisingly good *Hotel y Restaurante Royal* (②), and another very good option, *Hotel el Eden*, next to the old station (②), whose friendly owners also serve tasty food. Both simple hotels have rooms with or without private bathrooms.

On to the coast: Puerto Barrios

Heading on towards the Caribbean, another 15km brings you to **La Trinchera**, junction for the branch road to Mariscos (see p.250) on the shores of Lake Izabal. Further down the Motagua valley the road pushes on through a blooming landscape of cattle ranches and fruit trees, splitting again at the junction for the twin towns of **MORALES** and **BANANERA**, a ramshackle collection of wooden huts and railway tracks. These squalid towns are of no interest except as the transport hub of the lower Motagua, served by all the second-class buses for Petén and a regular shuttle of minibuses to and from Río Dulce. There's also, of course, a steady flow of buses for Puerto Barrios and Guatemala City. Note that most fast Litegua buses (see "Puerto Barrios Travel Connections", p.242) don't pass through Morales or Bananera. If, for whatever reason, you need **to stay** in Morales, the small *Hotel del Centro* (☎ & fax 9478054; ④) on Avenida Bandegua is the most comfortable option, and all rooms come with private bathrooms, while the *Pensión Montavlo*, next to the station (①), is very basic but reasonably clean.

A short distance beyond the turning for Morales/Bananera you pass the **Ruidosa junction**, from where the highway to Petén heads northwest, running out over the Río Dulce before being engulfed by the jungles. Another 51km brings you to the Caribbean, with the road dividing for the last time, right to the old port of Puerto Barrios and left to Puerto Santo Tomás de Castillo, the modern town and dock.

Puerto Barrios

At this last junction, unless you happen to be driving a banana truck, the turning for **PUERTO BARRIOS** is the one to take. Founded in the 1880s by President

BANANERA AND BANANAS

The unprepossessing town of Bananera has a special place in the history of Guatemala. It was here that the **United Fruit Company** made its headquarters and masterminded the growth of their massive empire. The company's land is now owned by Del Monte, who maintain a local headquarters in a neatly landscaped and well-sealed compound and continue to dominate the area. The town is still surrounded by a sea of banana plantations, with crop-dusting planes wafting overhead, a company store that supplies the faithful and a one-hole golf course (at the bottom of the airfield), testifying to the presence of foreign executives.

The United Fruit Company muscled in on the Motagua valley in the early part of this century, developing huge tracts of unused land, waging war on endemic diseases and making millions of dollars in the process. The company's fingers were in so many pies that it became known as "el pulpo", the octopus, and its political lobby was so powerful that it secured exemption from almost all taxes, controlling not only the banana industry but also the country's railways and the crucial port at Puerto Barrios. So profitable was the company that its assets multiplied fourteen times between 1900 and 1930. Its tentacles held Central America so firmly that when the socialist government of Arbenz proposed confiscating the company's unused lands in 1954, the United Fruit Company engineered a coup and replaced the government. Del Monte, as inheritors of the empire, have kept their hands relatively clean, limiting themselves to exporting around two billion bananas a year.

Rufino Barrios, the port soon fell into the hands of the United Fruit Company, who used their control of the railways to ensure that the bulk of trade passed this way. Puerto Barrios was Guatemala's main port for most of this century, and while the Fruit Company was exempt from almost all tax the users of its port were obliged to pay heavy duties. In the 1930s it cost as much to ship coffee to New Orleans from Guatemala as it did from Brazil. These days the boom is over and the town distinctly forlorn, although you'll still find all the services associated with ports, including an array of strip clubs, all-night bars and brothels. The streets are wide, but they're poorly lit and badly potholed, and the handful of fine old Caribbean houses are now outnumbered by grimy hotels and hard-drinking bars.

Across the bay is **Santo Tomás de Castillo**, the newest port facility in the country. To look at the concrete plaza, the planned housing and the fenced-off docks, you'd never guess that the place had a moment's history, but oddly enough it's been around for a while. It was originally founded by the Spanish in 1604, who inhabited it with some Black Caribs, the survivors of an expedition against pirates on Roatán Island. The pirates in turn sacked Santo Tomás, but it was revived in 1843, when a Belgian colony was established here. Today it's connected by a regular shuttle of local buses to Puerto Barrios, though other than the docks themselves there's nothing much to see.

Practicalities

Cheap **hotels** are plentiful in Puerto Barrios, and designed to accommodate a typically impoverished port population, although in amongst the squalor there is also a slice of Caribbean charm. Always check your room has a fan (or air-conditioning), as this is a very hot and sticky town. First choice should be the seafront *Hotel del Norte*, 7 C & 1 Av (☎ & fax 9480087; ③), a magnificent but faded colonial time warp

PUERTO BARRIOS: TRAVEL CONNECTIONS

There is no purpose-built **bus** station in Puerto Barrios; all Litegua pullmans arrive and leave from its terminal in the centre of town on 6 Av, between 9 and 10 Calles. Second class buses arrive and depart from very near here, at one of several bays grouped around the central market which occupies the streets around 8 and 9 Calles and 6 and 7 Avenidas.

Litegua **pullmans**, the country's finest and fastest buses, ply the Caribbean Highway from Puerto Barrios to Guatemala City nineteen times daily from 1am to 4pm (5hr). From the capital, the luxury buses leave hourly from 6am to 5pm from the plaza in front of the train station at 9 Av and 18 C. Tickets for pullmans can be bought in advance, although on the whole it's not necessary.

Second class buses go from Puerto Barrios to Chiquimula, via Zacapa, every hour or so from 4am to 3.45pm: if there's no direct connection take a Guatemala City bus as far as the Río Hondo junction, from where an endless stream of pullmans heads out to Esquipulas and all points in between, for connections to Copán (Honduras) and the border with El Salvador. A single daily bus to Mariscos (2hr) leaves from outside the market in Puerto Barrios at 3pm.

From the Muelle Municipal at the bottom of 12 C, a public **ferry** leaves Puerto Barrios for **Lívingston** daily at 10.30am and 5pm (90min; $1.50) returning at 5am and 2pm. Departure times are subject to sudden changes so it's worth checking on arrival in Puerto Barrios. This service is supplemented by a fleet of small **speedboats**, which leave when full (generally every thirty minutes or so); they are faster and more frequent than the ferries, charging around $3.50 a head for the forty-minute trip. For Punta Gorda in **Belize**, a boat leaves every day at 1pm from the same dock at the end of 12 C (1hr 30min; $10); an extra one on Tuesdays and Fridays leaves at 7am (2hr 30min; $6). You have to clear **immigration** before you can buy a ticket, and it's a good idea to do so the day before you leave. The immigration office is at the end of 9 C, two blocks north of the dock (7am–noon & 2–5pm); the ticket office is next to the dock. There's now a 24-hour immigration post in Entre Rios, on the jungle route to Honduras, but you can also get your Guatemalan exit stamp in Puerto Barrios.

built entirely from wood, with clapboard rooms, which come with or without private bathroom. There's a nice swimming pool, and a classy restaurant – all mahogany panelling, pristine white-starched tablecloths and old-school service, though the food fails to live up to the decor. For a more modern experience, try the excellent value, motel-style *Hotel Internacional*, 7 Av & 16 C (☎9480367; ③), where all the rooms have private showers and TV, and there's a small swimming pool – single travellers get a particularly good deal. If you're catching the ferry to Lívingston, the *Hotel Europa 2*, 3 Av & 12 C (☎9481292; ③), is ideally placed. It's a clean, safe, friendly place, and all the rooms have fans and private showers. The best of the budget options are the large and friendly *Hotel Caribeña*, 4 Av between 10 & 11 calles (☎ 9480384; ②), with good value double, triple and quadruple rooms, and a top-notch seafood restaurant, and the *Hotel Xelajú*, 9 C between 6 & 7 avenidas (☎9480482; ②), a reasonable budget joint that's handy for the buses; though it looks a little rough from the outside, the rooms are clean, and the place is safe. And finally, if you fancy a little luxury, the *Hotel Cayos del Diablo* across the bay, reached by a regular free boat service from the jetty (☎9480361; fax 9482364; ⑧), is a lovely hideaway hotel, discretely set above a secluded beach. The accommodation is in beautiful thatched *cabañas* and there's a swimming pool and a good restaurant.

When it comes to **eating**, Puerto Barrios boasts an abundance of cheap, rough *comedores* as well as a few better, more expensive options. Good, cheap food is always available in the market and at the 24-hour restaurants on its edges, including *Cafesama* and *El Punto*. The best place in town is the reasonably priced *Rincon Uruguayo*, 7 Av & 16 C, a ten-minute walk south of the centre of town. Its speciality is meat cooked on a giant *parrilla* (grill), South-American style, but you can also get vegetarian dishes, such as barbecued spring onions and *papas asados* (closed on Mondays). For good value fish and seafood, try the popular *Safari*, right on the seafront at the end of 5 Av, ten minutes north of the centre; the *Restaurant La Caribeña*, 4 Av between 10 & 11 calles, whose speciality is a superb *caldo de mariscos* (seafood soup); or the upmarket *La Fonda de Enrique*, on 9 C, opposite the market/bus terminal, which has a relaxed atmosphere and air-conditioning.

Puerto Barrios also has more than its fair share of **bars**, pool halls and nightclubs, with a lot of the action centring on 6 and 7 avenidas and 6 and 7 calles. Reggae and punta rock are the sounds on the street, and you'll catch a fair selection at weekends at *La Canoa*, a small club popular with Garifuna people, on 5 Av & 2 C – it's a bit of a hike from the town centre so you may want to take a taxi. **Taxis** seem to be everywhere in Barrios; drivers toot as they drive through the streets touting for customers.

As for other business: there's no Inguat office in town, despite the sign directing you towards one on 12 C, so you'll have to check at the Litegua terminal for bus connections, and at the port at the end of 12 C for boat schedules. The **Telgua** office is at the junction of 8 Av and 10 C (daily 7am–midnight), and the **post office** is at 6 C & 6 Av (Mon–Fri 8am–4.30pm). There are a number of **banks** scattered around the town: Lloyds is on the corner of 7 Av & 15 C (Mon–Fri 9am–3pm, Sat 9am–1am); Banco G&T (for Mastercard) is at 7 C & 6 Av (Mon–Fri 9am–7pm, Sat 9am–1pm); and Banco Industrial (with a 24-hour ATM which takes Visa) at 7 Av & 7 C.

The jungle route to Honduras

If you're heading for Honduras from Puerto Barrios there are two very different options: either the long haul by bus, through Chiquimula, which takes a day or so, or the more direct, adventurous **jungle route**, which involves a five-hour journey of bus, boat and **trek** through swamp and banana plantations to the border, then a further six hours or so by bus to San Pedro. The latter may seem more obvious, and indeed a longstanding treaty between Guatemala and Honduras provides for the construction of a road link along this route. The Hondurans fulfilled their part of the bargain, building a good road to the border, but Guatemala, afraid that the docks at Puerto Cortés would steal business from its own Santo Tomás de Castillo, backed out of the deal, though there has been talk recently of reviving the project.

In Puerto Barrios you need to catch a bus from 8 C between 6 and 7 avenidas for **Finca la Inca**: they leave at 6am, 7.45am and every 45 minutes after that, for the two-hour trip. It's not worth taking a bus after noon, because you'll probably get stuck in some tiny riverside hamlet in no man's land. After an hour or so, you'll pass the village of **Entre Ríos** and the **immigration** post (open 24 hours a day), where officials may ask you for an unofficial "tax" of Q10: this is, in fact, a bribe, but if you argue at length, the bus may leave without you. In another hour or so, the bus will stop by the Motagua river, just before Finca la Inca, where you'll find the odd moneychanger (from whom it's worth buying a few Honduran lempiras), and a boat to take you on the twenty-minute ride over the border. The trip will cost around $3 if there are a few of you, but if you're on your own you'll pay more. You'll arrive at a tiny settlement just inside Honduras, where a Honduran *lancha* will take you on the pretty fifty-minute trip (around $2 a head) up the Río Tinto – look out for kingfishers and terrapins on the way. Finally you'll arrive beside a grassy riverside verge, from where a pick-up will drive you to the village of **Tegucijalpita** (20min) for around $2.50 per person. Tegucijalpita has a basic *comedor* and the simple *Hospedaje Rosita* (①), and very little else.

From Tegucijalpita there are regular buses to Puerto Cortés (2hr) via the pretty Caribbean town of Omoa (1hr 30min): both have **immigration** posts. There are lots of ecotourism possibilities around **Omoa** and some good hotels, including the *Bahía de Omoa* (④) right on the beach, and *Roli and Berni's Place* (②). In **Puerto Cortés** immigration is at 3 Av & 5 C (upper floor), and is open 24 hours a day, despite the sign: just knock on the door if it appears closed. Just across the plaza from immigration is the Citul bus terminal, from where an excellent service runs to San Pedro Sula every thirty minutes between 5am and 7.30pm (1hr 15min).

During the dry season, there may be insufficient water in the river to get as far as Tegucijalpita, in which case you'll probably travel via the Honduran village of **Cuyamelito**, where you can stay at the simple *Hospedaje Monte Cristo* (①), if need be. The village is 15km before Tegucijalpita on the Omoa and Puerto Cortés road, and is also served by regular buses.

LÍVINGSTON AND THE RÍO DULCE

North of Puerto Barrios the **Bay of Amatique** is ringed with a bank of lush green hills, rising straight out of the Caribbean and coated in tropical rainforest. Halfway between Puerto Barrios and the border with Belize, at the mouth of the Río Dulce, is **LÍVINGSTON**. Reached only by boat, Lívingston not only enjoys a superb setting but is also the only **Carib** town in Guatemala, a strange hybrid of Guatemalan and Caribbean culture in which marimba mixes with Marley. While certainly affected by modernization, this is also the centre for a number of small and traditional villages strung out along the coast, and it has a powerful atmosphere of its own.

Arrival and information

The only way you can get to Lívingston is **by boat**, either from Puerto Barrios, the Río Dulce, Belize, or Omoa in Honduras. Wherever you come from, you'll arrive at the main dock on the south side of town. Straight ahead up the hill is the main drag with most of the restaurants, bars and shops, and the **immigration office** (daily 7am–9pm), where you can get an exit stamp if you're heading for Belize or an entrance stamp if you've just arrived, is on the left as you walk up the hill a block or so before the *Hotel Río Dulce*. For **money exchange**, the Banco de Comercio changes cash or travellers' cheques (Mon–Fri 9am–5pm & Sat 9am–1pm) – take the road on the left as you walk up the hill from the docks. Out of hours you can usually change travellers' cheques, at a fairly poor rate, in one of the shops along the main drag – try the Almacen Koo Wong. **Telgua** is on the main street up from the docks (daily 7am–midnight), with the **post office** next door.

The best **travel agent** in town is Exotic Travel, in the *Bahía Azul* restaurant on the main street, whose helpful owners can arrange a variety of trips around the

CARIB CULTURE

Along with several Belizean centres, Lívingston provides the focus for a displaced people who are now strung out across the Bay of Amatique and southern Belize. Their history begins on the island of St Vincent, where their pure ancestors intermarried with shipwrecked sailors and runaway slaves. In 1795 they staged a rebellion against British rule, were defeated, and resettled on the island of Roatán off Honduras, from where they migrated to the mainland.

Today the **Carib culture** incorporates elements of indigenous beliefs with African and *ladino* constituents, and in Belize in particular they have recently attempted to revive their independent cultural identity as "Garifuna" people. To Guatemala's *ladinos*, who've always had a problem accepting indigenous cultures, the Caribs are a mysterious and mistrusted phenomenon. They are not only subjected to the same prejudices that plague the Maya population, but also viewed with a strange awe that gives rise to a range of fanciful myths. Uninformed commentators have argued that their society is matriarchal, polygamous, and directed by a secret royal family. Accusations of voodoo and cannibalism are commonplace too, and it's often claimed that the women speak a language incomprehensible to the men, passing it on only to their daughters. The reality is more prosaic: though the Carib culture is certainly unique, it is fast being swamped by more modern twentieth-century rhythms. Most of the beliefs that underpin Garifuna traditions, such as the notion of the spirit house and the mythical journey from Roatán, mean far less to young Caribs than Marley, dreads and weed.

area. These include a boat trip up the Río Dulce, to the lovely, white sand Playa Blanca, as well as excursions further afield to the Cayos Sapodillas off the coast of Belize for **snorkelling**, and to the Punta Manabique reserve for game **fishing**. You can also buy tickets here for the public **boats**, which leave for Puerto Barrios daily at 5am and 2pm (90min; $1.50), plus regular **speedboat** departures (45min; $3.50), which leave when full. There are also boats to Punta Gorda in Belize on Tuesdays and Fridays at 8am (1hr; $12) and to Omoa in Honduras on the same days at 7.30am (2hr 30min; $36 each, minimum of four people). You can also get to Belize via Puerto Barrios, from where there are daily departures.

Accommodation

Hotel California, turn right just before the *Bahía Azul* restaurant. Clean, vivid green-painted hotel where the reasonable rooms all have private bathrooms. ②.

Hotel Caribe, along the shore to the left of the dock, as you face the town (☎9481073). Basic, budget hotel with bare rooms, some with private showers and fans. Avoid downstairs where things get a touch smelly. Doubles only. ①.

Hotel Casa Rosada, about 300m left of the dock, past the *Caribe* (☎ & fax 9027014). The *cabanas* are right on the water, with hand-painted ornaments, beautiful views and a relaxed atmosphere: the bathrooms are communal, but immaculate. Non-residents can come for the excellent vegetarian meals. ③.

Hotel Garifuna, follow the main street, turn left towards the *Ubafu* bar, then first right (☎9481091). Squeaky-clean new building with spotless rooms; very safe. All rooms have fans and private shower. ②.

Hotel Río Dulce, at the top of the hill as you walk into town. Impressive colonial-style wooden building with a newish extension. Not particularly friendly and with something of a reputation for theft – go for an upstairs room, if you can. The balcony is one of the best places in Lívingston for watching the world go by. ②.

Tucán Dugú, first on the right on the main street (☎ & fax 9481073). Lívingston's only luxury hotel, with great views of the bay and a very pleasant bar and swimming pool (small fee for non-residents). ⑦–⑧.

Hotel El Viajero, turn left after the dock, past the *Hotel Caribe*. Small, basic budget hotel; the slightly shabby rooms are safe and all have fans; some have private bathrooms. ①.

The town and around

Lívingston is a small town with only a handful of streets, and you can see most of it in an hour or so. While there's not much to do in town itself, other than relaxing in local style, there are a few places nearby that are worth a visit. The Garífuna **museum** (in theory, Mon–Fri 8am–noon & 2–4pm), in a lovely wooden house just of the main drag close to the *Bahía Azul* restaurant, is worth a look for its art and handicrafts displays, and cultural information. Sadly, the local **beaches** are not of the Caribbean dream variety, and tend to be strewn with seaweed, but there are plenty of pleasant places to take a swim. Everywhere you'll find that the sand slopes into the sea very gradually. It is not safe for women to walk alone along the beaches, however, as a number of **rapes** have been reported in recent years.

Eating and drinking

There are plenty of places to **eat** in Lívingston, one of the best being *The African Place*, which serves a good range of unusual dishes and some superb seafood, including delicious fish with curry sauce. It's on the far side of town from the dock in one of Guatemala's most outlandish buildings, designed and built in a Moorish style by its Spanish owner. The hotel itself is not recommended. For **vegetarian** meals, you can't beat the *Casa Rosada* (see above), though prices are not set for the budget traveller. The excellent *Bahía Azul*, on the main street, is probably the most popular place in town, with a great terrace for watching Lívingston street life. Other than this your best bet is one of the small *comedores* on the main street, all of which do a fantastic line in simple **fried fish**. The *Comedor Coni* and the *Lívingston* are two of the best, both very simple, friendly and inexpensive. For a good **fruit juice**, or a tropical breakfast, try the *MC Tropical*, opposite the *Río Dulce* hotel.

For evening entertainment there are plenty of funky **bars**, of which the central *Ubafu* is usually the most lively, and a **disco** on the beach, where you'll hear the deep bass rythms of Jamaican reggae and pure Garífuna punta rock.

The Río Dulce

In a few moments we entered the Río Dulce. On each side, rising perpendicularly from three to four hundred feet, was a wall of living green. Trees grew from the water's edge, with dense unbroken foliage, to the top; not a spot of barrenness was to be seen; and on both sides, from the tops of the highest trees, long tendrils descended to the water, as if to drink and carry life to the trunks that bore them. It was, as its name imports, a Río Dulce, a fairy scene of Titan land, combining exquisite beauty with colossal grandeur. As we advanced the passage turned, and in a few minutes we lost sight of the sea, and were enclosed on all sides by a forest wall; but the river, although showing us no passage, still invited us onward.

John Lloyd Stephens (1841).

Another very good reason for coming to Lívingston is to travel up the **Río Dulce**, a truly spectacular trip that takes you into the hills behind the town and eventually brings you to the main road about 30km upriver. The scenery is the main attraction, but along the way there are a couple of places where you can stop off for a while. If you really want to do it thoroughly, searching out the river's wildlife or exploring the inlets, then you'll certainly need to rent a boat – you can find them fairly easily in both Lívingston and the town of Río Dulce (see p.249), but make sure that you fix the price (around $10 per person) and schedule first, so that the boatmen don't try to hurry you.

From Lívingston the river heads into a daunting gorge, between sheer rock faces 100m or so in height. Clinging to the sides is a wall of tropical vegetation and cascading vines, and here and there you might see some white herons or flocks of squawking parakeets. A few kilometres into the gorge there's a spot, known to most boatmen, where warm sulphurous waters emerge from the base of the cliff – a great place for a swim. Afterwards, a friendly spot to stop for fried fish or a snack is the *Restaurante El Viajero*, about level with the mouth of the Río Tatin and with great views across the waters. Almost opposite is the **Ac'Tenamit Health Centre**, which caters to the needs of around forty newly established Quiché Indian villages, whose inhabitants have been driven off the land elsewhere. Until the American *Guatemala Tomorrow Fund* came to work here, the people had neither schools, medical care, nor much else. Now there is a 24-hour clinic, a primary school for ninety children, as well as a self-help programme to train adults in "income generating" crafts. Volunteer doctors, nurses and dentists who can commit themselves for at least one month are very welcome. For more information contact *Ac'Tenamit/Pueblo Nuevo*, Aptdo Postal 2675, Guatemala City, Guatemala, CA.

After another five or six kilometres the gorge opens out into a small lake, **El Golfete**, on whose northern shore is the **Biotopo de Chocón Machacas** (daily 7am–4pm; $5), a government-sponsored nature reserve designed to protect the habitat of the manatee or sea cow, a threatened species that's seen around here from time to time. The manatee is a massive seal-shaped mammal that lives in both sea and freshwater and, according to some, gave rise to the myth of the mermaid. Female manatees breastfeed their young clutching them in their flippers, but are not as dainty as traditional mermaids, weighing up to a ton. They are exceptionally timid too, so you're unlikely to see one.

The reserve also protects the forest that still covers much of the lake's shore, and there are some specially cut trails where you might catch sight of a bird or two, or if you've plenty of time and patience a tapir or jaguar – if not, you may well encounter a tame monkey kept by one of the reserve workers. The jetty where the boats dock is great to swim from. Visitors are welcome to **camp**, but you'll need to bring your own food and some form of water purification. Alternatively, if you have river transport, you could eat your meals at the *Los Palafitos Restaurant*, just outside the reserve. In a peaceful spot, this *comedor* does great fish and shrimp and sells beers at reasonable prices.

At the western end of the Golfete is another **charity operation**, this one an orphanage for children from the capital, who are referred here by the judicial system. *Casa Guatemala* is run entirely on donations and with the help of volunteers, who do anything from teach, nurse or instruct in carpentry, sewing or typing. There are between 80 and 150 children of all ages here at any one time and volunteers with the right background, who can stay at least one month (preferably three), are always desperately needed. The work is very stressful (starting at 5am daily) and conditions basic, to say the least, but for those who can take it, it's time well spent. For more information contact *Casa Guatemala*, 14 C 10–63, Zona 1, Guatemala City (☎2325517).

Lake Izabal and around

Heading on upstream, across the Golfete, the river closes in again and passes the marina and bridge at the squalid town of **Río Dulce** (sometimes also known as El Rellano), on the northern side of the river. This part of the Río Dulce is a favourite playground for wealthy Guatemalans, with boats and hotels that would put parts of California to shame; the shores of **Lake Izabal** beyond hide increasing numbers of elite properties behind high walls and dense foliage. Here also the road for Petén crosses the river and the boat trip comes to an end, although you might try and include a stop at the *castillo*, on the other side of the bridge.

The very beautiful area along the lush banks of the Río Dulce and Lake Izabal is fast becoming a tourist destination in its own right, with plenty to keep you occupied for at least a week and a genuinely relaxed atmosphere. A great way to explore these beautiful waterways is to take a three-day sailing trip (around $150 per person) on one of John Clarke's 46-foot catamarans, leaving every Friday around noon from *Bruno's* bar (see p.249); for more details, contact the Antigua office at 1 Av Sur 11B (☎ & fax 8323352). Staying close to Río Dulce, you will be at the hub of a small but lively social scene; if you really want to get away from it all, head for **Denny's Beach** on the southern shore of Lake Izabal, or the **Finca**

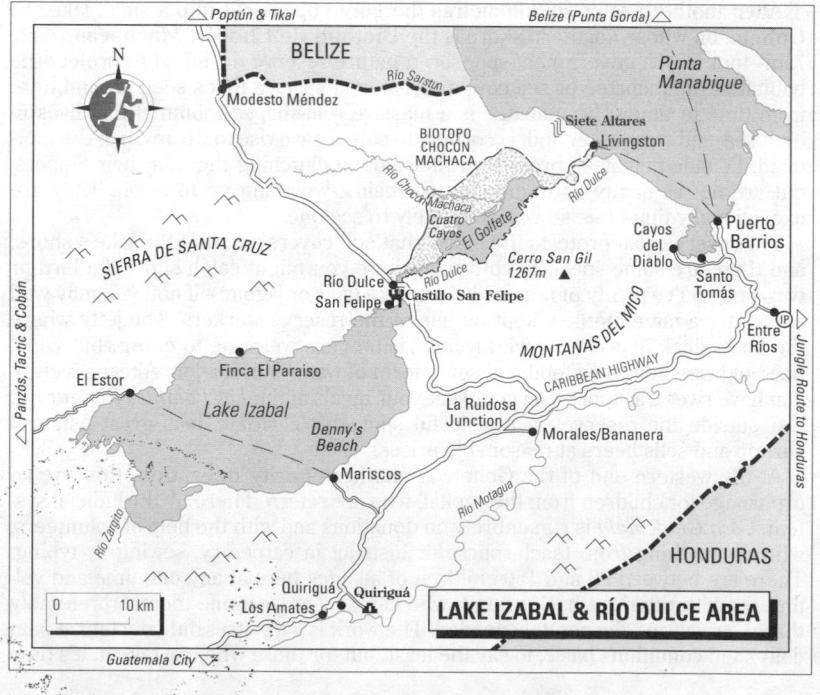

El Paraiso on the northern shore. The former is actually more conveniently reached from **Mariscos**, also on the southern shore of the lake, but you will have no trouble finding a boatman to take you to either place from Río Dulce. Before you arrange anything, however, ask around about going rates and make sure you fix a price before you set out. The *Hollymar* restaurant (see below) is a great place for gathering information.

Río Dulce town

The town of **RÍO DULCE** consists of a couple of older settlements, El Rellano to the north and Fronteras to the south side of the huge concrete road bridge that connects the two. It's little more than a truck stop for traffic to Petén, pausing at the line of cheap *comedores* and *tiendas*, before the long stretch north to Flores.

If you're heading towards Guatemala City or Puerto Barrios, your best bet is to take a minibus to the La Ruidosa junction or the town of Morales (every 30min), and catch a bus to Guatemala City or Puerto Barrios from there. If you're heading for Petén, there are regular buses until 5pm, then about every hour until 11pm, but as it's not recommended to travel at night you may want to sleep in Río Dulce and move on in the morning. It may also be possible to travel along a new road on the north side of the lake (scheduled to be completed before 2000), connecting the town of Río Dulce with the Finca El Paraiso, and on to El Estor (see p.300), for connections up the Polochic valley to Cobán and the Verapaces.

Practicalities in and around Rio Dulce town

If you're on a tight budget, the best place **to stay** is *Hotel Backpackers*, a new set-up right under the bridge on the south side in Río Dulce town (☎2081779; fax 3319408). Here there are a variety of rooms including dorm beds ($4 per person), private doubles (③), and also hammock space ($3 per person, $2 if you bring your own hammock). Marie, the manageress, is a great source of information, and the noticeboard has lots of good stuff about yacht-crewing opportunities and sailing courses; you can also rent canoes here. Another budget option is the *Hacienda Tijax*, a 500-acre working tropical farm and rubber plantation on the northeastern waterfront, two minutes by water taxi from the bridge (☎9027825; ①). This is a great spot to pitch a tent or stay in one of the rustic self-catering lodges; you can also rent horses and go riding in the hills beyond the river. Alcohol and soft drinks are sold on the farm, though provisions must be bought in the town. Slightly more comfortable is the *Hotel Río Dulce*, on the north side of the bridge in Río Dulce town (③), which has nice, clean double rooms with fans and showers. For something a little more upmarket, try *Suzanna's Laguna*, on the southwestern waterfront just outside Rio Dulce town (Guatemala City fax 3692681; ⑤), which has beautiful polished wood rooms, an open-air bar and a restaurant. If you prefer a stronger Guatemalan flavour and fewer foreign boaters, try one of the large hotels dotted around the river's shores, such as the *Hotel Marimonte* (☎9478585; Guatemala City fax 3344964; ⑥), or the *Hotel Catamaran* (☎9478801, Guatemala City fax 3318450; ⑥), which is set in a more attractive location, downriver from the bridge; both hotels, though, have seen better days.

In addition to the hotel **restaurants**, the *Bar/Restaurant Hollymar*, on the northside of the bridge, is a great place to meet other travellers and yachties, eat good food and drink the night away. You can also make radio contact with most places around the river and lake from here. A couple of minutes' walk from the *Hollymar, Bruno's*, under the shadow of the bridge, is very popular with the

American sailing fraternity. Here you can catch up with the latest news, and watch movies and US sports.

Castillo de San Felipe

If you have an hour or so to spare then it's worth taking a water taxi 1km upstream to the **Castillo de San Felipe** (daily 8am to 5pm; $1), which marks the entrance to Lake Izabal. Your entrance ticket doubles as a colourful information sheet (in English or Spanish) detailing the castle's history. San Felipe is a tribute to the audacity of English pirates, who used to sail up the Río Dulce and into the lake in order to steal supplies and harass mule trains. The Spanish were so infuriated by this that they built the fortress to seal off the entrance to the lake, and a chain was strung across the river. In later years the castle was used as a prison, but, since restoration and landscaping, looks exactly like a miniature medieval castle, with a maze of tiny rooms and staircases and fantastically thick walls. Alongside there's a café, swimming pool and tennis court.

About 300m away, the *Hotel Humberto* (②) is a good budget **hotel**, though it's looking rather dilapidated these days and is a little far from the road if you're just passing through. The quickest way to get there from the bridge is to take a water taxi to the *castillo*; returning you'll have to walk 3km if you can't hitch a lift on the dirt road leading back to the highway. Far nicer, though a little overpriced, is the nearby *Hotel Vinas del Lago* (☎9027505; fax 4763042; ⑦), which offers great views across the lake from its several terraces and also has its own private beach. Also in the waterside village of **SAN FELIPE**, a few kilometres from the *castillo*, is the *Rancho Escondido* (☎ & fax 3692681; ②), a friendly American-Guatemalan guest house and backpacker's retreat (with hammock space) and a restaurant. The only problem is the inconvenient location, though you can call or radio them from *Hollymar* and they'll come and pick you up.

Around Lake Izbal: Finca El Paraiso, Mariscos and Denny's Beach

Beyond the *castillo*, the broad sweep of **Lake Izabal** opens before you, with great views of the fertile highlands beyond the distant shores. Mornings are the best time for sailing or boat trips, before strong winds whip up dangerous waves later in the day. Local boatmen run trips to various places around the lake, including **Finca El Paraiso**, where there are six beautiful *cabañas* on the waterfront, sleeping up to four (make radio contact on VHF73, or phone Gabriella de la Vega Rodriguez in Guatemala City on ☎2532397; ⑤), and some nice bar-restaurants. The *finca* makes a great base for exploring the hidden treasures around the lake, including an amazing hot waterfall cascading into pools cooled by fresh river water (small fee). Beyond the pools, hidden in the surviving jungle, are a series of **caves** whose interiors are crowded with extraordinary shapes and colours, made even more memorable by the fact that you have to swim by torchlight to see them. Not for claustrophobes. A new bus or pick-up service is planned to the *finca* from Río Dulce and El Estor, but if it's not yet in operation you can hire a boat or hitch a bumpy ride on a tractor-drawn trailer.

MARISCOS is the main town on the south side of Lake Izabal, and most people visit only to catch the ferry across the lake to El Estor (see p.300), from where early morning buses run to Cobán in Alta Verapaz. In its day Mariscos was an important stopping-off point, where travellers heading for the capital would disembark and continue overland, but nowadays it's bypassed by modern transport routes. It's pretty much a one-street town, with three cheap, scruffy **hotels**, a police station, a pharmacy, a well-stocked supermarket at the pier, and of course the passenger **ferry** that leaves at noon, returning at 6am (1hr; $2). Small *lanchas* supplement the ferry service at other times when there are enough passengers (1hr; $3.50). One direct bus a day runs from Guatemala City to Mariscos, departing at 6am from outside the train station at 18 C and 9 Av; and one runs from Puerto Barrios at 3pm. Both return after the arrival of the boat from El Estor at 7am. At other times take any bus along the Caribbean Highway, ask to be dropped at La Trinchera, and a pick-up will take you from there to Mariscos. If you have **to stay** in Mariscos, the best place is *Hotel Karinlinda* (②), where some rooms have private bathrooms, or the more basic but still pretty clean *Hospedaje Los Almendras* (①).

If you're craving a good swim, you can't do better than head for **Denny's Beach**, an ideal place to get away from it all with nice *cabañas* above the sandy beach (Guatemala City ☎ & fax 3692681; VHF 09; ④); you can also camp or sling a hammock. The open-air bar and restaurant are a bit expensive, so bring as many provisions as you can with you. Denny's Beach is best approached from Mariscos – hiring a *lancha* will set you back around $25, but if you call or radio Dennis Gulck, the owner, someone will come and get you. Alternately, you could barter with a boatman in Río Dulce.

THE EASTERN HIGHLANDS

The eastern end of the highlands, connecting Guatemala City with El Salvador, ranks as the least-visited part of the entire country. In this stronghold of right-wing politics the population is almost entirely Latinized, speaking Spanish and wearing Western clothes, although many are by blood pure Maya. Only in a couple of isolated areas do they still speak Pokoman, the region's indigenous language, which is closely related to Kekchi, the language spoken around Cobán. The *ladinos* of the east have a reputation for behaving like cowboys, and violent demonstrations of macho pride are common.

The landscape lacks the immediate appeal of the western highlands. Not only are its peaks lower, but its features are generally less clearly defined. The volcanoes, unlike the neatly symmetrical cones of the west, are badly eroded, merging with the lower-lying hills. But the lower altitude does have a positive side: the hills are that much more fertile, and the broad valleys are lush with vegetation, similar in many ways to the highlands of El Salvador.

On the whole you're unlikely to head in this direction unless you're on your way to the border with El Salvador, in which case your best bet is to travel directly to **San Salvador** by pullman. It's a route that takes you through the southern side of the eastern highlands, and several companies can get you from one capital to the other in little over five hours. If, however, you decide to explore this part of the country, the best route takes you right through the central area, from **Jutiapa** to **Jalapa**, and then east to **Esquipulas**; near here, you'll find the spectacular vocanic crater lake of **Ipala** which can be climbed in just two hours. The roads are poor in this region but the scenery along the way is superb, taking you across vast valleys and over great ranges of hills.

Alternatively, you can head into the northern side of the eastern highlands, along a good road that branches off the Caribbean Highway and connects the towns of **Zacapa**, **Chiquimula** and Esquipulas. From here you can head on into

El Salvador, or make a short trip to the ruins of **Copán** in Honduras, the very best of the southern Maya sites. The landscape out this way is very different, with dry hills and dusty fields, but once again the population is very urban and Latinized.

From Guatemala City to El Salvador

Although there are several possible routes between the capital and the El Salvadorean border, it's the highland route, passing through Cuilapa, that draws the most traffic. This is not only the fastest connection between the two countries but also offers the most spectacular scenery, weaving through a series of lush valleys. The highway leaves Guatemala City through the southern suburbs of Zona 10, and climbs steeply out of the city, passing the hillside villas of the wealthy. It then reaches a high plateau from where you get a good view of the eastern side of the Pacaya volcano, its cone spraying out rocks and smoke. There are few towns out this way: the only place before **CUILAPA**, some 70km from the capital, is the small roadside settlement of Barberena. Cuilapa's claim to fame is that it is supposedly the very "centre of the Americas" – this doesn't, however, make it an interesting place to stop. There are a couple of hotels if you get stuck, and a branch road that heads south to the coastal town of **Chiquimulilla** (buses every hour or so; see p.231).

Eleven kilometres beyond Cuilapa the highway splits at the **El Molino junction**. The southern fork, highway CA8, is the most direct route to the border, heading straight for the crossing at **VALLE NUEVO**, less than 50km away. This road is straight, fast and scenic, but the border crossing is little more than a customs post and there's nowhere to stay when you get there or on the way.

The northern fork, CA1, is the continuation of the **Pan-American Highway**. This road is much slower, as it passes through most of the main towns and is served only by second-class buses, but it's also considerably more interesting. If you're heading directly for El Salvador, the southern branch is the one to stick with, and if you wait at the junction a pullman for San Salvador will turn up sooner or later.

The Pan-American Highway: Jutiapa

Heading west from El Molino, the Pan-American Highway turns towards the mountains, running through an isolated valley of sugar cane, then climbing onto a high plateau. Here the landscape is more characteristic of the eastern highlands, with its open valleys and low ridges overshadowed by huge eroded volcanoes.

Bypassing the small town of Quesada, the road arrives at **JUTIAPA**. The centre of trade and transport for the entire eastern region, this is a busy and not particularly attractive place, with a steady stream of buses to and from the border and the capital, and to all other parts of the east, from Jalapa to Esquipulas. If you decide **to stay**, there are plenty of places to choose from and if you need to **change money** there is a branch of the Banco del Ejercito on 5 C.

Hourly **buses** pass through Jutiapa heading for the border and for Guatemala City, pulling in at the bus terminal right in the middle of town. Jutiapa is also the starting point for a trip across the eastern highlands to Chiquimula or Esquipulas. The quickest route takes you directly to Esquipulas, through Ipala, and buses from Jutiapa head this way. But if you'd rather take your time and see the best of this part of the country then take a bus to Jalapa, spend the night there, and then press on to Chiquimula.

Asunción Mita and the border at San Cristóbal

Heading on from Jutiapa towards the border with El Salvador the Pan-American Highway runs through El Progreso, where the roads to Jalapa and to Ipala (for the direct route to Chiquimula or Esquipulas) branch off to the north. Beyond here the road drops into yet another vast open valley, and arrives at the small town of **ASUNCIÓN MITA**, 45 minutes from Jutiapa and thirty minutes from the border. Despite its jaded appearance, Asunción has a considerable past: founded, according to Maya records, in 1449, and captured by the Spanish in 1550, it was an important staging post on the royal route to Panamá in colonial times. Nowadays, its only real significance is as the last town before the border; if you arrive in the evening it's easiest to stay the night and cross into El Salvador the next day.

Archeology enthusiasts might want to visit the **ruins** about 4km to the east of Asunción Mita along the main road – opposite the INDECA building. There's not much to see, but if you rummage around in the fields you should be able to find a series of small mounds, which according to legend, were built as a monument to Quetzalcoatl by an old man and a young girl who rose out of a lake.

A stream of buses and minibuses connect Asunción Mita with the **border**, 21km south. The actual crossing point is marked by the small town of **SAN CRISTÓBAL**, where you'll find a couple of basic *pensiónes* (①–②) and an Inguat office. The last **bus** for Guatemala City leaves the border at around 3pm, and the last minibus for Asunción Mita leaves at around 5pm.

Jalapa to Ipala

Any trip through the eastern highlands should include the road **between Ipala and Jalapa**, which takes you through some truly breathtaking scenery. This is not actually on the way to anywhere, and it's a fairly long and exhausting trip, but if you've had enough of the tourist overkill of the western highlands and don't mind a bumpy ride, then it makes a refreshing change.

From Jutiapa direct buses run to Jalapa, passing over the shoulder of the Tahual volcano and through a huge bowl-shaped valley, thick with fields of sugar cane, tobacco and maize. The main towns along the way are **Monjas** and **Morazán**, two busy agricultural centres. **JALAPA** itself is a prosperous but isolated town, resting on a high plateau in the heart of the eastern highlands and surrounded by low peaks and cattle pasture. Set away from all the major roads, its busy bus terminal links all the area's smaller towns and villages. Chances are that you'll arrive here fairly late and have **to stay** the night; not a bad prospect as the *Hotel Casa del Viajero*, at 1 Av 0–70 (☎9224086; ②), is one of finest budget **hotels** in the country: charming, friendly and relaxed, with a good restaurant. If it's full, try *Hotel Mendez*, at 1 C A 1–27 (☎9224835; ②), overlooking the bus terminal; avoid all others. The town also boasts an astonishing three branches of the Banco G&T (all Mon–Fri 8am–7pm, Sat 10am–2pm).

A paved road runs from Jalapa to **Sanarate**, on the main road from Guatemala City to Puerto Barrios – much the fastest route back to the capital. Alternatively, there's a very rough road to Guatemala City via Mataquesquintla and San José Pinula – only recommended to the hardy and patient as it takes a couple of days.

Buses run every hour or so from Jalapa to Guatemala City from 3am until 3pm via Jutiapa, and until 4pm via Sanarate. Coming from Guatemala City, buses to Jalapa via Sanarate leave from 22 C 1–20, Zona 1, between 4am and 6pm, a journey of just over three hours. Buses leave Jalapa for Chiquimula (6hr) via Ipala every ninety minutes from 4am to 1pm.

San Luis Jilotepéque and Ipala

Heading on from Jalapa towards Chiquimula and Esquipulas the road climbs into the hills for the most beautiful section of the entire trip, leading up onto a high ridge with superb views, and then dropping down to the isolated villages of San Pedro Pinula and **SAN LUÍS JILOTEPÉQUE**, two outposts of Maya culture. The plaza of San Luis is particularly impressive, with two massive ceiba trees, a colonial church, and a couple of replica stelae from Copán – and on Sundays it's the scene of a vast Indian market. There are two fairly basic *pensiónes*.

Fourteen kilometres beyond San Luis, this back road joins the main road from Jutiapa at **IPALA**. This is an important crossroads, from where buses run to Jutiapa to the north, Jalapa in the west, Chiquimula to the north and Esquipulas in the east. The village itself is a pretty forlorn place with a few shops and a couple of **hotels**, the best of which is the basic *Hotel Ipala Real* (☎9237107; ②), where the rooms have cable TV and en-suite showers and toilets. Alternatively, try the basic, pretty dirty but cheap *Hospedaje Ipaleco* (①) or, as a last resort, the sleazy and squalid *Hospedaje Ana Maria Luz* (①).

Ipala is built on an open plain at the base of the **Ipala volcano** (1650m), which looks more like a rounded hill. The cone, inactive for hundreds of years, is now filled by a beautiful little **crater lake** ringed by dense tropical forest, and is similar in many ways to the cone of Chicabal near Quezaltenango. The lake is said to contain a unique species of fish, the *mojarra*, which apparently has six prominent spines on its back. It's beautifully peaceful up here and the shores of the lake, which you can walk around in a couple of hours, make a wonderful place to **camp**, though you'll have to bring all your own supplies.

You can climb the volcano from Ipala, a distance of around 10km, but the easiest ascent (2hr) is from the south, setting out from close to the village of **Agua Blanca**. If you're in your own transport, head for the tiny settlement of Sauce, at Km 26.5 on the Ipala to Agua Blanca road, park by the small *tienda* and follow the dirt track up to the summit. By public transport, take a bus from the Zona 4 bus terminal in Guatemala City to Agua Blanca: buses leave at 5am, 7am and noon, returning at 3am, 6am and noon. From here, it's a pretty straighforward route to the lake, ask the way to the Finca El Paxte, and continue to the top from there.

The north: Zacapa, Chiquimula and Esquipulas

What is true of the entire eastern highlands is particularly true of the string of towns that runs along the northern side of the mountains. Here eastern machismo is at its most potent and hardly anyone lives outside the towns. The vast majority of the population are *ladinos*, and furiously proud of it, with a reputation for quick tempers, warm hearts and violent responses. The trio of **Zacapa**, **Chiquimula** and **Esquipulas** are the most accessible towns in the eastern highlands, with a good road and fast bus service from the capital. They also offer access to two particularly interesting sites: the Maya ruins at **Copán** in Honduras, and the shrine of the **Black Christ** in Esquipulas.

The direct road branches off the Caribbean Highway at the Río Hondo junction, running through dry, dusty hills to Zacapa, and on through Chiquimula and Esquipulas to the three-way border with Honduras and El Salvador. Before Zacapa the road passes the small town of **ESTANZUELA**, which, oddly enough, has its own museum of paleontology, **El Museo de Paleontología Bryan Patterson** (daily 8am–5pm; free), dedicated to an American scientist who worked in the area for many years. The exhibits, which include the fossil of a blue whale, manatee bones, a giant armadillo shell, and the entire skeleton of a mastodon said to be some fifty thousand years old, are equally unexpected. There are also some more recent pieces such as a small Maya tomb, transported here from a site 66km away, and in the basement some copies of Copán stelae and one or two originals. The museum has a certain amateur charm and is well worth a look if you have an half an hour to spare. To get here take any bus between El Rancho and Zacapa – including all the buses heading between Guatemala City and Esquipulas – ask the driver to drop you at the village, and simply walk straight through it for ten minutes, along the main street. Since it's the only museum for hundreds of kilometres, it shouldn't prove too hard to find.

Zacapa

Just 13km from the Río Hondo junction, **ZACAPA** is reached from the main road by twin bridges across the Río Grande. In the dry months this is one of the hottest towns in the country, with maximum temperatures of 35–40°C. Its atmosphere is dominated by two things: *ladino* culture and the surrounding desert, which is irrigated to produce tobacco. There's not much to do in Zacapa, although it's pleasant enough, with a large, busy market, and some hot springs a few kilometres to the south. The town itself stretches out between the old train station and the plaza, a relaxed, tree-lined spot, that boasts some of the finest public toilets in Guatemala. The plaza is also where you'll find the Banco G&T (Mon–Fri 9am–7pm, Sat 9am–1pm), which will cash travellers' cheques, and the **post office** (Mon–Fri 8am–4.30pm); the **Telgua** office is nearby on 5 C (daily 7am–midnight). There are two **hotels** of note: the good value, eccentric Chinese-run *Hotel Wong*, 6 C 12–53 (②), where the rooms come with or without private bathrooms, and the vast chintzy *Hotel Miramundo*, 17 Av 5–41, Zona 3 (☎9412674; fax 9410157; ④), whose rooms have air-conditioning and TV. Zacapa has something approaching an epidemic of Chinese restaurants, most of which offer only fair food at inflated prices (around $5 a meal): the *Po Wing*, on the plaza, is a reasonable option and has an ice-cream parlour attached.

The **bus** terminal in Zacapa is a kilometre or so from the centre; take a local bus if you don't want to walk. From the terminal, buses leave hourly for Guatemala City, Chiquimula and Esquipulas. There are also minibuses that run between the junction at El Rancho and all of the towns out this way: in Zacapa pick them up on 13 Av between 6 and 7 calles, near the *Hotel Wong*; they don't run to any timetable but departures are regular. Coming from Guatemala City there are plenty of buses to Zacapa from the Zona 1 terminal at 19 C and 9 Av.

The hot springs of Santa Marta

The one good reason for stopping off in Zacapa is to take a trip to the **Aguas Thermales Santa Marta**, four or five kilometres south of town. There are no buses out this way so you'll either have to walk (you might be able to hitch some of the way) or go by taxi (around $3). To get to the hot springs on foot, walk up the street to the right of the church in Zacapa's plaza, past the Banco G&T. After four blocks you come to a small park where you want to take the first left, then the next right and then another left. This brings you onto a track that heads out of town across a small river – stick with this track as it continues through the fields and after about 3km it will start to drop into another small valley. Just as it does so take the left-hand fork, at the end of which you'll find the baths – if you get lost, just ask for *los baños*.

The bathing rooms are set off a small courtyard built in a vaguely colonial style. Inside each room there's a huge tiled tub, filled with naturally heated water and a couple of beds. The tubs cost $5 to hire, for as many people as you want to fit in, and the very friendly owner Rolando also sells beers, soft drinks and snacks. It's a superbly relaxing experience, sending you to the brink of sleep – if not beyond.

Chiquimula

From Zacapa the main road continues towards the border, heading up over a low pass and into a great open valley. Set to one side of this is the town of **CHIQUIM-ULA**, an ugly, bustling *ladino* stronghold. Chiquimula is the largest of the three northern towns and its dusty plaza is the main regional bus terminal, permanently congested by the coming and going of assorted traffic. Other than this, it is of little note but for a massive ruined colonial church, on the edge of town beside the main road. The church was damaged in the 1765 earthquake and its ruins have gradually been left behind as the town has shifted.

As Chiquimula is the starting point for routes to Copán in Honduras and back through Ipala to Jalapa, you might well end up **staying**. If so, the *Pensión Hernandez*, 3 C 7–41 (☎ & fax 9420708; ②), down the hill from the central plaza, is the best option, with safe parking, a pool, and plenty of clean, simple rooms, all with fan and some with showers. The helpful owner speaks good English, and you can also send **email** from here. A little further down the same road, at 8–30, *Hotel Central* (☎9420118; ④) has five pleasant rooms all with private bathrooms and cable TV, while *Hotel Victoria*, 2 C 9–99 (☎9422238; ③), half a block west of the bus terminal, is also reasonable value, and all rooms have a private shower and cable TV.

When it comes to **eating** there are plenty of good, inexpensive *comedores* in and around the market, behind the church, as well as *Magic Burger* and *Cafe Paiz*, both on 3 C, for predictable fast food and good fruit juices. For something a little more interesting try *Bella Roma*, 7 Av 5–31, which specializes in pizza and pasta, or *Lugar El Pason*, 8 Av 2–68, like a German beer garden without the noise, which has good, imaginative food. *Las Vegas*, on 7 Av off the plaza, is where the town's upwardly mobiles gather, but the prices are high, the decor garish, and the margaritas disappointing. The only other evening entertainment in Chiquimula is the *Cine Liv* on the plaza.

There's a branch of the Banco G&T at 7 Av 4–75 (Mon–Fri 9am–7pm, Sat 10am–2pm), and the largest sombrero shop in the market also **changes money** and travellers' cheques. The **Telgua** office is on the corner of the plaza (daily 7am–midnight). **Buses** to Guatemala City and Esquipulas leave every hour or so from the terminal midway between the plaza and the highway, and to Puerto Barrios until 3pm. There are hourly buses to Jalapa (6hr), via Ipala, from 5am to 6pm, and also to the border at El Florido (2hr 30min), for Copán in Honduras, at 6am, 9am, 10.30am, 11.30am, 12.30pm, 1.30pm, 3.30pm and 4.30pm.

Esquipulas

We returned to breakfast, and afterwards set out to visit the only object of interest, the great church of the pilgrimage, the Holy Place of Central America. Every year, on the fifteenth of January, pilgrims visit it, even from Peru and Mexico; the latter being a journey not exceeded in hardship by the pilgrimage to Mecca. As in the east, "it is not forbidden to trade during the pilgrimage", and when there are no wars to make the roads unsafe eighty thousand people have assembled among the mountains to barter and pay homage to "our Lord of Esquipulas".

John Lloyd Stephens (1841).

The final town on this eastern highway is **ESQUIPULAS**, which, now as in Stephens's day, has a single point of interest; it is almost certainly the most important Catholic shrine in Central America. Arriving from Chiquimula the bus winds through the hills, beneath craggy outcrops and forested peaks, emerging suddenly at the lip of a huge bowl-shaped valley centring on a great open plateau. On one side of this, just below the road, is Esquipulas itself. The place is entirely dominated by the four perfectly white domes of the church, brilliantly floodlit at night: beneath these the rest of the town is a messy sprawl of cheap hotels, souvenir stalls and overpriced restaurants. The pilgrimage, which continues all year, has generated numerous sidelines, creating a booming resort where people from all over Central America come to worship, eat, drink and relax, in a bizarre combination of holy devotion and indulgence.

The principal day of **pilgrimage**, when the religious significance of the shrine is at its most potent, is January 15. Even the smallest villages will save enough money to send a representative or two on this occasion, their send-off and return invariably marked by religious services. These plus the thousands who can afford to come in their own right ensure that the numbers attending are still as high as in Stephens's day, filling the town to bursting and beyond. Buses chartered from all over Guatemala choke the streets, while the most devoted pilgrims arrive on foot (some dropping to their knees for the last few kilometres). There's a smaller pilgrimage annually on March 9, and faithful crowds visit year-round.

Inside the **church** today there's a constant scurry of hushed devotion amid clouds of smoke and incense. In the nave pilgrims approach the image on their knees, while others light candles, mouth supplications or simply stand in silent crowds. The image itself is most closely approached by a separate, side entrance where you can join the queue to shuffle past beneath it and pause briefly in front before being shoved on by the crowds behind. Back outside you'll find yourself among swarms of souvenir and relic hawkers, and pilgrims who, duty done, are ready to head off to eat and drink away the rest of their stay. Many pilgrims also visit a set of nearby **caves** said to have miraculous powers; and there are some **hot baths** – ideal for ritual ablution.

THE ESQUIPULAS PILGRAMAGE

The history of the **Esquipulas pilgrimage** probably dates back to before the Conquest, when the valley was controlled by Chief Esquipulas. Even then it was the site of an important religious shrine, perhaps connected with the nearby Maya site of Copán. When the Spanish arrived the chief was keen to avoid the normal bloodshed and chose to surrender without a fight; the grateful Spaniards named the city they founded at the site in his honour. The famed colonial sculptor Quirio Cataño was then commissioned to carve an image of Christ for the church constructed in the middle of the new town, and in order to make it more likely to appeal to the local Indians he chose to carve it from balsam, a dark wood. (Another version has it that Cataño was hired by Maya after one of their number had seen a vision of a dark Christ on this spot.) In any event the image was installed in the church in 1595 and soon accredited with miraculous powers. But things really took off in 1737 when the bishop of Guatemala, Pardo de Figueroa, was cured of a chronic ailment on a trip to Esquipulas. The bishop ordered the construction of a new church, which was completed in 1758, and had his body buried beneath the altar.

While all this might seem fairly straightforward it doesn't explain why this figure has become the most revered in a country full of miracle-working saints. One possible explanation is that it offers the Maya, who until recently dominated the pilgrimage, a chance to combine pre-Columbian and Catholic worship. It's known that the Maya pantheon included several Black deities such as Ek Ahau, the black lord, who was served by seven retainers, and Ek-chuach, the tall black one, who protected travellers. When Aldous Huxley visited the shrine in 1934 his thoughts were along these lines: "So what draws the worshippers is probably less the saintliness of the historic Jesus than the magical sootiness of his image... numinosity is in inverse ratio to luminosity."

Practicalities

When it comes to staying in Esquipulas, you'll find yourself amongst hundreds of visitors whatever the time of year. **Hotels** probably outnumber private homes and there are new ones springing up all the time. Bargains, however, are in short supply, and the bulk of the budget places are grubby and bare, with tiny monk-like cells – not designed in a spirit of religiosity, but simply to up the number of guests. **Prices** are rarely in writing and are always negotiable, depending on the flow of pilgrims. Avoid **Saturdays** when prices double.

Many of the least expensive places are clustered opposite the church on the other side of the main road, 11 C. The family-run *Hotel Villa Edelmira* (②), and *La Favorita*, on 10 C and 2 Av (②), are two of the best simple budget hotels. For a touch more luxury, head for the *Hotel Los Angeles*, in the street opposite the church (☎9431254; ③), where some rooms have private bathrooms, or the *Hotel Esquipulao*, on 2 Av, next to the church (④), a cheaper annexe to the *Hotel Payaqui* (☎9431143; fax 9431371; ⑤), where there's a pool and all rooms come with a TV and fan. There are dozens of **restaurants** and **bars** in town, most of them overpriced by Guatemalan standards. Breakfast here is a great deal, though – you shouldn't have to pay more than $1.50 for a good feed. The *Hacienda Steak House*, a block from the plaza at 2 Av and 10 C is one of the smartest places in town, but there's no shortage of cheaper places on 11 C and the surrounding streets. Banco Industrial, at 9 C and 3 Av, has a 24-hour ATM that takes Visa, and there's also a lone cinema, the Cine Galaxia.

Rutas Orientales run a superb **bus** service between Guatemala City and Esquipulas, with departures every hour from 2am to 5pm (4hr). Its office in Guatemala City is at 19 C 8–18, Zona 1, and in Esquipulas it's on the main street, at 11 C and 1 Av. There are also buses across the highlands to Ipala and Jutiapa, and regular minibuses to the borders with El Salvador (every 30min, 6am–4pm; 1hr) and Honduras (every 30min, 6am–5.30pm; 30min). To get to Copán you'll need to catch a bus to Chiquimula and change there.

On to the borders: El Salvador and Honduras

The **Honduran** border crossing at **Aguacaliente** (24-hour), just 10km from Esquipulas, is served by a regular shuttle of minibuses from the main street, and taxis that will shuttle you back and forth for a dollar a time. The **El Florido** crossing, which is more convenient if you're heading for the ruins of Copán, is reached by bus from Chiquimula. There's a **Honduran consulate** (Mon–Fri 9am–5pm) in the *Hotel Payaqui* in Esquipulas, beside the church.

The border with El Salvador is about 24km from Esquipulas, down a branch road that splits from the main road just before you arrive at the town. Minibuses and buses serve this border too, but there's no Salvadorean consulate in Esquipulas.

COPÁN

Across the border in Honduras, less than a day's journey from Guatemala City, are the ruins of **Copán**, one of the most magnificent of all Maya sites. While the scale of Copán may not be as impressive as Tikal or Chichén Itzá, it has by far the greatest number of decorative carvings, stelae and altars of any of the Maya sites, including the longest Maya text in existence, the Hieroglyphic Stairway, which contains some two thousand glyphs carved onto a flight of sixty stone steps. Not suprisingly, the site is being heavily promoted by the Honduran government and tour operators and now ranks as the second most visited spot in the country after the Bay Islands.

Although it is just about possible to see the ruins as a day-trip from Guatemala, to really appreciate the splendours of the site it is best to spend a night in Honduras. If you set out early from Guatemala, to arrive at Copán by lunchtime, you can either spend the afternoon at the ruins and return the next morning, or settle in for a day – transport from the ruins to the border is much less regular in the afternoon. The guards at the El Florido border post operate a special system of temporary entry so as not to invalidate your Guatemalan visa (see below).

Getting to and from the ruins

Wherever you're coming from you first need to get to **Chiquimula**, around three and a half hours from Guatemala City (buses leave every hour or so from the terminal in Zona 1, at 18 C and 9 Av; any bus going to Esquipulas will pass through Chiquimula). From the terminal in Chiquimula eight second-class buses, usually packed, depart for **El Florido** and the border with Honduras (6am–4.30pm; at least 2hr 30min). Twenty minutes up the road, in the direction of Esquipulas, the road for the border branches off to the left at the **Vado Hondo junction**. The journey through the Sierra del Espíritu Santo to El Florido is rough and dusty: in the few small villages along the way the people are mostly Chortí-speaking Maya, the remnants of an isolated tribe who've largely abandoned traditional ways.

At **EL FLORIDO** there's the most rudimentary of **border posts** (7am–6pm). Here you'll be charged around $1 to leave Guatemala, and up to $3 to enter Honduras, depending on the mood of the day. Explain to the border guards that you intend to go no further than *las ruinas* (the ruins) and they'll give you a **temporary entrance stamp**, which saves a lot of hassle – they won't stamp your passport but instead give you a separate piece of paper which you simply give back to them when you return. Hence if you have a Guatemalan visa or tourist card it won't be invalidated. If, on the other hand, you're heading on into Honduras, make sure you get the real thing. Moneychangers operate on both sides of the border, but you can also find them, or rather they'll find you, in the village. On the Honduran side, buses run between the border and the town of **Copán Ruinas** every thirty minutes, taking around half an hour to complete the bumpy, twelve-kilometre journey; the last bus leaves the border at 4pm. Private pick-ups also run the journey, leaving when full; the fare in both cases is L.10 (75¢).

Trucks and buses head **back to El Florido** and the border throughout the morning, with the last departure at around 3pm. From El Florido to **Chiquimula**, there are nine buses a day (5.30am–3pm).

A more expensive, but much easier way of getting to the ruins is to go on a mini-bus shuttle with one of the **tour agents** based in Antigua or Guatemala City; Monarcas in Antigua (see p.108) charges $40 one-way, $70 return.

Copán Ruinas

A kilometre from the ruins, the town of **COPÁN RUINAS**, formerly a small tobacco farming village, is now a busy centre which derives most of its income from visitors to the site. Despite this influx of tourists, the town has remained largely unspoilt, with cobbled streets and red-tiled houses set among green hills.

You do not need an area **phone code** to call Copán or the Bay Islands. From Guatemala simply dial ☎00504 then the number required.

Arrival and information

Given its size, it is virtually impossible to get lost in Copán Ruinas, despite the fact that none of the streets are numbered or named. All **buses** arrive by the small football field on the eastern side of town, and sometimes, but not always, drive up a short hill to circle the central plaza. Banco Atlántida, on the plaza (Mon–Fri 9am–3.30pm, Sat 9am–noon), will **change Guatemalan quetzals** and travellers' cheques, and give cash advances on Visa cards. Hondutel, the Honduran **telephone** company (daily 7am–9pm), and the **post office** are next door to each other, just off the southwest corner of the plaza.

Accommodation

Many of the town's **hotels** have recently undergone refits and improved their standards, to attract the ever-booming organized tour market. Prices, consequently, are slightly higher than you'd pay for the equivalent accommodation elsewhere in Honduras, though there is still a reasonable range to suit most budgets.

Hotel Brisas de Copán, one block north of the plaza (☎614118). Clean, good-sized rooms, all with bath, hot water and TV. ④.

The **price codes** we've used for accommodation in Copán and the Bay Islands are the same as those used throughout the Guatemala section of the Guide: see p.25 for more details.

Hotel California, one block northeast of the plaza. A new, laid-back place with clean rooms set around a courtyard. Free drinking water. ②.

Hotel Camino Maya, southwest corner of the plaza (☎614446; fax 614518). A newly renovated hotel with reasonably sized rooms, all of which have baths and hot water. Ask for one at the front with a balcony overlooking the plaza. ⑥.

Casa de Café B&B, at the southwest edge of town, overlooking the Río Copán Valley (☎527274). A charming place, with a relaxing garden and comfortable, airy rooms, all with bath and hot water. Breakfast and free coffee all day are included. ⑤.

Hotel Los Gemelos, opposite the *California* (☎614077). A long-established backpacker's favourite; the rooms are basic but very clean, with communal bathrooms. The friendly owners will provide hot water if enough people ask. ①.

Iguana Azul, next to the *Casa de Café* and under the same ownership. Newly refurbished, nicely decorated dorms (under $5 per person) and private rooms. Has a communal area and laundry facilities, but no private bathrooms. ②.

Hotel Marina Copán, on east side of square (☎614070; fax 614477). The most luxurious place in town by a long shot. The stylish rooms have air-conditioning and TV, and there is a small pool, sauna, gym and bar on site. ⑧.

La Posada, just north of the plaza. A good value, recently renovated place with large, comfortable rooms, some with bath. ②.

Around town

Whilst the main reason for staying in the town of Copán Ruinas is to visit the ruins, it's a pleasant enough place to spend a few days drinking in the clean air and relaxing. On or around the plaza, you'll find a number of souvenir shops selling reasonably priced ceramics, and wood and leather crafts from the region, while the Tabacos y Recuerdos, just north of the plaza, next to *La Posada*, has a wide selection of Honduran cigars. The low-key **Museo Regional de Arqueología**, on the west side of the plaza (Mon–Sat 8am–noon & 1–4pm; $1.50), is worth a browse for its exhibition of statues, sculptures and other Maya artefacts.

For something a bit more energetic, head north up the hill to the old military barracks, five blocks from the plaza, from where the views over the town and surrounding countryside are impressive. Alternatively, you could take a day-trip to the nearby El Rubí waterfall, hot springs and caves, with Go Native Tours, a block past Hondutel on the other side of the street (☎ & fax 614432).

Eating and drinking

There's a wide variety of restaurants and bars in Copán Ruinas, many of which cater specifically for the tourist market, though almost all the restaurants stop serving at 10pm.

Café Elisa, in the *Hotel Camino Maya*, on the southwest corner of the plaza. Serves excellent local and European-style breakfasts, including fruit salads and waffles.

Café Isabel, a block past Hondutel. An unpretentious café serving a range of well-prepared local dishes; the vegetable soup is particularly good.

Café Welchez, on northwest corner of the plaza. Pleasant European-style café, serving slightly pricey coffees, juices, alcoholic drinks and light meals. The tables upstairs by the window are the best for people watching.

Llama del Bosque, two blocks past Hondutel. Has a large menu offering local breakfasts, meat and chicken dishes, and delicious *baleadas* (tortilla filled with beans, cheese and cream).

Tres Locos Bar, at the *Hotel California*, a block northeast of the plaza. A fun bar; and a good place to catch up on local news and information (closes at 9pm).

Tunkul Bar and Restaurant, opposite the *Llama del Bosque*. Prices are reasonable and the portions of meat, pasta and vegetarian dishes are large at this popular foreign-owned restaurant. The bar stays open until midnight.

Vamos a Ver Cafe, a block south of the plaza. European-owned café, serving huge portions of well-prepared food. The bread is homemade and the outdoor courtyard is very popular. Shows English-language films on video nightly.

A brief history of Copán

In recent years great strides have been made in understanding the history of Copán, although it's important to remember that the site lies at the southern limit of Maya civilization and was largely cut off from all the other sites except Quiriguá, forty miles to the north (see p.237), which is believed to have been a major outpost. Archeological evidence suggests that the Río Copán valley was first inhabited around 1000 BC, while graves dating from 900 BC have been found to contain a carved jade necklace from the Motagua valley, indicating the existence of trade with other parts of the country. Construction of the city is thought to have begun around 100 AD, and a stela found in the Papagayo temple in 1988 refers to Yak K'uk Mo', the first ruler and founder of the dynasty, who governed from at least 426 AD to 435 AD. Little is known about subsequent rulers, although both the third and fourth members of the dynasty are mentioned on Monument 26 at Quiriguá; the fifth and sixth rulers, however, are practically unknown.

It wasn't until the sixth century, however, that Copán emerged as a substantial city. Its golden era began in 553 AD with the accession to the throne of Moon Jaguar, the tenth ruler, and continued through the reigns of Smoke Serpent (578–628 AD), Smoke Jaguar (628–695 AD) and Eighteen Rabbit (695–738 AD). This period of stable and long-lasting government laid the basis for unprecedented political, social and artistic growth: the city flourished, growing both in population and size, with Smoke Jaguar in particular presiding over the construction of more stelae and monuments than any other ruler. Growth continued with Eighteen Rabbit's rule, when the style of shallow relief carving, for which Copán is famous, was developed. His reign also saw the construction of the Great Plaza, the final version of the Pelota Court and Temple 22 in the East Court.

This golden period was brought to an end in 738 AD by the capture and decapitation of Eighteen Rabbit by Cauac Sky, ruler of the ascendant and increasingly powerful Quiriguá. He was succeeded by a short-lived ruler, Smoke Monkey (738–749), and little new building took place during these uncertain years. Political stability returned in 749 with the succession of Smoke Shell, and the city prospered until his death in 763. During his reign the famous hieroglyphic stairway, perhaps the most impressive piece of Maya architecture anywhere, was built. Smoke Shell's son, Yax Pac, took office on July 2, 763, and despite his frantic attempts to maintain the building boom – including the construction of Altar Q illustrating the entire history of the dynasty – the city went into decline. Skeletal remains from this period indicate malnutrition and disease, with far-from-adequate food resources to support the population of around twenty thousand. Yax

Pac died in the winter of 820, and the seventeenth and final ruler, U Cit Tok' took the throne two years later: the date of his death and the end of the dynastic line of Copán remain unknown.

The site came to light again soon after the Conquest, though the Spanish showed scant interest in it: in a letter to King Felipe II in March 1576, Don Diego de Palacios commented "near here on the road to San Pedro Sula ... are certain ruins and vestiges of a grand population and magnificent buildings constructed with such skill that is seems that they could never have been made by people as coarse as the inhabitants of this province". It wasn't until the nineteenth century, however, and the publication of *Incidents of Travel in Central America, Chiapas and Yucatán* by John Lloyd Stephens and Frederick Catherwood, that Copán became known to the wider world. Stephens, the then acting US ambassador, had succeeded in buying the ruins in 1839 for fifty dollars, and spent several weeks at the site clearing the undergrowth, sketching buildings and taking measurements, with the intention of transporting the ruins back to the US. The success of his book, however, and the interest it sparked in Mesoamerican culture, guaranteed Copán's safety and resulted in it becoming a magnet for archeologists ever since.

The first of a long line of foreign historians to study the site was the Brit Alfred Maudsley, who – under the sponsorship of the Peabody Museum, Harvard – began a full-scale mapping, excavation and reconstruction project in 1891 that lasted for several years. A second major investigation was begun in 1935 by the Washington Carnegie Institute, which involved diverting the Río Copán to prevent it carving into the site. A breakthrough in understanding, not only of Copán but the whole Maya world, came in 1959 when archeologists Heinrich Berlin and Tatiana Proskouriakoff first began to decipher the hieroglyphics, leading to the realization that they are a record of the history of the cities and the Maya dynasties. It was not until 1977, however, that the Hondurans themsleves became involved in the investigations. Since then, the *Instituto Hondureño de Antropología e Historia* has been running a series of projects at the site in an attempt to uncover further secrets of the Maya world.

The site

The **site** (daily 8am–4pm; $10 including entry to Las Sepultras) lies 1km north of Copán Ruinas town, and is entered through the **visitor centre** (same hours as site), where there's an exhibition explaining Copán's place in the Maya empire and a small model of the city as it once was. On the other side of the car park from the visitor centre is the **Museum of Mayan Sculpture** (daily 8am–4pm; $10), which is dominated by a full-scale replica of the Rosalila Temple. Dating from 591 and discovered intact under Structure 16 in 1989, the temple has been brightly painted, as it was originally, but is exposed to the elements and intended to fade over time. The entire ground floor of the museum represents the Maya concept of a dark underworld, with exhibits signfiying death and violence, such as skulls and bats. The upper floor houses many of the finest original sculptures from the site showing comprehensively the ability and skill of the Maya craftsmen.

From the visitor centre, it's about a two-hundred-metre walk to the **warden's gate**, which marks the entrance to the site proper. Once inside the gate you can walk straight ahead to the Great Plaza or turn right and approach via the smaller East and West courts, saving the splendours of the plaza till last.

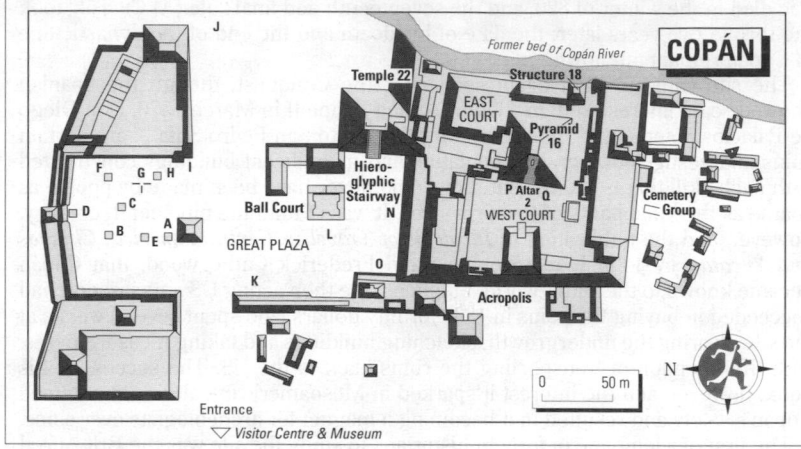

The East and West Courts

When you head to the right you'll arrive first in the **West Court**, a small, confined area that forms part of the main acropolis. The most famous feature here is **Altar Q**, at the base of Pyramid 16. Carved in 776, it's dedicated to Yax Pac (also known as New-Sun-at-Horizon), celebrating his ascension to the throne on July 2, 763. The top of the altar is carved with six hieroglyphic blocks while the sides are decorated with sixteen cross-legged figures, all seated on cushions. The most recent theories suggest that these figures represent previous rulers of Copán, pointing at a portrait of Yax Pac receiving a ceremonial staff from the city's first ruler, Yak K'uk Mo'. The monument, therefore, endorses Yax Pac's right to rule, and provides clear evidence of the importance of the dynastic power structures. Behind the altar, archeologists found a small crypt, containing the remains of a macaw and fifteen big cats, possibly sacrificed in honor of Yax Pac.

In 1989, archeologists working on **Pyramid 16**, behind Altar Q, made the most exciting discovery of recent years: the uniquely undamaged facade of the **Rosalila Temple**, which appears to have been purposely buried intact within the structure you see today and has been hidden for over a thousand centuries. It was usual for the Maya ritually to deface or destroy their obsolete temples or stelae, yet with this one they took great care not to damage the hand-modelled stucco sculptures that adorned it, making it possible to build a precise replica, which you can see in the Museum of Mayan Sculpture. (The original is to be re-sealed from the outside world once scientific studies are completed.) The temple was built to serve as a centre for worship during the reign of Butz'Chan, Copán's eleventh leader (578–628 AD), whose rule marked the apogee of 160 years of political, social and artistic growth.

Climbing the stairs behind Altar Q brings you into the **East Court**, slightly larger than the West Court and with more elaborate sides. Standing in the central dip, you're surrounded by austere carving, the best of which are the great jaguar heads, each as large as a human's, with hollows in the eyes that would once have held pieces of jade or polished obsidian. In the middle of the staircase, flanked by the jaguars, is a rectangular Venus mask, also carved in superb deep relief.

At the southern end of this court is **Structure 18**, a small square building with carved panels, although the process of reconstruction has revealed one or two gaps in the sequence. The floor of this structure has been dug up to reveal a magnificent tomb, possibly that of Yax Pac. Unfortunately, by the time the tomb was excavated by archeologists it was empty, having been looted on a number of occasions. South of Structure 18 is the **Cemetery Group**, so called because it was once thought to have been a burial site although current theories suggest that it was a residential complex, possibly home to the ruling elite. To date, little work has been done on this part of the site.

At the northernmost end of the court, separating it from the main plaza is **Temple 22**, one of Copán's most impressive buildings. While some of the stonework is astonishingly simple, other sections, particularly around the door frames, are superbly intricate and decorated with outlandish carving. Above the doorway is the body of a double-headed snake, its heads resting on two figures which in turn are supported by skulls. At the corners of the temple are portraits of the long-nosed rain god Chaac, a favourite Maya deity. The quality of the carving on this temple has led archeologists to suggest that the East Court may have been Copán's most important plaza. Such carving is unique in the southern Maya area with only the Yucatán sites such as Kabáh and Chicanna displaying craftsmanship of comparable quality.

The Great Plaza

The Great Plaza, Copán's hallmark, sums up its finest features and peculiar architectural attributes. At the southern end of the plaza, the **Hieroglyphic Court** is pressed up against the Central Acropolis. On one side is the **Temple of the Inscriptions**, a great towering stairway, and at its base is **Stela N**, another classic piece of Copán carving with portraits on the two main faces and glyphs down the sides. The Great Plaza is strewn with these stelae, all of them magnificently carved and exceptionally well preserved. The depth of the relief has protected the nooks and crannies, and in some of these you can still see flakes of paint; originally the carvings and buildings would have been painted in a whole range of bright colours, but only the red seems to have survived. The style of carving is similar to that of Quiriguá, and at both sites the portraits of assorted rulers dominate the decoration, with surrounding glyphs giving details of events and dates from the period of their rule. Here at Copán most of the carving has yet to be decoded: **Stela J** is perhaps the most unusual, decorated in a kind of woven pattern which is found at only one other place in the entire Maya world, Quiriguá.

On the left-hand side of the Hieroglyphic Court is the famed **Hieroglyphic Stairway**, the most astonishing work of all. The stairway is made up of some 63 stone steps, with every block carved to form part of the glyphic sequence – a total of between 1500 and 2200 glyphs. It forms the longest known Maya hieroglyphic text, but sadly attempted reconstruction by early archeologists left the sequence so jumbled that a complete interpretation is still some way off. The easiest part to understand is the dates, which range from 544 AD to 744 AD. At the base of the stairway is **Stela M**, which records a solar eclipse in 756 AD.

To the north of the Hieroglyphic Court, Copán's **Ball Court** is one of the few Maya courts that still has a paved floor. Again, the entire plaza would once have been paved like this and probably painted too. The court dates from 775 AD, and beneath it are two previous versions. The rooms that line the sides of the court, overlooking the playing area, would probably have been used by priests and members of the elite as they observed the ritual of the game.

As for the rest of the plaza, its main appeal lies in the various stelae, Copán's greatest feature. The vivid quality of the carving remains wonderfully clear, with the portraits still having an eerie presence, and it is these carvings, above all else, that separate Copán from all other sites. Most of these stelae (including A, B, C, D, F, H and 4) represent **Eighteen Rabbit**, Copán's "King of the Arts". **Stela A**, dating from 731 AD, has incredibly deep carving, although much is now eroded. Its sides include a total of 52 glyphs, better preserved than the main faces. **Stela B** is one of the more controversial stones, with a figure that some see as oriental, supporting theories of mass migration from the East. **Stela C** (730 AD) is one of the earliest stones to have faces on both sides, and like many of the central stelae it has an altar at its base, carved in the shape of a turtle. In fact, this stela represents two rulers: the one facing the turtle is Eighteen Rabbit's father, who lived well into his eighties (the turtle is a symbol of longevity), while the other is the young acceder to the throne. At the northern end of the plaza, **Stela D** depicts Eighteen Rabbit with long hair and a beard, a fashion that he may well have taken with him when he was captured by Cauac Sky, the ruler of Quiriguá, in 738 AD. The other stelae dotted around the main plaza all follow the same basic pattern, ranging from the fierce-looking **Stela F** to the faceless **Stela J**, entirely covered in glyphs.

Las Sepultras

The smaller **Las Sepultras**, a couple of kilometres to the northeast of the main site, has been the focus of much archeological interest in recent years. While nothing like as impressive as Copán itself, Las Sepultras is an interesting supplement, providing as it does the most complete picture to date of daily domestic life in Maya times. Eighteen of some forty residential compounds at the site have been excavated, yielding one hundred buildings which would have been inhabited by the Maya nobility. Smaller compounds on the edge of the site are thought to have housed the young princes, concubines and servants. More than 250 tombs have been excavated from around the compounds, demonstrating the Maya custom of burying the nobility close to their residences. Also, the large number of women found in these tombs suggests that the Maya elite practised polygamy. One of the most interesting finds – the tomb of a priest or shamán, dating from around 450 AD – is on display in the museum in Copán Ruinas, as is a carved bench, made in 780 AD, and dedicated to a high-ranking member of Yax Pac's court.

THE BAY ISLANDS
(ISLAS DE LA BAHÍA)

Just a day or so from Copán, the **Bay Islands**, with their clear, calm waters and abundant marine life, are Honduras's major tourist attraction. Strung along the world's second largest barrier reef, the islands are the ideal destination for cheap diving, sailing and fishing, while less active types can sling a hammock on one of the many palm-fringed, sandy beaches and snooze in the shade, watching the magnificent sunsets that paint the broad skies with colours as vibrant as the coral below.

A string of underwater mountain peaks extending from the mainland Sierra de Omoa, the three main Bay Islands, along with some 65 smaller cayes, sweep in a

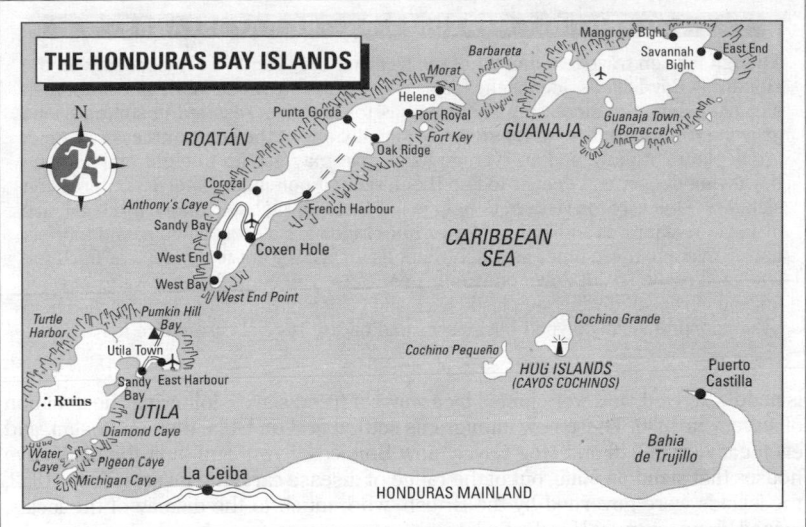

125-kilometre curve off the northern coast of Honduras. **Roatán** is the largest and most developed of the group, with **Guanaja**, to the east, being a more upmarket and exclusive resort destination, and **Utila**, the closest to the mainland, attracting budget travellers from all over the world. All three islands offer superb diving and snorkelling opportunites.

The best time to visit the islands is from March to September, when the water visibility is good, and the weather is clear and sunny with little rain; October and November are very wet, with rains being less heavy from December to February. Daytime temperatures range between 25 and 29°C all year, but the islands benefit from almost constant cooling east-southeasterly trade winds. Watch out for **mosquitoes** and **sandflies**, which are endemic on all the islands: lavish coatings of baby oil help to repel the latter.

A brief history

The **Paya Indians** were the most likely first inhabitants of the Bay Islands, leaving behind ruins and fractions of ceramics. On his fourth journey to the Americas, **Columbus** landed on Guanaja on June 11, 1502, naming it "Isla de los Pinosi" (Pine Island), and the islands were half-heartedly colonized by the Spanish soon after. The swampy shores and shallow reef, impassable for big vessels, made serious settlement impossible, but in the seventeenth and eighteenth centuries provided perfect cover for **pirates** and buccaneers. The notorious pirate Captain Henry Morgan is said to be buried somewhere on Utila; his treasure from the raid on Panamá in 1671 remains undiscovered beneath Roatán.

In 1797, around 3000 Garifuna were forcibly transported by the British from the island of St Vincent to Roatán. The Spanish soon persuaded the majority of these to move to Trujillo on the mainland, leaving only a small settlement, which still exists today, at Punta Gorda on the north coast. After 1821 an influx of white Cayman

ECO-FRIENDLY MEASURES ON THE BAY ISLANDS

Though foreign travellers delight in the fact that they can live very cheaply on the Honduras Bay Islands, life for the locals is not quite so sweet. With an economy in steady decline, the increasing shift towards tourism has resulted in some serious growing pains. Numbers of **lobster**, traditionally one of the best sources of income, are depleting rapidly, and an average fisherman may use up to eight tanks in one day diving deeper and deeper to find them, risking potentially fatal decompression sickness. One way for visitors to help is not to accept lobster under the legal size of 4oz in restaurants and stores. **Water shortages** are also a problem, and tourists use on average three times as much water as locals: try not to run taps or flush toilets needlessly. To cut down on **waste products**, you could bring a water purifier instead of repeatedly buying plastic jugs, and re-use plastic bags. You can also help by supporting locally owned businesses and taking special care not to leave litter.

islanders arrived, and were joined by a wave of freed slaves, following the abolition of slavery in 1830. These new immigrants settled first on Utila, then on Roatán, and eventually on Sheen and Hog Cayes, now Bonacca Town, and built the distinctive houses that stand on stilts, out of the range of disease-carrying insects. From 1852, the islands were governed by the British, who, much to the dismay of the locals, turned them over to Honduras because of pressure from North America, who feared British expansion. However, the islands remained culturally separate from the mainland, holding onto their language – English – and unique traditions. Even today, although Spanish is spoken in the schools and government offices, and is spreading further as growing numbers of mainlanders come in search of work, the language on the street is **English**, with a unique Creole-like accent. As in most of Central America, **religion** plays a significant role on the islands, with a large Catholic population as well as a considerable number of Seventh Day Adventists.

Although fishing and working away on cargo ships and oil rigs remain important sources of income for the islanders, the local economy is increasingly coming to rely on **tourism**. Since the early 1990s, there has been a huge growth in the number of visitors to the islands, which shows no signs of abating. Whilst the tourists have undoubtedly brought economic benefits, questions are now being raised about the environmental impact and the long-term wisdom of selling off the islanders' heritage.

Getting to the islands

The best way to get to all the islands is from the coastal city of La Ceiba in Honduras, 32km from Utila, from where there are regular flights and boats. From Copán to La Ceiba, the easiest route is via **San Pedro Sula**; direct fast buses leave from the small bridge by the football ground in Copán at 4am, 5am and 7am, taking around three hours, and arriving at 6a C, 6–7 Av SO in San Pedro. In addition, local buses leave from the same place in Copán every forty minutes or so for La Entrada (2hr), where you can pick up a Santa Rosa to San Pedro Sula bus (2hr). If you need **to stay** the night in San Pedro, the good value *Hotel Terraza*, 6a Av, 4–5 C SO (☎503108; ③), is close to the bus terminal, with private bathrooms, hot water and TV; alternatively, there's the *Hotel San Pedro*, 3a C, 1–2 Av SO (☎531513; ②), with a variety of rooms ranging from basic to comfortable.

However, if you have the option, you should press on to **La Ceiba**, which is much nicer and has a well-deserved reputation as party city of Honduras. From San Pedro, you can get the daily Cotraibal direct bus from 1a Av, 7–8 C SO to Trujillo, which stops at La Ceiba (3hr); these leave at 9am, noon and 3pm. If you miss the last Cotraibal bus, you can get one of the slower Catisa-Tupsa buses, which leave every hour until 5.30pm from 2a Av, 5–6 C SO (4hr). Buses arrive at a central terminal, about 1.5km from the centre of La Ceiba; taxis cost L.7 (50¢) per person to the city centre. If you need to stay overnight in La Ceiba, *Hotel Iberia,* Av San Isidro (☎430401; ③) is a good bet and has rooms with air-conditioning, bath and TV, some with balconies overlooking the street. For restaurants, bars and clubs, head for 1a Calle which runs along the seafront, and is the heart of the city's *Zona Viva*.

By air

Flights to the islands leave from **Golosón International Airport**, 11km west of La Ceiba on the road to Tela. Taxis to the airport from the city centre cost L.50 ($4), or take any bus from the terminal to Tela and get off at the airport access road. Outside peak holiday season, you can buy tickets to Roatán by simply turning up at the airport, though you'll need to buy tickets to the other islands in advance. Isleña and Sosa have offices on the central plaza in La Ceiba, while the other airline companies' offices are at the airport. Note that flights are sometimes cancelled with little or no notice, and delays are commonplace. Flight schedules are also liable to last minute change, so always doublecheck times.

To Guanaja: Caribbean flies once daily; Isleña has two flights a day (Mon–Sat) and one on Sunday; and Sosa flies once a day (Mon–Sat).

To Roatán: Caribbean Air flies four times a day; Isleña has eight flights daily (Mon–Sat); Sosa has four flights daily; and Rollins Air flies seven times a day.

To Utila: Isleña flies twice daily (Mon–Sat); Rollins has two flights daily (Mon–Sat); and Sosa flies three times a day (Mon–Sat).

By boat

The **Muralla de Cabotaje** municipal dock is about 5km to the east of the city: taxis from the city centre cost L.25 ($2) per person. The *MV Tropical* has regular, scheduled services to Roatán (2hr) and Utila (1hr); fares to both are around $10 one-way.

Monday: La Ceiba–Roatán 5am; Roatán–La Ceiba 7.30am; La Ceiba–Utila 10am; Utila–La Ceiba 11.30am; and La Ceiba–Roatán 3.30pm.

Tuesday–Friday: Roatán–La Ceiba 7am; La Ceiba–Utila 10am; Utila–La Ceiba 11.30pm; and La Ceiba–Roatán 3.30pm.

Saturday: Roatán–La Ceiba 7am; La Ceiba–Roatán 11am; and Roatán–La Ceiba 2pm.

Sunday: La Ceiba–Roatán 7am; and Roatán–La Ceiba 3.30pm.

In addition, the *MV Starfish* cargo supply boat leaves Utila for La Ceiba every Monday at around 5am, returning on Tuesday at around 11am; tickets can be bought at the dock ($8 one-way). You'll also find no shortage of unscheduled boats to take you to Roatán, Utila or Guanaja; ask around at the docks for details.

Utila

The smallest of the islands and closest to the mainland, **Utila** is famed for its multitude of **scuba diving** facilities – with ten or so dive schools teaching in up to eight languages – and for having some of the cheapest diving in the world. Even old-hands get excited about the waters here, where lizard fish and toadfish dart by, scarcely distinguishable from the coral; eagle rays glide through the water like huge birds flying through the air; tetchy damselfish get in your face if you invade their territory, and parrotfish chomp steadily away on the coral. Meanwhile, barracuda and nurse sharks circle the waters, checking you out from a distance. In addition, the world's largest fish, the whale shark, which can reach up to 16m long, is a regular visitor to the channel between Utila and Roatán in October and November; dive shops on both islands run trips to look for the marine giant.

Utila is still the cheapest of the islands, with the cost of living only slightly higher than on the mainland, although prices are gradually rising. Life is laid-back and people are on the whole friendly, although opportunistic crime is on the increase. Though most people on Utila are used to seeing travellers and their curious attire, it is more polite to wear long trousers and dresses. Note also that drinking from glass bottles on the street is prohibited.

Arrival, getting around and information

The vast majority of Utila's small population is concentrated in the east of the island around a large, curved harbour, paralleled by one of the island's two roads. If you arrive by air, you'll land at the airstrip in a region known as **the Point**, at the eastern end of the harbour. West of here is the main settlement, **East Harbour**, which is where you'll dock if you arrive by boat, and further west is the region known as **Sandy Bay**. The island's main road, a twenty-minute walk from end to end, runs along the seafront from the airstrip to Sandy Bay. The island's second road, **Cola de Mico Road**, heads inland from the dock then turns into a dirt track winding north across the island.

Wherever you arrive, you'll be met by representatives from the dive schools with **maps** and information on special offers. Many schools offer free accommodation during their courses, but it's worth checking out the various options before signing up for a course. For more objective **information**, the Utila branch of BICA (Bay Islands' Conservation Association) has a visitor and information office on the main street between the airstrip and the dock, though its opening hours are erratic (usually Mon–Fri 9am–noon and a couple of hours in the afternoon). You could also pick up a copy of the monthly *Utila Times*, from its office next to *Rubi Inn*, which provides useful information about local events.

Accommodation

Though Utila has more than 25 affordable guest houses and hotels, and a profusion of rooms for rent, they fill up fast especially at Christmas and Easter. Everywhere is within walking distance of the dock and airstrip, and we have listed accommodation in the order that you'll come to it, walking west along the road from the airstrip. It's easy to spend longer than you've planned here: the good news is that most places give a hearty discount by the month, and **apartments** are available for as little as $50 a month. There are few places to **camp** except on the cayes.

Despite interminable plans to install 24-hour **power**, the main generator for the island usually turns off at midnight and restarts at 5am, cutting out sporadically during the day. Many places have their own generators, however, so check before paying for a room.

ON THE ROAD FROM THE AIRSTRIP TO THE DOCK

Cooper's Inn (☎453184). One of the best budget places on the island, with clean, basic rooms and friendly management. ①.

Rubi's Inn, two minutes' walk from the dock (☎453240). Very clean, with airy rooms and views over the water; kitchen facilities are available. ②.

Sharkey's Cabins, behind *Sharkey's Reef Restaurant*, close to the airstrip (☎453212). Set in a peaceful garden, the rooms have air-conditioning, private bathrooms and big beds: there's also a terrace with great views over the lagoon. ④.

Trudy's (☎453103). A very popular place, with large, clean rooms, and you can swim from the dock at the back. ③.

COLA DE MICO ROAD

Blueberry Hill, just beyond Thompson's bakery, on the opposite side of the road (☎453141). Characterful cabins with basic cooking facilities: run by friendly owners. ①.

Mango Inn, five minutes' walk up the road (☎453335). A beautiful, well-run place built in local style and set in shady gardens. It has a range of rooms, from air-conditioned, thatched bungalows for two, to pleasant dorms ($3 per person). Also has a book exchange and laundry service, and the attached *Mango Café* is a lively spot serving good food. ②.

SANDY BAY

Utila Lodge, behind Hondutel (☎453143). Also a dive resort, the *Lodge* is the best hotel in town and offers daily rates as well as weekly packages for divers and non-divers. It has its own dock and can arrange fishing trips. ⑦.

Hotel Utila, two minutes' walk beyond the dock (☎453140). All the rooms in this large, modern building come with private baths and TV, and some have air-conditioning. ③.

Seaside Inn, opposite Gunter's Dive shop (☎453150). A reasonable place, though it fills up quickly: the newer rooms have private baths. ①.

Margaritaville Beach Hotel, ten minutes' walk west of the dock (☎453266). A new place with large, airy rooms, and a peaceful seafront location: all rooms have private baths. ②.

Diving

Diving is the main activity on Utila, where the water temperature stays around 27°C all year and is beautifully calm. Coral is still abundant, especially the regal pillar coral and sponges, and you'll see lots of marine life, too: the parrotfish are huge, and there are a fair amount of (non-threatening) nurse sharks, sea turtles and rays. The most dramatic diving is off the northern coast of the island. At night the water lights up with phosphorescence; shake your hand in the water to see tiny particles glow green.

Prices are pretty standard across all the dive schools. Currently, a 3–5-day PADI course costs around $140 in high season (Dec–April) and $125 in low season (May–Nov), including accommodation and tuition. **Safety standards** on Utila have been subject to debate in the past, with several – avoidable – diving accidents occurring in the last few years. When chosing a school, therefore, you should make sure you get along with and understand the instructors, check all the equipment and ensure that all the boats have working oxygen and a first-aid kit. Anyone with asthma or ear problems will not be allowed to dive. BICA sells diving insurance for $2 a day, a worthwhile investment, and has also been installing buoys on the dive sites to prevent boats anchoring on the reef. You should check that your school uses these when mooring. **Recommended schools** include the Utila Dive Centre (UDC), on the road between the dock and the airport; Gunter's Dive Shop, two minutes' walk west of the dock, which also rents out sea kayaks; Alton's, two minutes' walk west of the airstrip; and Underwater Vision, opposite *Trudy's*. Salty Dog's, a minute's walk west of the dock, has **underwater photography** equipment for rent, and many of the dive shops also rent out **snorkelling** equipment for around $10 a day.

Swimming, snorkelling and walks

Swimming in the water around Utila can be a bit of a hassle. Rather than jumping off any dock on the island, best head to **Blue Bayou**, a thirty-minute walk from town, where you can bathe in chest deep water and snorkel further out. Hammocks are slung in the shade of coconut trees and there's a food stand selling burgers and beers; snorkelling gear is also available for rent. The views are particularly breathtaking at sunset, but watch out for the sandflies. East of town, **Airport Beach,** at the end of the airstrip, offers good snorkelling just offshore, as does the little reef beyond the **lighthouse.** The path from the end of the airstrip up the east coast of the island leads to a couple of small coves, the second of which is good for swimming and sunbathing, though the piles of dumped garbage dilute the pleasure somewhat. Five minutes' beyond the coves, you'll come to the **Ironshores**, a mile-long stretch of low volcanic cliffs with lava tunnels cutting down to the water.

Another pleasant walk (about 5km) is along the Cola de Mico Road across the island to the 270ft **Pumpkin Hill**, a beautiful display of lava rocks surrounded by a small rocky beach with waves crashing all around. The look-out tower on top of the hill gives great views of the island. There is beautiful snorkelling beyond the beach, and several underwater caves and cliffs, though it is not safe to go into the caves. The walk to the beach takes about an hour from East Harbour, though in the wet season, the track is a sea of mud. On clear days any point on the southern edge of the island offers great views across to the mainland and the dark bulk of Pico Bonito.

The Cayes

Utila Cayes consist of eleven tiny outcrops strung along the southwestern edge of the island, which have been a designated wildlife refuge since 1992. **Suc Suc** (or Jewel) **Caye** and **Pigeon Caye**, connected by a narrow causeway, are both inhabited, and the pace of life here is slower even than in Utila. Small launches regularly shuttle between Suc Suc and Utila (75¢), or can be rented to take you across for a day's snorkelling, if you have your own equipment. If you want to **stay**, *Vicky's Rooms* on Suc Suc (①) offers basic accommodation, and there are a couple of reasonable restaurants and a good fish market.

Boats from Utila (prices are negotiable, and depend on the number of passengers) will take you to **Water Caye**, an idyllic stretch of white sand, coconut palms and a small coral reef. Camping is allowed (bring all your food, equipment for a camp fire and water), and a caretaker turns up every day to collect $1 for use of the island, plus another $1 if you want to rent a hammock. There are full moon parties here every month, and best of all, no sandflies. Most of the other cayes are privately owned, though the houses on **Morgan** and **Sandy cayes** can be rented through George Jackson, on Pigeon Key (☎453161).

Eating

Lobster and fish are staples on the islands, as are the usual Honduran dishes of rice, beans and chicken. In recent years, however, European foods, such as pasta, pizza and pancakes, have become widely available. For cheap snacks, head for the evening stalls near the dock, which do a thriving trade in *baleadas* (tortillas filled with beans, cheese and onions). Note that most of the island's restaurants stop serving at around 10pm.

Bundu Café, on the main street, east of the dock. Serves European-style breakfasts and lunches, and shows English-language films at night. Food served Mon–Wed, Fri & Sat 9am–3pm.

Golden Rose, just past the "7-11" in Sandy Bay. Dive instructors and locals rate this as the island's best restaurant for its tasty local dishes.

Jade Seahorse, on Cola de Mico Road. Serves great breakfasts and *licuados*, as well as good seafood.

Mango Café, in the *Mango Inn*. A popular place with an interesting selection of tasty European food and a lively bar. Closed Mondays.

Mermaid's Corner, at *Rubi's Inn*. Thre's a great atmosphere in this popular pasta and pizza restaurant, though service can be very slow.

Sharkey's Reef Restaurant, at *Sharkey's Cabins*. The nearest Utila gets to gourmet cuisine, specializing in delicious fish and vegetarian dishes. Prices are high, but worth it for the wonderful California-style and Caribbean food. Only serves dinner; closed Mon & Tues.

Thompson's Bakery, Cola de Mico Road. A popular place to hang out, read, drink coffee and meet other travellers, while sampling the good value breakfasts, or range of daily baked goods. The book exchange here is crammed with paperback romances. Open 6am–noon.

Utila's Cuisine, close to the dock. An unpretentious local place where you can feast on cheap chicken and meat dishes.

Utila Reef, on the airstrip road, close to Trudy's. Tasty local and international dishes are served on an upstairs terrace overlooking the water. The daily specials, such as lobster and rice salad, are particularly good.

Nightlife

The *Seabreaker* bar, opposite *Rubi's Inn*, on the waterfront, has a party every Tuesday, Thursday and Saturday night, with a cocktail hour, happy hour and music until 11pm. On Saturday nights, the party continues until 3am, at *07*, just west of *Rubi's Inn*, with a disco playing mainly reggae plus a little techno. The *Casino*, by the dock, attracts a more local crowd with reggae and a dash of salsa and merengue. During the rest of the week, the *Mango Café* is a popular spot for cheap beer and a quiet drink, while the *Bucket of Blood*, on Cola de Mico Road, has regular happy hours and late night drinking. If you fancy a game of billiards, the national sport in Honduras, there's a pool hall behind the *Bucket of Blood*, which stays open until 11pm.

Listings

Banks Banco Atlántida and Banchasa, both close to the dock, exchange money and offer advances on Visa cards (Mon–Fri 8–11.30am & 1.30–4pm, Sat 8–11.30am).

Bicycles can be rented for around $2 a day from the house next to Henderson's Grocery store, just west of the dock, and from other venues around town – look for the handwritten signs.

Book exchange The *Bundu Café*, on the main street, east of the dock, has a book exchange and offers information on diving.

Doctor The Medical Clinic is just beyond the immigration office in Sandy Bay (Mon–Fri 8–11.30am).

Immigration office is next to Hondutel in Sandy Bay (Mon–Fri 9am–noon & 2–4.30pm).

Port office in the large building in the main dock (Mon–Fri 8.30am–noon & 2–5pm, Sat 8.30am–noon).

Post office in the large building in the main dock (Mon–Fri 9am–noon & 2–4.30pm, Sat 9–11.30am).

Shopping Henderson's and Christina's stores, west and east of the dock respectively, sell basic groceries and clothes.

Telephones Hondutel is next to the immigration office in Sandy Bay (Mon–Fri 7am–noon & 2–5pm).

Travel agents Tropical Travel and Utila Tour Travel Centre, both east of the dock on the airstrip road, can book and confirm flights to La Ceiba, and elsewhere in Central America.

Roatán

Some 50km from La Ceiba, **Roatán** is the largest of the Bay Islands, more than 40km long and about 3km wide. Accommodation is geared towards wealthy vacationers staying in, luxury all-inclusive resorts and doing anything from scuba diving to nature hiking in the hardwood forests. **Coxen Hole** is the commercial centre, while **West End** is the place to head for absolute relaxation. The sandflies are worse here than on Utila, but not quite as bad as on Guanaja.

Arrival and getting around

Flights from La Ceiba, San Pedro Sula and occasionally further afield land regularly at the **airport**, 3km from Coxen Hole, the main town on the south side of the island. The airport is on the road to French Harbour, and collective taxis to Coxen Hole cost L.20 ($1.50). Alternatively, you could walk to the road and wait for one of the public minibuses which head to town every thirty minutes or so (L.10; 80¢). There's an information desk, a hotel reservation desk, car rental agencies and a bank at the airport. The **ferry dock** is in the centre of Coxen Hole.

A paved road runs west–east along the island connecting the major communities. **Minibuses** leave regularly from Main Street in Coxen Hole, heading west to Sandy Bay and West End (every 30min until late afternoon) and east to Brick Bay, French Harbour, Oak Ridge and Punta Gorda (every hour or so until late afternoon); fares are L.7–15 (50¢–$1). However, if you really want to explore, you'll need to **rent a car** or **motorbike**. In addition to the agencies at the airport, Sandy Bay Rent a Car has offices at Sandy Bay and West End, where you can rent jeeps for $45 per day, and motorbikes for $25 a day.

Coxen Hole

The capital of the Bay Islands, **Coxen Hole** (aka Roatán Town) is where the boats dock and the planes land; it's also the site of the immigration office, customs, the law courts for all the islands, and most of the island's shops. The town's two main roads are **Main Street**, which runs along the waterfront, and **Ticket Street**, which goes to West End. The town itself is dusty and run-down and most visitors come only to change money or to shop. Unless you have a very early flight you're unlikely **to stay** here, but if you do need to, the *Hotel Cayview*, on Main Street (☎451202; ⑤), has comfortable rooms with air-conditioning and private baths, whilst the *Hotel El Paso*, on Main Street (☎451059; ②), has clean rooms, but communal bathrooms. There are a number of cheap *comedores*, serving standard Honduran **food**, while the friendly *Pava Pizza* on Main Street sells decent pizzas, as well as sandwiches and snacks. *Que Pasa Cafe*, in Libreria Casi Todo 11, on Ticket Street, serves European-style breakfasts and snacks.

JAMIE MARSHALL, GUATEMALAN INDIAN CENTRE

Copán, Honduras

IAN OSBORNE, FOOTPRINTS

Tikal

IAIN STEWART

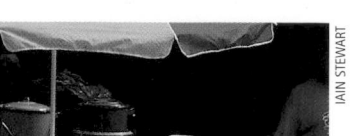

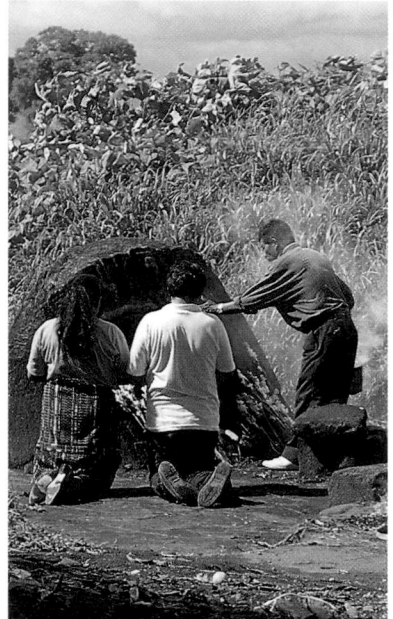

Fertility rite, El Baúl

IAIN STEWART

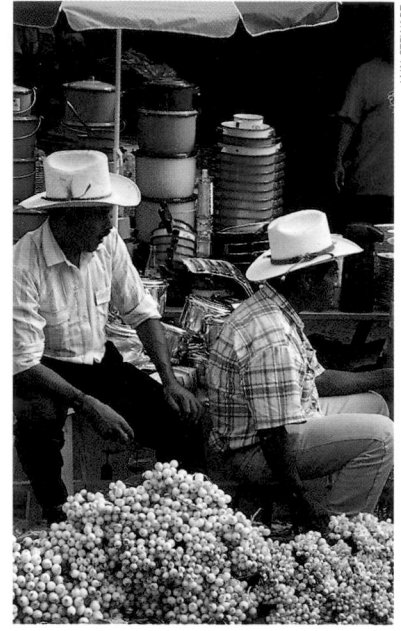

Market traders, Chiquimula

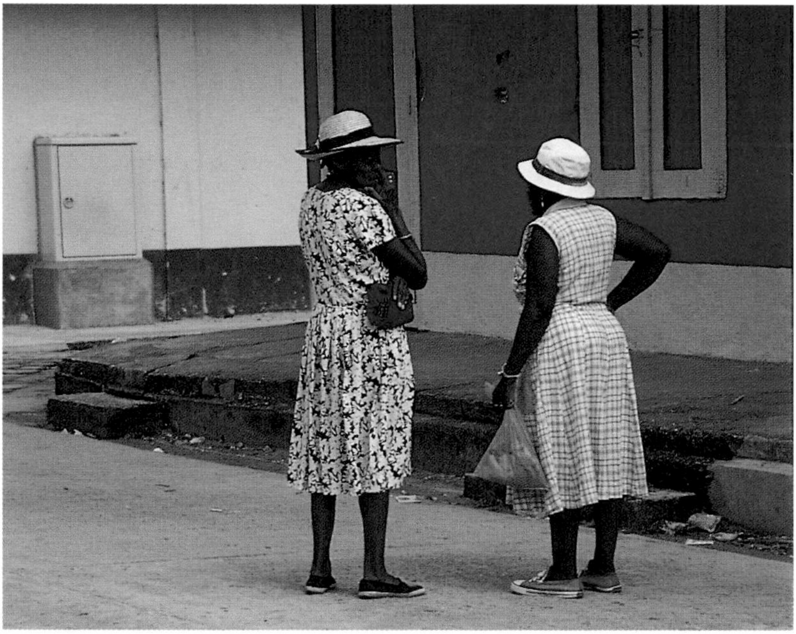
IAIN STEWART

Garifuna women, Lívingston

JOHN NOBLE

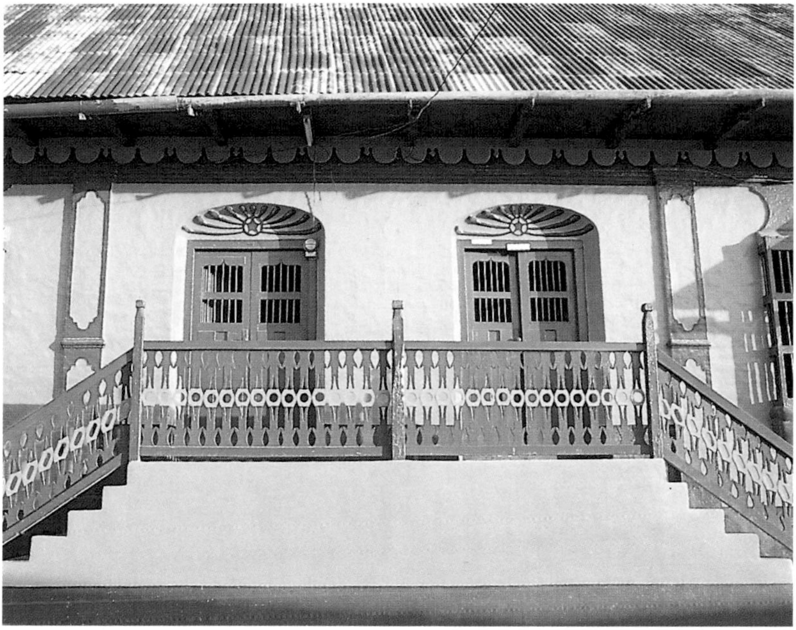

Flores, Petén

IAIN STEWART

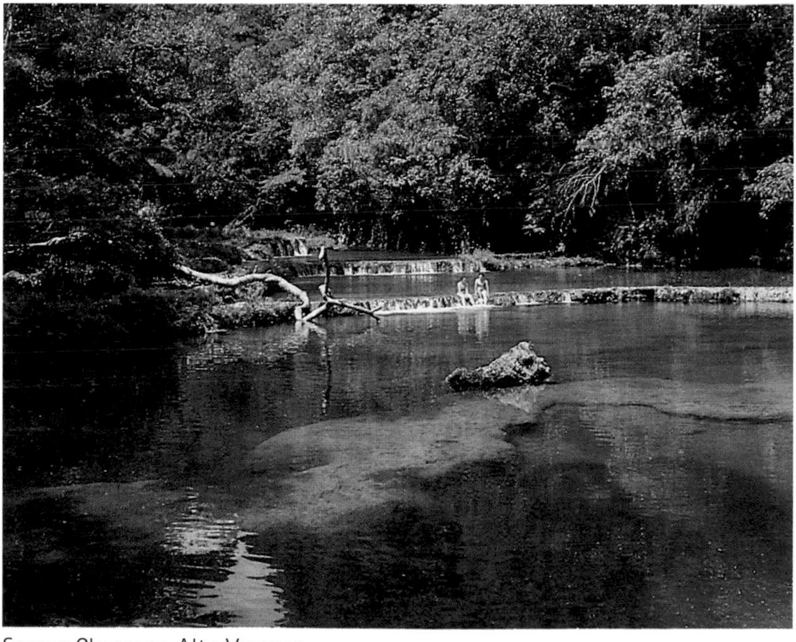

Semuc Champey, Alta Verapaz

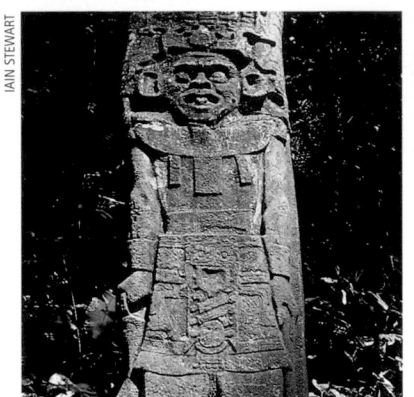

IAIN STEWART

Ceibal

IAIN STEWART

Quiriguá

IAIN STEWART

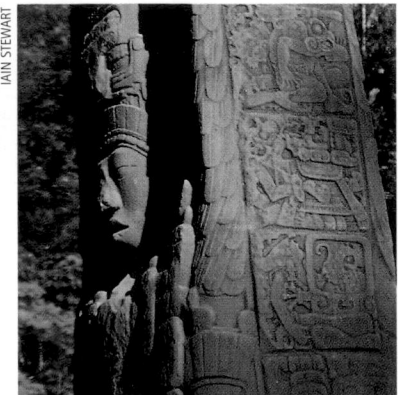

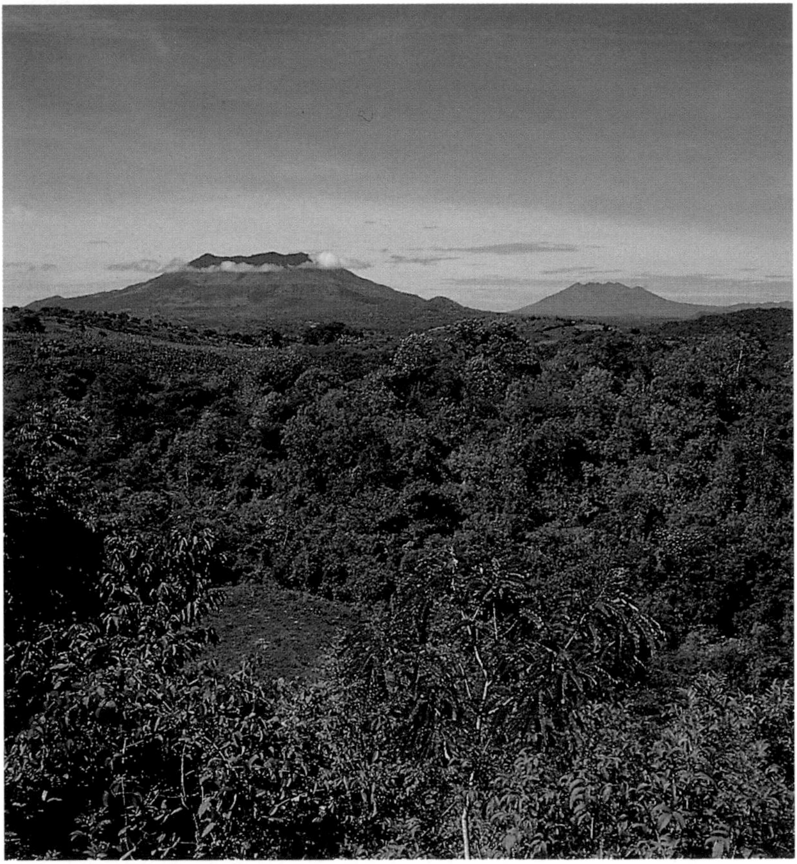

Eroded volcanoes in the eastern highlands

All the town's practical facilities, including the banks, offices, post office, immigration office and most shops, are on a hundred-metre strech of Main Street, near where the buses stop. For tourist **information**, pick up a copy of the *Coconut Telegraph*, an informative magazine about the island and its events from the Cooper Building. The headquarters of BICA (Mon–Fri 9am–noon & 2–5pm) also has information on places of interest on the island as well as its flora and fauna. For **changing travellers' cheques**, dollars and cash advances on Visa cards try Bancahsa, or Credomatic (both Mon–Fri 8.30am–11.30am & 1–4pm, Sat 8.30–11.30am). The **immigration office** (Mon–Fri 9am–noon & 2–4.30pm) and the **post office** (Mon–Fri 9am–noon & 2–4.30pm, Sat 9–11.30am) are both near the small square on Main Street, while **Hondutel** is behind Bancahsa. For **shopping**, HB Warren is the largest supermarket on the island and sells a wide range of groceries and foodstuffs, as well as clothes. Yaba Ding Ding and Mahchi both sell postcards and souvenirs, such as T-shirts and jewellery, and there is a small, not too impressive general market, just behind Main Street.

Sandy Bay

Midway between Coxen Hole and West End, **Sandy Bay** is an unassuming community that is home to a couple of interesting attractions. The **Institute for Marine Sciences** (9am–5pm; closed Wed; $4), based at *Antony's Key Resort*, has exhibitions on the marine life and geology of the islands and a museum with useful information on local history and archeology. You can also watch daily bottle-nosed dolphin shows (Mon, Tues, Thurs & Fri 10am & 4pm, Sat & Sun 10am, 1pm & 4pm; $4), and dive or snorkel with the dolphins ($100 and $75 respectively; must be booked in advance). Across the road from the institute, several short nature trails weave through the jungle at the **Cambola Botanical Gardens** (daily 8am–5pm; $3), a riot of beautiful flowers, lush ferns and tropical trees. A twenty-minute walk from the gardens up Monte Carambola brings you to the Iguana Wall, a section of cliff that acts as a breeding ground for iguanas and parrots. From the top of the mountain you can see across to Utila, on clear days.

There are a few places **to stay** in Sandy Bay, all of which are clearly signposted off the main road, or the dirt track that cuts off it to the sea. The cheapest option is the non-smoking *Beth's Place* (☎451266; ②), with clean rooms, and communal bathrooms and kitchen; snorkelling equipment is also available for rent. Slightly more upmarket is the *Oceanside Inn* (⑥), with large rooms and a good restaurant. More upmarket still is *Antony's Key Resort* (☎451003; fax 451140; only offers weekly packages), one of the smartest places on the island, with cabins set among the trees and on a small caye. All-inclusive dive packages start at $600 per person per week. The nicest place **to eat** is the popular bar and restaurant, *Rick's American Café*, set on the hillside above the road. It serves US-style burgers, seafood and snacks, and is open for dinner all week and brunch on Sundays.

West End

With its calm waters and incredible soft white beaches, **West End** makes the most of its ideal setting, gearing itself mainly towards travellers who can afford to pay that bit more for their own little slice of heaven. Set in the southwest corner of the island, round a shallow bay, the village has retained a laid-back charm, and the gathering pace of tourist development has done little to dent the friendliness of the villagers.

The paved road from Coxen Hole finishes at the northern end of the community, by **Half Moon Bay**, one of the village's best beaches. A sandy track runs alongside the water's edge, ending at a small bridge at the far end of the village, beyond which is another good beach. At the end of the paved road, the Coconut Tree store sells a good selection of groceries, and just beyond on the left, the Libreria Casi Todo has a book exchange and **travel agency**, where you can book or change flights. The best place for **renting** bicycles, motorbikes, inflatable boats, snorkelling gear and other water equipment is the little stall under the trees just past the Libreria, whilst Joanna's Gift Shop, about five minutes' walk from the Libreria, sells handicrafts and swimwear. About a ten-minute walk back up towards Coxen Hole, you can send and receive **faxes and email** at the *Online Café* (closed Sundays), which also has a small book exchange.

ACCOMMODATION

Accommodation is listed in the order that you'll come to it, as you arrive in the village. During low season (May–Nov) it's worth negotiating a discount, particularly for longer stays.

Coconut Tree Cabins, on the paved road at the entrance to the village. Comfortable, spacious cabins all with covered porches, fridges and hot water. ⑥.

Chilie's, turn right at the end of the paved road, and walk for about 100m. A new, English-owned place with dorm beds and private rooms in a two-storey house. At the back is a kitchen for guests' use; camping is also possible in the large garden. ②.

Half Moon Bay Cabins, at the northern edge of Half Moon Bay; follow the track for about 300m past *Chilie's* (☎451075). One of the original upmarket places, with a lively restaurant and bar. The secluded cabins are scattered around wooded grounds, close to the water's edge, and all have fan or air-conditioning. ⑥.

Dolphin Resort, turn left onto the dirt track, and it's about 200m down on the left. Small, clean rooms in a brick building, all with air-conditioning, private baths and hot water. ④.

Pinnochio's, continue 200m past the *Dolphin Resort*, then turn left at the signed turn for Stanley's Island restaurant (fax 451841). This new wooden building, set on a hillside above the village, has clean, airy rooms with bath and hot water. The owners are very friendly and there's a good restaurant downstairs. ④.

Jimmy's Lodge, at the southern end of the village, ten minutes' walk from the paved road. Extremely basic backpackers' institution, with mattresses on the floor in a large dorm and a hose shower; under $3 per person. Hammocks can also be slung, if there's room, and the beach location is great.

EATING

Cannibal Café, in front of the *Dolphin Resort*. One of the cheapest places to eat, though serves mostly snacks. The *baleadas* and *quesadillas* (large tortillas filled with cheese) are good value and come in huge portions.

Pinocchio's. Serves an eclectic range of meat, fish and pasta dishes at reasonable prices. The chicken and vegetable risotto for $5 is particularly tasty. Closed Wed.

Rudy's Coffee Stop, just before Joanna's Gift Shop on the paved road. Serves great breakfasts of banana pancakes, omlettes, fresh coffee and juices. Closed Sun.

Salt and Pepper, above the Coconut Tree Store. A wide-ranging gourmet menu, which includes French, Italian, Indian and Mexican dishes. Expect to pay upwards of $10 a head, with wine, but the relaxed atmosphere and excellent cooking make it worth the money.

Seaview Restaurant, halfway along the main drag. A popular joint, with a nicely laid-out eating area. The large, well-prepared pizzas are good value, through service can be appallingly slow.

WATERSPORTS IN AND AROUND WEST END

Diving courses for all levels, and in several languages, are on offer in West End. Most places charge similar prices, with a standard four-day open-water course costing around $200. Some schools include basic accommodation in the price. Most schools offer optional dive insurance for around $2 per day, which is well worth having: see p.271 for details of safety precautions when choosing a dive school. Tyll's Dive and West End Divers, next to each other on the main drag about 100m south of the paved road, are two of the more popular shops with good safety records, while Sueño del Mar, 50m further on, rents out underwater cameras.

The reef lying just offshore provides some suberb **snorkelling**, with the best spots being at the mouth of Half Moon Bay and just offshore from *Jimmy's Lodge* (see above). You can also rent out **sea-kayaks** from Sea Blades, at the Libreria Casi Todo: expect to pay around $12 for a half-day, and $20 for a full-day. Belvedere's, on the waterfront about 30m south of Librería Casi Todo, runs popular, hour-long **glass-bottomed boat** tours for $8, while Flame & Smoke, on the beach beyond *Jimmy's Lodge* charters boats for half- or full-day **fishing trips**.

Stanley's Island Restaurant, up the hill behind *Pinocchio's*. A locally owned restaurant serving good food at reasonable prices. The *tapado* (fish stew) and coconut bread are particularly delicious.

DRINKING
Drinking can drain your pocket fast in West End. It's best to seek out the half-price **happy hours** at many of the restaurants and bars; starting at around 4.30pm, many of them last until 10pm. The *Blue Mango Bar*, on the seafront 200m beyond Librería Casi Todo, has a nightly happy hour from 5pm to 7pm, while *Foster's Restaurant/Bar*, built out over the sea opposite Joanna's Gift Shop, has a party every Thursday night; at other times it's a good place for a quiet drink and to enjoy the superb views over the ocean. The *Cool Lizard* on the beach just past *Jimmy's Lodge* is another fine spot for the sunset-watching.

West Bay
Two kilometres west of West End, towards the tip of Roatán, is **West Bay**, a stunning, white sand beach, fringed by coconut palms. Its waters are crystal clear, and there's great snorkelling at the southern end of the beach where the reef meets the shore. The beach and water come under the protection of the Sandy Bay and West End Marine Reserve, though this hasn't been able to prevent a rash of *cabañas* and restaurants being built in the vicinity over recent years. Most are low-key, however, only slightly detracting from the tranquility of the place, and, provided you avoid the sandflies by sunbathing on the jettys, you'll be as near to paradise as you can get.

You can walk to West Bay from West End, a pleasant 45 minute stroll south along the beach and over a few rock outcrops, or take one of the small launches that leave *Foster's Restaurant* regularly; the last one returns to West End at 9pm. A dirt road also runs here: from West Bay, head up the road to Coxen Hole and take the first turning on the right. If you want **to stay**, the *Bananarama Dive School* (⑤) and *Cabaña Roatána* (⑥) are both halfway along the beach and rent out pleasant cabins. For **food**, try the *Bite on the Beach* (closed Mon & Tues) or *Neptuno's Seafood Grill*, both at the north end of the beach and serving good, but pricey, seafood meals.

East of Coxen Hole

From Coxen Hole, the paved road runs east, giving glimpses of wrecked ships, and passing the small secluded cove of **Brick Bay**. After about 10km, it reaches **French Harbour**, a busy fishing port and the island's second largest town. This is where most of the Roatán's money comes and goes – not from tourism, but from shrimp and lobster packaging. More attractive than Coxen Hole and less run-down, it makes a lively place **to stay** for a couple of days, with all the accommodation being right in the centre. *Harbour View Hotel* (☎455390; ④) has reasonable rooms with bath and hot water, whilst the more upmarket *Buccaneer Hotel* (☎455032; ⑦) has a pool, a large wooden deck overlooking the water and a disco at the weekends. The best place **to eat** is at *Gio's*, by the Credomatic building, on the waterfront, where you can dine on excellent but pricey seafood; for more local fare, try *Pat's Place*, 50m further on.

From French Harbour the road cuts inland, running along a central ridge with superb views of both the north and south coasts of the island. After about 14km it reaches **Oak Ridge**, a quaint fishing port of wooden houses strung along a harbour. There are some nice unspoilt beaches to the east of town, which are accessible by launches from the main dock. The best place **to stay** is at the clean and pleasant *Hotel San José* (☎452328; ④), on a small caye a short distance across the water from the dock. The terrace restaurant at the nearby *Reef House Resort* has great sea views but rather pricey meals. Launches run from the main dock to the caye on demand (50¢).

About 5km from Oak Ridge, on the northern coast of the island, is **Punta Gorda**, the oldest Garifuna community in Honduras and the oldest settlement on Roatán. The best time to visit is for the anniversary of the founding of the village (April 6–12) when Garifuna from all over the country attend the celebrations. If you want **to stay**, *Ben's Dive Resort*, on the waterfront (☎451916; ⑤), has comfortable cabins, while *Los Cincos Hermanos*, in the centre, has basic, clean rooms (②). The *Hello Hello*, close by, serves great local **food** at good prices, while the *Paradise Bar,* at the entrance to the village, is the place to head for Sunday lunchtime barbeques.

From Punta Gorda, a dirt road continues east along the island, passing a turning to the secluded **Paya Beach**, after about 1.5km. A further 5km or so beyond here, you'll find **Camp Bay Beach**, an unspoilt stretch of tropical white sand. The road ends at **Port Royal**, on the southern edge of the island, where the remains of a fort built by the English can be seen on the caye offshore. The village lies within the boundaries of the **Port Royal Park and Wildlife Reserve**, the largest refuge on the island, which protects the water supply and birds and mammals such as the opossum and agouti. Pirates loved the sheltered coast here, and you may well stumble across the forlorn remains of forts and shipwrecks on the beautiful beaches.

Guanaja

The easternmost Bay Island, **Guanaja** is the most beautiful, undeveloped and expensive of all the islands, designated a Marine National Park. It actually consists of two islands, separated by a narrow canal, with the main settlement, **Bonacca** or **Guanaja Town**, sitting on a small caye, a few hundred metres offshore from the larger island. It is here that you'll find the island's shops and main residential area, as well as the bulk of the reasonably priced accommodation. All the houses in Bonacca are built on stilts above the water – vestiges of early settlement by the Cayman islanders – and the only way to get around is by water taxi, which adds both to the atmosphere and to the cost of living.

The larger island boasts the highest point of the entire Bay Islands, Michael's Peak (412m), which is covered with Caribbean pine forest and hardwoods. More than 50km long, and about 6km wide, it's a stunning, untouched place, with lovely waterfalls and incredible views of sea and jungle; unfortunately, there are more sandflies here than on any of the other islands. The only villages of any substance on the island are **Savanah Bight** (on the west coast) and **Mangrove Bight** (on the north coast), though these are both much smaller than Bonacca. A superb trail leads from Mangrove Bight up Micheal's Peak and down to Sandy Bay (on the south coast), affording stunning views of the island and surrounding reef; fit walkers can do the trail in a day, although it is possible to camp at the summit, provided you bring all your provisions with you.

Arrival and information

Guanaja **airstrip** is in the heart of the big island, next to the canal, and is served by daily flights from the mainland (see p.269 for details). Aside from a couple of dirt tracks there are no roads, the main form of transport being small launches. Boats from the main dock in Bonacca meet all flights, and there are collective services from the airstrip to Savanah Bight at 7am and 11am. Rides can be hitched on private boats to Mangrove Bight for a nominal fee.

If you arrive **by boat**, you'll come in at the main dock in Bonacca. The Capitania de Puerto, on the main pier has information on unscheduled boat services to the other islands and points on the Honduran mainland.

Bonacca itself is built on wooden causeways over the canals, many of which have now been filled in. The main causeway, running for about 500m east–west along the caye with a maze of small passages branching off it, is where you'll find all the shops, **banks** and businesses. You can change dollars and travellers' cheques at Banco Atlántida, on the main causeway to the left of the dock, and Bancahsa, on the main causeway to the right of the dock (both Mon–Fri 9am–noon); Bancahsa also gives cash advances on Visa cards.

Accommodation

Most of the hotels on Guanaja are luxury all-inclusive dive resorts offering weekly packages, which need to be booked in advance: the resorts are all reached by launch from the airstrip. In contrast, Bonacca has a small number of reasonably priced hotels, and a private house, just before the *Hotel Alexander*, which **rents out rooms** for under $10 per person.

BONACCA

Hotel Alexander, at the eastern end of the main causeway, to the right of the dock (☎454326). The best location in Bonacca, whose the large, comfortable rooms have private bathrooms and balconies overlooking the water. ⑥.

Hotel Miller, halfway along the main causeway (☎454327). The building is slightly run-down, but the rooms are in reasonable condition. Most rooms have hot water and, for a little extra, air-conditioning. ③.

Hotel Rosario, opposite the *Hotel Miller* (☎454240). A modern building, with comfortable rooms, all with private bath, air-conditioning and TV. ⑤.

Casa Sobre El Mar, on Pond Caye, just south of Bonacca (☎454269). Has three bright, breezy rooms for $85 per person including all meals.

BIG ISLAND

Unless otherwise stated, all prices are per person for a week-long package.

Bahía Resort, on the south side of the island across from Bonacca (☎454212). One of the smaller resorts, with accommodation in comfortable bungalows and a pool. Packages start at $800.

Bayman Bay Club, on the north side of the island (☎454179). Has well-furnished cabins set on a wooded hillside above the beach. Packages including dives and all meals cost $700–750.

Hillton Hotel, by the airstrip (☎45 4299). The clean rooms all have private baths and TV. Though its location is not as scenic as some of the other resorts, it is the cheapest option on the main island, and lets rooms by the night. ⑤.

The Island House Resort, on the north side of the island (☎454196). A very pleasant resort, close to several expanses of beautiful beach. Packages start at $590.

Posada del Sol, on the south side of the island (☎454186). The cabins are scattered around sixty acres of ground, and the amenities here include pool, tennis courts, sea kayaks and snorkelling equipment. Packages start from $340 for three nights.

SMALL ISLAND

West Peak Inn, towards the western tip of the Small Island (fax 454219; email *david@vena.com*). A relaxed place with comfortable cabins close to good, deserted beaches and a trail up to the 94-metre-high West Peak. Prices include all meals. ⑥.

Around the big island

Marble Hill, on the northern side of the big island has great caves and beautiful beaches in almost complete seclusion; volcano and black rock **underwater caves** also abound. The small rocky headland of **Michael's Rock**, west of the Island House, is a surrounded by stretches of beautiful white beach, with good snorkelling close to the shore. **Diving** is excellent all around the island and particularly on the southern shore, where you'll find clear water and intriguing natural formations such as caves, walls and tunnels – there's even a cave entrance said to have been the hideout for nineteenth-century filibuster William Walker during his ill-fated attempt to take over Honduras. You can also get down to the *Jado Trader*, a huge ship wrecked in 1987: it's lodged 28m below the surface, and surrounded by coral. Diving can be difficult if you don't go through a resort package; if you want to do it independently, Dive Freedom in the Coral Café building, on the main causeway in Bonacca, rents out equipment and runs courses.

Fishing and **snorkelling** can be fixed with local boatmen who charge $10–15 to take you out on the water. In many areas, however, the reef is close enough to swim to if you have your own snorkel gear.

Eating and drinking

There are several **restaurants** in Bonacca, most of which stay open till around 9pm and close on Sundays. None are particularly cheap, however, as most of the supplies have to be shipped in from the mainland, and the real gourmet eating experiences are reserved for the package resorts on the big island. In Bonacca itself, try *Bonacca's Garden*, halfway along the main causeway, or the restaurant at the *Hotel Alexander*, both of which serve reasonably priced local dishes. The *Up and Down Restaurant*, close to *Bonacca's Garden*, serves good pizza and pasta, while the *Coral Café* is a popular spot to hang out, though the drinks are better than the food.

Cayos Cochinos (Hog Islands)

The **Hog Islands**, set in emerald waters 17km northeast of La Ceiba, comprise two small islands – **Cochino Grande** and **Cochino Pequeño** – and thirteen palm-fringed **cayes**. All are privately owned and see few tourists, but it's well worth making the effort to get out here. With a vast expanse of unexplored reef, the entire area is a marine reserve, with anchoring on the reef and commercial fishing strictly prohibited in order to maintain the coral and fish in its natural state. On land the hills are studded with hardwood forests, palms and cactus, with Cochino Grande having a number of trails across its interior, and a small peak rising to 145m.

Organized **accommodation** on the islands is limited to the *Plantation Beach Resort* on Cochino Grande (☎420974), which only does weekly dive packages for around $800, including all meals and three dives a day. The resort will pick you up by launch from the Muralla de Cabotaje in La Ceiba for $30 one-way. Far more rewarding is to stay in the Garifuna fishing village of **Chachauate** on Lower Monitor Caye, in the south of Cochino Grande. The villagers have allocated a hut for visitors to sling their hammocks for a minimal charge, and will cook meals for you. Basic groceries are available in the village, though you should bring water and major food supplies with you from the mainland.

Getting to Cayos Cochinos

The easiest way to get to the Cayos Cochinos is to take a direct **bus** from La Ceiba to the village of **Nueva Armenia** (daily at 11am; 2hr), from where boats leave in the early morning for **Chachauate** (1hr; $10–15 one-way). If you arrive after midday you may want to try bargaining to secure your own launch, though this is likely to be expensive. In order to get the early morning boats, you'll need **to stay** the night in Nueva Armenia – there's a basic hotel, in the centre of the village (①), which cooks meals on request. To avoid spending the afternoon in Nueva Armenia, you could take any of the more regular buses from La Ceiba to Trujillo, Tocoa or Olanchito, which all pass through Jutiapa, from where you can hitch or walk the 8km to Nueva Armenia.

FIESTAS

JANUARY
El Progreso (near Jutiapa) kicks off the fiesta year in the eastern highlands. The action lasts from the 12th to 15th; the final day is the most important. **Cabañas** (near Zacapa) has a fiesta from the 19th to 21st, in honour of San Sebastian; the 19th is the main day. **Ipala**'s fiesta, which includes some traditional dances and bullfighting, is from the 20th to 26th: the 23rd is the main day. There's also the great pilgrimage to **Esquipulas** on the 15th.

FEBRUARY
San Pedro Pinula, one of the most traditional places in the east, has a fiesta from the 1st to 4th, in which the final day is the main one. **Monjas** has a fiesta from the 5th to 10th, with the 7th as the main day. **Río Hondo** (on the main road near Zacapa) has its fiesta from the 24th to 28th; the 26th is the principal day. Both **Pasaco** (in the department of Jutiapa) and **Huite** (near Zacapa) have moveable fiestas around carnival time.

Continues over

MARCH

Jerez (in the department of Jutiapa) has a fiesta in honour of San Nicolas Tolentino from the 3rd to 5th, with the last day as the main one. There's a smaller day of pilgrimage to the Black Christ of Esquipulas on the 9th. **Moyuta** (near Jutiapa) and **Olapa** (near Chiquimula) both have fiestas from the 12th to 15th. **Morales**, a town with little to celebrate but its lust for life, has a fiesta from the 15th to 21st, with the main day on the 19th. **Jocotán** (halfway between Chiquimula and El Florido) has a moveable fiesta in March.

APRIL

April is a quiet month in the east but **La Unión** (near Zacapa) has a fiesta from the 22nd to 25th.

MAY

Jalapa has its fiesta from the 2nd to 5th, with the 3rd the main day. **Gualán** (which is near Zacapa) has a fiesta from the 5th to 9th.

JUNE

The only June fiesta out this way is in **Usumatlán**, from the 23rd to 26th.

JULY

Puerto Barrios has its fiesta from the 16th to 22nd, with the main day on the 19th: this has something of a reputation for its (enjoyably) wild celebrations. **Jocotán** (near Chiquimula) has its fiesta from the 22nd to 26th. **Esquipulas** has a fiesta in honour of Santiago Apostol from the 23rd to 27th.

AUGUST

Chiquimula has its fiesta from the 11th to 18th, with the main day on the 15th: sure to be a good one, this also includes bullfighting. Over on the other side of the highlands, **Asunción Mita** has a fiesta from the 12th to 15th. **San Luis Jilotepéque** has its one-day fiesta on the 25th.

SEPTEMBER

Sansare (between Jalapa and Sanarate) has its fiesta from the 22nd to 25th, with the 24th as the main day.

NOVEMBER

Sanarate celebrates from the 7th to 14th and **Jutiapa** from the 10th to 16th, with the middle day as the main day. **Quesada** (near Jutiapa) has a fiesta from the 26th to 30th.

DECEMBER

Zacapa has its fiesta from the 4th to 9th, with the main day on the 8th, and **San Luis Jilotepéque** from the 13th to 16th. **Cuilapa** goes wild from the 22nd to 27th, and **Lívingston** has a Caribbean carnival from the 24th to 31st: one of the best places in the country to spend Christmas.

travel details

BUSES

Bus is the best way to get around the eastern highlands. For the northeastern area simply take a bus to either **Puerto Barrios** or **Esquipulas**, as these pass through all the main towns in between. To travel into the central highlands you need to catch a bus heading for **Jutiapa**, and change buses there.

The Motagua valley and Lake Izabal/Río Dulce area

Buses for **Puerto Barrios** leave Guatemala City hourly from the terminal at 9 Av and 18 C in Zona 1. The very best of these, luxury pullmans, are run by Litegua (5.30am–5pm; $6), whose office is at 15 C 10–40. From Puerto Barrios, Litegua runs 19 buses daily (including nine *especiales*) **to Guatemala City** (1am–4pm) from its office on 6 Av, between 9 & 10 calles. The trip takes about 5hr and tickets can be bought in advance. All buses run past the entrance road for **Quiriguá** (about 3hr 30min from Guatemala City), and virtually everywhere else along the way except **Morales** and **Bananera**: for these you can change at the **Ruidosa junction** where the road to Petén turns off.

From Puerto Barrios there are also buses to **Morales and Bananera** every hour or so; to **Esquipulas** during the morning; to **Mariscos** at 3pm daily; and to Finca La Inca for the **jungle route to Honduras** at 6am, 7.45am then every 45 min until 4pm (2hr).

From Morales and Bananera there are regular buses and minibuses **to Río Dulce**, where you can pick up buses to Petén.

To Mariscos there's a direct bus from 18 C and 9 Av in Guatemala City at 6am, and one from Puerto Barrios at 3pm – there are also pick-ups to Mariscos from the **La Trinchera** junction on the main Caribbean Highway.

The eastern highlands

To Esquipulas hourly pullman buses, run by Rutas Orientales, leave from 19 C and 9 Av, Zona 1, in Guatemala City (4am–6pm; 4hr). Buses from Esquipulas **to Guatemala City** (hourly, 2am–6pm) call in at **Zacapa** and **Chiquimula**. If you're coming from Puerto Barrios or Petén and want to head out this way, you can pick up one of these at the **Río Hondo junction** on the Caribbean highway.

From Esquipulas there is also a regular flow of minibuses and buses to the borders with El Salvador (1hr) and Honduras (30min). There are also buses to **Jutiapa** and **Jalapa**.

From Chiquimula there are regular daily buses between 6am and 4.30pm to the **El Florido** border crossing (2hr 30min), from where trucks and buses run to **Copán** in Honduras. There's also a regular service to **Ipala** (1hr) and on to **Jalapa** (6hr) between 5am and 6pm.

To Jutiapa buses leave every hour or so from the Zona 4 bus terminal in Guatemala City between 6am and 4pm; most of them go on to **Asunción Mita** and **San Cristóbal Frontera** – the border with El Salvador. The last bus from the border to Guatemala City is at around 3pm. All buses between Guatemala City and Jutiapa pass through **Cuilapa**, from where there are hourly buses to **Chiquimulilla**.

From Jutiapa there are buses to all parts of the eastern highlands, including **Esquipulas**, **Ipala** and **Jalapa**.

To San Salvador several companies run a direct service from Guatemala City via the **Valle Nuevo** border crossing (hourly; 8hr). Companies serving this route include Mermex, Taca and Trascomer, whose offices are all at the junction of 1 C and 5 Av, Zona 4, in Guatemala City. Tica Bus also serves this route, with its buses leaving from 11 C 2–38, Zona 9, Guatemala City.

BOATS

From Puerto Barrios to Lívingston there's a daily ferry service at 10.30am and 5pm (1hr 30min; $1.50), returning at 5am and 2pm. In addition, a steady shuttle of speedboats operates between Puerto Barrios and Lívingston, leaving when they are full ($3).

From Puerto Barrios to Punta Gorda in **Belize** the Maria Eugenia boat leaves daily at 1pm (1hr 30min; $9), plus a ferry on Tues and Fri at 7am (2hr 30min; $8).

From Lívingston up the Río Dulce there are daily sightseeing boats (around 3hr; $8).

From Lívingston to Omoa in **Honduras** a boat leaves on Tues and Fri (minimum of 6 people; 2hr 30min; $36).

From Mariscos to El Estor a ferry leaves daily at noon, returning at 6am (1hr; $2).

CHAPTER FIVE

COBÁN AND THE VERAPACES

While essentially a continuation of Guatemala's western highlands, the mountains of Alta (Upper) and Baja (Lower) Verapaz have always been set apart in a number of ways: certainly, the flat-bottomed Salamá valley and the mist-soaked hills of Cobán are physically unlike any of the country's other mountainous areas. **Baja Verapaz**, the more southerly of these two departments, is sparsely populated, a mixture of deep river valleys, dry hills and lush tropical forest, dotted with tiny hamlets. Just two roads cross the department; one connects the fiesta towns of **Salamá**, **Rabinal** and **Cubulco**, while the other runs from the Eastern Highway up to Cobán. **Alta Verapaz**, the wettest and greenest of Guatemala's highlands, occupies the higher land to the north. Local people say it rains for thirteen months a year here, alternating between straightforward downpour and the drizzle of the *chipi-chipi*, a misty rain that hangs interminably on the hills, although the mountains are now being deforested at such a rate that weather patterns may soon be disrupted. For the moment, however, the area's alpine terrain remains almost permanently moist, coated in resplendent vegetation and vivid with greenery. The capital of Alta Verapaz is **Cobán**, from where roads head north into Petén, west to El Quiché, and east to Lake Izabal.

The **history** of the Verapaces is also quite distinct. Long before the Conquest local Achi Indians had earned themselves a unique reputation as the most blood-thirsty of all the tribes, said to sacrifice every prisoner that they took. Their greatest enemies were the Quiché, with whom they were at war for a century. So ferocious were the Achi that not even the Spanish could contain them by force. Alvarado's army was unable to make any headway against them, and eventually he gave up trying to control the area, naming it *tierra de guerra*, the "land of war".

ACCOMMODATION PRICE CODES

All accommodation listed in this guide has been graded according to the following price scales. These refer to the price in US dollars of the cheapest double room in high season. For more details see p.25.

① Under $5	④ $15–25	⑦ $60–80
② $5–10	⑤ $25–40	⑧ $80–100
③ $10–15	⑥ $45–60	⑨ over $100

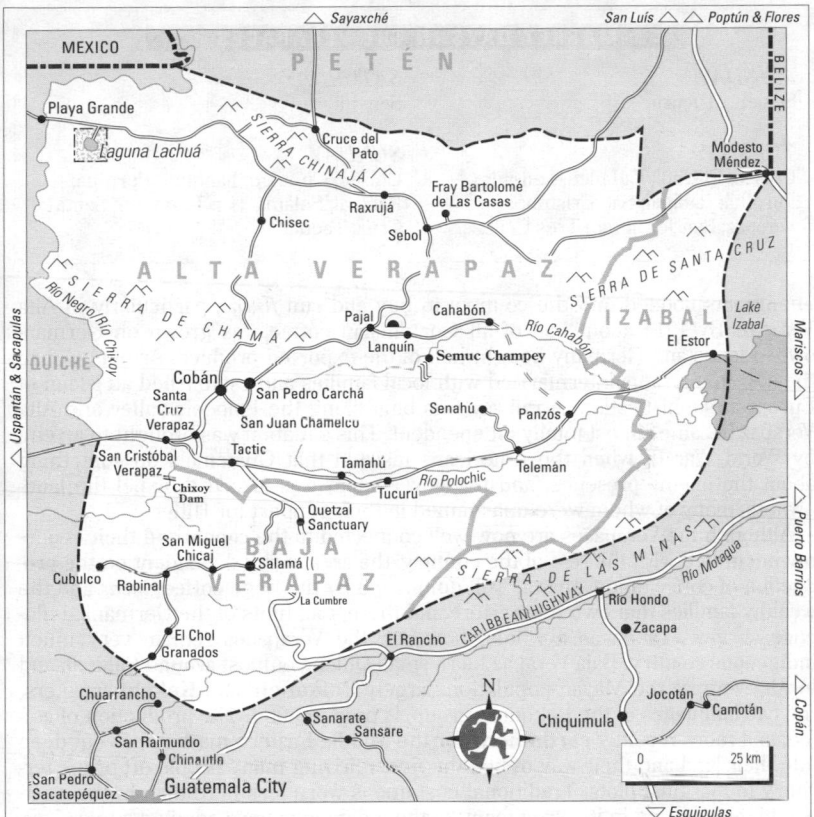

The church, however, couldn't allow so many heathen souls to go to waste, and under the leadership of **Fray Bartolomé de Las Casas**, the so-called apostle of the Indians, they made a deal with the conquistadors. If Alvarado would agree to keep all armed men out of the area for five years, the priests would bring it under control. In 1537 Las Casas himself, accompanied by three other Dominican friars, set out into the highlands. Here they befriended the Achi chiefs, and learning the local dialects they translated devotional hymns and taught them to the bemused Indians. By 1538 they had made considerable progress, converting large numbers of Indians and persuading them to move from their scattered hillside homes to the new Spanish-style villages. At the end of the five years the famous and invincible Achi were transformed into Spanish subjects, and the king of Spain renamed the province *Verapaz*, "True Peace".

Since the colonial era the Verapaces have remained isolated and in many ways independent: all their trade bypassed the capital by taking a direct route to the Caribbean, along the Río Polochic and out through Lake Izabal. The area really started to develop with the **coffee boom** at the turn of the century, when German

MARKET DAYS IN THE VERAPACES

MONDAY
Senahú; Tucurú.

SATURDAY
Senahú.

TUESDAY
Chisec; El Chol; Cubulco; Lanquín; Purulhá; Rabinal; San Cristóbal Verapaz; San Jerónimo; Tres Cruces.

SUNDAY
Chisec; Cubulco; Lanquín; Purulhá; Rabinal; Salamá; San Jerónimo; Santa Cruz; Tactic.

immigrants flooded into the country to buy and run *fincas*, particularly in Alta Verapaz. By 1914 about half of all Guatemalan coffee was grown on German-owned lands and Germany bought half of the exported produce. Around Cobán the new immigrants intermarried with local families and established an island of European sophistication. A railway was built along the Polochic valley and Alta Verapaz became almost totally independent. This situation was brought to an end by World War II, when the Americans insisted that Guatemala do something about the enemy presence, and the government was forced to expel the land-owners, many of whom were unashamed in their support for Hitler.

Although the Verapaces are now well connected to the capital and their economy integrated with the rest of the country, the area is still dependent on the production of coffee, and Cobán is still dominated by the huge coffee *fincas* and the wealthy families that own them. Here and there, too, hints of the Germanic influence survive. Taken as a whole, however, the Verapaces remain very much indigenous country: Baja Verapaz has a small Quiché outpost around Rabinal, and in Alta Verapaz the Mayan population, largely **Pokomchí** and **Kekchí** speakers, the two languages of the Pokoman group, is predominant. The production of coffee, and more recently **cardamom** for the Middle Eastern market, has cut deep into their land and their way of life, the *fincas* driving many people off prime territory to marginal plots. Traditional costume is worn less here than in the western highlands, and in its place many of the indigenous have adopted a more universal Kekchí costume, using the loose hanging *huipile* and locally made *cortes*.

The northern, flat section of Alta Verapaz includes a slice of Petén rain forest, and in recent years Kekchí Mayans have fanned out into this empty expanse, reaching the Río Salinas in the west, heading up into the Petén and making their way across the border into Belize. Here they carve out sections of the forest and attempt to farm, a process that threatens the future of the rain forest and offers little long-term security for the migrants.

Where to go

Few tourists make it out this way, possibly because the Maya tradition and costumes are not so evident as in the western highlands, but if you've time and energy to spare then you'll find these highlands astonishingly beautiful, with their unique limestone structure, moist, misty atmosphere and boundless fertility. The hub of the area is **Cobán**, an attractive mountain town with good accomodation, coffee houses and restaurants; it's a little subdued once the rain sets in, but is still the place from which to explore and the starting point for several adventurous trips. In August Cobán hosts the **National Folklore Festival**; in Baja Verapaz, the towns of **Salamá**, **Rabinal** and **Cubulco** are also renowned for their fiestas.

From Cubulco you can continue on foot, over the Sierra de Chuacús, to Joyabaj, a spectacular and exhausting hike.

In an isolated patch of cloud forest in the north of Baja Verapaz is one of the region's main attractions, the **quetzal sanctuary**, where you can occasionally see one of Central America's rarest birds, prized since the earliest of times. Heading out to the east of Cobán you can reach the exquisite natural bathing pools of **Semuc Champey**, surrounded by lush tropical forest and fed by the azure waters of the river **Cahabón**, which boasts spectacular white-water rafting possibilities. Cobán is also the starting point for three seldom-travelled back routes: east down the Río Polochic to **Lake Izabal**; north through Pajal and Raxrujá towards **Petén**; and west to **Uspantán** for Santa Cruz del Quiché and Nebaj (or all the way across to Huehuetenango).

Baja Verapaz

A strange but dramatic mix of dry hills and verdant, fertile valleys, Baja Verapaz is crossed by a skeletal road network. The historic towns of **Salamá**, **Rabinal** and **Cubulco** are all regularly served by buses, and have interesting markets as well as being famed for their fiestas, where you'll see some unique traditional dances. The other big attraction is the **quetzal sanctuary**, set to one side off the main road between Cobán and the El Rancho.

The main approach to both departments is from the Caribbean Highway, where the road to the Verapaz highlands branches off at the **El Rancho** junction. Lined with scrub bush and cacti, the road climbs steadily upwards, the dusty browns and dry yellows of the Motagua valley soon giving way to an explosion of green as dense pine forests and alpine meadows grip the mountains. The views from up here are superb, though the mountains can often be shrouded in a blanket of cloud. Some 48km beyond the junction is **La Cumbre de Santa Elena**, where the road for the main towns of Baja Verapaz turns off to the west, immediately starting to drop towards the floor of the Salamá valley. Surrounded by steep hillsides, with a level flood plain at its base, the valley appears entirely cut off from the outside world.

At the valley's eastern end lies the village of **SAN JERÓNIMO**, which is bypassed by the road for Salamá. In the early days of the Conquest Dominican priests built a church and convent here and planted vineyards, eventually producing a wine that earned the village something of a reputation. In 1845, after the religious orders were abolished, an Englishman replaced the vines with sugar cane and began brewing an *aguardiente* that became equally famous. These days the area still produces cane, and a fair amount of alcohol, although the English connection is long gone. Minibuses connect Salamá and San Jerónimo, but there's no particular reason to visit the village unless you're exceptionally keen on *aguardiente*.

Salamá, Rabinal and Cubulco

At the western end of the valley is **SALAMÁ**, capital of the department of Baja Verapaz. The town has a relaxed and prosperous air, and like many of the places out this way its population is largely *ladino*. There's not much to do outside **fiesta time** (September 17 to 21), other than browse in the Sunday market, though a couple of things are worth looking out for. On the edge of town lies a crumbling colonial bridge, now used only by pedestrians, and the old church is also interesting, with huge altars, darkened by age, running down either side. If you decide **to stay**, the pick of the hotels is the *Hotel Tezulutlán* (☎ & fax 9400141; ④), a gorgeous old building just off the plaza with rooms set around a leafy courtyard. A cheaper option is the basic budget *Pensión Juarez*, at the end of 5 C past the police station (☎9400055; ②), which has plenty of hot water. Salamá also has a branch of the Banco del Café (Mon–Fri 9am–5pm, Sat 10am–2pm), and a post office (Mon–Fri 8am–4.30pm).

Buses from Guatemala City to Salamá (3hr 30min), Rabinal (4hr 30min) and Cubulco (5hr 30min) depart hourly, between 5am and 5pm, from outside the redundant train station in Zona 1, at 19 C and 9 Av. They return from Cubulco between 1am and 2.30pm. If you're only going as far as Salamá there's a steady shuttle of minibuses to and from La Cumbre for connections with pullman buses running between Cobán and Guatemala City.

To the west of Salamá the road climbs out of the valley over a low pass and through a gap in the hills, to San Miguel Chicaj, a small, traditional village clustered around a colonial church. Beyond here the road climbs again, this time to a greater height, reaching a pass with magnificent views across the surrounding hills, which step away into the distance.

An hour or so from Salamá you arrive in **RABINAL**, another isolated farming town that's also dominated by a large colonial church. Here the proportion of indigenous inhabitants is considerably higher, making both the Sunday market and the fiesta well worth a visit. Founded in 1537 by Bartolomé de Las Casas himself, Rabinal was the first of the settlements in his peaceful conquest of the Achi nation: about 3km northwest are the ruins of one of their fortified cities, known locally as Cerro Cayup. Nowadays the place is best known for its oranges, claimed to be the best in the country – and they certainly taste like it.

Rabinal's **fiesta**, January 19 to 25, is famous above all for its dances. The most notorious of these, an extended dance drama known as the *Rabinal Achi*, was last performed in 1856, but many other unique routines are still performed. The *patzca*, for example, is a ceremony calling for good harvests, using masks that portray a swelling below the jaw, and wooden sticks engraved with serpents, birds and human heads. If you can't make it for the fiesta, at least try and get to the Sunday market. Rabinal has a reputation for producing high-quality *artesanía*, including carvings made from the *arbol del morro*, the Calabash tree, and traditional pottery. There are several fairly basic **hotels** in Rabinal, the best of which is the excellent *Posada San Pablo*, 3 Av 1–50 (②), a superb budget hotel with spotless rooms. If you can't get in there, try the *Hospedaje Caballeros*, 9 C 4–02 (①).

Leaving Rabinal the road heads on to the west, climbing yet another high ridge with fantastic views to the left, into the uninhabited mountain ranges. To the north, in one of the deep river valleys, lies the **Chixoy** hydroelectric plant (see p.291) where over three-quarters of Guatemala's electricity is generated.

Another hour of rough road brings you down into the next valley and to **CUBULCO**, an isolated, Ladino town, surrounded on all sides by steep, forested mountains. Cubulco is again best visited for its fiesta, this being one of the few places where you can still see the *Palo Volador*, a pre-Conquest ritual in which men throw themselves from a thirty-metre pole with a rope tied around their legs, spinning down towards the ground as the rope unravels, and hopefully landing on their feet. It's as dangerous as it looks, particularly when you bear in mind that most of the dancers are blind drunk: in 1988 an inebriated dancer fell from the top of the pole, killing himself. The fiesta still goes on, though, as riotous as ever, with the main action taking place on July 23. The best place **to stay** is in the large *farmacia* (①), in the centre of town, and there are several good *comedores* in the market.

On from Cubulco: the back routes

If you'd rather not leave the valley the same way that you arrived, there are two other options. One bus a day leaves Cubulco at around 9am, heads back to Rabinal and then, instead of going to La Cumbre and the main road, turns to the south, crossing the spine of the Sierra de Chuacús and dropping directly down towards Guatemala City. The trip takes you over rough roads for around eight hours, through El Chol, Granados and San Juan Sacatepéquez, but the mountain views and the sense of leaving the beaten track help to make the journey more appealing.

Hiking from Cubulco to Joyabaj

If you'd rather leave the roads altogether, an even less travelled route takes you out of the valley on foot, also over the Sierra de Chuacús, to Joyabaj in the department of Quiché. The hike takes between eight and ten hours, but if you have a tent it's probably best to break the trip halfway at the village of **TRES CRUCES** (if you don't have one, you'll probably be able to find a floor to sleep on). The views, as you tramp over a huge ridge and through a mixture of pine forest and farmland, are spectacular.

The hills around Cubulco are covered in a complex network of paths so it's worth getting someone to point you in the right direction, and asking plenty of people along the way – for the first half of the walk it's better to ask for Tres Cruces rather than Joyabaj. Broadly speaking the path bears up to the right as it climbs the hillside to the south of Cubulco, crossing the mountain range after about three hours. On the other side is an open, bowl-shaped valley, where to reach Tres Cruces you walk along the top of the ridge that marks the right-hand side of the valley – heading south from the pass. Don't drop down into the valley until you reach Tres Cruces. The village itself is the smallest of rural hamlets, perched high on the spine of the ridge, and far from the reach of the nearest road. On Thursday mornings the tiny plaza is crammed with traders who assemble for the market, but otherwise there's nothing save a couple of simple *tiendas*. Beyond Tres Cruces you drop down into the valley that cuts in to the right (west) of the ridge, and then follow the dirt road out of the valley, onto the larger Joyabaj to Pachalum road – turn right for Joyabaj (p.130).

Towards Alta Verapaz: the quetzal sanctuary

Heading for Cobán, and deeper into the highlands, the main road sweeps straight past the turning for Salamá and on around endless tight curves below forested hillsides. Just before the village of Purulhá is the **Biotopo del Quetzal** (daily 6am–4pm; $5), a 1153-hectare nature reserve designed to protect the habitat of the endangered quetzal. The reserve covers a steep area of dense rain/cloud forest, through which the Río Colorado cascades towards the valley floor, forming waterfalls and natural swimming pools. It is also known as the **Mario Dary**

THE RESPLENDENT QUETZAL

The **quetzal**, Guatemala's national symbol (after which the country's currency is named) has a distinguished past but an uncertain future. The bird's feathers have been sacred from the earliest of times, and in the strange cult of Quetzalcoatl, whose influence spread throughout Mesoamerica, it was incorporated into the plumed serpent, a supremely powerful deity. To the Maya the quetzal was so sacred that killing one was a capital offence, and the bird is also thought to have been the *nahual*, or spiritual protector, of the Maya chiefs. When Tecún Umán faced Alvarado in hand-to-hand combat, his headdress sprouted the long green feathers of the quetzal; when the conquistadors founded a city adjacent to the battleground they named it **Quetzaltenango**, the place of the quetzals.

In modern Guatemala the quetzal's image saturates the country, appearing in every imaginable context. Citizens honoured by the president are awarded the Order of the Quetzal, and the bird is also considered a symbol of freedom, since caged quetzals die from the rigours of confinement. Despite all this, the sweeping tide of deforestation threatens the very existence of the bird, and the sanctuary is about the only concrete step that has been taken to save it.

The more resplendent of the birds, and the source of the famed feathers, is the male. Their heads are crowned with a plume of brilliant green, the chest and lower belly is a rich crimson, and trailing behind are the unmistakeable oversized, golden-green tail feathers, though these are only really evident in the mating season. The females, on the other hand, are an unremarkable brownish colour. The birds nest in holes drilled into dead trees, laying one or two eggs at the start of the rainy season, usually in April or May.

Reserve, in honour of one of the founders of Guatemala's enviromental movement. A lecturer from San Carlos University, Mario Dary pioneered the establishment of nature reserves in Guatemala and spent years campaigning for a cloud forest sanctuary to protect the quetzal, causing great problems for the powerful timber companies in the process. He was murdered in 1981.

Visiting the reserve

Paths through the undergrowth from the road complete a circuit that takes you up into the woods above the reserve headquarters (maps are available). Although there are reasonable numbers of quetzals hidden in the forest, they're extremely elusive. The **best time of year to visit** is just before and just after the nesting season (between March and June), and the best time of day is **sunrise**. In general the birds tend to spend the nights up in the high forest and float across the road as dawn breaks, to spend the days in the forest below, and they can be easily identified by their strange jerky, undulating flight. A good place to look out for them is at one of their favoured feeding trees, the broad-leaved *aguacatillo* which produces a small avocado-like fruit. Whether or not you see a quetzal, the forest itself, usually damp with the *chipi-chipi*, a perpetual mist, is well worth a visit: a profusion of lichens, ferns, mosses, bromeliads and orchids, spread out beneath a towering canopy of cypress, oak, walnut and pepper trees.

Camping is no longer permitted at the reserve, but a kilometre or so past the entrance you can **stay** in either wooden cabins or rooms at the rustic *Hospedaje Los Ranchitos del Quetzal* (☎3313579; ②). There's no electricity and the *comedor's* menu is usually limited to eggs and beans, although the one major compensation is that quetzals can often be seen in the patch of forest around the hotel; staff sometimes insist on charging an entrance fee even if you just want to come in and look around. If you're after more luxurious accommodation, try the *Hotel Posada Montaña del Quetzal* (☎3351805; ⑤), 4.5km before the reserve on the way from Guatemala City, which offers pleasant rooms with warm water and private showers and has its own restaurant.

Buses from Cobán pass the entrance hourly, but make sure they know you want to be dropped at the *biotopo* as it's easy to miss. Those arriving by car will find the reserve at Km 161 on the highway between Cobán and the Caribbean Highway.

Alta Verapaz

Beyond the quetzal sanctuary the main road crosses into the department of Alta Verapaz, and another 13km takes you beyond the forests and into a luxuriant alpine valley of cattle pastures hemmed in by steep, perpetually green hillsides.

The first place of any size is **TACTIC**, a small mainly Pokomchí-speaking town adjacent to the main road, which most buses pass straight through. Tactic has earned its share of fame as the site of the **pozo vivo**, the living well. A sign points the way to this decidedly odd attraction, opposite the northern entrance road. The well itself is a small pool that appears motionless at first, until your eye catches the odd swirl in the mud. Legend has it that the water only comes to life when approached, because it harbours the restless soul of a dead Mayan beauty who fell in love with a Spanish soldier. After the soldier had died fighting to protect her from the less than honorable attentions of his companions, she chose to be stoned to death rather than marry another.

The colonial church in the village is also worth a look, as is the Chi-ixim chapel, high above the town. If you fancy a cool swim, then head for the *Balneario Cham-che*, a crystal-clear spring-fed pool, on the other side of the main road, opposite the centre of town. The simple *Pensión Central* (①), on the main street north of the plaza, has a pair of beautiful resident macaws; alternatively, the *Hotel Villa Linda* (☎9539216; ③) offers a little more comfort.

Further towards Cobán, the turning for **SAN CRISTÓBAL VERAPAZ** peels off to the left. A pretty town surrounded by fields of sugar cane and coffee, it's set on the banks of **Lake Cristóbal**, a favourite spot for swimming and fishing, although a shoe factory on the shore has now badly polluted the water. Legend has it that the lake was formed in 1590 as a result of a dispute between a priest and local Indians over the celebration of pagan rites. According to one version the earth split and swallowed the Indians, sealing their graves with the water, while another has it that the priest fled, hurling maledictions so heavy that they created a depression which then filled with water. The Pokomchí-speaking Indians of San Cristóbal are among the last vestiges of one of the smallest and oldest highland tribes. If you're thinking of visiting the village, though, make enquiries at the tourist office in Cobán first. It was here, in 1994, that an American tourist was beaten up so viciously that she died, and the US State Department issued a travel warning against Guatemala.

South of San Cristóbal is the billion-dollar disaster known as the **Chixoy dam** and hydroelectric plant, financed with money borrowed from the World Bank. Though the dam provides Guatemala with a large proportion of its electricity needs, the price of the project has been high. Unchecked deforestation in the area has increased sediment in the river thus reducing the efficiency of the power plant, and the cost of constructing the dam now accounts for up to fifty percent of all Guatemala's foreign debt payments. West from San Cristóbal the rough road continues to **Uspantán** (in the western highlands) from where buses run to Santa Cruz del Quiché, via Sacapulas, for connections to Nebaj and Huehuetenango. To head out this way you can either hitch from San Cristóbal or catch one of the buses that leave San Pedro Carchá at 10am and noon, passing just above the terminal in Cobán ten minutes later, and reaching San Cristóbal after about another half hour.

Cobán

The heart of these rain-soaked hills and the capital of the department is **COBÁN**, where the paved highway comes to an end. If you're heading up this way, stay in town for a night or two and sample some of the finest coffee in the world in one of Cobán's many genteel cafés. Cobán is not a large place; its suburbs fuse gently with outlying meadows and pine forests, giving the town the air of an overgrown mountain village. When the rain sets in, it has something of a subdued atmosphere and in the evenings the air is usually damp and cool. That said, the sun does put in an appearance most days, and the town makes a useful base to recharge, eat well, sleep well and for all kinds of **ecotourism** possibilities in the spectacular mountains and rivers nearby.

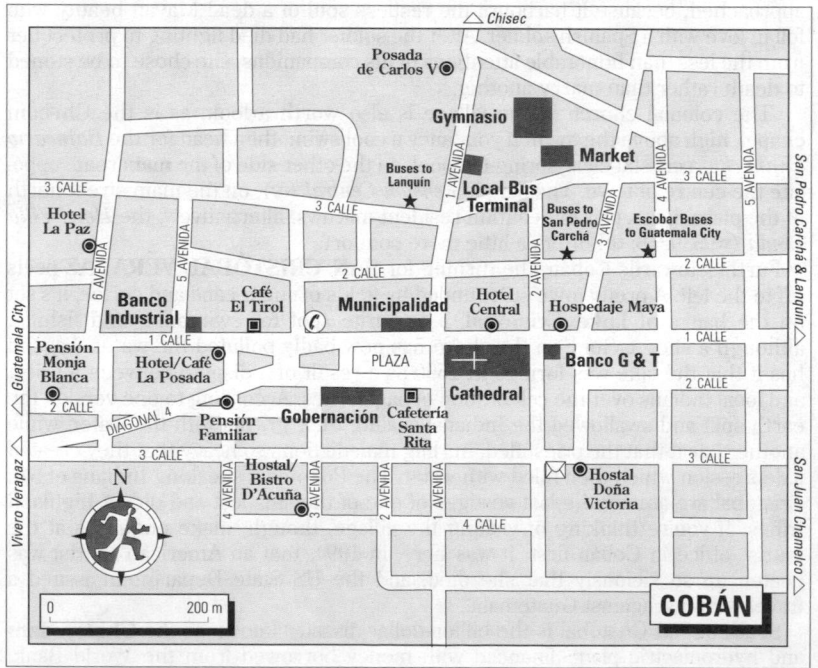

Arrival and information

Transportes Escobar Monja Blanca, one of Guatemala's best **bus** services (their latest *especiales* boast onboard TV and video), has regular departures between Guatemala City and Cobán (hourly, 2.30am–4pm; 4–5hr). In the capital, the office is at 8 Av 15–16, Zona 1, and even has a Wimpy inside the waiting room, though plans are afoot to move to the new Meta del Norte bus terminal on the outskirts of Guatemala City (see p.53). In Cobán, you'll find them on the corner of 2 C and 4 Av, Zona 4. Buses to **local destinations** such as Senahú, El Estor, Lanquín and Cahabón leave from the main bus terminal, down the hill behind the town hall. There are also regular departures from **San Pedro Carchá** (see p.296), a few kilometres away.

Although Inguat has no tourist office in Cobán, a couple of hotels more than adequately fill the **information** gap: the *Hostal d'Acuña* (see below) has helpful staff, a good folder with maps and bus times and a handy noticeboard, while *Hostal Doña Victoria* also provides useful information and arranges tours. Another source is Access, in the same complex as *Café Tirol*, where both the owners are bilingual and you can send **email**. Telgua's main office is in the plaza (daily 7am–midnight).

Accommodation

Unless you're here for one of the August fiestas you'll probably only pause for a day or two before heading off into the hills, out to the villages, or on to some other part of the country. There are, however, plenty of **hotels** in town, and there's free **camping** at the Parque National Las Victorias, on the northwest side of town; it lacks showers, though there are toilets and running water.

Hostal d'Acuña, 4 C 3–17 (☎9521547). Undoubtedly the most popular budget choice, offering spotless rooms for 2–6 people, with comfortable bunks. Dorms are built in the garden of a colonial house, on whose verandah guests and visitors can enjoy excellent home-cooking, including blueberry pie – many a budget is destroyed here sipping capuchino and munching cake. Highly recommended. ②.

Hotel Central, 1 C 1–74 (☎9521442). Germanic decor and friendly staff, but rooms, set round a nice little garden, are a little gloomy and overpriced though they do have hot water and private bathrooms. ④.

Hostal Doña Victoria, 3 C 2–38, Zona 3 (☎9522214; fax 9522213). Beautiful, refurbished colonial house dripping with antiques and oozing character. Comfortable bedrooms are all individually furnished and come with hot water and private bathroom, though you should avoid the noisy streetside rooms. There's a lovely garden, and a good café/bar and restaurant. ⑤.

Pensión Familiar, Diagonal 4 2–49, Zona 2. At the sharp end of the plaza and at the rough end of the quality scale. Cell-like rooms, simple and bare, are bleached every morning. Two lovely toucans help lift the spirits. ②.

Hospedaje Maya, 1 C 2–33 (☎9522380), opposite the Cine Norte. Large, basic hotel used by local travellers and traders. Bargain rates, warm showers and friendly staff help combat the nasty smell emanating from the toilets. ①.

Pensión Monja Blanca 2C 6–37, Zona 2 (☎9521358). There's a wonderfully old-fashioned atmosphere in this hotel, where all the rooms are set around a stunning courtyard garden. Some are nicely refurbished with private bath, and many are decorated with ecclesiastical art; all are very quiet. ②.

Hotel la Paz, 6 Av 2–19, Zona 1 (☎9521358). Safe, pleasant budget hotel run by a very vigilant *señora*. Some rooms have private bathroom. ②.

Hotel la Posada, 1 C 4–12, at the sharp end of the plaza (☎ & fax 9521495). Probably the city's finest hotel, in an elegant colonial building, said to be the oldest in the city, with a beautiful, antique-furnished interior. The rooms, many with wooden Moorish-style screens and some with four-poster beds, are set around two leafy courtyards and offer all the obvious luxuries without compromising the sedate and civilized atmosphere. Its excellent restaurant and café are frequented by Cobán's elite. ⑤.

Posada de Carlos V, 1 Av 3–44 (☎ & fax 9521780). Mountain chalet-style hotel with pine-trimmed rooms and modern amenities, close to the market. Comfortable, but not memorable. Check out the lobby photographs of old Cobán. ④.

The Town

Cobán's imperial heyday, when it stood at the centre of its own isolated world, is long gone, and its glory faded. The **plaza**, however, remains an impressive triangle, from which the town drops away on all sides. It's dominated by the **cathedral**, which is worth peering into to see the remains of a massive ancient cracked church bell. A block behind, the **market** bustles with trade during the day and is surrounded by food stalls at night. Life in Cobán revolves around **coffee**: the sedate restaurants, tearooms, trendy nightclubs and overflowing supermarket are a tribute to the town's affluent elite, while the crowds that sleep in the market and plaza, assembling in the bus terminal to search for work, are migrant labourers heading for the plantations. Since the fast road linked Cobán with the capital, the *finqueros*, wealthy owners of the coffee plantations, have mostly moved to Guatemala City, but a small residue still base themselves in Cobán. Hints of the days of German control can also be found here in the architecture, which incorporates the occasional suggestion of Bavarian grandeur.

One of the nicest things to do in Cobán is to walk out to the church of **El Calvario** (daily 7am–7pm), which dates from 1559. It's a short, but pleasant stroll from the town centre – head west out of town on 1 Calle, then turn right up 7 Av until you reach the cobbled path heading upwards. On the way up, you'll pass a number of small Mayan crosses blackened by candle smoke and decorated with scattered offerings. There's a commanding view over the town from the church, and next door is the green, wooded expanse of the **Parque National Las Victorias**.

Another place worth visiting lies just outside town: the **Vívero Verapaz** (Mon–Sat 9am–noon & 2–5pm, Sun 9am–noon; $1), a former coffee *finca* now dedicated to the growing of orchids, which flourish in these sodden mountains. The export of the blooms is illegal in Guatemala but the farm produces some seven hundred indigenous varieties, as well as a handful of hybrids which they've put together themselves, all of which are sold within Guatemala. The plants are nurtured in a wonderfully shaded environment, and a farm worker will show you around and point out the most spectacular buds, which are at their best between November and January. The farm is on the old road to Guatemala City, which you reach by leaving the plaza on Diagonal 4. At the bottom of the hill turn left, go across the bridge and follow the road for 3–4km. A taxi here from the plaza will cost around $3.

Eating and drinking

When it comes to **eating** in Cobán you have a choice between fancy European-style restaurants and very basic, inexpensive *comedores*. For really cheap food, your best bet, as always, is the **market**, but remember that it's closed by dusk, after which street stalls set up in the plaza selling barbecued meat and warm tortillas.

Bistro Acuña, 4 C 3–17. The most relaxed place to eat in town: a stunning period setting, uplifting classical music, attentive service and a good place to meet other travellers. A full scale blowout will cost around $8 a head but there are many cheaper options including great cannelloni. Leave room to delve into the calorific cake cabinet.

Kam Mun, 1 C 8–12. Excellent, hyper-hygenic Chinese restaurant, offering a good line-up of economical oriental choices. Daily noon–9.30pm.

Hotel La Posada, 1 C 4–12, at the sharp end of the plaza. The smartest restaurant in town, serving traditional Guatemalan specialities as well as international cuisine. The café, on the verandah outside, does superb breakfasts, coffee, tea and snacks. It's an excellent place to watch life and traffic go by, and is fairly kind on the wallet.

Cafetería Santa Rita, 2 C, on the plaza close to the cathedral. Good *comedor* with friendly service and decent Guatemalan food, in case you're sick of all those European style cafés.

Café Tirol 1C, on the north side of the plaza. Relatively upmarket by Guatemalan standards, though cheaper than the *Posada*. Serves 22 different types of coffee and pretty good breakfasts, hot chocolates, pancakes and sandwiches. Service can be distracted. Tues–Sun 7am–8.30pm.

Nightlife and entertainment

Generally speaking Cobán is a pretty quiet place, particularly so in the evenings, although behind closed doors people do indulge in some very metropolitan pleasures. There are two **cinemas**, the CineTuria in the plaza, and the Cine Norte, on 1 C. In addition to the usual cantinas, there are two half-decent **bars**: *La Tasca* in *Hostal Doña Victoria* with a good happy hour, and *Kikoe's*, on 2 Av, close to the *Hostal d'Acuña*. Strange though it may seem, the town also has several **nightclubs** – try *Oasis*, on 6 Av, just off 1 C, or *Le Bon*, on 2 C and 3 Av, both of which serve up the usual disco mix of merengue and handbag house laced with a dash of salsa.

Listings

Banks Banco del Café, 1 Av 2–68 (Mon–Thurs 8.30am–8pm, Fri 8am–8pm, Sat 10am–2pm); Banco G&T, 1 C & 2 Av, for Mastercard transactions (Mon–Fri 9am–7pm, Sat 9am–1pm); & Banco Industrial, 1 C & 2 Av, with an ATM which accepts Visa (Mon–Fri 8.30am–7pm, Sat 8.30am–5.30pm).

Car rental Local outfit Geo Rentals (☎9521650) is in the same building as *Café Tirol* and Access; Tabarini is on 7 Av 2–27, Zona 2 (☎ & fax 9521504).

Dentist Centro Dental Cristal , 5 Av 1–55, Zona 3 (☎9521777).

Doctor Dr Franco, 2 C 4–41, Zona 3 (☎9521069).

Hospital The private Centro Médico Galeno is on 2 C 2–08 Zona 3 (☎9513175), the state Hospital Regional, is on 8 C 1–24, Zona 4 (☎9521315).

Laundry At Lavendería La Providencia, at the sharp end of the plaza on Diagonal 4, you can wash and dry a machine-load for around $3 (Mon–Sat 8am–noon & 2–5pm).

Post office 2 C & 2 Av (Mon–Fri 8am–4.30pm).

Spanish Schools The Instituto Cobán International (INCO Int) on 2 C 6–23, Zona 2 (☎ & fax 9521727), offers twenty hours of teaching, two excursions and full board for around $110 per week. The Active Spanish School on 3 C 6–12, Zona 1 (☎9521432) is even cheaper at $85 a week including full board.

Travel Agents Epiphyte Adventures, 2 Av & 2 C (☎9522213), aims to promote "low impact tourism as a vehicle for rural development and biological conservation" and offers highly informative tours around Alta Verapaz, including Semuc Champey, the Laguna Lachuá National Park (see p.302), and a French-owned eco-lodge near the remote Candelaria caves (see p.301), where twenty indigenous families receive over 60 percent of the tour price. Other ecotourism operators are the *Hostal d'Acuña* and *Hostal Doña Victoria*, both of whom run trips to Semuc Champey and other destinations and well as providing travel information.

San Pedro Carchá

A few kilometres away, **SAN PEDRO CARCHÁ** is a smaller version of Cobán, with silver rather than coffee money firing the economy, and a greater percentage of Mayan people. These days the two towns are merging into a single urban sprawl, and many of the buses that go on towards Petén, or even over to Uspantán, leave from Carchá. Some of the Escobar buses from Guatemala City continue to Carchá; others stop at Cobán, in which case you can catch one of the regular shuttle buses between the two. These leave from the terminal in Cobán and from the plaza in Carchá.

In San Pedro Carchá itself the **regional museum** (Mon–Fri 9am–noon & 2–5pm) in a street beside the church, is worth a visit. It houses a collection of Maya artefacts, dolls dressed in local costumes, and a mouldy collection of stuffed birds and animals, including the inevitable moulting quetzal. Another excursion takes you a couple of kilometres from the centre of town to the **Balneario Las Islas**, a stretch of cool water that's popular for swimming and **camping**, though there are no formal facilities. To get here walk along the main street beside the church and take the third turning on the right. Follow this street for about a kilometre, then take the right-hand fork at the end.

If you want **to stay** in Carchá, try the *Pensión Central*, just off the plaza, or the *Hotel La Reforma*, 4 C 8–45 (both ②). For **changing money**, there's a branch of the *Banco del Ejercito* on the plaza (Mon–Fri 9am–1pm & 2.30–5.30pm, Sat 10am–2pm). **Moving on**, buses to local destinations such as Senahú, El Estor, Lanquín and Cahabón leave from the plaza. Two buses a day (at 10am and noon) leave from beside the *bomberos* for **Uspantán** (pausing just above the terminal in Cobán), where you can get connections to Sacapulas, Nebaj and Quiché. They return from Uspantán at 3am and 3.30am.

San Juan Chamelco

A few kilometres southeast of Cobán, easily reached by regular local buses from the terminal, **SAN JUAN CHAMELCO** is the most important Kekchí settlement in the area. Most of your fellow bus passengers are likely to be women dressed in traditional costume, wearing beautiful cascades of old coins for earrings, and speaking Kekchí rather than Spanish. Chamelco's focal point is a large colonial church, whose facade is rather unexpectedly decorated with a Mayan version of the Habsburg double eagle – undoubtedly a result of the historic German presence in the region. Inside, you will find the usual hushed devotional tones and flickering candles around the altars. The most significant treasure, the church bell, is hidden in the belfry; it was a gift to the Indian leader Juan Matalbatz from no less than the Holy Roman Emperor Charles V.

The large market around the church sells anything from local farm produce to blue jeans, but very little in the way of crafts, and the best time to visit the village is for its annual **fiesta**, on June 16. A special feature of the festival is the procession, during which participants dress up in a variety of outfits from pre-Conquest Maya costumes to representations of local wildlife, in celebration of the local Kekchí culture and environment.

If you enjoy Chamelco's peaceful atmosphere, and would like to explore the beautiful countryside, a great **place to stay** is *Don Jeronimo's* (⑤ full board), a vegetarian guest house/retreat run by an eccentric American, who has been living off the land for a good twenty years, and is possibly the only grower of blueberries in Guatemala. You'll find him either by walking 5km from Chamelco to the Aldea Chajaneb, or by catching a bus from outside the *Tienda Maranatha*, on the street running behind the church. Ask to be dropped off at the appropriate footpath.

East to Lanquín, Semuc Champey and beyond

Northeast of Cobán and San Pedro Carchá a rough, badly maintained road heads off into the hills, connecting a string of coffee *fincas*. For the first few kilometres the hills are closed in around the road, but as it drops down into the richer land to the north the valleys open out. Their precipitous sides are patched with cornfields and the level central land is saved for the all-important coffee bushes. As the bus lurches along, clinging to the sides of the ridges, there are fantastic views of the valleys below.

The road divides at the **Pajal** junction (43km and up to three hours by bus from Cobán), where one branch turns north to Sebol and Fray Bartolomé de Las Casas and the other cuts down deep into the valley to **LANQUÍN** (another 12km and 45min). This sleepy, modest Kekchí village, where little Spanish is spoken, shelters beneath towering green hills, whose lower slopes are planted with coffee and cardamom bushes. There's a good, cheap one-stop *hospedaje*-cum-*tienda*-cum-*comedor*, the *Divina Providencia* (①), with good grub, steaming hot showers, and the only cold beers in town. Its clapboard rooms are comfortable enough, though you may hear more of your neighbours' nocturnal pursuits than you would wish. For a touch more luxury, try *Hotel El Recreo*, on the road into the village (☎9522160; fax 9522333; ④), where there's a choice of rooms in wooden huts, a restaurant and a pool, but electricity only between 6pm and 9pm; prices rise at weekends.

The Lanquín caves
Just a couple of kilometres from the village, the **Lanquín caves** are a maze of dripping, bat-infested chambers, stretching for at least 3km underground (daily 8am–noon & 1.30–5pm; Q10). To find them, simply walk along the road heading back to Cobán and turn right along a signposted dirt road which turns off towards the river, five minutes after you pass the *Recreo* hotel. A walkway, complete with ladders and chains, has been cut through the first few hundred metres and electric lights have been installed, which makes access substantially easier, though it remains dauntingly slippery. Before you set out from the village ask in the *municipalidad* if they can turn on the lights, but fix the fee before you set off. It's also well worth dropping by at dusk, when thousands of bats emerge from the mouth of the cave and flutter off into the night. A small car park near the entrance to the caves has a covered shelter where you're welcome to **camp** or sling your hammock.

Semuc Champey
The other attraction around Lanquín, the extraordinary pools at **Semuc Champey** are harder to reach than the caves, but a great deal more spectacular. If you're lucky and there are enough tourists in town, you can catch a pick-up which leaves from outside the *municipalidad* at about 8am, comes back around noon, and costs Q3. Alternatively, you can hire Rigoberto Fernandez's pick-up for a $10 return trip, including two hours at the pools. You can find him in the

unnamed shop painted a vivid green beneath the park in Lanquin. From Cobán, you can book a tour (around $30 per person; see p.295), or take the *Hotel d' Acuña* shuttle bus (Wed & Sat, but only if they have enough people). The hardest option is to walk. It takes around three hours from Lanquín, and can be extremely tough going if the sun is out – take plenty of water. To get there, set out from the village along the gravel road that heads to the south, away from the river. Beyond the houses, this starts to climb back and forth, out of the valley and down into another, then wanders through thick tropical vegetation where bananas, coffee and cardamom plants grow beside scruffy thatched huts. Just as you start to lose hope, the river appears below the road, which heads upstream for a kilometre or so before crossing a suspension bridge. Once you're over the bridge, follow the track uphill for a little way, then bear right and you'll soon come to a car park where you may be asked for $1 entry. Finally, follow the muddy track that brings you, at long last, to the pools.

This staircase of turquoise waters suspended on a natural limestone bridge has a series of idyllic pools in which you can swim – watch out for the odd sharp edge. The bulk of the Río Cahabón runs underground beneath this natural bridge but, if you walk a few hundred metres upstream via a slippery obstacle course of rocks and roots, you can see the aquatic frenzy, where the river plunges into a cavern, cutting under the pools to emerge downstream. If you have a tent or a hammock it makes sense to **stay** the night – there's a thatched shelter, and the altitude is sufficiently low to keep the air warm in the evenings. Be warned, though, it is not safe to leave your belongings unattended.

Beyond Lanquín

Beyond Lanquín the road continues another 24km east to **Cahabón** (which has a basic *pensión*), from where a very rough road heads south to Panzós (see below), cutting high over the mountains through superb scenery. In the unlikely event of the road being in a good enough state of repair, there's an occasional bus between these two places, but normally transport is by pick-ups that carry people and property between the two, though even these are increasingly rare. Another extremely rough trail connects Cahabón with Senahú (see below), which is sometimes negotiable in a four-wheel drive; ask around in Cahabón about current conditions.

Buses leave Cobán daily at 6am, 12.30pm, 1pm & 3pm for Lanquín (3hr), then continue on to Cahabón (4hr). Return buses to Cobán depart from Lanquín at 5am, 7am and 3pm, leaving Cahabón an hour earlier. On Sundays there may only be the 3pm service to Cobán and it will be packed. Buses for **Fray Bartolomé de Las Casas** and **Raxrujá** (see p.301) pass Pajal each morning at around 6.30am and 8.30am.

Down the Polochic valley to Lake Izabal

If you're planning to head out towards the Caribbean from Cobán, or simply interested in taking a short trip along backroads, then the **Polochic valley** is an ideal place to spend the day being bounced around inside a bus. Travelling the length of the valley you witness an immense transformation as you drop down through the coffee-coated mountains and emerge into lush, tropical lowlands. To reach the head of the valley you have to travel south from Cobán along the main road to Guatemala City; shortly after Tactic at the San Julián junction, you leave the luxury of tarmac and head off into the valley. The scenery is pure Alta Verapaz: V-shaped valleys where coffee commands the best land and fields of maize cling to the upper slopes wherever they can. The villages are untidy-looking places where the Kekchí and Pokomchí Maya are largely *ladinized* and seldom wear the brilliant red *huipiles* that used to be traditional here.

The first village at the upper end of the valley is Tamahú, 15km below which the village of Tucurú marks the point where the valley starts to open out and the river loses its frantic energy. High above Tucurú, in the mountains to the north, is the **Chelemá Quetzal Reserve**, a large protected area of pristine cloud forest which contains one of the highest concentrations of quetzals anywhere in the world, not to mention an array of other birds and beasts, including some very vocal howler monkeys. The reserve is extremely difficult to reach and you really need a four-wheel drive to get you up there – if you'd like to drop by for a couple of days, contact the reserve's office in Cobán at 6 Av, Zona 1 (☎9513238), opposite the *Hotel La Paz*.

Beyond Tucurú the road plunges abruptly, with cattle pastures starting to take the place of the coffee bushes, and both the villages and the people have a more tropical look about them. Next comes La Tinta, and then Telemán, the largest of the squalid trading centres in this lower section of the valley.

A side trip to Senahú

From Telemán a side road branches off to the north and climbs high into the lush hills, past row upon row of neatly ranked coffee bushes. As it winds upwards a superb view opens out across the level valley floor below, exposing the river's swirling meanders and a series of oxbows and cut-offs.

Set back behind the first ridge of hills, the small coffee centre of **SENAHÚ** sits in a steep-sided bowl. The village itself is a fairly unremarkable farming settlement, but the setting is spectacular to say the least, and it is the ideal starting point for a short wander in the Alta Verapaz hills. **Buses** connect Senahú and Cobán daily, leaving the terminal in Cobán at 6.30am, 11.30am and 2.30pm; the first bus returns from Senahú at 4pm (always ask the drivers for the latest timetable). Alternatively, you could easily hitch a ride on a truck from Telemán. Senahú boasts a couple of simple *pensiones,* as well as the more comfortable *Hotel Senahú* in the centre of the village, with six pleasant rooms (☎9522160; ④).

Two kilometres to the east of Senahú a gravel road, occasionally served by buses, runs to the *Finca El Volcán,* beyond which you can continue towards Semuc Champey (see above), passing the *Finca Arenal* en route. The walk takes at least three days, and with the uncertainty of local weather conditions you can expect to be regularly soaked, but the dauntingly hilly countryside and the superb fertility of the vegetation make it all worthwhile. The best way to find the route is to hire a guide in Senahú, though you do pass several substantial *fincas* where you can ask directions. Another hike takes you to Cahabón through some equally stunning lush mountain terrain – ask at the *Hotel Senahú* for directions. Sometimes you can make this trip in a four-wheel drive.

Panzós

Heading on down the Polochic valley you reach **PANZÓS**, the largest of the valley villages. Its name means "place of the green waters", a reference to the swamps that surround the river, infested with alligators and bird life. It was here in Panzós that the old Verapaz railway from the Caribbean coast ended, and goods were transferred to boats for the journey across Lake Izabal. These days you have to go all the way to the lakeshore at El Estor to find the ferry. In 1978, Panzós briefly hit international headlines when a group of *campesinos* attending a meeting to settle land disputes were gunned down by the army and local police, in one of the earliest and most brutal massacres of General Lucas García's regime. The day before the atrocity, bulldozers had prepared mass graves at two sites outside the town before the demonstrators even arrived. About a hundred men, women and children were killed, and the event is generally regarded as a landmark in the history of political violence in Guatemala, after which the situation deteriorated rapidly. García's interest in the dispute, however, may have been more personal than political, as he owned 78,000 acres of land in the area around Panzós.

El Estor

Beyond Panzós, the road pushes east towards Lake Izabal. Just before the lakeside town of **EL ESTOR**, it passes a huge and deserted **nickel plant**, yet another monument to disastrous foreign investment. In the mid-1960s, prompted by a chance discovery of high-grade nickel deposits, the International Nickel Company of Canada formed *Exmibal* (*Exploraciones y Explotaciones Mineras de Izabal*), which then built and developed the mine and processing plant. After thirteen years of study and delay the plant opened in 1977, functioned for a couple of years at reduced capacity, and was then shut down as a result of technical problems and the plummeting price of nickel. Today the great, ghost-like structure stands deserted, surrounded by the prefabricated huts that would have housed its workforce. There is, however, some prospect of a revival as the owners of the plant are considering reopening it to mine cobalt from the surrounding hills.

El Estor itself, a kilometre or so beyond the plant, settled back into provincial stupor after the mine closed down, but is now undergoing a revival, at the centre of a regional development boom. Fresh farmlands are being opened up all the time, a new road is due to be completed before the year 2000 to connect the town with the Río Dulce along the north shore of the lake, and oil companies have discovered a large oil field beneath the lake itself. The prospect of oil wells in the lake has prompted a mixed reaction among locals as eager entrepreneurs squabble with environmentalists. Shell, meanwhile, who will operate the rigs, has promised huge compensation should they blacken the water or wipe out a species or two. Shell is by no means the first foreign presence here: the town's name is said to have derived from a local mispronunciation of the name given to it by English pirates, who came up the Río Dulce to buy supplies ("The Store"). These days the only boat that drops by is the **ferry for Mariscos**, which leaves daily at 6am, returning at noon. On the other side it's met by two buses, one to Guatemala City and the other for Puerto Barrios.

Apart from the pool in the plaza, which harbours fish, turtles and alligators, there's not a lot to see in El Estor. However, it does have a friendly, relaxed atmosphere, particularly in the warmth of the evening when the streets are full of activity, and you could easily spend a few days exploring the surrounding area, much of which remains undisturbed. An excellent place for a swim is at **El Boquerón canyon**, in the hills to the east of El Estor; to get there, follow the road to the east of town for 8km. **Bikes** can be rented from 6 Av 4–26, for Q3 an hour, or ask for the owner at *Hugo's Restaurant*, on the main plaza, who will take you there by boat for around $10 a person (minimum two). The delta of the **Río Polochic**, now a wildlife reserve, is also particularly beautiful, a maze of swamp, marsh and forest which is home to alligators, monkeys, tapirs and an abundance of bird life, while the lake itself abounds with fish, including tarpon and snook. The irrepressible Oscar Paz, who runs the *Hotel Vista del Lago* (see below) is an enthusiastic promoter of the area and will arrange a boat and guide to explore any of the surrounding countryside, go fishing in the lake or visit the hot springs at *Finca Paraiso*.

The best **hotel** in El Estor is the *Hotel Vista del Lago* (☎9497205; ②), a beautiful colonial-style wooden building beside the dock, which the owner claims was the original "store" that gave the village its name. All rooms have private bathrooms, and second-floor rooms have superb views of the lake. A little cheaper, but still very pleasant, is the *Hotel Villela*, on 6 Av 2–06 (②), a block up from the *Vista del Lago*, which is surrounded by a beautiful garden and has private showers. Simpler still, the *Hospedaje Santa Clara*, 5 Av 2–11 (☎9487244; ②), has basic, clean rooms, some with their own shower. For a delicious French **meal**, not too expensive, check out *Restaurante El Dios del Sol*, on the eastern side of town, or *Hugo's Restaurant* for fresh fish and delicious grilled meat.

Ten **buses** leave El Estor daily between 1.30am and 3.30pm for the bumpy but beautiful ride to Cobán (8hr); see "Travel Details" on p.305 for details of the return journey.

North towards Petén

In the far northern section of the Alta Verapaz, the lush hills drop away steeply onto the limestone plain that marks the frontier with the department of Petén. The road network here is rough and ready, to say the least, and each year roads return to jungle while others are cut and repaired. Understandably, then, all existing maps of the area are riddled with errors. At present, two roads head north: the first from Cobán via **Chisec**, the second from San Pedro Carchá, via Pajal. From the **Pajal** junction it's a slow, very beautiful journey through typical alpine scenery, a verdant landscape of impossibly green mountains, tiny adobe-built hamlets, pasture and pine forests. After three hours or so of twists and turns you'll reach **Sebol**, a beautiful spot on the Río Pasión where waterfalls cascade into the river and a road heads off for **Fray Bartolemé de las Casas**. For some reason, this small village has been left off most maps but boasts three hotels – the best is *Pensión Ralios* (①) – and buses to San Pedro Carchá (8hr) and Cobán. Back on the main road, the next stop is the small settlement of **Raxrujá**, where the buses from Cobán terminate with only pick-ups and trucks continuing north to **Cruce del Pato** and then on, either up to Sayaxché and Petén or west into the Ixcán.

Raxrujá and the Candelaria caves
RAXRUJÁ (spelt locally Raxruhá), 26km southeast of Cruce del Pato, is the best place to get a pick-up, truck or, if you're very lucky, a bus north to Sayaxché and Flores or west to Playa Grande and the Ixcán. Little more than a few streets and an army base straggling round the bridge over the Río Escondido, a tributary of the Pasión, it has the only **accommodation** for miles around. With buses leaving daily for Cobán at 4am and 8am, you may end up staying at one of the basic *pensiones* in order to get an early start – *Hotel Raxruha*, next to the Texaco garage (①), is the best bet.

The limestone mountains to the west of Raxrujá are full of caves. Some of the best are the **Candelaria caves**, 10km west. The most impressive cave mouths are on pri-

---

THE XAMÁN MASSACRE

Since 1992, communities of refugees, mainly highland Maya, have been settling in pockets of land in the "frontier" country of northern Alta Verapaz. On the whole, the *repatriados*, some of whom have been in exile in Mexico for decades, have reintegrated peacefully, with one notable exception. In 1994 a group of 206 Mam-, Ixil-, Kekchí-, Q'anjobal- and Quiché-speaking Maya families established a settlement in **Xamán**, near Chisec, as part of a government-sponsored programme. A year later, soldiers entered the community and opened fire indiscriminately, killing eleven and wounding thirty others. Both Amnesty International and MINUGUA (the UN Guatemalan peace mission) hold soldiers from Military Barracks Zona 21 responsible for the massacre. Though the Minister of Defence resigned and the Commander of Military Zone 21 was dismissed days after the killing, no-one has yet been brought to trial, despite recent arrests. As so often in these cases, judicial investigations have been thwarted by intimidation and threats against witnesses.

---

vate property, a short walk from the road, jealously guarded by Daniel Dreux who has built the **Complex Cultural de Candelaria** conservation area. Though he also offers wonderful **accommodation** in wooden dorms and a bungalow, the complex is often block-booked by French tour groups, and there's little, if any, chance of getting a place by turning up on spec. Contact STP travel agency in Guatemala City, 2 Av 7–78, Zona 10 (☎3346235), or Epiphyte Adventures in Cobán (see p.295) in advance. Up the hill behind the cabins are some huge cave entrances, though you'll only be allowed to see them as part of a tour. It's also possible to raft or kayak through the caves on the beautiful jade green river but, again, you'll need to organize this with a specialist travel agency in Guatemala City, or through Epiphyte Adventures.

The area beyond Raxrujá, where the rolling foothills of the highlands give way to the flat expanse of southern Petén, is known as the **Northern Transversal Strip** and is the source of much contentious political debate in Guatemala. In the 1970s it was earmarked for development as a possible solution to the need for new farmland and pressures for agrarian reform, but widespread corruption ensured that huge parcels of land, complete with their valuable mineral resources, were dispersed no further than the generals: the land was dubbed "Generals' Strip". Since then oil reserves have been developed around Playa Grande, in the west of the strip and the area has seen heavy fighting between the army and guerrillas.

Playa Grande (Cantabál, Ixcán)

Continuing west from Raxrujá, trucks regularly make the 90km journey over rough roads to **Playa Grande** (6hr or more), a bridging point over the Río Negro. There's nothing here but the bridge, a huge army base and a couple of *comedores*, but it's a loading point for grain travelling downriver, so you might get a boat.

The town formerly known as **PLAYA GRANDE** (also referred to as **CANTABÁL** or **IXCÁN**), 7km west of the river crossing, is an authentic frontier settlement with cheap hotels, rough bars and brothels. It's also the administrative and transport centre of the region. The best **place to stay** is the *Hospedaje Reyna* (①), which is basic but clean and has at least some semblance of a courtyard.

One point of interest in this area is the **Laguna Lachuá National Park**, a beautiful little lake 8km to the east of Playa Grande. Any truck driver will drop you off at the entrance, which is signposted right by the road, and it's a four-kilome-

FIESTAS

The Verapaces are famous for their fiestas, and in Baja Verapaz especially you'll see an unusual range of traditional dances. In addition, Cobán hosts the **National Fiesta of Folklore**, at the start of August, which is attended by indigenous groups from throughout the country.

JANUARY
Rabinal's fiesta, famed for its traditional dances, runs from the 19th to 25th, with the most important events taking place on the 21st. **Tamahú** has a fiesta from the 22nd to 25th, with the 25th being the main day.

MAY
Santa Cruz Verapaz has a fiesta from the 1st to 4th, including the dances of *Los Chuntos*, *Vendos* and *Mamah-Num*. **Tucurú** celebrates from the 4th to 9th, with the main day on the 8th.

JUNE
Senahú has its fiesta from the 9th to 13th, with the main day on the 13th. In **Purulhá** the action is from the 10th to 13th, which is the principal day. **San Juan Chamelco** has a fiesta from the 21st to 24th, in honour of San Juan Bautista. In **San Pedro Carchá** the fiesta is from the 24th to 29th, with the main day on the 29th: here you may witness the dances of *Moros y Cristianos* and *Los Diablos*. **Chisec** has a fiesta from the 25th to 30th; the main day is the 29th.

JULY
Cubulco has a very large fiesta from the 20th to 25th, in honour of Santiago Apostol. Dances include the *Palo Volador*, *Toritos*, *Los 5 Toros* and *El Chico Mudo*, among others. **San Cristóbal Verapaz** has a fiesta from the 21st to 26th, also in honour of Santiago.

AUGUST
The fiesta in **Cobán** lasts from July 31 to August 6, and is immediately followed by the **National Fiesta of Folklore**. **Tactic** has a fiesta from the 11th to 16th, with the main day on the 15th. In **Lanquín** the fiesta runs from the 22nd to 28th, with the last day as the main day. In **Chajal** the fiesta takes place from the 23rd to 28th, and in **Panzós** it lasts from the 23rd to 30th.

SEPTEMBER
Cahabón has a fiesta from the 4th to 8th, with the main day on the 6th. **Salamá** has its fiesta from the 17th to 21st, with the principal day on the 17th. In **San Miguel Chicaj** the fiesta runs from the 25th to 29th, and in **San Jerónimo** it lasts from the 27th right through until October 10.

DECEMBER
Santa Cruz El Chol has a fiesta from the 6th to 8th, with the main day on the 8th.

tre walk from here to the lake. One of the least visited national parks in Central America, this is a beautiful, tranquil spot, the clear, almost circular lake completely surrounded by dense tropical forest. Though it smells slightly sulphurous, the water is good for swimming, with curious horseshoe-shaped limestone formations by the edge that make perfect individual bathing pools. You'll see otters and an abundance of bird life, but watch out for mosquitoes. There's a large thatched *rancho* by the shore, ideal for camping or slinging a hammock (available for rent). Though fireplaces and wood are provided, you'll need to bring food and drinking water. Canoes are also available for rent.

You can get to Playa Grande **from Cobán** on one of the endless streams of trucks setting out from the corner of the bus terminal – a journey of at least eight hours. Heading south **from Sayaxché** you need to catch a bus or pick-up to Playitas via Cruce del Pato and take another pick-up or truck from there. There are also regular flights from the airstrip in Cobán.

Into the Ixcán

The Río Negro marks the boundary between the departments of Alta Verapaz and Quiché; the land to the west is known as the **Ixcán**. This huge swampy forest, some of which was settled in the 1960s and 1970s by peasants migrating from the highlands, became a bloody battleground in the 1980s. In the last few years, the Ixcán has become a focal **repatriado** settlement as refugees who fled to Mexico in the 1980s are resettled in a string of "temporary" camps west of the river. Travelling further west, across the Ixcán and into northern Huehuetenango, though no longer hazardous, is still fairly ardous, taking at least two or three days to get from Playa Grande to Barillas (see p.196). **Veracruz**, 20km (1hr 30min) from Playa Grande, is the first place of note, a *repatriado* settlement at the crossroads beyond the Río Xalbal. Some buses continue to Mayalan, 12km away, across the presently unbridged Río Piedras Blancas. Here the road ends and you'll have to walk the next 15km to **Altamirano** on the far bank of the Río Ixcán – if you're in good shape it'll take about four or five hours. The path is easy to follow, and passes several tiny villages. At the last village, **Rancho Palmeras**, ask for directions to the crossing point on the Ixcán, where boys will pole you across the flowing river. Once across, Altamirano is still a few kilometres away up the hill. From here a regular flow of trucks make the thirty-kilometre journey to Barillas, taking at least four hours over some of the worst roads in the country. It's a spectacular journey, though, especially as you watch the growing bulk of the Cuchumatanes rising ever higher on the horizon. You can also get trucks over the border into **Mexico**, taking you to Chajul on the Río Lacantún in Chiapas, but you need a Guatemalan exit stamp first, probably best obtained in Cobán or Flores.

travel details

BUSES

Baja Verapaz

Transportes Dulce María, 19 C 9 Av, Zona 1, Guatemala City (☎2500082), runs hourly buses from **Guatemala City to Cubulco** (5hr 30min) via **Salamá** (3hr 30min) and **Rabinal** (4hr 30min) between 5am and 5pm, returning hourly from Cubulco to the capital between 1.30am and 2pm.

A daily bus from **Guatemala City to Cubulco via El Chol** leaves the Zona 4 terminal at about 4am, and from Cubulco on the return journey at 9am (about 9hr).

Heading for Baja Verapaz **from Cobán** or from Guatemala City you can also take any bus between Cobán and the capital (see below) and get off at **La Cumbre** (de Santa Elena) from where minibuses run to Salamá.

Alta Verapaz

Cobán to El Estor (around 8hr). Buses leave daily from the terminal in Cobán at 4am, 5am, 6.30am, 8am, 8.30am, 10.30am, 11.30am, 12.30pm, 1pm, 2pm and 3pm. For the return journey, ten buses leave El Estor daily between 1.30am and 3.30pm.

Cobán to Guatemala City (4–5hr). First-class pullman services (hourly 4am–5pm) calling at all points in between including the Biotopo and Tactic, are run by the efficient Transportes Escobar y Monja Blanca, at 8 Av 15–16, Zona 1, Guatemala City (☎2324949), and at 2 C 3–77, Zona 4, Cobán (☎9521536 or 9521498). Return journeys from Cobán to Guatemala City leave hourly (2.30am–4pm).

Cobán to Tactic (40min) and **San Cristóbal Verapaz** (30min). Hourly from the terminal (see p.293) or take any bus bound for Guatemala City.

Cobán to Senahú (around 7hr). Departures from the terminal leave at 6.30am, 11.30am and 2.30pm. From Senahú to Cobán the first bus leaves at 4am, but you should always check these the night before.

San Pedro Carchá to Uspantán (5hr). Two daily at 10am and noon. From Uspantán there's a connecting bus to Santa Cruz del Quiché, which passes through Sacapulas, for connections to Nebaj. Buses for San Pedro Carchá and Cobán leave Uspantán at 3am and 3.30am.

San Pedro Carchá to Fray Bartolomé de Las Casas (7hr). Daily buses leave from 6am, with an occasional extra service at midday. The first return bus leaves Las Casas for Carchá at 6am.

San Pedro Carchá to Raxrujá (9hr). Two departures daily at 6am and 8am to Raxrujá, from where there are pick-ups to **Sayaxché**. If you miss the morning Raxrujá buses, take a bus to Las Casas, get off at Sebol and get a pick-up from there.

San Pedro Carchá to Cahabón (4hr). Four buses leave daily at 6am, 12.30pm, 1pm and 3pm, passing through **Lanquín** (3hr). The return buses leave Cahabón for San Pedro Carchá and Cobán at 4am, 6am and 2pm, reaching Lanquín a hour later.

CHAPTER SIX

PETÉN

T he vast northern department of **Petén** occupies about a third of
Guatemala but contains less than three percent of its population. This
huge expanse of swamps, dry savannahs and tropical rain forest forms
part of an untamed wilderness that stretches into the Lacandon forest of
southern Mexico and across the Maya Mountains to Belize. Totally unlike any
other part of the country, much of it is virtually untouched, with ancient ceiba and
mahogany trees that tower 50m above the forest floor. Undisturbed for so long,
the area is also extraordinarily rich in **wildlife**. Some 285 species of bird have
been sighted at Tikal alone, including a wide range of hummingbirds, toucans,
blue and white herons, hawks, buzzards, wild turkeys, motmot (a bird of paradise) and even the elusive quetzal, revered since Maya times. Many of these can

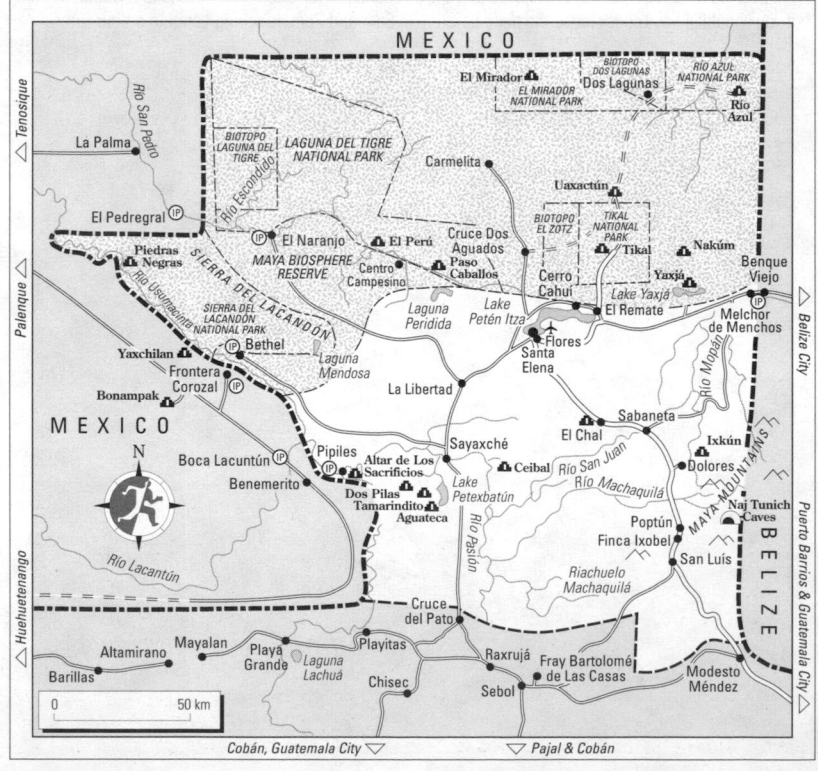

be seen quite easily in the early morning and evening, when their cries fill the air. Beneath the forest canopy lurk many other species that are harder to locate. Among the mammals are the massive tapir or mountain cow, ocelots, deer, coat-is, jaguars, monkeys, plus crocodiles and thousands of species of plants, snakes, insects and butterflies.

Recently, however, this position of privileged isolation has been threatened by moves to colonize the country's final frontier. Waves of **settlers**, lured by offers of free land, have cleared enormous tracts of jungle, while oil exploration and commercial logging have brought with them mountains of money and machinery, cutting new roads deep into the forest. The population of Petén, in 1950 just 15,000, is today estimated at 350,000, a number which puts enormous pressure on the remaining forest. Various attempts have been made to halt the tide of destruction and in 1990 the government declared that forty percent of Petén would be protected by the **Maya Biosphere Reserve**, although little is done to enforce this. In late 1997 a new campaign to highlight the threat to the remaining jungle was launched with support from the likes of Bianca Jagger, and backed by President Arzú, though how effective this will be remains to be seen.

The Petén rain forests also provided shelter for some of Guatemala's guerrilla armies, in particular the FAR (Rebel Armed Forces) during the civil war. This led to many of the settlers being driven across the border into Mexico and becoming refugees, while the oil industry, too, had to withdraw from some of the worst-hit areas. Today most of the refugees have returned, though there are still small pockets of tension in the region. Many disputes are over land rights, with Belizean troops evicting Guatemalan *campesinos* from the disputed border area and mass occupations of privately owned *fincas* by peasant groups. Drug traffickers have also moved into Petén to set up marijuana plantations and fly cocaine in from South American to the region's remote airstrips.

The new interest in the region is in fact something of a reawakening, as Petén was once the heartland of the **Maya civilization**, which reached here from the highlands some 2500 years ago. More than 200 Maya sites have been reported in the Petén area: many of them completely buried in the jungle, and some known only to locals. Here Maya culture reached the height of its architectural, scientific and artistic achievement during the Classic period, roughly 300–900 AD. Great cities rose out of the forest, surrounded by smaller satellite centres and acres of raised and irrigated fields. Tikal and El Mirador are among the largest and most spectacular of all **Maya ruins** – Tikal alone has some 3000 buildings – but they represent only a fraction of what was once here. At the close of the tenth century the cities were mysteriously abandoned, and many of the people moved north to the Yucatán where Maya civilization continued to flourish until the twelfth century.

THE MAYA BIOSPHERE RESERVE

The idea behind biosphere reserves, conceived in 1974 by UNESCO, is an ambitious attempt to combine the protection of natural areas and the conservation of their genetic diversity with scientific research and sustainable development. The **Maya Biosphere Reserve**, created in 1990, covers 16,000 square kilometres of northern Petén: in theory it is the largest tropical forest reserve in Central America.

On the premise that conservation and development can be compatible, land use in the reserve has three designations: **core areas** include the national parks, major archeological sites and the *biotopos*, areas of scientific investigation. The primary role of core areas is to preserve biodiversity; human settlements are prohibited though tourism is permitted. Surrounding the core areas are **multiple use areas** where inhabitants, aided and encouraged by the government and NGOs, are able to engage in sustainable use of the forest resources and small-scale agriculture. The **buffer zone**, a fifteen-kilometre wide belt along the southern edge of the reserve, is intended to prevent further human intrusion while containing many existing villages.

Fine in theory, particularly when you consider that much of the northern reserve skirts the Calakmul Biosphere Reserve in Mexico and that protected land in Belize forms much of the reserve's eastern boundary. In practice, however, the destruction of Petén's **rain forest** proceeds virtually unchecked. Less than fifty percent of the original cover remains and illicit logging, often conducted from Mexico with the complicity of Guatemalan officials, is reducing it further. Although the soil is thin, poor migrant families from Guatemala's agriculturally impoverished southeastern departments arrive daily to carve out *milpa* – slash-and-burn – holdings in the sparsely settled buffer and multiple-use zones. Oil extraction takes place in core areas in the northwest and new roads are being built. Some areas of the reserve are being allocated for *repatriado* – returning refugee – settlement, causing acrimony between those government departments whose task is to assist the refugees and those whose job it is to protect the reserve.

Although alarming and very real, the threats to the integrity of the reserve are being tackled by a number of government agencies and NGOs, both Guatemalan and international. Foreign funding, from aid programmes and conservation organizations, provides much of the finance for protection, and people living in remote villages realize that their future depends on sustainable use of forest resources. Tourism is an accepted part of the plan and, though most visitors see little outside Tikal and Flores, a trip to the more remote *biotopos* and national parks is possible as guides and the basic infrastructure become more organized.

By the time the Spanish arrived the area had been partially recolonized by the Itzá, a group of Toltec-Maya (originally from the Yucatán) who inhabited the land around Lake Petén Itzá. The forest proved so impenetrable that it wasn't brought under Spanish control until 1697, more than 150 years after they had conquered the rest of the country. Although the Itzá resisted persistent attempts to Christianize them, their lakeside capital was eventually conquered and destroyed by Martín de Ursúa and his army, thus bringing about the defeat of the last independent Maya tribe. The Spanish had little enthusiasm for Petén, though, and under their rule it remained a backwater, with nothing to offer but a steady trickle of chicle – the basic ingredient of chewing gum, which is bled from sapodilla trees. Independence saw no great change, and it wasn't until 1970 that Petén became genuinely accessible by car. Even today the network of roads is skeletal, and many routes are impassable in the wet season.

The hub of the department is **Lake Petén Itzá** where the three adjacent towns of **Flores**, **Santa Elena** and **San Benito** together form the only settlement of any size. You'll probably arrive here, if only to head straight out to the ruins of **Tikal**, Petén's prime attraction. But the town is also the starting point for buses to the **Belize border** and for **routes to Mexico** along the Río San Pedro and the Río Usumacinta from Bethel. Arriving from Belize it's probably better to base yourself at the small lakeside village of **El Remate**, halfway between Flores and Tikal. If you plan to reach any of the more distant ruins – **El Mirador**, **Yaxjá**, **Nakúm** or **Río Azul** – then Flores is again the place to be based. To the south is **Sayaxché**, surrounded by yet more Maya sites including **Ceibal**, which boasts some of the best preserved carvings in Petén. From Sayaxché you can set off down the Río Pasión to **Mexico** and the ruins of **Yaxchilán**, or take an alternative route back to Guatemala City – via Cobán in Alta Verapaz.

Getting to Petén

Most visitors arrive in Petén by bus or plane directly **from Guatemala City**: by air it's a short fifty-minute hop; by bus it can take anywhere between ten and twenty hours and is a gruelling experience, despite the recent upgrading of the road between Río Dulce and Flores.

Air tickets can be bought from any travel agent in Guatemala City, Antigua, Panajachel or Quetzaltenango. You can also get them direct from the airline but this is a great deal more expensive. Four domestic airlines – Aerovias, Avcom, TAPSA, Tikal Jets – and the national airline, Aviateca, fly daily to Petén. The domestic airlines depart from their offices inside the airport perimeter (entrance on Av Hincapie). Aviateca departs from the **international side** – make sure your taxi driver knows which flight you're on. Flights depart at 6.30am and 7am and *Aviateca* also has an afternoon flight at 5.30pm. Although cut-throat competition between the airlines means that return tickets currently cost around a bargain $60 or so, many flights are heavily in demand and overbooking is common. Of the domestic carriers Tikal Jets offers the best service and has the largest craft; it also has a connection in Flores with Tropic Air of Belize. Aviateca and Aerocaribe have connections from Flores to Cancún, the latter via Chetumal.

Buses from Guatemala City **to Flores** are run by six companies, all operating from a sleazy and dangerous part of Zona 1 between 16 and 17 calles and 8 and 10 avenidas. Between them they operate around twenty buses a day, all of which pass Río Dulce (for **Lívingston**) bridge after about five hours on a fast paved road. The best buses are the extremely comfortable pullmans run by Linea Dorada which leave daily from 16 C 10–55, Zona 1, at 7pm (10hr), though as the price is around $22 one-way you may prefer to fly. If you want a reasonably comfortable ride, try Fuente del Norte (☎2513817) and Maxima (☎2324684), both of which run decent buses, from the corner of 9 Av and 17 C for $12 one-way (10–12hr). Fares are about forty percent cheaper on the standard *corriente* services, but the journey takes between fourteen and eighteen hours.

Coming from the **highlands**, you can get to Petén along the backroads from Cobán in Alta Verapaz, a long, exhausting and adventurous route covered in more detail on p.301. You can also enter Guatemala **from Belize** or **Mexico** via Petén. The most obvious route is from Belize, through the border at Melchor de Mencos (see p.345), but there are also two river routes that bring you through from Palenque (see p.339) or Tenosique (see p.342) in Mexico.

Guatemala City to Flores

If you don't want to do the 554-kilometre trip from the capital to Flores in one go, it's easy enough to do it in stages. Just past the village of **El Lobo**, *La Ceiba* (②), at Km 175, 100m east of the Río Lobo bridge, is a friendly, relaxing place to break the journey, run by an English-Guatemalan couple. Offering good food, budget rooms and camping on the banks of the river, it's ideal if you're visiting the Quiriguá ruins (see p.237). Most buses make a stop in **Morales** on the Caribbean Highway (see p.240). Shortly afterwards, the road to Petén turns north at the **Ruidosa junction**, soon crossing the **Río Dulce** at the stopping-off place for the boat to Lívingston. From here it continues through Modesto Méndez and on through San Luís to **Poptún**, about 100km short of Flores and the best place to break the trip. Alternatively, you could fly to Poptún from Guatemala City with Koppsa (☎3606354).

Finca Ixobel

A couple of kilometres walk south of Poptún is the *Finca Ixobel* (☎9277363) a working farm that provides **accommodation** to tourists. The farm was originally operated by Americans Mike and Carole DeVine, but on June 8, 1990, Mike was murdered by the army. This prompted the American government to suspend military aid to Guatemala, and after a drawn-out investigation, which cast little light on their motives, five soldiers were convicted of the murder in September 1992. Two others have managed to evade capture and their commanding officer, Captain Hugo Contreras, escaped from jail shortly after his arrest. Carole remains in Guatemala running the *finca*, having fought the case for years, while recent revelations hint that the CIA knew in advance of a plot to kill her husband. The *finca* remains as popular as ever – record occupancy is now well over a hundred, with latecomers bedding down in hammocks in *champas*, large circular thatched huts.

In the cool foothills of the Maya Mountains, surrounded by lush pine forests, *Finca Ixobel* is a beautiful and relaxing place, where you can swim in the pond, walk in the forest, dodge the parrot attacks and stuff yourself with delicious home-grown food. They arrange four-day hikes into the jungle, plus horse-riding, rafting, four-wheel drive jungle trips, and short excursions to nearby caves, though you should check the current security situation with *finca* staff, since an armed attack on a group visiting the caves in late 1997. The *finca* has attractive bungalows with private bathrooms (④), rooms (②), dorms, camping and hammock space, and tree houses (②). The latter are very popular, although only one is actually in a tree: the rest are on high stilts among the pines. You run up a tab for accommodation, food and drink, paying when you leave – which can be a rude awakening. To get to the *finca* ask the bus driver to drop you at the gate (marked by a large sign), from where it's a walk of about 1km through the pine trees.

Poptún and around

The dusty frontier town of **POPTÚN** makes a useful stop off on the way to Flores, with a Telgua office, banks, and several *pensiones*. The best is the friendly *Hotel Posada de los Castellanos*, in the centre of town (☎9277222; fax 9277365; ②), where all rooms have hot water and a bathroom, with the nearby *Pensión Izalco* (①) being a decent second choice. The best food in town is at the *Fonda Ixobel 2*, which serves good bread and cakes, or the *Comedor los Claveles*.

The limestone hills surrounding Poptún are riddled with **caves** and coated in lush tropical forest. The largest cave contains an underground river and waterfall that you can swim through, if you don't mind leaping into a chilly pool in total darkness. The most impressive, however, is the remote **Naj Tunich** (Stone House) near the Belizean border, which was discovered in 1980. Unfortunately it's difficult to see the wonders within, as it has been officially closed to visitors since being severely vandalized in 1989, though it may reopen again soon. Its walls are decorated with extensive hieroglyphic texts (400 glyphs in total) and **Maya murals**, which, in addition to depictions of religious ceremonies and ball games, include several graphic and well-preserved drawings of erotic scenes, a feature found nowhere else in Maya art. Caves were sacred to the ancient Maya, who believed them to be entrances to Xibalba, the dreaded underworld. The glyphs and pottery found here all date to a relatively short period from 733 to 762 AD. If you're very keen to visit Naj Tunich, ask around at the *Finca Ixobel*, or check with Carlos at the *Villa de las Castellanos* (see below), who will have the latest information and can organize a four-wheel drive excursion.

Four kilometres north of Poptún, just past the village of **Machaquilá**, is *Cocay Camping* (①), set in peaceful isolation on the banks of the river. It's run by Christina and Paco, former employees at the *Finca Ixobel*, who offer very simple huts, camping, and vegetarian and European food. Get off the bus at the south side of the river bridge and follow the signs west for ten minutes. Over the bridge to the right, attractively set in a patch of forest, are the new *cabañas* of the *Villa de los Castellanos* (☎9277541; fax 9277542; ⑤, but ask about the special backpacker rates), which offer a comfortable base for adventurous visitors to explore the forests, rivers and caves of central Petén. Carlos, the owner, is also an excellent source of information, botanical, historical and logistical. One amazing five-day horseback trip heads west through an area seldom visited by outsiders, across the Machaquilá Forest Reserve, camping at San Miguel caverns and the ruins of Machaquilá, before descending the Río Pasión to Ceibal (see p.355).

Dolores and El Chal

Most buses call in at the village of **Dolores**, set back from the road about 20km north of Poptún. Founded in 1708 as an outpost for missionaries working out of Cobán, these days it's a growing town and the area around is becoming settled by returning refugees. An hour's walk to the north are the unrestored Maya ruins of **Ixkún**, a mid-sized site made up of eight plazas. Fifteen kilometres north of Dolores a road branches northeast at the village of Sabaneta, making a short cut to the **Belize border**. Some buses from Guatemala to Melchor use this route, though it's liable to flooding and often in bad condition.

A further 30km brings you to the ruins of **El Chal**, signed on the west side of the village of the same name, and less than 500m from the road. Call in at the small hut by the entrance to the ruins for a free tour with the guard. The ruins include several plazas and a ball court, and the palace complex, built on a ridge, gives a view of the surrounding countryside. Although some bush has been cleared, the buildings are largely unrestored – the most remarkable features are a couple of stelae and nearby altars with clearly visible glyphs and carved features. If you need **to stay**, there are a couple of basic hotels in the village, the *Medina* and the *Bienestar* (both ①).

Flores

Although it's the capital of Petén, **FLORES** is an easy-going, sedate place with an old-fashioned atmosphere, quite unlike most towns in the region where commerce and bustle dominate. A cluster of cobbled streets and ageing houses built around a twin-domed church, it sits beautifully on a small island in Lake Petén Itzá, connected to the mainland by a causeway. The modern emphasis lies across the water in the twin towns of **SANTA ELENA** and **SAN BENITO**, both of which are ugly, chaotic and sprawling towns, dusty in the dry season and mud-bound during the rains. Santa Elena, opposite Flores at the other end of the causeway, is strung out between the airport and the market, and takes in several hotels, the offices of the bus companies, and a well-established residential area. San Benito, further west, is at the forefront of the new frontier, complete with rough bars, villains, prostitutes, sleazy hotels and mud-lined streets. The three once distinct towns are now often lumped together under the single name of Flores.

The **lake** is a natural choice for settlement, and its shores were heavily populated in Maya times. The city of **Tayasal**, capital of the Itzá, lay on the island that was to become modern Flores. Cortes passed through here in 1525, on his way south to Honduras, and left behind a sick horse which he promised to send for. In 1618 two Franciscan friars arrived to find the people worshipping a large white idol in the shape of a horse called "Tzimin Chac", the thunder horse. Unable to persuade the Indians to renounce their religion they smashed the idol and left the city. Subsequent visitors were less well received; in 1622 a military expedition of twenty men was invited into the city by Canek, chief of the Itzá, where they were set upon and sacrificed to the idols. The town was eventually destroyed by Martín de Ursúa and an army of 235 in 1697. The following year the island was fortified in order to be used as an outpost of the Spanish Empire on the Camino Real (Royal Road) to Campeche. For the entire colonial period (and indeed up to the 1960s) Flores languished in virtual isolation, having more contact with neighbouring Belize than the capital.

Today, despite the steady flow of tourists passing through for Tikal, the town retains a genteel air, with residents greeting one another courteously as they meet in the streets. Though it has little to detain you in itself – a leisurely thirty-minute stroll around the cobbled streets and alleyways is enough to become entirely familiar with the place – Flores does offer the most pleasant surroundings in which to stay, eat and drink.

Arrival

Arriving by bus from Guatemala City you'll be dropped on or near C Principal in Santa Elena, just a few blocks from the causeway to Flores. Coming from the Belize border on Pinita you'll probably be dropped at the *Hotel San Juan*, round the corner from the causeway. The **airport** is 3km east of the causeway; a $2 taxi-ride from town. **Local buses**, known here as *urbanos,* cover the route for Q0.50, but this entails a time-consuming change halfway. These buses also run across the causeway about every ten minutes. Getting **back** to the airport, local buses leave from the Flores end of the causeway about every twenty minutes.

Information

The knowledgeable staff at the **Inguat** desk in the arrivals hall at the airport (Mon–Sat 6–10am & 3–6pm – sometimes also on Sun) can give you reasonable

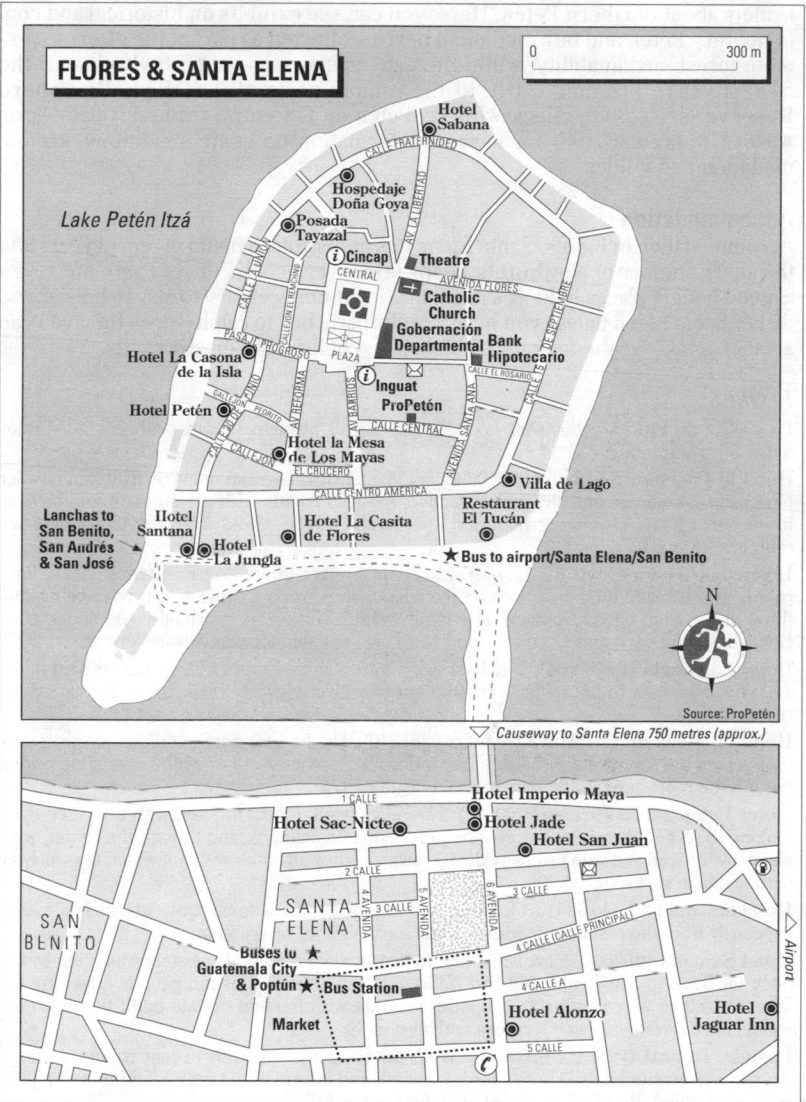

FLORES & SANTA ELENA

Lake Petén Itzá

Hotel Sabana

Hospedaje Doña Goya

Posada Tayazal

i Cincap

Theatre

Catholic Church

Gobernación Departmental

Bank Hipotecario

Hotel La Casona de la Isla

i Inguat ProPetén

Hotel Petén

Hotel la Mesa de Los Mayas

Villa de Lago

Restaurant El Tucán

Lanchas to San Benito, San Andrés & San José

Hotel Santana

Hotel La Jungla

Hotel La Casita de Flores

★ Bus to airport/Santa Elena/San Benito

N

Source: ProPetén

▽ *Causeway to Santa Elena 750 metres (approx.)*

Hotel Imperio Maya

1 CALLE

Hotel Sac-Nicte

Hotel Jade

Hotel San Juan

2 CALLE

SAN BENITO

SANTA ELENA

3 AVENIDA

4 AVENIDA

5 AVENIDA

6 AVENIDA

3 CALLE

Airport ▷

Buses to Guatemala City & Poptún ★

★ Bus Station

4 CALLE (CALLE PRINCIPAL)

4 CALLE A

Market

Hotel Alonzo

Hotel Jaguar Inn

5 CALLE

maps and information, as well as the useful free listings magazine, *Petén*. There's another Inguat office on the central plaza in Flores (Mon–Fri 8am–4pm; ☎9260669), whose staff are helpful but will probably direct you across the plaza to **CINCAP** (*Centro de Información sobre la Naturaleza, Cultura y Artesanías de Petén*; Tues–Sat 9am–1pm & 2–8pm, Sun 2–6pm), in the *Castillo de Arismendi*, to examine their more detailed maps, books and leaflets about northern Petén. Here, you can see exhibits on historical and contemporary Petén and buy medicinal herbs, collected as part of the effort to promote forest sustainability, while the café upstairs has superb views over the lake. If you're planning a trip to the remote parts of the **Maya Biosphere Reserve** (see p.308), check with ProPetén on C Central (Mon–Fri 8am–5pm; ☎9261370; fax 9260495) for current information on route conditions, accommodation and guides.

Accommodation

Accommodation in Flores/Santa Elena has undergone a boom in recent years and the sheer number of new **hotels** keeps prices very competitive. There are several good budget places in Flores itself, making it unnecessary to stay in noisier and dirtier Santa Elena unless you have a really early bus to catch – even then you can arrange a taxi. All the top-range hotels listed below take **credit cards**.

FLORES

La Casita de Flores (☎3600000; fax 9260032). Small, attractive rooms and very good rates in the low season. ③.

Hotel la Casona de la Isla (☎9260692; fax 9260593). An arresting citrus fruit and powder blue paint job on the outside, and attractive, modern rooms with private bath and air/con inside. Also has a swimming pool and spectacular sunset views from the terrace restaurant/bar. ⑤.

Hospedaje Doña Goya (no phone). Excellent budget guest house, offering clean, light rooms with fan, and the best prices on the island. Some rooms come with private baths, and those at the front have balconies. The family who run it are very friendly and speak good English, some Dutch and German; good rates are available for single travellers. ②.

Hotel La Jungla (☎9260634). The best value in this price range, with gleaming tiled floors and private baths with hot water. A rooftop *mirador* gives views over the town and lake. Good restaurant. ③.

Hotel La Mesa de Los Maya (☎ & fax 9261240). The hotel is a new addition to the restaurant, which is a longstanding Flores institution. It's a pleasant place with reasonable prices, though the rooms are a little dark and old-fashioned. ④.

Hotel Petén (☎9260593; fax 9260692). Friendly, small, modern hotel, with a terrace overlooking the lake. It's run by the ever-helpful Pedro Castellanos, and though the rooms are a shade overpriced and won't win any design awards, they all come with hot water, fans, private bath and lake views. ⑤.

Hotel Sabana (☎ & fax 9261248). Large, modern place with a small pool and nice lake views, especially from the restaurant. Some rooms have air-con, all are good value. ④.

Hotel Santana (☎9260492; fax 9260662). Recently modernized, three-storey building by the dock for boats to San Benito and San Andrés. It has a small pool and patio overlooking the lake, as well as very comfortable, spotless rooms with fan and private bath; the first floor rooms have private lakeside terraces and air-con. ⑤.

Posada Tayazal (☎ & fax 9260568). Well-run budget hotel, with decent rooms, some of which have private baths. There's a roof terrace and information service, and tours to Tikal can be arranged. Best budget option if *Doña Goya* is full. ②.

Villa del Lago (☎ 9260629; fax 9260508). Modern, two-storey building with pretty, comfortable rooms – granny would like the flowery decor. The small breakfast terrace at the rear is a great place to enjoy the sunrise. ②.

SANTA ELENA

Hotel Alonzo, 6 Av 4–99 (☎9260105). A new budget hotel with clean rooms. Some have balconies, and a few come with private bathrooms, though the communal bathroom is a little grubby. There's a public telephone and a reasonable restaurant, and it's on the Fuente del Norte bus route. ②.

Hotel Imperio Maya, 6 Av & 1 C. Cleanish, street-level rooms with fan, right by the causeway to Flores. ①.

Hotel Jade, 6 Av. A shambolic, backpackers' stronghold, but the cheapest beds in town. ①.

Hotel Jaguar Inn, Calzada Rodríguez Macal 8–79 (☎9260002). Comfortable rooms with choice of air-con or fan, but situated a little out of town near the airport. ④.

Hotel Sac-Nicte, 1 C 4–45 (☎ & fax 9260092). Clean rooms with fans and private shower; those on the second floor have views of the lake. The flexible owners will serve breakfast before the 4am trip to Tikal. ②.

Hotel San Juan, 2 C & 6 Av, a block from the causeway (☎ & fax 9260042). Doubles as the Pinita bus terminal and travel agent, organizing trips to Tikal, but it's not particularly good value, and is distinctly unfriendly. Most guests are captives straight off the Pinita bus; head elsewhere if you can, as it's very noisy with buses in the early morning. Some air-con rooms, and some with bath. ②.

Eating and drinking

Good, cheap places to eat are in short supply in Santa Elena and Flores, although a couple of good restaurants cater specifically to tourists. Flores boasts a handful of **comedores**, and a number of **cafés** on the main square and in the surrounding streets.

FLORES

La Canoa, C Centro America. Popular, good value place, serving pasta, great soups, and some vegetarian and Guatemalan food, as well as excellent breakfasts.

The Chaltunhá, opposite *Hotel Santana*, right on the water. Great spot for lunch, snacks and sandwiches, and not too expensive.

Café-Bar Gran Jaguar, Central Plaza. Flores' most popular café.

Restaurant Gran Jaguar, Av Barrios. Guatemalan restaurant geared up for tourists. Good value complete meals include soup, salad, tea, coffee and a pastry.

Jungla, a couple of blocks left of the causeway. The *Mesa*'s chief rival: a little cheaper but a lot less interesting.

El Kóbena, across the street from the *Tucán*. Small restaurant serving everything from breakfast to *enchiladas*.

La Mesa de los Maya, see hotel listings above. International and Guatemalan food, with local specialities such as armadillo, wild turkey, deer and local river fish.

Pizzeria Picasso, across the street from the *Tucán*, next door to *El Kóbena*. Run by the same family as the *Tucán*, serving great pizza under cooling breezes from the ceiling fans.

Las Puertas, signed off C Santa Ana. Paint-splattered walls, live music and some very good pasta and healthy breakfasts. Worth it for the atmosphere.

Hotel Santana, see hotel listings above. The usual mix of meat, pasta and fish dishes.

El Tucán, a few metres east of the causeway, on the waterfront. Excellent fish, enormous chef's salads, very good Mexican food and the best waterside terrace in Flores.

Vegetarianos, further along the street from *El Kóbena*. Uninspired veggie food in a *comedor*-style setting.

SANTA ELENA

Restaurant los Amigos, 6 Av, opposite Telgua. Santa Elena's best restaurant, with a fairly extensive menu that caters for vegetarians.

Restaurant Leo Fu Lo, next door to the *Hotel Jade*. Delicious, but expensive Chinese food.

Restaurant Petenchel, 2 C, beyond *Hotel San Juan*, past the park. Simple, good food: the nicest place to eat around the main street. You can leave your luggage here while checking on buses or looking for a room.

Listings

Banks Banks in Flores – try Banco de Guatemala or Bank Hipotecario – only change travellers' cheques. The best place for changing cash is Banora (Mon–Sat 8.30am–8pm), on 4 C in Santa Elena. For credit card cash advances, use Banco Industrial, 4 C in Santa Elena for Visa (they also have a 24-hour ATM), and Banco G&T, on the main road between Santa Elena and San Benito (Mon–Fri 9am–8pm, Sat 10am–2pm) for Mastercard. Otherwise, Flores and Santa Elena are full of sharks offering to change money, often at poor rates.

Bike rental Cahuí, 30 de Junio, Flores (daily 7am–7pm; ☎ & fax 9260494) rents bikes for Q5 an hour.

Car rental Several firms, including Budget, Hertz, San Juan and Koka, operate from the airport. Hertz also has an office in the *Hotel Tziquinaha*, on the airport road, and San Juan in the *Hotel San Juan* in Santa Elena. All offer cars, minibuses and jeeps, with prices starting at around $70 a day for a jeep.

MOVING ON FROM FLORES

All the Guatemala City **bus companies** have offices on C Principal in Santa Elena, and there are more than twenty departures daily to the capital. As a rule the more comfortable buses leave in the evening, with Fuente del Norte (☎9260517) having a good number of departures, but Linea Dorada (☎9260070), which also has an office in Flores, is the very best, leaving at 7.30pm every evening. For travel **around Péten** Rosita, Pinita, and Del Rosio have basic buses, which are always crowded. The latter two hike their rates for tourists, so before buying a ticket be sure to pick up the list of regulated fares at Inguat or CINCAP; it also details departure times. It's best to get on Pinita buses in the market, as they are often full by the time they pass the San Juan hotel.

Travelling on **to Belize**, Pinita buses leave for the border at Melchor de Mencos at 5am, 8am and 11am. Rosita, departing from the market in Santa Elena, runs buses at 5am, 7am, 9.30am, 11am, 2pm 3pm and 6pm. Mundo Maya operates an air-con express service leaving daily at 5am, which gets to Belize City at 10am and continues to the **Mexican border** at Chetumal for connections north to Cancún – this service is about three times more expensive than the public bus but very much faster and more comfortable. For **Naranjo** (and **boats** to La Palma, Mexico), Pinita buses leave at 5am, 8am, 11am, 1pm and 2pm, and Del Rosio services at 11.30 and 2.30pm (5hr). Along with the regular stream of minibuses that **Tikal** run by almost every hotel in Flores and Santa Elena (1hr 30min; $3.50), there's a daily service run by Pinita leaving at 1pm (2hr) and continuing on to Uaxactún. Pinita also runs buses to **Bethel**, on the Río Usumacinta at 5am and 1pm (4hr), **San Andrés** at 7am, 8am, noon and 1pm, and **Sayaxché** (2hr) at 6am, 9am, 10am, 1pm and 4pm; Del Rosio buses also leave for Sayaxché at 5am and noon. If you're heading for **Cobán**, there are currently no buses via Raxrujá so you'll have to head for Cruce del Pato (4hr 30min) on Del Rosio's 5am bus for Playitas via Sayaxché, and hitch south from Cruce del Pato on a series of pick-ups.

Tickets for **flights** to Guatemala City can be bought at the airport, at hotels *San Juan* and *Petén*, or at any of the travel agents in Santa Elena and Flores. Other flights include the Aviateca service to Cancún (daily 5pm), Tropic Air to Belize City (Mon–Fri 9.30am & 4.30pm), and Aerocaribe to Cancún via Chetumal (Mon–Fri 5.30pm).

For details on getting to **Mexico** along the Río San Pedro, see p.342.

Doctor Centro Medico Maya, 2 Av & 4 C (☎9260180), by the *Hotel Diplomatico* in Santa Elena, are helpful and professional, though no English is spoken.

Email There are two places in Flores where you can send messages: *C@fénet* on Av Barrios (daily 9am–9pm), and *Arpa* on C Centro America. Make sure you see the messages sent yourself, as there have been instances of email not getting through.

Language school The Eco-Escuela in San Andrés offers individual tuition in a classroom overlooking the lake; see p.318.

Laundry Try Lavandería Amelia, behind CINCAP in Flores, or Petenchel, on the street that encircles Flores (both $3 to wash and dry).

Phone and faxes The Telgua office is on 5 C in Santa Elena, but you're better off using one of the private telephone and fax services; try *Hotel Alonzo*, 6 Av in Santa Elena or, Cahuí, 30 de Junio in Flores (daily 7am–7pm; ☎ & fax 9260494), which is also a good place to leave messages and pick up information.

Post office In Flores it's two doors away from the Inguat office; in Santa Elena it's on 2 C & 7 Av, two blocks east of the *Hotel San Juan* (Mon–Fri 8am–4.30pm).

Travel agents The most helpful is Arco Iris in Flores (☎9260786), who sells flights, and has the best prices for tours to the ruins and around the lake. For tailor-made tours to ruins throughout Petén, use Expedicion Panamundo, 2 C 4–90 in Santa Elena (☎ & fax 9260501), whose manager, Julio Alvarado, provides guides with archeological expertise. Explore, on C Central America, Flores (☎9260665; fax 9260550) has specialist knowledge of the Petexbatún area, while Agencia de Viajes Tikal, in Santa Elena (☎9260758), is a small friendly agency which books tickets and tours and will let you leave luggage while you look for a room.

Voluntary work ARCAS, in Santa Elena (*Asociación de Rescate y Conservación de Vida Silestre*, or Wildlife Conservation and Rescue Association; ☎9260077), runs a rescue service for animals taken illegally as pets from the forests, and always needs volunteers. The work, while rewarding, can be very demanding and you'll need to commit yourself for at least three weeks.

Around Flores

For most people Flores is no more than an overnight stop, but if you have a few hours to spare, the lake and surrounding hills offer a couple of interesting diversions. The most obvious excursion is a **trip on the lake**. Boatmen can take you on a circuit that includes a *mirador* and small ruin on the peninsula opposite, and the **Peténcito zoo** (daily 8am–5pm) with its small collection of sluggish local wildlife, pausing for a swim along the way. (Note, though, that the concrete waterslide by the zoo can be dangerous and has caused at least one death.) The fee is negotiable but it's cheaper if you can get together a group of four or five people. On weekdays, you'll find the boatmen behind the *Hotel Santana*, in the southwestern corner of Flores; at weekends and holidays they gather at the start of the causeway. If you'd rather paddle around under your own steam you can rent a canoe for around $2 an hour.

Of the numerous **caves** in the hills behind Santa Elena, the most accessible is **Aktun Kan** – simply follow the Flores causeway through Santa Elena, turn left when it forks in front of a small hill, and then take the first right. Otherwise known as *La Cueva de la Serpiente*, the cave is the legendary home of a huge snake: there's a small entrance fee (daily 8am–5pm; $1), for which the guard will turn on the lights and explain to you some of the bizarre names given to the various shapes inside.

San Andrés and San José

Though accessible by bus and boat, the traditional villages of **San Andrés** and **San José**, across the lake from Flores, have until recently received few visitors. The pace of life is slower here even than in Flores and the people even more courteous and friendly. The streets, sloping steeply up from the shore, are lined with one-storey buildings, some of *palmetto* sticks and thatch, some coated with plaster, and others hewn in brightly painted concrete. Pigs and chickens wander freely.

In the past the mainstay of the economy was the arduous and poorly paid collection of **chicle**, the sap of the sapodilla tree, for use in the manufacture of chewing gum. This involves setting up camps in the forest, and working for months at a time in the rainy season when the sap is flowing. Today, natural chicle has largely been superseded by artificial substitutes, but there is still a demand for the original product, especially in Japan. Other forest products are also collected, including *xate* (pronounced *shatay*), palm leaves used in floral arrangements and exported to North America and Europe, and *pimienta de jamaica*, known as allspice. Harvesters *(pimenteros)* use spurs to climb the trees and collect the spice, then dry it over a fire. Since the creation of the Maya Biosphere Reserve (see p.308), however, efforts have been made to provide villagers with alternative sources of income.

Getting to the villages is no problem during daylight. *Lanchas* leave from the beach next to the *Hotel Santana* in Flores (6.15am & 5.15pm; Q2), or you can go by boat across to San Benito and pick up *lanchas* there. Once off the boat head left 45° and look for the *Coca-Cola* stand; *lanchas* leave when full, and you'll usually catch one around midday. If you're desperate to get across from Flores or San Benito a chartered *expreso* will cost Q40. **Buses** leave for San Andrés from the market in Santa Elena at 7am, 8am, noon and 1pm; if they don't continue to San José it's an easy downhill walk. **Returning** is simple in the mornings, with *lanchas* at 6am, 7am and noon, and there are regular buses throughout the day.

San Andrés

Most outsiders in **SAN ANDRÉS** are students at the only **language school** in Petén, the Eco-Escuela. Since nobody in the village speaks English a course here is an excellent opportunity to immerse yourself in Spanish, without the distractions of Antigua, though it may be daunting for absolute beginners. For more information, check at ProPetén in Flores or call ☎9288106 (Spanish only), or ☎9261370 (Spanish and English). In the USA you can contact Conservation International Eco-Escuela (☎202/973-2264; fax 887-5188).

The best of San Andrés' few simple **comedores** is the *Angelita*, at the top of the hill next to the road junction. Nearby, the only **hotel** in the village, the *Hospedaje El Reposo* (①) offers simple, clean budget rooms, a few with private bath; all have electricity but power cuts are common, so bring a flashlight or candles. Far more luxurious is the *Hotel Nitún* (☎9288132; fax 9288113; ⑤ including transport from Flores), 3km west of the village. Thatched stone *cabañas* with hardwood floors have large bedrooms and private bathrooms, and the restaurant serves superb food. This is also the base for Monkey Eco Tours, who organizes well-equipped expeditions to remote archeological sites (☎ & fax 9260494 in Flores, or contact José Antonio Gonzalez of Mesoamerica Explorers, 7 Av 13–01, Edificio La Cúpula, Zona 9, Guatemala City; ☎ & fax 3325045).

San José

Just 2km east along the shore from San Andrés, above a lovely bay, **SAN JOSÉ** is even more relaxed than its neighbour. The village is undergoing something of a cultural revival: Itzá, the pre-Conquest Maya tongue is being taught in the school, and you'll see signs in that language dotted all around. Over the hill beyond the village is a secluded rocky beach where there's a shelter to sling a hammock and a couple of cabins to rent. A kilometre inland from here, at Nueva San José, the *Posada Yaxni'k* (☎ & fax 9265229; ④) boasts simple, clean rooms with homemade furniture and private bath (no hot water) in a restored *finca* that's now part of a **women's co-operative**; guests can also learn about the use of traditional medicinal plants. Beyond San José, a signed track on the left leads 4km to the Classic period **ruins of Motúl**. The site is fairly spread out and little visited (though there should be a caretaker about), with four plazas. In plaza B a large stela in front of a looted temple depicts dancing Maya lords. Plaza C is the biggest, with several mounds and courtyards, while plaza D has the tallest pyramid. It's a secluded spot, ideal for bird-watching, and probably best visited by bicycle from either of the villages. With your own vehicle or bike you could follow the dirt road round the north shore to meet the Tikal road at El Remate.

El Remate and around

On the eastern shore of Lake Petén Itzá, 30km from Santa Elena on the road to Tikal, **EL REMATE** offers a pleasant alternative to staying in Flores. Just 2km north of the junction with the road to Belize/Melchor, it's a quiet, friendly village, growing in popularity as a convenient base for Tikal, and with several worthwhile places to visit nearby, such as the **Ruins of Ixlú** and the **Biotopo Cerro Cahuí**.

Getting to El Remate is easy: every minibus to Tikal passes through the village, while local buses from the market in Santa Elena run to Jobompiche, a village on the lake near the Biotopo Cerro Cahuí (see below), and to Socotzal on the way to Tikal (every 2hr, 8am–5pm). Coming from the Belize border, get off at Puente Ixlú – from here you can walk or hitch the 2km to El Remate. Heading to Flores, local buses pass through El Remate at 5.30am, 7.30am and 8am, and a swarm of minibuses from Tikal ply the route from midday onwards.

Accommodation around El Remate

The range of accommodation in and around El Remate has expanded in recent years, yet each place listed below is well spaced, with no sense of overcrowding. None is more than 5km from the junction with the Tikal road. There are no private **phone numbers**: to contact any of the places below leave a message on the community telephone (☎9260269). All the hotels below are listed in the order you approach them from the village of Puente Ixlú: beyond *La Casa de Don David* the route follows the road to Jobompiche, along the north shore of the lake.

El Mirador del Duende, on the Tikal road, El Remate. High above the lake and reached by a stairway cut into the cliff, this incredible collection of whitewashed stucco *cabañas* that look like igloos, is decorated with Maya glyphs. The owner was born nearby, and is an expert on jungle lore, leading hikes to all Petén's archeological sites. Hammock slingers and campers are welcome. The restaurant, high above the lake, serves cheap vegetarian food including stewed yucca. ①.

La Mansión del Pajaro Serpiente, just below *El Mirador del Duende* on the Tikal road (☎ & fax 9260065 in Flores). The most comfortable accommodation in the area, these stone-built and thatched, two-storey *cabañas* sit in a tropical garden. Each suite has a living room, bedroom and immaculate bathroom plus superb lake views. When available, the smaller *cabañas*, usually used by tour guides or drivers, are just as comfortable and about a third of the price. ④.

John's Lodge, at the junction with the road to Cerro Cahuí and Jobompiche. Hammock space only and the water supply can be irregular. ②.

La Casa de Don David, at the junction with the road to Cerro Cahuí, 300m beyond *La Mansión*. Probably the most atmospheric place in El Remate. Owner David Kuhn is a mine of information about Petén, and provides great home cooking and near-legendary after-dinner "tarantula tours". He also sells bus tickets and will pick you up from Puente Ixlú if you let him know in advance. ③.

Casa Mobego, 500m down the road to Cerro Cahuí on the right. A good budget deal and right by the lake: the simple, well-constructed stick and thatch *cabañas* have great lake views. Swimming, canoe rental and camping are all available, and there's a good, inexpensive restaurant. ②.

El Gringo Perdido, 3km from the road in the Cerro Cahuí *biotopo* (contact Viajes Mundial in Guatemala City on ☎2320605; fax 2538761). Long-established place offering expensive rooms with a mosquito-netted bunk-bed and bath, as well as some better value basic *cabañas*, camping and a fine restaurant. The setting, in the forest leading to the lake, is supremely tranquil; guided canoe tours are also available. ② for *cabañas*, ⑤ for rooms.

Hotel Camino Real Tikal, on the Jobompiche road, 4km from the highway, beyond Cerro Cahuí (☎9260209; in Guatemala City ☎3334633; fax 3374313). A luxury option set in extensive lakeside grounds. The rooms are a bit unimaginative and corporate and there are attendant luxury trappings like buggies and a souvenir shop, but the views of the lake are excellent, there's a private beach and guests have free use of kayaks, rowing boats and a complimentary guided tour of the *biotopo*. There's also a superb pool and restaurant, as well as car rental and a travel agency.⑨.

Ixlú and the Biotopo Cerro Cahuí

Two kilometres south of El Remate, at the Belize/Melchor road junction, formerly known simply as El Cruce, is the tiny village of **Puente Ixlú**, where you'll find a thatched information hut with toilets. Inside, a large map of the area shows the little restored **ruins of Ixlú**, 200m down a signed track from the road, on the shore of **Lake Salpetén**. The *Zac Petén* restaurant, on the Melchor side of the junction, is the best place to eat; they'll also let you store your bags. A very basic **campsite** has been built on the lakeshore where you can rent canoes.

On the north shore of the lake, 2km from the main road, the **Biotopo Cerro Cahuí** (daily 7am–5pm; $5) is a 650-hectare wildlife conservation area comprising lakeshore, ponds and some of the best examples of undisturbed tropical forest in Petén. The smallest and most accessible of Petén's *biotopos*, it contains a rich diversity of plants and animals, and is especially recommended for birdwatchers. There are hiking trails, a couple of small ruins and two thatched *miradores* on the hill above the lake; pick up maps and information at the gate where you sign in.

Tikal

Just 65km from Flores, towering above the rain forest, lies **Tikal**, possibly the most magnificent of all Maya sites. The ruins are dominated by five enormous temples: steep-sided granite pyramids that rise up to 60m from the forest floor. Around them are literally thousands of other structures, many still hidden beneath mounds of earth.

The site itself is surrounded by the **Tikal National Park**, a protected area of some 370 square kilometres, and is on the edge of the even larger Maya Biosphere Reserve. The trees around the ruins are home to hundreds of species including howler and spider monkeys, toucans and parakeets. The sheer scale of the place is overwhelming, and its atmosphere spellbinding. Whether you can spare as little as an hour or as long as a week, it's always worth the trip.

Getting there

The best way to reach the ruins is in one of the **tourist minibuses** – VW combis known as *colectivos* – that meet flights from the capital and are operated by just about every hotel in Flores and Santa Elena. *Hotel San Juan* is the largest operator, with departures at 6am, 8am and 10am, returning at 2pm, 4pm and 5pm (1hr; $6 return). In addition a **local bus**, run by Pinita, leaves Santa Elena market at 1pm, passes the *Hotel San Juan* and arrives at Tikal about two hours later; it then continues to Uaxactún (see p.330), returning at 6am. There are also tourist minibus departures at 4am – useful if you want to see the ruins at dawn but would rather not stay at the site. It's usually billed as the "**sunrise at Tikal**" trip, though the appearance of the sun is generally delayed by mist rising from the humid forest and many find the experience slightly disappointing. From Río Dulce, the Mundo Maya express bus runs daily to Tikal.

If you're travelling **from Belize**, there is usually no need to go all the way to Flores: instead change buses at **Puente Ixlú**, the three-way junction at the eastern end of Lake Petén Itzá (see p.319). The local bus from Santa Elena to Tikal and Uaxactún arrives at about 2pm, and there are plenty of passing minibuses all day long. There have been occasional **robberies** along the road between Tikal and the Belizean border at Melchor, with most of the targets being the tourist minibuses. These robbers are not usually violent but they are determined – be especially careful when changing buses. That said, they tend to leave the local "chicken buses" alone, and the risk overall, while real, is small.

Site practicalities

Plane and local bus schedules are designed to make it easy to visit the ruins as a day trip from Flores or Guatemala City, but if you can spare the time it's well worth staying overnight. Partly because you'll need the extra time to do justice to the ruins themselves, but more importantly, to spend dawn and dusk at the site, when the forest canopy bursts into a frenzy of sound and activity. The air fills with the screech of toucans and the roar of howler monkeys, while flocks of parakeets wheel around the temples, and bats launch themselves into the night. With a bit of luck you might even see a grey fox sneak across one of the plazas.

Entrance to the national park costs $8.50 a day and you're expected to pay again if you stay overnight, although this is not strictly enforced. If you arrive after dusk you will automatically be issued with a ticket for the next day. The ruins themselves are open from 6am to 6pm, and extensions to 8pm can be obtained from the *inspectoría* (7am–noon & 2–5pm), a small white hut on the left at the entrance to the ruins.

Accommodation, eating and drinking

There are three **hotels** at the ruins, all of them fairly expensive and not especially good value for money, though you can often get discounts out of season. The

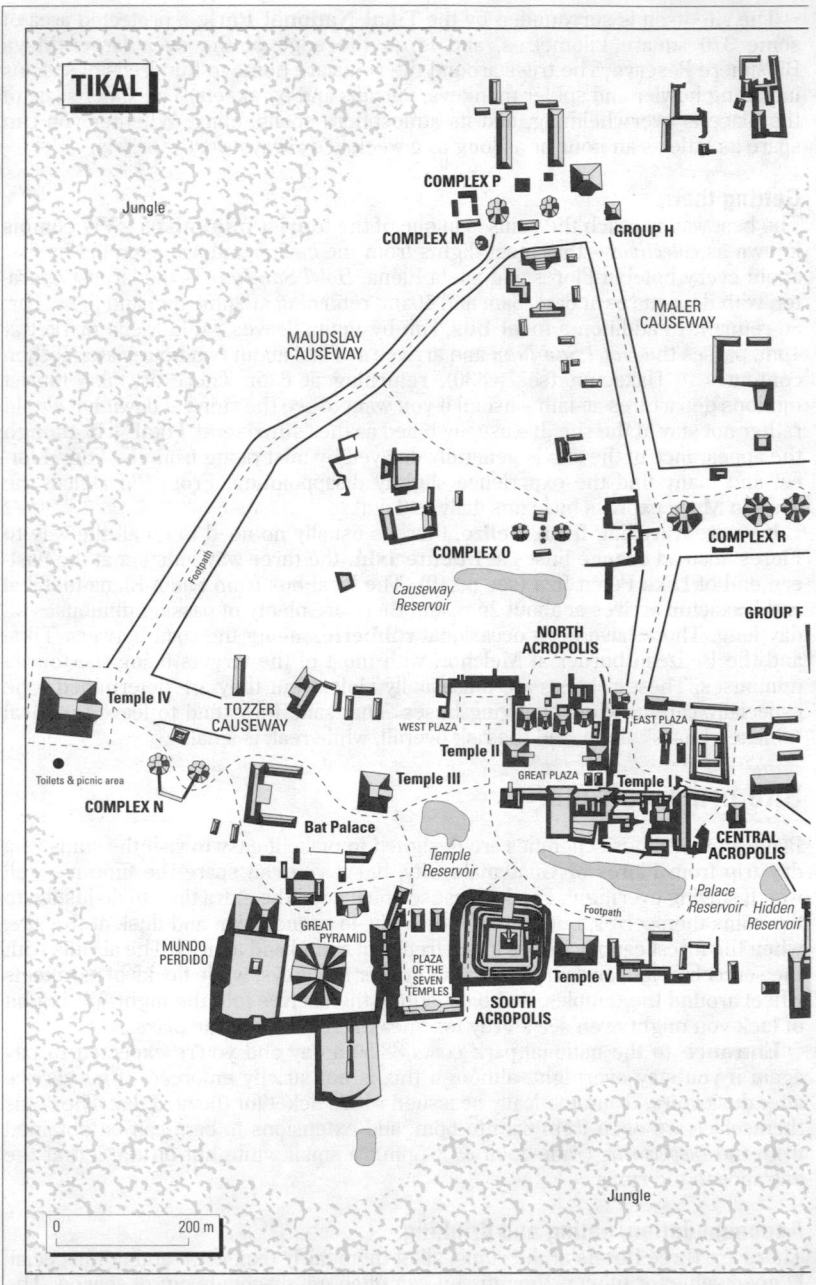

TIKAL

Jungle

COMPLEX P

COMPLEX M

GROUP H

MAUDSLAY CAUSEWAY

MALER CAUSEWAY

COMPLEX O

Causeway Reservoir

COMPLEX R

GROUP F

NORTH ACROPOLIS

Temple IV

TOZZER CAUSEWAY

WEST PLAZA

EAST PLAZA

Temple II

Toilets & picnic area

COMPLEX N

Temple III

GREAT PLAZA

Temple I

CENTRAL ACROPOLIS

Bat Palace

Temple Reservoir

Palace Reservoir

Hidden Reservoir

Footpath

MUNDO PERDIDO

GREAT PYRAMID

PLAZA OF THE SEVEN TEMPLES

Temple V

SOUTH ACROPOLIS

Jungle

0   200 m

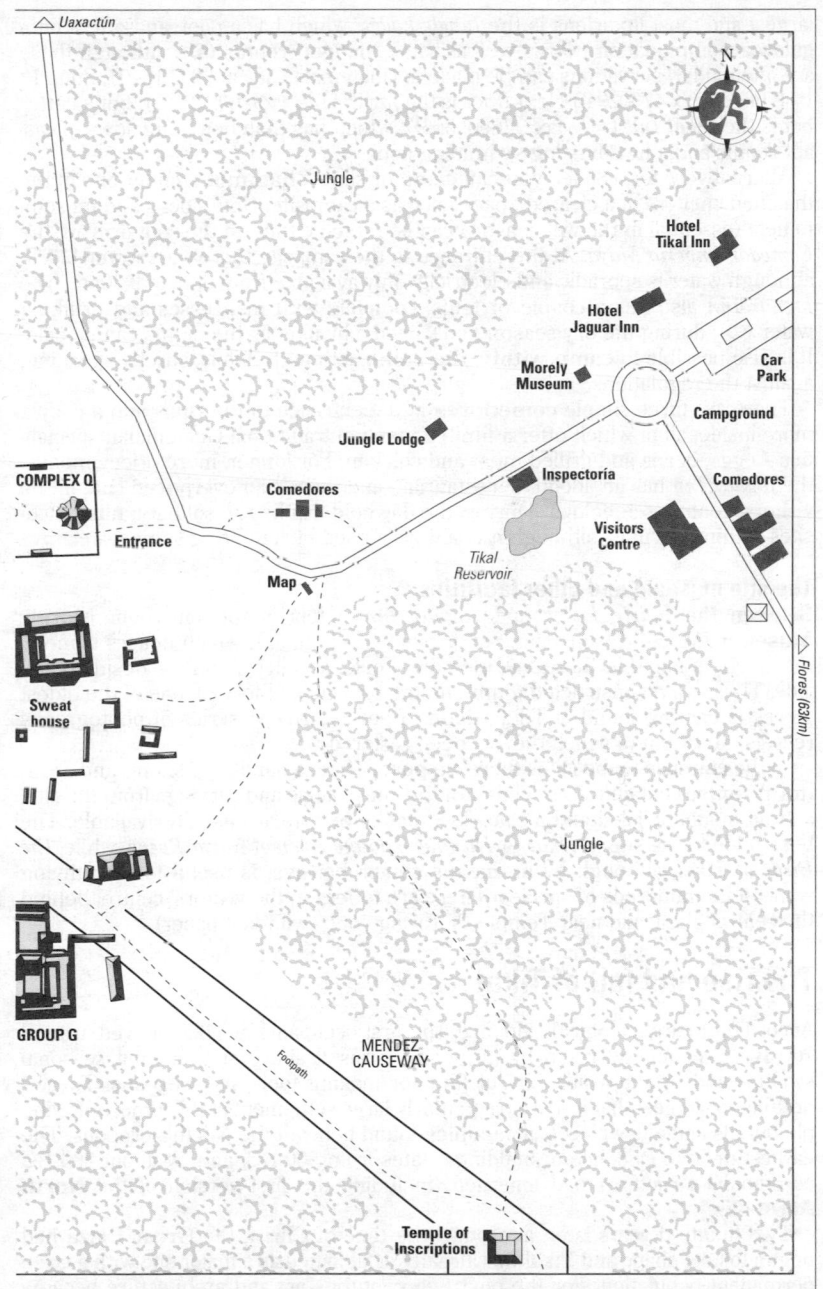

largest and most luxurious is the *Jungle Lodge*, which has a pool, and offers bungalow accommodation (⑥) as well as some "budget" rooms (④), although these are often full; reservations can be made in Guatemala City, at 29 C 18–01, Zona 12 (☎4768775; fax 4760294.) Next door is the *Jaguar Inn* (☎9260002; ⑥), but a better bet is the *Tikal Inn* (☎ & fax 9260065; ⑤), which has thatched bungalows, pleasant rooms and a heat-busting swimming pool.

Alternatively, for a $6 fee you can **camp** or sling a **hammock** under one of the thatched shelters in a cleared space used as a campsite. Hammocks and mosquito nets (essential in the wet season) can be rented either on the spot or from the *Comedor Imperio Maya*. At the entrance to the campsite there's a shower block, although water is sporadic and electricity only available from 6pm to 9.30pm. The *Jaguar Inn* also has a couple of tents, complete with mattresses and drinking water (②); during the dry season you'll need a blanket as the nights can be cold. It is also possible to **camp within the ruins**, although this is, strictly speaking, against the regulations.

There are three simple **comedores** at the entrance to the ruins and a couple more inside, all of which offer a limited menu of traditional Guatemalan specialities – eggs, beans and grilled meat and chicken. For longer, more pricey menus, the *Jaguar Inn* has an adequate restaurant, and there's an overpriced café in the visitors' centre (see below). During the day cold drinks are sold at a number of sites within the ruins, although it is always a good idea to bring some water.

The site museum and other facilities

Between the *Jungle Lodge* and *Jaguar Inn* hotels is the one-room **Morely Museum** (Mon–Fri 9am–5pm, Sat & Sun 9am–4pm; $2), which houses some of the artefacts found in the ruins, including tools, jewellery, pottery, obsidian and jade. There's a reconstructed tomb and the remains of Stela 29, one of the oldest pieces of carving found at Tikal, dating from 292 AD. A series of photographs reveals the extent to which they've been restored.

At the entrance to the ruins there's a **post office**, a handful of shops, and a **visitors' centre** containing a selection of the finest stelae and carvings from the site, a scale model of Tikal and a café. Two books of note are usually available. The best guide to the site is *Tikal, A Handbook to the Ancient Maya Ruins*, while *The Birds of Tikal*, although by no means comprehensive, is useful for identifying some of the hundreds of species. There are **toilets** in the visitors' centre, behind the central plaza, and near Temple IV (bring your own toilet paper).

The rise and fall of Tikal

According to archeological evidence, the first occupants of Tikal arrived around 700 BC, probably attracted by its position raised above surrounding seasonal swamps and by the availability of flint for making tools and weapons. There's nothing to suggest that it was a particularly large settlement at this time, only simple burials and a few pieces of ceramics found beneath the North Acropolis. The earliest definite evidence of buildings dates from 500 BC, and by about 200 BC ceremonial structures had emerged, including the first version of the **North Acropolis**.

Two hundred years later, at around the time of Christ, the **Great Plaza** had begun to take shape and Tikal was already established as a major site with a large permanent population. For the next two centuries art and architecture became increasingly ornate and sophisticated. The styles that were to dominate throughout the Classic period were perfected in these early years, and by 250 AD all the major architectural traits were established. Despite this, Tikal remained very much a secondary centre, dominated, along with the rest of the area, by **El Mirador**, a massive city about 65km to the north.

The closing years of the **Preclassic** era were marked by the eruption of the Ilopango volcano in El Salvador, which smothered a huge area of the highlands, including much of Guatemala and Honduras, in a thick layer of volcanic ash. Trade routes were disrupted and alliance patterns altered. The ensuing years saw the decline and abandonment of El Mirador, creating a power vacuum and opening the way for the expansion of several smaller sites. To the south of El Mirador the two sites of Tikal and Uaxactún emerged as substantial centres of trade, science and religion. Less than a day's walk apart and growing rapidly, the cities engaged in a heated competition which could have only one winner. Matters finally came to a head on January 16, 378 AD, when, under the inspired leadership of Great Jaguar Paw, Tikal's warriors overran Uaxactún. The secret of Tikal's success appears to have been its alliance with the powerful highland centre of **Kaminaljuyú** – on the site of modern Guatemala City – which was itself allied with **Teotihuacán**, the city that dominated what is now central Mexico.

The victory over Uaxactún enabled Tikal's rulers to dominate central Petén for the next three centuries, during which time it became one of the most elaborate and magnificent of all Maya city states monopolizing the crucial lowland trade routes, its influence reaching as far as Copán in Honduras and Yaxchilán on the Usumacinta. The elite immediately launched an extensive rebuilding programme, including a radical remodelling of the North Acropolis and the renovation of most of the city's finest temples.

It is clear that Tikal's alliance with Kaminaljuyú and Teotihuacán remained an important part of its continuing power: stelae and paintings from the period show that Tikal's elite adopted Teotihuacán styles of clothing, pottery and weaponry. The paintings on some vases are even thought to show the arrival of traders and emissaries from Teotihuacán in Tikal. This extended period of prosperity saw the city's population grow to somewhere between 50,000 and 100,000, expanding to cover an area of around thirty square kilometres. Debate still rages about the exact function of Tikal, but it's now widely accepted that it was a real city, surrounded by farmland rather than forest. The elite lived in the centre, possibly housed in the area around the Central Acropolis, and the ordinary people in small residential compounds dotted around the core of the site and out in the fields.

In the middle of the sixth century, however, Tikal suffered a major setback. Already weakened by upheavals in Mexico, where Teotihuacán was in decline, the city now faced a major challenge from the east, where the city of **Caracol** (in the Maya Mountains of Belize) was emerging as a major regional power. Caracol's ambitious leader, Lord Water, launched his first attack on Tikal in April 556 AD, but failed to take the city; a year later he was back, this time managing to assume control and subdue Tikal's powerful elite. Between September 17, 557 and March 18, 692, no new monuments were erected at Tikal, and most of the previous stelae were deliberately erased. During this period of subjugation Tikal was probably not occupied by an invading army but it was almost certainly overshadowed by the new power of Caracol.

The effect of Caracol's assault was to free many smaller centres throughout Petén from Tikal's influence, creating fresh and disruptive rivalry. By the middle of the seventh century, however, Caracol's stranglehold had begun to relax and Tikal embarked upon a dramatic renaissance under the formidable leadership of **Ah Cacaw**, Lord Chocolate. At 1.67m tall, this dynamic leader was a giant among the Maya people, who on average reached just 1.57m. During his reign the main ceremonial areas, the East Plaza and the North Acropolis, were completely remodelled, reclaimed from the desecration suffered at the hands of Caracol. Tikal regained its position among the most important of Petén cities under Ah Cacaw and, as a tribute, his son Caan Chac (who ascended the throne on December 12, 734 AD, and is known as Ruler B), had the leader's body entombed in the magnificent Temple I. Ah Cacaw's strident approach gave birth to a revitalized and powerful ruling dynasty: the site's five main temples were built in the hundred years following his death, and magnificent temples were still under construction at Tikal as late as 889 AD.

What brought about Tikal's final **downfall** remains a mystery, but what is certain is that around 900 AD almost the entire lowland Maya civilization collapsed. Possible causes range from earthquake to popular uprising, but the evidence points in no particular direction. We do know that Tikal was abandoned by the end of the tenth century. Afterwards, the site was used from time to time by other groups, who worshipped here and repositioned many of the stelae, but it was never occupied again.

Rediscovery

After its mysterious decline little is known of Tikal until 1695 when Father Avendano, lost in the maze of swamps, stumbled upon a "variety of old buildings". The colonial powers were distinctly unimpressed by Petén and for the next 150 years the ruins were left to the jungle. In 1848 they were rediscovered by a government expedition led by Modesto Méndez. Later in the nineteenth century a Swiss scientist visited the site and removed the beautifully carved wooden lintels from the tops of Temples I and IV – they are currently in a museum in Basel – and in 1881 the English archeologist Maudslay took the first photographs of the ruins, showing the main temples cloaked in tropical vegetation.

Until 1951 the site could only be reached – with considerable difficulty – on horseback, and although there was a steady trickle of visitors the ruins remained mostly uncleared. Then the Guatemalan army built an airstrip, paving the way for an invasion of archeologists and tourists. In 1956 the Tikal project was started in order to mount one of the most comprehensive investigations ever carried out at a Maya site. By the time it was completed in 1970 the report stretched to 28 volumes and included the work of 113 archeologists. Despite this, astonishingly little is known for certain about the ruins or their history.

The ruins

The sheer scale of the ruins at Tikal can at first seem daunting. But even if you make it only to the main plaza, and spend a hour relaxing on top of a temple, you won't be disappointed. The **central area**, with its five main temples, forms by far the most impressive section; if you start to explore beyond this you can wander seemingly forever into the maze of smaller structures and outlying complexes.

From the entrance to the Great Plaza

Walking into the ruins the first structures that you come to are the evocatively named **Complex Q** and **Complex R**, two of the seven sets of twin pyramids that were built to mark the passing of each *katun*, a period of twenty 360-day years. This is an architectural feature found only at Tikal and Nakúm, a site to the east. Only one of the pyramids is restored, with the stelae and altars re-erected in front of it. The stelae at the base of the pyramid are blank, as a result of erosion, but there's a copy of a superbly carved example, Stela 22 (the original of which can be seen in the visitors' centre at the entrance to the site) in the small enclosure set to one side. The carvings on Stela 22 record the ascension to the throne of **Chitam**, Tikal's last known ruler, in the month of the parrot, 768 AD. He is portrayed in full regalia, complete with an enormous sweeping headdress and the staff of authority. Q and R were Chitam's main contribution to Tikal's architectural heritage and the last great structures to be built at the site.

Following the path as it bears around to the left, you approach the back of Temple I through the **East Plaza**. On the left side, behind a small ball court, is a broad platform supporting a series of small buildings known as the **Marketplace**, and in the southeast corner of the plaza stands an imposing temple, beneath which were found the remains of several severed heads, the victims of human sacrifice. Behind the marketplace is the **Sweat House**, which may have been a kind of sauna similar to those used by highland Indians today. It's thought that Maya priests would take a sweat bath in order to cleanse themselves before conducting religious rituals.

From here a few short steps bring you to the **Great Plaza**, the heart of the ancient city. Surrounded by four massive structures, this was the focus of ceremonial and religious activity at Tikal for around a thousand years, and was still in use long after the rest of the city had been abandoned. The earliest part is the North Acropolis; the two great temples, which disrupted its original north–south axis, weren't built until the eighth century. The plaza covers an area of one and a half acres, and beneath today's grass lie four layers of paving, the oldest of which dates from about 150 BC and the most recent from 700 AD. Temple II can be climbed, and although the ascent can be a hair-raising experience, it's well worth it for the views from the top. At present the steeper stairway on Temple I is roped off, though it may be reopened in the future.

Temple I, towering 44m above the plaza, is the hallmark of Tikal – it's also known as the Jaguar Temple because of the jaguar carved in its door lintel, though this is now in a museum in Basel. The temple was built as a burial monument to contain the magnificent **tomb of Ah Cacaw**, one of Tikal's most impressive rulers, who ascended the throne in 682 AD (see p.326). It was constructed shortly after his death in 721 AD, under the direction of Ah Cacaw's son and successor Caan Chac. Within the tomb at the temple's core, the skeleton was found facing north, surrounded by an assortment of jade, pearls, seashells and stingray spines, which were a traditional symbol of human sacrifice. There was also some magnificent pottery, depicting a journey to the underworld made in a canoe rowed by mythical animal figures. A reconstruction of the tomb is on show at the site museum. Hundreds of tons of flint and rubble were poured on top of the completed tomb and the temple was built around this, with a staircase of thick plastered blocks running up the front. The staircase was a skeleton structure, over which the final surface would have been built. The whole thing is topped by a three-room building and a hollow roof comb that was originally painted in cream, red and possibly green. On the front of the comb it's just possible to make out a seated figure and a stylized serpent. The view from the top of the temple, raised just above the forest canopy, is incredible; the great plaza spread out below you, with the complex structures of the North Acropolis to the right and the Central Acropolis to the left. Standing opposite, like a squat version of Temple I, is **Temple II**, known as the Temple of the Masks for the two grotesque masks, now heavily eroded, that flank the central stairway. As yet no tomb has been found beneath this temple, which now stands 38m high, although with its roof comb intact it would have equalled Temple I. It's an easy climb up the staircase to the top, from where the echo is fantastically clear and crisp.

The **North Acropolis**, which fills the whole north side of the plaza, is one of the most complex structures in the entire Maya world. In traditional Maya style it was built and rebuilt on top of itself, and beneath the twelve temples that can be seen today are the remains of about a hundred other structures. As early as 100 BC the Maya had constructed elaborate platforms supporting temples and tombs here; in about 250 AD the entire thing was torn down and rebuilt as a platform and four vaulted temples, each of which was rebuilt twice during early Classic times. Archeologists have removed some of the surface to reveal these earlier structures, including two four-metre-high **masks**. One facing the plaza, protected by a thatched roof, is clearly visible; the other can be reached by following the dark passageway to the side – you'll need a torch. In 1959 a trench was dug deep beneath the platform of the North Acropolis, unearthing a bizarre burial chamber in which the body of a ruler lay surrounded by nine retainers killed for the occasion, along with turtles, a crocodile and a mass of pottery.

In front of the North Acropolis are two lines of **stelae** with circular altars at their bases, all of which were originally painted a brilliant red. These were once thought to show images of the gods, but archeologists now believe the carvings are of members of Tikal's ruling elite. This elite was certainly obsessive in its recording of the city's dynastic sequence, linking it with great historical moments and reaching as far back into the past as possible. Many of the stelae, throughout the site, bear the marks of ritual defacement, which was carried out when one ruler replaced another to erase any latent powers that the image may have retained. Many of the stelae now in the main plaza were set up in their current positions long after the decline of the city by people who still worshipped here.

The Central Acropolis and Temple V

On the other side of the plaza is the **Central Acropolis**, a maze of tiny interconnecting rooms and stairways built around six smallish courtyards. The buildings here are usually referred to as palaces rather than temples, although their precise use remains a mystery. Possibilities include law courts, temporary retreats, administrative centres, and homes for Tikal's elite. What we do know is that they were constantly altered and adapted, with rooms, walls and doorways added and repositioned on a regular basis. The large two-storey building in Court 2 is known as **Maler's Palace**, named after the archeologist Teobert Maler who made it his home during expeditions in 1895 and 1904.

Behind the acropolis is the palace reservoir, one of at least twelve clay-lined pools that were fed by a series of channels with rainwater from all over the city. Further behind the Central Acropolis is **Temple V** (58m) which supports a single tiny room and is thought to be a mortuary shrine to an unknown ruler. The temple is currently undergoing a huge restoration project, partly financed by Spain; work is expected to be completed by the year 2000 when the view from the top should be superb, with a great profile of Temple I and a side view of the central plaza.

From the West Plaza to Temple IV

Behind Temple II is the **West Plaza**, dominated by a large Late Classic temple on the north side, and scattered with various altars and stelae, which, like those in the Great Plaza, owe their present position to Postclassic people, who rearranged many of the smaller monuments. From here the **Tozzer Causeway** – one of the raised routes that connected the main parts of the city – leads west to **Temple III** (55m), covered in jungle vegetation. A fragment of Stela 24, found at the base of the temple, dates it at 810 AD. Around the back of the temple is a huge palace complex, of which only the **Bat Palace** has been restored. Further down the causeway, on the left-hand side, is **Complex N**, another set of twin pyramids. In the northern enclosure of the complex, the superbly carved **Stela 16** shows the ruler Ah Cacaw, who was buried beneath Temple I. The altar at its base bears a sculpted scene and a text that possibly refers to the death of his wife.

At the end of the Tozzer Causeway is **Temple IV**, the tallest of all the Tikal structures at a massive 64m. Built in 741 AD, it is thought by some archeologists to be the resting place of the ruler Coon Chac, whose image was depicted on wooden lintels built into the top of the temple. At the top are three rooms, separated by walls 12m thick: to reach them you have to scramble over more roots and rocks, and finally up a metal ladder around the side of the pyramid. Slow and exhausting as this is, it's always worth it, offering one of the finest views of the whole site. All around you the green carpet of the canopy stretches out to the horizon, interrupted only by the great roof combs of the other temples. At any time this view is enthralling – at sunset or sunrise it's unbeatable.

From Temple IV the **Maudslay Causeway** leads to **Group H**, which includes two more twin-pyramid structures, and from here the **Maler Causeway** takes you back down to the East Plaza, past yet another set.

The Mundo Perdido, the Plaza of the Seven Temples and the Temple of the Inscriptions

The other main buildings in the centre of Tikal are to the south of the Central Acropolis. Here, reached by a trail from Temple III, you'll find the **Plaza of the Seven Temples**, which forms part of a complex dating back to before Christ. There's an unusual triple ball court on the north side of the plaza, and to the east is the unexcavated South Acropolis. To the west of here is the **Mundo Perdido**, or Lost World, another magical and very distinct section of the site with its own atmosphere and architecture. Little is known about the ruins in this part of the site, but archeologists hope that further research will help to explain the early history of Tikal. The main feature is the **Great Pyramid**, a 32-metre-high structure whose surface hides four earlier versions, the first dating from 700 BC. The top of the pyramid offers awesome views towards Temple IV and the Great Plaza and makes an excellent base to watch the dramatic sunrise or sunset.

Finally there's the **Temple of the Inscriptions**, reached along the Méndez Causeway from the East Plaza behind Temple I. The temple (only discovered in 1951) is about 1km from the plaza. It's famous for its twelve-metre roof comb, on the back of which is a huge hieroglyphic text, only just visible these days.

Outside the main area are countless smaller **unrestored structures**. Compared to the scale and magnificence of what you've seen already they're not that impressive, but armed with a good map (the best is in Coe's guide to the ruins), it can be exciting to explore some of the rarely visited outlying sections. Tikal is certain to exhaust you before you exhaust it.

Uaxactún and around

Twenty-four kilometres north of Tikal, strung out by the side of an airstrip, are the village and ruins of **UAXACTÚN**. With a couple of places to stay, several *comedores* and a daily bus to Santa Elena, the village is an ideal jumping-off point for the remote northern ruins of **El Zotz**, **Río Azul** and **El Mirador**. Substantially smaller than Tikal, the site is thought to date from the same period, although there's also evidence of much earlier occupation and the main group of structures is known to have been rebuilt over a period of five hundred years. During the Preclassic period Uaxactún and Tikal coexisted in relative harmony, all hopes of expansion overshadowed by the presence of El Mirador to the north. By the first century AD, however, El Mirador was in decline and rivalry between Tikal and Uaxactún took off as both cities began to expand, embarking on grand building programmes. The two finally clashed on January 16, 378 AD, when Tikal's warriors conquered Uaxactún, forcing it to accept subordinate status.

The overall impact of Uaxactún may be a little disappointing after the grandeur of Tikal, but if you're planning a stroll through the forest then this is an excellent spot to make for. You'll probably have the site to yourself, giving you the chance to soak up the atmosphere. The most interesting buildings are in **Group E**, east of the airstrip, where three reconstructed temples, built side by side, are arranged to function as an observatory. Viewed from the top of a fourth temple, the sun rises behind the north temple on the longest day of the year and behind the southern one on the shortest day. It's an architectural pattern that was first discovered here but has since been found at a number of other sites. Beneath one of these temples the famous **E-VII** was unearthed, the oldest building ever found in Petén. Its three phases of construction probably date back to 2000 BC, but still seem connected with much later Maya architecture. The original pyramid had a simple staircase up the front, flanked by two stucco masks, and post holes in the top suggest that it may have been covered by a thatched shelter. Over on the other side of the airstrip is **Group A**, a series of larger temples and residential compounds, some of them reconstructed, spread out across the high ground. In amongst the structures are some impressive stelae, each sheltered by a small thatched roof.

Practicalities

Several tour companies in Flores run **day-trips** to Uaxactún, and it's easy enough to get there independently. A dirt road, recently improved, links Tikal with Uaxactún, passing the entrance to the ruins at Tikal and skirting around the side of the site before heading north. A daily **bus** from the market in Santa Elena passes through Tikal en route for Uaxactún at around 3.30pm.

Staying overnight you have three options. The *EcoCampamento*, run jointly by ARCAS and Uaxactún's guide association (☎9260077 in Flores), has tents and hammocks, protected by mosquito nets, under a thatched shelter (Q20 per person; Q15 if you bring your own gear), while the welcoming *Hotel y Campamento El Chiclero* (③), where the bus stops and parks overnight, offers clean rooms without bath. Owner Antonio Baldizón organizes four-wheel-drive trips to Río Azul, and his wife Neria prepares excellent home-cooked food. You can also camp or sling a hammock for Q15. Manuel Soto, who built *Mirador del Duende* in El Remate (see p.319), operates *Tecomate* (①), a similar camping, *cabaña* and hammock place at the entrance to the village; he also offers guided walking trips to the more remote Maya sites.

Uaxactún's **guide association** has a small **information office** at the end of the airstrip and will organize **camping trips** to any of the remote northern sites, into the jungle, east to Nakum, and to Yaxha, towards Belize. Equipment is carried on horseback; price ($25 per person per day for a group of three or more) includes guide, horses, camping gear and food. Check in CINCAP or ARCAS in Flores.

El Zotz, Río Azul and El Mirador

Away to the north of Tikal, lost in a sea of jungle, are several other substantial **ruins** – unrestored and for the most part uncleared, but with their own unique atmosphere. The bulk of the temples lies beneath mounds of earth, their sides coated in vegetation, and only the tallest roof combs are still visible. Doubtless in a year or two they'll be reached by road – today dirt tracks go as far as Río Azul and El Zotz – but for the moment they remain well beyond the reach of the average visitor. Perfect if you're in search of an adventure and want to see a virtually untouched Maya site.

El Zotz

Thirty kilometres west of Uaxactún, along a rough jeep track, sometimes passable in the dry season (with four-wheel drive), is **El Zotz**, a large Maya site in the *biotopo* of El Zotz/San Miguel. To **get there** you can rent vehicles in Uaxactún, or rent a pack horse, guide, food and camping equipment from Uaxactún's guide association (see above). After about four hours – almost halfway – you come to **Santa Cruz**, now almost abandoned, where Pablo Perez makes a living from selling honey and crocodile skins. He'll direct you to the *aguada* for water (you'll need a filter) and will let you camp if you decide to split the journey. At the site itself you'll be welcomed by the guards who look after the *biotopo* headquarters. You can camp here, and, with permission, use the kitchen and drinking water. Remember to bring some food to share with the guides.

Totally unrestored, El Zotz has been systematically looted, although there are guards on duty all year. The three main temples are smothered in soil and vegetation, but using the workers' scaffold you can climb to the top of the tallest structure, spectacular in itself. Zotz means "bat" in Maya and each evening at dusk you'll see tens, perhaps hundreds of thousands of **bats** of several species emerge from a cave near the campsite. It's especially impressive in the moonlight, the beating wings sounding like a river flowing over rapids – one of the most remarkable natural sights in Petén.

Walking on, it takes about four and a half hours to get to **Cruce Dos Aguadas**, a crossroads village on a bus route to Santa Elena (bus leaves at 7am). There are a couple of basic *tiendas* and *comedores* here, the best of which is the *Comedor Patojas* where they'll let you sling a hammock or camp. Northwards the road goes to Carmelita (see p.333) for El Mirador and west to Pasos Caballos for El Perú (see p.343; not possible in the rainy season). You could do this trip in reverse by taking the noon bus from Santa Elena to Dos Aguadas, and heading to El Zotz the next morning. While this route is shorter, entailing less walking, there's also less forest cover than on the route from Uaxactún, and less chance of seeing wildlife.

Río Azul

Río Azul, a remote site in the northeast corner of Petén, 177km from Flores, was discovered in 1962. The city and its suburbs are thought to have had a population of around five thousand, scattered over 750 acres. Although totally unrestored, the core of the site is similar in many ways to Tikal, only smaller. The tallest temple (AIII) stands some 47m above the forest floor, poking its head out above the treetops and giving magnificent views across the jungle. Investigations suggest that the site peaked in the late Preclassic era but remained an important centre well into the Classic period.

Several incredible **tombs** have been unearthed, lined with white plaster and painted with vivid red glyphs. Tomb 19 is thought to have contained the remains of one of the sons of Stormy Sky, Tikal's great expansionist ruler (who ruled Tikal shortly after it conquered Uaxactún), suggesting that the city may have been founded by Tikal to consolidate the border of its empire. Nearby tombs contained bodies of warriors dressed in clothing typical of the ancient city of Teotihuacán in central Mexico, further supporting the theory that Tikal may have derived much of its power from an alliance with this mighty city.

Extensive **looting** occurred after the site's discovery, with a gang of up to eighty men plundering the tombs once the archeological teams had retreated to Flores in the rainy season. During the late 1960s and early 1970s when the looting business reached its height, Río Azul supplied the international market with unique treasures, including some incredible green jade masks and pendants. The gangs stripped the tombs bare, hacking away many of their elaborately decorated walls and removing some of the finest murals in the Maya world. Despite its chamber being looted in 1981, Tomb 1's walls escaped the worst of the damage and remain mercifully intact. Working with simple tools, several of the robbers are thought to have died when tombs caved in on them, and in due course, the bodies, buried alongside their Maya ancestors, will probably be unearthed by archeologists. More recently, several new tombs have been discovered, probably those of noblemen rather than royalty, though, and their murals don't compare with those that have been removed. Today there are two resident guards.

The **road** that connects Tikal and Uaxactún continues for another 95km north to reach Río Azul (a total of 115km from Tikal). This route is only passable in the dry season, and even then it's by no means easy. The three-day round trip by **jeep** (a day each way and a day at the site) involves frequent stops to clear the road. **Walking** or on **horseback** it's four days each way – three at a push. Trips (around $300 per person) can be arranged through a number of agents: check with the Inguat representative at Flores airport; at CINCAP or ProPetén in Flores (see p.313); Avinsa, 4 C 8–15, Santa Elena; *Hotel el Chiclero* in Uaxactún (see p.330); or Aventuras Sin Limites, which has offices in the *Hotel Frontera Palace* (☎9265196) at the Belize border (see p.345). Once you arrive at Río Azul you'll be welcome to **stay** at the guard's camp and may even encounter a lonely group of archeologists. The campsite at Ixcán Río, on the far bank of the Río Azul, is 6km from the main ruins, and during rainy periods vehicles may not be able to ford the river; fortunately, a dugout canoe is provided to carry you and the supplies. For much of the year the river is reduced to a series of pools, and the road continues another 12km to **Tres Banderas**, where the borders of Guatemala, Mexico and Belize meet. Eventually, you'll be able to get your exit stamp in Uaxactún and continue to Mexico using this route: check in Flores or El Remate.

El Mirador

El Mirador is perhaps the most exotic and mysterious of all Petén's Maya sites. Still buried in the forest, this massive city matches Tikal's scale, and may even surpass it, although little is known about its history. Rediscovered in 1926, it dates from an earlier period than Tikal, and was almost certainly the first great city in the Maya world. It flourished between 150 BC and 150 AD, and was unquestionably the dominant city in Petén, being home to tens of thousands of Maya, and occupying a commanding positon above the rain forest, at an altitude of 250 metres. Little archeological work has been done here but it's clear that the site represents the peak of Preclassic Maya culture, which was perhaps far more sophisticated than was once believed.

The core of the site covers some sixteen square kilometres, stretching between two massive pyramids that face each other across the forest on an east–west axis. The site's western side is marked by the massive **Tigre Complex**, made up of a huge single pyramid flanked by two smaller structures, a triadic design that's characteristic of El Mirador's architecture. The base of this complex alone would cover around three football fields, while the height of the main pyramid touches 70m, making it the tallest structure anywhere in the Maya world. In front of the Tigre Complex is El Mirador's sacred hub: a long narrow plaza, the **Central Acropolis**, and a row of smaller buildings. Burial chambers unearthed in this central section had been painted with ferric oxide to prevent corrosion and contained the bodies of priests and noblemen, surrounded by the obsidian lancets and stingray spines used to pierce the penis, ears and tongue in ritual bloodletting ceremonies. The spilling of blood was seen by the Maya as a method of summoning and sustaining the gods, and was clearly common at all the great ceremonial centres.

To the south of the Tigre Complex is the **Monos Complex**, another triadic structure and plaza, named after the local howler monkeys that roar long into the night and after heavy rainfall. To the north, the **León Pyramid** and the **Casabel Complex** mark the boundary of the site. Heading away to the east, on the other side of the main plaza and the Central Acropolis, the Puleston Causeway runs some 800m to the smaller East Group, the largest of which (about 2km from the Tigre Complex) is the **Danta Complex**. Another triadic structure, it rises in three stages to a height just below that of the Tigre pyramid, but gives even better views since it was built on higher land.

The area **around El Mirador** is riddled with smaller Maya sites, and as you look out across the forest from the top of either of the main temples you can see others rising above the horizon on all sides – including the largest (as opposed to the tallest) Maya pyramid, Calakmul in Mexico. Raised **causeways**, ancient trading routes, connect many of these smaller sites to El Mirador and some are currently being investigated by visiting archeologists. Among the most accessible are **Nakbé**, 10km south, where a huge Maya mask (5m by 8m) was found in September 1992, and **El Tintal**, around 21km southwest, which you'll pass on your way in from Carmelita.

GETTING TO EL MIRADOR

Any journey to El Mirador is a substantial undertaking, involving an arduous sixty-kilometre truck ride north from San Andrés to **Carmelita**, a *chicle* and *x'ate* gathering centre at the end of the road, followed by two days of hard jungle hiking, during which you'll need a horse to carry your food and equipment. If you don't mind basic living conditions, the trip offers an exceptional chance to see virtually untouched forest, and perhaps some of the creatures inhabiting it. The first night after leaving Carmelita is spent – in a simple thatched shelter if you've no tent – by an *aguada* (a waterhole of dubious quality) near the ruins of **Tintal**, a large site which you'll be able to explore on the way back. Another day's walking brings you to the guards' huts at **El Mirador**, where you are welcome to stay, using their hearth to cook on. You should bring along food or drink for the guards, who spend forty days at a time in the forest, subsisting on beans and tortillas. The journey, impossibly muddy in the rainy season, is best attempted from mid-January to August; February to April is the driest period. The only other serious hazards are the *garraptas* (ticks), for which you'll need a pair of tweezers and a trusty companion. Whether you take a tour or go independently you're advised to examine the information and maps in ProPetén and in CINCAP first.

ProPetén (see p.314) organizes a five-day **tour** ($85 each for two people) from Carmelita to El Mirador, which includes guide, packhorse, and a night at the *Campamento Nakbe* in Carmelita – you need to bring your own food and water purification system. Other tour companies in Flores also offer trips, almost certainly more expensive. It's also perfectly feasible to travel **independently**, arranging a guide and horse in Carmelita (about $25 a day), and bringing your own food and camping gear. To get to Carmelita, take a bus from Santa Elena to San Andrés (see p.318); the noon service continues to Cruce Dos Aguadas (see p.331), a third of the way to Carmelita. From either place trucks will take you the rest of the way, although the road is appalling, making progress unpredictable – expect to pay around $4–5 for the ride. Check with ProPetén in Flores before setting out – they often have vehicles going to Carmelita and will know the road conditions. When you arrive at Carmelita ask for Luis Morales, president of the Tourism Committee, who can arrange guides for the trip and accommodation at the *campamento*.

Sayaxché and around

Southwest of Flores, on a lazy bend in the Río Pasión, is **SAYAXCHÉ**, an easygoing settlement that's an ideal base for exploring the forest and its huge collection of archeological remains. A frontier town at the junction of road and river, Sayaxché is an important point of storage for grain and cattle and the source of supplies for a vast surrounding area which is being steadily cleared and colonized. The complex network of rivers and swamps that cuts through the forested wilderness here has been an important trade route since Maya times, and there are several interesting ruins in the area. Upstream is **Ceibal**, a small but beautiful site in a wonderful jungle setting; to the south is **Lake Petexbatún**, on the shores of which are the small ruins of **Dos Pilas**, **Aguateca** and **Tamarindito**. A visit to these offers great opportunities to wander in the forest and watch the wildlife.

Sayaxché practicalities

Getting to Sayaxché from Flores is very straightforward, with several Pinita **buses** (6am, 9am, 10am, 1pm & 4pm; 2hr) and one Del Rosio service (5am) leaving from Santa Elena market to ply the fairly smooth 62-kilometre dirt road. Hitching a ride in a **pick-up** at other times is not too difficult. The bus brings you as far as the north bank of the Río Pasión, directly opposite Sayaxché. Del Rosio buses cross the river on the ferry; Pinita services stop on the north bank, from where passengers are ferried across by motorized canoes or a large, flat-bottomed barge.

The best **hotel** in Sayaxché is the *Guayacan* (☎9268777; ②), a modern building right beside the river, whose basement floods in the wet season. The owner, Julio Godoy, is one of the great patriarchs of Sayaxché. He used to guide big-game hunters until hunting was outlawed, and knows the area extremely well. For a cheaper room, head left down the street above the *Hotel Guayacan* to the cleanish *Hospedaje Mayapan* (①). If that's full then try the *Hospedaje Sayaxché* (①) or the *Hospedaje Margot* (①), though both are very much last resorts. There are plenty of reasonable places to eat, the best being the *Restaurant Yaxkin* (closes at 8pm); though it's a little pricey the portions are huge. Alternatively, try the restaurant at the *Hotel Guayacan,* where there's good food and fine views of the river. *La Montaña* is another solid option, owned by the knowledgable and helpful Julián Mariona, who arranges **trips** for groups of six or more to all the places mentioned above (around $40 a day), or to anywhere else you might care to visit. If he can't help you, he'll direct you to someone who can, whether you want to rent a fishing rod or a jeep.

Plenty of **boatmen** are eager to take you up- or downriver, though they tend to drive a hard bargain and quote all prices in dollars. A good bet is to try Pedro Mendez Requena, of *Viajes Don Pedro* (☎ & fax 9286109), who offers **tours** of the area from his office on the riverfront. Prices are again high, though it can be fun to shoot the breeze and subtly negotiate a deal. Don Pedro knows the captains of all the *tiendas aquaticas* (trading boats) heading downstream to Benemérito (see p.339), and is a good man to discuss your plans with. Though generally you'll need a horse or a boat to get to the remote sites of **Aguateca** and **Dos Pilas**, during the dry season a four-wheel drive truck runs from Sayaxché to both, leaving at 4am and taking around three hours.

Changing dollars is relatively easy in Sayaxché and you can change travellers' cheques at Banora, a block up from the *Hotel Guayacan*. They may also have facilities for cash advances.

The ruins of Ceibal

The most accessible and impressive of the sites near Sayaxché is **Ceibal**, which you can reach by land or river. By boat it's easy enough to make it there and back in an afternoon. Not much commercial river traffic heads upstream, however, so you'll probably have to **rent a boat** – ask around at the waterfront and be prepared to haggle: boats take up to six people and generally charge around $40. The one- to two-hour boat trip is followed by a short walk through towering rain forest. **By road** Ceibal is just 17km from Sayaxché. Any transport heading south out of town towards Cruce del Pato passes the entrance road to the site, from where it's an eight-kilometre walk through the jungle to the ruins. About halfway along the road, you'll pass a sign denoting the start of the protected area of the Ceibal cultural monument, though this status hasn't prevented some *campesinos* clearing a chunk of forest. Visiting Ceibal should be a day-trip, but if you're unlucky you may end up stranded at the entrance road waiting for a truck back. If you haven't hired a boat and decide to try and return by river, be prepared to wait a long time for a ride. If you have a tent or hammock (with mosquito net), you might as well stay – bring food to share with the guards and you'll always be welcome.

Surrounded by forest and shaded by huge ceiba trees, **the ruins** of Ceibal are partially cleared and restored, and beautifully landscaped into a mixture of open plazas and untamed jungle. Although it can't match the enormity of Tikal, and many of the largest temples lie buried under mounds, Ceibal does have some outstanding carving, superbly preserved due to the use of hard stone. The two main plazas are dotted with lovely **stelae**, centred on two low platforms. Fragments of stucco found on these platforms suggest that they were originally decorated with ornate friezes and painted in brilliant shades of red, blue, green, pink, black and beige. During the Classic period Ceibal was a relatively minor site, but it grew rapidly between 830 and 930 AD, apparently after falling under the control of colonists from what is now Mexico. In this period it was the largest southern lowland site, with an estimated population of around 10,000. Outside influence is clearly visible in the carving here: speech scrolls, straight noses, waist-length hair and serpent motifs are all decidedly non-Maya. The architecture is also very different from that of the Classic Maya sites, including the round platforms that are usually associated with the Quetzalcoatl cult, which spread from the north at the start of the Postclassic period, around 1000 AD. The monkey-faced Stela 2 is particularly striking, beyond which, straight ahead down the path, lies Stela 14, another impressive sculpture. If you turn right here and walk for ten minutes, you'll reach the only other restored site, a massive circular stone **observation** platform, used for astromomy and superbly set in a clearing in the forest.

Lake Petexbatún

A similar distance to the south of Sayaxché is **Lake Petexbatún**, a spectacular expanse of water ringed by dense forest and containing plentiful supplies of snook, bass, alligator and freshwater turtle. The shores of the lake abound with wildlife and Maya remains and though the ruins themselves are small and unrestored, they do make interesting goals as part of a trip into the forest. Their sheer number suggests that the lake was an important trading centre for the Maya.

If you can get together a group of three or four it's well worth arranging a boat and guide to take you on a **two- or three-day trip** around the lake. The simplest way to do this is to ask Julián at *La Montaña* in Sayaxché. There are plenty of options – touring the lake on foot, by boat or on horseback, wandering in the jungle, fishing or bathing in the natural warm springs on the lakeshore – but whichever you opt for you'll need a guide. It's cheapest to **stay** at the sites themselves, camping or sleeping in a hammock, although if you do feel the need for a little luxury there are **hotels** around the lake. Owned by Julián, the *Posada Caribe*, on the river before it enters the lake (☎ & fax 9286114; ⑦, including full board) offers clean, screened cabins, reasonable food and boat trips to Aguateca; negotiate rates in advance. Of the other hotels, try *Mahogany Lodge*, set in forest on a peninsula jutting into the lake (☎3317646; ⑦, including full board), with wooden *cabañas*, and camping in comfortable beds under a thatched roof with screens ($20). The nearby *Posada San Mateo* caters for upmarket tours and is of little use to independent travellers, though its bar is a great place to stop off for an ice-cold beer.

Aguateca

Of the two main sites on Lake Petexbatún, **Aguateca**, perched on a high outcrop at the southern tip of the lake, is the more accessible. Discovered in 1957, the site remains completely unrestored, although in recent years it has been the subject of intense archeological investigation. Throughout the Classic period Aguateca was dominated by the nearby city of Dos Pilas, and reached its peak at the beginning of the eighth century, when the latter was developing an aggressive policy of expansion, mounting military campaigns against nearby centres. Stela 2, dated 741 AD, records an attack on Tikal that was mounted in alliance with Ceibal and Dos Pilas, while Stela 1 records the capture of a ruler from Piedras Negras in the same year. After 761 AD Dos Pilas began to lose control of its empire and members of the elite moved their headquarters to Aguateca, attracted by its strong defensive position. Their enemies, however, soon caught up with them, and sometime after 790 Aguateca itself was overrun.

Surrounded by dense tropical forest and with superb views of the lake, Aguateca has a magical atmosphere. You can clearly make out the temples and plazas, dotted with well-preserved stelae. The carving is superbly executed, the images including rulers, captives, hummingbirds, pineapples and pelicans. If you ask the two guards who live here, they'll give you an enthusiastic and well-informed tour, explaining the meaning of the various images and showing you the stelae shattered by looters who hoped to sell the fragments. Aguateca is also the site of the only known **bridge** in the Maya world, which crosses a narrow gash in the hillside, but it's not that impressive in itself.

The guards always welcome company and if you want to **stay** they'll find some space for you to sling a hammock or pitch a tent, but you'll need to bring a mosquito net and food. To reach the site from Sayaxché by boat takes a couple of hours, but as the boatmen usually charge around $130 for the round trip you'll either need a large group or deep pockets. Aguateca is also accessible by truck in the dry season (see p.335).

Dos Pilas and around

A slightly closer (and therefore cheaper) option is **Dos Pilas**, another unreconstructed site, buried in the jungle a little way west of the lake. This was the centre of a formidable empire in the early part of the eighth century and again boasts some superb carving. From Sayaxché a 45-minute speedboat trip takes you to Rancho El Caribe, at the northern tip of the lake, from where it's a further 12km on foot to the ruins. Again, it may be possible to get there by truck during the dry months (see p.335). Two guards live at the site and it's certainly possible to stay here – as always, you should bring a tent or hammock and mosquito net, and enough food to share with the guards. Otherwise you can make a day-trip of it and return to Sayaxché in the evening, or stay at the nearby *Posada Caribe* (see p.336).

If you are interested in further exploration, ask the guards to guide you to the nearby sites of **Tamarindito** (which was responsible for the rebellion against Dos Pilas in 761 AD) and **Arroyo de Piedras**, both of which can be reached on foot from Dos Pilas.

South to the Ixcán

The road south from Sayaxché skirts round the edge of the **Ceibal natural reserve**, at first slicing through a stretch of jungle, then through a flat scrubland of lone tree stumps, cattle pasture and thatched *cabañas* where indigenous families and their swollen-bellied children live. These Kekchí, many of whom are returning refugees, struggle to eke out a meagre existence from the land.

Half an hour before **Cruce del Pato**, where the road splits (see p.301), the magnificent bulk of the Cuchumatanes mountain range comes into view, with the looming, forested ridges rising abruptly from the plain. A Del Rosio bus runs daily along this road between Sayaxché and Playitas.

Routes to Mexico

River trade between Guatemala and Mexico is increasing rapidly, as are the number of tourists making obscure border crossings. The most common routes use cargo boats which make the trip **from Sayaxché** to Benemérito, on the Mexican bank of the Río Usumacinta, several times a week. Also popular is the trip **from Flores** to El Naranjo by bus, then along the Río San Pedro to La Palma in Mexico, while increasing numbers are travelling the backroads and using the **Bethel–Frontera Corozal** route, the best way to visit the ruins of Yaxchilán (see p.346) and Bonampak. All are reasonably well organized and the people along the way are now used to seeing foreign faces.

Border formalities are relatively straightforward on the San Pedro route, where there's a Guatemalan immigration office in El Naranjo and a Mexican one along the river at El Pedregal. On the Río Usumacinta there is a Guatemalan immigration post at the riverside army base in Pipiles and a new one at Bethel. On the Mexican side there are immigration posts at a number of places along the Usumacinta, including Boca Lacantún, just outside Benemérito, and Frontera Corozal. Though it's easy enough to cross the border without getting your passport stamped, if you are caught you'll almost certainly live to regret it and could well end up in a Mexican police station for hours, while they leaf through FBI photographs and try to identify you. The Mexican army is usually the first official organization to greet you and anywhere in this part of Chiapas you can expect to have your papers examined by patrols; that said, officials are always very polite and never give tourists any cause for concern.

From Sayaxché to Benemérito and into Mexico

Downriver from Sayaxché the **Río Pasión** snakes its way through an area of forest and swamp that is gradually being occupied by a mixture of well-organized farming cooperatives and impoverished migrants. Along the way tiny river turtles bask on exposed rocks, white herons fish in the shallows and snakes occasionally slither across the surface of the river. There are two main landmarks: a slick American mission on the left-hand bank and the army post at **Pipiles** on the right, which marks the point where the rivers Salinas and Pasión merge to form the Usumacinta. All boats have to stop at Pipiles, where passengers present their papers at the immigration post and luggage may be searched.

On the south bank of the river not far from Pipiles is the small Maya site of **Altar de los Sacrificios**, discovered by Teobert Maler in 1895. Commanding an important river junction, this is one of the oldest sites in Petén, but these days there's not much to see beyond a solitary stela. The beach below, which is exposed in the dry season, is often scattered with tiny fragments of Maya pottery, uncovered as the river eats into the base of the site, carving into ancient burials.

From Pipiles it's possible to head **up the Río Salinas**, south along the Mexican border, through an isolated area visited only by traders buying maize and selling soft drinks and aspirin. Between trips these entrepreneurial geniuses can be found in Sayaxché, loading and unloading their boats, and for a small fee they might take a passenger or two. Most boats only go part of the way up the Salinas, but if you're really determined you can travel all the way to Playitas or Playa Grande (see p.302), and there join the road east to Raxrúja and Fray Bartolomé de Las Casas, or head west across the Ixcán (p.304). This is a rough trip for which you'll need a hammock, a mosquito net, a week or two, and a great deal of patience.

Following the **Usumacinta** downstream from Pipiles you arrive at **BENEMÉRITO** in Mexico, a sprawling frontier town at the end of a dirt road from Palenque. Passengers from Sayaxché are charged $8–10 for what is usually an eight-hour trip, although boats with business along the way can take a couple of days to get this far. Benemérito is the destination of most of the cargo traffic, but if you're in a hurry, or want to go further down the Usumacinta to Yaxchilán, you can rent a fast boat – expect to pay around $150 from Sayaxché to Benemérito (3–4hr), or double that to Yaxchilán (8hr). From Benemérito you can head on to Yaxchilán by boat or, much cheaper, by bus to Frontera Corozal and then by boat (see below). Benemérito has a few basic **hotels** and *comedores*. The best **restaurant** in town is the *A y D* on the main road, parallel to the river and about a kilometre from it; the owner speaks some English, changes dollars, and can give bus information.

By road from Benemérito to Frontera Corozal

Between Benemérito and Palenque there's a twenty kilometre branch road off the main route to the riverside village of **FRONTERA COROZAL**, the nearest settlement to Yaxchilán. There are at least five **buses** a day from Benemérito to Palenque (9hr), which pass by the junction for Corozal – otherwise, hitching is possible, though traffic is scarce. The first **immigration post** on this route is a couple of kilometres outside Benemérito at Boca Lacantún, where the road crosses the Río Lacantún – ask the bus driver to stop for you while you go in and pick up a tourist card. The last minibus *colectivos* leave for Palenque around 2.30pm. In Frontera Corozal itself there's very basic accomodation and if you ask around you'll be able to find somewhere to sling a hammock; you should be able to **camp** on the football pitch once the evening game has drawn to a close. The village does have a couple of simple *comedores* and an **immigration post** – so if you arrive directly by boat from Sayaxché, or across the river from Bethel (see below), you can get a tourist card here. If you want to visit Yaxchilán you *must* register at the immigration post. For details of the river trip from Benemérito to Frontera Corozal, see below.

From Bethel to Frontera Corozal

Very few commercial boats do the trip between Sayaxché and Frontera Corozal, but if you're in a group of five or more you could always rent a boat to take you there, which should take about six or seven hours. The cheapest and best way to get there from the Guatemala side, however, is along the rough road to **BETHEL** on the Río Usumacinta, where there's a Guatemalan immigration post. Although there is officially no road, travellers may be charged Q10 to cross the border. Two buses a day leave Flores for Bethel (5am & 1pm), passing the junction north of Sayaxché a couple of hours later. It's a tough and exhausting bus ride (4–5hr from Flores), but at Bethel it's relatively easy to find a *lancha* heading downstream, or you can rent one ($25 for three people to Frontera Corozal; $100 to Yaxchilán).

Bethel itself is a pleasant village with wide grassy streets and plenty of trees to provide shade. You can **camp** above the river bank and there are several **comedores** – try the *Café el Ranchito* for good food and useful information – and *tiendas*. Though clearly the remains of an important Maya city, today the **Bethel ruins**, 1.5km from the village, are little more than tree-covered mounds, their existence unknown to archeologists until 1995. There's an **eco-campamento** set among them – the *Posada Maya* – with thatched shelters for tents and hammocks on top of a wooded cliff high above the river. Prices are relatively high for camping ($5 per person) but this includes comfortable beds (with sheets) in mosquito-proof tents. The men of the village can guide you through the jungle to a cenote and can arrange trips to other ruins.

By river to Yaxchilán and Piedras Negras

As you head downriver from Benemérito, the **Río Usumacinta** marks the border between Guatemala and Mexico, passing through dense tropical rainforest, occasionally cleared to make way for pioneer villages and cattle ranches, particularly along the Mexican bank. Seven-day **trips down the Usumacinta**, from Bethel to Tenosique, are run by Maya Expeditions at 15 C 1–91, Zona 10, Guatemala City (☎3634955; fax 3374666).

Below Benemérito the first place of any interest on the river is the **Planchon de Figuras**, at the mouth of the Lacantún, a river that feeds into the Usumacinta from the Mexican side. One of the least known and most unusual of all Maya sites (though hardly a site in the conventional sense), this consists of a superb collection of graffiti carved into a great slab of limestone that slopes into the river. Its origin is completely unknown, but the designs, including birds, animals, temples and eroded glyphs, are certainly Maya. A little further downriver is the Chorro waterfall, a series of beautiful cascades some 30km before Frontera Corozal.

Yaxchilán

Boats to the Maya **ruins of Yaxchilán**, 15km beyond Frontera Corozal, can be rented in Sayaxché, Benemérito and Frontera Corozal. Rates are high: if you're on your own or in a small group, it's cheaper to get on a boat that's being used by a tour group, or to get a lift with one of the local boats that can sometimes be persuaded to go on to the ruins. If you're coming from Guatemala and plan to travel all the way to Yaxchilán by boat then it's cheaper to rent one for the whole trip – speak to Julián in Sayaxché (see p.335).

The ruins are undeniably the most spectacular on the Usumacinta, superbly positioned on the Mexican bank, spread out over several steep hills within a great loop in the river. This is an important location, and carvings at Yaxchilán, like those at the neighbouring sites of Bonampak and Piedras Negras, tell of repeated conflict with the surrounding Maya centres. By 514 AD, when its emblem glyph was used for the first time, Yaxchilán was already a place of some size, but its era of greatness was launched by the ruler Shield Jaguar, who came to power in 682 and extended the city's sphere of influence through a campaign of conquest. At this stage it was sufficiently powerful to form a military alliance that included not only the Usumacinta centres but also Tikal and Palenque. Shield Jaguar was succeeded by Bird Jaguar III, possibly his son, who seems to have continued the campaign of military expansion. Less is known about the later years in Yaxchilán, although building continued well into the Late Classic period so the site was probably occupied until at least 900 AD.

What you see today is a collection of plazas, temples and ball courts strung out along the raised banks of the river, while the low hills in the centre of the site are topped with impressive palaces. The structures are all fairly low, but each of the main temples supports a massive honeycombed roof, decorated with stucco carvings. The quality of this carving is yet again exceptional, though many of the best pieces have been removed to museums around the world: one set of particularly fine lintels is displayed in the British Museum in London.

More recent finds, however, including some incredibly well-preserved carving, remain on site. When the layers of vegetation are peeled back the original stonework appears unaffected by the last thousand years, with flecks of red paint still clinging to the surface. Yaxchilán's architecture focuses heavily on the river, and the remains of a built-up bank suggest that it might have been the site of a bridge or toll gate. At low water you can see a pyramid, about 8m square at the base, 6m high, with a carved altar on top. Built on the river bed and completely submerged at high water, it is believed by archeologists to be a bridge abutment.

Until fairly recently the site was still used by Lacandon Indians, who came here to burn incense, worship, and leave offerings to their gods. The whole place still has a bewitching atmosphere, with the energy of the forest, overwhelming in its fertility, threatening to consume the ruins. The forest here is relatively undisturbed and buzzes with life; toucans and spider monkeys loiter in the trees, while bats are now the main inhabitants of the palaces and temples.

Arriving at the site by boat you'll be met by one of the guards who live here to ward off the ever-present threat of looting. They are happy to show you round the site, though they generally ask a small fee for their labours. You're welcome to camp too, though mosquitoes can be a problem – whether you're staying or not – particularly in the rainy season.

Piedras Negras

Downstream from Yaxchilán, the ruins of **Piedras Negras** stand on the Guatemalan side of the river. Despite being possibly as extensive as Tikal, this is one of the least accessible and least visited of Maya sites. Though many of the very best carvings are on display in the National Museum of Archeology in Guatemala City, where they're a great deal easier to see, there's still plenty to experience on site. Piedras Negras, whose name refers to the stones lining the river bank here, was closely allied with Yaxchilán and probably under its rule at various times. Maps of this area often show an airstrip alongside the site, but this has long been lost to the jungle, so don't count on landing here.

Upon arrival, the most immediately impressive monument is a large rock jutting over the river bank with a carving of a seated, male figure presenting a bundle to a female figure. This was once surrounded by glyphs, now badly eroded and best seen at night with a torch held at a low angle. Continuing up the hill, across plazas and over the ruins of buildings you get some idea of the city's size. Several buildings are comparatively well preserved, particularly the **sweat baths**, used for ritual purification; the most imposing of all is the **Acropolis**, a huge complex of rooms, passages and courtyards towering 100m above the river bank. A **megalithic stairway** at one time led down to the river, doubtless a humbling sight to visitors (and captives) before the forest invaded the city. Another intriguing sight is a huge double-headed turtle glyph carved on a rock overhanging a small valley. This is a reference to the end of a *katun*; inside the main glyph is a giant representation of the day sign Ahau (also signifies Lord), recalling the myth of the birth of the maize god. During research carried out at Piedras Negras in the 1930s the artist and epigrapher Tatiana Proskouriakoff noticed that dates carved on monuments corresponded approximately to a human life span, indicating that the glyphs might refer to events in one person's lifetime, possibly the rulers of the city. Refuted for decades by the archeological establishment, the theory was later proved correct.

Traditionally, the presence of FAR guerrillas in the region protected the ruins from systematic looting – neither looters nor the army dared enter. Now the guerrillas are just a memory and access from the Mexican bank is becoming easier, it remains to be seen how long Piedras Negras can maintain its relatively untouched state.

Below Piedras Negras the current quickens and the river drops through two massive canyons. The first of these, **Cañon de San José**, is a narrow corridor of rock sealed in by cliffs 300m high; the second, the **Cañon de las Iguanas**, is less dramatic. Travel on this part of the river is treacherous and really only possible on white-water rafts: smaller craft have to be carried around the two canyons, and under no circumstances is it possible to travel upriver.

El Naranjo and the San Pedro river route into Mexico

The most direct and popular route **from Flores to Mexico** takes you along the Río San Pedro, through a remote, deforested area. The river trip starts in **EL NARANJO**, a small settlement in the northwest of Petén. Pinita buses from Flores run to El Naranjo at 5am, 8am, 11am, 1pm and 2pm; there are also Del Rosio services at at 11.30am and 2.30pm. The trip, over rough roads, takes between four and five hours. El Naranjo is a rough spot, consisting of little more than an army base, an immigration post and a main street leading to the ferry, with a few shops, *comedores* and basic hotels. Once you arrive you'll need to confirm the **boat schedule**; there's usually a service to La Palma in Mexico at around 1pm ($20 per person), returning at 8am the next day. The Guatemalan immigration post is next to the dock, and you'll be charged a fee to leave; generally $5 for Americans and Q5 for Europeans, with "regulations" often depending on the whim of the official. You can change money with the boatmen or at the *tienda*, but rates are poor. If you miss the boat, there's little to do here, though you could wander around the ruins near the dock; the army has machine-gun posts on top of the pyramids but the soldiers are friendly enough.

The *Hotel Quetzal* (①) by the boat dock is the most convenient **place to stay**, but it's basic and uncomfortable with dark cramped rooms and filthy toilets, and the restaurant serves poor, overpriced meals. Across the river, a few minutes by boat upstream from the ferry, the friendly, family-run *Posada San Pedro* has much better accommodation in *cabañas* with private bath and mosquito-netted beds (☎9261276 in Flores; Guatemala City ☎3341823; ④). It is mostly used by tour groups but if you're in a small group it may be worthwhile seeing if they have space. You could also try the CECON headquarters, across from the ferry 150m downstream – a boy in a canoe will take you for a couple of quetzals. This is the administrative centre for the *biotopo* Laguna del Tigre, and if not in use by students and scientists there may be dorm space. They'll also let you use the kitchen.

Heading downriver, the next port of call is the Mexican immigration post, about an hour away. Beyond that another three hours bring you to **LA PALMA** in Mexico, a small riverside village with bus connections to Tenosique, a good transport hub. There's nothing much in La Palma, but at a hut beside the river you can buy cold beer and food, and sling your hammock if you miss the bus. The hut's owner also changes money – at a bad rate, but if you're in need of pesos or quetzals it may be the best you'll get. If you miss the last (5pm) bus to Tenosique (and coming from Guatemala most people do), it's best to refuse Nicolás's offer of a taxi, as the last bus out of Tenosique is at 7pm and you're likely to miss that too. Resign yourself to staying the night and making an early start – the first bus out is at 6am. You can **camp** in the shelter at restaurant *Parador Turistico* by the river bank, which has the best **food** in town; they also have a couple of basic **rooms to rent**.

If you're entering Guatemala from La Palma you'll be able to catch a bus to Flores (4–5hr) from the immigration post in El Naranjo at about 2pm.

The Ruta Guacamaya and the ruins of El Perú

To the east of El Naranjo, in the upper reaches of the Río San Pedro, is **El Perú**, a seldom-visited and unreconstructed archeological site buried in some of the wildest rain forest in Petén. The temple mounds are still coated in vegetation but the site is perhaps most famous for its many well-preserved **stelae**. The two guards welcome visitors, particularly if you bring along a little spare food. You can get there by boat from El Naranjo, travelling upriver for a day, spending a day at the site and then heading back the next day, but a more practical route is being developed by ProPetén in Flores. Known as **La Ruta Guacamaya**, this is an exciting five-day trip by truck, horse and boat along rivers and through primary forest, taking in remote ruins and the largest concentrations of scarlet macaws in northern Cental America. Contact ProPetén for full details.

From Flores to Belize

The 100km from Flores to the border with Belize takes you through another sparsely inhabited section of Petén, a journey of around three hours by bus. **Buses** leave from the *Hotel San Juan* in Santa Elena at 5am, 8am and 11am, and Rosita buses from the market at 5am, 7am, 9.30am, 11am, 2pm, 3pm and 6pm. You'll need to set out early in order to get to San Ignacio or Belize City the same day: if you catch the 5am service you can make it straight through to Chetumal, in Mexico. Along the way the bus passes through Puente Ixlú (p.319), halfway between **Tikal** and Flores, so if you're coming directly from the site you can pick it up there. Once again you should set off as early as you can to avoid getting stranded.

Linea Dorada also operates a 5am **express service** to Belize City (5hr; $20) and on to Chetumal (8hr; $30), leaving from its offices on Calle Principal in Santa Elena. More than twice as expensive as the public bus, this service is quicker and smoother and also connects with services in Chetumal to Cancún. The *Hotel San Juan* mafiosi also operates a similar service.

Lake Yaxhá and the ruins of Yaxhá and Nakúm

About halfway to the border, **Lake Yaxhá** is a shallow limestone depression similar to Lake Petén Itzá, ringed by dense rain forest. The lake is home to two Maya sites and offers access to a third, **Nakúm**, to the north. The first two can be visited by car in a day, but Nakúm is more remote, demanding a couple of days or more, for which you'll need a hammock and food at the very least.

The Yaxhá ruins

The main Flores–Belize road passes about 8km to the south of the lake – ask the driver to drop you at the turning, from where it's a sweltering two-hour walk along the branch road to the lake. Here the road heads around to the right towards a *finca*, but to make it to **the ruins of Yaxhá** you want to bear off to the left, along a smaller track. At the ruins you'll find a couple of guards, who are permanently stationed here to ward off potential looters. Stuck out in the wilderness they're always pleased to see strangers and will be glad to show you around.

The ruins, rediscovered in 1904, are spread out across nine plazas. Though clearing and restoration work have recently begun, don't expect any of the manicured splendour of Tikal, but do count on real atmosphere as you attempt to discover the many features still half hidden by the forest. The most unusual aspect of Yaxhá is that the town appears to have been laid out on a grid pattern, more typical of Teotihuacán than of the less systematic growth of a Maya centre.

There is another small site, known as **Topoxte**, on the lakeshore, reached by dirt road from the eco-camp. It's not particularly impressive, but again there's one very unusual feature: everything is built on a miniature scale, including tiny temples and stelae. Inevitably an American archeologist has suggested that the site is evidence of a race of pygmy Maya.

If you want to **stay**, the wonderful solar-powered *El Sombrero Eco-Campamento* (☎9265299; fax 9265198; in Guatemala City ☎4482428; in San Ignacio, Belize ☎092/3508; ④), on the south side of the lake just off the road, has no-smoking rooms in wooden jungle lodges and space for camping. Meals – somewhat pricey – are served in the open-air restaurant, and there's a library of books on wildlife and the Maya. They can also organize boat trips and horseback tours to ruins as distant as Tikal. There's another *eco-campamento*, run by Inguat, on the far side of the lake, below the ruins, where you can pitch a tent or sling a hammock beneath a thatched shelter for free.

The ruins of Nakúm

About 20km north of Lake Yaxhá are the unrestored **ruins of Nakúm**, a somewhat larger site. The road between Yaxhá and Nakúm is rarely passable so if you plan to visit both sites you'll probably have to walk to Nakúm. The most impressive structure is the residential-style palace, which has forty rooms and is similar to the North Acropolis at Tikal. It's thought that Nakúm was a trading post in the Tikal empire, funnelling goods to and from the Caribbean coast, a role for which it is ideally situated at the headwaters of the Río Holmul. Once again there are a couple of guards permanently posted at the site and they'll be more than willing to show you around and find a spot for you to sling a hammock or pitch a tent.

If you'd rather not walk back to the road from Nakúm then it's also possible to walk from here **to Tikal** in a day, a distance of around 25km. To do this you'll need to persuade one of the guards to act as a **guide** as there's nothing marking the route. Alternatively, you could bring a guide with you for the entire trip, which is certainly the best course of action if you're in a group. To arrange a guide, speak to Inguat or see CINCAP in Flores; expect to pay around $40 per day for a guided trip from Flores to Yaxhá, Nakúm and Tikal. *El Sombrero* offers a horse-riding adventure along this route, which can include a day's fishing in the lake. It's also possible to make the trip the other way round, from Tikal to Yaxhá, if you ask around amongst the guards at the site. Approached from this direction, however, the circuit is somewhat anti-climactic, as the sites get smaller and smaller.

FIESTAS

Petén may not offer Guatemala's finest fiestas, but those there are abound with typical *ladino* energy, featuring fireworks and heavy drinking. In some of the smaller villages you'll also see traditional dances and hear the sounds of the marimba – transported here from the highlands along with many of the inhabitants of Petén.

JANUARY
Flores has its fiesta from the 12th to 15th; the final day is the most dramatic.

MARCH
San José has a small fiesta from the 10th to 19th.

APRIL
Poptún's fiesta, from April 27 to May 1, is held in honour of San Pedro Martír de Merona.

MAY
San Benito has a fiesta from the 1st to 9th, which is sure to be wild and very drunken. The border town of **Melchor de Mencos** has its fiesta from the 15th to 22nd, with the main day being the 22nd. **Dolores** has a fiesta from the 23rd to 31st, with the principal day on the 28th.

JUNE
Sayaxché has a funfair on the 16th, in honour of San Antonio de Padua.

JULY
Santa Ana's action runs from the 18th to 26th.

AUGUST
San Luís has a fiesta from the 16th to 25th, with the main day on the last day.

OCTOBER
San Francisco's fiesta runs from the 1st to 4th.

NOVEMBER
San Andrés, across the lake from Flores, has a fiesta from the 21st to 30th, with the last day the main day.

DECEMBER
Finally **La Libertad** has its fiesta from the 9th to 12th.

Melchor de Mencos and the border

MELCHOR DE MENCOS marks the Guatemalan side of the Belize–Guatemala border. There are several cheap **hotels** and *comedores*, though only one place worth staying, the *Hotel Frontera Palace* (☎ & fax 9265196; ④), just over the bridge on the river bank. The rooms, in pleasant thatched cabins, have the luxury of hot water, and there's also a restaurant. The owner, Marco Gross, who runs a small gift shop and travel agency, knows Petén extremely well and can organize trips to any of the Maya sites. The next best place to stay is the *Hilton* (①), overlooking a rather smelly creek at the far end of the street.

The Guatemalan and Belizean **border posts** are on the eastern bank of the river. Despite the countries' differences, border formalities are fairly straightforward; you have to pay a small departure tax on leaving Guatemala. **Moneychangers** will pester you on either side of the border and will give a fair rate, once you've bargained with a couple. There's also a **bank** (Mon–Fri 8.30am–2pm) just beyond the immigration building next to the *Frontera Palace*.

Buses leave **for Belize City** every hour or so, right from the border. Indeed, most actually begin their journey from the market in Melchor; for others you may have to take a shared taxi to Benque Viejo or to San Ignacio (Bz$4 per person; 20min). The journey takes a little over three hours along a good, fast, paved road.

If you can muster a small group and are in a real hurry to get to Belize City, or beyond into Mexico, then you might consider renting a minibus, which will enable you to make it right through to Mexico in a day: contact the *Hotel Petén* in Flores. Heading in the other direction, buses leave Melchor **for Flores** at 3am, 5am, 8am, 11am, 1pm and 3pm (sometimes also 5pm), and there's also a fairly regular supply of pick-ups and trucks. As usual it's well worth setting out early, when the bus service is at its best.

travel details

Buses

This is a rundown of the **scheduled bus services** available: for details of other options, see the relevant accounts in the text.

Guatemala City to Flores (10–15hr). Fuente del Norte buses leave six or seven times daily from a clean, safe terminal at 17 C 8–46, Zona 1, Guatemala City (☎2513817, 2538169). Maya Express runs buses at 4pm, 6pm and 8pm from 17 C 9–36, Zona 1, Guatemala City (☎2321914), but the best option is the daily Linea Dorada bus which leaves at 7.30pm from 16 C 10–55, Zona 1 (☎2329658). All buses pass through Poptún and past the Río Dulce bridge for **Lívingston**. On the return journey, there are at least 20 departures per day, including Fuente del Norte at 8am, 11am, 5pm and 8pm; Maya Express at 4pm, 6pm and 8pm; and Linea Dorada at 7.30pm. All buses leave from C Principal.

From Flores to Tikal (less than 2hr). A fleet of minibuses leaves hourly from the *Hotel Petén* and *Hotel San Juan* (4am–10am), returning hourly from 2pm. Minibuses also leave from the airport to Tikal, connecting with planes from Guatemala City. The Pinita bus leaves at 1pm (3hr) and continues to Uaxactún; it returns from Uaxactún at 6am.

From Flores to Sayaxché (2hr). Pinita (at the *Hotel San Juan*) has buses at 6am, 9am, 10am, 1pm and 4pm; in addition the Del Rosio buses at 5am and noon stop at Sayaxché at around 7am and 2pm en route to **Cruce del Pato**.

From Flores to Melchor de Mencos (3hr). Pinita runs buses at 5am, 8am, 11am; Rosita at 5am, 7am, 9.30am, 11am, 2pm, 3pm and 6pm. From **Melchor to Flores** buses and minibuses run every hour or so from 3am until around 4pm.

From Flores to Belize. Linea Dorada runs a daily luxury bus from its offices on Calle Principal in Santa Elena to Belize City at 5am (5hr), which continues on to the Mexican border at Chetumal (8hr) and connnects with another service up the coast to Cancún.

Flores to El Naranjo (5hr). Pinita buses run daily at 5am (to connect with the boat), 9.30am, 11.30am and 2pm, returning at the same times.

Boats

Flores to San Andrés (25min). Boats stopping at San Benito leave when full in daylight hours only, and there are direct services at 6.15am and 5.15pm. On the return journey, direct boats leave at 6am, 7am and noon.

El Naranjo to La Palma in Mexico (4hr). One boat leaves daily at 1pm.

Sayaxché to Benemérito, Mexico. A trading boat leaves most days (at least 12hr); rented speedboats take 2hr 30min–3hr.

Sayaxché to Rancho el Caribe on the Río Petexbatun. There's a daily *lancha* around noon (2hr).

Planes

Guatemala City to Flores (50min). Aerovias, Avcom, Tikal Jets and Tapsa each fly once daily with outward flights in the early morning, between 6.30am and 7am, returning at around 4pm. Aviateca flies twice daily in both directions, once in the morning and once in the afternoon.

From Flores to Belize City (35min). Flights with Tropic Air leave Mon–Fri at 9am & 4pm.

From Flores to Cancún (1hr 20min). Aviateca flights leave on Tues, Wed, Fri, Sat & Sun, and Aerocaribe flies on Mon, Wed & Fri. You can also charter flights from Flores to Uaxactún, Dos Lagunas, El Naranjo, Sayaxché, Poptún, Río Dulce, Lívingston and to the Honduras border.

PART THREE

THE
CONTEXTS

HISTORY

Prior to the advent of the Maya civilization very little is known about the area that is now called Guatemala, and even the Maya remain fairly mysterious. Set out here is a brief overview of many separate theories, none of which can claim to dominate the academic debate. Over the last few years the situation has, if anything, become even more confused, as excavations of important new sites throw up information that casts doubt on many accepted notions. At any moment our whole understanding could be overturned by new discoveries, and there is certainly still a great deal to learn.

PREHISTORY

The earliest inhabitants of the Americas are thought to have crossed the Bering land bridge from Siberia to Alaska during the Fourth Ice Age, around 60,000 years ago, when sea levels were considerably lower than they are today. Successive waves of Stone Age hunters, travelling south along an ice-free corridor, had reached Central and South America by 15,000 BC. The first recognizable culture, known as **Clovis**, had emerged by 10,000 BC, and worked stone tools, including spearpoints, blades and scrapers, dating from 9000 BC, have been found in the Guatemalan highlands.

In **Mesoamerica**, an area defined as stretching from north central Mexico through Central America to Panamá, the first settled pattern of development took place around 8000 BC, as a warming climate forced the hunter-gatherers to adapt to a different way of life. The glaciers were in retreat and the big game, which the hunters depended upon, became scarce due to the warmer, drier climate and possibly over-hunting. This period, in which the hunters turned to more intensive use of plant foods, is known as the **Archaic** and lasted until about 2000 BC. During this time the food plants vital to the subsequent development of agriculture, such as corn, beans, peppers, squash and probably maize, were domesticated, and research on ancient pollen samples indicates that the Petén region was an area of savannahs and broad-leaved woodlands. Current theory suggests that tropical forest did not appear until the Classic period, by which time the Maya could more easily control its profuse growth.

An early language, known as Proto-Maya, was in use at the time in the western highlands, and probably other places too.

THE EARLY MAYA

Somewhere between 2000 and 1500 BC we move into the **Preclassic**, a name used by archeologists to describe the earliest developments in the history of the **Maya**, marking the first phase on a long road of evolution and increasing sophistication which culminates with the Classic (300–900 AD).

The names given to archeological periods are often confusing. Current excavations seem to be pushing back the dates when the earliest breakthroughs were made, and the dates of each period vary according to what you read; but in general terms the tail end of the Archaic (5000–1500 BC) becomes the **Formative** or **Preclassic** (1500 BC–300 AD), in which the early Maya settled in villages, practised agriculture and began making pottery. Many of the temple mounds at Kaminaljuyú, on the outskirts of Guatemala City, are Preclassic, although thorough excavation is impossible as the mounds are now largely covered by sprawling suburbs. Further evidence, from a site near Ocós on the Pacific coast of Guatemala, shows groups of between three and twenty family huts, some of which include small temples.

By the **Middle Preclassic** (1000–300 BC) similar pottery and artefacts, including red and orange jars, dishes of the *Mamon* style and stone *metates*, for grinding corn, are found throughout the Maya lands, from southern

Guatemala to northern Yucatán. Temple mounds are still at their most basic and the entire culture remains village-based. However, it's thought that some kind of Maya language was spoken throughout the area and that there was a substantial increase in the population. Religion, practised from a very early date, may have provided the stimulus and social cohesion to build bigger towns and, as in all early agricultural communities, food surpluses freed some to eventually become seers, priests and astronomers. However, the Middle Preclassic is primarily marked by the spread of stable village life, with little in the way of sophisticated cultural advances.

Elsewhere in Mesoamerica, however, big changes were taking place that were to have a far-reaching impact throughout the region. The first great culture to emerge was the **Olmec** civilization, originating in the coastal plain of Veracruz, in Mexico. The Olmecs, often regarded as the true ancestors of Maya culture, developed a complex polytheistic religion, an early writing system and a calendar known as the "Long Count", which was later adopted by the Maya.

Among the Maya, real advances in architecture came in the **Late Preclassic** (300 BC–300 AD), when the **Chicanel culture** dominated the northern and central areas. Large pyramids and temple platforms were built at Tikal, El Mirador, Río Azul, Kaminaljuyú and many other sites in Guatemala, in what amounted to an explosion of Maya culture. Traditionally, these early Maya were painted as peaceful peasant farmers led by astronomer-priests, but in fact these new cities were bloodthirsty, warring rivals, with trade being of vital importance. The famous Maya corbelled arch (which was not a true arch, with a keystone, but consisted of two sides, each with stones overlapping until they eventually met, and thus could only span a relatively narrow gap) was developed in this period, and the whole range of buildings became more ambitious. The question of what sparked this phase of rapid development is a subject of much debate. Some archeologists argue that the area was injected with ideas from across the Pacific, while others see the catalyst as the Olmec culture from the Gulf of Mexico. Both groups agree, however, that writing and calendar systems spread south along the Pacific coast, which developed before the Petén area: in the

archeological sites around the modern town of Santa Lucía Cotzumalguapa there is much evidence of Olmec-style carving.

Rivalling the developments on the Pacific coast was the city of **Kaminaljuyú**, on the site of the modern capital of Guatemala, which dominated the central highlands in the early Preclassic. The principal centre in Petén during this period was **El Mirador**, where the tallest temples in the Maya world were built at around the time of Christ. El Mirador remains one of the least understood of the great Maya cities and its ruins will doubtless yield some important information on Preclassic Maya civilization.

THE CLASSIC MAYA

The development that separates the Late Preclassic from the early **Classic period** (300–900 AD) is the introduction of the Long Count calendar and a recognizable form of writing. This appears to have taken place by the fourth century AD and marks the beginning of the greatest phase of Maya achievement.

During the Classic period all the cities we now know as ruined or restored sites were built, almost always over earlier structures. Elaborately carved **stelae**, bearing dates and emblem-glyphs, were erected at regular intervals. These tell of actual rulers and of historical events in their lives – battles, marriages, dynastic succession and so on. As these dates have come to be deciphered they have provided confirmation (or otherwise) of archeological evidence and offered a major insight into the nature of Maya dynastic rule.

Developments in the Maya area were still powerfully influenced by events to the north. The overbearing presence of the Olmecs was replaced by that of **Teotihuacán**, which dominated Central Mexico during the early Classic period. Armed merchants, called *pochteca*, operated at this time, spreading the influence of Teotihuacán as far as Petén and the Yucatán. They brought new styles of ceramics and alternative religious beliefs and perhaps preceded a complete military invasion. Whatever happened around 400 AD, the overwhelming power of Teotihuacán radically altered life in Maya lands. Influence spread south, via the Pacific coast, first to Kaminaljuyú on the site of modern Guatemala City and thence to Petén, where Tikal's rise to power must have been helped by close links with Teotihuacán. Both cities prospered greatly: Kaminaljuyú was rebuilt in the style of Teotihuacán, and Tikal has a stela depicting a lord of Tikal on one side and a warrior from Teotihuacán on the other.

Exactly how the various centres related to one another is unclear, but it appears that large cities dominated specific regions though no city held sway throughout the Maya area. Broadly speaking the culture was made up of a federation of city states, bound together by a coherent religion and culture and supporting a sophisticated trade network. The cities jostled for power and influence, a struggle that occasionally erupted into open warfare.

Intense wars were fought as rival cities sought to dominate one another, with no ruler appearing to gain ascendancy for very long. There were clearly three or four main centres that dominated the region through an uncertain process of alliances. Tikal was certainly a powerful city, but at one time Caracol in Belize defeated Tikal, as shown by a Caracol ball-court marker. Detailed carvings on wooden lintels and stone monuments depict elaborately costumed lords trampling on captives and spilling their own blood at propitious festivals, staged according to the dictates of the intricate and precise Maya calendar. Copán and Quiriguá were certainly important centres in the southern area, while the cities of the highlands were still in their infancy.

At the height of Maya power, advances were temporarily halted by what is known as the **Middle Classic Hiatus**, a period during which there was little new building at Tikal and after which many smaller centres, once under the control of Tikal, became independent city states. The victory of Caracol over Tikal, some time around 550 AD, may have been a symptom or a cause of this, and certainly the collapse of Teotihuacán in the seventh century caused shock waves throughout the civilizations of Mesoamerica. In the Maya cities no stelae commemorating events were erected, and monuments and statues were defaced and damaged. In all likelihood the Maya centres suffered revolts, and warfare raged as rival lords strove to win political power.

However, as the new kings established dynasties, now free of Teotihuacán's military or political control, the Maya cities flourished as never before. Architecture, astronomy and art reached degrees of sophistication unequalled

by any other pre-Columbian society. Trade prospered and populations grew: Tikal had an estimated 40,000 people. Many Maya centres were larger than contemporary Western European cities, then in their "Dark Ages".

The prosperity and grandeur of the **Late Classic** (600–800 AD) reached all across the Maya lands: from Bonampak and Palenque in the west, to Labná, Sayil, Calakmul and Uxmal in the north, Altun Ha and Cerros in the east, and Copán and Quiriguá in the south, as well as hundreds of smaller centres. Masterpieces of painted pottery and carved jade (their most precious material) were created, often to be used as funerary offerings. Shell, bone and, occasionally, marble were also exquisitely carved; temples were painted in brilliant colours, inside and out. Most of the pigments have faded long ago, but vestiges remain, enabling experts to reconstruct vivid images of the appearance of the ancient cities.

THE MAYA IN DECLINE

The days of glory were not to last very long, however. By 750 AD political and social changes began to be felt; alliances and trade links broke down, wars increased and stelae recording periods of time were carved less frequently. Cities gradually became depopulated and new construction ceased in the central area after about 830 AD. Bonampak was abandoned before its famous murals could be completed, while many of the great sites along the River Usumacinta (now part of the border between Guatemala and Mexico) were occupied by militaristic outsiders.

The reason for the decline is not (and may never be) known. Probably, several factors contributed to the downfall of the Maya. The growth and demands of the unproductive elite may have led to a peasant revolt, while the increase in population put great strains on food production, possibly exhausting the fertility of the soil, and epidemics may have combined to cause the abandonment of city life. At the end of the Classic period there appears to have been strife and disorder throughout Mesoamerica. The power vacuum left by the departing elite could have been partially filled by Putun or Chontal Maya moving into Petén from Tabasco and Campeche in Mexico.

By the tenth century, the Maya had abandoned their central cities and those few Maya that remained were reduced to a fairly primitive state. But not all Maya cities were entirely deserted: those in northern Belize, in particular, survived to some degree, with Lamanai and other cities in the area remaining occupied throughout the **Postclassic** period (900 AD to Spanish Conquest); the Yucatán peninsula, which appears to have escaped the worst of the depopulation, was conquered by the militaristic Toltecs who came from central Mexico in 987 AD. The invaders imposed their culture on the Maya, possibly introducing human sacrifice and creating a hybrid of Classic Maya culture.

The decline of Maya civilization in the Petén lowlands meant a rapid depopulation of the heartland of the Maya, an event which prompted an influx of population into the surrounding areas, and in particular into the Yucatán peninsula in the north and the Guatemalan highlands to the south. These areas, formerly peripheral regions of relatively little development, now contained the last vestiges of Maya culture, and it's at this time that the Guatemala area began to take on some of the local characteristics which are still in evidence today. By the end of the Classic period there were small settlements throughout the highlands, usually built on open valley floors and supporting large populations with the use of terraced farming and irrigation. Little was to change in this basic village structure for several hundred years.

PRE-CONQUEST: THE HIGHLAND TRIBES

Towards the end of the thirteenth century, however, the great cities of the Yucatán, such as Chichén Itzá and Uxmal, which were now inhabited by groups of Toltec-Maya from the gulf coast of Mexico, were also abandoned. At around the same time there was an invasion of the central Guatemalan highlands, also by a group of **Toltec-Maya**, although whether they came from the Yucatán or from the Gulf of Mexico remains uncertain. Some argue that they travelled due south into the highlands along the Usumacinta and Chixoy river valleys, while others claim that they came from further west and entered the area via the Pacific coast, which has always been a popular route for invading armies. Their numbers were probably small but their impact was profound, and following their arrival life in the highlands was radically altered.

What once had been a relatively settled, peaceful and religious society became, under the influence of the Toltecs, fundamentally secular, aggressive and militaristic. The Toltec invaders were ruthlessly well organized and in no time at all they established themselves as a ruling elite, founding a series of competing empires. The greatest of these were the **Quiché**, who dominated the central area and had their capital, **Utatlán**, to the west of the modern town of Santa Cruz del Quiché. Next in line were the **Cakchiquel**, who were originally based to the south of the Quiché, around the modern town of Chichicastenango, but later moved their capital to **Iximché**. On the southern shores of Lake Atitlán the **Tzutujil** had their capital on the lower slopes of the San Pedro volcano. To the west the **Mam** occupied the area around the modern town of Huehuetenango, with their capital at **Zaculeu**, while the northern slopes of the Cuchumatanes were home to a collection of smaller groups such as the **Chuj**, the **Kanjobal**, and further to the east the **Aguatec** and the **Ixil**. The eastern highlands, around the modern city of Cobán, were home to the notoriously fierce **Achi** nation, with the **Kekchi** to their north, while around the modern site of Guatemala City the land was controlled by the **Pokoman**, with their capital at **Mixco Viejo**. Finally, along the Pacific coast the **Pipil**, a tribe that had also migrated from the north, occupied the lowlands.

The sheer numbers of these tribes give an impression of the extent to which the area was fragmented, and it's these same divisions, now surviving on the basis of language alone, that still shape the highlands today (see map on p.377).

The Toltec rulers probably controlled only the dominant tribes – the Quiché, the Tzutujil, the Mam and the Cakchiquel – while their lesser neighbours were still made up entirely of people indigenous to the area. Arriving in the later part of the thirteenth century, the Toltecs must have terrorized the local Quiché-Cakchiquel highlanders and gradually established themselves in a new, rigidly hierarchical society. They brought with them many northern traditions – elements of a Nahua-based language, new gods and an array of military skills – and fused these with local ideas. Many of the rulers' names are similar to those used in the Toltec heartland to the north, and they claimed to trace their ancestry to Quetzalcoatl, a mythical ruling dynasty from the Toltec city of Tula. Shortly after the Spanish Conquest the Quiché wrote an account of their history, the *Popol Vuh*, in which they lay claim to a Toltec pedigree, as do the Cakchiquel in their account, *The Annals of the Cakchiquel*.

The Toltec invaders were not content with overpowering just a tribe or two, so under the dircction of their new rulers the Quiché began to expand their empire by conquering neighbouring tribes. Between 1400 and 1475 they embarked on a campaign of conquest that brought the Cakchiquel, the Mam and several other tribes under their control. At the height of their power around a million highlanders bowed to the word of the Quiché king. But in 1475 the man who had masterminded their expansion, the great Quiché ruler **Quicab**, died, and the empire lost much of its authority. The Cakchiquel were the first to break from the fold, anticipating the death of Quicab and moving south to a new and fortified capital, Iximché, in around 1470. Shortly afterwards the other tribes managed to escape the grip of Quiché control and assert their independence. For the next fifty years or so the tribes were in a state of almost perpetual conflict, fighting for access to the inadequate supplies of farmland. All the archeological remains from this era give evidence of this instability; gone are the valley-floor centres of pre-Toltec times, and in their place are fortified hilltop sites, surrounded by ravines and man-made ditches.

When the Spanish arrived, the highlands were in crisis. The population had grown so fast that it had outstripped the food supply, forcing the tribes to fight for any available land in order to increase their agricultural capacity. With a growing sense of urgency both the Quiché and the Cakchiquel had begun to encroach on the lowlands of the Pacific coast. The situation could hardly have been more favourable to the Spanish, who fostered this intertribal friction, playing one group off against another.

THE SPANISH CONQUEST

While the tribes of highland Guatemala were fighting it out amongst themselves, their northern neighbours, in what is now Mexico, were confronting a new and ruthless enemy. In 1521 the Spanish conquistadors had captured the Aztec capital at Tenochtitlan and were starting to cast their net further afield. Amidst the horrors of the Conquest there was one man, **Pedro de Alvarado**, whose evilness stood out above the rest. He could hardly have been better suited to the job – ambitious, cunning, intelligent, ingenious, dashingly handsome and ruthlessly cruel.

In 1523 Cortés despatched Alvarado to Guatemala, entreating him to use the minimum of force "and to preach matters concerning our Holy Faith". His army included 120 horsemen, 173 horses, 300 soldiers and 200 Mexican warriors, largely Tlaxcalans who had allied themselves with Cortés in the conquest of Mexico. Marching south they entered Guatemala along the Pacific coast, where they met with the first wave of resistance, a small army of Quiché warriors. These were no match for the Spaniards, who cut through their ranks with ease. From here Alvarado turned north, taking his troops up into the highlands and through a narrow mountain pass to the Quetzaltenango valley, where they came upon the deserted city of **Xelajú**, a Quiché outpost.

Warned of the impending arrival of the Spanish, the Quiché had struggled to build an alliance with the other tribes, but old rivalries proved too strong and the **Quiché** army stood alone. Three days later, on a nearby plain, they met the Spaniards in open warfare. It's said that the invading army was confronted by some 30,000 Quiché warriors, led by **Tecún Umán** in a headdress of quetzal feathers. Despite the huge disparity in numbers, sling-shot and foot soldiers were no match for cavalry and gunpowder, and the Spaniards were once again able to wade through the Maya ranks. Legend has it that the battle was brought to a close when Alvarado met Tecún Umán in hand-to-hand conflict – and cut him down.

Accepting this temporary setback, the Quiché decided to opt for a more diplomatic solution and invited the Spaniards to their capital **Utatlán**, where they planned to trap and destroy them. But when Alvarado saw their city he grew suspicious and took several Quiché lords as prisoners. When hostilities erupted once again he killed the captives and had the city burnt to the ground.

Having dealt with the Quiché, Alvarado turned his attention to the other tribal groups. The **Cakchiquel**, recognizing the military superiority of the Spanish, decided to form some kind of alliance with them and as a result of this the Spaniards established their first headquarters, in 1523, alongside the Cakchiquel capital of **Iximché**. From here they ranged far and wide, overpowering the countless smaller tribes. Travelling east, Alvarado's army met the **Tzutujil** on the shores of Lake Atitlán. Here the first battle took place at a site near the modern village of Panajachel, and the second beneath the Tzutujil capital, at the base of the San Pedro volcano, where the Spaniards were helped by a force of Cakchiquel warriors who arrived on the scene in some 300 canoes. Moving on, the Spanish travelled south to the Pacific coast, where they overcame the **Pipil** before making their way back to Iximché.

In 1524 Alvarado sent his brother Gonzalo on an expedition against the **Mam**, who were conquered after a month-long siege during which they holed up in their fortified capital **Zaculeu**. In 1525 Alvarado himself set out to take on the **Pokoman**, at their capital **Mixco Viejo**, where he came up against another army of some 3000 warriors. Once again they proved no match for the well-disciplined Spanish ranks.

Despite this string of relatively easy gains it wasn't until well into the 1530s that Alvarado managed to assert control over the more remote parts of the highlands. Moving into the Cuchumatanes his forces were beaten back by the **Uspantec** and met fierce opposition in the **Ixil**. And while Alvarado's soldiers were struggling to contain resistance in these isolated mountainous areas, problems also arose at the very heart of the campaign. In 1526 the Cakchiquel rose up against their Spanish allies, in response to demands for tribute; abandoning their capital the Cakchiquel moved into the mountains, from where they waged a guerrilla war against their former partners. As a result of this the Spanish were forced to abandon their base at Iximché, and moved instead to a site near the modern town of Antigua.

Here, on St Cecilia's Day, November 22, 1527, they established their first permanent capital, the city of **Santiago de los Caballeros**. For ten years indigenous labourers toiled in the construction of the new city, neatly sited at the base of the Agua volcano, putting together a cathedral, a town hall, and a palace for Alvarado. The land within the city was given out to those who had fought alongside him, and plots on the edge of town were allocated to his remaining Maya allies.

Meanwhile, one particularly thorny problem for the Spanish was presented by the **Achi** and **Kekchi** Indians, who occupied what are now the Verapaz highlands. Despite all his efforts Alvarado was unable to conquer either of these tribes, who fought fiercely against the invading armies. In the end he gave up on the area, naming it *Tierra de Guerra* and abandoning all hopes of controlling it. The situation was eventually resolved by the Church. In 1537 **Fray Bartolomé de Las Casas**, the "protector of the Indians", travelled into the area in a bid to persuade the locals to accept both Christianity and Spanish authority. Within three years the priests had succeeded where Alvarado's armies had failed, and the last of the highland tribes was brought under colonial control in 1540. Thus did the area earn its name of *Verapaz*, true peace.

Alvarado himself grew tired of the Conquest, disappointed by the lack of plunder, and his reputation for brutality began to spread. He was forced to return to Spain to face charges of treason, but returned a free man with a young wife at his side. Life in the New World soon sent his bride to an early grave and Alvarado set out once again, in search of the great mineral wealth that had eluded him in Guatemala. First he travelled south to Peru, where it's said that Pizarro paid him to leave South America. He then returned to Spain once again, where he married **Beatriz de la Cueva**, his first wife's sister, and the two of them made their way back to Guatemala, where he dropped off his new bride before setting sail for the Spice Islands. Along the way he stopped in Mexico, to put down an uprising, and was crushed to death beneath a rolling horse.

From 1524 until his death in 1541 Alvarado had ruled Guatemala as a personal fiefdom, desperately seeking adventure and wealth and enslaving and abusing the local population in order to finance his urge to explore. By the time of his death all the Maya tribes had been overcome, although local uprisings, which have persisted to this day, had already started to take place.

COLONIAL RULE

The early years of colonial rule were marked by a turmoil of uprisings and political wrangling, and while the death of Alvarado might have been expected to bring a degree of calm, it was in fact followed by fresh disaster. When Alvarado's wife, Beatriz de la Cueva, heard of his death she plunged the capital into a period of prolonged mourning. She had the entire palace painted black, both inside and out, and ordered the city authorities to appoint her as the new governor. Meanwhile, the area was swept by a series of storms, and on the night of September 10, 1541, it was shaken by a massive earthquake. The sides of the Agua volcano shuddered, undermining the walls of the cone and releasing its contents. A great wall of mud and water swept down the side of the cone, and the city of Santiago was buried beneath it.

The surviving colonial authorities moved up the valley to a new site, where a second **Santiago de los Caballeros** was founded in the following year. This new city served as the administrative headquarters of the **Audiencia de Guatemala**, which was made up of six provinces: Costa Rica, Nicaragua, San Salvador, Honduras, Guatemala and Chiapas (now part of Mexico). With Alvarado out of the way the authorities began to build a new society, re-creating the splendours of the homeland. Santiago was never endowed with the same wealth or freedom as Mexico City and Lima, but it was nevertheless the centre of political and religious power for two hundred years, accumulating a superb array of arts and architecture. By the mid-eighteenth century its population had reached some 80,000. Here colonial society was at its most developed, rigidly structured along racial lines with pure-blood Spaniards at the top, indigenous slaves at the bottom, and a host of carefully defined racial strata in between. The city was regularly shaken by scandal, intrigue and earthquakes, and it was eventually destroyed in 1773 by the last of these, after which the capital was moved to its modern site.

Perhaps the greatest power in colonial Central America was the **Church**. The first religious order to reach Guatemala was the **Franciscans**, who arrived with Alvarado himself, and by 1532 the **Mercedarians** and **Dominicans** had followed suit, with the **Jesuits** arriving shortly after. **Francisco Marroquín**, the country's first bishop, rewarded these early arrivals with huge concessions, including both land and indigenous people, which later enabled them to earn fortunes from sugar, wheat and indigo, income boosted by the fact that they were exempt from tax. In later

years a whole range of other orders arrived in Santiago, and religious rivalry became an important shaping force in the colony. The wealth and power of the Church fostered the splendour of the colonial capital while ruthlessly exploiting the native people and their land. In Santiago alone there were some eighty churches, and alongside these were schools, convents, hospitals, hermitages, craft centres and colleges. The religious orders became the main benefactors of the arts, amassing a wealth of tapestry, jewels, sculpture and painting, and staging concerts, fiestas and endless religious processions. Religious persecution was at its worst between 1572 and 1580, when the office of the **Inquisition** set up in Santiago, seeking out those who had failed to receive the faith and dealing with them harshly. Not much is known about the precise nature of the Guatemalan inquisition, however, as no written records have survived.

By the eighteenth century the power of the Church had started to get out of control, and the Spanish kings began to impose taxes on the religious orders and to limit their power and freedom. The conflict between Church and State came to a head in 1767, when Carlos III banished the Jesuits from the Spanish colonies.

The Spanish must have been disappointed with their conquest of Central America as it offered none of the instant plunder that had been found in Mexico and Peru. They found small amounts of silver around the modern town of Huehuetenango and a few grains of gold in the rivers of Honduras, but nothing that could compare with the vast resources of Potosí (a huge silver mine in Bolivia) or highland Mexico. In Central America the **colonial economy** was based on agriculture. The coastal area produced cacao, tobacco, cotton and, most valuable of all, indigo; the highlands were grazed with sheep and goats; and cattle, specially imported from Spain, were raised on coastal ranches. In the lowlands of Petén and the jungles of the lower Motagua valley, the mosquitoes and forests remained unchallenged, although here and there certain aspects of the forest were developed; chicle, the raw material of chewing gum, was bled from the sapodilla trees, as was sarsaparilla, used to treat syphilis.

At the heart of the colonial economy was the system of *repartamientos*, whereby the ruling classes were granted the right to extract labour from the indigenous population. It was this that established the system whereby the Maya population were transported to the Pacific coast to work the plantations, a pattern that is still a tremendous burden today (see box on p.214).

Meanwhile, in the capital it was graft and corruption that controlled the movement of money, with titles and appointments sold to the highest bidder. All of the colony's wealth was funnelled through the city, and it was only here that the monetary economy really developed.

The impact of the Conquest was perhaps at its most serious in the highlands, where the **Maya population** had their lives totally restructured. The first stage in this process was the *reducción*, whereby scattered native communities were combined into new Spanish-style towns and villages. Between 1543 and 1600 some 700 new settlements were created, each based around a Catholic church. Ostensibly, the purpose of this was to enable the Church to work on its new-found converts, but it also had the effect of pooling the available labour and making its exploitation that much easier. The highland villages were still bound up in an ancient system of subsistence farming, although its pattern was now disturbed by demands for tribute.

Maya **social structures** were also profoundly altered by post-Conquest changes. The great central authorities that had previously dominated were now eradicated, replaced by local structures based in the new villages. *Caciques* (local chiefs) and *alcaldes* (mayors) now held the bulk of local power, which was bestowed on them by the Church. In the distant corners of the highlands, however, priests were few and far between, only visiting the villages from time to time. Those that they left in charge developed not only their own power structures but also their own religion, mixing the new with the old. By the start of the nineteenth century the Maya population had largely recovered from the initial impact of the Conquest, and in many places these local structures became increasingly important. In each village *cofradía* (brotherhood) groups were entrusted with the care of saints, while *principales*, village elders, held the bulk of traditional authority, a situation that still persists today. Throughout the highlands, village uprisings became increasingly commonplace as the new indigenous culture became stronger and stronger.

Perhaps even more serious for the indigenous population than any social changes were the **diseases** that arrived with the conquistadors. Waves of plague, typhoid and fever swept through a population without any natural resistance to them. In the worst-hit areas the native population was cut by some ninety percent, and in many parts of the country their numbers were halved.

Two centuries of colonial rule totally reshaped the structure of Guatemalan society, giving it new cities, a new religion, a transformed economy and a racist hierarchy. Nevertheless, the impact of colonial rule was perhaps less marked than in many other parts of Latin America. Only two sizeable cities had emerged and the outlying areas had received little attention from the colonial authorities. While the indigenous population had been ruthlessly exploited and suffered enormous losses at the hands of foreign weapons and imported diseases, its culture was never eradicated. It simply absorbed the symbols and ideas of the new Spanish ideology, creating a dynamic synthesis that is neither Maya nor Catholic.

INDEPENDENCE

The racist nature of colonial rule had given birth to deep dissatisfaction amongst many groups in Central America. Spain's policy was to keep wealth and power in the hands of those born in Spain (*chapetones*), a policy that left growing numbers of Creoles (including those of Spanish blood born in Guatemala) and Mestizos (of mixed blood) resentful and hungry for power and change. (For the majority of the indigenous people, both power and wealth were way beyond their reach.) As the Spanish departed, Guatemalan politics was dominated by a struggle between **conservatives**, who sided with the Church and the Crown, and **liberals**, who advocated a secular and more egalitarian state. One result of the split was that independence was not a clean break, but was declared several times.

The spark, as throughout Spanish America, was Napoleon's invasion of Spain and the abdication of King Fernando VII. In the chaos that followed a liberal constitution was imposed on Spain in 1812 and a mood of reform swept through the colonies. At the time Central America was under the control of **Brigadier Don Gabino Gainza**, the last of the Captains

General. His one concern was to maintain the status quo, in which he was strongly backed by the wealthy landowners and the church hierarchy. Bowing to demands for independence, but still hoping to preserve the power structure, Gainza signed a formal **Act of Independence** on September 15, 1821, enshrining the authority of the Church and seeking to preserve the old order under new leadership. Augustín de Iturbide, the short-lived emperor of newly independent Mexico, promptly sent troops to annex Guatemala to the Mexican empire, a union which was to last less than a year.

A second Declaration of Independence, in 1823, joined the Central American states in a loose **federation**, adopting a constitution modelled on that of the United States, abolishing slavery and advocating liberal reforms. The federation, however, was doomed by the struggle between and within each of the countries. The first president of the federation was **General Manuel José Acre**, a Salvadorean, who fought bitterly with his party and then founded a government of his own. This prompted others to do the same and the liberals of Salvador, Honduras and Guatemala united under the leadership of **Francisco Morazon**, a Honduran general. Under his rule **Mariano Galvez** became the chief of state in Guatemala: religious orders were abolished, the death penalty done away with, and trial by jury, a general school system, civil marriage and the Livingston law code were all instituted.

The liberal era, however, lasted little longer than the Mexican empire, and the reforming government was overthrown by a revolt from the mountains. Throughout the turmoil of independence, life in the highlands remained harsh, with the indigenous population still bearing the burdens imposed on them by two centuries of colonial rule. In 1823 a cholera epidemic swept through the entire country, killing thousands and only adding to the misery of life in the mountains. Seething with discontent, the Maya were united behind an illiterate but charismatic leader, the 23-year-old **Rafael Carrera**, under whose command they marched on Guatemala City.

Carrera respected no authority other than that of the Church, and his immediate reforms swept aside the changes instituted by the liberal government. The religious orders were restored to their former position and traditional Spanish titles were reinstated. The conservatives had little in common with Carrera but they could see that he offered to uphold their position with a tremendous weight of popular support, and hence they sided with him. Under Carrera Guatemala fought a bitter war against Morazon and the federation, eventually establishing itself as an independent republic in 1847. Carrera's other great challenge came from the state of **Los Altos**, which included much of the western highlands and proclaimed itself an independent republic in defiance of him: it was a short-lived threat, however, and the state was soon brought back into the republic.

In 1865 Carrera died, at the age of 50, leaving the country ravaged by the chaos of his tyranny and inefficiency. He was succeeded by **Vicente Cerna**, another conservative, who was to rule for the next six years.

Meanwhile, the liberal opposition was gathering momentum yet again and 1867 saw the first **liberal uprising**, led by **Serpio Cruz**. His bid for power was unsuccessful but it inspired two young liberals, Justo Rufino Barrios and Francisco Cruz, to follow suit. In the next few years they mounted several other unsuccessful revolts, and in 1870 Serpio Cruz was captured and hanged.

RUFFINO BARRIOS AND THE COFFEE BOOM

1871 marked a major turning point in Guatemalan politics. In that year Rufino Barrios and Marcia Garcia Ganados set out from Mexico with an army of just 45 men, entering Guatemala via the small border town of Cuilco. The **liberal revolution** thus set in motion was an astounding success, the army growing by the day as it approached the capital, which was finally taken on June 30, 1871. Ganados took the helm of the new liberal administration but held the presidency for just a few years, surrounding himself with ageing comrades and offering only very limited reforms.

Meanwhile, out in the district of Los Altos, **Rufino Barrios**, now a local military commander, was infuriated by the lack of action. In 1872 he marched his troops to the capital and installed them in the San José barracks, demanding immediate elections. These were granted and he won with ease. Barrios was a charismatic leader with tyrannical tendencies (monuments throughout the country testify to his sense of his own importance) who regarded himself as the great reformer and was intent on making sweeping changes. Above all he was a man of action. His most immediate acts were classic liberal gestures: the restructuring of the education system and an attack on the Church. The University of San Carlos was secularized and modernized, while clerics were forbidden to wear the cloth and public religious processions were banned. The Church was outraged and excommunicated Barrios, which prompted him to expel the archbishop in retaliation.

The new liberal perspective, though, was instilled with a deep arrogance and Barrios would tolerate no opposition, regarding his own racial and economic outlook as absolute. In order to ensure the success of his reforms he developed an effective network of secret police and struggled to make the army increasingly professional. In later years he founded the *politecnica*, an academy for young officers, and the army became an essential part of his political power base.

Alongside all this Barrios set about reforming agriculture, in which he presided over a boom period, largely as a result of the cultivation of **coffee**. It was this more than anything else that distinguished the era and was to fundamentally reshape the country. When the liberals came to power coffee already accounted for half the value of the country's exports, and by 1884 the volume of output had increased five times. To foster this expansion Barrios founded a Ministry of Development, which extended the railway network (begun in 1880), established a national bank, and developed the ports of Champerico, San José and Iztapa to handle the growth in exports. Between 1870 and 1900 the volume of foreign trade increased twenty times.

All this had an enormous impact on Guatemalan **society**. Many of the new plantations were owned and run by German immigrants, and indeed the majority of the coffee eventually found its way to Germany. The newcomers soon formed a powerful elite, and although most of the Germans were later forced out of Guatemala (during World War II), their impact can still be felt: directly in the Verapaz highlands, and more subtly in the continuing presence of an extremely powerful clique, their wealth based on the income from plantation farming, who are still central to political life in Guatemala. The new liberal perspective maintained that foreign ideas were superior to indigenous ones, and while immigrants were welcomed with open arms the Maya population was still regarded as hopelessly inferior.

Indigenous society was also deeply affected by the needs of the coffee boom, and it was here that the new crop had the most damaging and lasting effect. Under the previous regime landowners had complained that the native population was reluctant to work on the plantations and that this endangered the coffee crop. Barrios was quick to respond to their needs and instituted a system of **forced labour**. In 1876 he ordered local political chiefs to make the necessary workers available: up to one-quarter of the male population could be despatched to work on the *fincas*; in addition to this the landowners continued to employ their old methods and debt peonage spread throughout the highlands. Conditions on the *fincas* were appalling and the workforce was treated with utter contempt.

As a result of the coffee boom many Maya lost not only their freedom but also their land. From 1873 onwards the government began confiscating land that was either unused or communally owned, and selling it to the highest bidder. In some instances villages were given small tracts of land taken from unproductive *fincas*, but in the vast majority of cases it was the Maya who lost their land to large coffee plantations. Huge amounts of the country were seized, and land that had been communally owned for centuries was gobbled up by the new wave of agribusiness. In many areas the villagers rose up in defiance, and there were significant **revolts** throughout the western highlands. In Momostenango some 500 armed men faced the authorities, only to find their village overrun by troops and their homes burnt to the ground. In Cantel troops shot all of the village officials, who were campaigning against plans to build a textile factory on their land. Throughout the latter years of the nineteenth and the early ones of the twentieth century, villages continued to rise up in defiance of demands on their land and labour. At the same time the loss of their most productive land forced the Maya to become dependent on seasonal labour, while attacks on their communities drove them into increasing introspection.

JORGE UBICO AND THE BANANA EMPIRE

Rufino Barrios was eventually killed in 1885 while fighting to re-create a unified Central America, and was succeeded by a string of short-lived, like-minded presidents. The next to hold power for any time was **Manuel Estrada Cabrera**, a stern authoritarian who restricted union organization and supported the interests of big business. He ruled from 1898 until he was overthrown in 1920, by which time he was on the verge of insanity.

Meanwhile, a new and exceptionally powerful player was becoming involved: the **United Fruit Company**, whose influence asserted itself over much of Central America in the early decades of the twentieth century and which was to exercise tremendous power over the next fifty years. The story of the United Fruit Company starts in Costa Rica, where a man named Minor Keith was contracted to build a railway from San José to the Pacific coast. Running short of money he was forced to plant bananas on land granted as part of the railway contract. The business proved so profitable that Keith merged his own Tropical Trading and Transport Company with his main rival The Boston Fruit company, to form the United Fruit Company.

The Company first moved into Guatemala in 1901, when it bought a small tract of land on which to grow bananas, and in 1904 it was awarded a contract to complete the railway from Guatemala City to Puerto Barrios. The company was also granted 100 feet on either side of the track, exempted from paying any tax for the next 99 years, and assured that the government wouldn't interfere with its activities. In 1912 ownership of the Pacific railway network fell to the company and, as it already controlled the main Caribbean port, this gave it a virtual monopoly over transport. It was around this time that large-scale banana cultivation really took off, and by 1934 United Fruit controlled a massive amount of land, exporting around 3.5 million bunches of bananas annually and reaping vast profits. In 1941 some 25,000 Guatemalans were employed in the banana industry.

The power of the United Fruit Company was by no means restricted to agriculture, and its influence was so pervasive that the company earned itself the nickname *El Pulpo*, "the octopus". Control of the transport network brought with it control of the coffee trade: by 1930 28 percent of the country's coffee output was handled by the company's Caribbean port, Puerto Barrios. During the 1930s it cost as much to ship coffee from Guatemala to New Orleans as it did from Río de Janeiro to New Orleans.

Against this background the power of the Guatemalan government was severely limited, with the influence of the United States increasing alongside that of the United Fruit Company. In 1919 Guatemala faced a financial crisis and President Cabrera was ousted by a coup the following year. He was replaced by **Carlos Herrera**, who represented the Union Party, a rare compromise between liberal and conservative politicians. Herrera refused to use the traditional weapons of tyranny and his reforms threatened to terminate United Fruit Company contracts. As a result of this Herrera was to last barely more than a year, replaced by **General José Maria Orellano** in December 1921. Orellano had no qualms about repressive measures and his minister of war, Jorge Ubico, killed some 290 opponents in 1926, the year in which Orellano died of a heart attack. His death prompted a bitter power struggle between Jorge Ubico, a fierce radical, and **Lazaro Chacon**, who won the day and was elected as the new liberal president. In the next few years indigenous farmers began to express their anger at the United Fruit Company monopoly, while the company demanded the renewal of longstanding contracts, squeezing Chacon from both sides. His rule came to an end in 1930, when he suffered a stroke.

The way was now clear for **Jorge Ubico**, a charismatic leader who was well connected with the ruling and land-owning elite. Ubico had risen fast through the ranks of local government as *jefe politico* in Alta Verapaz and Retalhuleu (greatly assisted by the patronage of his godfather Rufino Barrios), earning a reputation for efficiency and honesty. As president, however, he inherited financial disaster. Guatemala had been badly hit by the Depression, accumulating debts of some $5 million: in response Ubico fought hard to expand the export market for Guatemalan produce, managing to sign trade agreements that exempted local coffee and bananas from import duties in the United States. But increased trade with the great

American power was only possible at the expense of traditional links with Europe.

Within Guatemala Ubico steadfastly supported the United Fruit Company and the interests of US business. This relationship was of such importance that by 1940 ninety percent of all Guatemalan exports was being sold in the United States. Trade and diplomacy drew Guatemala ever closer to the United States, a relationship exemplified when Ubico, against his will, was forced to bow to US pressure for the expulsion of German landowners in the run-up to World War II.

Internally, Ubico embarked on a radical programme of reform, including a sweeping drive against corruption and a massive road-building effort, which bought him great popularity in the provinces. Despite his liberal pretensions, however, Ubico sided firmly with big business when the chips were down, always offering his assistance to the United Fruit Company and other sections of the landowning elite. The system of debt peonage was replaced by the **vagrancy law**, under which all landless peasants were forced to work 150 days a year. If they weren't needed by the *fincas* then their labour was used in the road-building programme or some other public works scheme. The power of landowners was further reinforced by a 1943 law that gave them the power to shoot poachers and vandals, and in effect landowners were given total authority over their workforce. Throughout his period of office Ubico ignored the rights and needs of the peasant population, who were still regarded as ignorant and backward, and as a result of this there were continued uprisings in the late 1930s and early 1940s.

Internal security was another obsession that was to dominate Ubico's years in office, as he became increasingly paranoid. He maintained that he was a reincarnation of Napoleon and was fascinated by all aspects of the military: he operated a network of spies and informers whom he regularly used to unleash waves of repression, particularly in the run-up to elections. In 1934, when he discovered an assassination plan, three hundred people were killed in just two days. To prevent any further opposition he registered all printing presses in the country and made discipline the cornerstone of state education.

But while Ubico tightened his grip on every aspect of government, the rumblings of opposition grew louder. In 1944 discontent erupted in a wave of student violence, and Ubico was finally forced to resign after fourteen years of tyrannical rule. Power was transferred to **Juan Frederico Ponce Viades**, who attempted to continue in the same style, but by the end of the year he was also faced with open revolt, and finally the pair of them were driven into exile.

TEN YEARS OF "SPIRITUAL SOCIALISM"

The overthrow of Jorge Ubico released a wave of opposition that had been bottled up throughout his rule. Students, professionals and young military officers demanded democracy and freedom. It was a mood that was to transform Guatemalan politics and was so extreme a contrast to previous governments that the handover was dubbed **the 1944 revolution**.

Power was initially passed to a joint military and civilian junta, elections were planned, and in March 1945 a new constitution was instituted, extending suffrage to include all adults and prohibiting the president from standing for a second term of office. In the elections **Juan José Arévalo**, a teacher, won the presidency with 85 percent of the vote. His political doctrine was dubbed "spiritual socialism", and he immediately set about effecting much-needed structural reforms. Under a new budget, a third of the government's income was allocated to social welfare, to be spent on the construction of schools and hospitals, a programme of immunization, and a far-reaching literacy campaign. The vagrancy laws were abolished, a national development agency was founded, and in 1947 a labour code was adopted, granting workers the right to strike and union representation.

The expulsion of German plantation owners during World War II had placed several large *fincas* in the hands of the state, and under Arévalo some of these were turned into cooperatives, while new laws protected tenant farmers from eviction. Other policies were intended to promote industrial and agricultural development: technical assistance and credit were made available to peasant farmers and there was some attempt to colonize Petén.

In Arévalo's final years the pace of reform slackened somewhat as he concentrated on consolidating the gains made in early years and evading various attempts to overthrow him. Despite his popularity Arévalo was still wary of the traditional elite: church leaders, old-school army officers and wealthy landowners all resented the new wave of legislation, and there were repeated coup attempts.

Elections were scheduled for 1950 and during the run-up the two main candidates were **Colonel Francisco Arana** and **Colonel Jacobo Arbenz**, both military members of the junta that had taken over at the end of the Ubico era. But in 1949 Arana, who was favoured by the right, was assassinated. Suspicion fell on Arbenz, who was backed by the peasant organizations and unions, but there was no hard proof. For the actual vote Arana was replaced by **Brigadier Ydigoras Fuentes**, an army officer from the Ubico years.

Arbenz won the election with ease, taking 65 percent of the vote, and declared that he would transform the country into an independent capitalist nation and raise the standard of living. But the process of "overthrowing feudal society and ending economic dependency" was to lead to a direct confrontation between the new government and the American corporations that still dominated the economy.

Aware of the size of the task that faced him, Arbenz enlisted the support of the masses, encouraging the participation of peasants in the programme of agrarian reform and inciting the militancy of students and unions. He also attempted to break the great monopolies, building a state-run hydroelectric plant to rival the American-owned generating company and a highway to compete with the railway to the Caribbean, and planning a new port alongside Puerto Barrios, which was still owned by the United Fruit Company. At the same time Arbenz began a series of suits against foreign corporations, seeking unpaid taxes. Internally, these measures aroused a mood of national pride, but they were strongly resented by the American companies whose empires were under attack.

The situation became even more serious with the **law of agrarian reform** passed in July 1952, which stated that idle and state-owned land would be distributed to the landless. Some of this land was to be rented out for a lifetime lease, but the bulk of it was handed over outright to the new owners, who were to pay a small percentage of its market value. The former owners of the land were to be compensated with government bonds, but the value of the land was calculated on the basis of the tax

they had been paying, usually a fraction of its true value.

The new laws outraged landowners, despite the fact that they were given the right to appeal. Between 1953 and 1954 around 884,000 hectares were redistributed to the benefit of some 100,000 peasant families. It was the first time since the arrival of the Spanish that the government had responded to the needs of the indigenous population, although some studies suggest that the whole issue confused them, and they were unsure how to respond. The landowner most seriously affected by the reforms was the United Fruit Company, which only farmed around fifteen percent of its land holdings, and lost about half of its property.

As the pace of reform gathered, Arbenz began to take an increasingly radical stance. In 1951 the Communist Party was granted legal status, and in the next election four party members were elected to the legislature. But the Arbenz government was by no means a communist government, although it remained staunchly anti-American.

In the United States the press repeatedly accused the new Guatemalan government of being a communist beachhead in Central America, and the US government attempted to intervene on behalf of the United Fruit Company. Allen Dulles, the new director of the CIA, happened also to be a member of the company's board.

In 1953 President Eisenhower finally approved plans to overthrow the government. The CIA set up a small military invasion of Guatemala to depose Arbenz and install an alternative administration more suited to their tastes. A rag-tag army of exiles and mercenaries was put together in Honduras, and on June 18, 1954, Guatemala City was bombed with leaflets demanding the resignation of Arbenz. Aware that the army would never support him, Arbenz had bought a boat-load of Czechoslovakian arms, hoping to arm the people; but the guns were intercepted by the CIA before they reached Puerto Barrios. On the night of June 18, Guatemala was strafed with machine-gun fire while the invading army, described by Arbenz as "a heterogeneous Fruit Company expeditionary force", was getting closer to the city by the hour.

On June 27 Arbenz declared that he was relinquishing the presidency to **Colonel Carlos**

Enrique Díaz, the army chief of staff. And on July 3 John Peurifoy, the American Ambassador to Guatemala, flew the new government to Guatemala aboard a US Air Force plane. Guatemala's attempt to escape the clutches of outside intervention and bring about social change had been brought to an abrupt end.

COUNTER-REVOLUTION AND MILITARY RULE

Following the overthrow of Arbenz it was the army that rose to fill the power vacuum, and they were to dominate politics for the next thirty years, sending the country into a spiral of violence and economic decline. Since the time of Jorge Ubico the army had become increasingly professional and political, and now it began to receive increasing amounts of US aid, expanding its influence to include a wide range of public works and infrastructure projects.

In 1954 the American ambassador had persuaded a provisional government to accept **Castillo Armas** as the new president, and the gains of the previous ten years were immediately swept away. Hardest hit was the indigenous population, who had enjoyed the greatest benefits under the Arbenz administration, as *ladino* rule was firmly reinstated. The constitution of 1945 was revoked and replaced by a more restrictive version; all illiterates were disenfranchised, left-wing parties were outlawed, and large numbers of unionists and agrarian reformers were simply executed. Restrictions placed on foreign investment were lifted and all the land that had been confiscated was returned to its previous owners. Meanwhile, Armas surrounded himself with old-style Ubico supporters, attempting to reinstate the traditional elite and drawing heavily on US assistance in order to develop the economy.

To lend a degree of legitimacy to the administration Armas held a referendum in which voters were given the chance to support his rule (though what else was on offer was never made clear). With or without popular support, however, the new government had only limited backing from the armed forces, and coup rumblings continued throughout his period of office, which was brought to a close in 1957, when he was shot by his own bodyguard.

The assassination was followed by several months of political turmoil, out of which **Ydigoras** (who had stood against Arbenz in 1954, but declined an offer to lead the CIA invasion) emerged as the next president, representing the National Democratic Renovation Party. Ydigoras was to rule for five years, a period that was marked by corruption, incompetence, outrageous patronage and economic decline caused by a fall in coffee prices, although as some compensation the formation of the Central American Common Market helped to boost light industry. The government was so disastrous that it prompted opposition even from within the ranks of the elite. In 1960 a group of young military officers, led by **Marcos Yon Sosa** and **Turcios Lima**, attempted, without success, to take control, while in 1962 a large section of the Congress withdrew its support from the government.

Ydigoras was eventually overthrown when Arévalo threatened to return to Guatemala and contest the 1963 elections, which he might well have won. The possibility of another socialist government sent shock waves through the establishment in both Guatemala and the United States, and John F. Kennedy gave the go-ahead for another coup. In 1963 the army once more took control, under the leadership of **Perlata Azurdia**.

Perlata was president for just three years, during which he fiddled with the constitution and took his time in restoring the electoral process. Meanwhile, the authoritarian nature of his government came up against the first wave of armed resistance. Two failed coupsters from 1960, Turcios Lima and Marcos Yon Sosa, both army officers, took to the eastern highlands and waged a **guerrilla war** against the army. Trained in counter-insurgency by the US army in Panamá and both in their early twenties, they began to attack local army posts. A second organization, FAR, emerged later that year, and the Guatemalan Labour Party (PGT) formed a shaky alliance with the guerrillas, attempting to represent their grievances in the political arena and advocating a return to Arévalo's rule.

Perlata finally lost control in the 1966 elections, which were won by **Julio Cesar Montenegro** of the centre-left *Partido Revolucionario*. Before taking office, however, Montenegro was forced to sign a pact with the military, obliging him to obey their instructions and giving the army a totally free hand in all affairs of national security. Montenegro was elected on July 1, and his first act was to offer an amnesty to the guerrillas: when this was rejected a ruthless counter-insurgency campaign swung into action (a pattern of events that was repeated in the early 1980s under Ríos Montt).

Under the command of Colonel Arana Osorio, "the Jackal of Zacapa", specially trained units, backed by US advisers, undermined peasant support for the guerrillas by terrorizing the local population. The guerrillas were soon forced to spend much of their time on the move, and further damage was done to the movement by the death of Turcios Lima, in a car crash. By the end of the decade the guerrilla movement had been virtually eradicated in the eastern highlands, and its activities, greatly reduced, shifted to Guatemala City.

Meanwhile, Montenegro declared his government to be "the third government of the revolution", aligning it with the socialist administrations of Arévalo and Arbenz. But despite the support of reformers, students, professionals and a large section of the middle classes, his hands were tied by the influence of the army. Above all else the administration was marked by the rise of political violence and the increasing power of an alliance between the army and the MLN, a right-wing political party. Political assassination became commonplace as "**death squads**" such as the *Mano Blanco* and *Ojo por Ojo* operated with impunity, killing peasant leaders, students, unionists and academics.

ECONOMIC DECLINE AND POLITICAL VIOLENCE

The history of Guatemala since 1970 has been dominated by electoral fraud and political violence. At the heart of the crisis is the injustice and inequality of Guatemalan society: for while the country remains fairly prosperous the benefits of its success never reach the poor, who are denied access to land, education or health care and are forced instead to work in the coastal plantations that fuel the capital's affluence. The victims of this system have little to lose, while the ruling elite refuses to concede any ground.

In the 1970 elections the power of the military and the far right (represented by the MLN and PID) was confirmed, and **Colonel Arana Osorio**, who had directed the counter-insurgency campaign in the east, was elected president. The turnout was under fifty percent, of which Arana polled just under half, giving him the votes of around four percent of the popula-

tion (bearing in mind that only a small percentage was enfranchised).

Once in power he set about eradicating armed opposition, declaring that "if it is necessary to turn the country into a cemetery in order to pacify it, I will not hesitate to do so". The reign of terror, conducted by both the armed forces and the "death squads", reached unprecedented levels. Once again the violence was to claim the lives of students, academics, opposition politicians, union leaders and agrarian reformers. According to one estimate there were 15,000 political killings during the first three years of Arana's rule.

The next round of presidential elections was held in 1974, and was contended by a broad coalition of centre-left parties under the banner of the National Opposition Front (FNO), headed by General Efraín Ríos Montt. The campaign was marked by manipulation and fraud on the part of the right, who pronounced their candidate, **Kjell Laugerud**, as the winner. The result caused uproar, and for several days the situation was extremely tense. Ríos Montt was eventually persuaded to accept defeat and packed off to a diplomatic post in Spain, although many had hoped that reforming elements within the armed forces would secure his right to the presidency.

Meanwhile, the feared severity of the Laugerud regime never materialized and instead he began to offer limited reforms, incorporating Christian Democrats into his government. Greater tolerance was shown towards union organizations and the cooperative movement, and the government launched a plan for the colonization of Petén and the Northern Transversal Strip in an attempt to provide more land. The army, though, continued as ever to consolidate its authority, spreading its influence across a wider range of business and commercial interests and challenging Laugerud's moderation.

All of this was interrupted by a massive **earthquake** on February 4, 1976. The quake left around 23,000 dead, 77,000 injured and a million homeless. For the most part it was the homes of the poor, built from makeshift materials and on unstable ground, that suffered the most, while subsistence farmers were caught out just as they were about to plant their corn. On the Caribbean coast Puerto Barrios was almost totally destroyed and remained cut off from the capital for several months.

In the wake of the earthquake, during the process of reconstruction, fresh centres of regional control emerged on both sides of the political spectrum. The electoral process seemed to offer no respite from the injustice that was at the heart of Guatemalan society, and many of the victims felt the time had come to take action. A revived trade union organization championed the cause of the majority, while a new guerrilla organization, the Guerrilla Army of the Poor (EGP), emerged in the Ixil area, and army operations became increasingly ferocious. In 1977 President Carter suspended all military aid to Guatemala because of the country's appalling human rights record.

In the following year, 1978, Guatemala's elections were once again dominated by the army, who engineered a victory for **Brigadier General Fernando Lucas García**, who had served as defence minister in the Laugerud administration. The run-up to the elections was marred by serious disturbances in Guatemala City, after bus fares were doubled. Lucas García promised to bring the situation under control, and things took a significant turn for the worse as the new administration unleashed a fresh wave of violence. All opposition groups met with severe repression, as did journalists, trade unionists and academics. Conditions throughout the country were deteriorating rapidly, and the economy was badly affected by a fall in commodity prices, while several guerrilla armies were developing strongholds in the highlands.

As chaos threatened, the army resorted to extreme measures, and within a month there was a major massacre. In the village of **Panzós**, Alta Verapaz, a group of local people arriving for a meeting were cut down by soldiers, leaving a hundred of them dead (see p.299). In Guatemala City the situation became so dangerous that political parties were driven underground. Two leading members of the Social Democrats, who were expected to win the next election, lost their lives in 1979. Once they were out of the way the government turned on the Christian Democrats, killing more than a hundred of their members and forcing Vinicio Cerezo, the party's leader, into hiding.

Throughout the Lucas administration the **army** became increasingly powerful and the death toll rose steadily. In rural areas the war against the guerrillas was reaching new heights as army casualties rose to 250 a month, and the demand for conscripts grew rapidly. The four main guerrilla groups had an estimated 6000 combatants and some 250,000 unarmed collaborators. Under the Lucas administration the horrors of **repression** were at their most intense, both in the highlands and in the cities. The victims again included students, journalists, academics, politicians, priests, lawyers, teachers, unionists, and above all peasant farmers, massacred in their hundreds. Accurate figures are impossible to calculate but it's estimated that around 25,000 Guatemalans were killed during the four years of the Lucas regime.

But while high-ranking officers became more and more involved in big business and political wrangling, the officers in the field began to feel deserted. Here there was growing discontent as a result of repeated military failures, inefficiency and a shortage of supplies, despite increased military aid from Israel.

RÍOS MONTT

The 1982 elections were again manipulated by the far right, who ensured a victory for **Aníbal Guevara**. However, on March 23 a group of young military officers led a successful coup, which installed **General Efraín Ríos Montt** (who had been denied the post in 1974) as the head of a three-member junta. The coup leaders argued that they had been left with no option as the ruling elite had overridden the electoral process three times in the last eight years, and the takeover was supported by the majority of the opposition parties.

Ríos Montt was a committed Christian, a member of the *Iglesia del Verbo*, and throughout his rule Sunday night television was dominated by presidential sermons. Above all he was determined to restore law and order, eradicate corruption, and defeat the guerrillas, with the ultimate aim of restoring "authentic democracy". Government officials were issued with identity cards inscribed with the words "I do not steal. I do not lie."

In the immediate aftermath of the coup things improved dramatically. Repression dropped overnight in the cities, a welcome relief after the turmoil of the Lucas regime. Corrupt police and army officers were forced to resign, and trade and tourism began to return.

However, in the highlands the war intensified, as Ríos Montt declared that he would defeat the guerrillas by Christmas. Throughout

June they were offered **amnesty** if they turned themselves in to the authorities, but once the month had passed (and only a handful had accepted) the army descended on the highlands with renewed vigour. Montt had instituted a new "code of conduct" for the army, binding soldiers not to "take a pin from the villagers" and not to "make romantic overtures to the women of the region". The army set about destroying the guerrillas' infrastructure by undermining their support within the community. In those villages that had been "pacified" the local men were organized into Civil Defence Patrols (PACs), armed with ancient rifles, and told to patrol the countryside. Those who refused were denounced as "subversives". Thus the people of the villages were forced to take sides, caught between the attraction of guerrilla propaganda and the sheer brutality of the armed forces.

Ríos Montt's bizarre blend of stern morality and ruthlessness was as successful as it was murderous, and the army was soon making significant gains against the guerrillas. In late 1982 President Reagan, deciding that Ríos Montt had been given a "bum rap", restored American military aid. Meanwhile, the "state of siege" became a "state of alarm", under which special tribunals were given the power to try and execute suspects. By the middle of 1983 Ríos Montt was facing growing pressure from all sides. Leaders of the Catholic Church were outraged by the influx of evangelical preachers, while politicians, businesspeople, farmers and professionals were angered by the lack of progress towards democratic rule, and landowners were frightened by rumours of land reform.

In August 1983 Ríos Montt was overthrown by yet another military coup, this one backed by a US government keen to see Guatemala set on the road to democracy. The new president was **General Mejía Víctores**, and although the death squads and disappearances continued, elections were held for an 88-member Constituent Assembly, which was given the task of drawing up a new constitution in preparation for presidential elections.

Under Víctores there was an upturn in the level of rural repression, though the process of reconstruction initiated by Ríos Montt continued. Internal refugees were rehoused in "model villages", where they were under the control of

the army. Scarcely any money was available for rebuilding the devastated communities, and it was often widows and orphans who were left to construct their own homes. In the Ixil Triangle alone the war had displaced 60,000 people (72 percent of the population), and nine model villages were built to replace 49 that had been destroyed. Nationwide a total of 440 villages had been destroyed and around 100,000 had lost their lives.

In 1985 presidential elections were held, the first free vote in Guatemala for thirty years.

CEREZO AND THE RETURN TO DEMOCRATIC RULE

The elections were won by **Vinicio Cerezo**, a Christian Democrat whose father had served in the Arbenz administration. Cerezo was by no means associated with the traditional ruling elite and had himself been the intended victim of several assassination attempts. His election victory was the result of a sweeping wave of popular support, and in the run-up to the election he offered a programme of reform that he claimed would rid the country of repression.

Once in office, however, Cerezo was aware that his room for manoeuvre was subject to severe limitations, and he declared that the army still held 75 percent of the power. From the outset he could promise little: "I'm a politician not a magician. Why promise what I cannot deliver? All I commit myself to doing is opening up the political space, giving democracy a chance."

Throughout his six-year rule Cerezo offered a **non-confrontational approach**, seeking above all else to avoid upsetting the powerful alliance of business interests, landowners and generals. To protect himself, he courted the support of a group of sympathetic officers, and with their aid survived several coup attempts. But the administration remained trapped in the middle; the right accused Cerezo of communist leanings, while the left claimed that he was evading his commitment to reform.

Political killings dropped off a great deal under civilian rule, although they by no means stopped. Murder was still a daily event in Guatemala in the late 1980s and the war between the army and the guerrillas still raged in remote corners of the highlands. In Guatemala City the death squads continued to operate freely. No one accused Cerezo of involvement in the killings but it was clear that they were often carried out by policemen or soldiers as the right continued to use violent repression to direct and control the political situation.

In many ways the Cerezo administration was a bitter disappointment to the Guatemalan people. Although these early years of civilian rule did create a breathing space, by the time the decade drew to a close it was clear that the army was still actively controlling political opposition. Having forsaken the role of government, the generals allowed Cerezo to take office, presenting an acceptable face to the world, but the army continued to control the countryside and the economy continued to serve a small but potent elite. By 1988 violence was again on the increase, and in the village of El Aguacate, in the department of Chimaltenango, 22 corpses were found in a shallow grave. Army and guerrillas have blamed each other for the massacre, by far the most serious under Cerezo's rule, but no real proof has emerged (which may in itself be an indication of official involvement). Urban killings and **"disappearances"** were also on the increase in the final years of Cerezo's rule. In February 1989 there were 220 killings, of which 82 were politically motivated. It now appears that the Cerezo administration failed to stem the tide of violence or to alter the country's distorted balance of power.

The country's leading **human rights organization**, the Mutual Support Group (GAM), hoped that civilian rule would present them with a chance to investigate the fate of the "disappeared" and to face up to the country's horrific recent history. Cerezo, however, chose to forget the past, and ongoing abuses went largely uninvestigated and unpunished. GAM's leaders, meanwhile, became victims of the death squads.

Nevertheless, the promise of civilian rule created a general thaw in the political climate, fostering the growth of numerous pressure groups and fresh demands for reform, making protests and strikes a regular feature of Guatemalan life. Real change, however, never materialized. Despite the fact that at least 65 percent of the population were still living below the official poverty line, little was done to meet their needs in terms of education, health care or employment. The thirst for land reform reared its head once again, and under the leadership of Padre Andrés Girón, some 35,000 peasants demanded action. Girón's approach was direct.

He accused business interests of "exploiting and killing our people. We want the south coast, that's where the wealth of Guatemala lies." Cerezo avoided the issue and in a bid to appease the business community steered clear of any significant tax reform or privatization policy. (Padre Girón was the intended victim of an assassination attempt.) The population became increasingly frustrated with the Cerezo regime; teachers, postal workers and farm labourers all came out on strike, demanding action on human rights and economic reform, while the threat of a military coup continued to restrict the government's room for manoeuvre.

Meanwhile, the economy was hit badly by falling commodity prices (most notably the price of coffee), further restricting the president's position. Despite the fact that Guatemalan income tax is among the lowest in the world, any move to increase tax receipts was met with bitter resistance from the landowning classes. However, Cerezo did successfully negotiate a loan from the IMF and instituted a series of austerity measures designed to revitalize the economy after decades of decline.

Acknowledging that his greatest achievement had been to survive, Cerezo organized the country's first civilian transfer of power for thirty years in 1990.

THE 1990 ELECTION AND THE SERRANO ADMINISTRATION

The **1990 elections** were dogged by controversy. The constitution prevented Cerezo from standing for re-election, while another former president, General Ríos Montt, who retained much popularity in the countryside, was prevented from running for office since he had previously come to power as the result of a military coup. In the end twelve candidates contested the election, and it was won by a former minister in the Ríos Montt government, **Jorge Serrano**. However, with a third of the population not registered to vote and an abstention rate of 56 percent, Serrano had the support of less than a quarter of the people.

An engineer and evangelical, Serrano emphasized his centre-right economic goals and attempted to negotiate a final solution to the country's thirty-year civil war. But once again the government appeared both uninterested and incapable of effecting any real reform. The level of human rights abuse remained high, death squad activity continued, the economy remained weak and the army was still a powerful force, using intimidation and murder to stamp out opposition. (Five hundred Guatemalans either disappeared or were killed in extrajudicial executions in 1992.)

Despite the fact that Guatemala remained one of the richer nations in the region, **economic growth** was slow and the economy remained largely dependent on commodities, US aid and tourism. The Serrano administration, unable to act decisively, faced a growing wave of strikes and protests in 1993, following a series of price rises and wage freezes. Economic activity was still controlled by a tiny elite; 60 percent of the workforce were employed in agriculture and less than two percent of landowners owned more than 65 percent of the land, leaving some 85 percent of the population living in poverty, with little access to health care or education.

Nevertheless, Guatemala's dispossessed and poor continued to clamour for change. Out in the countryside the **indigenous population** became increasingly organized and influential, denouncing the continued bombardment of villages and rejecting the presence of the army and the system of civil patrols. Matters were brought into sharp focus in 1992, when Rigoberta Menchú was awarded the Nobel Peace Prize for her campaigning work on behalf of Guatemala's indigenous population. In spite of the efforts of the Serrano administration the country's civil war still rumbled on and three main guerrilla armies, united as the URNG, continued to confront the army. (The guerrillas were thought to have between 1000 and 3000 armed regulars, while the army numbered some 43,000.)

One of the most pressing problems for the indigenous people was the return of some 45,000 **refugees** who had been living in camps in Mexico. In January 1993 a first group of 2500 refugees returned home after more than a decade in Mexico, resettling in villages in the Ixcán region in the north of the department of Quiché. Prior to their return other villages in the area were bombarded and two were destroyed by the army after their inhabitants had fled, a move that was frighteningly reminiscent of the worst days of the country's civil war. As the remaining refugees started to make their way home, hardened by ten years in exile, their resettlement was a great test of how far Guatemala had come since those days. The refugees insisted upon their right to establish free civil communities, while the army argued that they were linked with the guerrillas.

THE OUSTING OF SERRANO

In **May 1993**, much to the surprise of the international community, President Serrano responded to a wave of popular protest with an *auto-golpe* or **self-coup**. Suspending the constitution he stated that he would rule by decree. Following the example of Peru's President Fujimori, Serrano argued that the country was endangered by civil disorder and corruption. "I had to put a stop to it", he claimed, arguing that the drug mafia planned to take over Guatemala. Few were convinced, and the US responded by suspending its annual $67 million of aid.

Serrano's claims about the "drug mafia" masked a more self-serving purpose, that of holding onto power. Throughout the early part of 1993 his popularity was in steep decline; price rises met with violent protest, human rights abuses remained commonplace and negotiations with the guerrillas were deadlocked. As his former supporters deserted him Serrano was forced to rely increasingly upon the support of the army and it was the generals who backed and orchestrated the coup. However, within a couple of days they had decided that Serrano's fumbling wasn't really serving their purposes and on June 1 he was removed from office. Into his shoes stepped the Defence Minister, **General José Domingo Carcia Samayoa**, but in the face of further widespread protests, from both left and right, congress finally appointed **Ramiro de León Carpio**, the country's human rights ombudsman, as the new president.

In some ways the crisis drew back the curtains on Guatemala's flirtation with civilian rule to reveal that the army retained the controlling hand, although for the generals the coup had a bitter sting in its tail. Serrano, like Cerezo before him, was a useful front man, but certain key issues such as human rights, tax and land reform, remained unassailable. Guatemalan society maintained its hopelessly imbalanced structure, dominated by an alliance of the army, big business and landowners, who allowed civilians to run the government so that they could get on with the more serious business of running the country. Coup rumblings reminded the presidents that the troops were waiting in the wings.

However, the generals clearly underestimated the force of popular protest and even they couldn't sustain Serrano or control the appointment of his successor. While the coup was going on de León Carpio's home was surrounded by troops. His subsequent appointment as president suggests that Serrano's backers themselves were replaced. One of de León Carpio's first moves was a reshuffle of the senior military command, although he rejected calls for revenge. In an interview with *El Pais* he said "My task is to attain stability. ... We are a people that has scarcely experienced democracy. It has arrived overnight, without us having the culture or education that goes with it. Couple that with the terrible violence rooted in this country and you see there is a lack of political consciousness. But we will come out ahead."

ARZÚ AND THE PEACE ACCORDS

In January 1996, polls to elect a new president demonstrated the country's increasing lack of faith in the electoral process, which had failed to bring any real change after the much-heralded return to civilian rule in 1986. Some 63 percent of registered voters stayed at home and it was only a strong showing in Guatemala City that ensured the success of **Alvaro Arzú**, a former mayor of the capital. Blond, blue-eyed and somewhat bland, Arzú represents Guatemala's so-called modernizing right. His party, the PAN or National Advancement Party, has strong oligarchic roots and is committed to private-sector-lead growth and the free market, though his early adoption of a relatively progressive stance, appointing new defence, foreign and economic ministers and shaking up the armed forces' power structure, surprised many.

Once in power, he moved quickly to bring an end to the 36-year civil war, meeting with leaders of the URNG (an umbrella organization of the four major former guerrilla groups), and working towards a final settlement. He was the major force behind the signing of the **Peace Accords**, on December 29, 1996, which finally ended a conflict that had claimed more than 150,000 lives and concluded almost a decade of talks. The core of the Peace Accords includes measures to recognize the identity of indigenous people and eliminate discrimination against them; to promote socio-economic development for all Guatemalans; and to set up a MINUGUA-overseen truth commission to investigate previous human rights violations.

Despite the country's early enthusiasm for Arzú's initiatives, faith in his administration has since waned. **Land reform** and **Maya issues** are perhaps the most politically delicate of the problems he faces. With around five percent of the population owning seventy percent of the cultivatable land, bitter disputes resulting in deaths have arisen, as squatters clash with security forces. Large swathes of the Petén jungle continue to be cut down by *campesinos* and timber companies, with more and more marginal plots being farmed throughout the country. The indigenous Maya, who number more than half of Guatemala's population, are still grossly disadvantaged, subject to institutional racial discrimination and, despite the Indigenous Rights Accord of 1995 (see p.389), have little hope of improvement within the foreseeable future.

The **rising cost of living** throughout 1997 and 1998 has been another problem for virtually the entire population, with many day-to-day essentials now costing only a little less than in the US or Europe. **Unemployment** is also on the up: Guatemala has little industry of its own, and much of the work available to unskilled Guatemalans is in foreign-owned textile factories where garments are assembled for export to the US and Korea. These factories rarely pay tax or import/export duty and workers earn a typical daily wage of around $3. In 1997, more than 70,000 Guatemalans (mainly women) were working in these factories.

Guatemalans have also had to contend with a nationwide increase in the **crime rate**, over the last decade or so. Despite a population of only twelve million, the country has the fourth highest incidence of kidnapping in the world (around 1000 people in 1997). Petty theft, muggings and armed robbery are all on the increase, affecting every social class including the weathly elite and tourists. Despite the introduction of a new police force, **corruption** is still endemic, and few Guatemalans expect change in the near future.

Cases of **politically related violence** have decreased dramatically under Arzú's administration, with the exception of the assassination of human rights campaigner, Bishop Juan Gerardi in April 1998, and left-wing and Maya rights groups now have more freedom to protest and participate in mainstream life, than ever before. Despite this, the difficult job of tackling the many problems Guatemala has been left with after years of inequality, violence, corruption and poverty, has only just begun.

CHRONOLOGY OF THE MAYA

25,000 BC Paleo-Indian period.
First waves of nomadic hunters from the north.

9000 BC Stone tools found in Guatemalan highlands.

7500 BC Archaic period.
Evidence of settled agricultural communities throughout Mesoamerica, maize cultivated and animals domesticated.

4500 BC First Maya-speaking groups settle in western Guatemala, around Huehuetenango.

1500 BC Preclassic or Formative period.
Divided into: Early: 1500–1000 BC Middle: 1000–300 BC; Late: 300 BC–300 AD.
During this period the Maya began building the centres which developed into the great cities of the Classic period. Trade, of vital importance, increased, and contact with the **Olmec**people of Mexico brought many cultural developments, including a calendar and new gods.
Kaminaljuyú dominates high-land Guatemala, while **El Mirador** is the most important city in the north.

300 AD Classic period.
Maya culture reaches its high point – introduction of the Long Count **calendar**, used to mark events on carved stelae and monuments. The central lowlands are thickly populated, with almost all the sites now known flourishing. In the Early Classic the influence of **Teotihuacán** was strong: client cities like **Kaminaljuyú** and **Tikal** were particularly suc cessful. Later, and especially after the fall of Teotihuacán, more and more cities flourish: Tikal remains important but is defeated in battle at least once by **Caracol** (in Belize). The great buildings today associated with the Maya almost all date from the Classic period.

900 AD Postclassic period.
Decline of Classic civilizations in Mexico as well as Guatemala, for reasons which remain unclear. Population decline and abandonment of many important Maya centres in Guatemala, though some survive in neighbouring countries and remain relatively prosper ous throughout the Postclassic period.

987 AD Toltec invasion of Yucatán, results in Toltec culture being grafted onto Maya: possible Mexican influence on the Maya in Guatemala.

c.1200 Cities of the Yucatán abandoned – major movement south of Toltec-Maya population. Toltecs come to dominate many of the Guatemalan highland tribes. The village-based highland society that is familiar today begins to develop.

1400–75 Quiché overrun much of highland Guatemala, conquering their rivals. After 1475 their power declines and tribes splinter again. Quiché capital is built at **Utatlán**; Cakchiquel version is constructed at **Iximché**.

1519 Cortés lands in Mexico.

1521 Aztec capital of Tenochtitlán falls to Spanish.

1523 Alvarado arrives in Guatemala.

1523–40	**Spanish Conquest** of Guatemala proceeds: first Spanish capital founded 1527.
1541	Alvarado dies; new capital founded at **Antigua**.
17th c.	**Colonial rule** is gradually established throughout the country. Antigua is the capital of the whole of Central America, and the power of the Church grows.
1697	Conquest of the Itzá at Tayasal on Lake Petén Itzá: the last of the independent Maya.
18th c.	Colonial Guatemala remains a backwater, with no great riches for the Spanish.
1821	Mexico and Central America gain **independence** from Spain; Guatemala annexed by Mexico, then joins Central American Federation.
1847	Guatemala becomes republic, independent of Central America under **Rafael Carrera**.
1850	Guatemala and Britain continue to squabble over Belize.
1862	Belize becomes part of the British empire.
1867	First **liberal uprising** under Serpio Cruz.
1871	Liberal revolution; **Rufino Barrios** becomes president. Start of coffee boom.
1930	**Jorge Ubico** president – banana boom and height of **United Fruit Company** power.
1944–54	"Spiritual Socialism" presidencies of **Arévalo** and **Arbenz:** ended by CIA-backed military coup.
1954	**Castillo Armas** president: the start of **military rule** and a series of military-backed dictators.
1960s	First **guerrilla** actions, rapidly followed by repressive clampdowns and rise of **death squads** under **Colonel Carlos Arana**.
1970	**Colonel Arana Osorio** president.
1974	Electoral fraud wins presidency for **Kjell Laugerud**.
1976	**Earthquake** leaves 23,000 dead, a million homeless.
1978	**Lucas García** president: thousands die through repression.
1982	**Ríos Montt** president: situation improves. Belize becomes independent.
1986	**Vinicio Cerezo** elected: return to civilian rule though power of military remains great.
1990	**Jorge Serrano** elected on less than 25 percent of vote.
1991	Guatemala recognizes Belizean independence.
1993	Serrano ousted by generals – **Ramiro de León Carpio** appointed.
1996	**Alvaro Arzú** and the PAN elected.

THE MAYA ACHIEVEMENT

For some three thousand years before the arrival of the Spanish, Maya civilization dominated Central America, leaving behind some of the most impressive and mysterious architecture in the entire continent. At their peak, around 300 AD, Maya cities were far larger and more elaborate than anything that existed in Europe at the time. Their culture was complex and sophisticated, fostering the highest standards of engineering, astronomy, stonecarving and mathematics, as well as an intricate writing system.

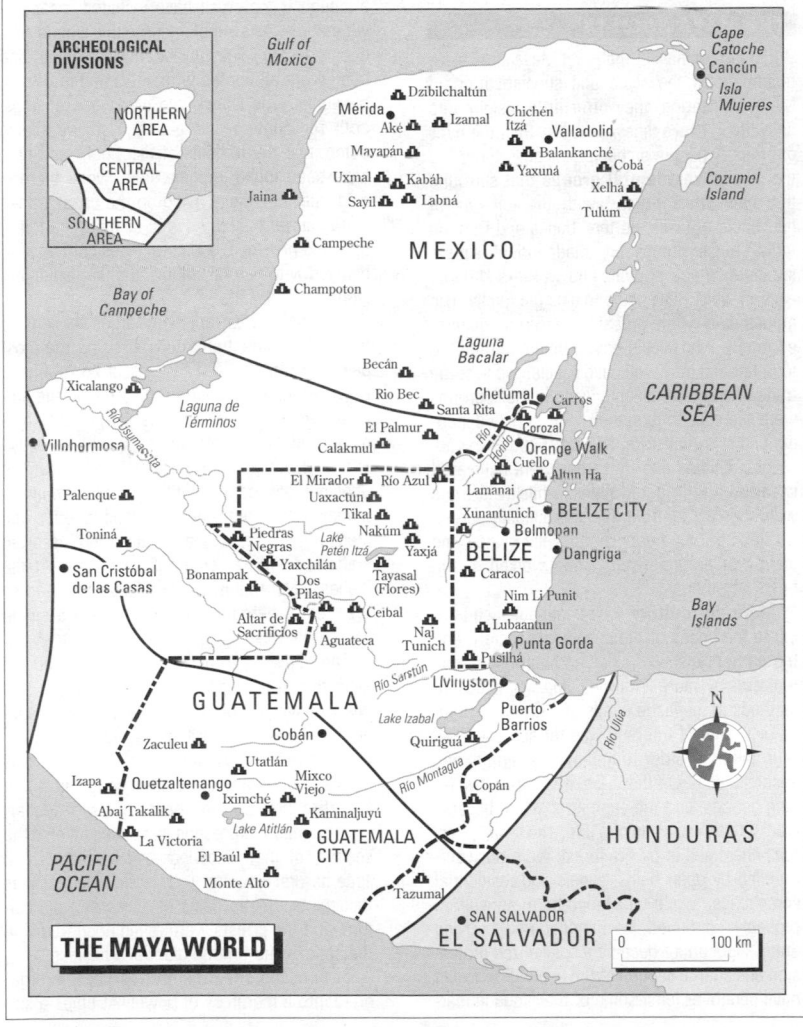

THE MAYA WORLD

To appreciate all this you have to see for yourself the remains of the great centres. Despite centuries of neglect and abuse they are still astounding, their main temples towering above the forest roof. Stone monuments, however, leave much of the story untold, and there is still a great deal that we have to learn about Maya civilization. What follows is the briefest of introductions to the subject, hopefully just enough to whet your appetite for the immense volumes that have been written on it.

THE MAYA SOCIETY

While the remains of the great Maya sites are a testament to the scale and sophistication of Maya civilization, they offer little insight into daily life in Maya times. To reconstruct the lives of ordinary people archeologists have turned to the smaller **residential groups** that surround the main sites, littered with the remains of household utensils, pottery, bones and farming tools. These groups are made up of simple structures made of poles and wattle-and-daub, each of which was home to a single family. The groups as a whole probably housed an extended family, who would have farmed and hunted together and may well have specialized in some trade or craft. The people living in these groups were the commoners, their lives largely dependent on agriculture. Maize, beans, cacao, squash, chillies and fruit trees were cultivated in raised and irrigated fields, while wild fruits were harvested from the surrounding forest. Much of the land was communally owned and groups of around twenty men worked in the fields together.

Maya **agriculture** was continuously adapting to the needs of the developing society, and the early practice of slash-and-burn was soon replaced by more intensive and sophisticated methods to meet the needs of a growing population. Some of the land was terraced, drained or irrigated in order to improve its fertility and ensure that fields didn't have to lie fallow for long periods, and the capture of water became crucial to the success of a site. The large cities, today hemmed in by the forest, were once surrounded by open fields, canals and residential compounds, while slash-and-burn agriculture probably continued in marginal and outlying areas. Agriculture became a specialized profession and a large section of the population would have bought at least some of their food in mar-

kets, although all households still had a kitchen garden where they grew herbs and fruit.

Maize has always been the basis of the Maya **diet**, in ancient times as much as it is today. Once harvested it was made into *saka*, a corn-meal gruel, which was eaten with chilli as the first meal of the day. During the day labourers ate a mixture of corn dough and water, and we know that *tamales* were also a popular speciality. The main meal, eaten in the evenings, would have been similarly maize-based, although it may well have included meat and vegetables. As a supplement to this simple diet, deer, peccary, wild turkeys, duck, pigeons and quail were all hunted with bows and arrows or blowguns. The Maya also made use of dogs, both for hunting and eating. Fish were also eaten, and the remains of fish hooks and nets have been found in some sites, while there is evidence that those living on the coast traded dried fish far inland. As well as food, the forest provided firewood, and cotton was cultivated to be dyed with natural colours and then spun into cloth.

The main sites represent larger versions of the basic residential groups, housing the most powerful families and their assorted retainers. Beyond this these centres transcended the limits of family ties, taking on larger political, religious and administrative roles, and as Maya society developed they became small cities. The principal occupants were a small number of priestly rulers, but others included bureaucrats, merchants, warriors, architects and assorted craftsmen – an emerging middle class. At the highest level this **hierarchy** was controlled by a series of hereditary positions, with a single chief at its head.

The relationship between the cities and the land, drawn up along feudal lines, was at the heart of Maya life. The peasant farmers supported the ruling class by providing labour – building and maintaining the temples and palaces – food and other basic goods. In return the **elite** provided the peasantry with leadership, direction, protection and above all else the security of their knowledge of calendrics and supernatural prophecy. This knowledge was thought to be the basis of successful agriculture, and the priests were relied upon to divine the appropriate time to plant and harvest.

In turn, the sites themselves became organized into a hierarchy of power. At times a single city, such as Tikal or El Mirador, dominated vast areas, controlling all of the smaller sites, while at other times smaller centres operated independently. A complex structure of **alliances** bound the various sites together and there were periodic outbursts of open **warfare**. The distance between the larger sites averaged around 30km, and between these were myriad smaller settlements, religious centres and residential groups. The structure of these alliances can be traced to the use of emblem glyphs. Only those of the main centres are used in isolation, while the names of smaller sites are used in conjunction with those of their larger patrons. Trade and warfare between the large centres was commonplace as the cities were bound up in an endless round of competition and conflict.

THE MAYA CALENDAR

The cornerstone of all Maya thinking was an obsession with **time**. For both practical and mystical reasons the Maya developed a highly sophisticated understanding of arithmetics, calendrics and astronomy, all of which they believed gave them the power to understand and predict events. All great occasions were interpreted on the basis of the Maya calendar, and it was this precise understanding of time that gave the ruling elite its authority. The majority of carving, on temples and stelae, records the exact date at which rulers were born, ascended to power, and died.

The basis of all Maya **calculation** was the vigesimal counting system, which used multiples of twenty. All figures were written using a combination of three symbols – a shell to denote zero, a dot for one and a bar for five – which you can still see on many stelae. When calculating calendrical systems the Maya used a slightly different notation known as the head-variant system, in which each number from one to twenty was represented by a deity, whose head was used to represent the number.

When it comes to the Maya **calendar** things start to get a little more complicated as a number of different counting systems were used, depending on the reason the date was being calculated. The basic unit of the Maya calendar was the day, or *kin*, followed by the *uinal*, a group of twenty days roughly equivalent to our month; but at the next level things start to get more complex as the Maya marked the passing of time in three distinct ways. The **260-day**

almanac (16 *uinals*) was used to calculate the timing of ceremonial events. Each day was associated with a particular deity that had strong influence over those born on that particular day. This calendar wasn't divided into months but had 260 distinct day names. (This system is still in use among the Cakchiquel Indians who name their children according to its structure and celebrate fiestas according to its dictates.) A second calendar, the so-called **"vague year"** or *haab*, was made up of eighteen *uinals* and five *kins*, a total of 365 days, making it a close approximation of the solar year. These two calendars weren't used in isolation but operated in parallel so that once every 52 years the new day of the solar year coincided with the same day in the 260-day almanac, a meeting that was regarded as very powerful and marked the start of a new era.

Finally the Maya had another system for marking the passing of history, which is used on dedicatory monuments. The system, known as the **long count**, is based on the great cycle of thirteen *baktuns* (a period of 5128 years). The current period dates from 3116 BC and is destined to come to an end on December 10, 2012. The dates in this system simply record the number of days that have elapsed since the start of the current great cycle, a task that calls for ten different numbers – recording the equivalent of years, decades, centuries, etc. In later years the Maya sculptors obviously tired of this exhaustive process and opted instead for the short count, an abbreviated version.

ASTRONOMY

Alongside their fascination with time the Maya were interested in the sky and devoted much time and energy to unravelling its patterns. Several large sites such as Copán, Uaxactún and Chichén Itzá have **observatories** carefully aligned with solar and lunar sequences.

The Maya showed a great understanding of **astronomy** and with their 365-day "vague year" were just half a day out in their calculations of the solar year, while at Copán, towards the end of the seventh century AD, Maya astronomers had calculated the lunar cycle at 29.53020 days, not too far off our current estimate of 29.53059. In the Dresden Codex their calculations extend to the 405 lunations over a period of 11,960 days, as part of a pattern that set out to predict eclipses. At the same time

MAYA TIME – THE UNITS

1 *kin* = 24 hours

20 *kins* = 1 *uinal*, or 20 days

18 *uinals* = 1 *tun*, or 360 days

20 *tuns* = 1 *katun*, or 7200 days

20 *katuns* = 1 *baktun*, or 144,000 days

20 *baktun* = 1 *pictun*, or 2,880,000 days

20 *pictuns* = 1 *calabtun*, or 57,600,000 days

20 *calabtuns* = 1 *kinchiltun*, or 1,152,000,000 days

20 *kinchiltuns* = 1 *alautun*, or 23,040,000,000 days

they had calculated with astonishing accuracy the movements of Venus, Mars and perhaps Mercury. Venus was of particular importance to the Maya as they linked its presence with success in war, and there are several stelae that record the presence of Venus prompting the decision to attack.

RELIGION

Maya **cosmology** is by no means straightforward as at every stage an idea is balanced by its opposite and each part of the universe is made up of many layers. To the Maya this is the third version of the earth, the previous two having been destroyed by deluges. The current version is a flat surface, with four corners, each associated with a certain colour; white for north, red for east, yellow for south, and black for west, with green at the centre. Above this the sky is supported by four trees, each a different colour and species, which are also sometimes depicted as gods, known as *Bacabs*. At its centre the sky is supported by a ceiba tree. Above the sky is a heaven of thirteen layers, each of which has its own god, while the very top layer is overseen by an owl. Other attested models of the world include that of a turtle (the land) floating on the sea. However, it was the underworld, *Xibalda*, "The Place of Fright", which was of greater importance to most Maya, as it was in this direction that they passed after death, on their way to the place of rest. The nine layers of hell were guarded by the "Lords

of the Night", and deep caves were thought to connect with the underworld.

Woven into this universe the Maya recognized an incredible array of **gods**. Every divinity had four manifestations based upon colour and direction and many also had counterparts in the underworld and consorts of the opposite sex. In addition to this there was an extensive array of patron deities, each associated with a particular trade or particular class. Every activity from suicide to sex had its representative in the Maya pantheon.

RELIGIOUS RITUAL

The combined complexity of the Maya pantheon and calendar gave every day a particular significance, and the ancient Maya were bound up in a demanding **cycle of religious ritual**. The main purpose of ritual was the procurement of success by appealing to the right god at the right time and in the right way. As every event, from planting to childbirth, was associated with a particular divinity, all of the main events in daily life demanded some kind of religious ritual and for the most important of these the Maya staged elaborate ceremonies.

While each ceremony had its own format there's a certain pattern that binds them all. The correct day was carefully chosen by priestly divination, and for several days beforehand the participants fasted and remained abstinent. The main ceremony was dominated by the expulsion of all evil spirits, the burning of incense before the idols, a sacrifice (either animal or human), and blood-letting.

In divination rituals, used to foretell the pattern of future events or account for the cause of past events, the elite used various **drugs** to achieve altered states of consciousness. Perhaps the most obvious of these was alcohol, either made from fermented maize or a combination of honey and the bark of the balnche tree. Wild tobacco, which is considerably stronger than the modern domesticated version, was also smoked. The Maya also used a range of hallucinogenic mushrooms, all of which were appropriately named, but none more so than the *xibalbaj obox*, "underworld mushroom" and the *k'aizalah obox*, "lost judgement mushroom".

INDIGENOUS GUATEMALA

A vital indigenous culture is perhaps Guatemala's most unique feature. It's a strange blend of contradictions, and while the Maya people may appear quiet and humble, their costumes, fiestas and markets are a riot of colour, creativity and celebration. In many ways the Maya live in a

Throughout this Guide we have used the terms Maya or indigenous people to refer to those Guatemalans of Maya origins. You may also hear them called *Indio* (or Indian), though in Guatemala this term has racially pejorative connotations.

world of their own, responding to local traditions and values and regarding themselves as *indígena* first and Guatemalans second.

GUATEMALA'S INDIGENOUS LANGUAGES

N

MEXICO

BELIZE

ÍTZA

MOPÁN

Gulf of Honduras

CHUJ

San Mateo Ixtatán
Solomá   IXIL

JACALTECA

KANJOBAL

KEKCHÍ

GARIFUNA

Nebaj

Cobán

Huehuetenango   AGUATECA   USPANTECA

Tactic

POCOMCHI

MAM   Sta. Cruz del Quiché   QUICHÉ

CHORTÍ

San Marcos

Totonicapán

HONDURAS

Quetzaltenango

Sololá

CAKCHIQUEL

TZUTUJIL   Antigua   GUATEMALA CITY

Palín   POKOMAN

PACIFIC OCEAN

EL SALVADOR

It's generally accepted that indigenous Maya, the vast majority of whom live in the western highlands, make up about half of Guatemala's population, although it's extremely hard to define exactly who is Maya. For the sake of the national census, people who consider themselves indigenous are classed as such, regardless of their parentage. And when it comes to defining Maya as a group, culture is more important than pedigree, as the Maya define themselves through their relationships with their land, gods, villages and families. Holding aloof from the melting pot of modern Guatemalan society, Maya people adhere instead to their traditional *costumbres*, codes of practice that govern every aspect of life.

As a result of this the only way to define Maya culture is by describing its main characteristics, acknowledging that all indigenous Guatemalans will be a part of some of them, and accepting that many are neither *indigena* nor *ladino*, but combine elements of both.

INDIGENOUS CULTURE

When the Spanish set about destroying the Maya tribes of Guatemala they altered every aspect of life for the indigenous people, uprooting their social structures and reshaping their communities. Before the Conquest the bulk of the population had lived scattered in the hills, paying tribute to a tribal elite, and surviving through subsistence farming and hunting. Under Spanish rule they were moved into new **villages**, known as *reducciónes*, where their homes were clustered around a church and a marketplace. Horizons shrank rapidly as allegiances became very localized and tribal structures were replaced by the village hierarchies that still dominate the highlands today.

For the last 450 years the Maya population has suffered repeated **abuse**, as the predominantly white elite have exploited indigenous land and labour, regarding the Maya as an expendable commodity. But within their own communities indigenous Guatemalans were left pretty much to themselves and developed an astoundingly introspective culture that is continually adapting to new threats, reshaping itself for the future. **Village life** has been insulated from the outside world and in many areas only a handful of the population speak fluent Spanish, the remainder speaking one of the 28 indigenous languages and dialects (see map on

p.377). Today's indigenous culture is a complex synthesis including elements of Maya, Spanish and modern American cultures.

The vast majority of the indigenous population still live by **subsistence farming**, their homes either spread across the hills or gathered in small villages. The land is farmed using the *milpa* system to produce beans, chillies, maize and squash – which have been the staple diet for thousands of years. To the Maya, land is sacred and the need to own and farm it is central to their culture, despite the fact that few can survive by farming alone. Most are now forced to migrate to the coast for several months a year, where they work in appalling conditions on the **plantations**, in order to supplement their income. In some villages the economy is boosted by a local **craft**: in Momostenango they produce wool and blankets, around Lake Atitlán the villagers make reed mats, in Cotzal and San Pablo la Laguna they make rope, while other villages specialize in market gardening, pottery, flowers or textiles.

Family life is also rigidly traditional with large families very much a part of the indigenous culture. Marriage customs vary from place to place but in general the groom is expected to pay the bride's parents, and the couple may well live with their in-laws. If things don't work out separation isn't a great problem and men often take more than one wife (nor is it totally unheard of for a woman to live with two men). A man's place is in the fields and a woman's in the home, where she cooks, tends to the children, and weaves. Authority within the village is usually given to men, although in the Ixil area women are involved in all decision making.

INDIGENOUS RELIGION

Every aspect of Maya life – from the birth of a child to the planting of corn – is loaded with religious significance, based on a complicated **fusion of the Maya pantheon and the Catholic religion**. Christ and the saints have taken their place alongside *Dios Mundo*, the God of the World, and *Hurakan*, the Heart of Heaven. The two religions have merged to form a hybrid, in which the outward forms of Catholicism are used to worship the ancient pantheon, a compromise that was probably fostered by Spanish priests. The symbol of the cross, for example, was well known to the Maya, as used to signify the four winds of heav-

EVANGELISM IN GUATEMALA

One of the greatest surprises awaiting first-time travellers in Guatemala is the number of evangelical churches in the country, with fundamentalist, Pentecostal or neo-Pentecostal services taking place in most towns and villages. Although early Protestant missions came to Guatemala as far back as 1882, the impact of US-based churches remained marginal and largely unnoticed until the 1950s, when **state repression** and the subsequent **guerrilla war** began to weaken the power of the Catholic church. Up until this time, more than 95 per cent of the population was officially Catholic, though the rural Maya had their own hybrid forms of worship which mixed Catholic ceremony with pagan rites.

While the hierarchy of the Catholic church remained fervently anti-communist and closely aligned with the economic, political and military elite, during the early 1960s many rural Catholic priests became increasingly active in supporting peasant leagues and development projects, with some even joining the guerrillas. Consequently, the generals, politicians and big landowners began to consider the Catholic church as being riddled with communist sympathizers, and targeted troublemakers accordingly. By the early 1980s, so many Catholic priests had been murdered by the state-sponsored death squads, that the Catholic church pulled out of the entire department of Quiché in protest. In contrast, most of the evangelical missionaries preached the importance of an army victory over the guerrillas, and, with their pro-business, anti-communist rhetoric, attracted many converts anxious to avoid suspicion and survive. In addition, the early evangelicals had made it a priority to learn the native Maya languages, and had the Bible translated into Quiché, Mam, Caquichel and other tongues.

However, the devastating **1976 earthquake** was the catalyst that unleashed a tidal wave of US evangelists into Guatemala with church-backed disaster relief programmes. Millions of dollars of medicine, food and toys were distributed as handouts to those prepared to convert, and shattered villages were rebuilt with new schools and health centres. In the eyes of the impoverished rural villagers, Protestantism became linked with prosperity, and its lively church services, where dancing, music and singing were the norm, gained huge popularity.

The movement received another boost in 1982, when **General Ríos Montt** seized power in a military coup to become Guatemala's first evangelical president. The population was treated to Montt's maniacal, marathon Sunday sermons, and a new flood of mission teams entered the country from the US. For many Guatemalans, Ríos Montt represented the best and worst of evangelism: he was frenzied and fanatical on one hand, but honest and strict on the other. Though Ríos Montt himself was ousted after just seventeen months in power, he retains a reputation among many Guatemalans as an honourable politican untainted by corruption. In the 1990 elections he was leading all the polls before his candidature was declared invalid (as a former president), and another *evangelico*, Jorge Serrano won instead.

Whilst Guatemala is currently the least Catholic country in Latin America, with around sixty percent of the population looking to the Vatican for guidance and about forty percent supporting the evangelicals, it is doubtful whether the Protestants can retain this level of worship. For years, some denominations have been promising devotees miracles, such as bumper harvests, which have failed to materialize, and their popularity looks to be on the wane.

---

en, the four directions, and everlasting life. Today many of the deities have both Maya and Hispanic names, and are usually associated with a particular saint. All the deities remain subordinate to a mighty and remote supreme being, and Christ takes a place in the upper echelons of the hierarchy.

For the Maya, **God** is everywhere, bound up in the seasons, the mountains, the crops, the soil, the air and the sky. Every important event is marked by prayer and offerings, with disasters often attributed to divine intervention. Even

more numerous than the gods are the **spirits** that are to be found in every imaginable object, binding together the universe. Each individual is born with a *nagual*, or spiritual counterpart, in the animal world, and his or her destiny is bound up with that particular animal. The spirits of dead ancestors are also ever-present and have to be looked after by each successive generation.

Traditionally, **worship** is organized by the community's religious hierarchy. All office-holders are male and throughout their lives they progress through the system, moving from post to post. The various posts are grouped into **cofradías**, ritual brotherhoods, each of which is responsible for a particular saint. Throughout the year the saint is kept in the home of an elder member, and on the appointed date, in the midst of a fiesta, it's paraded through the streets, to spend the next year somewhere else. The elder responsible for the saint will have to pay for much of the fiesta, including costumes, alcohol and assorted offerings, but it's a responsibility, or *cargo*, that's considered a great honour. In the traditional village hierarchy it's these duties that give the elders a prominent role in village life and through which they exercise their authority. Spending money on **fiestas** is really the only way that wealthy villagers can use their money in an acceptable way. (In some villages, such as Chichicastenango and Sololá, a *municipalidad indígena*, or indigenous council, operates alongside the *cofradías*, and is similarly hierarchical. As men work their way up through the system they may well alternate between the civil and religious hierarchies.) The *cofradías* don't necessarily confine themselves to the traditional list of saints, and have been known to foster "evil" saints, such as San Simón or **Maximón**, a drinking, smoking *ladino* figure, sometimes referred to as Judas or Pedro de Alvarado.

On a more superstitious level, personal religious needs are catered for by **brujos**, native priests who communicate with the gods and spirits. This is usually done on behalf of an individual client who's in search of a blessing, and often takes place at shrines and caves in the mountains, with offerings of *copal*, a type of incense, and alcohol. They also make extensive use of old Maya sites, and small burnt patches of grass litter many of the ruins in the highlands. *Brujos* are also credited with the ability to cast spells, predict the future and communicate with the dead. For specific medical problems, the Maya appeal to *zahorins*, who practise traditional medicine with a combination of invocation and herbs, and are closely associated with the *brujo* tradition.

Until the 1950s, when Catholic **missionaries** became active in the highlands, many indigenous Guatemalans had no idea that there was a gulf between their own religion and orthodox Catholicism. To start with the missionaries drew most of their support from the younger generation, many of whom were frustrated by the rigidity of the village hierarchy. Gradually, this has eroded the authority of the traditional religious system, undermining the *cofradías*, disapproving of traditional fiestas, and scorning the work of the *brujos*. As a part of this reforming movement Catholic Action, combining the drive for orthodoxy with an involvement in social issues, has also had a profound impact.

After the 1976 earthquake, waves of Protestant missionaries, known as **evangelicos**, arrived in Guatemala, and their presence has also accelerated the decline of traditional religion (see box above). In the 1980s their numbers were greatly boosted by the influence of Ríos Montt, at a time when the Catholic Church was suffering severe repression. These days there are at least three hundred different sects in operation, backed by a huge injection of money from the US, and offering all sorts of incentives to fresh converts. But indigenous religion is no stranger to oppression and despite the efforts of outsiders the *brujos* and *cofradías* are still in business, and fiestas remain drunken and vaguely pagan.

MARKETS AND FIESTAS

At the heart of the indigenous economy is the **weekly market**, which remains central to life in the highlands and provides one of the best opportunities to see Maya life at close quarters. The majority of the indigenous population still lives by subsistence farming but spares a single day to gather together in the nearest village and trade their surplus produce. The market is as much a social occasion as an economic one and people come to talk, eat, drink, gossip and have a good time. In some places the action starts the night before with marimba music and heavy drinking.

On market day itself the village is filled by a steady flow of people, arriving by bus, on foot, or by donkey. In no time at all trading gets under way, and the plaza is soon buzzing with activity and humming with conversation, although raised voices are a rarity, with bargains struck after long and tortuous negotiations. Markets certainly don't operate in the way that "westerners" might expect and rival traders will happily set up alongside one another, more concerned about the day's conversation than the volume of trade.

The scale and atmosphere of markets varies from place to place. The country's largest is in **San Francisco el Alto**, on Friday, and draws traders from throughout the country. Other famous ones are the Friday market in Sololá, and the Thursday and Sunday markets in Chichicastenango, but almost every village has its day. Some of the very best are in tiny, isolated hamlets, high in the mountains.

Once a year every village, however small, indulges in an orgy of celebration in honour of its patron saint – you'll find a list of them at the end of each chapter. These **fiestas** are a great swirl of dance, music, religion, fireworks, eating and outrageous drinking, and express the vitality of indigenous culture. They usually centre on religious processions, in which the image of the local patron saint is paraded through the streets, accompanied by the elders of the *cofradía*, who dress in full regalia. (All members of a *cofradía* usually have special ceremonial costumes, superbly woven and beautifully decorated.) The larger fiestas also involve funfairs and week-long markets. Traditional music is played with marimbas, drums and flutes; or professional bands may be hired, blasting out popular tunes through crackling PA systems.

Dance, too, is very much a part of fiestas, and incorporates routines and ideas that date from ancient Maya times. Dance costumes are incredibly elaborate, covered in mirrors and sequins, and have to be rented for the occasion. Despite the cost, which is high by highland standards, the dancers see their role both as an obligation – to tradition and the community – and an honour. Most of the dances form an extension of some vague dramatic tradition where local history was retold in dance dramas, and are loosely based on historical events. The *Dance of the Conquistadors* is one of the most popular, modelled on the *Dance of the Moors* and introduced by the Spanish as a re-enactment of the Conquest, although in some cases it's been instilled with a significance that can never have been intended by the Spanish. The dancers often see no connection with the Conquest, but dance instead to release the spirits of the dead, a function perhaps closer to Maya religion than Catholicism. The *Palo Volador*, a dramatic dance in which men swing perilously to the ground from a twenty-metre pole, certainly dates from the pre-Columbian era (these days you'll only see it in Cubulco,

Chichicastenango and Joyabaj), as does the *Dance of the Deer*, while the *Dance of the Bullfight* and the *Dance of the Volcano* relate incidents from the Conquest itself. Most of the dances do have steps to them, but the dancers are usually blind drunk and sway around as best they can in time to the music, sometimes tumbling over each other or even passing out – so don't expect to see anything too dainty.

MAYA COSTUME

To outsiders the most obvious and impressive feature of indigenous culture is the **hand-woven cloth** that's worn by the majority of the women and some of the men. This, like so much else in the Maya world, is not simply a relic of the past but a living skill, responding to new ideas and impulses and re-created by each generation.

Nevertheless, **weaving** is one of the oldest of Maya skills, and was practised for centuries before the arrival of the Spanish. We know that it was a highly valued talent, and the Maya goddess Ix Chel, "she of the rainbow", who presided over childbirth, divination and healing, is often depicted at her loom. In pre-Columbian times the majority of the population probably wore long white cotton tunics, similar to those worn by the Lacandon Indians today. In the highlands it's a style that has been largely superseded, although in some villages, such as Soloma and San Mateo Ixtatán, the basic format is still the same, now embellished with magnificent embroidery. We also know, from Maya tombs and sculptures, that the nobility wore elaborate headdresses and heavily decorated cloth, using blues and reds created with vegetable dyes. Here it seems that tunics and robes were also the fashion of the day.

After the Conquest, the indigenous nobility was virtually eradicated and the focus was shifted from large regional centres to small village communities. Meanwhile, silk and wool were introduced by the Spanish, as were a whole range of new dyes. Not much is known about the development of Maya costume in colonial times, and it's impossible to say when or why each village developed a distinctive style of dress. Some argue that the styles were introduced by the Spanish as a means of control, rather like the branding of sheep, while others claim that they developed naturally from the introspective nature of village culture. The truth is probably to be found somewhere between the two: we know that Spanish symbols were introduced into traditional costume designs, but that at times the Spanish had little influence over life in the villages.

WOMEN'S CLOTHING

Today there are around 150 villages where women still wear **traditional costume**, each with its own patterns, designs and colours. What little we know of their development shows that designs are constantly changing, adopting new patterns and ideas. The advent of literacy, a recent development in most areas, means that modern *huipiles* might include the word *escuela* (school), the name of the village, or even the words *Coca Cola*. Synthetic thread, including garish silvers and golds, has also been absorbed into many of the patterns, and as village society starts to open up, some designs, once specific to a single village, are coming to be used throughout the country.

Nevertheless, the basic style of the clothing worn by women has changed little since Maya times. The most significant development is simply that the *huipil*, which once hung loose, is now tucked into the skirt. Only in one or two places have the women added sleeves, or gathered their skirts, although in recent times young women have responded to outside influences and the latest generation of costumes tends to emphasize the shape of the body. But in defiance of modern fashion Maya women still wear their hair in an assortment of bizarre styles, ranging from the halos of Santiago Atitlán to the pompoms of Aguacatán. Ceremonial *huipiles*, which are always the most spectacular, are still worn loose, in classic Maya style.

The basic element of a Maya woman's costume is the *huipil*, a loose-fitting blouse, normally woven by the women themselves on a **back-strap loom**. All *huipiles* are intricately decorated, either as a part of the woven pattern or with complex embroidery, and these designs are specific to each village. To protect the embroidery some women wear their *huipiles* inside out, saving the full splendour for market days. Ceremonial *huipiles*, reserved for fiestas, are usually more extravagant, often hanging low in the most traditional style. Under the *huipil* a skirt, or *corte*, is worn, and these are becoming increasingly standardized. Usually woven on a foot loom, it is a simple piece of cloth, up to five metres long, joined to form a tube into which the women step. Most common are the *jaspeado cortes* woven on looms in Salcajá, San Francisco Totonicapán and Cobán by commercial weavers, and tie-dyed in universally worn patterns. In some cases there are distinct styles, but these tend to be used in a general region rather than in specific villages: the brilliant reds of Nebaj and Chajul, the yellows of San Pedro and San Marcos, and the blues of the Huehuetenango area, for example. To add individuality to their skirts the women decorate them with thin strips of coloured embroidery, known as *randa*. And to hold them up they use elaborate **sashes**, woven in superb colours and intricate patterns, and often including decorative tassels. Perhaps the most outlandish part of women's costume is the headdress, which varies widely and seems to have no connection with modern styles. The most famous of these are the halos of Santiago Atitlán – twelve-metre strips of cloth – while the turbans of Nebaj and Aguacatán are some of the finest. In addition to the cloth that they wear the women also weave **tzutes**, used to carry babies or food, and shawls that ward off the highland chill.

MEN'S CLOTHING

Highland men have always had greater contact with the outside world that the women, and as a result have been more susceptible to change. From the outset their costume was influenced to a greater extent by the arrival of the Spanish, and today **men's traditional costume** is worn in only a few villages. The more traditional styles are generally reflected in ceremonial costume, while everyday clothes are heavily influenced by non-traditional "western" styles. If you're around for a fiesta you'll probably see some fantastic costumes worn by men who wear jeans every other day of the year.

On the whole even "traditional costumes" now have more in common with shirt and trousers than the ancient loose-hanging tunic. Nevertheless, men's costumes do include superb weaving and spectacular designs. Their jackets are particularly unusual, ranging from the superb reds of Nebaj, modelled on those worn by Spanish officers, to the ornate tuxedo-style of Sololá. (Those worn in Sololá seem to undergo regular changes, and the greys of late have now been superseded by a very ornate white version.) In the Cuchumatanes the men wear **capixays**, small ponchos made from wool, and in San Juan Atitlán these bear a remarkable similarity to monks' habits. Other particularly unusual features are the **ponchitos**, short woollen skirts, worn in Nahualá and San Antonio Palopó; the superbly embroidered shorts of Santiago Atitlán and Santa Catarina Palopó; and the astounding cowboy-style shirts of Todos Santos and Sololá.

Although fewer men wear traditional costume the styles that remain are astonishingly diverse, their scarcity making them appear all the more outlandish. The **tzute**, a piece of cloth worn either on the head or folded on the shoulder, is of particular significance, often marking out an important member of the *cofradía*. In some villages the mayor, dressed in jeans and a T-shirt, will still wear a woven *tzute* on his shoulder as a symbol of office.

DESIGNS

The **designs** used in the traditional costume of both men and women are as diverse as the costumes themselves, an amazing collection of sophisticated patterns, using superb combinations of colour and shape. They include a range of animals, plants and people, as well as abstract designs, words and names. Many of them probably date from long before the Conquest: we know that the snake, the double-headed eagle, the sun and the moon were commonly used in classic Maya design, while the peacock, horse and chicken can only have been introduced after the arrival of the Spanish. The **quetzal** is perhaps the most universal feature and is certain to date from pre-Conquest times, when the bird was seen as the spiritual protector of Quiché kings. The significance of the designs is as imprecise as their origins, although according to Lily de Jongh Osborne, an expert on Maya culture, designs once expressed the weaver's position within the social hierarchy, and could also indicate marital status. One particularly interesting design is the bat on the back of the jackets of Sololá, which dates back to the bat dynasty, among the last Cakchiquel rulers. In days gone by each level of the village hierarchy wore a different style of jacket, although today fashion is the prime consideration, and each generation is simply more outrageous than the last.

HUMAN RIGHTS IN GUATEMALA

Since the arrival of the Spanish, Guatemalan history has been characterized by political repression and economic exploitation, involving the denial of the most basic human rights. A horrifying catalogue of events stretches across the last 450 years, but reached levels as barbaric as any previously seen in the late 1970s and the early 1980s. The chief victims have always been the indigenous Maya, generally regarded as backward, ignorant and dispensable. Today the story of Guatemalan repression is very much an unfinished history, although the level of violence has declined significantly in the last few years.

THE EARLY YEARS

When **Pedro de Alvarado** arrived in Guatemala in 1523 he brought with him the notions of violent conquest and racist exploitation that have dominated the country to the present day. In the early years of the Conquest towns were burnt to the ground and huge numbers of indigenous people were massacred and enslaved. At the same time they had to contend with repeated epidemics that were to halve their numbers. Once the initial Conquest was over the survivors were systematically herded into villages, deprived of their land, and forced to work in the new plantations: a pattern that seems all too familiar in modern Guatemala.

Equally familiar is the response of the indigenous population, who rose in defiance. It took almost two centuries for their numbers to recover from the devastation of the Conquest, but by the start of the eighteenth century uprisings were common. There were **revolts** in 1708, 1743, 1760, 1764, 1770, 1803, 1817, 1818, 1820, 1838, 1839, 1898 and 1905, all of which met with severe repression.

Independence brought little change. Under **Rufino Barrios** (1873–85) the demands of the coffee industry put fresh strains on the indigenous population, as their land and labour were once again exploited for the benefit of foreign investors and the ruling elite. Under **Jorge Ubico** (1931–44) laws were introduced that obliged Maya men to work on the plantations, and for the first time the government developed a network of spies and informers, giving it the capacity to deal directly with dissenting voices: a capacity it demonstrated in 1934, when Ubico discovered a plot to assassinate him and had some 300 people killed in just two days.

The most significant developments, at least in terms of human rights, came during the socialist governments of **Arévalo** and **Arbenz** (1945–55) which, for the first time, sought to meet the needs of the indigenous population. Local organizations such as unions and cooperatives were free to operate, suffrage was extended to include all adults, health and schooling were expanded, and land was redistributed to the dispossessed. For the first time in the country's history the issues of inequality and injustice were taken by the horns.

However, in 1954 the government was overthrown by a CIA-backed coup, which cleared the stage for military rule and ushered in the modern era of repression.

MILITARY RULE

Since the 1954 coup the army has dominated the government, operating in alliance with the landowning elite and foreign business interests to consolidate the power of the right. Large-scale repression wasn't to begin until the mid-1960s, but directly after the takeover the army began gathering the names of those who had been active under the socialist administration. In association with the CIA they put together a list of some 70,000 people – a much-used reference source once the killing began.

The **guerrilla** movement, which developed out of an army revolt in 1960, was first active in the eastern highlands. Throughout the 1960s political violence was on the increase, aimed not just at the guerrillas, but at all political opponents and left-wing sympathizers. In the war against the guerrillas the army was unable to strike directly at its enemy and opted instead to eradicate their support in the community. Between 1966 and 1977 some 10,000 noncombatants were killed in a bid to destroy a guerrilla force that numbered no more than 500; and by the early 1970s the guerrillas were on the run, unable to mount attacks or add to their numbers.

In other parts of the country there was a brutal clampdown on a range of "suspect" organi-

EYEWITNESS TESTIMONY

The following account, of a massacre in San Francisco Nentón that took place on July 17, 1982, was related to a priest in a Mexican refugee camp by survivors; the account is taken from an Amnesty International report.

At 11am on Saturday 17 July the army arrived in San Francisco having passed through the nearby villages of Bulej and Yalambojoch. The army had previously visited the village on 24 June and had told the inhabitants that they could be killed if they were found not to be peacefully working in their homes and their fields. Soldiers had also said, however, that the villagers should not run away from the army, as it was there to defend them. On 17 July some 600 soldiers arrived on foot. A helicopter circled nearby and eventually landed. The military were accompanied by an ex-guerrilla, now in military uniform, who was apparently acting as the army's informer. The people were told to assemble for a discussion with the colonel. It was the first day on which the village's new civil defense patrol was to have begun its duties. Some of the survivors said that the patrol, of 21, was taken away shortly after the arrival of the army and had not been seen since. They are presumed dead.

According to testimonies collected by priests, the villagers first sensed they were in danger when a man who survivors said had been "tied up like a pig" was brought before them by the soldiers. They knew he had not been involved in anything, and yet saw that he was being "punished". They also saw how "angry" the commander appeared to be and began to fear for themselves. They were first asked to unload the soldiers' supplies from the helicopter, which they did. The men were then shut up in the courthouse to begin praying "to make peace with God", as they were about to suffer. A survivor described how: "We pray, 11 o'clock, 12 o'clock passes. By now, everyone has come into town and been shut up. At 1 o'clock, it began: a blast of gunfire at the women, there in the church. It makes so much noise. All the little children are crying."

This witness went on to tell how the women who survived the initial gunfire were taken off in small groups to different houses by soldiers where they were killed, many apparently with machetes. After they had been killed, the houses were set on fire. This witness and the others interviewed described a particularly atrocious killing they had seen, the murder of a child of about three. The child was disembowelled, as were several others, but kept screaming, until a soldier smashed his

head with a pole, then swung him by his feet and threw him into a burning house. "Yes", said the witness, "yes, I saw it. Yes, I saw how they threw him away, threw him into the house."

The witness continued: "At 2 o'clock, they began with all the men. They ordered them out of the courthouse in small groups, and then blasted them with gunfire. It went on and on. They tied up the men's hands and then 'bang, bang'. We couldn't see, we could only hear the noise of the guns. The killing took place in the courtyard outside the courthouse, then they'd throw the bodies into the church. They killed the three old people with a blunt machete, the way you would kill sheep."

Another witness described how the old were killed: "The old people said, 'What have we done, no, we are tired and old. We're not thinking of doing anything. We're not strong. We can't do anything any more.' But they said, 'You're not worth anything any more, even if you're tired, get out of there.' They dragged them out, and knifed them. They stabbed and cut them as if they were animals and they were laughing when they killed them. They killed them with a machete that had no teeth. They put one man on the table and cut open his chest, the poor man, and he was still alive, and so they started to cut his throat. They cut his throat slowly. He was suffering a lot. They were cutting people under the ribs, and blood came rushing out and they were laughing." Another survivor continued: "When they got to the end, they killed six people in the courthouse. One was a military commissioner. They didn't care. They killed him there at his table with his three policemen."

"By now it was 6.30pm. It was getting dark outside. They threw a bomb into the corner of the courthouse. It was bloody, two were killed. How the blood ran! It ran all over me. Then they fired at the remaining bodies in the courthouse. Then they threw all the bodies in a heap. They dragged people by the feet, as if they were animals. They threw me on top of the dead bodies."

One witness ended his testimony: "Father my heart is so heavy with pain for the dead, because of what I have seen. I saw how my brothers died. All of them: friends, godparents, everyone, as we are all brothers. My heart will cry for them the rest of my life. But they had committed no crime. Nobody said: 'This is your crime. Here is the proof.' They just killed them, that's all. That's how death came."

A list of the dead was compiled in Mexico on September 5. It included 302 people, 92 of whom were under twelve, and the youngest less than two months old.

zations. In Guatemala City this campaign gave birth to the **"death squads"**, put together by the right-wing MLN (National Liberation Movement) and the army. The first to emerge was *Mano Blanco*, who swore "to eradicate national renegades and traitors to the fatherland". Today the death squads have become a permanent feature of Guatemalan politics, and they were active throughout the 1960s, 1970s and 1980s, assassinating unionists, left-wing politicians and students. Victims were usually abducted by men in unmarked cars, and later their bodies were found, dumped by the roadside, mutilated and tortured. Between 1970 and 1974, 15,325 people "disappeared".

By 1975 the guerrilla movement was once again on the rise, as were peasant organizations, cooperatives and unions, all inspired by the move towards **liberation theology**, under which the Catholic Church began to campaign on social issues. The experience of 1954 proved to the Guatemalan people that their political options were severely restricted, and in the 1970s and 1980s they directed their energies towards grass-roots organization and eventually armed uprising. But in response to this the repression continued, and in 1976 Amnesty International stated that a total of 20,000 Guatemalans had been killed in the previous decade.

The closing years of the 1970s saw a rapid polarization of the situation that gave birth to a fresh wave of violence. The **guerrilla movements** were by now well established in many different parts of the country, as repression in the highlands drove increasing numbers to seek refuge in their ranks. At this stage there were four main organizations: the PGT (Guatemalan Workers Party), who operated in Guatemala City and on the Pacific coast; FAR (the Rebel Armed Forces), who fought throughout Petén; EGP (the Guerrilla Army of the Poor), who had several fronts in northern Quiché; and ORPA (Organization of People in Arms), who functioned in San Marcos and Quetzaltenango.

The election of **Lucas García** in 1978 marked the onset of unprecedented mass repression. Once again the list of victims included left-wing politicians, labour leaders, lawyers, priests, nuns, teachers, unionists, academics and students, all of whom were regarded as subversive. In the highlands the war against the guerrillas also reached a new inten-

sity, as selective killings were replaced by outright massacres. Once again the army found itself pitched against an elusive enemy and resorted to indiscriminate killings in a bid to undermine peasant support for the guerrillas.

Repression was so widespread that human rights organizations found it almost impossible to keep track of the situation, although certain incidents still came to light. In 1980 36 bodies were found in a mass grave outside Comalapa; in early 1981 17 people were killed in Santiago Atitlán; and in April 1981 Oxfam estimated that 1500 had been killed in Chimaltenango in the previous two months. Precise numbers are impossible to calculate, but according to some estimates 25,000 died during the first four years of the Lucas administration, the vast majority killed either by the security forces or by the death squads, which were often operated by off-duty soldiers or policemen and directed from an annexe of the National Palace.

RÍOS MONTT

In March 1982 Lucas was replaced by **General Efrían Ríos Montt**, and the situation improved significantly. The guerrillas were offered amnesty, death squad activity dropped off, and an office was set up to investigate the fate of the disappeared. But Ríos Montt had vowed to defeat the guerrillas by Christmas and in rural areas the level of violence did increase as the army began to make big gains in the fight against the guerrillas. In the early months of Ríos Montt's rule massacres were still commonplace as it took him some time to reshape the armed forces and provide an alternative to the brutal approach they had adopted under Lucas García. The campaign still claimed a heavy death toll, despite the downturn in indiscriminate slaughter. According to Amnesty International there were 2186 killings in the first four months of the new administration, and by now some 200,000 refugees had fled the country. Amnesty's report on the Ríos Montt administration (see box on previous page) is a catalogue of horror, though in many ways the events described were more typical of the Lucas García regime. However, its eyewitness accounts of army campaigns capture the full extent of repression in the highlands.

Under Ríos Montt the army campaign was much more successful and the guerrillas were driven into the remote corners of the highlands.

REPRESSION OF THE MAYA DURING THE 1970S AND 1980S

Throughout their history Guatemala's Maya have been severely victimized and exploited, with the situation being particularly serious during the 1970s and 1980s, and threatening the future of the entire indigenous population. Guatemala's Maya have always been the victims of racism, malnutrition and poor health care, suffering through the neglect of central government. However, Guatemala's undeclared civil war increased their burden immeasurably. In 1983 Survival International published an account of the repression of the Maya population, which examined the way the Maya were selected for particularly brutal treatment. What follows is an extract from that report, which describes the situation in the late 1970s and early 1980s, when it was at its worst. Since that time things have improved significantly and, whilst the indigenous Maya still suffer from institutionalized racism, exploitation, inferior health care and bitter poverty, the countryside is at least peaceful again, and an awaking cultural confidence is beginning to develop. In this account the term Indian has been used to refer to the indigenous Maya.

1883 Survival International Report: Indians are reportedly bearing the brunt of the Guatemalan army's efforts to root out subversion. In May, *El Gráfico*, Guatemala's second largest newspaper, condemned the "genocide being carried out in the Indian regions of the country". A western European diplomat quoted on June 3 by the *New York Times* said, "Indians are systematically being destroyed as a group. . . . There is no break with the past." A priest in Huehuetenango told John Dinges in July that "the army is trying to kill every Indian alive". Guatemalan security forces do not always distinguish between innocent civilians and guerrillas, acknowledges General Ríos Montt. "Look, the problem of war is not just a question of who is shooting. For each one who is shooting there are ten behind him." His press secretary, Francisco Bianchi, adds: "The guerrillas won over many Indian collaborators. Therefore, the Indians

were subversives, right? And how do you fight subversion? Clearly you had to kill Indians because they were collaborating with subversion. And then they say, "You're massacring innocent people." But they weren't innocent. They had sold out to subversion."

According to some reports, the government is also seeking to destroy once and for all the traditional Indian way of life. Measures are being aimed at the elimination of the several Indian languages still spoken in rural Guatemala. Young men conscripted into the army are stationed in regions where different languages are spoken and are forbidden to speak to each other in their own language. The army is said to aggressively discourage the use of Indian language by everyone else, whether in their own community or relocated in strategic hamlets (model villages). The Indians' distinctive traditional costume, which is such an important expression and symbol of their ethnic identity and pride, is taken from them and burned. The religious fiestas which used to be a feature of Indian life in rural Guatemala are forbidden with the claim that food prepared for these occasions will be given to the guerrillas. The musical instruments used in these fiestas are destroyed. The linkages between generations which permit and channel the transmission and continuation of cultural traditions are broken as the people are made orphans, losing their children, their parents, and their grandparents. Community solidarity is undermined by forcing men conscripted into the "civil patrols" to attack and kill their neighbours or fellow villagers.

Not only are Indian customs, beliefs and traditions under attack but the economic and ecological basis for Indian existence is being destroyed. It is reported that when the army attacks an Indian community, the people's houses, belongings and crops are burned and their domestic animals are killed or illegally confiscated. Rivers and streams, sources of drinking water, are said to be poisoned. In certain areas extensive pine forests are being burned down, in some cases set on fire by incendiary bombs thrown from helicopters.

Soldiers swept through the mountains, rounding up those who had fled from previous campaigns and herding them into refugee camps, while villagers were forced to defend their own communities in Civil Defence Patrols. Those who returned from the mountains were put to work by the army, who fed and "re-educated" them. Accounts of the army campaign under Ríos

Montt are deeply divided. Some commentators see him as a significant reformer, who saved the rural population by transforming the approach of the army. On the other hand there are those who regard him as the most brutal of all Guatemala's rulers. Most Guatemalans, particularly those in the highlands, do seem to speak very highly of him and say that when he came to power he managed to put a stop to the indiscriminate violence which had plagued the country.

Ríos Montt was replaced by **Mejía Víctores** in August 1983, and under the new administration there was a significant drop in the level of rural repression, although selective killings were still an everyday event. In 1984, however, the number of urban disappearances rose once again, with around fifty people abducted each month. In the highlands the process of reconstruction began. Guerrilla forces had dropped to around 1500, and although military campaigns continued, "model villages" were now being built to replace those that had been destroyed. Even so the conditions for refugees and survivors were still highly restricted and many large and impoverished communities are now made up entirely of widows and orphans.

Towards the end of 1985 the country faced its first free elections in thirty years, after a period that had seen eighteen different administrations and cost the lives of 100,000 people. Another 38,000 had "disappeared", 440 villages had been destroyed, and 100,000 Guatemalans had fled to Mexico.

CIVILIAN RULE

In 1986 the election of **Vinicio Cerezo** as Guatemala's first civilian president for almost thirty years was widely regarded as a major opportunity to improve the human rights situation within the country. Cerezo himself had, on several occasions, come close to assassination, and members of his party, the Christian Democrats, have always been a favourite target of the death squads.

Following Cerezo's inauguration there was a marked decrease in the quantity of human rights violations although in a matter of months things started to deteriorate once again. Abductions, killings and intimidation remained widespread, with the victims drawn from the same groups as before. Between February 1986 and January 1987 there were at least one thousand killings, the vast majority attributable to "death squads". No one accused Cerezo of involvement in the murders, but it does seem that they were carried out by members of the security forces, which was a measure of his inability to control them.

In rural areas the level of violence dropped off significantly. With guerrilla forces estimated at 1000 to 3000, the army had little need to use the same heavy-handed tactics it had employed in the past. Many observers felt that the reduction in human rights abuse was simply a reflection of a more refined strategy by the army, who had already established control and could now use a more subtle but no less effective form of repression – killing selective targets rather than destroying entire communities. Abuses of the indigenous population remained common, and they were often exploited and undernourished, with little access to education or health care. In many areas the indigenous population was forced to participate in civil patrols (despite assurances that they would have the option not to), which themselves became important in the system of repression and were responsible for intimidation, murder and abduction.

In 1988, just two years after the return to civilian rule, the level of violence began to increase sharply. Many people's worst fears were confirmed in November of that year when 22 bodies were found in a shallow grave near El Aguacate, a small village in the department of Chimaltenango. As yet there is no clear evidence to indicate who carried out the massacre, although testimonies suggest that the army was responsible: they blame the guerrillas.

The killing continued throughout Cerezo's term in office and there was no real effort either to find the bodies of the disappeared – despite the pleas of their relatives – or to bring the guilty to trial. Cerezo himself remained preoccupied with holding onto power, fending off several coup attempts and trying to build some kind of power base. As president he adopted a non-confrontational approach which not only ensured a reprieve for the guilty but also allowed for the continued abuse of human rights. In his more candid moments Cerezo admitted that the continuing power of the army restricted his room for manoeuvre and argued that any investigation of past abuses would be impossible as he would have to put the entire army on trial.

TOWARDS THE MILLENNIUM

In 1990 Cerezo handed the reins of power to **President Serrano**, but the situation remained bleak, with abductions, torture, intimidation and extrajudicial executions still commonplace. According to several US human rights groups, five hundred Guatemalans either "disappeared" or were killed in extrajudicial executions in 1992 alone. That said, the administration was forced to tackle several high-profile cases, including the murder of street children and the assassinations of US citizen Michael Devine and the anthropologist Myrna Mack Chang, and for the first time members of the armed forces were convicted of human rights violations. A number of defiant local groups were very vocal in denouncing violations, particularly the Mutual Support Group (**GAM**), many of whose members and leaders were kidnapped and murdered. By contrast the government's Human Right Commission received over one thousand complaints of human rights violations and acted on none of them.

Meanwhile out **in the highlands** a number of new factors emerged. In December 1990 the people of Santiago Atitlán expelled the army from their village, after troops shot and killed thirteen people (see p.391). In the wake of this incident a number of other villages called for army bases to be closed. The confidence of the Maya population was further boosted in 1992, when the Nobel Peace Prize was awarded to Rigoberta Menchú (see over), briefly focusing world attention on the plight of Guatemala's indigenous population. In early 1993 the first **refugees** began returning from Mexico to settle in the Ixcán region of northern Quiché. Their return provoked a fresh crisis in the countryside and the army bombarded nearby villages and resorted to familiar tactics to terrorize those returning. As more refugees have come home, the shortage of land and the uncertainty surrounding their future provided additional tension and resulted in a fresh wave of human rights abuses by the armed forces. The most serious case was the massacre of eleven people (and the wounding of thirty more) by soldiers in the village of **Xamán** in Alta Verapaz on October 5, 1995 (see p.302). Since then thousands more refugees have returned, including ex-guerrillas, and relations have generally been good with other established communities, though unemployment is very high amongst the returning refugees.

The **Indigenous Rights Accords of 1995** (see p.370) sought to tackle these outstanding issues, with commitments to educate Maya children in their native tongue, to promote the use of indigenous languages at national and local level, to encourage greater political participation for the Maya, and to preserve their sacred areas. However, little progress has been made to date: Arzú's government has delayed the imposition of a Children Code to ensure that schools teach Maya and Garifuna children in their native languages, while the other central commitments will take decades to implement, even if the will is still there.

One of the most crucial strands of the **Peace Accords of December 1996** was the establishment of a Truth Commission, overseen by MINUGUA (the UN mission to Guatemala), to investigate human rights abuses committed during the civil war. However, the Commission's lack of legal teeth, a short lifespan, and a stipulation that only abuses "linked to the armed conflict" should be investigated, has led Guatemalans to have little faith in it. Few expect more from the Commission than a slap on the wrist for the army (who have already refused to hand over documents that might threaten "national security") and a reprimand for certain guerrilla actions.

Whilst MINUGUA's presence has undoubtedly helped keep the army in check, and there now is little evidence of systematic military and state-backed repression (Guatemala was removed from the United Nations human rights blacklist in September 1997), **violence** continues, particularly in the cities. Death squads still harass, injure and murder street children and "undesirables", and research carried out by PRODEN (the Child's Rights Commission) in late 1997 estimated there were up to five thousand children living rough in the country, mainly in the capital. Human Rights Watch documented 55 "social cleansing" attacks in 1996, resulting in twelve deaths. Child kidnapping rings have also been operating in Guatemala, stealing babies to sell to the USA.

In the late 1990s, relative calm exists in the countryside, following the signing of the peace accords, though major human rights issues remain and the odd atrocity, such as the assaination of Bishop Juan Gerardi still occurs. The most serious human rights problems affect the **Maya population**, who remain discriminated against, largely live in extreme poverty

For more information on human rights in Guatemala contact Amnesty International, 1 Easton St, London WC1X 0DW (☎0171/413 5500); The Guatemalan Committee for Human Rights, 83 Margaret St, London (☎0171/631 4200); or Human Rights Watch, at 33 Islington High St, London N1 9LH (☎0171/713 1995), or 1522 K St, NW #910, Washington DC 20005–1202 (☎202/3716592)

(81 percent, according to government estimates), suffer appalling health care and education (75 percent are illiterate), and have the lowest life expectancy in the western hemisphere. A Maya man will live on average to around 47 years of age, a woman to 48, up to 17 years less than their *mestizo* compatriots. Non-Spanish speakers rarely get court translaters or bilingual state defence lawers and, despite forming over fifty percent of the population, only six out of eighty Congressional deputies are indigenous.

Since the peace settlements a crime wave has swept the country, with thefts, kidnapping and random robberies being commonplace. Due to an almost universal lack of faith in the justice system, public **lynchings** of suspected criminals are a common response, though in numerous cases the suspects are later found to be innocent and the criminals go unpunished. It remains to be seen whether the newly formed PNC (civilian police force) will be successful in tackling this problem.

RIGOBERTA MENCHÚ AND THE NOBEL PEACE PRIZE

Five hundred years after Columbus reached the Americas the Nobel committee awarded their peace prize to **Rigoberta Menchú**, a 33-year-old Maya woman who has campaigned tirelessly for peace in Guatemala. In their official statement the Nobel committee described Menchú as "a vivid symbol of peace and reconciliation across ethnic, cultural and social dividing lines."

Within Guatemala, however, the honour provoked controversy. There can be little doubt that Menchú had firm connections and deep sympathies with Guatemala's guerrillas, although after she was awarded the prize she distanced herself from the armed struggle. Nevertheless, many people argued that her support for armed uprising made her an inappropriate winner of a peace prize. A couple of days before the announcement the army's chief spokesman Captain Julio Yon Rivera said she "defamed the fatherland", although once the prize was awarded he claimed to have been expressing a personal opinion that was not the official view of the Guatemalan army. The foreign minister, Gonzalo Mendez Park, was equally dismissive, describing Menchú as "tied to certain groups that have endangered Guatemala". Others feared that the prize would be interpreted as a vindication of the guerrillas and only serve to perpetuate the civil war.

Menchú's own words, however, show her to be essentially a pacifist and suggest that her unspoken support for the guerrillas was very much a last resort. "For us, killing is something monstrous. And that's why we feel so angered by all the repression. ... Even though the tortures and kidnappings had done our people a lot of harm, we shouldn't lose faith in change. This is when I began working in a peasant organization and went on to another stage of my life. There are other things, other ways."

Menchú's story is undeniably tragic and her account of it offers a real insight into the darkest years of Guatemalan history and their impact on the indigenous people. Born in the tiny hamlet of Chimel, in the hills south of Uspantán, Menchú is the sixth of nine children. By the age of eight she was working on the coastal plantations picking coffee, where one of her brothers died of malnutrition and her best friend died from pesticide poisoning. Her father was an activist who campaigned for the defence of peasants' land, although his role within the community probably made the family an obvious target for repression. In 1979 one of Menchú's brothers was kidnapped by the army and allegedly burnt alive, along with several other prisoners, though recent investigations have cast some doubt on this version of events. In early 1980 her father was part of a delegation of Maya leaders who peacefully occupied the Spanish embassy in Guatemala City in order to draw attention to their plight. The Guatemalan army, however, set fire to the building, killing all those inside (an action which precipitated Spain to break off diplomatic relations for more than five years). Three months after her father's death, Menchú's mother was kidnapped by the army, raped, tortured and murdered.

In 1980 Menchú fled the country for Mexico, where she collaborated with a Venezuelan journalist to write her autobiography, *I, Rigoberta Menchú – An Indian Woman In Guatemala*, and campaigned tirelessly for the cause of indigenous people in Guatemala and throughout the Americas. Since leaving, Menchú has returned to Guatemala on a number of occasions, although she faces the constant threat of assassination.

Today Menchú remains the most visible international campaigner for the rights of Guatemala's indigenous people and provides a clear focus for what is a fairly diverse movement. Her role is both difficult and dangerous; in November 1995, when she was becoming heavily involved in the campaign for a proper investigation into the Xamán massacre, Menchú's nephew was abducted in Guatemala City. In an interview at the time, Menchú expressed her confidence in a gradual but important process of change. "In Guatemala human rights continue to be violated every day. You only have to look at the summaries every weekend to see the number of people killed. But on the other hand, the population is coping with the situation in an exemplary way. Every day the vote against fear is gathering strength and this is the foundation for change in the future. What has already changed is the participation of the population in human rights activism."

LANDSCAPE AND WILDLIFE

Guatemala embraces an astonishingly diverse collection of environments, ranging from the permanently moist rain forests and mangroves of the Caribbean coast to the exposed central highlands, where the ground is often hard with frost. Its wildlife is correspondingly varied; undisturbed forests provide a home to both temperate species from the north and tropical ones from the south, as well as a number of indigenous species found nowhere else in the world.

THE PACIFIC COAST

Guatemala's **Pacific coastline** is marked by a thin strip of black volcanic sand, pounded by the surf. There are no natural harbours and boats have to take their chances in the breakers or launch from one of the piers (though the purpose-built Puerto Quetzal now takes large, ocean-going ships). The sea itself provides a rich natural harvest of shrimp, tuna, snapper and mackerel, most of which go for export. The coastal waters are also ideal for sport fishing. A couple of kilometres offshore, dorado, which grow to around forty pounds, are plentiful, while further out there are marlin, sailfish, wahoo and skipjack.

The **beach** itself rises from the water to form a large sandbank, dotted with palm trees,

behind which the land drops off into low-lying mangrove swamps and canals. In the east, from San José to the border, the **Chiquimulilla Canal** runs behind the beach for around 100km. For most of the way it's no more than a narrow strip of water, but here and there it fans out into swamps, creating a maze of waterways that are an ideal breeding ground for young fish, waterfowl and a range of small mammals. The sandy shoreline is an ideal nesting site for three species of **sea turtles**, including the giant leatherback (see box on p.228), which occasionally emerge from the water, drag themselves up the beach and deposit a clutch of eggs before hauling their weight back into the water. At Monterrico, to the east of San José, a nature reserve protects a small section of the coastline for the benefit of the turtles, and with luck you might see one here. **The Monterrico Reserve** (p.229) is in fact the best place to see wildlife on the Pacific coast as it includes a superb mangrove swamp, typical of the area directly behind the beach, which you can easily explore by boat.

The **mangroves** are mixed in with water lilies, bulrushes and tropical hardwoods, amongst which you'll see **herons**, **kingfishers** and an array of **ducks** including **muscovies** and **white whistling ducks**. In the area around Monterrico flocks of **wood stork** are common, and you might also see the **white ibis** or the occasional **great jabiru**, a massive stork that nests in the area. With real perseverance and a bit of luck you might also catch a glimpse of a **racoon**, **anteater** or **opossum**. You'll also be able to see **alligators** and **iguanas**, if not in the wild then at the reserve headquarters where they are kept on a breeding programme. Other birds that you might see almost anywhere along the coast include **plovers**, **coots** and **terns**, and a number of winter migrants including **white** and **brown pelicans**.

Between the shore and the foothills of the highlands, the **coastal plain** is an intensely fertile and heavily farmed area, where the volcanic and alluvial soils are ideal for sugar cane, cotton, palm oil, rubber plantations and cattle ranches. In recent years soya and sorghum, which require less labour, have been added to this list. Guatemala's coastal **agribusiness** is high cost and high yield: the soils are treated chemically and the crops regularly sprayed with a cocktail of pesticides, herbicides and fertilizers. There's little land that remains untouched by the hand of commercial agriculture so it's hard to imagine what this must once have looked like, but it was almost certainly very similar to Petén, a mixture of savannah and rain forest supporting a rich array of wildlife. These days it's only the swamps, steep hillsides and towering hedges that give any hint of its former glory, although beautiful flocks of white **snowy** and **cattle egrets** feed alongside the beef cattle.

Finally, one particularly interesting lowland species is the **opendula**, a large oriole which builds a long woven nest hanging from trees and telephone wires. They tend to nest in colonies and a single tree might support fifty nests. You'll probably notice the nests more than the birds, which thrive throughout Guatemala and neighbouring countries.

THE BOCA COSTA

Approaching the highlands, the coastal plain starts to slope up towards a string of volcanic cones, and this section of well-drained hillside is known as the **Boca Costa**. The volcanic soils, high rainfall and good drainage conspire to make it ideal for growing **coffee**, and it's here that Guatemala's best crop is produced, with rows of olive-green bushes ranked beneath shady trees.

Where the land is unsuitable for coffee, lush tropical forest still grows, clinging to the hills. As you head up into the highlands, through deeply cleft valleys, you pass through some of this superb forest, dripping with moss-covered vines, bromeliads and orchids. The full value of this environment had remained unexplored for many years and the foundation of the **Faro Field Station**, on the southern slopes of the **Santiaguito** volcano, revealed an amazing, undisturbed ecosystem, protected by the threat of volcanic eruption. Over 120 species of bird have been sighted here, including some real rarities such as **solitary eagles**, **quetzals** and **highland guans**. The **azure-rumped tanager**, seen here in June 1988, hadn't previously been sighted in Guatemala since the mid-nineteenth century.

THE HIGHLANDS

The highlands proper begin with a chain of **volcanoes**. There are 33 in all, running in a direct line from the southwest to the northeast. Most can be climbed in five or six hours and the view from the top is always superb. The highest is **Tajumulco** (4210m), which marks the Mexican border, and there are also three active cones: **Fuego**, **Pacaya** and **Santiaguito**, all of which belch sulphurous fumes, volcanic ash, and the occasional fountain of molten rock. Beneath the surface their subterranean fires heat the bedrock and there are several places where spring water emerges at near boiling point, offering the luxury of a hot bath (for the best of these see Almolonga, p.174).

On this southern side of the central highlands there are two large lakes, set in superb countryside and hemmed in by volcanic peaks. Both tell a sad tale of environmental mismanagement. **Lake Amatitlán**, to the south of Guatemala City, is further down the road to contamination, its waters already blackened by pollution and its shores ringed with holiday homes. It remains a popular picnic spot for the capital's not so rich. Further to the west is **Lake Atitlán**, still spectacularly beautiful, with crystal blue water, but increasing tourist development threatens to damage its delicate ecological balance. The greatest damage so far was done by the introduction of the **black bass** in 1958, in a bid to create sport fishing. The bass is a greedy, thuggish beast and in no time at all its presence had reshaped the food chain. Smaller fish became increasingly rare, as did crabs, frogs, insects and small mammals. Worst hit was the **Atitlán grebe**, a small, flightless water bird unique to the lake. Young grebes were gobbled up by the hungry bass, and by 1965 just eighty of them survived. By 1984, falling water levels caused by the 1976 earthquake, combined with tourist development of the lakeshore, cut their numbers by another thirty, and today the bird is officially extinct. Meanwhile the beauty of Lake Atitlán remains under threat from overdevelopment, population growth and soil erosion.

On the northern side of the volcanic ridge are the **central valleys** of the highlands, a complex mixture of sweeping bowls, steep-sided valleys, open plateaux and jagged peaks. This central area is home to the vast majority of Guatemala's population and all the available land is intensely farmed, with hillsides carved into workable terraces and portioned up into a patchwork of small fields. Here the land is farmed by *campesinos* using techniques that predate the arrival of the Spanish. The *milpa* is the mainstay of Maya farming practices: a field is cleared, usually by slash and burn, and is planted with maize as the main crop, with beans, chillies and squash grown beneath it at ground level. Traditionally, the land is rotated between *milpa* and pasture, and also left fallow for a while, but in some areas it's now under constant pressure, the fertility of the soil is virtually exhausted and only with the assistance of fertilizer can it still produce a worthwhile crop. The pressure on land is immense and each generation is forced to farm more marginal territory, planting on steep hillsides where exposed soil is soon washed into the valley below.

Some areas remain off limits to farmers, however, and there are still vast tracts of the highlands that are **forested**. In the cool valleys of the central highlands pine trees dominate, intermixed with oak, cedar and fir, all of which occur naturally. To the south, on the volcanic slopes and in the warmth of deep-cut valleys, lush tropical forest thrives in a world kept permanently moist – similar in many ways to the forest of Verapaz, where constant rain fosters the growth of "high rain forest".

Heading on to the north the land rises to form several **mountain ranges**. The largest of these are the Cuchumatanes, a massive chain of granite peaks that reach a height of 3790m above the town of Huehuetenango. Further to the east there are several smaller ranges such as the Sierra de Chuacús, the Sierra de las Minas and the Sierra de Chama. The high peaks support stunted trees and open grassland, used for grazing sheep and cattle, but are too cold for maize and most other crops.

Bird life is plentiful throughout the highlands; you'll see a variety of **hummingbirds**, flocks of screeching **parakeets**, **swifts**, **egrets** and the ever-present **vultures**. Slightly less commonplace are the **quails** and **wood partridges**, **white-tailed pigeons**, and several species of doves including the **little Inca** and the **white-winged dove**. Last but by no means least is the **quetzal**, which has been revered since Maya times. The male quetzal has fantastic green tail-feathers which snake behind it through the air as it flies: these have always been prized by hunters and even today the bird is very rare indeed. Near Copán is the **Biotopo del Quetzal**, a protected area of high rain forest in the department of Baja Verapaz, where quetzals breed.

The highlands also support a number of small **mammals**, including foxes and small cats, although your chances of seeing these are very slim indeed.

THE RAIN FORESTS OF PETÉN

To the north of the highlands the land drops away into the **rainforests** of Petén, a huge chunk of which remain miraculously undisturbed, although recent oil finds, guerrilla war and migrant settlers are all putting fresh strain on this ecological wonderland. The forest of Petén extends across the Mexican border, where it merges with the Lacandon rain forest, and into Belize, where it skirts around the lower slopes of the Maya Mountains, reaching to the Caribbean coast.

Around seventy percent of Petén is still covered by **primary forest**, with a canopy that towers 50m above the forest floor, made up of hundreds of species of trees, including ceiba, mahogany, aguacate, ebony and sapodilla. The combination of a year-round growing season, plenty of moisture and millions of years of evolution have produced an environment that supports literally thousands of species of plants and trees. While temperate forests tend to be dominated by a single species – fir, oak or beech, say – it's diversity that characterizes the tropical forest. Each species is specifically adapted to fit into a particular ecological niche, where it receives a precise amount of light and moisture.

It's a biological storehouse that has yet to be fully explored although it has already yielded some astonishing **discoveries**. Steroid hormones, such as cortisone, and diosgenin, the active ingredient in birth control pills, were developed from wild yams found in these forests; and tetrodoxin, which is derived from a species of Central American frog, is an anesthetic 160,000 times stronger than cocaine.

Despite its size and diversity the forest is surprisingly **fragile**. It forms a closed system in which nutrients are continuously recycled and decaying plant matter fuels new growth. The forest floor is a spongy mass of roots, fungi, mosses, bacteria and micro-organisms, in which nutrients are stored, broken down with the assistance of insects and chemical decay, and gradually released to the waiting roots and fresh seedlings. The thick canopy prevents much light reaching the forest floor, ensuring that the soil remains damp but warm, a hotbed of chemical activity. The death of a large tree prompts a flurry of growth as new light reaches the forest floor, and in no time at all a young tree rises to fill the gap. But once the trees are removed the soil is highly vulnerable, deprived of its main source of fertility. Exposed to the harsh tropical sun and direct rainfall, an area of cleared forest soon becomes prone to flooding and drought. Recently cleared land will contain enough nutrients for four or five years of good growth, but soon afterwards its usefulness declines rapidly and within twenty years it will be almost completely barren. If the trees are stripped from a large area soil erosion will silt the rivers and parched soils disrupt local rainfall patterns

However, **settlement** needn't mean the end of the rain forest, and in the past this area supported a huge population of Maya, who probably numbered several million. (Some archeologists, however, argue that during Maya occupation Petén was a mixture of savannah and grassland, and that relatively recent climatic changes have enabled it to evolve into rain forest.) Only one small group of Maya, the Lacandon, still farm the forest using traditional methods. They allow the existing trees to point them in the right direction, avoiding areas that support mahogany, as they tend to be too wet, and searching out ceiba and ramon trees, which thrive in rich, well-drained soils. In April a patch of forest is burnt down and then, to prevent soil erosion, planted with fast-growing trees such as bananas and papaya, and with root crops to fix the soil. A few weeks later they plant their main crops: maize and a selection of others, from garlic to sweet potatoes. Every inch of the soil is covered in growth, a method that mimics the forest and thereby protects the soil. The same land is cultivated for three or four years

and then allowed to return to its wild state, although they continue to harvest from the fruit-bearing plants and in due course return to the same area. The whole process is in perfect harmony with the forest, extracting only what it can afford to lose and ensuring that it remains fertile. Sadly, the Lacandon are a dying breed and the traditional farming practices are now used by very few. In their place are waves of new settlers, burning the forest and planting grass for cattle. Neither the cattle, the farmers or the forest will survive long under such a system.

In its undisturbed state the rain forest is still superbly beautiful and is home to an incredible range of wildlife. Amongst the birds the **ocellated turkey**, found only in Petén, is perhaps the most famous. But the forest is also home to **toucans**, **motmots**, several species of **parrots** including **Aztec** and **green parakeets**, and the endangered **scarlet macaw**, which is said to live to at least fifty. As in the highlands, **hummingbirds**, **buzzards** and **hawks** are all common. A surprising number of these can be seen fairly easily in the **Tikal National Park**, particularly if you hang around until sunset.

Amongst the mammals you'll find **jaguars** (referred to as *tigre* in Guatemala), **peccary** (a type of wild boar), **brocket deer**, **opossums**, **weasels**, **porcupines**, **pumas**, **ocelots**, **armadillos** and several different species of **monkey**, including **spiders** and **howlers**, which emit a chilling deep-throated roar. The massive **tapir** (mountain cow) plunder through the forests, and the river banks are occupied by tiny **ridge-backed turtles** and **crocodiles**, while **egrets** and **kingfishers** fish from overhanging branches. The rivers and lakes of Petén are correspondingly rich, packed with **snook**, **tarpon** and **mullet**.

BOOKS

In the past Guatemala has never inspired a great deal of literature, but in recent years the country's political turmoil has spawned a boom in non-fiction. Politics overshadows almost all books about Guatemala, and most travel, historical and cultural accounts deal with Central America as a whole, offering only a small slice of the country.

Many of the books listed below are difficult to find outside the US, though they may be imported by specialist bookshops. Useful sources include the *Interhemispheric Education Research Center* in the US (☎505/842-8288; fax 246-1601) and the *Latin American Bureau*, 1 Amwell St, London EC1R 1UL (☎0171/278 2829; fax 278 0165; email *lab@gn.apc.org*). Where possible, we have given both the US and UK publishers, with the US publisher first (US/UK); o/p means a book is out of print.

TRAVEL

Stephen Connoly Benz *Guatemalan Journey* (University of Texas Press in US). A contemporary perspective on the complexities of Guatemalan society, and the impact of US culture and evangelism, with particularly good accounts of life in the capital and the textile factories.

Anthony Daniels *Sweet Waist of America* (Trafalgar Square/Arrow; both o/p). A delight to read. Daniels takes a refreshingly even-handed approach to Guatemala and comes up with a fascinating cocktail of people and politics, discarding the stereotypes that litter most books on Central America. The book also includes interesting interviews with prominent characters from Guatemala's recent history.

Thomas Gage *Travels in the New World* (University of Oklahoma Press in US and UK). Unusual account of a Dominican friar's travels through Mexico and Central America between 1635 and 1637, including some fascinating insights into colonial life as well as some great attacks on the greed and pomposity of the Catholic Church abroad.

Aldous Huxley *Beyond the Mexique Bay* (Flamingo in UK; o/p). Huxley's travels, in 1934, took him from Belize through Guatemala to Mexico, swept on by his fascination for history and religion, and sprouting bizarre theories on the basis of everything he sees. There are some great descriptions of Maya sites and Indian culture, with superb one-liners summing up people and places.

Patrick Marnham *So far from God . . .* (Viking Penguin; o/p/Bloomsbury). A saddened and vaguely right-wing account of Marnham's travels through the Americas from the US to Panamá (missing out Belize). Dotted with amusing anecdotes and interesting observations, the book was researched in 1984, and its description of Guatemala is dominated by the reign of terror. The Paraxtut massacre, mentioned by Marnham, has since been unmasked as a fabrication.

Jonathan Evans Maslow *Bird of Life, Bird of Death* (Dell/Penguin; both o/p). Again travel and political comment are merged as Maslow sets out in search of the quetzal, using the bird's uncertain future as a metaphor for contemporary Guatemala and contrasting this with the success of the vulture. It's a sweeping account, very entertaining, but more concerned with impressing the reader than representing the truth. A great yarn, set in a country that's larger than life, but in the end a naive and stereotypical image of Central American horror.

Jeremy Paxman *Through the Volcanoes* (Paladin in the UK; o/p). Similar in many ways to Patrick Marnham's book, this is another political travel account investigating the turmoil of Central America and finding solace in the calm of Costa Rica. Paxman's travels take him through all seven of the republics, and he offers a good overview of the politics and history of the region.

Nigel Pride *A Butterfly Sings to Pacaya* (Constable in the UK; o/p). The author, accompanied by his wife and four-year-old son, travels south from the US border in a Jeep, heading through Mexico, Guatemala and Belize. A large section of the book is set in Maya areas and illustrated by the author's drawings of landscapes, people and animals. Though the travels took place nearly twenty years ago the pleasures and privations they experience rarely appear dated: the description of the climb of the Pacaya volcano is one of the highlights of the book.

John Lloyd Stephens *Incidents of Travel in Central America, Chiapas, and Yucatán* (Dover/Prentice Hall). Stephens was a classic nineteenth-century traveller. Acting as American ambassador to Central America, he indulged his own enthusiasm for archeology; while the republics fought it out among themselves he was wading through the jungle stumbling across ancient cities. His journals, told with superb Victorian pomposity punctuated with sudden waves of enthusiasm, make great reading. Some editions include fantastic illustrations by Catherwood of the ruins overgrown with tropical rain forest.

Paul Theroux *The Old Patagonian Express* (Houghton Mifflin/Penguin). An epic train journey from Boston to Patagonia that takes in a couple of miserable train trips in Guatemala. Theroux doesn't have much time for Guatemalans, dismissing them as unhelpful and taciturn, but as usual, his way with words paints a vivid picture. See p.47 for a taster.

Marcus McPeek Villatoro *Walking to the Milpa* (Moyer Bell in US and UK). Engaging but disturbing account of a lay missionary's three-year stint in the frontier settlement of Poptún in Petén, giving an insight into the superstitions, dangers and celebrations of life in rural Guatemala.

Ronald Wright *Time Among the Maya* (Henry Holt/Abacus). A vivid and sympathetic account of travels from Belize through Guatemala, Chiapas and Yucatán, meeting the Maya of today and exploring their obsession with time. The book's twin points of interest are the ancient Maya and the recent violence. An encyclopedic bibliography offers ideas for exploration in depth, and the author's knowledge is evident in the superb historical insight he imparts through the book. Certainly one of the best travel books on the area.

FICTION, AUTOBIOGRAPHY AND POETRY

Miguel Angel Asturias *Hombres de Maiz* (Macmillan; o/p/Verso). Guatemala's most famous author, Asturias is deeply indebted to Guatemalan history and culture in his work. "Men of Maize" is generally regarded as his masterpiece, classically Latin American in its magic realist style, and bound up in the complexity of indigenous culture. His other works include *El Señor Presidente*, a grotesque portrayal of social chaos and dictatorial rule, based on Asturias's own experience; *El Papa Verde*, which explores the murky world of the United Fruit Company; and *Weekend en Guatemala*, describing the downfall of the Arbenz government. Asturias died in 1974, after he had won the Nobel prize for literature.

Paul Bowles *Up Above the World* (Ecco Press/Peter Owen). Paul Bowles is at his chilling, understated best in this novel based on experiences of Guatemala in the late 1930s. **Jane Bowles** used the same visit for her fiction in *A Guatemalan Idyll* and other tales, recently republished in *Everything is Nice: Collected Stories of Jane Bowles* (Peter Owen in UK).

Francisco Goldman *The Long Night of White Chickens* (Grove-Atlantic/Faber). Drawing on the stylistic complexity of Latin American fiction, this novel tells the tale of a young Guatemalan orphan who flees to the US and works as a maid. When she finally returns home she is murdered. It's an interesting and ambitious story flavoured with all the bitterness and beauty of Guatemala's natural and political landscape.

Gaspar Pedro Gonzales *A Mayan Life* (The Yax Te' Press in US). Absorbing story about the personal and cultural conflicts facing a K'anjobal Maya in the Cuchumanantes mountains as he seeks a higher education. Gonzales claims this is the first novel ever written by a Maya author, though it is obviously highly autobiographical.

Norman Lewis *The Volcano Above Us* (Penguin in the UK; o/p). Vaguely historical novel published in 1957 that pulls together all the main elements of Guatemala's recent history. The image that it summons is one of depressing drudgery and eternal conflict, set against a background of repression and racism. In the light of what's happened it has a certain prophetic quality, and remains gripping despite its miserable conclusions.

Victor Perera *Rites: A Guatemalan Boyhood* (Mercury House/Eland). Autobiographical account of a childhood in Guatemala City's Jewish community. It may not cast much light on the country, but it's an interesting read, pulling together an unusual combination of cultures.

Rodrigo Rey Rosa *Dust on her Tongue; The Beggar's Knife* (both City Lights/Peter Owen). Two collections of stories by a young Guatemalan writer, translated by Paul Bowles. The tales are brutal and lyrical, concerned, as Bowles comments, with "a present-day Central America troubled by atavistic memories of its sanguinary past". Recommended.

GUATEMALAN HISTORY, POLITICS AND HUMAN RIGHTS

Tom Barry *Guatemala A Country Guide* (Interhemispheric Research Center in US and UK). A comprehensive and concise account of the political, social and economic situation in Guatemala, with a mild left-wing stance. Currently the best source for a good overview of the situation.

Phillip Berryman *Christians in Guatemala's Struggle* (Catholic Institute for International Relations in UK). Well-informed and written slim volume, covering 1944–84. Even if you're not particularly interested in the Christian angle, it offers a concise account of the political situation, seen through the eyes of the oppressed. It includes a great deal of information about the development of opposition to the oligarchy, particularly union organization.

George Black *Garrison Guatemala* (Monthly Review Press/Zed Books). An account of the militarization of Guatemalan politics up to 1982. Black's condemnation is total: the conflict in Guatemala is seen as a battle to the death, with armed uprising the only possible solution and the probable outcome.

Jim Handy *Gift of the Devil* (South End Press in US). The best modern history of Guatemala, concise and readable with a sharp focus on the Indian population and the brief period of socialist government. Don't expect much detail on the distant past, which is only explored in order to

set the modern reality in some kind of context, but if you're interested in the history of Guatemalan brutality then this is the book to read. By no means objective, it sets out to expose the development of oppression and point the finger at those who oppress.

Margaret Hooks *Guatemalan Women Speak* (EPICA/Catholic Institute for International Relations). An interesting collection of interviews with Guatemalan women, ranging from the wife of a *finca* owner to an impoverished indigenous highlander. The book embraces a wide range of topics, including work, family, sexuality, politics and religion, and gives voice to a seldom heard perspective on the nation's problems.

In Focus: Guatemala – A Guide to the People, Politics and Culture (Latin American Bureau in UK). Published in 1998, this is part of an excellent series of country studies that summarize concisely the historical, political, economic and social situation throughout Latin America and the Caribbean.

George Lovell *A Beauty that Hurts: Life and Death in Guatemala* (Between the Lines in Canada). A good contemporary analysis enlivened by interviews with exiles and activists. The book also scrutinizes recent political events through newspaper articles, and reviews the historical context that has shaped modern Guatemala.

Victor Montejo *Testimony: Death of a Guatemalan Village* (Curbstone Press in US and UK). Yet another horrifying account of murder and destruction. In this case it's the personal testimony of a school teacher, describing the arrival of the army in a small highland village and the killing that follows.

James Painter *Guatemala: False Hope, False Freedom* (Latin American Bureau/Monthly Review Press). Another deeply depressing analysis of the situation in Guatemala today. First published in 1987, and revised in 1989, it deals with the failure of civilian rule. It also includes an investigation into the roots of inequality and a summary of the main forces that help perpetuate it. Read it alongside Jean-Marie Simon's book (see below).

Mario Payeras *Days of the Jungle* (Monthly Review Press/Casa de las Americas; o/p). A slim volume written under the auspices of the EGP, one of Guatemala's main guerrilla armies. In this sense it's unique, as the voice of the guerrillas is rarely heard. Here one of their number tells of the early days of the organization, as they enter Guatemala through the jungles of the northwest and attempt to establish contacts amongst the local population. There are, however, serious doubts about the accuracy of the story.

Victor Perera *Unfinished Conquest* (University of California Press in US and UK). Superb, extremely readable account of the civil war paying particular attention to the political, social and economic inequalities affecting the author's native country. Immaculately researched, the book's strength comes from extensive interviews with ordinary and influential Guatemalans.

Stephen Schlesinger and Stephen Kinzer *Bitter Fruit: The Untold Story of the American Coup In Guatemala* (Doubelday/Sinclair Browne; both o/p). As the title says, this book traces the American connection in the 1954 coup, delving into the murky water of United Fruit Company politics and proving that the invading army received its orders from the White House.

Jean-Marie Simon *Eternal Spring – Eternal Tyranny* (Norton in US and UK). Of all the books on human rights in Guatemala, this is the one that speaks with blinding authority and the utmost clarity. Combining the highest standards in photography with crisp text, there's no attempt to persuade you – the facts are allowed to speak for themselves, which they do with amazing strength. If you want to know what happened in Guatemala over the last twenty years or so there is no better book, though Simon clearly takes sides, aligning herself with the revolutionary left – there's no mention of abuses committed by the guerrillas.

Guatemala in Rebellion. Fascinating historical snippets and eyewitness accounts tracing Guatemalan history from the arrival of the Spanish to 1983, in which the people involved are allowed to speak for themselves. They range from conquistadors to priests and indigenous peoples.

CENTRAL AMERICAN POLITICS

Tom Barry *Central America Inside Out* (Grove-Atlantic in US). Well-informed background reading on the entire region. By the same author, *Inside Guatemala* (InterHemispheric Education Resource Center in US and UK) is part of a series of guides covering the history, politics, ecomomy and society of Central America; packed with accessible facts and analysis.

James Dunkerley *Power in the Isthmus* (Norton/Verso Editions). Detailed account of Central American politics offering a good summary of the contemporary situation, albeit in turgid academic style. His later book, *The Pacification of Central America* (Verso Editions In US and UK), published in 1994, is a similar well-researched account with plenty of statistics. It covers more recent events, in particular the region's civil wars, up to the beginning of the peace process.

Ralph Lee Woodward Jr *Central America: A Nation Divided* (Oxford University Press in US and UK). A good general summary of the Central American situation, despite its daft title.

INDIGENOUS CULTURE

Linda Asturias de Barrios *Comalapa: Native Dress and its Significance* (Ixchel Museum, Guatemala). Only available in Guatemala, this is a work of skilled academic research, investigating weaving skills and their place within modern Indian communities.

Krystyna Deuss *Indian Costumes from Guatemala* (K Deuss in UK; o/p). A useful survey of the traditional costumes worn in Guatemala, and one of the best introductions to the subject.

Guisela Mayen de Castellanos *Tzute and Hierarchy in Sololá* (Ixchel Museum, Guatemala). Only available within Guatemala, this is a detailed and academic account of indigenous custome and the complex hierarchy that it embodies. Somewhat dry in its approach, but the research is superb and some of the information is fascinating.

Rigoberta Menchú *I, Rigoberta Menchú – An Indian Woman in Guatemala* (Norton/Verso). Unusual and fascinating account of life in the highlands, by Nobel Peace Prize winner Rigoberta Menchú. The book traces the abuse of the Maya population and the rising tide of violence. It includes a chilling description of the military campaign and of the power and complexity of Quiché culture, homing in on the enormous gulf between *ladinos* and the Maya.

Hans Namuth *Los Todos Santeros* (Nishen in UK; o/p). Splendid book of black-and-white photographs taken in the village of Todos Santos, to the north of Huehuetenango. The book was inspired by the work of anthropologist Maud Oakes (see below).

Maud Oakes, *Beyond the Windy Place; The Two Crosses of Todos Santos* (Gollancz in UK; o/p). An anthropologist who spent many years in the Mam-speaking village of Todos Santos, north of Huehuetenango. Oakes' studies of life in the village were published in the 1940s and 1950s and still make fascinating reading.

The Popol Vuh (Touchstone/Scribner's). The great poem of the Quiché, written shortly after the Conquest and intended to preserve the tribe's knowledge of its history. It's an amazing swirl of ancient mythological characters and their wandering through the Quiché highlands, tracing Quiché ancestry back to the beginning. There are several versions on offer though many of them are half-hearted, including only a few lines from the original. The best is translated by Dennis Tedlock.

James D Sexton (ed) *Son of Tecún Umán* (Waveland Press/University of Arizona Press); *Campesino* (Univeristy of Arizona Press in US and UK); and *Ignacio* (University of Pennsylvania Press in US and UK). Three excellent autobiographical accounts written by an anonymous Maya from the south side of Lake Atitlán. The books give an impression of life inside a modern Maya village, bound up in poverty, local politics and a mixture of Catholicism and superstition, and manage to avoid the stereotyping that usually characterizes description of the indigenous population. The earliest is *Son of Tecún Umán*, which takes us from 1972–77, while the second account, *Campesino*, leads up to 1982 and includes the worst years of political violence. *Ignacio* completes the tale. *Casa Andinista*, in Antigua, sometimes has copies.

Philip Werne *The Maya of Guatemala* (Minority Rights Group in UK; o/p). A short study of repression and the Maya of Guatemala. The latest edition (published in 1994) is now a little out of date but interesting none the less.

ARCHEOLOGY

Robert Carmack *Quichean Civilization* (University of California Press in US and UK).

Thorough study of the Quiché and their history, drawing on archeological evidence and accounts of the Conquest. A useful insight into the structure of highland society at the time of the Conquest.

Michael Coe *The Maya* (Thames and Hudson in US and UK). Now in its fifth edition, this clear and comprehensive introduction to Maya archeology is certainly the best on offer. Coe has also written several more weighty, academic volumes. His *Breaking the Maya Code* (Thames and Hudson/Penguin), a personal history of the decipherment of the glyphs, owes much to the fact that Coe was present at many of the important meetings leading to the breakthrough. While his criticism of J Eric Thompson may provoke controversy, this book demonstrates that the glyphs did actually reproduce Maya speech.

William Coe *Tikal: A Handbook to the Ancient Maya Ruins* (University of Pennsylvania Press in US). Superbly detailed account of the site, usually available at the ruins. The detailed map of the main area is essential for in-depth exploration.

Charles Gallenkamp *Maya* (Viking Penguin/Penguin; o/p). Perhaps a touch over-the-top on the sensational aspects of Maya archeology, this is none the less another reasonable introduction to the subject. An overview of the history of Maya archeology, the book takes you through the process of unravelling the complexity of the Maya world.

Orellana *The Tzutujil Mayas*. A study of highland tribes, which goes into great depth when it comes to events since the Conquest.

Linda Schele and David Freidel *A Forest of Kings: The Untold Story of the Ancient Maya* (Morrow in US). The authors, in the forefront of the "new archeology", have been personally responsible for decoding many glyphs. This book, in conjunction with *The Blood of Kings*, by Linda Schele and Mary Miller (Braziller/Thames and Hudson), shows that far from being governed by peaceful astronomer-priests, the ancient Maya were ruled by hereditary kings, lived in aggressive city states, and engaged in continuous alliances and war. *The Maya Cosmos*, by Schele, Freidel and Joy Parker (Morrow in US), is more difficult to read, dense with copious notes, but examines Maya ritual and religion in a unique and far-reaching way.

Robert Sharer *The Ancient Maya* (Stanford University Press). If you want to dig deep try this weighty account of Maya civilization, now in its fourth edition. More concerned with being scientifically accurate than readable, it's a long, dry account, but if you can spare the time you'll end up well informed.

J Eric Thompson *The Rise and Fall of the Maya Civilization* (University of Oklahoma Press in UK). A major authority on the ancient Maya, Thompson has produced many academic studies. This is one of the more approachable. He is also the author of an interesting study of Belizean history in the first two centuries of Spanish colonial rule, which casts some light on the tribes that weren't immediately conquered by the Spanish.

WILDLIFE AND THE ENVIRONMENT

Louise H Emmons *Neotropical Rainforest Mammals*, illustrated by Francois Feer (University of Chicago Press in US and UK). Highly informative, with colour illustrations, written by experts for non-scientists. Local and scientific names are given, along with plenty of interesting snippets.

Steve Howe and Sophie Webb *The Birds of Mexico and Northern Central America* (Oxford University Press in US and UK). A tremendous work, the result of years of research, this is the definitive book on the region's birds. Essential for all serious ornithologists.

John C Kricher *A Neotropical Companion* (Princeton University Press in US and UK). Subtitled "An Introduction to the Animals, Plants and Ecosystems of the New World Tropics", this contains an amazing amount of valuable information for nature lovers. Researched mainly in Central America, so there's plenty that's directly relevant.

Don Moser *The Jungles of Central America* (Time-Life Books in US). Glossy trip through the wildernesses of Central America. By no means a comprehensive account of the region's wildlife but a good read nonetheless, with several useful sections on Guatemala.

Frank B Smythe, *The Birds of Tikal* (Natural History Press in US). This is sadly all that's on offer for budding ornithologists in Guatemala,

but we should be thankful for small mercies. The book can usually be bought in Tikal.

GUIDES

Bruce Hunter *A Guide to Ancient Maya Ruins* (University of Oklahoma Press in US and UK). The only guide that focuses exclusively on Maya ruins, this offers an account of all the most important sites in Mexico, Guatemala and Belize. Many of the more obscure ruins are ignored, but it's well worth reading.

Barbara Balchin de Koose *Antigua for You* (Watson in Guatemala). The latest in a line of guides focusing on Guatemala's most popular tourist city, this book gives a very good and comprehensive account of the colonial architectural wonders, but not much else.

Trevor Long and Elizabeth Bell *Antigua Guatemala* (Filmtrek in Guatemala). This is the best guide to Antigua, replacing an older version by Mike Shawcross which is now out of print. The book is available from several shops in Antigua.

Lily de Jongh Osborne *Four Keys to Guatemala* (Mayflower Publishing Co in UK; o/p). One of the best guides to Guatemala ever written, including a short piece on every aspect of the country's history and culture. Osborne also wrote a good book on indigenous arts and crafts in Guatemala. Sadly, both books are now out of print.

Carlos E. Prahl Redondo *Guia de los Volcanes de Guatemala* (Club Andino Guatemalteco). A very comprehensive and systematic account of the nation's 37 volcanoes and how to get to the top of them, put together by a local teacher.

COOKBOOKS

Copeland Marks *False Tongues and Sunday Bread: A Guatemalan and Maya Cookbook* (Donald I Fine in US). Having travelled in Guatemala and suffered the endless onslaught of beans and tortillas, you may be surprised to find that the country has an established culinary tradition. Copeland Marks, an American food writer, has spent years unearthing the finest Guatemalan recipes, from hen in chocolate sauce to the standard black beans. The book is a beautifully bound celebration of Guatemalan food as it should be.

LANGUAGE

Guatemala takes in a bewildering collection of languages, but fortunately for the traveller Spanish will get you by in all but the most remote areas. Some middle class Guatemalans speak English but it's essential to learn at least a few Spanish phrases or you're in for a frustrating time.

The Spanish spoken in Guatemala has a strong Latin American flavour to it, and if you're used to the dainty intonation of Madrid or Granada then this may come as something of a surprise. Gone is the soft s, replaced by a crisp and clear version. If you're new to Spanish it's a lot easier to pick up than the native version. Everywhere you'll find people willing to make an effort to understand you, eager to speak to passing gringos.

The rules of **pronunciation** are pretty straightforward and, once you get to know them, strictly observed. Unless there's an accent, words ending in d, l, r and z are **stressed** on the last syllable, all others on the second last. All **vowels** are pure and short.

A somewhere between the A sound of back and that of father.

E as in get.

I as in police.

O as in hot.

U as in rule.

C is soft before E and I, hard otherwise: *cerca* is pronounced serka.

G works the same way, a guttural H sound (like the *ch* in loch) before E or I, a hard G elsewhere – *gigante* becomes higante.

H is always silent.

J is the same sound as a guttural G: *jamon* is pronounced hamon.

LL sounds like an English Y: *tortilla* is pronounced torteeya.

N is as in English unless it has a tilde (accent) over it, when it becomes NY: *mañana* sounds like manyana.

QU is pronounced like an English K.

R is rolled, RR doubly so.

V sounds more like B, *vino* becoming beano.

X is slightly softer than in English – sometimes almost SH – *Xela* is pronounced shela.

Z is the same as a soft C, so *cerveza* becomes servesa.

Below is a list of a few essential words and phrases (and see p.32 for food lists), though if you're travelling for any length of time a **dictionary** or **phrase book** is obviously a worthwhile investment. Any good Spanish phrasebook or dictionary should see you through in Guatemala, but specific Latin American ones are the most useful. The *University of Chicago Dictionary of Latin-American Spanish* is a good all-rounder, while *Mexican Spanish: A Rough Guide Phrasebook*, has a menu reader, rundown of colloquialisms and a number of cultural tips that are relevant to many of the Latin American countries, including Guatemala. If you're using a dictionary, remember that in Spanish CH, LL, and Ñ count as separate letters and are listed after the Cs, Ls, and Ns respectively.

A SPANISH LANGUAGE GUIDE

BASICS

Yes, No	*Si, No*	Open, Closed	*Abierto/a, Cerrado/a*
Please, Thank you	*Por favor, Gracias*	With, Without	*Con, Sin*
Where, When	*Donde, Cuando*	Good, Bad	*Buen(o/a), Mal(o/a)*
What, How much	*Qué, Cuanto*	Big, Small	*Gran(de), Pequeño/a*
Here, There	*Aqui, Alli*	More, Less	*Mas, Menos*
This, That	*Este, Eso*	Today, Tomorrow	*Hoy, Mañana*
Now, Later	*Ahora, Mas tarde*	Yesterday	*Ayer*

GREETINGS AND RESPONSES

Hello, Goodbye	*Ola, Adios*	Not at all/You're welcome	*De nada*
Good morning	*Buenos dias*	Do you speak English?	*¿Habla (usted) Ingles?*
Good afternoon/night	*Buenas tardes/noches*	I don't speak Spanish	*(No) Hablo Español*
See you later	*Hasta luego*	My name is . . .	*Me llamo . . .*
Sorry	*Lo siento/disculpeme*	What's your name?	*¿Como se llama usted?*
Excuse me	*Con permiso/perdón*		
How are you?	*¿Como está (usted)?*	I am English/	*Soy/Ingles(a)/*
I (don't) understand	*(No) Entiendo*	Australian	*Australiano(a).*

NEEDS – HOTELS AND TRANSPORT

I want	*Quiero*	How do I get to . . . ?	*¿Por donde se va a . . . ?*
I'd like	*Quisiera*		
Do you know . . . ?	*¿Sabe . . . ?*	Left, right, straight on	*Izquierda, derecha, derecho*
I don't know	*No se*	Where is . . . ?	*¿Donde esta . . . ?*
There is (is there)?	*(¿)Hay(?)*	. . . the bus station	*. . . el terminal de camionetas*
Give me . . . (one like that)	*Deme . . . (uno asi)*	. . . the train station	*. . la estación de ferrocarriles*
Do you have . . . ?	*¿Tiene . . . ?*	. . . the nearest bank	*. . el banco mas cercano*
. . . the time	*. . . la hora*		
. . . a room	*. . . un cuarto*	. . . the post office	*. . . el correo/la oficina de correos*
. . . with two beds/ double bed	*. . . con dos camas/ cama matrimonial*	. . . the toilet	*. . . el baño/sanitario*
It's for one person (two people) . . . for one night (one week)	*Es para una persona (dos personas) . . . para una noche (una semana)*	Where does the bus to . . . leave from?	*¿De donde sale la camioncta para . . . ?*
		Is this the train for Puerto Barrios?	*¿Es este el tren para Puerto Barrios?*
It's fine, how much is it?	*¿Está bien, cuanto es?*	I'd like a (return) ticket to . . .	*Quisiera un boleto (de ida y vuelta) para . . .*
It's too expensive	*Es demasiado caro*		
Don't you have anything cheaper?	*¿No tiene algo más barato?*	What time does it leave (arrive in . . .)?	*¿A qué hora sale (llega en . . .)?*
Can one . . . ? . . . camp (near) here?	*¿Se puede . . . ? ¿ . . . acampar aqui (cerca)?*	What is there to eat?	*¿Qué hay para comer?*
		What's that?	*¿Qué es eso?*
Is there a hotel nearby?	*¿Hay un hotel aquí cerca?*	What's this called in Spanish?	*¿Como se llama este en Español?*

NUMBERS AND DAYS

1	un/uno/una	20	veinte	1990	mil novocientos
2	dos	21	veintiuno		noventa
3	tres	30	treinta	1991	. . . y uno
4	cuatro	40	cuarenta	2000	dos mil
5	cinco	50	cincuenta		
6	seis	60	sesenta	first	primero/a
7	siete	70	setenta	second	segundo/a
8	ocho	80	ochenta	third	tercero/a
9	nueve	90	noventa		
10	diez	100	cien(to)	Monday	lunes
11	once	101	ciento uno	Tuesday	martes
12	doce	200	doscientos	Wednesday	miercoles
13	trece	201	doscientos uno	Thursday	jueves
14	catorce	500	quinientos	Friday	viernes
15	quince	1000	mil	Saturday	sabado
16	diez y seis			Sunday	domingo

GLOSSARY

AGUARDIENTE Raw alcohol made from sugar cane.

AGUAS Bottled fizzy drinks.

ALCADE Mayor

ALDEA Small settlement.

ALTIPLANO Highland area of central Guatemala.

ATOL Drink usually made from maize dough, cooked with water, salt, sugar and milk. Can also be made from rice.

BARRANCA Steep-sided ravine.

BARRIO Slum or shantytown.

BIOTOPO Protected area of ecological interest, usually with limited tourist access.

BOCA COSTA Western slopes of the Guatemalan highlands, prime coffee-growing country.

BRUJO Maya priest who can communicate with the spirit world .

CAKCHIQUEL Indigenous highland tribe occupying an area between Guatemala City and Lake Atitlán.

CAMIONETA Second-class bus. In other parts of Latin America the same word means a small truck or van.

CANTINA Local hard-drinking bar.

CHAPÍN Nickname for a citizen of Guatemala.

CHICLE Sapodilla tree sap from which chewing gum is made.

CLASSIC Period during which ancient Maya civilization was at its height, usually given as 300–900 AD.

COFRADÍA Religious brotherhood dedicated to the protection of a particular saint. These groups form the basis of religious and civil hierarchy in traditional highland society and combine Catholic and pagan practices.

COMEDOR Basic Guatemalan restaurant, usually with just one or two things on the menu, and always the cheapest places to eat.

CORRIENTE Another name for a second-class bus.

CORTE Traditional Guatemalan skirt.

COSTUMBRE Guatemalan word for traditional customs of the highland Maya, usually of religious and cultural significance. The word often refers to traditions which owe more to paganism than to Catholicism.

CREOLE Guatemalan of mixed Afro-Caribbean descent.

DCG *Democracia Cristiana Guatemalteca* (Guatemalan Christian Democratic Party).

EFECTIVO Cash.

EGP *Ejército Guerrillero de los Pobres* (Guerrilla Army of the Poor). A Guatemalan guerrilla group that operated in the Ixil triangle and Ixcán areas.

EVANGÉLICO Christian evangelist or fundamentalist, often missionaries. Name given to numerous Protestant sects seeking converts in Central America.

FAR *Fuerzas Armadas Rebeldes* (Revolutionary Armed Forces). Guatemalan guerrilla group that was mainly active in Petén.

FINCA Plantation-style farm.

GARIFUNA Black Guatemalan of mixed African and native American blood.

GLYPH Element in Maya writing and carving, roughly the equivalent of a letter or numeral.

GRINGO/GRINGA Any white-skinned foreigner, not necessarily a term of abuse.

HOSPEDAJE Another name for a small basic hotel.

HUIPIL Woman's traditional blouse, usually woven or embroided.

INDÍGENA Indigenous person of Maya descent.

INDIO Racially abusive term to describe someone of Maya descent. The word *indito* is equally offensive.

INGUAT Guatemalan tourist board.

I.V.A. Guatemalan sales tax of ten percent.

IXIL Highland tribe grouped around the three towns of the Ixil triangle – Nebaj, Chajul and San Juan Cotzal.

KEKCHI Maya tribal group based around Cobán, the Verapaz highlands and Lake Izabal.

LADINO A vague term – at its most specific defining someone of mixed Spanish and Maya blood, but more commonly used to describe a person of "Western" culture, or one who dresses in "Western" style, be they pure Maya or of mixed blood.

LENG Slang for *centavo*.

MAM Maya tribe occupying the west of the western highlands, the area around Huehuetenango.

MARIACHI Mexican musical style popular in Guatemala.

MARIMBA Xylophone-like instrument used in traditional Guatemalan music.

MAYA General term for the large tribal group who inhabited Guatemala, southern Mexico, Belize, western Honduras and a slice of El Salvador since the earliest times, and still do.

MESTIZO Person of mixed native and Spanish blood, more commonly used in Mexico.

METATE Flat stone for grinding maize into flour.

MILPA Maize field, usually cleared by slash-and-burn.

MINUGUA United Nations mission, in Guatemala to oversee the peace process.

MLN *Movimiento de Liberacion Nacional* (National Liberation Movement). Right-wing political party in Guatemala.

NATURAL Another term for an indigenous person.

PENSIÓN Simple hotel.

PISTO Slang for cash.

PGT *Partido Guatemalteco de Trabajadores* (Guatemalan Labour Party, also known as the Guatemalan Communist Party).

PIPIL Indigenous tribal group which occupied much of the Pacific coast at the time of the Conquest, but no longer survives.

POSTCLASSIC Period between the decline of Maya civilization and the arrival of the Spanish, 900–1530 AD.

PRECLASSIC Archeological era preceding the blooming of Maya civilization, usually given as 1500 BC–300 AD.

PULLMAN Fast and comfortable bus, usually an old Greyhound.

QUICHÉ Largest of the highland Maya tribes, centred on the town of Santa Cruz del Quiché.

SIERRA Mountain range.

STELA Freestanding carved monument. Most are of Maya origin.

TECÚN UMÁN Last king of the Quiché tribe, defeated in battle by Alvarado.

TIENDA Shop.

TíPICA Clothes woven from multicoloured textiles, usually geared towards the Western customer.

TRAJE Traditional costume.

TZUTE Headcloth or scarf worn as a part of traditional Mayan costume.

TZUTUJIL Indigenous tribal group occupying the land to the south of Lake Atitlán.

URNG *Unidad Revolucionaria Nacional Guatemalteca* (Guatemalan National Revolutionary Unity). Umbrella organization of the four former guerrilla groups, now making moves to become a political party.

USAC *Universidad de San Carlos* (National University of San Carlos, Guatemala).

XATE Decorative palm leaves harvested in Petén for export to the US, to be used in flower arrangements.

INDEX

Stay in touch with us!

ROUGH*NEWS* **is Rough Guides' free newsletter. In three issues a year we give you news, travel issues, music reviews, readers' letters and the latest dispatches from authors on the road.**

I would like to receive ROUGH*NEWS*: please put me on your free mailing list.

NAME . . . .

ADDRESS . . . .

Please clip or photocopy and send to: Rough Guides, 1 Mercer Street, London WC2H 9QJ, England or Rough Guides, 375 Hudson Street, New York, NY 10014, USA.

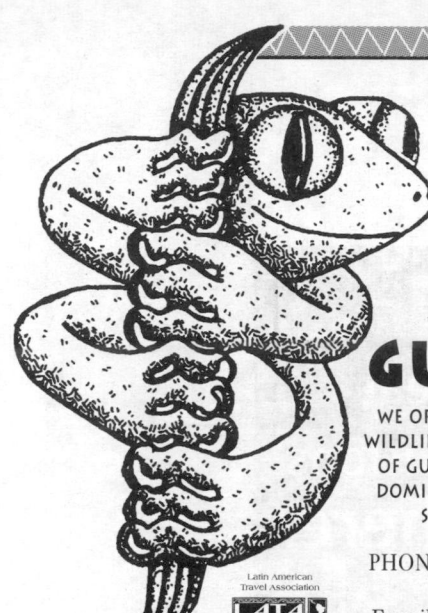

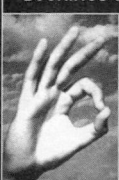